BIO-INSPIRED COMPUTATIONAL ALGORITHMS AND THEIR APPLICATIONS

Edited by **Shangce Gao**

Bio-Inspired Computational Algorithms and Their Applications
Edited by Shangce Gao

Published by InTech
Janeza Trdine 9, 51000 Rijeka, Croatia

Publishing Process Manager Marina Jozipovic

Technical Editor Teodora Smiljanic

Cover Designer InTech Design Team

Additional hard copies can be obtained from orders@intechopen.com

Bio-Inspired Computational Algorithms and Their Applications, Edited Shangce Gao
p. cm.
ISBN 978-953-51-0214-4

For EU product safety concerns:
IN TECH d.o.o., Prolaz Marije Krucifikse Kozulić 3, 51000 Rijeka, Croatia,
info@intechopen.com or visit our website at intechopen.com.

Meet the editor

Shangce Gao received his BS degree from Southeast University, Nanjing, China, in 2005, and his MS and PhD degrees in Intellectual Information Systems and Innovative Life Science from the University of Toyama, Japan in 2008 and 2011 respectively. From 2005 to 2006, he was a technical support engineer in Microsoft Co. Ltd., Shanghai, China. He has received the Outstanding Academic Performance Award of IEICE Hokuriku Branch in 2008, the Outstanding Self-Financed Students Abroad Award of Chinese Government from China Scholarship Council in 2009, the Outstanding Academic Achievement Award of IPSJ Hokuriku Branch in 2011, and the Outstanding Doctoral Award of University of Toyama in 2011. He is currently an associate research fellow at the Key Laboratory of Embedded System and Service Computing, Ministry of Education, Tongji University, Shanghai 200092, China. His main research interests are intelligent computing and brain cognition.

Contents

Preface

In recent years, there has been a growing interest in the use of biology as a source of inspiration for solving practical problems. These emerging techniques are often referred to as "bio-inspired computational algorithms". The purpose of bio-inspired computational algorithms is primarily to extract useful metaphors from natural biological systems. Additionally, effective computational solutions to complex problems in a wide range of domain areas can be created. The more notable developments have been the genetic algorithm (GA) inspired by neo-Darwinian theory of evolution, the artificial immune system (AIS) inspired by biological immune principles, and the swarm intelligence (SI) inspired by social behavior of gregarious insects and other animals. It has been demonstrated in many areas that the bio-inspired computational algorithms are complementary to many existing theories and technologies.

In this research book, a small collection of recent innovations in bio-inspired computational algorithms is presented. The techniques covered include genetic algorithms, artificial immune systems, particle swarm optimization, and hybrid models. Twenty-four chapters are contained, written by leading experts from researchers of computational intelligence communities, practitioners from industrial engineering, the Air Force Academy, and mechanical engineering. The objective of this book is to present an international forum for the synergy of new developments from different research disciplines. It is hoped, through the fusion of diverse techniques and applications, that new and innovative ideas will be stimulated and shared.

This book is organized into four sections. The first section shows seven innovative works that give a flavor of how genetic algorithms can be improved from different aspects. In Chapter 1, a sophisticated variant of genetic algorithms was presented. The characteristic of the proposed successive zooming genetic algorithm was that it can predict the possibility of the solution found to be an exact optimum solution which aims to accelerate the convergent speed of the algorithm. In the second chapter, based on the newly introduced data structure named "network operator", a genetic algorithm was used to search the structure of an appropriate mathematical expression and its parameters. In the third chapter, two kinds of newly developed mechanisms were incorporated into genetic algorithms for optimizing the trajectories generation in closed chain mechanisms, and planning the effects that it had on the mechanism by relaxing some parameters. These two mechanisms are as follows: the forced inheritance mechanism and the regeneration mechanism. The fourth chapter examines an empirical investigation on the roles of crossover and mutation operators in real-coded genetic algorithms. The fifth chapter summarizes custom processing architectures for genetic algorithms, and it presents a proposal for a scalable parallel array, which is adequate enough for implementation on field-programmable gate array technology. In the sixth chapter, a novel genetic algorithm with splicing and decomposable encoding representation was proposed. One very interesting characteristic of this representation is that it can be spliced and decomposed to describe potential solutions of the problem with different precisions by different numbers of uniform-salient building-blocks. Finally, a comprehensive overview on genetic algorithms, including the algorithm history, the algorithm architecture, a classification of genetic algorithms, and applications on evolvable hardware as examples were well summarized in the seventh chapter.

The second section is devoted to ten different real world problems that can be addressed by adapted genetic algorithms. The eighth chapter shows an effective clustering tool based on genetic algorithms to group documentary collections, and suggested taxonomy of parameters of the genetic algorithm numerical and structural. To solve a well-defined project portfolio selection problem, a hybrid model was presented in the ninth chapter by combining the genetic algorithm and functional-normative (multi-criteria) approach. In the 10th chapter, wide applications on astrophysics, rocket engine engineering, and energy distribution of genetic algorithms were illustrated.These applications proposed a new formal methodology (i.e., the inverted model of input problems) when using genetic algorithms to solve the abundances problems. In the 11th chapter, a continuous genetic algorithm was investigated to integrate a pair of registered and enhanced visual images with an infrared image. The 12th chapter showed a very efficient and robust self-adaptive genetic algorithm to build linear modeling of time series. To deal with the restricted vocabulary speech recognition problem, the 13th chapter presented a novel method based on the genetic algorithm and the fisher's linear discriminate ratio (FLDR). The genetic algorithm was used to handle the optimal feature generation task, while FLDR acted as the separability criterion in the feature space. In the 14th chapter, a very interesting application of genetic algorithms under the dynamic online auctions environment was illustrated. The 15th chapter examines the use of a parallel genetic algorithm for finding frequent itemsets over recent data streams investigated, while a breeder genetic algorithm, used to design power system stabilizer for damping low frequency oscillations in power systems, was shown in the 16th chapter. The 17th chapter discusses genetic algorithms utilized to optimize pulse patterns in synchronous machines at high power ratings.

The third section compiles two artificial immune systems and a particle swarm optimization. The 18th chapter in the book proposes a negative selection scheme, which mimics the self/non-self discrimination of the natural immune system to solve the change detection problem in dynamic fitness landscapes. In the 19th chapter, the dynamics of the innate immune response to Lipopolysaccharide in a microscopic section of tissue were formulated and modelled, using a set of partial differential equations. The 20th chapter analyzes swarm intelligence, i.e. the particle swarm optimization was used to deal with the identical parallel machine scheduling problem. The main characteristic of the algorithm was that its search strategy is perturbed by stochastic factors.

The fourth section includes four hybrid models by combing different meta-heuristics. Hybridization is nowadays recognized to be an essential aspect of high performing algorithms. Pure algorithms are always inferior to hybridizations. This section shows good examples of hybrid models. In the 21st chapter, three immune functions (immune memory, antibody diversity, and self-adjusting) were incorporated into the genetic algorithm to quicken its search speed and improve its local/global search capacity. The 22nd chapter focuses on the combination of genetic algorithm and culture algorithm. Performance on multidimensional knapsack problem verified the effectiveness of the hybridization. Chapter 23 studies the genetic algorithm that was incorporated into the Benders' Decomposition Algorithm to solve the capacitated plant location problem. To solve the constrained multiple-objective supply chain optimization problem, two bio-inspired algorithms, involving a non-dominated sorting genetic algorithm and a novel multi-objective particle swarm optimizer, were investigated and compared in the 24th chapter.

Because the chapters are written by many researchers with different backgrounds around the world, the topics and content covered in this book provides insights which are not easily accessible otherwise. It is hoped that this book will provide a reference to researchers, practicing professionals, undergraduates, as well as graduate students in artificial intelligence communities for the benefit of more creative ideas.

The editor would like to express his utmost gratitude and appreciation to the authors for their contributions. Thanks are also due to the excellent editorial assistance by the staff at InTech.

Shangce Gao
Associate Research Fellow
The Key Laboratory of Embedded System and Service Computing,
Ministry of Education
Tongji University
Shanghai

Part 1

Recent Development of Genetic Algorithm

1

The Successive Zooming Genetic Algorithm and Its Applications

Young-Doo Kwon[1] and Dae-Suep Lee[2]
[1]*School of Mechanical Engineering & IEDT, Kyungpook National University,*
[2]*Division of Mechanical Engineering, Yeungjin College, Daegu,*
Republic of Korea

1. Introduction

Optimization techniques range widely from the early gradient techniques [1] to the latest random techniques [16, 18, 19] including ant colony optimization [13, 17]. Gradient techniques are very powerful when applied to smooth well-behaved objective functions, and especially, when applied to a monotonic function with a single optimum. They encounter certain difficulties in problems with multi optima and in those having a sharp gradient, such as a problem with constraint or jump. The solution may converge to a local optimum, or not converge to any optimum but diverge near a jump.

To remedy these difficulties, several different techniques based on random searching have been developed: full random methods, simulated annealing methods, and genetic algorithms. The full random methods like the Monte Calro method are perfectly global but exhibit very slow convergence. The simulated annealing methods are modified versions of the hill-climbing technique; they have enhanced global search ability but they too have slow convergence rates.

Genetic algorithms [2-5] have good global search ability with relatively fast convergence rate. The global search ability is relevant to the crossover and mutations of chromosomes of the reproduced pool. Fast convergence is relevant to the selection that takes into account the fitness by the roulette or tournament operation. Micro-GA [3] does not need to adopt mutation, for it introduces completely new individuals in the mating pool that have no relation to the evolved similar individuals. The pool size is smaller than that used by the simple GA , which needs a big pool to generate a variety of individuals.

Versatile genetic algorithms have some difficulty in identifying the optimal solution that is correct up to several significant digits. They can quickly approach to the vicinity of the global optimum, but thereafter, march too slowly to it in many cases. To enhance the convergence rate, hybrid methods have been developed. A typical one obtains a rough optimum using the GA first, and then approaches the exact optimum by using a gradient method. Other one finds the rough optimum using the GA first, and then searches for the exact optimum by using the GA again in a local domain selected based on certain logic [7].

The SZGA (Successive Zooming Genetic Algorithm) [6, 8-12] zooms the search domain for a specified number of steps to obtain the optimal solution. The tentative optimum solutions are corrected up to several significant digits according to the number of zooms and the zooming rate. The SZGA can predict the possibility that the solution found is the exact optimum solution. The zooming factor, number of sub-iteration populations, number of zooms, and dimensions of a given problem affect the possibility and accuracy of the solution. In this chapter, we examine these parameters and propose a method for selecting the optimal values of parameters in SZGA.

2. The Successive Zooming Genetic Algorithm

This section briefly introduces the successive zooming genetic algorithm [6] and provides the basis for the selection of the parameters used. The algorithm has been applied successively to many optimization problems. The successive zooming genetic algorithm involves the successive reduction of the search space around the candidate optimum point. Although this method can also be applied to a general Genetic Algorithm (GA), in the current study it is applied to the Micro-Genetic Algorithm (MGA). The working procedure of the SZGA is as follows. First, the initial solution population is generated and the MGA is applied. Thereafter, for every 100 generations, the elitist point with the best fitness is identified. Next, the search domain is reduced to ($X_{OPT}-\alpha^k/2$, $X_{OPT}+\alpha^k/2$), and then the optimization procedure is continued on the reduced domain (Fig. 1). This reduction of the search domain increases the resolution of the solution, and the procedure is repeated until a satisfactory solution is identified.

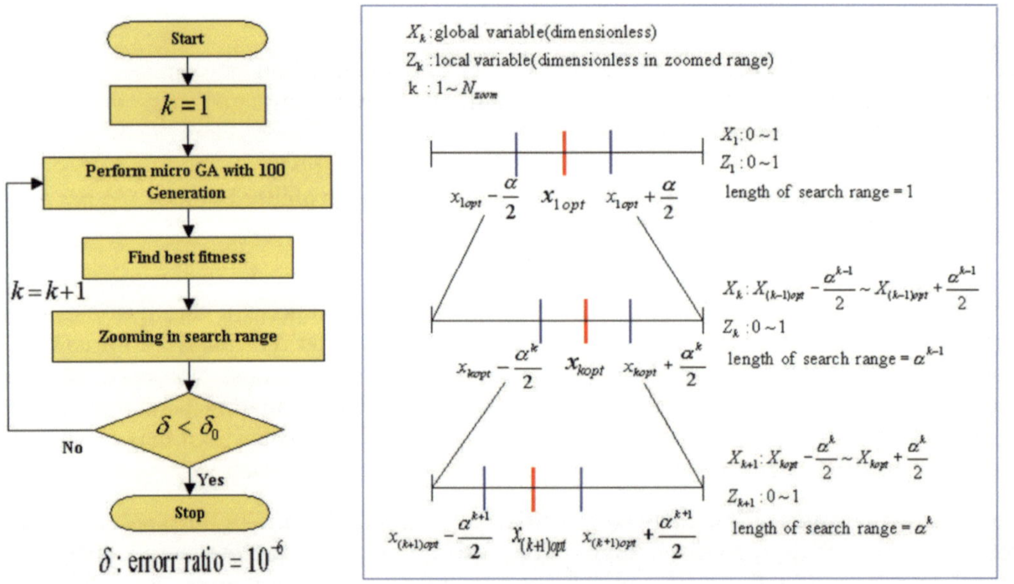

Fig. 1. Flowchart of SZGA and schematics of successive zooming algorithm

The SZGA can assess the reliability of the obtained optimal solution by the reliability equation expressed with three parameters and the dimension of the solution N_{VAR}.

$$R_{SZGA} = [1-(1-(\alpha/2)^{N_{VAR}} \times \beta_{AVG})^{N_{SP}}]^{N_{ZOOM}-1} \tag{1}$$

where,

α: zooming factor, β: improvement factor
N_{VAR}: dimension of the solution, N_{ZOOM}: number of zooms
N_{SUB}: number of sub-iterations, N_{POP}: number of populations
N_{SP}: total number of individuals during the sub-iterations ($N_{SP}=N_{SUB}\times N_{POP}$)

Three parameters control the performance of the SZGA: the zooming factor α, number of zooming operations N_{ZOOM}, and sub-iteration population number N_{SP}. According to previous research, the optimal parameters for SZGA, such as the zooming factor, number of zooming operations, and sub-iteration population number, are closely related to the number of variables used in the optimization problem.

2.1 Selection of parameters in the SZGA

The zooming factor α, number of sub-iteration population N_{SP}, and number of zooms N_{ZOOM} of SZGA greatly affect the possibility of finding an optimal solution and the accuracy of the found solution. These parameters have been selected empirically or by the trial and error method. The values assigned to these parameters determine the reliability and accuracy of the solution. Improper values of parameters might result in the loss of the global optimum, or may necessitate a further search because of the low accuracy of the optimum solution found based on these improper values. We shall optimize the SZGA itself by investigating the relation among these parameters and by finding the optimal values of these parameters. A standard way of selecting the values of these parameters in SZGA, considering the dimension of the solution, will be provided. .

The SZGA is optimized using the zooming factor α, number of sub-iteration population N_{SP}, and the number of zooms N_{ZOOM}, for the target reliability of 99.9999% and target accuracy of 10^{-6}. The objective of the current optimization is to minimize the computation load while meeting the target reliability and target accuracy. Instead of using empirical values for the parameters, we suggest a standard way of finding the optimal values of these parameters for the objective function, by using any optimization technique, to find the optimal values of these parameters which optimize the SZGA itself. Thus, before trying to solve any given optimization problem using SZGA, we shall optimize the SZGA itself first to find the optimal values of its parameters, and then solve the original optimization problem to find the optimal solution by using these parameters.

After analyzing the relation among the parameters, we shall formulate the problem for the optimization of SZGA itself. The solution vector is comprised of the zooming factor α, the number of sub-iteration population N_{SP}, and the number of zooms N_{ZOOM}. The objective function is composed of the difference of the actual reliability to the target reliability, difference of the actual accuracy to the target accuracy, difference of the actual N_{SP} to the proposed N_{SP}, and the number of total population generated as well.

$$F(\alpha,\ N_{SP},\ N_{ZOOM}) = \Delta R_{SZGA} + \Delta A + \Delta N_{SP} + (N_{SP} \times N_{ZOOM}) \quad (2)$$

where,

ΔR_{SZGA} : difference to the target reliability

ΔA : difference to the target accuracy
ΔN_{SP} : difference to the proposed N_{SP}

The problem for optimzation of SZGA itself can be formulated by using this objective function as follows:

$$\text{Minimize } F(X) \tag{3}$$

where,

$$X = \{\alpha, N_{SP}, N_{ZOOM}\}^T$$

$$0 < \alpha < 1$$
$$N_{SP} \sim 100$$
$$N_{ZOOM} > 1$$

The difference of the actual reliability to the target reliability is the difference between R_{SZGA} and 99.9999%, where reliability R_{SZGA} is rewritten with an average improvement factor as

$$R_{SZGA} = [1 - (1 - (\alpha / 2)^{N_{VAR}} \times \beta_{AVG})^{N_{SP}}]^{N_{ZOOM}-1} \tag{4}$$

Here, we can see the average improvement factor β_{AVG}, which is to be regressed later on. The difference of realized accuracy to the target accuracy is the difference between accuracy A and 10^{-6}, where accuracy A is actually the upper limit and may be written as,

$$A = \alpha^{N_{ZOOM}-1} \tag{5}$$

The difference of the actual N_{SP} to the proposed N_{SP} is difference between N_{SP} and 100 [7] . In organizing the optimization algorithm, each element in the objective function is given different weights according to its importance. Thus, the target reliability and target accuracy are met first, and then the number of total population generated is minimized. Although any optimization technique could have been used to slove eq.(3), one can adopt the SZGA in optimizing the SZGA itself to obtain a solution fast and accurately.

The parameters in SZGA have been optimized by using the objective function and improvement factor averaged after regression for a test function [9]. The target reliability is 99.9999% and target accuracy of solution is 10^{-6}. The proposed number of sub-iteration population N_{SP} is 100. Table 1 shows the optimized values for the SZGA parameters for four cases of different number of design variables.

We found a similar tendency to Table 1 for test functions of various numbers of design variables. We also found that the recommended number of sub-iteration population N_{SP} would no longer be acceptable to assure reliability and accuracy for the cases whose number of design variables is over 1. A much greater number of sub-iteration population is needed to obtain an optimal solution with the proper reliability (99.9999%) and accuracy (10^{-6}).

To confirm our optimized result, we fixed two parameters in the feasible domain that satisfy the target reliability and target accuracy, and checked the change in the objective function as a function of the remaining parameter. Examples of the change in the objective function for the case of four design variables showed the validity of the obtained optimal values of the parameters. Although these values may not be valid for all the other cases, they can be used as a good reference for new problems. Some other ways of choosing the values of these parameters will be given later on.

No. of Variables	2	4	8	16
Zooming Factor α	.02573	.1303	.4216	.5176
N_{ZOOM}	5	8	17	22
N_{SP}	1,000	2,000	9,510	1,479,230
No. of Function Evaluation	5,000	16,000	161,670	32,543,060

Table 1. Result of optimized parameters in SZGA for different number of design variables

2.2 Programming for successive zooming and pre-zoning algorithms

Programming the SZGA is simple, as explained below. This zooming philosophy may not be confined only in GA, but can be applied to most other global search algorithms. Let Y(I) be the global variables ranging YMIN(I) ~ YMAX(I), where I is the design variable number. Z(I) consists of local normalized variables ranging 0~1. Thus, the relation between them is as follows in FORTRAN;

```
      DO 10 I=1,NVAR ! NVAR=NO. of VARIABLES
   10 Y(I)=YMIN(I)+(YMAX(I)-YMIN(I))*Z(I)
```

The relation between local variable Z(I) and local variable X(I) (0~1) in the zoomed region is as follows;

```
      DO 12 I=1,NVAR
   12 Z(I)=ZOPT(I,JWIN)+ALP**(JWIN-1)*(X(I)-0.5)
```

Where, ZOPT(I,JWIN) is the elitist in the zoom step (JWIN-1), and ALP is the zooming factor. Note that ZOPT(I,JWIN-1) is more logical. However, the argument is increased by one to meet old versions of FORTRAN, which require a positive integer as a dimension argument. Based on the elitist in step (JWIN-1), we are seeking variables in step JWIN. Please note that ZOPT(I,1)=0.

A pre-zoning algorithm adjusts the gussed initial zone to a very reasonable zone after one set of generation.

```
      DO 14 I=1,NVAR
      YMIN(I)=YINP(I)-BTA*ABS(YINP(I))
   14 YMAX(I)=YINP(I)+BTA*ABS(YINP(I))
```

Where, YINP(I)is the elitist obtained after one set of generation. Thus, we eliminate the assumed initial boundary, and establish a new reasonable boundary. The coefficient BTA may be properly selected, say 0.5.

2.3 Hybrid genetic algorithm

Genetic algorithms are stochastic global search methods based on the mechanism of natural selection and natural reproduction. GAs have been applied to structural optimization problems because they can solve optimization problems that involve mixing continuous, discontinuous, and non-convex regions etc. The SGA (simple GA) has been improved to MGA by using some techniques like tournament selection as well as the elitist strategy. Yet, GAs have some difficulty in fast searching the exact optimum point at a later stage. The DPE (Dynamic Parameter Encoding) GA [4] uses a digital zooming technique, which does not change a digit of a higher rank further after a certain stage. The SZGA (Successive Zooming GA) zooms the searching area successively, and thus the convergence rate is greatly increased. A new hybrid GA technique, which guarantees to find the optimum point, has been proposed [7, 14].

The hybrid GA first identifies a quasi optimal point using an MGA, which has better searching ability than the simple genetic algorithm. To solve the convergence problem at the later stage, we employed hybrid algorithms that combine the global GA with local search algorithms (DFP [1] or MGA). The hybrid algorithm using the DFP (Davidon Fletcher Powell) method incorporates the advantages of both a genetic algorithm and the gradient search technique. The other hybrid algorithm of global GA and local GA at the zoomed area is called LGA (Locally zoomed GA), checks the concavity condition near the quasi minimum point. The enhancement of the above hybrid algorithms is verified by application of these algorithms to the gate optimization problem.

In this hybrid algorithm of minimization problem, an MGA is performed generation-by-generation until there is no further change of the objective function, and then the approximate optimum solution is found at $\mathbf{Z}_{MCA}$. The gradients of the objective function as a function of the design variables are checked, if the concavity condition [1] is satisfied at the boundary of a small zoomed area (Fig. 2). If the condition is not satisfied, the small zoomed area is increased by δ. After several iterations, concavity conditions are finally achieved at the boundary of the final zoomed area ($\kappa\delta \times \kappa\delta$) centered at $\mathbf{Z}_{MCA}$. With the elitist solution from the global GA (approximate optimum solution, $\mathbf{Z}_{MCA}$) and the concavity condition, the optimum point is found within the final zoomed area [$Z(i)$: ($Z_{MCA}(i) - \kappa\delta$) ~ ($Z_{MCA}(i) + \kappa\delta$)]. From this point, a local GA is performed for the small finally zoomed area, which probably contains the optimum point. Usually, this area is much smaller than the original are, so the convergence rate increases considerably (note that the first approximate solution prematurely converged to an inexact but near optimum point).

Water gates need to be installed in dams to regulate the flow-rate and to ensure the containing function of dams. Among these gates, the radial gate is widely used to regulate the flow-rate of huge dams because of its accuracy, easy opening and closing, endurance etc. Moreover, 3-arm type radial gate has better performance than 2-arm type, in connection with the section size of girders and the vibration characteristics during discharging operation. Table 2 compares the optimized results for a 3-arm type radial gate, which considers the reactions to the minimized main weight of the structure including vertical girders with or without arms. The hybrid algorithm (MGA+DFP, MGA+LGA) obtained the exact optimal solution of 0.690488E+10 after far fewer generations of 4100 than the 9000 by MGA, which result in a close but not the exact solution of 0.690497E+10.

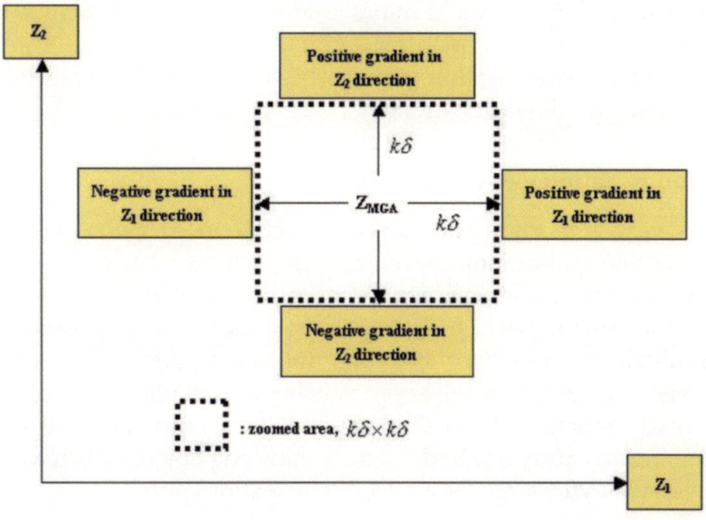

Fig. 2. Confirmed zoomed region after checking the concavity condition

3-arm type	Micro GA	MGA+DFP	MGA+LGA
Convergence Generation	9000	4000+α	4100
Objection Function	0.690497E+10	0.690488E+10	0.690488E+10

Table 2. Comparison of results: MGA, MGA+DFP, MGA+LGA

3. Example of the SZGA

The value of the zooming factor α, an optimal parameter was obtained in reference [8], and was found to show good match with the empirical one. Using this zooming factor in SZGA, the displacement of a truss structure was derived by minimizing the total potential energy of the system. The capacity of the servomotor, which operates the wicket gate mounted in a Kaplan type turbine of the electric power generator, was optimized using SZGA with the value of zooming factor [8].

This is just one parameter among the full optimal parameters discussed in sec.2.1 [9]. Therefore, the analysis done with this factor [8] is a simplified analysis. As commented in section 2.1, the values of the parameters of a well-behaved test model suggested in the Table 1 can be used for an optimization, or the values of the parameters obtained in another way as discussed in the next section can be used.

Several additional examples of SZGA optimization are presented in the following sections to provide more insight on SZGA and to find another way of choosing the values of the SZGA parameters. The first example finds the Moony-Rivlin coefficients of a rubber material to compare with those from the least square method. The second example is a damage detection problem in which the difference between the measured natural frequencies and those of the assumed damage in the structure is minimized. The third example finds the optimal link specification (lengths and initial angular positions of members) to control the double link system with one motor in an automotive diesel engine. The fourth and last example finds an optimal specification (parametric sizes at specified positions) of a ceramic jar that satisfies the required holding capacity.

3.1 Determination of Mooney-Rivlin coefficients

The rubber is a very important mechanical material in everyday life, used widely in mechanical engineering and automotive engineering. Rubber has low production cost and many advantages such as its characteristic softness, processability, and hyper-elasticity. The development of the rubber parts including most process of the shape design, product process, test evaluation, ingredient blending for the required property has used the empirical methods. CAE based on advances in computer-aided structural analysis software is applied to many products. FEM method is applied on various models of rubber parts to evaluate the non-linearity property and the theoretical hyper-elastic behavior of rubber, and to develop analysis codes for large, non-linear deformation.

The structure of rubber-like materials are difficult to analyze because of their material non-linearity and geometric non-linearity as well as their incompressibility. Furthermore, unlike other linear materials, rubber materials have hyper-elasticity, which is expressed by the strain energy function. The representative strain energy functions in the finite element analysis of rubber are the extension ratio invariant function (Mooney-Rivlin model) and the principal extension ratio function (Ogden model). This case uses the Mooney-Rivlin model to investigate the behavior of a rubber material.

The value of the zooming factor changes according to the number of variables and the population number of a generation. If the population number is large, more exact solution can be obtained than the approach with smaller one. For a large population number, which is inevitable in the case of many design variables, longer computation time is needed. In this case, because six design valuables are used to solve the six material properties, nine hundred population units per one generation are used. At this time, whenever zooming is needed, the function is calculated 90,000 times, where, 900 is the population number per one generation and 100 is generation number per one zooming because zooming is implemented after 100 generations . So the point number searched per one valuable is 6 units ($=90{,}000^{1/6}$). To search the optimum point, the zooming factor must be not less than 1/6. Therefore, the zooming factor of 0.2 is used.

The maximum generation number must be decided after the zooming factor is chosen. If the zooming factor is large, the exact solution can be solved as increasing zooming step. Generation numbers have to be decided by the user because they affect the amount of calculation like the population numbers do. For example, when zooming factor of 0.3 is chosen and Maxgen (maximum allowed generation number) is decided as 1000 (N_{ZOOM} = 10), the accuracy of the final searching range becomes $Z_{RANGE} = \alpha^{(Nzoom-1)} = 0.3^{(10-1)}$ = 1.97E-05, and if Maxgen is decided by 1500 (N_{ZOOM} = 15) the final searching range becomes $Z_{RANGE} = \alpha^{(Nzoom-1)} = 0.3^{(15-1)}$ = 4.78E-08, where Z_{RANGE} is the value related with the resolution of solution and is the searching range after N steps of zooming. The smaller this value is, the more exact the solution becomes. In this case, Maxgen=900 is adopted. SZGA minimized the total error better than the other two methods.

Errors to be minimized	Haines & Wilson	Least Square	SZGA
Simple extension	0.757932	0.709209	0.921277
Pure shear	0.702015	0.620089	0.370579
Equi-biaxial	13.2580	0.242475	0.139983
Total error	14.7180	1.57177	1.43184

Table 3. Comparisons of errors among the different methods for obtaining Mooney-Rivlin 6 coefficients

3.2 Damage detection of structures

Structures can sometimes experience failures far earlier than expected, due to fabrication errors, material imperfections, fatigue, or design mistakes, of which fatigue failure is perhaps the most common . Therefore, to protect a structure from any catastrophic failure, regular inspections that include knocking, visual searches, and other nondestructive testing are conducted. However, these methods are all localized and depend strongly on the skill and experience of the inspector. Consequently, smart and global ways of searching for damages have recently been investigated by using rational algorithms, powerful computers, and FEM.

The objective function of the difference between the measured data and the computed data is minimized according to an assumed structural damage to find the locations and intensities of possible damages in a structure. The measured data can be the displacement of certain points or the natural frequencies of the structure, while the computed data are obtained by FEM using an assumed structural damage, whose severity is graded between 0 and 1. For example, Chou et al. used static displacements at a few locations in a discrete structure composed of truss members, and adopted a kind of mixed string scheme as an implicit redundant representation. Meanwhile, Rao adopted a residual force method, where the fitness is the inverse of an objective function, which is the vector sum of the residual forces, and Koh adopted a stacked mode shape correlation that could locate multiple damages without incorporating sensitivity information [11].

Yet, a typical structure can be sub-divided into many finite elements and has many degrees of freedom. Thus, FEM for a static analysis, as well as for a frequency analysis, takes a long time. For a GA, the analysis time is related to the number of functions used for evaluating fitness. This number can become uncontrollable when monitoring a full structure, and as a result, the RAM or memory space required becomes too large and the access rate too slow when handling so much data.

Accordingly, the proposed SZGA is very effective in this case, as it does not require so many chromosomes, even as few as 4, thereby overcoming the slow-down of the convergence rate of the conventional GA, which need many chromosomes in determining the extent of a damage. Furthermore, the issue of many degrees of freedom can also be solved by sub-dividing the monitoring problem into smaller sub-problems because the number of damages will likely be between 1~4, as long as the structure was designed properly. Moreover, the fact that cracks usually initiate at the outer and tensile stressed locations of a structure is also an advantage. As a result, the number of sub-problems becomes manageable, and the required time is much reasonable.

Several tests were performed first to determine the effectiveness of the SZGA for structure monitoring, where regional zooming is not necessary. Next, the procedure used to sub-divide the monitoring problem is presented, along with a comparison of the amount of computation required between a full-scale monitoring analysis and a sub--divide monitoring analysis according to the number of probable damage sites. The optimization problem for various cases of structural damage detection was solved by using three or six variables, zooming factor of 0.2 or 0.3, and total number of function evaluations of 100,000 or 150,000, which is $N_{ZOOM} \times$ sub-iteration population number. The sub-iteration population number means the total population number in a sub-generation of one zooming.

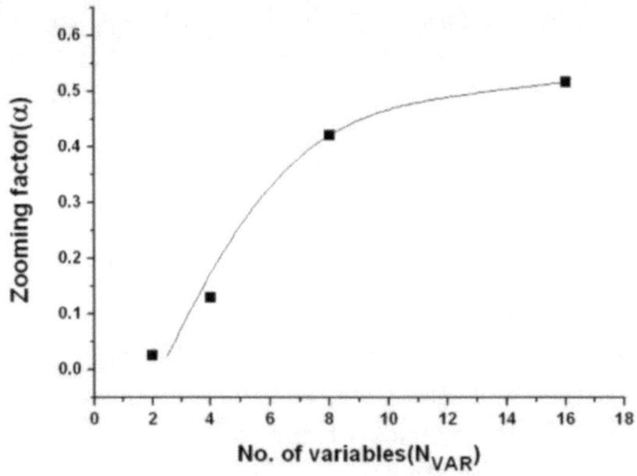

Fig. 3. Zooming factor with respect to the number of variables

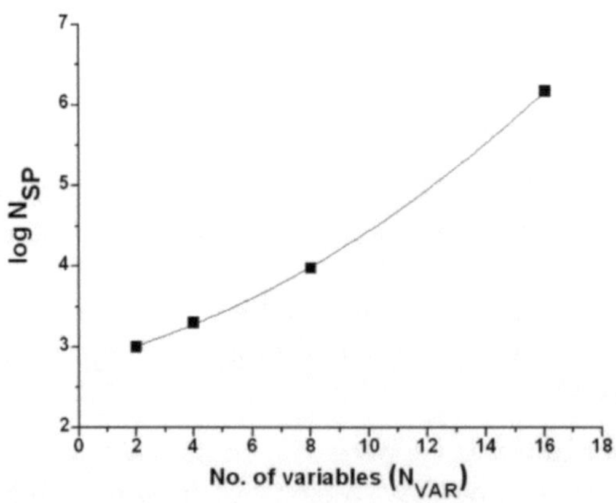

Fig. 4. Number of sub-iteration population with respect to the number of variables

Fig. 3, Fig. 4 and Fig. 5 are the fitting curves of 'N_{VAR} - α', 'N_{VAR} - N_{SP}' and 'N_{VAR} - Number of function calculation' relationship data, respectively, based on Table 1. These figures are prepared for the data point not shown in Table 1 for interpolation purpose.

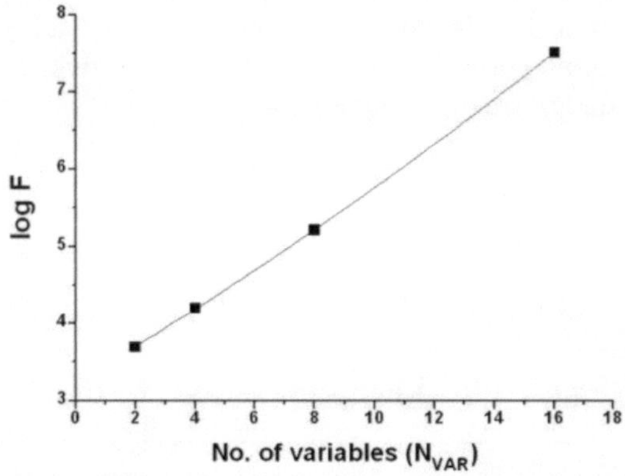

Fig. 5. Number of function calculations with respect to the number of variables

The SZGA can pinpoint an optimal solution by searching a successively zoomed domain. Yet, in addition to its fine-tuning capability, the SZGA only requires several chromosomes for each zoomed domain, which is a very useful characteristic for structural damage detection of a large structure that has a great number of solution variables. In the present study, just four or six digits of chromosomes were used. The accuracy of optimal solution is guaranteed by the successively zoomed infinitesimal range.

Most structures have few cracks, which may exist at different locations. Therefore, a combinational search method is suggested to search for separate cracks by choosing probable damage site as ${}_nC_k$. n denotes the number of total elements and k denotes the number of possible crack sites (1~4). Thus, up to four cracks (k) were considered in a continuum structure modelled with n (=20) elements, and the number of function calculations between the combinational search and the full scale search was compared.

$$ {}_nC_k = \frac{n!}{k!(n-k)!} \tag{6} $$

No. of cracks	${}_nC_k$	No. of function calculation		Ratio (Combinational/Full)
		Combinational search	Full scale search	
1	20	0.580671×10^{5}	0.578096×10^{9}	0.100445×10^{-3}
2	190	0.950000×10^{6}	0.578096×10^{9}	0.164332×10^{-2}
3	1140	0.990843×10^{7}	0.578096×10^{9}	0.171398×10^{-1}
4	4845	0.740788×10^{8}	0.578096×10^{9}	0.128143

Table 4. Result of combinational searching method to reduce amount of calculation in SZGA

When monitoring the entire structure, the number of function calculations became about six hundred million based on the relation between the number of variables and the number of function calculations. However, when the combinational searching method was used, the number of function calculations was reduced by about 10^{-1}~10^{-4} times when compared to the full-scale monitoring case, as shown in Table 4. Table 5 shows the good detection of the damage using the combination method and SZGA.

Element No.	19	20	25	26	31	32
Actual soundness factor	1	1	0.5	1	1	1
Damage detection result	1.0	1.0	0.499999	1.0	1.0	1.0

Table 5. Result of structural damage detection using the combination method and SZGA

3.3 Link system design using weighting factors

This section presents a procedure involving the use of a genetic algorithm for the optimal designs of single four-bar link systems and a double four-bar link system used in diesel engines. Studies concerning the optimal design of the double link system comprised of both an open single link system and a closed single link system which are rare, and moreover the application of the SZGA in this field is hard to find, where the shape of objective function have a broad, flat distribution [12].

During the optimal design of single four-bar link systems, one can find that for the case of equal IO angles, the initial and final configurations show certain symmetry. In the case of open single link systems, the radii of the IO links are the same and there is planar symmetry. In the case of closed single systems, the radii of the IO links are the same and there is point symmetry.

To control the Swirl Control Valve in small High Speed Direct Injection engines, there are two types of actuating systems. The first uses a single DC motor controlled by Pulse Width Modulation, while the second uses two DC motors. However, this study uses the first type of actuator for the simultaneous control of two Swirl Control Valves using a double link system. When two intake valves in a diesel engine are controlled by a single motor, they usually exhibit quite different angular responses when the design variables for the control link system are not properly selected. Therefore, in order to ensure balanced performance in diesel engines with two intake valves, an optimization problem needs to be formulated and solved to find the best set of design variables for the double four-bar link system, which in turn can be used to minimize the different responses to a single input.

Two weighting factors are introduced into the objective function to maintain balance between the multi-objective functions. The proper ratios of weighting factors between objective functions are chosen graphically. The optimal solutions provided by the SZGA and developed FORTRAN Link programs can be confirmed by monitoring the fitness. The reduction in the objective functions is listed in the tables. The responses of the output links that follow the simultaneously acting input links are verified by experiment and the Recurdyn 3-D kinematic analysis package. The experimental and analysis results show good correspondence.

The proposed optimal design process was successfully applied to a recently launched luxury Sports Utility Vehicle model. Table 6 shows the original response and that of the optimized model. The optimal model exhibits almost the exact left and right outputs, and the difference between the left and right responses of 0.603 is thought to be a least value for the given positions of the link centers and the double control system adopting a single input motor.

Model	Input (degree)	Output(degree)		
		Left	Right	Max. Difference
Original	0-90	0-89.144	0-91.958	2.044
Optimal	0-90	0-89.999	0-89.999	0.603

Table 6. Comparison of original and optimal models

3.4 Proper band width for equality constraints

In a problem having an equality constraint, it is not so simple for GA to satisfy the constraint while maintaining efficiency. Optimal solution lies on the line of equality constraint. It is very important to gernerate individuals on or near the equality line. However, the desirable narrow area including the equality line is very small compared with the whole area. The number of individual generated in this narrow area is much less than those in the outer area of the desirable narrow area including the equality line. Therefore, the convergence rate of GA or SZGA is significantly slow for the problems with equality constraints. The bandwidth method is proposed to overcome this kind of slow convergence rate.

For the minimization problems, we added a basic penalty function to meet the equality constraint, which will be explained soon. For this problem with the basic constraint, we can not expect a rapid convergence rate as mentioned above. Therefore, we added an additional penalty function to the region, located out of the desirable narrow area including the equality line, to make an infeasible area of a very highly increased objective function. The bandwidth denotes the half width of the narrow region with the basic penalty only.

There are three methods to handle the equality constraints using GA. One is to give both sides the penalty functions along the equality condition. The other is to give one side the monotonic function and other side the even (jump) penalty function along the equality constraint. However, the one side with the monotonic penalty should be feasible. And, the final one is to apply one side with no penalty function and the other side with the even (jump) penalty function along the equality constraint, and the one side of no penalty function should be feasible.

The penalty methods provided in Fig. 6 only with original penalty, is the basic technique for handling the equality constraint [15]. With this kind of basic technique only, however, the convergence rate would be too slow to reach the optimal point. Many generated individuals are wasted because they mostly too far from the equality constraint line. Therefore we need an additional penalty function to increase the effectiveness of GA. That is an additional penalty to the objective function if the condition is located in outer region of a certain bandwidth centered with the equality constraint.

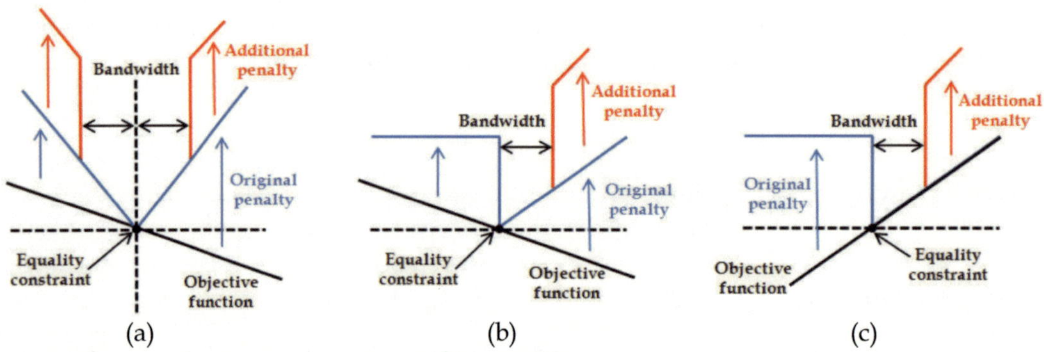

Fig. 6. Three methods to handle the equality constraint in GA.

Using the type (c) equality constraint and additional bandwidth penalty, the design of a ceramic jar was optimized for three values of zooming factors and various bandwidths of equality constraint, as shown in Fig. 7 and Table 7. The result showed a proper range of bandwidth for the equality constraint. In Table 7, the optimal solutions were found for the jar, satisfying the equality constraint of 2 liter volume.

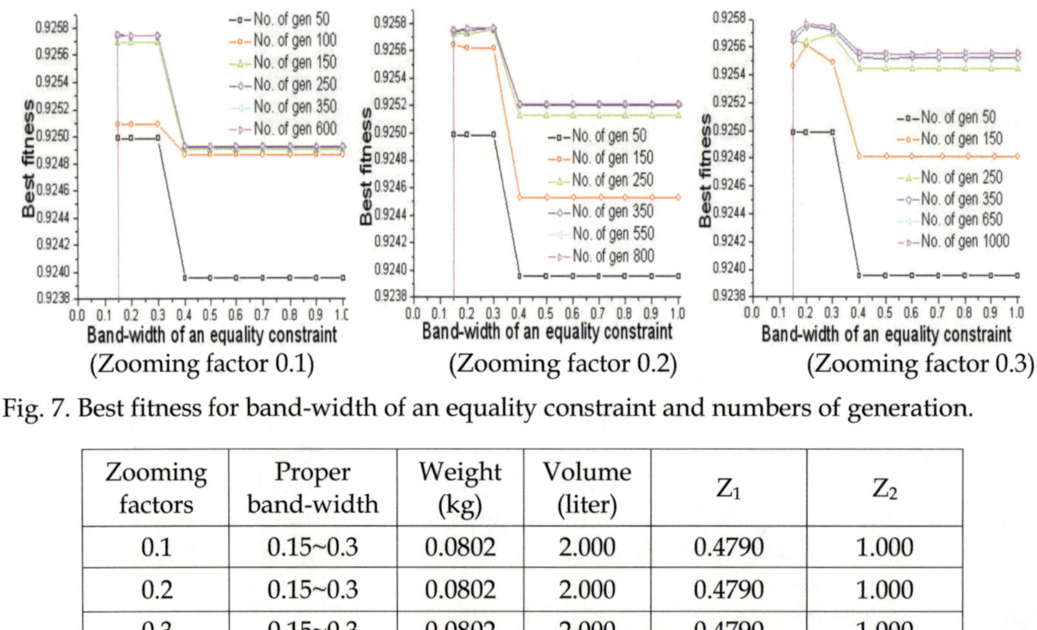

Fig. 7. Best fitness for band-width of an equality constraint and numbers of generation.

Zooming factors	Proper band-width	Weight (kg)	Volume (liter)	Z_1	Z_2
0.1	0.15~0.3	0.0802	2.000	0.4790	1.000
0.2	0.15~0.3	0.0802	2.000	0.4790	1.000
0.3	0.15~0.3	0.0802	2.000	0.4790	1.000

Table 7. Proper bandwidths and the optimal solutions for three zooming factors

This optimization problem does not converge below 0.15 of the band-width of an equality constraint, because the objective function is rather complicated and the band-width is relatively too narrow to give the most candidated optimal individual out of feasible region.

When the band-width is bigger than about 0.3, the best fitness dropped rapidly. In other words, if we open the full range as the feasible solution range, the optimal ridge would be too narrow to be chosen by GA. In conclusion, a too narrow bandwidth may lead to a divergence and a too wide bandwidth may result in inefficiency.

4. Further studies and concluding remarks

The SZGA explained in the foregoing sections may be applied to more fields of interest, such as, the optimal design of ceramic pieces considering important factors like beauty, usage, stability, strength, lid, and exact volume. Prediction of a long -term performance of a rubber seal installed in an automotive engine is another possible application.

The most dominant characteristics of SZGA are its accuracy up to the required significant digits, and its rapid convergence rate even in the later stage. However, users have to properly select the parameters, namely, the zooming factor, number of zooms, and number of sub-domain population. A useful reference can be found in Table 1, Fig. 3, Fig. 4, and Fig. 5. The number of zooms can be determined by eq.(5) for a given upper limit of accuracy. The number of sub-domain population has been recommended as a fixed number until now, however, it may be varied as a function of the zooming step.

5. References

[1] D.M. Himmelblau, 1972, *Applied Nonlinear Programming*, McGraw-Hill.

[2] D.E. Goldberg, 1989, *Genetic Algorithms in Search, Optimization, and Machine Learning*, Addison-Wesley.

[3] K. Krishnakumar, 1989, “Micro-genetic algorithms for stationary and non-stationary function optimization,” SPIEP, Intelligent Control and Adaptive Systems, Vol. 1196, pp. 289~296.

[4] N.N. Schraudolph, R.K. Belew, 1992, "Dynamic parameter encoding for genetic algorithms," Journal of Machine Learning, Vol. 9, pp. 9-21.

[5] D.L. Carroll, 1996, “Genetic algorithms and optimizing chemical oxygen-lodine lasers,” Developments in Theoretical and Applied Mechanics, Vol. 18, pp. 411~424.

[6] Y.D. Kwon, S.B. Kwon, S.B. Jin and J.Y. Kim, 2003, “Convergence enhanced genetic algorithm with successive zooming method for solving continuous optimization problems,” Computers and Structures, Vol. 81, Iss. 17, pp. 1715~1725.

[7] Y.D. Kwon, S.B. Jin, J.Y. Kim, and I.H. Lee, 2004, “Local zooming genetic algorithm and its application to radial gate support problems,” Structural Engineering and Mechanics, An International Journal, Vol. 17, No. 5, pp. 611~626.

[8] Y.D. Kwon, H.W. Kwon, J.Y. Kim, S.B. Jin, 2004, “Optimization and verification of parameters used in successive zooming genetic algorithm,” Journal of Ocean Engineering and Technology, Vol. 18, No. 5, pp. 29~35.

[9] Y.D. Kwon, H.W. Kwon, S.W. Cho, and S.H. Kang, 2006, “Convergence rate of the successive zooming genetic algorithm using optimal control parameters,” WSEAS Transactions on Computers, Vol. 5, Iss. 6, pp. 1200~12007.

[10] Y.D. Kwon, J.Y. Kim, Y.C. Jung, and I.S. Han, 2007, “Estimation of rubber material property by successive zooming genetic algorithm,” JSME, Journal of Solid Mechanics and Materials Engineering, Vol. 1, Iss. 6, pp. 815-826.

[11] Y.D. Kwon, H.W. Kwon, W.J. Kim, and S.D. Yeo, 2008, "Structural damage detection in continuum structures using successive zooming genetic algorithm," Structural Engineering and Mechanics, An International Journal, Vol. 30, No. 2, pp. 135~146.

[12] Y.D. Kwon, C.H. Sohn, S.B. Kwon, and J.G. Lim, 2009, "Optimal design of link systems using successive zooming genetic algorithm," SPIE, Progress in Biomedical Optics and Imaging, Vol. 7493, No. 1~3, pp. 17-1~8.

[13] O. Baskan, S. Haldenbilen, Huseyin Ceylan, Halim Ceylan, 2009, "A new solution algorithm for improving performance of ant colony optimization," Applied Mathematics and Computation, Vol. 211, Iss. 1, pp. 75~84.

[14] N. Tutkun, 2009, "Optimization of multimodal continuous functions using a new crossover for the real-coded genetic algorithms," Expert Systems with Applications, Vol. 3, Iss. 4, pp. 8172~8177.

[15] Y.D. Kwon, S.W. Han, and J.W. Do, 2010, "Convergence rate of the successive zooming genetic algorithm for band-widths of equality constraint," International Journal of Modern Physics B, Vol. 24, No. 15&16, pp. 2731~2736.

[16] Z. Ye, Z. Lee, M. Xie, 2010, "Some improvement on adaptive genetic algorithms for reliability-related applications," Reliability Engineering and System Safety, Vol. 95, Iss. 2, pp. 120~126.

[17] K. Wei, H. Tuo, Z. Jing, 2010, "Improving binary ant colony optimization by adaptive pheromone and commutative solution update," IEEE, 5th International Conference on Bio Inspired Computing: Theory and Applications (BIC-TA), pp. 565~569.

[18] S. Babaie-Kafaki, R. Ghanbari, N. Mahdavi-Amiri, 2011, "Two effective hybrid metaheuristic algorithms for minimization of multimodal functions," Computer Mathematics, Vol. 88, Iss. 11, pp. 2415~2428.

[19] M.A. Ahandani, N.P. Shirjoposh, R. Banimahd, 2011, "Three modified version of differential evolution for continuous optimization," Soft Computing, Vol. 15, Iss. 4, pp. 803~830.

2

The Network Operator Method for Search of the Most Suitable Mathematical Equation

Askhat Diveev[1] and Elena Sofronova[2]
[1]*Institution of Russian Academy of Sciences Dorodnicyn Computing Centre of RAS,*
[2]*Peoples' Friendship University of Russia*
Russia

1. Introduction

For many applied and research problems it is necessary to find solution in the form of mathematical equation. These problems are the selection of function at approximation of experimental data, identification of control object model, control synthesis in the form of state space coordinates function, the inverse problem of kinetics and mathematical physics, etc. The main method to receive mathematical equations for solution of these problems consists in analytical transformations of initial statement formulas of the problem. A few problems have the exact analytical solution, therefore mathematicians use various assumptions, decomposition, and special characteristics of solutions. Usually mathematicians set the form of mathematical equation, and the optimal parameters are found using numerical methods and PC. Such methods as the least-square method have been applied to the problems of approximation for many years (Kahaner D. et al., 1989).

Recently the neural networks have been used to solve complex problems when the mathematical equation cannot be found analytically. The structure of any neural network is also given within the values of parameters or weight coefficients. In problems of function approximation and the neural network training the form of mathematical equation is set by the researcher, and the computer searches for optimum values of parameters in these equations (Callan, 1999; Demuth et al., 2008).

In 1992 a new method of genetic programming was developed. It allows to solve the problem of search of the most suitable mathematical equation. In genetic programming mathematical equations are represented in the form of symbol strings. Each symbol string corresponds to a computation graph in the form of a tree. The nodes of this graph contain operations, and the leaves contain variables or parameters (Koza, 1992, 1994; Koza, Bennett et al., 1999 & Koza, Keane et al., 2003).

Genetic programming solves the problems by applying genetic algorithm. To perform the crossover it is necessary to find symbol substrings that correspond to brunches of trees. The analysis of symbol strings increases the operating time of the algorithm. If the same parameter or variable is included in the required mathematical equation several times, then to solve the problem effectively the genetic programming needs to crossover the trees so that the leaves contain no less than the required number of parameters or variables.

Limitations of the genetic programming revealed at the solution of the problem of suitable mathematical equation search, have led to creation of the network operator.

In this work we introduce a new data structure which we called a network operator. Network operator is a directed graph that contains operations, arguments and all information for calculations of mathematical equation.

Network operator method was used for the problems of control synthesis (Diveyev & Sofronova, 2008; Diveev, 2009; Diveev & Sofronova, 2009a,b).

2. Program notations of mathematical equations

Mathematical equations consist of variables, parameters, unary and binary operations that form four constructive sets.

Set of variables

$$\mathrm{X} = (x_1,\dots,x_N),\ x_i \in \mathrm{R}^1,\ i = \overline{1,N}. \tag{1}$$

Set of parameters

$$\mathrm{Q} = (q_1,\dots,q_P),\ q_i \in \mathrm{R}^1,\ i = \overline{1,P}. \tag{2}$$

Unary operations set

$$\mathrm{O}_1 = (\rho_1(z) = z, \rho_2(z),\dots,\rho_W(z)). \tag{3}$$

Binary operations set

$$\mathrm{O}_2 = (\chi_0(z',z''),\dots,\chi_{V-1}(z',z'')). \tag{4}$$

Unary operations set must have an identity operation

$$\rho_1(z) = z. \tag{5}$$

Binary operations must be commutative

$$\chi_i(z',z'') = \chi_i(z'',z'),\ i = \overline{0,V-1}, \tag{6}$$

associative

$$\chi_i((z',z''),z''') = \chi_i(z',(z'',z''')),\ i = \overline{0,V-1}, \tag{7}$$

and have a unit element

$$\exists e_i \Rightarrow \chi_i(e_i,z) = z,\ i = \overline{0,V-1}. \tag{8}$$

A program notation of mathematical equation is a notation of equation with the help of constructive sets (1) – (4).

3. Graphic notations of mathematical equations

To present mathematical equation as a graph we use a program notation. Let us enlarge the program notation by additional unary identity operation $\rho_1(z)=z$ and binary operation with a unit element $\chi_i(e_i,z)=z$. These operations do not influence the result of calculation but they set a definite order of operations in the notation, so that binary operations have unary operations or unit elements as their arguments, and unary operations have only binary operations, parameters or variables as their arguments.

A graphic notation of mathematical equation is a notation of binary operation that fulfills the following conditions:

a. binary operation can have unary operations or unit element of this binary operation as its arguments;
b. unary operation can have binary operation, parameter or variable as its argument;
c. binary operation cannot have unary operations with the same constants or variables as its arguments.

Any program notation can be transformed into a graphic notation.

4. Network operator of mathematical expression

To construct a graph of the mathematical expression we use a graphic notation. The graphic notation can be transformed into the graph if unary operations of mathematical expression correspond to the edges of the graph, binary operations, parameters or variables correspond to the nodes of the graph.

Suppose that in graphic notation we have a substring where two unary operations are arguments to binary operation $\ldots\chi_k(\rho_l(\ldots),\rho_m(\ldots))\ldots$ This substring is presented as a graph on Fig. 1

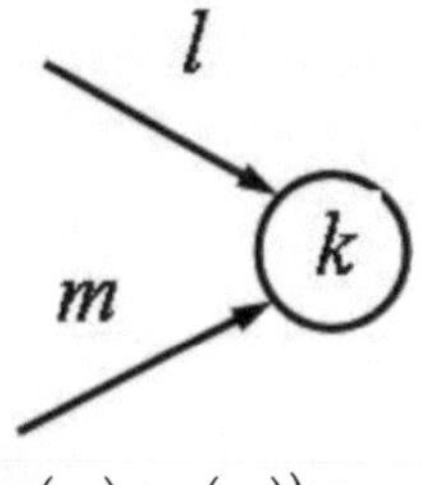

Fig. 1. The graph for substring $\ldots\chi_k(\rho_l(\ldots),\rho_m(\ldots))\ldots$

Suppose we have a substring where binary operation is an argument to unary operation $\ldots\rho_k(\chi_l(\ldots))\ldots$. This substring is presented as a graph on Fig. 2.

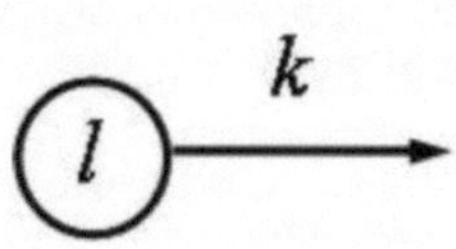

Fig. 2. The graph for substring $\ldots\rho_k(\chi_l(\ldots))\ldots$

Let us have a substring where parameter or variable is an argument to unary operation $\ldots\rho_k(a)\ldots$, where a is an argument or parameter of mathematical equation, $a \in X \cup Q$. The graph for this substring is presented on Fig. 3.

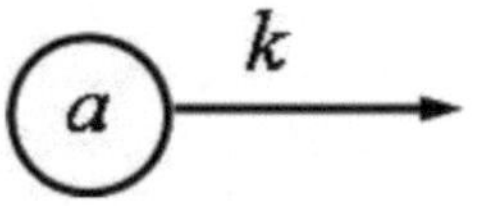

Fig. 3. The graph for substring $\ldots\rho_k(a)\ldots$, $a \in X \cup Q$

If graphic notation contains a substring where binary operation with a unit element is an argument to unary operation $\ldots\rho_k(\chi_l(\rho_m(\ldots),0))\ldots$ We do not depict this unit elements and the node has only one incoming edge as shown on Fig. 4.

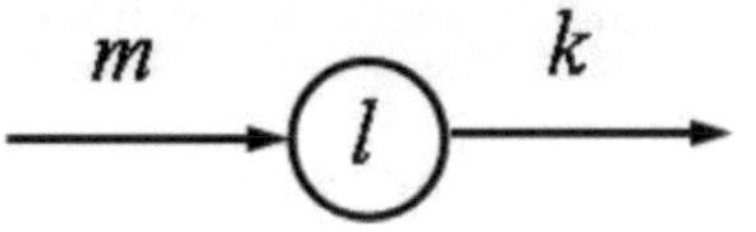

Fig. 4. The graph for substring $\ldots\rho_k(\chi_l(\rho_m(\ldots),0))\ldots$

5. Properties of network operators

Network operator is a directed graph that has the following properties:

a. graph has no loops;
b. any nonsource node has at least one edge from the source node;
c. any non sink node has at least one edge to sink node;
d. every source node corresponds to the element from the set of variables X or the set of parameters Q;
e. every node corresponds to binary operation from the set of binary operations O_2;
f. every edge corresponds to unary operation from the set of unary operations O_1.

To calculate mathematical expression we have to follow certain rules:

a. unary operation is performed only for the edge that comes out from the node with no incoming edges;
b. the edge is deleted from the graph once the unary operation is performed;
c. the binary operation in the node is performed right after the unary operation of the incoming edge is performed;
d. the calculation is terminated when all edges are deleted from the graph.

To construct most of mathematical expressions we use the sets of unary and binary operations that are given in Table 1 and Table 2.

Consider the construction of the network operator for the following mathematical equation

$$y = x_1 + \sin(x_1) + q_1 x_1 e^{-x_2}.$$

$\rho_1(z)=z$	$\rho_{13}(z)=\arctan(z)$
$\rho_2(z)=\begin{cases}\varepsilon^{-1}, & \text{if } \lvert z\rvert>\frac{1}{\sqrt{\varepsilon}}\\ z^2, & \text{otherwise}\end{cases}$	$\rho_{14}(z)=\begin{cases}\frac{\operatorname{sgn}(z)}{\varepsilon}, & \text{if } \lvert z\rvert>\frac{1}{\sqrt[3]{\varepsilon}}\\ z^3, & \text{otherwise}\end{cases}$
$\rho_3(z)=-z$	$\rho_{15}(z)=\begin{cases}\sqrt[3]{\varepsilon}, & \text{if } \lvert z\rvert<\varepsilon\\ \sqrt[3]{z}, & \text{otherwise}\end{cases}$
$\rho_4(z)=\operatorname{sgn}(z)\sqrt{\lvert z\rvert}$	$\rho_{16}(z)=\begin{cases}z, & \text{if } \lvert z\rvert<1\\ \operatorname{sgn}(z), & \text{otherwise}\end{cases}$
$\rho_5(z)=\begin{cases}\frac{\operatorname{sgn}(z)}{\varepsilon}, & \text{if } \lvert z\rvert<\varepsilon\\ \frac{1}{z}, & \text{otherwise}\end{cases}$	$\rho_{17}(z)=\operatorname{sgn}(z)\ln(\lvert z\rvert+1)$
$\rho_6(z)=\begin{cases}\varepsilon^{-1}, & \text{if } z>-\ln(\varepsilon)\\ e^z, & \text{otherwise}\end{cases}$	$\rho_{18}(z)=\begin{cases}\frac{\operatorname{sgn}(z)}{\varepsilon}, & \text{if } \lvert z\rvert>-\ln(\varepsilon)\\ \operatorname{sgn}(z)\left(e^{\lvert z\rvert}-1\right), & \text{otherwise}\end{cases}$
$\rho_7(z)=\begin{cases}\ln(\varepsilon), & \text{if } -\ln\lvert z\rvert>\frac{1}{\varepsilon}\\ \ln\lvert z\rvert, & \text{otherwise}\end{cases}$	$\rho_{19}(z)=\begin{cases}0, & \text{if } \lvert z\rvert>-\ln(\varepsilon)\\ \operatorname{sgn}(z)e^{-\lvert z\rvert}, & \text{otherwise}\end{cases}$
$\rho_8(z)=\begin{cases}\operatorname{sgn}(z), & \text{if } \lvert z\rvert>-\ln(\varepsilon)\\ \frac{1-e^{-z}}{1+e^{-z}}, & \text{otherwise}\end{cases}$	$\rho_{20}(z)=\begin{cases}1, & \text{if } z>\varepsilon\\ 0, & \text{if } z<0\\ \frac{3z^2}{\varepsilon^2}-\frac{2z^3}{\varepsilon^3}, & \text{otherwise}\end{cases}$
$\rho_9(z)=\begin{cases}1, & \text{if } z\ge 0\\ 0, & \text{otherwise}\end{cases}$	$\rho_{21}(z)=\begin{cases}1, & \text{if } z>\frac{\varepsilon}{2}\\ -1, & \text{if } z<-\frac{\varepsilon}{2}\\ \frac{3z}{\varepsilon^2}-\frac{4z^3}{\varepsilon^3}, & \text{otherwise}\end{cases}$
$\rho_{10}(z)=\operatorname{sgn}(z)$	$\rho_{22}(z)=\begin{cases}0, & \text{if } \lvert z\rvert>-\ln(\varepsilon)\\ e^{-\lvert z\rvert}, & \text{otherwise}\end{cases}$
$\rho_{11}(z)=\cos(z)$	$\rho_{23}(z)=\begin{cases}-\frac{\operatorname{sgn}(z)}{\varepsilon}, & \text{if } \lvert z\rvert>\frac{1}{\sqrt[3]{\varepsilon}}\\ z-z^3, & \text{otherwise}\end{cases}$
$\rho_{12}(z)=\sin(z)$	$\rho_{24}(z)=\begin{cases}\frac{\varepsilon}{1+\varepsilon}, & \text{if } z>-\ln(\varepsilon)\\ \frac{1}{1+e^{-z}}, & \text{otherwise}\end{cases}$

Table 1. Unary operations

Operation	Unit element
$\chi_0(z',z'')=z'+z''$	0
$\chi_1(z',z'')=z'z''$	1
$\chi_2(z',z'')=\max\{z',z''\}$	$-\frac{1}{\varepsilon}$
$\chi_3(z',z'')=\min\{z',z''\}$	$\frac{1}{\varepsilon}$
$\chi_4(z',z'')=z'+z''-z'z''$	0
$\chi_5(z',z'')=\mathrm{sgn}(z'+z'')\sqrt{(z')^2+(z'')^2}$	0
$\chi_6(z',z'')=\mathrm{sgn}(z'+z'')(\lvert z'\rvert+\lvert z''\rvert)$	0
$\chi_7(z',z'')=\mathrm{sgn}(z'+z'')\max\{\lvert z'\rvert,\lvert z''\rvert\}$	0

Table 2. Binary operations

First we set parentheses to emphasize the arguments of functions. Then using Table 1 and Table 2 we find appropriate operations and replace functions by operations

$$\begin{aligned} y=x_1+\sin(x_1)+q_1x_1e^{-x_2} &=\left((x_1+\sin(x_1))+q_1x_1e^{-x_2}\right)=\chi_0\left((x_1+\sin(x_1)),q_1x_1e^{-x_2}\right)\\ &=\chi_0\left(\chi_0(x_1,\sin(x_1)),q_1x_1e^{-x_2}\right)=\chi_0\left(\chi_0(x_1,\rho_{12}(x_1)),\chi_1(q_1x_1,\rho_6(-x_2))\right)\\ &=\chi_0\left(\chi_0(x_1,\rho_{12}(x_1)),\chi_1(\chi_1(q_1,x_1),\rho_6(\rho_3(x_2)))\right). \end{aligned}$$

As a result we obtain a program notation of mathematical equation

$$y=\chi_0\left(\chi_0(x_1,\rho_{12}(x_1)),\chi_1(\chi_1(q_1,x_1),\rho_6(\rho_3(x_2)))\right).$$

We can see that this program notation does not meet the requirements to graphic notation. These requirements are necessary for further construction of the graph. According to the definition of the network operator binary operations correspond to the nodes of the graph, unary operations correspond to the edges, thus binary and unary operations must be arguments of each other in the graphic notation of mathematical equation.

When a binary operation has as its argument in program notation then we cannot construct the graph, because there is no edge, in other words no unary operation, between two nodes.

To meet the requirements for graphic notation let us introduce additional unary identity operations. For example in the given program notation we have a substring

$$y=\chi_0(\chi_0(\ldots),\chi_1(\ldots)).$$

Here binary operation has two binary operations as its arguments. It does not satisfy condition «a» of graphic notation. If we use additional identity operation, then we have

$$y=\chi_0(\rho_1(\chi_0(\ldots)),\rho_1(\chi_1(\ldots))).$$

Unary identity operation $\rho_1(z)$ does not change the value of argument and this operation is necessary for the construction of the graph by graphic notation.

Since graphic notation should contain binary operations with unary operations as their arguments then we additional unary identity operations. We get

$$y=\chi_0\left(\rho_1\left(\chi_0\left(\rho_1(x_1),\rho_{12}(x_1)\right)\right),\ \rho_1\left(\chi_1\left(\rho_1\left(\chi_1\left(\rho_1(q_1),\rho_1(x_1)\right)\right),\rho_6\left(\rho_3(x_2)\right)\right)\right)\right).$$

This notation is not a graphic one, because it does not satisfy condition «b» of graphic notation. Here unary operation has unary operation as its argument

$$\ldots\rho_6(\rho_3(x_2))\ldots$$

We use additional binary operation with a unit element as its second argument, for example $\chi_0(\ldots,0)$. According to Table 2 binary operation $\chi_0(z',z'')$ is addition. A unit element for addition is 0 and it does not influence the result of calculation. Thus we get

$$\ldots\rho_6\left(\chi_0\left(\rho_3(x_2),0\right)\right)\ldots$$

We obtain the graphic notation of mathematical equation

$$y=\chi_0\left(\rho_1\left(\chi_0\left(\rho_1(x_1),\rho_{12}(x_1)\right)\right),\ \rho_1\left(\chi_1\left(\rho_1\left(\chi_1\left(\rho_1(q_1),\rho_1(x_1)\right)\right),\rho_6\left(\chi_0\left(\rho_3(x_2),0\right)\right)\right)\right)\right).$$

This notation does not satisfy condition «c» of graphic notation, because it contains a substring where binary operation has two unary operations with the same variable as its arguments

$$\ldots\chi_0\left(\rho_1(x_1),\rho_{12}(x_1)\right)\ldots$$

We add a binary operation with a unit element and a unary identity operation to the substring

$$\ldots\chi_0\left(\rho_1\left(\chi_0\left(\rho_1(x_1),0\right)\right),\rho_{12}(x_1)\right)\ldots$$

As a result we get the following notation of mathematical equation

$$y=\chi_0\left(\rho_1\left(\chi_0\left(\rho_1\left(\chi_0\left(\rho_1(x_1),0\right)\right),\rho_{12}(x_1)\right)\right),\ \rho_1\left(\chi_1\left(\rho_1\left(\chi_1\left(\rho_1(q_1),\rho_1(x_1)\right)\right),\rho_6\left(\chi_0\left(\rho_3(x_2),0\right)\right)\right)\right)\right).$$

This notation has all properties of graphic notation and we can construct the graph of equation by this notation. To construct the graph we use the rules presented on Fig. 1 - 4. The graph is shown on Fig. 5.

Fig. 5 shows the numeration of nodes on the top of each node in the graph. We see that the numbers of the nodes where the edges come out from are less than the numbers of nodes where the edges come in. Such numeration is always possible for directed graphs without loops.

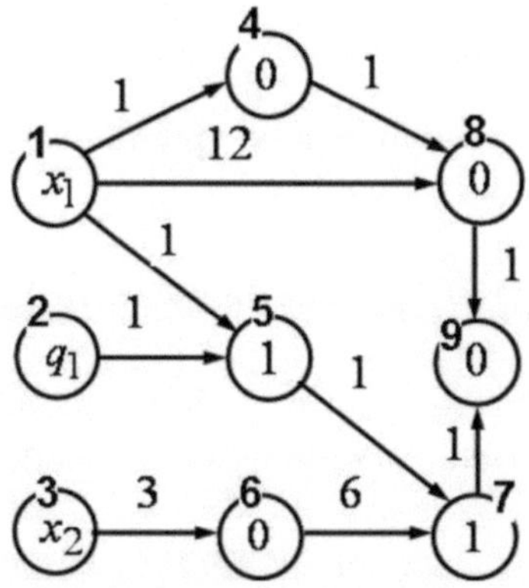

Fig. 5. Graph of mathematical equation

To calculate the mathematical equation which is presented as a graph we use additional vector of nodes $\mathbf{z}$ for storage of intermediate results. Each element of vector $\mathbf{z}$ is associated with the definite node in the graph. Initially elements of vector z_i that are associated with the source nodes have the values of variables and parameters. For example for the graph presented at Fig. 5 we have

$$\mathbf{z} = [z_1 \quad \dots \quad z_9]^T,$$

where 9 is the number of nodes in the graph. For the source nodes we set $z_1 = x_1$, $z_2 = q_1$, $z_3 = x_2$. Values of other elements z_i are equal to the unit elements for binary operations. As a result we get an initial value of vector of nodes

$$\mathbf{z} = [x_1 \quad q_1 \quad x_2 \quad 0 \quad 1 \quad 0 \quad 1 \quad 0 \quad 0]^T.$$

In the given example we use addition and multiplication. Unit element for addition is 0 and for multiplication is 1.

According to the rules of calculation, we calculate unary operation that corresponds to the edge that comes out from the node that has no incoming edges. For the edge (i, j) node i has no incoming edges at the moment. Unary operation ρ_k corresponds to the edge (i, j). Binary operation χ_l corresponds to the node j. Then we perform the following calculations

$$z_j = \chi_l\left(z_j, \rho_k(z_i)\right), \tag{9}$$

where z_j in the right part of the equation is the value on the previous step.

After calculation of (9) we delete the edge (i, j) from the graph.

If we numerate the nodes so that the number of the node where the edge comes out from is less than the number of the node that it comes in, then the calculation can be done just following the numbers of the nodes.

For the given example we have the following steps:

- edge (1,4), $z_4 = \chi_0(\rho_1(z_1), z_4) = x_1 + 0 = x_1$;
- edge (1,8), $z_8 = \chi_0(\rho_{12}(z_1), z_8) = \sin(x_1) + 0 = \sin(x_1)$;
- edge (1,5), $z_5 = \chi_1(\rho_1(z_1), z_5) = x_1 1 = x_1$;
- edge (2,5), $z_5 = \chi_1(\rho_1(q_1), z_5) = q_1 x_1$;
- edge (3,6), $z_6 = \chi_0(\rho_3(x_2), z_6) = -x_2 + 0 = -x_2$;
- edge (4,8), $z_8 = \chi_0(\rho_1(z_4), z_8) = x_1 + \sin(x_1)$;
- edge (5,7), $z_7 = \chi_1(\rho_1(z_5), z_7) = q_1 x_1 1 = q_1 x_1$;
- edge (6,7), $z_7 = \chi_1(\rho_6(z_6), z_7) = e^{-x_2} q_1 x_1$;
- edge (7,9), $z_9 = \chi_0(\rho_1(z_7), z_9) = e^{-x_2} q_1 x_1 + 0 = e^{-x_2} q_1 x_1$;
- edge (8,9), $z_9 = \chi_0(\rho_1(z_8), z_9) = x_1 + \sin(x_1) + e^{-x_2} q_1 x_1$.

When the calculations on the edge (8,9) are performed we obtain the result of initial mathematical expression.

Nodes 8 and 9 in the graph can be united since binary operations are associative and commutative. A reduced graph of mathematical equation is given on Fig. 6.

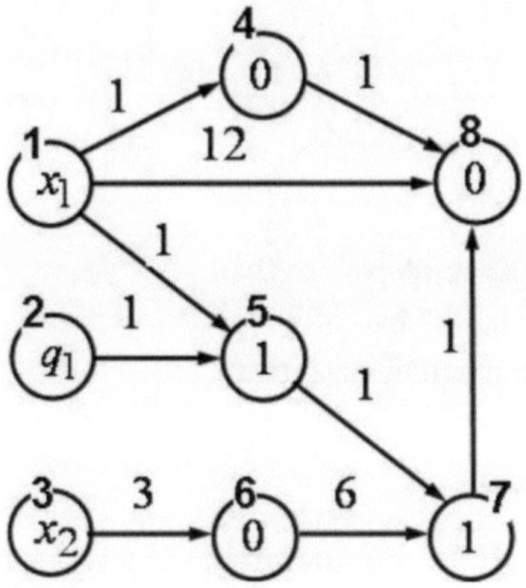

Fig. 6. Reduced graph of mathematical equation

The results of calculation for graphs presented on Fig. 5 and Fig. 6 are the same.

The result of calculation will not change if we unite two nodes that are linked by the edge that corresponds to unary identical operation and the edges that are linked to that nodes do not come in or out from the same node.

To construct the graph of mathematical equation we need as many nodes as the sum of parameters, variables and binary operations in its graphic notation. This number is enough for construction but not minimal.

The result of calculation will not change if to the sink node of the graph we add an edge with a unary identical operation and a node with binary operation and a unit element. An enlarged graph for given example is shown on Fig. 7.

A directed graph constructed form the graphic notation of mathematical equation is a network operator. One network operator can be associated with several mathematical equations. It depends on the numbers of sink nodes that are set by the researcher. In the given example if we numerate the sink nodes with numbers 7, 8, 9 then we will get three mathematical equations

$$y_1 = z_7 = e^{-x_2} q_1 x_1 ,$$

$$y_2 = z_8 = x_1 + \sin(x_1) ,$$

$$y_3 = z_9 = x_1 + \sin(x_1) + e^{-x_2} q_1 x_1 .$$

This feature of the graphic notation allows using the network operator for presentation of vector functions.

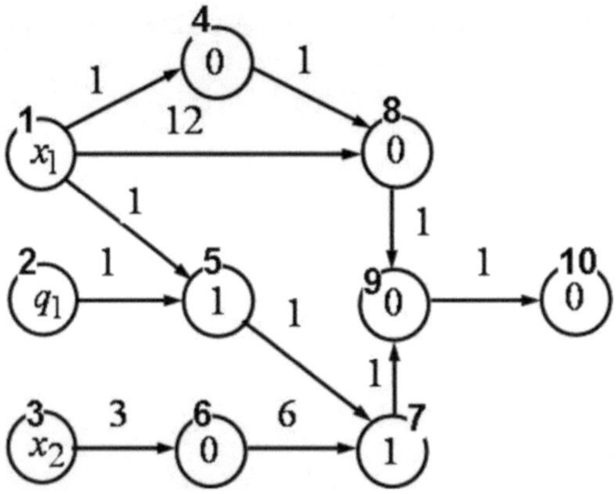

Fig. 7. Enlarged graph of mathematical equation

6. Network operator matrices

To present a network operator in the PC memory we use a network operator matrix (NOM). NOM is based on the incident matrix of the graph $\mathbf{A} = \left[a_{ij} \right]$, $a_{ij} \in \{0,1\}$, $i,j = \overline{1,L}$, where L is the number of nodes in the graph.

If we replace diagonal elements of the incident matrix with numbers of binary operations that correspond to appropriate nodes and nonzero nondiagonal elements with numbers of unary operations, we shall get NOM $\mathbf{\Psi} = \left[\psi_{ij} \right]$, $i,j = \overline{1,L}$.

For the network operator shown on the Fig. 6 we have the following NOM

$$\mathbf{A} = \begin{bmatrix} 0 & 0 & 0 & 1 & 1 & 0 & 0 & 1 \\ 0 & 0 & 0 & 0 & 1 & 0 & 0 & 0 \\ 0 & 0 & 0 & 0 & 0 & 1 & 0 & 0 \\ 0 & 0 & 0 & 0 & 0 & 0 & 0 & 1 \\ 0 & 0 & 0 & 0 & 0 & 0 & 1 & 0 \\ 0 & 0 & 0 & 0 & 0 & 0 & 1 & 0 \\ 0 & 0 & 0 & 0 & 0 & 0 & 0 & 1 \\ 0 & 0 & 0 & 0 & 0 & 0 & 0 & 0 \end{bmatrix} .$$

NOM for the graph on Fig. 6 is the following

$$\mathbf{\Psi} = \begin{bmatrix} 0 & 0 & 0 & 1 & 1 & 0 & 0 & 12 \\ 0 & 0 & 0 & 0 & 1 & 0 & 0 & 0 \\ 0 & 0 & 0 & 0 & 0 & 3 & 0 & 0 \\ 0 & 0 & 0 & 0 & 0 & 0 & 0 & 1 \\ 0 & 0 & 0 & 0 & 1 & 0 & 1 & 0 \\ 0 & 0 & 0 & 0 & 0 & 0 & 6 & 0 \\ 0 & 0 & 0 & 0 & 0 & 0 & 1 & 1 \\ 0 & 0 & 0 & 0 & 0 & 0 & 0 & 0 \end{bmatrix}.$$

NOM $\mathbf{\Psi} = \left[\psi_{i,j}\right]$, $i,j = \overline{1,L}$ is upper-triangular because of the numeration of nodes. NOM is not enough for calculation of mathematical equation since it does not contain information about parameters and variables. This information is kept in the initial values of vector of nodes

$$\mathbf{z} = [z_1 \ \ldots \ z_L]^T . \tag{10}$$

Then the calculation of mathematical equation can be done by

$$z_j = \chi_{\psi_{ij}}\left(\rho_{\psi_{ij}}(z_i), z_j\right), \text{ if } \psi_{ij} \neq 0 , \ i = \overline{1,L-1} , \ j = \overline{i+1,L} . \tag{11}$$

To calculate the mathematical equation by its NOM we need to look through all rows consequently, $i = \overline{1,L-1}$. In each row i we consider the elements that follow the diagonal element, $j = \overline{i+1,L}$. If among them we find nonzero element then we perform calculation according equation (11).

For the given NOM we get

$$\mathbf{z} = [x_1 \ q_1 \ x_2 \ 0 \ 1 \ 0 \ 1 \ 0]^T ,$$

$\psi_{1,4} = 1$, $\psi_{4,4} = 0$, $z_4 = \chi_0(\rho_1(z_1), z_4) = x_1 + 0 = x_1$;
$\psi_{1,5} = 1$, $\psi_{5,5} = 1$, $z_5 = \chi_1(\rho_1(z_1), z_5) = x_1 1 = x_1$;
$\psi_{1,8} = 12$, $\psi_{8,8} = 0$, $z_8 = \chi_0(\rho_{12}(z_1), z_8) = \sin(x_1) + 0 = \sin(x_1)$;
$\psi_{2,5} = 1$, $\psi_{5,5} = 1$, $z_5 = \chi_1(\rho_1(q_1), z_5) = q_1 x_1$;
$\psi_{3,6} = 3$, $\psi_{6,6} = 0$, $z_6 = \chi_0(\rho_3(x_2), z_6) = -x_2 + 0 = -x_2$;
$\psi_{4,8} = 1$, $\psi_{8,8} = 0$, $z_8 = \chi_0(\rho_1(z_4), z_8) = x_1 + \sin(x_1)$;
$\psi_{5,7} = 1$, $\psi_{7,7} = 1$, $z_7 = \chi_1(\rho_1(z_5), z_7) = q_1 x_1 1 = q_1 x_1$;
$\psi_{6,7} = 6$, $z_7 = \chi_1(\rho_6(z_6), z_7) = e^{-x_2} q_1 x_1$;
$\psi_{7,8} = 1$, $\psi_{8,8} = 0$, $z_8 = \chi_0(\rho_1(z_7), z_8) = e^{-x_2} q_1 x_1 + x_1 + \sin(x_1)$.

7. Variations of network operators

Similar network operators are network operators that satisfy the following conditions:

a. have the same source nodes;
b. have the same constructive sets.

Alike network operators are similar network operators that have equal numbers of nodes.

Network operators of alike structure are alike network operators that differ in unary and binary operations.

Variation of network operator is the change of network operator that leads to a similar network operator.

Simple variation of network operator is a variation that cannot be presented as a complex of other variations.

Simple variations of network operator are given in Table 3.

Number of simple variation	Simple variation
0	replacement of unary operation on the edge
1	replacement of binary operation in the node
2	addition of the edge with a unary operation
3	deletion of the edge if the node where this edge comes in has at least one more incoming edge
4	Increase of the node number
5	Decrease of the node number
6	addition of the node with a binary operation and incoming edge with unary operation
7	deletion of the sink node with incoming edge if this edge is single.

Table 3. Simple variations of network operator

Structural variation of network operator is a variation that changes the set of edges of network operator.

Structural variations change the incident matrix of the graph. In the Table 3 structural variations are 2 – 5. Variations 0, 1 do not change the incident matrix and lead to network operators of alike structure.

A complete network operator is a network operator in which we cannot perform variation 2.

A complete network operator contains L nodes in which the number of source nodes is $N+P$, maximum number of edges is equal to

$$|C| = \frac{(L-N-P)(L+N+P-1)}{2}. \tag{12}$$

If we apply variation 2, addition of an edge, to any network operator, then we can construct a full network operator which is alike initial network operator.

If we apply variation 3, deletion of an edge, to the complete network operator, then we can construct any alike network operator.

Any variation of network operator can be performed by a finite number of simple variations.

An eigen variation of network operator is a variation that does not change the number of nodes in the network operator.

In the Table 3 eigen variations are 0 – 5.

Any eigen variation of the network operator can be performed by a finite number of simple eigen variations.

To present any simple variation we use a variation vector

$$\mathbf{w} = [w_1 \, w_2 \, w_3 \, w_4]^T , \tag{13}$$

where w_1 is the number of variation from Table 3, w_2, w_3, w_4 are elements that integer values depend on the number of variation.

Values of elements of variation vector are given in Table 4. In case the values of elements are not defined they can take any values. For example when $w_1 = 1$ element w_2 can keep the number of the node where this edge comes in $w_2 = w_3$.

Variation of network operator is presented as

$$\tilde{\mathbf{\Psi}} = \mathbf{w} \circ \mathbf{\Psi} ,$$

where $\mathbf{\Psi}$ is the NOM before variation is performed, $\tilde{\mathbf{\Psi}}$ is the NOM after variation was performed.

Number of variation w_1	Number of the node where the edge comes out	Number of the node where the edge comes in	Number of unary operation	Number of binary operation
0	w_2	w_3	w_4	-
1	-	w_3	-	w_4
2	w_2	w_3	w_4	-
3	w_2	w_3	-	-
4	w_2	-	-	-
5	w_2	-	-	-
6	w_2	-	w_3	w_4
7	-	w_3	-	-

Table 4. Elements of variation vector

Consider examples of variations of network operator. We have a network operator that describes mathematical equation

$$y = \frac{q_1 x_1^3}{\sqrt[3]{x_1^2 + x_2^2}} .$$

Network operator matrix for the given equation is

$$\mathbf{\Psi} = \begin{bmatrix} 0 & 0 & 0 & 1 & 0 & 0 & 0 \\ 0 & 0 & 0 & 14 & 2 & 0 & 0 \\ 0 & 0 & 0 & 0 & 2 & 0 & 0 \\ 0 & 0 & 0 & 1 & 0 & 0 & 1 \\ 0 & 0 & 0 & 0 & 0 & 15 & 0 \\ 0 & 0 & 0 & 0 & 0 & 0 & 5 \\ 0 & 0 & 0 & 0 & 0 & 0 & 1 \end{bmatrix}.$$

Suppose we have a variation vector $\mathbf{w} = [2\ 4\ 6\ 2]^T$. Element $w_1 = 2$ shows that we perform addition of the edge. According to Table 3 a new edge should come out from the node 4, come in the node 6 and have unary operation 2.

As a result we have NOM

$$\tilde{\mathbf{\Psi}} = \mathbf{w} \circ \mathbf{\Psi} = \begin{bmatrix} 0 & 0 & 0 & 1 & 0 & 0 & 0 \\ 0 & 0 & 0 & 14 & 2 & 0 & 0 \\ 0 & 0 & 0 & 0 & 2 & 0 & 0 \\ 0 & 0 & 0 & 1 & 0 & 2 & 1 \\ 0 & 0 & 0 & 0 & 0 & 15 & 0 \\ 0 & 0 & 0 & 0 & 0 & 0 & 5 \\ 0 & 0 & 0 & 0 & 0 & 0 & 1 \end{bmatrix}.$$

NOM $\tilde{\mathbf{\Psi}}$ corresponds to the following mathematical equation

$$y = \frac{q_1 x_1^3}{\sqrt[3]{x_1^2 + x_2^2 + \left(q_1 x_1^3\right)^2}}.$$

Suppose variation vectors $\mathbf{w}^1 = [0\ 4\ 7\ 11]^T$ and $\mathbf{w}^2 = [0\ 6\ 7\ 1]^T$ are given. The first component of these vectors $w_1 = 0$ shows the replacement of unary operation on the edge. The second and the third components show the edge between the nodes. The first vector points to the edge $(4,7)$, the second – to the edge $(6,7)$. The forth element contains the number of new unary operation. According to Table 1 this operation for vector $\mathbf{w}^1$ is $\rho_{11}(z) = \cos(z)$, for vector $\mathbf{w}^2$ is $\rho_1(z) = z$. As a result we obtain NOM

$$\tilde{\mathbf{\Psi}} = \mathbf{w}^2 \circ \mathbf{w}^1 \circ \mathbf{\Psi} = \begin{bmatrix} 0 & 0 & 0 & 1 & 0 & 0 & 0 \\ 0 & 0 & 0 & 14 & 2 & 0 & 0 \\ 0 & 0 & 0 & 0 & 2 & 0 & 0 \\ 0 & 0 & 0 & 1 & 0 & 0 & 11 \\ 0 & 0 & 0 & 0 & 0 & 15 & 0 \\ 0 & 0 & 0 & 0 & 0 & 0 & 1 \\ 0 & 0 & 0 & 0 & 0 & 0 & 1 \end{bmatrix}.$$

NOM $\tilde{\mathbf{\Psi}}$ corresponds to

$$y = \cos\left(q_1 x_1^3\right)\sqrt[3]{x_1^2 + x_2^2}.$$

Consider the examples of improper variations that change the number of nodes in the network operator. We have a variation vector $\mathbf{w} = [6\ 4\ 7\ 0]^T$. Number of variation $w_1 = 6$ shows that we add the node with binary operation $w_4 = 0$ and an outcoming edge with unary operation $w_3 = 7$. After variation we obtain the NOM

$$\tilde{\mathbf{\Psi}} = \mathbf{w} \circ \mathbf{\Psi} = \begin{bmatrix} 0 & 0 & 0 & 1 & 0 & 0 & 0 & 0 \\ 0 & 0 & 0 & 14 & 2 & 0 & 0 & 0 \\ 0 & 0 & 0 & 0 & 2 & 0 & 0 & 0 \\ 0 & 0 & 0 & 1 & 0 & 0 & 1 & 7 \\ 0 & 0 & 0 & 0 & 0 & 15 & 0 & 0 \\ 0 & 0 & 0 & 0 & 0 & 0 & 5 & 0 \\ 0 & 0 & 0 & 0 & 0 & 0 & 0 & 0 \\ 0 & 0 & 0 & 0 & 0 & 0 & 0 & 0 \end{bmatrix}.$$

This NOM corresponds to the graph with two sink nodes and it presents at least two mathematical equations

$$y_1 = \frac{q_1 x_1^3}{\sqrt[3]{x_1^2 + x_2^2}},\ y_2 = \ln\left|q_1 x_1^3\right|.$$

Let us given variation vectors $\mathbf{w}^1 = [3\ 6\ 7\ 0]^T$ and $\mathbf{w}^2 = [5\ 7\ 0\ 0]^T$. In the first vector $w_1^1 = 3$, that is why we delete the edge between nodes $w_2^1 = 6$ and $w_3^1 = 7$. In the second vector $w_1^2 = 5$, and we delete the node $w_2^2 = 7$ with its incoming edge. As a result we have

$$\tilde{\mathbf{\Psi}} = \mathbf{w}^2 \circ \mathbf{w}^1 \circ \mathbf{\Psi} = \begin{bmatrix} 0 & 0 & 0 & 1 & 0 & 0 \\ 0 & 0 & 0 & 14 & 2 & 0 \\ 0 & 0 & 0 & 0 & 2 & 0 \\ 0 & 0 & 0 & 1 & 0 & 0 \\ 0 & 0 & 0 & 0 & 0 & 15 \\ 0 & 0 & 0 & 0 & 0 & 0 \end{bmatrix}.$$

This NOM corresponds to two mathematical equations

$$y_1 = q_1 x_1^3,\ y_2 = \sqrt[3]{x_1^2 + x_2^2}.$$

Since we have changed the graph we obtain two mathematical equations. Network operator is presented on Fig. 8.

Performance of variations is not always possible. If variation cannot be done then it is omitted. For example we have a variation vector $\mathbf{w} = [0\ 4\ 6\ 2]^T$. The first component shows variation 0, replacement of unary operation. However there is no edge between nodes $w_2 = 4$ and $w_3 = 6$, that is why this variation is not performed and NOM is not changed

$$\mathbf{\Psi} = \mathbf{w} \circ \mathbf{\Psi}.$$

For proper variations variation $w_1 = 3$ is not performed if one of the following conditions is fulfilled:

- edge (w_2, w_3) is absent;
- there are no other incoming edges to the node where the edge (w_2, w_3) comes in;
- there are no other outcoming edges from the node where the edge (w_2, w_3) comes out.

A structural distance between two similar network operators is a minimal number of single variations that should be performed to obtain one network operator from the other. A structural distance between network operator $\mathbf{\Psi}^1$ and network operator $\mathbf{\Psi}^2$ is equal to a structural distance between network operators $\mathbf{\Psi}^2$ and $\mathbf{\Psi}^1$.

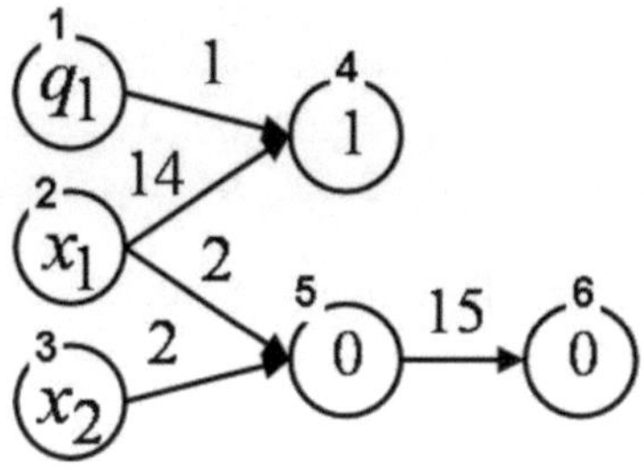

Fig. 8. Network operator after variations

8. Search of optimal mathematic equation

Let us formulate the problem of search of optimal mathematical equation $\mathbf{g}(\mathbf{x},\mathbf{q})$. It is necessary to find mathematical equation $\mathbf{g}(\mathbf{x},\mathbf{q})$, that provides minimums of object functions with restrictions

$$\min f_i(\mathbf{x},\mathbf{g}(\mathbf{x},\mathbf{q})),\ i = \overline{0,D}, \tag{14}$$

$$f_j(\mathbf{x},\mathbf{g}(\mathbf{x},\mathbf{q})) \le 0,\ j = \overline{D+1,K}, \tag{15}$$

where $\mathbf{x}$ is a vector of variables, $\mathbf{q}$ is a vector of parameters.

The solution to the problem (14), (15) is a mathematical equation $\tilde{\mathbf{g}}(\mathbf{x},\tilde{\mathbf{q}})$. Mathematical equation $\mathbf{g}(\mathbf{x},\mathbf{q})$ is a function

$$\mathbf{g}(\mathbf{x},\mathbf{q}) = \left[g_1(\mathbf{x},\mathbf{q}) \ldots g_M(\mathbf{x},\mathbf{q})\right]^T. \tag{16}$$

If $D \ge 1$, then the solution of the problem is a Pareto set

$$\Pi = \left\{\tilde{\mathbf{g}}^{i_k}(\mathbf{x},\tilde{\mathbf{q}}):\ k = \overline{1,s}\right\},$$

where $\forall \mathbf{g}^k(\mathbf{x},\mathbf{q}) \notin \Pi\ \ \exists \tilde{\mathbf{g}}^j(\mathbf{x},\tilde{\mathbf{q}}) \in \Pi$, $\mathbf{f}^0(\tilde{\mathbf{g}}^j(\mathbf{x},\tilde{\mathbf{q}})) \le \mathbf{f}^0(\mathbf{g}^k(\mathbf{x},\mathbf{q}))$, $0 \le j \le D$, $\mathbf{f}^0(\mathbf{g}(\mathbf{x},\mathbf{q})) = \left[f_0(\mathbf{g}(\mathbf{x},\mathbf{q})) \ldots f_D(\mathbf{g}(\mathbf{x},\mathbf{q}))\right]^T$, $\mathbf{f}^0(\mathbf{g}^j(\mathbf{x},\mathbf{q})) \le \mathbf{f}^0(\mathbf{g}^k(\mathbf{x},\mathbf{q}))$, if $f_i(\mathbf{g}^j(\mathbf{x},\mathbf{q})) \le f_i(\mathbf{g}^k(\mathbf{x},\mathbf{q}))$, $i = \overline{0,D}$, and $\exists f_l(\mathbf{g}^j(\mathbf{x},\mathbf{q})) < f_l(\mathbf{g}^k(\mathbf{x},\mathbf{q}))$.

To solve the problem (14), (15) we need to define a finite set of network operators, and in this set find the best solution accoding to (14).

In the set of network operators we choose a basic network operator. Basic network operator corresponds to the basic NOM $\mathbf{\Psi}^0$ and the basic mathematical equation $\mathbf{g}^0(\mathbf{x},\mathbf{q}^0)$, where $\mathbf{q}^0 = \left[q_1^0 \ldots q_P^0\right]^T$ is a vector of parameters.

Let us introduce a finite ordered set of variation vectors

$$\mathrm{W} = \left(\mathbf{w}^1,\ldots,\mathbf{w}^l\right), \tag{17}$$

where l is a cardinal number of W, $\mathbf{w}^i = \left[w_1^i \ldots w_4^i\right]^T$ is a variation vector, $i = \overline{1,l}$.

To construct the set of network operators we use a basic matrix $\mathbf{\Psi}^0$ and all possible sets W of variation vectors.

9. Genetic algorithm for method of variations of basic solution

Consider genetic algorithm that searches both structure and parameters of mathematical equation.

Initially we set the basic solution

$$\mathbf{\Psi}^0 = \left[\psi_{ij}^0\right], \; i,j = \overline{1,L}. \tag{18}$$

We generate the ordered sets of variation vectors

$$\mathrm{W}^i = \left(\mathbf{w}^{i,1},\ldots,\mathbf{w}^{i,l}\right), \; i = \overline{1,H}, \tag{19}$$

$$\mathbf{w}^{i,j} = \left[w_1^{i,j} \quad w_2^{i,j} \quad w_3^{i,j} \quad w_4^{i,j}\right]^T, \; i = \overline{1,H}, \; j = \overline{1,l}, \tag{20}$$

where H is a number of possible solutions in the population.

We generate bit strings for parameters

$$\mathbf{s}^i = \left[s_1^i \ldots s_{P(c+d)}^i\right]^T, \; i = \overline{1,H}, \tag{21}$$

where P is the number of parameters, c is the number of bits for the integer part of the value, and d is the number of bits for the fractional part.

For each chromosome $\left(\mathrm{W}^i,\mathbf{s}^i\right)$, $1 \le i \le H$, we define the values of object functions. We construct NOM using $\mathrm{W}^i = \left(\mathbf{w}^{i,1},\ldots,\mathbf{w}^{i,l}\right)$ and $\mathbf{\Psi}^0$

$$\mathbf{\Psi}^i = \mathbf{w}^{i,l} \circ \ldots \circ \mathbf{w}^{i,1} \circ \mathbf{\Psi}^0. \tag{22}$$

We present parametrical part of the chromosome $\mathbf{s}^i = \left[s_1^i \ldots s_{P(c+d)}^i\right]^T$, $1 \le i \le H$, as a vector of parameters. We present a bit string $\mathbf{s}^i$ from the Gray code to the binary code

$$\mathbf{b}^i = \left[b_1^i \ldots b_{P(c+d)}^i\right]^T, \tag{23}$$

$$b_j^i = \begin{cases} s_j^i, & \text{if } (j-1) \bmod (c+d) = 0 \\ s_j^i \oplus b_{j-1}^i, & \text{otherwise} \end{cases}, \quad j = \overline{1, P(c+d)}. \tag{24}$$

From the binary code we obtain the vector of parameters

$$\mathbf{q}^i = \left[q_1^i \dots q_P^i\right]^T, \tag{25}$$

$$q_k^i = \sum_{j=1}^{c+d} 2^{c-j} b_{j+(k-1)(c+d)}^i, \quad k = \overline{1, P}. \tag{26}$$

To estimate each possible solution $\mathbf{\Psi}^i$ and $\mathbf{q}^i$ we use parameter which is called a distance to a Pareto set.

A distance to a Pareto set is a number of possible solutions that are better in terms of Pareto than the current solution.

For each solution $\left(\mathrm{W}^j, \mathbf{s}^j\right)$, $1 \le j \le H$ we find mathematical equation $\mathbf{g}^j\left(\mathbf{x}, \mathbf{q}^j\right)$ and calculate the values of object functions (14)

$$\mathbf{f}^j = \left[f_0^j \dots f_D^j\right]^T, \tag{27}$$

In the set we find the number of possible solutions that are better than the solution $\left(\mathrm{W}^j, \mathbf{s}^j\right)$

$$\Lambda_j = \sum_{i=1}^{H} \lambda_i\left(\mathbf{f}^j\right), \tag{28}$$

where

$$\lambda_i\left(\mathbf{f}^j\right) = \begin{cases} 1, \text{ if } \mathbf{f}^i \le \mathbf{f}^j \\ 0, \text{ otherwise} \end{cases}. \tag{29}$$

To construct new solutions we perform genetic operations of selection, crossover and mutation.

We randomly choose two solutions $\left(\mathrm{W}^{i_1}, \mathbf{s}^{i_1}\right)$, $\left(\mathrm{W}^{i_2}, \mathbf{s}^{i_2}\right)$ and perform a crossover with probability

$$p_c = \max\left\{\frac{1+\gamma\Lambda_{i_1}}{1+\Lambda_{i_1}}, \frac{1+\gamma\Lambda_{i_2}}{1+\Lambda_{i_2}}\right\}, \tag{30}$$

where γ is a given crossover parameter, $0 < \gamma < 1$.

After crossover is performed in two points k_p, k_s we obtain four new solutions $\left(\mathrm{W}^{H+1}, \mathbf{s}^{H+1}\right)$, $\left(\mathrm{W}^{H+2}, \mathbf{s}^{H+2}\right)$, $\left(\mathrm{W}^{H+2}, \mathbf{s}^{H+3}\right)$, $\left(\mathrm{W}^{H+4}, \mathbf{s}^{H+4}\right)$

$$\mathrm{W}^{H+1} = \mathrm{W}^{i_1}, \tag{31}$$

$$\mathbf{s}^{H+1} = \left[s_1^{i_1} \ldots s_{k_p}^{i_1} s_{k_p+1}^{i_2} \ldots s_{P(c+d)}^{i_2} \right]^T , \quad (32)$$

$$W^{H+2} = W^{i_2} , \quad (33)$$

$$\mathbf{s}^{H+2} = \left[s_1^{i_2} \ldots s_{k_p}^{i_2} s_{k_p+1}^{i_1} \ldots s_{P(c+d)}^{i_1} \right]^T , \quad (34)$$

$$W^{H+3} = \left(\mathbf{w}^{i_1,1}, \ldots, \mathbf{w}^{i_1,k_s-1}, \mathbf{w}^{i_2,k_s}, \ldots, \mathbf{w}^{i_2,l} \right) , \quad (35)$$

$$\mathbf{s}^{H+3} = \left[s_1^{i_1} \ldots s_{k_p}^{i_1} s_{k_p+1}^{i_2} \ldots s_{P(c+d)}^{i_2} \right]^T , \quad (36)$$

$$W^{H+4} = \left(\mathbf{w}^{i_2,1}, \ldots, \mathbf{w}^{i_2,k_s-1}, \mathbf{w}^{i_1,k_s}, \ldots, \mathbf{w}^{i_1,l} \right) , \quad (37)$$

$$\mathbf{s}^{H+4} = \left[s_1^{i_2} \ldots s_{k_p}^{i_2} s_{k_p+1}^{i_1} \ldots s_{P(c+d)}^{i_1} \right]^T . \quad (38)$$

For each new solution $\left(W^{H+i}, \mathbf{s}^{H+i} \right)$, $i = \overline{1,4}$, we perform a mutation with probability $p_m \in [0,1]$. We find the points of mutation m_s, m_p for both parts of new solutions. In the new chromosome $\left(W^{H+i}, \mathbf{s}^{H+i} \right)$, $1 \le i \le 4$, we randomly generate a variation vector $\mathbf{w}_{m_s}^{H+i}$ with structural and parametric parts. For each new solutions we calculate the functions (14)

$$\mathbf{f}^{H+i} = \left[f_0^{H+i} \ldots f_D^{H+i} \right]^T , \; i = \overline{1,4} . \quad (39)$$

For a new solution j we find the distance to Pareto set Λ_{H+j} according to (28). Then we find the solution with a maximum distance to Pareto set

$$\Lambda_{i_+} = \max\left\{ \Lambda_i, i = \overline{1,H} \right\} , \quad (40)$$

where i_+ is a number of solution with maximum distance to Pareto set.

We compare new solution to the solution that has maximum distance to Pareto set

$$\Lambda_{H+j} < \Lambda_{i_+} . \quad (41)$$

If (41) is fulfilled then we replace the solution with a maximum distance by the first new solution $W^{i_+} = W^{H+j}$, $\mathbf{s}^{i_+} = \mathbf{s}^{H+j}$, $\mathbf{f}^{i_+} = \mathbf{f}^{H+j}$, and recalculate the distances for all solutions in the set.

These steps are performed for each new possible solution $\left(W^{H+j}, \mathbf{s}^{H+j} \right)$, $j = \overline{1,4}$.

The steps are repeated starting from the selection of possible solutions. After several given E iterations, where E is called epoch, we change basic solution $\mathbf{\Psi}^0$.

As a new basic solution we can take the solution that has minimum of function

$$\tilde{\mathbf{f}}^{i_-} = \min\left\{ \sqrt{\sum_{j=0}^{D} \left(\tilde{f}_j^i \right)^2} \right\} , \quad (42)$$

where i_- is the number of new basic solution, $\tilde{\mathbf{f}}^i = \left[\tilde{f}_0^i \dots \tilde{f}_D^i\right]^T$, $i = \overline{1,H}$, $\tilde{f}_j^i = \frac{f_j^i - f_j^-}{f_j^+ - f_j^-}$, $j = \overline{0,D}$, $f_j^+ = \max\left\{f_j^i, i = \overline{1,H}\right\}$, $f_j^- = \min\left\{f_j^i, i = \overline{1,H}\right\}$, $j = \overline{0,D}$.

For the more rapid search we use a subset of elite solutions $\left(\mathrm{W}^{i_e}, \mathbf{s}^{i_e}\right)$, $1 \le i_e \le H$. In this subset we calculate the values of functional after each variation $\mathbf{f}^{i_e}\left(\mathbf{\Psi}^{i_e,k}, \mathbf{s}^{i_e}\right)$,

$$\mathbf{\Psi}^{i_e,k} = \mathbf{w}^{i_e,k} \circ \dots \circ \mathbf{w}^{i_e,1} \circ \mathbf{\Psi}^0,\ 1 \le k \le d. \tag{43}$$

We find variation of the solution that leads to minimum distance to Pareto set $\Lambda_{i_e}\left(\mathbf{f}^{i_e,k}\right)$.

$$\Lambda_{i_e}\left(\mathbf{f}^{i_e,k_-}\right) = \min\left\{\Lambda_{i_e}\left(\mathbf{f}^{i_e,k}\right), k = \overline{1,d}\right\}, \tag{44}$$

where k_- is the number of desired variation. Other variations for possible solution i_e are replaced by zeros. The calculation is terminated after given number of loops.

Consider an example. It is necessary to find inverse function for mathematical equation

$$x = \cos\left(y^2\right) + \sqrt[3]{y}\ .$$

The solution is presented in the form $y = g(x, \mathbf{q})$, where $\mathbf{q}$ is a vector of parameters.

After substitution of found mathematical equation $g(x, \mathbf{q})$ in initial function we should obtain the identity

$$x \equiv \cos\left(g^2(x, \mathbf{q})\right) + \sqrt[3]{g(x, \mathbf{q})}\ .$$

Let us set a finite number of points

$$T = \left\{x^j : j = \overline{1,S}\right\}$$

and define two object functions

$$f_1 = \sqrt{\sum_{j=1}^{S}\left(x^j - \cos\left(g^2\left(x^j, \mathbf{q}\right)\right) - \sqrt[3]{g\left(x^j, \mathbf{q}\right)}\right)^2} \to \min,$$

$$f_2 = \max_j\left\{\left|x^j - \cos\left(g^2\left(x^j, \mathbf{q}\right)\right) - \sqrt[3]{g\left(x^j, \mathbf{q}\right)}\right| : j = \overline{1,S}\right\} \to \min.$$

Note that for exact solution we have $f_1 = 0$ and $f_2 = 0$.

Let us choose the following basic solution

$$y = q_1 x + q_2,$$

where $q_1 = 1$, $q_2 = 1$.

Network operator for basic solution is presented on Fig. 9.

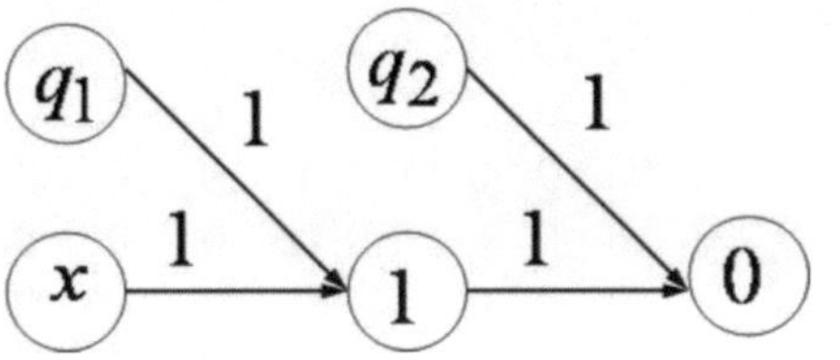

Fig. 9. Example of basic network operator

To construct a basic network operator we need 5 nodes, but if we want to enlarge the search space we add 3 nodes with addition operations and its unit elements. We get the network operator presented on Fig. 10.

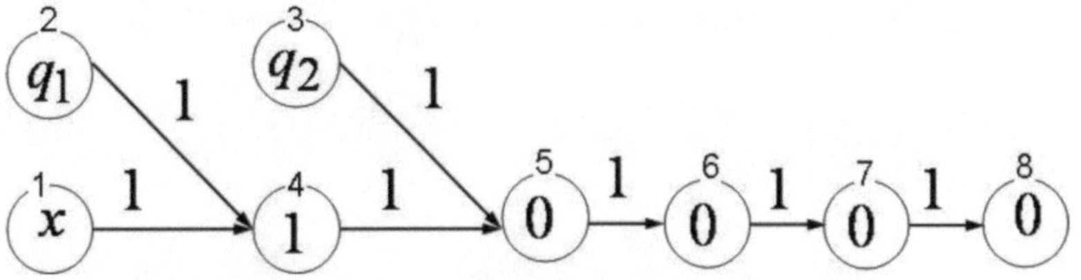

Fig. 10. An expanded basic network operator

NOM for graph shown on Fig. 10 is

$$\mathbf{\Psi}^0 = \begin{bmatrix} 0 & 0 & 0 & 1 & 0 & 0 & 0 & 0 \\ 0 & 0 & 0 & 1 & 0 & 0 & 0 & 0 \\ 0 & 0 & 0 & 0 & 1 & 0 & 0 & 0 \\ 0 & 0 & 0 & 1 & 1 & 0 & 0 & 0 \\ 0 & 0 & 0 & 0 & 0 & 1 & 0 & 0 \\ 0 & 0 & 0 & 0 & 0 & 0 & 1 & 0 \\ 0 & 0 & 0 & 0 & 0 & 0 & 0 & 1 \\ 0 & 0 & 0 & 0 & 0 & 0 & 0 & 0 \end{bmatrix}.$$

A genetic algorithm had the following values of parameters: number of chromosomes in initial population $H = 1024$, number of crossing couples in one generation 256, number of generations 128, number vectors of variations in one chromosome 8, number of generations between the change of basic solutions 22, number of elite chromosomes 8, probability of mutation $p_m = 0.8$, parameter for crossing $\gamma = 0.4$, number of parameters 2, number of bits for integer part $c = 2$, number of bits for fractional part $d = 6$, number of points $S = 11$. We obtained a Pareto set which is represented on Fig 11 and in the Table 5.

For example we take the solution no 310.

$$f_1\left(g^{310}(x,\mathbf{q})\right) = 0.32447275,\; f_2\left(g^{310}(x,\mathbf{q})\right) = 0.121647.$$

For this solution we have obtained the following values of parameters $q_1 = 3.14063$, $q_2 = 0.84375$.

The solution 310 is the network operator

$$\mathbf{\Psi}^{310} = \begin{bmatrix} 0 & 0 & 0 & 1 & 0 & 0 & 0 & 0 \\ 0 & 0 & 0 & 11 & 0 & 0 & 0 & 0 \\ 0 & 0 & 0 & 0 & 1 & 0 & 0 & 0 \\ 0 & 0 & 0 & 1 & 12 & 0 & 0 & 0 \\ 0 & 0 & 0 & 0 & 0 & 12 & 15 & 0 \\ 0 & 0 & 0 & 0 & 0 & 0 & 1 & 15 \\ 0 & 0 & 0 & 0 & 0 & 0 & 1 & 1 \\ 0 & 0 & 0 & 0 & 0 & 0 & 0 & 1 \end{bmatrix}.$$

or the function

$$g^{310}(x,\mathbf{q}) = \sin\left(\sin\left(x\cos\left(q_1\right)\right) + q_2\right)\sqrt[3]{\left(\sin\left(x\cos\left(q_1\right)\right) + q_2\right)^2}.$$

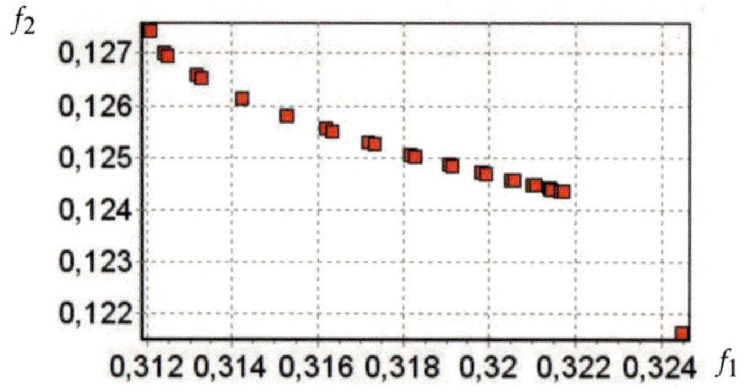

Fig. 11. A Pareto set

If we substitute our solution in initial mathematical expression then we have to obtain identity,

$$\tilde{x} = \cos\left(\left(g^{310}(x,\mathbf{q})\right)^2\right) + \sqrt[3]{\left(g^{310}(x,\mathbf{q})\right)}.$$

The graphs of the functions $\tilde{x}$ and identity function are represented on the Fig 12

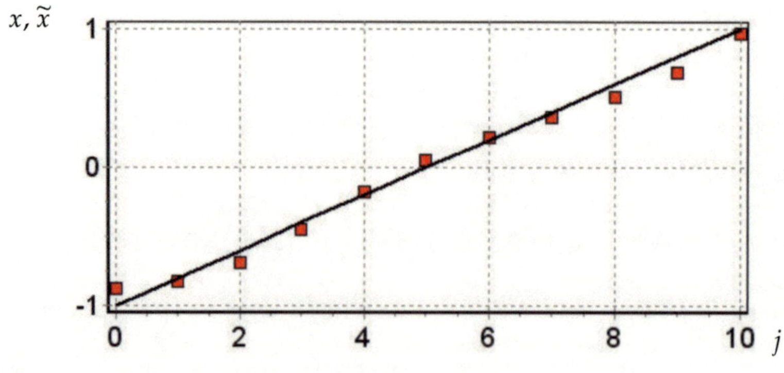

Fig 12. The graph of the function for the solution no 310

No	No of solution	f_1	f_2
1	27	0.31208313	0.12743371
2	469	0.3124092	0.12701286
3	36	0.31248842	0.12695655
4	366	0.31317121	0.12657987
5	492	0.3132807	0.12652959
6	122	0.31423625	0.12614932
7	412	0.31526313	0.12581255
8	173	0.31617553	0.12555099
9	868	0.31630362	0.12551643
10	472	0.31719342	0.12528834
11	494	0.31731617	0.12525837
12	18	0.31815508	0.12506176
13	106	0.31826894	0.1250361
14	624	0.31903468	0.12486921
15	54	0.31981169	0.12470895
16	180	0.31989995	0.12469127
17	132	0.32046985	0.12457951
18	560	0.32054244	0.12456557
19	539	0.32099647	0.12447971
20	205	0.32105204	0.12446936
21	288	0.321382	0.12440861
22	141	0.32141958	0.12440176
23	696	0.32161979	0.12436553
24	658	0.32163874	0.12436213
25	621	0.32170585	0.12435009
26	310	0.32447275	0.121647

Table 5.

10. Conclusion

In this work the new approach to the problem of automatic search of mathematical equations was considered. The researcher defines the sets of operations, variables and parameters. The computer program generates a number of mathematical equations that satisfy given restrictions. Then the optimization algorithm finds the structure of appropriate mathematical expression and its parameters. The approach is based on the new data structure the network operator.

If we replace the set of unary and binary operations in the network operator by the set of logic operations, then we can perform the search of the most suitable logic function (Alnovani et al. 2011).

11. Limitations & development

Presentation of the network operator as a matrix is limited by its dimension.

In the problems where mathematical equations have many variables and parameters, it is necessary to use big network operator matrices with many zero elements.

To exclude this limitation it is possible to divide one network operator with a considerable number of nodes into some small network operators. We receive the multilayer network operator and some matrices of smaller dimensions. Each layer of the network operator describes a part of mathematical equation.

Further development of the network operator is a creation of a special data structure for presentation of the network operator in memory of the computer. Such structure can be multilayered and provide effective parallel calculation.

12. References

Alnovani G.H.A., Diveev A.I., Pupkov K.A., Sofronova E.A. (2011) Control Synthesis for Traffic Simulation in the Urban Road Network, *Preprints of the 18-th IFAC World Congress.* Milan (Italy) August 28 – September 2. pp. 2196-2201.

Callan R. (1999) *The essence of neural networks.* The Prentice Hall Europe, 1999, ISBN 0-13-908732-X, 978-013-9087-32-5. 232 p.

Demuth, H.; Beale, M.; Hagan, M. (2008) *Neural Network Toolbox™ User's Guide.* The MathWorks, Inc. ISBN 0-9717321-0-8. 907 p.

Diveev A.I. (2009) A multiobjective synthesis of optimal control system by the network operator method. *Proceedings of international conference «Optimization and applications»* (OPTIMA) Petrovac, Montenegro, September 21-25, pp. 21-22.

Diveev A.I., Sofronova E.A. (2009) Numerical method of network operator for multi-objective synthesis of optimal control system, *Proceedings of Seventh International Conference on Control and Automation* (ICCA'09) Christchurch, New Zealand, December 9-11. pp. 701-708. ISBN 978-1-4244-4707-7.

Diveev A.I., Sofronova E.A. (2009) The Synthesis of Optimal Control System by the Network Operator Method, *Proceedings of IFAC Workshop on Control Applications of Optimization CAO'09*, 6 - 8 May, University of Jyväskylä, Agora, Finland.

Diveyev A.I., Sofronova E.A. (2008) Application of network operator method for synthesis of optimal structure and parameters of automatic control system, *Proceedings of 17-th IFAC World Congress*, Seoul, 05. - 12. July . pp. 6106 – 6113.

Kahaner, D.; Moler, C.; Nash, S. (1989) *Numerical methods and software* Prentice Hall Incorporation ISBN 0-13-6272-58-4. 504p.

Koza, J.R. (1992). *Genetic Programming: On the Programming of Computers by Means of Natural Selection*, MIT Press. ISBN 0-262-11170-5. 840 p.

Koza, J.R. (1994). *Genetic Programming II: Automatic Discovery of Reusable Programs*, MIT Press. ISBN 0-262-11189-6. 768 p.

Koza, J.R.; Bennett, F.H.; Andre, D. & Keane, M.A. (1999). *Genetic Programming III: Darwinian Invention and Problem Solving*, Morgan Kaufmann. ISBN 1-55860-543-6. 1154 p.

Koza, J.R.; Keane, M.A.; Streeter, M.J.; Mydlowec, W.; Yu, J.; Lanza, G. (2003). *Genetic Programming IV: Routine Human-Competitive Machine Intelligence*, Springer. ISBN 1-4020-7446-8. 590 p.

3

Performance of Simple Genetic Algorithm Inserting Forced Inheritance Mechanism and Parameters Relaxation

Esther Lugo-González, Emmanuel A. Merchán-Cruz,
Luis H. Hernández-Gómez, Rodolfo Ponce-Reynoso,
Christopher R. Torres-San Miguel and Javier Ramírez-Gordillo
Instituto Politécnico Nacional Escuela Superior de Ingeniería Mecánica y Eléctrica
México

1. Introduction

Genetic Algorithms (GA) are powerful tools to solve large scale design optimization problems. The research interests in GA lie in both its theory and application. On one hand, various modifications have been made to allow them to solve problems faster, more accurately and more reliably.

Genetic Algorithms are a search paradigm that applies principles of evolutionary biology (crossover, mutation, natural selection) in order to deal with intractable search spaces. The power and success of GA are mostly achieved by the diversity with the individuals of a population which evolve, in parallel, following the principle of the survival of the fittest. In general, the genetic algorithms resolve combinatorial optimization problems that in (Goldberg, 1989) are mentioned, this implies a large number of responses associated with an exponential growth in solutions potentially feasible according to the magnitude of the problem. In a standard GA the diversity of the individuals is obtained and maintained using the genetic operators crossover and mutation which allow the GA to find feasible solutions and avoid premature convergence to a local maximum (Holland, 1975).

The performance of a genetic algorithm, like any global optimization algorithm, depends on the mechanism for balancing the two conflicting objectives, which are exploiting the best solutions found so far and at the same time exploring the search space for promising solutions. The power of genetic algorithms comes from their ability to combine both exploration and exploitation in an optimal way (Holland, 1975). However, although this optimal utilization may be theoretically true for a genetic algorithm, there are problems in practice. These arise because of Holland assumed that the population size is infinite, that the fitness function accurately reflects the suitability of a solution, and that the interactions between genes are very small (Beasley et al., 1993).

The evolutionary algorithm proposed in this paper is composed by a classic genetic algorithms along with the forced inheritance mechanism proposed by (Merchán-Cruz, 2005, Merchán-Cruz et al., 2008, Merchán-Cruz et al., 2007) and the regeneration mechanisms by

(Ramírez-Gordillo, 2010, Lugo González, 2010), for optimizing the trajectory generation in closed chain mechanisms and planning the effects that it has on the mechanism by relaxing some parameters. The objective is to show the behavior of relaxing the parameters of the GA's, observing what advantages and disadvantages appear when varying some parameter exceeding the recommended values established in the literature.

2. Genetic Algorithm description

Once the problem encoding and the fitness functions have been chosen, the evolution process begin. To evolve new solutions, an initial population of encoded solutions is created randomly or using some problem-specific knowledge. This population is subjected to genetic operators to create new promising solutions.

A typical genetic algorithm starts with a randomly generated population composed by genes, locus, allele, chromosome, genotype, variables and phenotype (Holland, 1975, Goldberg, 1989, Michalewicz, 1999, Coello-Coello, 2007), figure 1.

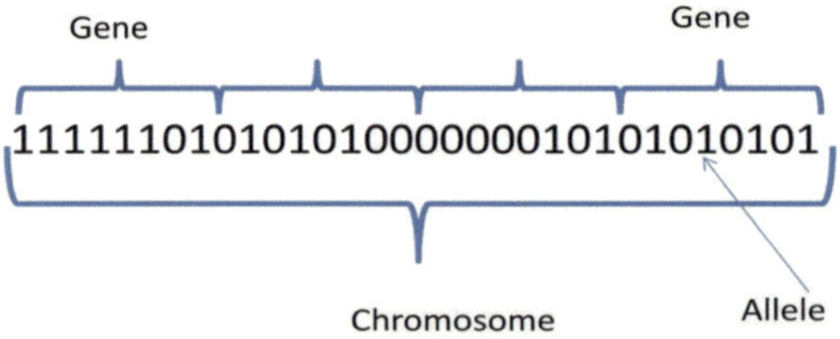

Fig. 1. Chromosome binary representation.

Individuals are probabilistically selected by evaluating the objective function. This gene has converged when at least 95% of individuals in the population share the same value of that genes. The population converges when all the genes have converged.

Different operators exist in GA´s, being the most popular (1) *selection*, (2) *crossover*, and (3) *mutation*, The steps to make a genetic algorithm, as defined in (Goldberg, 1989), are shown in the diagram of figure 2.

Initial Population is created randomly and it is encoded within the chromosome of an array with variable length. The coding can be done in a binary representation (Goldberg, 1989), based on the domain of each variable (figure 3).

In the *decodification* is necessary to have a representation of the genotype to assign the parameters within a chain of symbols known as genes. The *evaluation* uses the fitness function that reflect the value of the individual in terms of the real value of the variable in the problem's domain, but in many optimization combinatorial cases, where a great amount of restrictions exists; there is a probability in which part of the points of the search space represents no valid individuals. For example, the equation for the synthesis of planar mechanisms are:

$$F = \left(C_{xd}^{i}(v) - C_{xg}^{i}(v)\right)^{2} + \left(C_{yd}^{i}(v) - C_{yg}^{i}(v)\right)^{2} \tag{1}$$

Where C^i_{xd} is a set of specific points indicated by the designer and $C^i_{x\sigma}$ are the points generated by the coupler of the mechanism, and $v = r_1, r_2, r_3, r_4, r_{cx}, r_{cy}, \theta_0, x_0, y_0$, the angles $\theta_2^1, \theta_2^2, \ldots \theta_2^N$ are values for the variable θ_2, i is the rest of the quotient. The genetic algorithm maximizes solely, but the minimization can be made easily using the reciprocal of the function to avoid singularity problems (2):

$$fitnessoptimum = \frac{1}{fitness} \tag{2}$$

In order to improve the results, approaches such as elitism, regeneration stages and the forced inheritance mechanism can be inserted in the process of the algorithms:

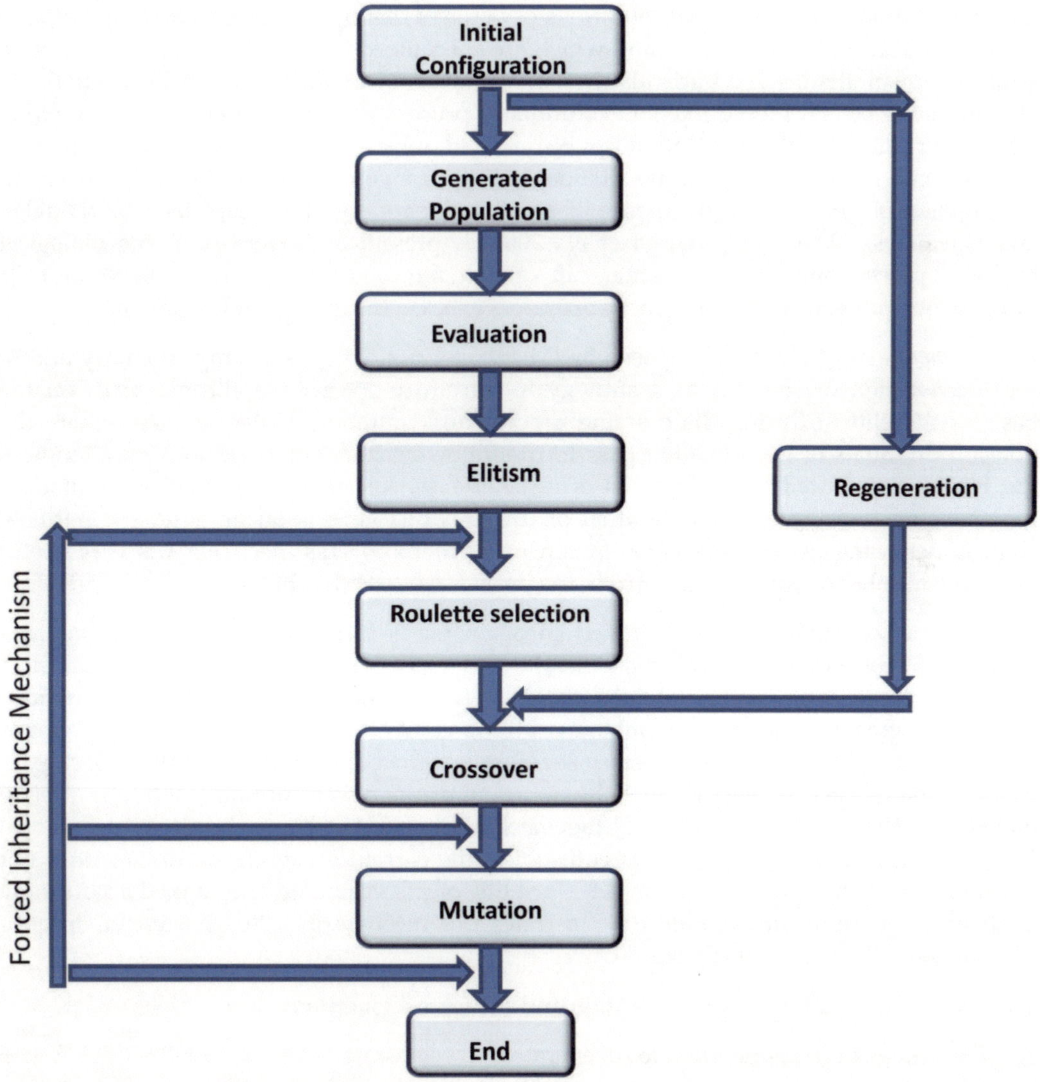

Fig. 2. Flowchart of genetic algorithms.

Domain=[-60 60 -60 60 0 60 ....0 360]

[X_{0min} X_{0max} Y_{0min} Y_{0max}............ $\theta_{min}\theta_{max}$]

Fig. 3. Structure Chromosome.

Elitism: In this case the best individual of the population at a certain time is selected like father, this reserve two slots in the next generation for the highest scoring chromosome of the current generation, without allowing that chromosome to be crossed over in the next generation. One of those slots, the elite chromosome will also not be subject to mutation in the next generation.

Regeneration Mechanism: The investigations on some alive organisms that use strategies for their renovation in physiological conditions or before a damage, demonstrate the possibility of incorporating cells that appear and which are specialized in providing reserve cells of an adult organism, thanks to a particular hereditary mechanism and, under this condition, the algorithm can be considered like an evolutionary process within the population. Therefore, a small percentage of the population can be renewed, which allows increasing the formation of construction blocks with better possibilities of finding an optimal value, but as inconvenient the problem of premature convergence of an evolutionary algorithm explained by (Hidalgo and Lanchares, 2000) and (Wen-Jyi et al., 2003) is presented. Nevertheless, the biological evolution process and its mimetization, can validate the use of a regeneration factor and its fundamental preservation in the genetic operators of selection, crosses and mutation.

Forced Inheritance Mechanism: Proposed by (Merchán-Cruz, 2005), is a complementary part of the regeneration mechanism as a strategy to introduce specialized chromosomes on the basis of the elitism during the crossing process and mutation. Unlike elitism, where the aptest individuals of a population pass to the following generation without no alteration, the FIM is introduced in the process of regeneration, selection, crossover and mutation, guaranteeing that the aptest individual of the previous generation undergoes a minimal change increasing its aptitude value of consistent method. This mechanism is very useful when the number of variables to solve in the problem is considerably large.

In the same way that the best obtained chromosome is carried among generations in a simple GA, the best set of chromosomes is also carried to the GA search for the next trajectory parameters. By introducing the best set of chromosomes from the previous trajectory segment of the initial population of the current GA search, the required number of generations to produce a new trajectory segment is reduced, provided that the trajectory is stable in that particular instant, since the optimum or the near optimum solution is already coded into the initial population. If the mechanism has to change its trajectory due to kinematic constrains or any other circumstance, the carried set of chromosomes does not affect the search for a new optimum set since this one is evaluated and ranked accordingly to its corresponding fitness. Figure 4 illustrates this mechanism called Forced Inheritance Mechanism, FIM, (Merchán-Cruz, 2005).

The necessary operations for regeneration and the forced inheritance are:

1. Percentage of the population to regenerate.
2. Chose again the number of individuals, the length of the chromosome and therefore the size of the population.

3. Regeneration takes the value from the individuals by the percentage to be regenerated.
4. This population is converted to binary representation.
5. The position that will occupy the regenerated ones in the original population is determined without altering the number of individuals.
6. Reinsert the regenerated population into a sector of the original population.
7. The best individual in the regenerated population introduces itself, looking forward not to alter the number of individuals.

Following the development of the genetic algorithm, taking the best individuals from the population will pay the selection of those who have been outfitted as parents of the new generations.

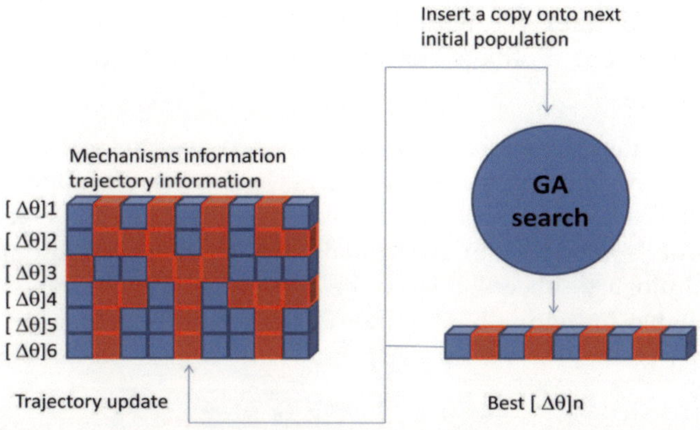

Fig. 4. Forced Inheritance Mechanism (Merchán-Cruz, 2005).

For the Parent Selection exists several techniques, but the most used is the proportional selection proposed by (Goldberg, 1989) in this each individual have a probability of being selected like parents, that is proportional to the value estimated by means of the objective function.

Crossover is based on taking two individuals correctly adapted to obtain descendants that share genes of both. There are several types of crossover mechanisms that are used depending on the scheme that is analyzed. According to (Kuri-Morales and Galaviz-Casas, 2002) the most popular are: single point crossover, two points and uniform crossover.

Mutation is an operator that is applied with probability *pm* and has the effect to invert a single bit using a probability of mutation of bit l^{-1}, being l the length of the chain of the chromosome.

While crossover needs large populations to effectively combine the necessary information, mutation works best when applied to small populations during a large number of generations. Mutation is usually a secondary search operator which performs a random search locally around a solution and therefore has received far less attention. However, in evolutionary strategies where crossover is the primary search operator, significant attention has been paid to the development of mutation operators. Several mutation operators, including adaptive techniques, have been proposed by (Lima, 2005). Clearly, mutation cannot perform this role as well as crossover.

By other hand *Crossover Probability* indicates how often will be crossover performed. If there is no crossover, offspring is an exact copy of parents. If there is a crossover, offspring is made from parts of parent's chromosome. If crossover probability is 100%, then all offspring is made by crossover. If it is 0%, a whole new generation is made from exact copies of chromosomes from old population (but this does not mean that the new generation is the same). Crossover is made expecting that new chromosomes will have good parts of old chromosomes and perhaps this will be better. However it is good to allow some part of the population survive to next generation.

Mutation probability says how often will be parts of chromosome mutated. If there is no mutation, the offspring is taken after crossover (or copy) without any change. If mutation is performed, part of a chromosome is changed. If mutation probability is *100%*, whole chromosome is changed, if it is 0%, nothing is changed. Mutation is made to prevent falling GA into local extreme, but it should not occur very often, because then GA will in fact change to *random search.*

Each operator allows that the evolutionary process progress toward promising regions in the area of search and can carry on diversity within the population and inhibit the premature convergence to an optimal local by means of new individuals sampled randomly. On the other hand is required to manipulate the information through a metric that quantifies the evolutionary process, this can be done through the design of a function that gets the more suitable individuals. This metric is known as a function of ability and it increases the ability of this individual to operate with a good performance and to get an unbeatable quality.

Problems typically contain restrictions, such as the non-linearity and inequality, which makes necessary to incorporate information on the violation of restrictions on some of the functions and the most known are *Criminalization role,* this restricts the fitness role by extending its domain by a factor of criminalization to any restriction raped. It can penalize for not being feasible or to make feasible an individual. The penalty function design must take into account how distant is an individual from the feasible area, the cost of fulfillment and the cost of expected compliance. Some of these penalties are:

- **Death Penalty.** It assigns a suitability of zero to the individual not feasible, avoiding calculate again restrictions or objective function. However, the algorithm may be truncated if the initial population does not contain any feasible individual.
- **Static Criminalization.** It defines levels of violation and chooses a coefficient of violation to each one of them.
- **Dynamic Criminalization.** The factors of criminalization change with time; they are susceptible to the values of the parameters and converge prematurely when these are not selected properly.
- **Adaptive Criminalization:** Adjusting the penalty on the basis of a feedback process.

The adaptive criminalization is used in this work.

2.1 Efficiency enhancement of GA

Goldberg categorized the efficiency enhancement techniques of GA into four broad classes: parallelization, hybridization, time continuation, and evaluation relaxation (Goldberg, 2002):

1. **Parallelization:** GAs are executed on several processors and the computational load is distributed among these Processors (Cantu-Paz, 2000). This leads to significant speed-up when solving large scale problems. Parallelization can be achieved through different ways. A simple way is to have part of the GA operations such as evaluation running simultaneously on multiple processors (Bethke, 1976). Another way is to create several subpopulations and allow them evolve separately at the same time, while spreading good solutions across the subpopulations (Grosso, 1985).
2. **Hybridization:** Local search methods or domain-specific knowledge is coupled with GA. This are powerful in global search. However, they are not as efficient as local search methods in reaching the optimum on micro-scale. Therefore, hybridization which incorporates local search methods into GA will facilitate local convergence. A common form of hybridization is to apply a local search operator to each member of the population after each generation in GA (Sinha, 2002).
3. **Time Continuity**: The capabilities of both mutation and recombination are utilized to obtain a solution of as high quality as possible with a given limited computational resource (Srivastava, 2002). Time continuation exploits the tradeoff between the search for solutions with a large population and a single convergence epoch or using a small population with multiple convergence epochs.
4. **Relaxation Evaluation**: An accurate, but computationally expensive fitness evaluation is replaced with a less accurate, but computationally inexpensive fitness estimate. The low-cost, less-accurate fitness estimate can either be 1) exogenous, as in the case of surrogate (or approximate) fitness functions, where external means that it can be used to develop the fitness estimate; or 2) endogenous, as in the case of fitness inheritance (Smith, 1995) where the fitness estimate is computed internally and is based on parental fitness.

3. Adjustment in the performance of the parameters of the GA

Some authors such as (Holland, 1975), have looked into the effect of varying GA's parameters which have to be taken into account to exploit the full potential in particular applications. Accordingly to this, for a search algorithm to perform well online, one has to decide quickly which are the most promising search regions in order to concentrate the search efforts there, the off-line performance does not penalize the search algorithm to explore poor regions of the search space, provided that this will help to achieve the best possible solutions (in terms of fitness), abig generation interval and the use of an elitist strategy also improve the performance of the GA's, in which the usual recommended mutation rates between 0.001 and 0.01 for the binary representation (Goldberg, 1989), or in general, much smaller value of the crossover probability (Cabrera et al., 2002).

The main parameters that can be adjusted, by the degree of importance within the GA are:

- Population size
- Percentage of crosses
- Percentage of mutation

The design of the algorithm is limited to choose and determine the degree of control or the strategies of parameters such as the ranges and the likelihood of a mutation, crossing and extent of the population. (Sanchéz-Marín, 2000) supported their research in the determination of control parameters, experimenting with different values and selecting those that gave better results. (De Jong, 1975) recommended, after experimenting, values for the probability of the interbreeding of simple point and the movement of a bit in the mutation. In this work, the following parameters are defined: a population-based measure of 50 individuals, probability of crossing 0.6, probability of mutation of 0.001 and elitist selection; however, it presents the disadvantage that these parameters only worked for a particular problem with very specific restrictions.

(De Jong, 1975) described that the operation on-line is based on the monitoring of the best solution in every generation, while the operation off-line takes into account all the solutions in the population to obtain the optimum value. (Grefenstette, 1986) used the meta-algorithms as a method of optimization, in order to obtain values with similar parameters for the operation on-line and off-line of the algorithm.

In order to have a good performance on-line of a search algorithm, it must quickly decide where the most promising search region is and concentrate their efforts there. The performance off-line does not always penalize the search algorithm to explore poor regions of the search space, since this will contribute to achieving the best possible solutions (in terms of fitness). The best sets of parameters analyzed on and off- line were population of 30 and 80 individuals, probability of crossing 0.95 and 0.45, probability of mutation 0.01 for both, either using a strategy of elitist selection for the on-line case or not elitist for the off-line case .

(Smith, 1993) proposes a genetic algorithm which adjusts the extent of the population taking into account the likelihood of error. This is linked with the number of generations, if under the conditions of little use is determined a small value (20 to 50) to the number of evaluations, the convergence will be quick, but it is not ensured an optimum result.

(Endre Eiben et al., 1999) expose technical drawbacks of the analysis of parameters on the basis of experimentation, observing the following points:

- Parameters are not independent, but trying all possible combinations of these systematically it is almost impossible.
- The process of tuning parameters is time-consuming, but if the parameters are optimized one by one, it is possible to handle their interactions.
- For a given problem, the values for the selected parameters are not necessarily the best, but if they are used to analyze uniformly, more meaningful values will be obtained.

In general, here are listed some important observations made by authors such as (Holland, 1975),with respect to the genetic algorithms that must be considered for the use of this tool, such as:

- A high generational interval and the use of an elitist strategy also improve the performance of the GA.
- The use of large populations *(> 200)* with a high percentage of mutation *(> 0.05)* does not improve the performance of a GA.
- The use of small populations *(< 20)* with low percentage of mutation *(< 0.002)* does not improve the performance of a GA.
- The mutation seems to have greater importance in the performance of a GA.
- If the size of the population is increased, the effect of crosses seems to be diluted.

With reference to the mutation, it has been deeply analyzed the value of the probability, but the results vary with each researcher, for example (De Jong, 1975) recommend *pm=0.001*, (Grefenstette, 1986, Goldberg, 1989) recommend *0.1*, (Fogarty, 1989) indicates *0.005 to 0.01*.

In the research of (Fogarty, 1989) and (Coello-Coello, 2007) have been developed some formulas in order determine the mutation, where its main contribution is considering the time and making a change of this during the execution of the GA. If the mutation percent is *0*, does not exist any alteration, if is *1*, the mutation creates always add-ons of the original individual and if it is 0.5, there is a high probability of altering strongly the schema of an individual. In conclusion, it is possible to control the power of alteration of the mutation and its capabilities for exploration, to have an equivalent weight within the AG as the crossing.

On the other hand for the crossing some common values for this are 0.6 indicated by (De Jong, 1975), *0.95 by* (Grefenstette, 1986), *0.75 to 0.95 by* (Fogarty, 1989). (Endre Eiben et al., 1999) specify that is more common to use the results obtained in own experimentation and is rarely used a value less than 0.6. When it is looking for locating the global optimum of a problem, the mutation may be more useful, but when it is in the cumulative gain, crossing offers greater benefits. From these research works it can be said that there are needs of large populations in the crossing, to combine effectively the necessary information, but in mutation best results are obtained when applied to small populations in a large number of generations.

Evolutionary strategies, where the mutation is the principal search operator, include several operators of mutation, as well as technical adaptation, proposed by (Lima et al., 2005, Rechenberg, 1973). (Whitley et al., 1998) reported comparative studies between the operators of crossover and mutation, demonstrating that there were important features of each operator that were not captured by the other.

In this work is demonstrated, through experimentation, that the maximum limit for individuals have an acceptable performance of the GA is 3000, this depends completely on study cases, since as it increases the number of variables in the problem to be analyzed it is necessary an increase in the population. With this amount of individuals the process of analysis is very slow, but it is in direct function of the mechanism type, the trajectory and the precision points required, in addition to the restrictions on the domain to get the angles and the links dimensions.

4. Study cases

The case of study is based on mechanisms synthesis, for that reason the basic concepts are presented.

A mechanism is a set of rigid members that are jointed together in order to develop a specific function. The mechanisms design, which is described by (Varbanov et al., 2006), consists of two parts: the analysis and synthesis. The first one consists of techniques to determine position, velocities and accelerations of points onto the members of mechanisms and the angular position, velocities and accelerations of those members. The second type explains the determination of the optimal length of the bars and the spatial disposition that best reproduces the desired movement of the coupler link. The optimal dimensional synthesis problem of mechanisms can be seen as a minimization process, since it is required that the structural error being as small as possible. The point of the coupler link will have to be able to generate a trajectory defined through separate points, with a minimum error. The generation of a desired trajectory consists controlling a point of the coupler link, figure 5 (case I four-bar mechanism and case II six-bar mechanism), so that its described trajectory drives the coupler through a discreet set of giving points, known as precision points (Norton, 1995). In order to determine this point it is necessary to obtain the open and close chain mechanism.

In the last century, have been developing a variety of mechanisms synthesis methods. These are usually based on graphical procedures originally developed by (Freudenstein, 1954); or on analytical methods of research of (Denavit and Hartenberg, 1964). Other techniques include the application of least squares in the finite synthesis of four-bar spatial synthesis proposed by (Levitski and Shakvazian, 1960), or on the mathematical model and simulation for the exact mechanisms synthesis as is described in (A. K. Mallik and A. Ghosh, 1994) and (Tzong-Mou and Cha'o-Kuang, 2005). However while these works have represented major contributions in the area, the principal restriction are the number of points of precision that can be taken into account to define the desired path. The foregoing refers to the fact that each point of precision defined for the desired path represents a new set of equations to be solved. For example, the synthesis of a four- bar mechanism involves a set of 7 holonomics restrictions that describe the kinematic relationship of the links that make it up; if the designer consider 4 points of accuracy, the problem to be solved is a set of 28 non-linear equations with 29 unknowns, which represents a non-linear indeterminate problem with an infinite number of possible solutions.

With all these arguments in mind and taking into account that exist a wide variety of applications that require a large number of precision points to define more accurately the trajectory to be reproduced by the mechanism, the synthesis of these can be seen as an optimization multi-objective problem. For this purpose, researchers have developed different methodologies that include non-linear optimization (Levitski and Shakvazian, 1960), genetic algorithms (Quintero-R et al., 2004, Laribi et al., 2004, Cabrera et al., 2002, Michalewicz, 1999, Roston and Sturges, 1996), neuronal networks (Vasiliu and Yannou, 2001), (Starosta, 2006), (Walczak, 2006)), Monte Carlo optimization (Kalnas and Kota, 2001), or the controlled method (Bulatovic and Djordjevic, 2004). All the above methods have been used for four-bar mechanisms synthesis and have helped to identify the constraints of space that lead to the synthesis of mechanisms and programs developed for applications.

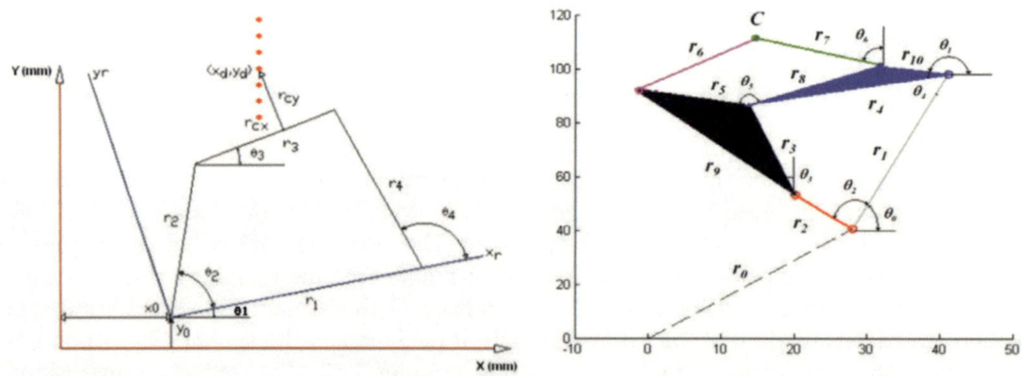

a) Coupler point on the coupler link of a four bar linkage

b) Type 6-bar Watt mechanism.

Fig. 5. Diferent mechanisms configuration.

4.1 Optimal design in the mechanisms synthesis

The formulation of this problem demands the definition of several aspects like the space of design, the objective function, the algorithm of optimization and the restrictions (Lugo-Gonzalez et al., 2010). In the case corresponding to the synthesis of mechanisms, it is desired to diminish the error between the desired and generated trajectories besides analyzing the changes in the response of the algorithm when modifying parameters like the probability of mutation and crossing, the number of individuals and the maximum of generations, that will be evaluated by the proposed equation (3) that has characteristics applied to the approximated evaluation of the function, that involves the addition of the penalty to the presented original version in the works of (Goldberg, 1989), which is:

$$F = \frac{1}{N} * \sqrt{\frac{\sum_{i=1}^{N}\left(C_{xd}^{i}(v) - C_{xg}^{i}(v)\right)^{2} + \left(C_{yd}^{i}(v) - C_{yg}^{i}(v)\right)^{2}}{ni}} \tag{3}$$

Applying a division of the number of individuals *ni* in addition to a factor of division by the reciprocal of *N*, that is the number of precision points, it adds a penalty whose objective is to recover the individuals that do not fulfill the initial restrictions known as the conditions of Grashof.

In order to finalize, the optimization algorithm uses four criteria of convergence that are defined as:

reng= Is the first restriction, this one is the first evaluation in which it is verified if the population fulfills the restrictions of Grashof (specific condition of mechanism synthesis).

maximogen = Defines the maximum number of times that the algorithm can evaluate the objective function. An additional call to this implies the conclusion of the search without reaching a solution.

minimerror = Defines the minimum value of error allowed in the objective function to being compared with the generated function. A change of value in the parameter of minimum error implies the conclusion of the search without reaching a solution.

condrep = Defines the number of times that the same value can be repeated into the evaluation before proceeding to the following operation.

Being fulfilled these last conditions to the evaluation; the algorithm will stop its search having presented the optimal values that better satisfy the restrictions and conditions.

4.2 Elliptical trajectory with parameters optimization of GA, 18 precision points, and a four- bar mechanism

The obtained research results in (Cabrera et al., 2002, Laribi et al., 2004, Starosta, 2006) are taken as a basis for describing an elliptical path with a four-link mechanism. The study case was proposed for the first time by (Kunjur and Krishnamurty, 1997). The synthesis was carried out using some variants of application using genetic algorithms or combining these with tools such as fuzzy logic. In the table 1 is shown the desired precision points to be followed by the mechanism. In the figure 6 is showed the corresponding graphic.

Point	1	2	3	4	5	6	7	8	9
X	0.5	0.4	0.3	0.2	0.1	0.005	0.02	0.0	0.0
Y	1.1	1.1	1.1	1.0	0.9	0.75	0.6	0.5	0.4
Point	10	11	12	13	14	15	16	17	18
X	0.03	0.1	0.15	0.2	0.3	0.4	0.5	0.6	0.6
y	0.3	0.25	0.2	0.3	0.4	0.5	0.7	0.9	1.0

Table 1. Precision points of desired elliptical trajectory by(Kunjur and Krishnamurty, 1997).

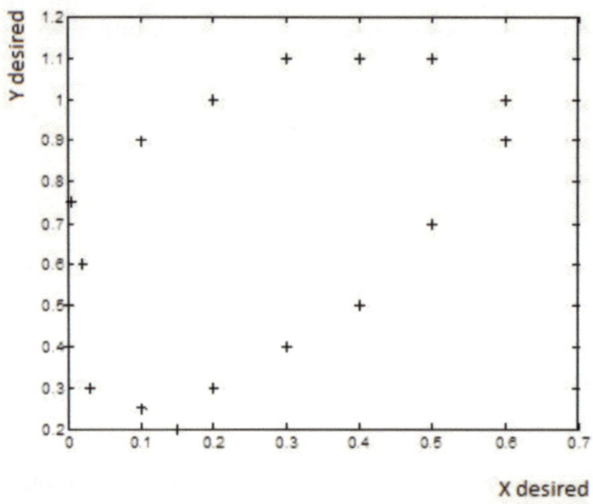

Fig. 6. Elliptical trajectory, by(Kunjur and Krishnamurty, 1997).

The realized parameters change is presented in table 2 and the results obtained by (Kunjur and Krishnamurty, 1997, Cabrera et al., 2002, Laribi et al., 2004, Starosta, 2006) and our results are shown in table 3. The analysis procedure is shown in figures 7 and 8. But this indicates that is necessary to make a change of value in the parameters of crossover and mutation. The changes are the number of individuals, crossover and mutation, affecting with this time and the number of generations for the convergence. It has a maximum number of 1500 generations and a precision of 6 digits.

Of this series of tests one concludes that:

The individual number is an important factor for the convergence, since although a response time with a small number of individuals is obtained, it does not make sure that the result is the optimal one. With a greater number of individuals the response time increases but the possibility of obtaining a better result also increases. As it has been mentioned previously, the program will have an optimal rank of individuals to operate satisfactorily, but this must be verified by trial and error, being a program that has as a basis the random generation of the population. However, the performance of the algorithm when the FIM is implemented only registers a minor reduction compared with the one obtained for the previously considered systems.

Do not exist a rule to determine the optimal value for the crossing and the mutation probability. Not always the maximum values, that produce a total change in the individual, give the best results, as it is observed in table 2. For this study case, the best result appears in interjection ***k*** with the value of minimum error. This value is affected directly by the dominion of the variables and in addition to the number of individuals.

The dominion is a determining value to obtain the optimal result, since all the variables are related to each other by the calculations required for the synthesis. For example if the restriction of some angles are modified, it changes the value of lengths of the links and by consequence the value of the error, since perhaps the bars must increase or decrease them length to cover the specified trajectory. Although the parameters are designed well, if this definition of variables are incorrect, it does not fulfilled the objective.

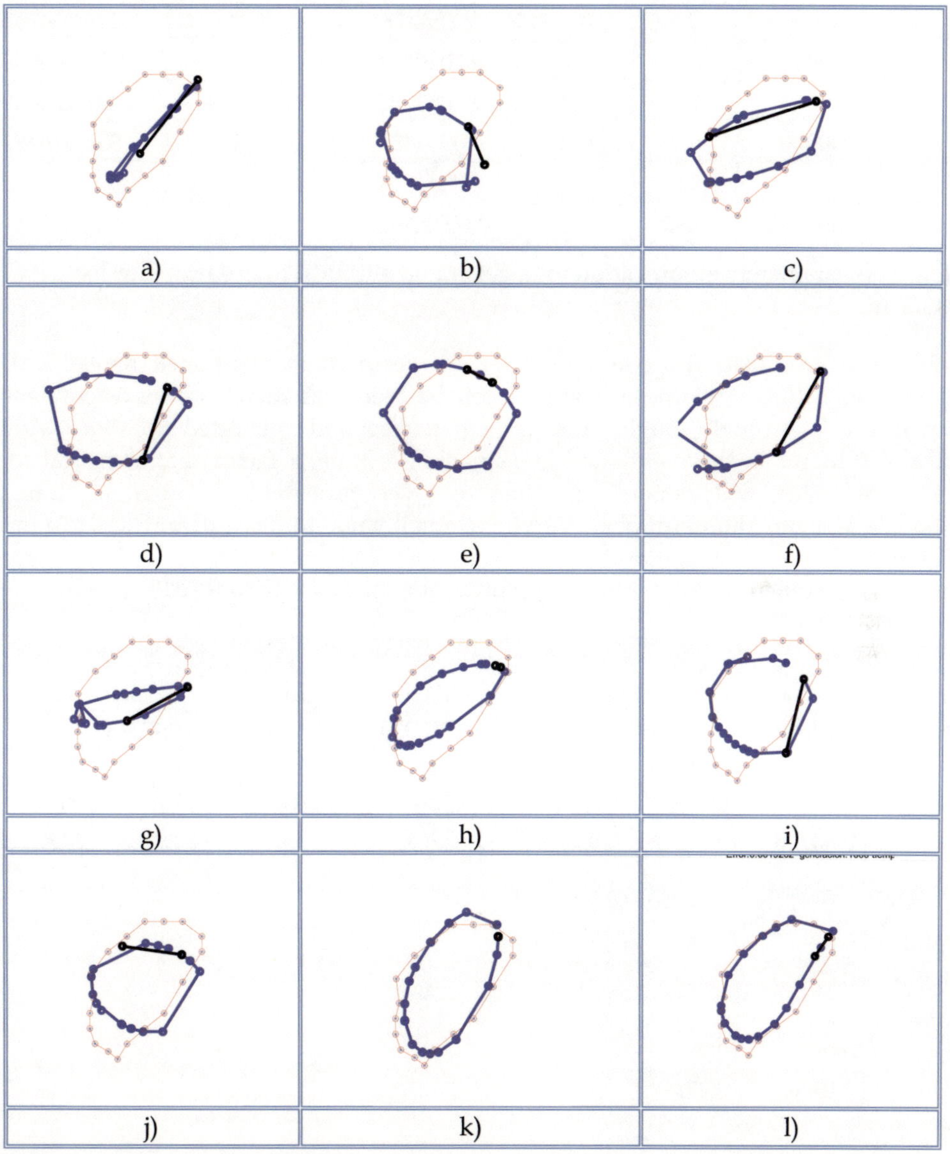

Fig. 7. Different parameters in elliptical trajectory.

	Population number	*Pc*	*Pm*	*Error*	*Generation*	*Time (S)*
a)	500	0.6	0.01	0.12607	974	124.70116
b)	1000	0.6	0.01	0.116874	992	200.83390
c)	1000	0.8	0.8	0.146653	994	281.61255
d)	1000	0.8	0.7	0.140036	992	318.54909
e)	1500	0.8	0.7	0.128140	992	499.81671
f)	1500	0.85	0.85	0.113155	979	384.667514
g)	2000	0.3	0.1	0.253548	992	416.934751
h)	2000	0.6	0.2	0.2020683	988	374.043950
i)	2000	0.6	0.4	0.1852588	991	431.125409
j)	2000	0.7	0.2	0.0986130	988	335.516387
k)	2000	0.7	0.4	0.0854537	995	402.078071
l)	2000	0.85	0.85	0.09922667	989	776.17100

Table 2. The parameters modification for a generated elliptical figure by a four bar mechanism.

In table 3 is presented the comparison of the researchers mentioned above with the proposed algorithm. With these results it can be seen that there is a correspondence of values in the bars length, angles and among desired and generated trajectory. Another variable not found in the mentioned investigation is time, a factor that is critical for the optimization. This will depend on the crossover probability, mutation parameters, individuals and generation number. Varying a small value to these parameters can mean a short time in convergence but not always the optimal value is guaranteed. With the specific parameters, the time elapsed by the GA optimization analysis is 280.508318 seconds.

Autor	*Xo*	*Yo*	*R2*	*R1*	*R4*	*R3*	*R5*
Kunjur	1.132062	0.663433	0.274853	1.180253	2.138209	1.879660	0.91
Cabrera	1.776808	-0.641991	0.237803	4.828954	2.056456	3.057878	2
Laribi	-3.06	-1.3	0.42	2.32	3.36	4.07	3.90
Starosta	0.074	0.191	0.28	0.36	0.98	1.01	0.36
A-G prop.	3.88548	0.907087	0.286753	4.52611	3.59121	4.29125	3.613847

Autor	*Error*	*No. Eval.*
Kunjur	0.62	5000
Cabrera	0.029	5000
Laribi	0.20	
Starosta	0.0377	200
A-G prop.	0.0152	2000

Table 3. Dimensions and angles definition of an elliptical path obtained by some authors.

In spite of applying more generations that in the last researcher work, satisfactory results are obtained. Due to the high amount of generations, computation time is more demanding, but this offers less error among the generated and desired path, and therefore, greater precision.

Figure 8 shows how the error behavior decreases at the beginning of the path and at the end of the evaluation in each generation (*a* and *b*). Figures *c* and *d* illustrates the four-bar mechanism along the path, covering the first and sixth precision point, which were randomly chosen to display the specified path.

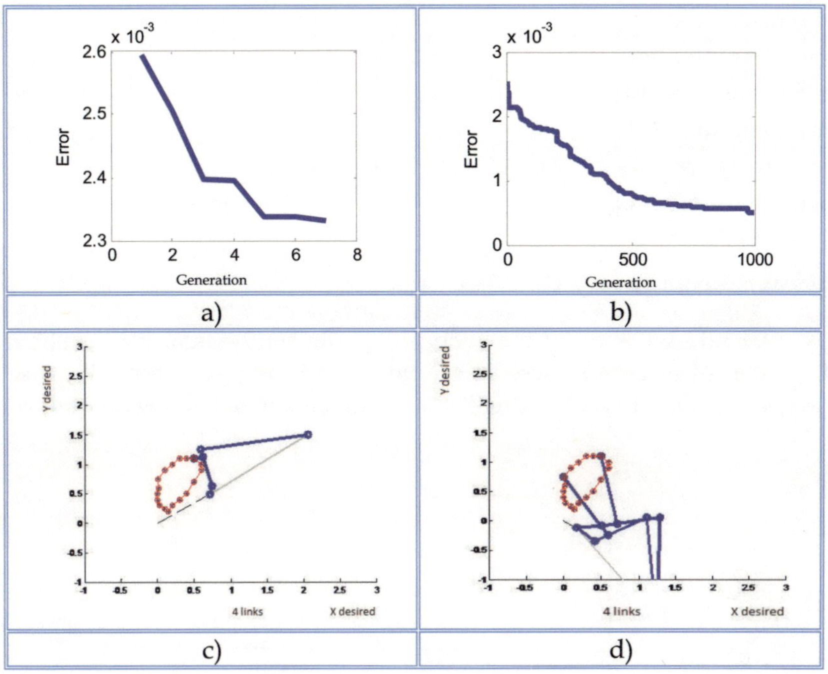

Fig. 8. Four-bar mechanism evolution to cover 18 precision points.

4.3 Six bar mechanisms optimization

There are two main six-link configuration mechanisms Watt and Stephenson type, whose features make them suitable for the manufacture of polycentric prostheses such as (Radcliffe, 1977, Dewen et al., 2003).

The first example illustrates a six-bar mechanism for covering 21 precision points. To evaluate the effectiveness of the analyzed mechanism a Watt-I type will follow a path with arbitrarily proposed restrictions on the initial 18 points, being the conditions reported in table 4.

Figure 9 presents the proposed path to be followed by the Watt-I type mechanism. As in the previous cases, settings in population, crossing and mutation probability, time and number of generation analysis, will be varied in order to demonstrate that these adjustments are not independent and that they are affected each other.

Polycentric Mechanisms	Description	
Characteristic		
Desired points Variables limits	x_d=[25 10 5 10 20 10 5 10 15 25 40 43 50 55 50 40 50 55 50 40 25]	
	y_d=[[130 120 100 80 65 55 35 20 15 10 10 15 20 40 55 65 80 100 120 130 130]	
Restriction for each links	$r1,r2,r3,r4,r5,r6,r7,r8,r9,r10 \in [-60,60]$ *inmm*	
	$x0,y0 \in [-60,60]$ *in mm*	
Movements range	0° *to* 360° degrees	
Population numbers	niindividuals	200
Crossover probability	Proportional type	varied
Mutation probability	Only one point	varied
Precision	Digits after point	6
Maximum number of generations	1000 generations	

Table 4. Six-bar mechanism restriction.

The path is obtained as a result of the evolution of the synthesis of the genetic mechanism (figure 10). In the subsequent figures and in table 5 it can be seen how decrease the error, while passing generations and changing some parameters to obtain the best adjustment.

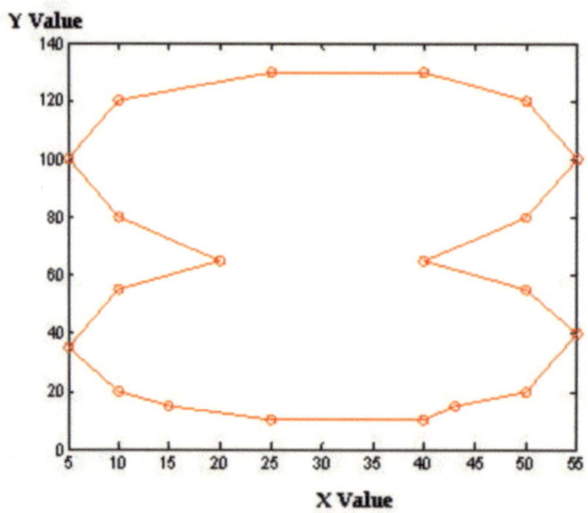

Fig. 9. Trajectory of 20 points for a six-bar Watt-I type mechanism.

This path was proposed with the objective of demonstrating that a six-link mechanism can follow paths that would be difficult to follow by a four-bar mechanism.

From this analysis it is concluded that:

- An increase in precision points is directly proportional to the number of individuals in the population, since to obtain a minor error, it is necessary to have a greater field of search.

- A small number of individuals decreases the search and does not offer satisfactory results.
- In order to obtain the optimal values is necessary to increase the value of the probability of crossing at least greater than 0.6.
- The rate of mutation can vary up to a maximum of 0.9, because if it increases to 1, it would be completely changing the individual without having a real meaning of the best for the evaluation, which was obtained with the elitism and the forced inheritance mechanism.
- High values of probability of crossover and mutation do not ensure that the best value of convergence is achieved.

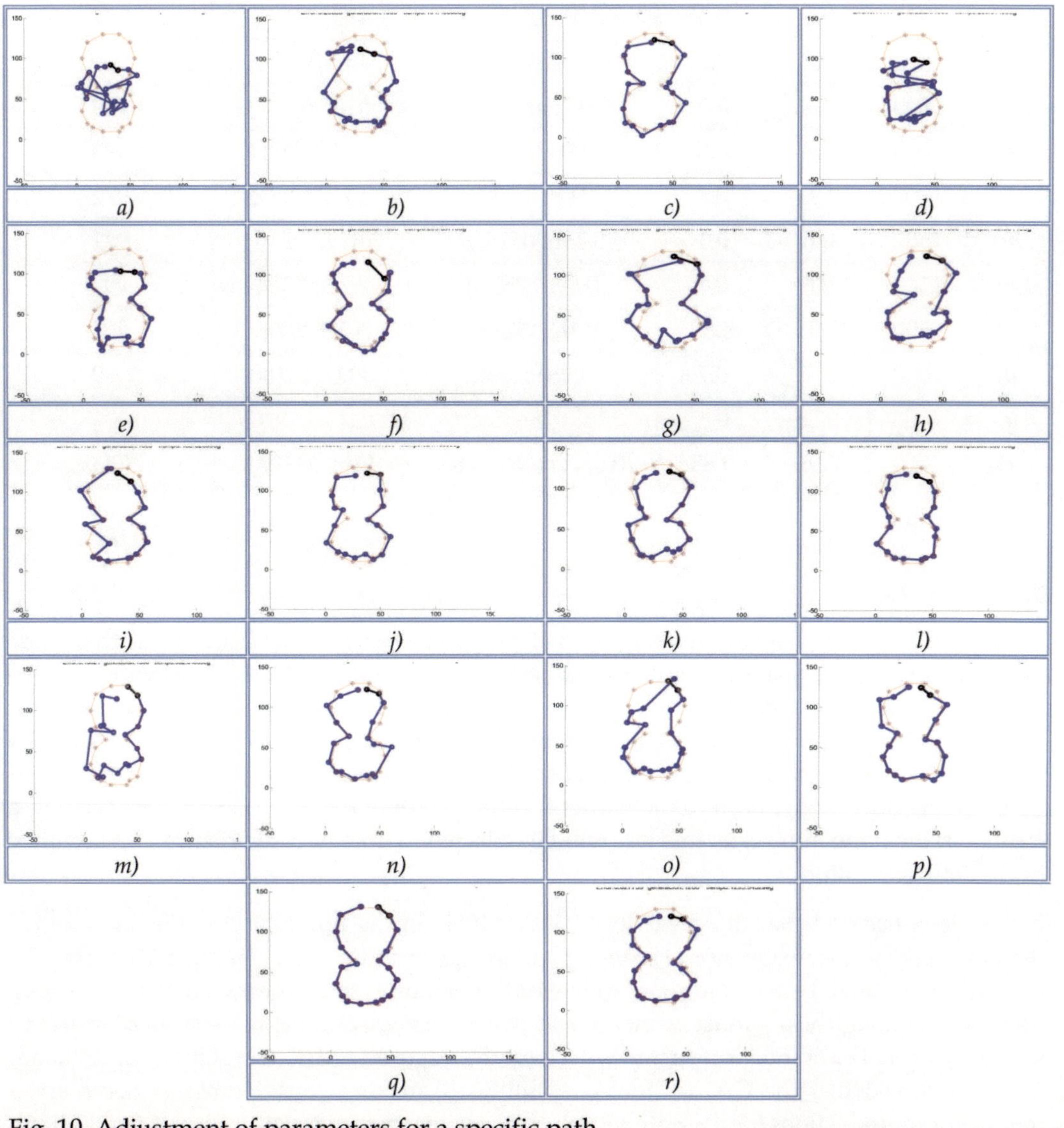

Fig. 10. Adjustment of parameters for a specific path.

	ni	*Pc*	*Pm*	*error*	*time*	*generations*
a)	200	0.6	0.01	0.4530713342399	180.693674	978
b)	200	0.6	0.4	0.2088516234	162.480752	991
c)	200	0.8	0.8	0.1039548356200	168.681711	996
d)	500	0.6	0.01	0.1441113	250.446997	981
e)	500	0.6	0.4	0.07266868	282.191	960
f)	500	0.8	0.8	0.0558228894	290.697	987
g)	1000	0.6	0.01	0.059796068	468.693084	999
h)	1000	0.6	0.4	0.0532988776	480.819397	947
i)	1000	0.7	0.5	0.119467646451	457.490696	999
j)	1000	0.7	0.7	0.03260650948	524.067239	989
k)	1000	0.8	0.5	0.099396876739	536.369984	993
l)	1000	0.85	0.8	0.0311870033413	550.612374	972
m)	1500	0.6	0.1	0.1962062488	619.52535	981
n)	1500	0.6	0.4	0.090105144	672.77304	990
o)	1500	0.95	0.85	0.163192355	1046.2808	968
p)	2000	0.7	0.7	0.08380448	1116.16188	999
q)	2000	0.85	0.8	0.0114246856933	1295.874818	987
r)	2000	0.95	0.85	0.0277589482798	1306.641231	1000

Table 5. Adjustment of six-bar mechanism parameters for a specific path.

5. Discussion

The optimization process is iterative, and it was demonstrated with the tests that were realized varying the parameters of the genetic algorithm to analyze the behavior of the system, which means that they can be modified until finding a system whose behavior satisfies the expectations and requirements of the designer. The parameters of the GA usually interact with each other in a nonlinear relation, that's why they cannot be optimized in an independent way, been demonstrated in the presented study cases. When existing a change in the population size, this fact will be reflected in time of convergence and accuracy in the path generation.

It was demonstrated that the diversity of individuals in the population is obtained and it remains along with the operator of crossing and the genetic mutation, since in all the analysis, they allow to find better solutions and avoid premature convergence to the maximum premises. Although also it must be mentioned that the elitism and the forced inheritance help to limit the number of individuals that will cover the imposed restrictions. On the other hand, it was observed that the GA has few possibilities of making considerable or necessary a number of reproductions for the optimal solution if it has an insufficient or small population.

Besides, the excessive population causes that the algorithm requires of a greater time of calculation to process and to obtain a new generation. In fact, there is not a limit wherein it is inefficient to increase the size of the population since it neither obtains a faster speed in the resolution of the problem, nor the convergence makes sure. For the referred study cases in this chapter, when increasing the population to 3500 individuals no acceptable results are presented and the program became extremely slow. If the population remains so large, like for example 1000 individuals, this means that it can improve the performance of the algorithm, although this is affected by slower initial responses. It is important to do emphasis on the relation that exists among the population size and the probabilistic relation in the solution space of the problem.

The study cases of this work are over determined and nonlinear type, which implies by necessity a space of multidimensional, nonlinear and non-homogenous solution, therefore, large initial values cover different regions of the solution space wherein the algorithm could converge prematurely to a solution that implies optimal premises costs, but when maintaining a low probability of mutation is not possible to assure that the population, although extensive in the number of individuals, continues being probabilistic representative of the problem solution. With this in mind and considering that the computation time to evaluate and to generate a new population of individuals from the present initial or, directly is the bound to the number of individuals of this one, requires a greater number of operations to obtain a new generation of possible solutions.

6. Conclusions

When operating with a population reduced in number of individuals, a sufficient representative quantity of the different regions of the solution space is not achieved, but the necessary computation time to create a new generation of possible solutions diminishes dramatically. When considering a high percentage of the probability of mutation in the algorithm, one assures a heuristic search made in different regions of the solution space, this combined with the forced inheritance mechanism has demonstrated that for the problem treated in this work, it is a strategy that power the heuristic capacities of the GA, for nonlinear multidimensional problems, non-homogenous, becoming the algorithm meta-heuristic; it is demonstrated then that an important improvement in the diminution of the error is obtained, around 20% with respect to the reported works previously. Also it was observed that the increase in the percentage of mutation improves the off-line performance, since all the solutions in the population are taken into account to obtain the optimal value. The off-line performance does not penalize the algorithm to explore poor regions of the search space, as long as it contributes to reach the best possible solutions in terms of aptitude.

It was verified that for the crossover the rule is fulfilled of which applying values smaller to 0.6, the performance is not optimal and it does not change the expected result for a specific problem. In the case of mutation, one demonstrated that this one can change no mattering the number of times and increasing its value to obtain optimal results, reaching almost at the unit, but avoiding to muter totally all the chromosomes eliminating the benefits created by the elitism and the forced inheritance mechanism.

By means of the trial and error, also one concludes that the parameters are not independent, and searching systematically to obtain all the possible combinations of these, is almost impossible; but if the parameters were optimized one at the time, it is then possible to handle its interactions and, for a given problem, the values of the selected parameters are not necessarily the optimal ones, but if they are analyzed uniformly they will generate more significant values.

7. Acknowledgment

The authors thank to Instituto Politécnico Nacional, Project Number. 20113426, for the facilities and means for the development of this research.

8. References

A. K. Mallik & A. Ghosh 1994. Kinematic Analysis and Synthesis of Mechanisms. *CRC-Press*, 688.

Beasley, D., Bull, D. R. & Martin, R., And R. 1993. An overview of genetic algorithms: part 1, fundamentals. *University Computing*, 15, 58-69.

Bethke, A. 1976. Comparison of Genetic Algorithms and Gradient-Based Optimizers on Parallel Processors: Efficiency of Use of Processing Capacity. *Tech. Rep. No. 197, Logic of Computers Group, University of Michigan*.

Bulatovic, R. R. & Djordjevic, S. R. 2004. Optimal Synthesis of a Four-Bar Linkage by Method of Controlled Deviation. *The first international conference on computational mechanics (CM'04)*, 31,No.3-4, 265-280.

Cabrera, J. A., Simon, A. & Prado, M. 2002. Optimal synthesis of mechanisms with genetic algorithms. *Mechanism and machine theory (Mech. mach. theory)*, 37 No10, 1165-1177.

Cantu-Paz, E. 2000. Efficient and Accurate Parallel Genetic Algorithms. *Kluwer, Boston, MA*.

Coello-Coello, C. A. 2007. Introducción a la computación evolutiva. *In:* CINVESTAV-IPN (ed.). Mèxico.

De Jong, K. A. 1975. *An analysis of the behaviour of a class of genetic adaptive systems*. Tesis doctoral, University of Michigan.

Denavit, J. & Hartenberg, R. S. 1964. Kinematic Synthesis of Linkages. *USA: Mc. Graw Hill*.

Dewen, J., Ruihong, Z., Ho, D., Rencheng, W. & Jichuan, Z. 2003. Kinematic and dynamic performance of prosthetic knee joint using six-bar mechanism *Journal of Rehabilitation Research and Development*, 40,No. 1, 39–48.

Endre Eiben, A., Hinterding, R. & Michalewicz, Z. 1999. Parameter Control in Evolutionary Algorithms. *IEEE Transactions on Evolutionary Computation*, 3, No. 2.

Fogarty, T. 1989. Varying the probability of mutation in the genetic algorithm. *Proc. 3rd Int. Conf. Genetic Algorithms, J. D. Schaffer, Ed. San Mateo, CA: Morgan Kaufmann*.

Freudenstein, F. 1954. An analitical approach to the design of four link mechanism. *Transactions of the ASME 76*, 483-492.

Goldberg, D. 2002. Lessons from and for Competent Genetic Algorithms. *Kluwer, Boston, MA*.

Goldberg, D. E. 1989. *Genetic algorithms in search, optimization, and machine learning*, USA, Addison - Wesley.

Grefenstette, J. J. 1986. Optimization of control parameters for genetic algorithms. *IEEE Trans. Systems, Man, Cybern*, 16, no. 1, 122-128.

Grosso, P. 1985. Computer Simulations of Genetic Adaption: Parallel Subcompnent Interaction in a Multilocus Model. *Ph.D Dissertation, University of Michigan.*

Hidalgo, J. I. & Lanchares, H. R. 2000. Partitioning and placement for multi-fpga systems using genetic algorithms. *In Proceedings of the Euromicro DSD 2000.*

Holland, J. H. 1975. Adaptation in natural and artificial system. *Ann Arbor, The University of Michigan Press.*

Kalnas, R. & Kota, S. 2001. Incorporating Uncertaintly intoMechanism Synthesis. *Mechanism and machine theory (Mech. mach. theory),* 36, No.3, 843-851.

Kunjur, A. & Krishnamurty, S. 1997. Genetic Algorithms in Mechanism Synthesis. *Journal of Applied Mechanisms and Robotics,* 4 No. 2, 18-24.

Kuri-Morales, A. & Galaviz-Casas, J. 2002. Algoritmos Genéticos. *Instituto Politécnico Nacional, Universidad NAcional Autonoma de México, Fondo de Cultura Económica,,* 202.

Laribi, M. A., Mlika, A., Romdhane, L. & Zeghloul, S. 2004. A combined genetic algorithm-fuzzy logic method (GA-FL) in mechanisms synthesis. *Mechanism and machine theory (Mech. mach. theory),* 39, 717-735.

Levitski, N. L. & Shakvazian, K. K. 1960. Synthesis of four element spatial mechanisms with lower pairs. *International Journal of Mechanical Sciences* 2, 76-92.

Lima, C. A. F. 2005. Combining Competent Crossover and Mutation Operators:a Probabilistic Model Building Approach. *GECCO'05.*

Lima, C. F., Sastry, K., Goldberg, D. E. & Lobo, F. G. 2005. Combining Competent Crossover and Mutation Operators: a Probabilistic Model Building Approach. *GECCO'05,* ACM 1595930108/ 05/0006.

Lugo-González, E., Hernández-Gómez, L. H., Ponce-Reynoso, R., Velázquez-Sánchez, A. T., Urriolagoitia-Sosa, G., Merchán-Cruz, E. A. & Ramírez-Gordillo, J. 2010. Performance Optimization of GA Based Planar Mechanism Synthesis. *In Proceedings of the 2010 IEEE Electronics, Robotics and Automotive Mechanics Conference (September 28 - October 01, 2010). IEEE Computer Society, Washington, DC,* 126-131.

Lugo González, E. 2010. *Diseño de mecanismos utilizando algoritmos genéticos con aplicaciòn en prótesis para miembro inferior.*Doctorado, Instituto Politécnico Nacional.

Merchán-Cruz, E. A. 2005. *Soft-computing techniques in the trajectory planning of robot manipulators sharing a common workspace.* Doctor of Philosophy, Sheffield.

Merchán-Cruz, E. A., Hernández-Gómez, L. H., Velázquez-Sánchez, A. T., Lugo-González, E. & Urriolagoitia-Sosa, G. 2007. Exploiting monotony on a genetic algorithm based trajectory planner (GABTP) for robot manipulators.). F. *In the 16th IASTED international Conference on Applied Simulation and Modelling (Palma de Mallorca, Spain, August 29 - 31, 2007,* De Felice, Ed. ACTA Press, Anaheim, CA, 300-305.

Merchán-Cruz, E. A., Urriolagoitia-Sosa, G., Ramírez-Gordillo, J., Rodríguez-Cañizo, R., Campos-Padilla, I. Y., Muñoz-César, J. J. & Lugo-González, E. 2008. GA Based Trajectory Planner for Robot Manipulators Sharing a Common Workspace with Adaptive *Population Size. In Proceedings of the 2008 Electronics, Robotics and Automotive Mechanics Conference (September 30 - October 03, 2008). IEEE Computer Society, Washington, DC,* 520-525.

Michalewicz, Z. 1999. Genetic Algorithms + Data Structure = Evolution Programs. *tercera ed. Nueva York: Springer.*

Norton, R. L. 1995. *Diseño de Maquinaria,* Impreso en México, Mc. Graw Hill.

Quintero-R, H., Calle-Trujillo, G. & Dáz-Arias, A. 2004. Síntesis de generación de trayectorias y de movimiento para múltiples posiciones en mecanismos, utilizando algoritmos genéticos. *Scientia et Technica,* 10 No.25.

Radcliffe, C. 1977. The knud Jansen lecture:above-knee mechanisms: kinematics, alignment and prescription criteria.: Prosthetic and orthetic practice.

Ramírez-Gordillo, J. 2010. *Planeación de trayectorias en sistemas de manipuladores robóticos múltiples.*Doctorado, Instituto Politécnico Nacional.

Rechenberg, I. 1973. Evolutionsstrategie Optimierung technischer systeme nach prinzipien der biologischen evolution. *Friedrich Frommann Verlag, Stuttgart-Bad Cannstatt.*

Roston, G. P. & Sturges, R. H. 1996. Genetic Algorithm Synthesis of Four-bar Mechanisms. *Artificial Intelligence for Engineering Design,Analysis and Manufacturing,* 10, pp. 371-390.

Sanchéz-Marín, F. T. 2000. *Contribución a la Síntesis Dimensional de Mecanismos Planos para Generación de Trayectorias.*Doctor en Ciencias, Universitat Jaume-I.

Sinha, A. 2002. Designing Efficent Genetic and Evolutionary Algorithm Hybrids. *M.S. Thesis, University of Illinois-Urbana-Champaign.*

Smith, B. D. A. S. S., R. 1995. Fitness Inheritance in Genetic Algorithms. *in: Proc. of the ACM Symposium on Applied Computing,* 345-350.

Smith, R. 1993. Adaptively resizing populations: An algorithm and analysis. *Proc. 5th Int. Conf. Genetic Algorithms, S. Forrest Ed. San Mateo, CA: Morgan Kaufmann,* 653.

Srivastava, R. 2002. Time Continuation in Genetic Algorithms. *M.S. Thesis, University of Illinois-Urbana-Champaign.*

Starosta, R. 2006. On some application of genetic algorithm in mechanism synthesis. *Annual Meeting of GAMM, Book of Abstracts, 77.*

Tzong-Mou, W. & Cha'o-Kuang, C. 2005. Mathematical model and its simulation of exactly mechanism synthesis with adjustable link. *Applied Mathematics and Computation,* 160, 309-316.

Varbanov, H., Yankova, T., Kulev, K. & Lilov, S. 2006. S&AExpert system for planar mechanism design. *Expert Systems with Applications,* 31, 558-569.

Vasiliu, A. & Yannou, B. 2001. Dimensional Synthesis of planar Mechanism Using Neural Network: Application to path generator lnkages. *Mechanism and machine theory (Mech. mach. theory,* 36 No. 2, 229-310.

Walczak, T. 2006. Mechanism synthesis with the use of neural network. *in Annual Meeting of GAMM, Book of Abstracts.Berlin, 77.*

Wen-Jyi, H., Chien-Min, O. & Chin-Ming, Y. 2003. Robust Vector Quantization for Burst Error Channels Using Genetic Algorithm. *European Symposium on Artificial Neural Networks,* 267-274.

Whitley, D., Rana, S. & Heckendorn, R. 1998. Representation Issues in Neighborhood Search and Evolutionary Algorithms. *In D. Quagliarella, J. P´eriaux, C. Poloni, and G. Winter, editors, Genetic Algorithms and Evolution Strategies in Engineering and Computer Science. Recent Advances and Industrial Applications, chapter* 3, 39-57.

4

The Roles of Crossover and Mutation in Real-Coded Genetic Algorithms

Yourim Yoon[1] and Yong-Hyuk Kim[2*]
[1]*School of Computer Science and Engineering, Seoul National University, Seoul*
[2]*Department of Computer Science and Engineering, Kwangwoon University, Seoul*
Republic of Korea

1. Introduction

We recognized that the roles of crossover and mutation in real encoding are quite different from those in binary encoding during performing previous work with real-coded genetic algorithms (Yoon et al., 2012). In this study, we are to argue the distinct roles of genetic operators in real encodings.

Recently many studies on evolutionary algorithms using real encoding have been done. They include ant colony optimization (Socha & Dorigo, 2008), artificial bee colony algorithm (Akay & Karaboga, 2010; Kang et al., 2011), evolution strategies (ES) (Beyer, 2001), differential evolution (Das & Suganthan, 2011; Dasgupta et al., 2009; Kukkonen & Lampinen, 2004; 2005; Mezura-Montes et al., 2010; Noman & Iba, 2005; Rönkkönen et al., 2005; Storn & Price, 1997; Zhang et al., 2008), particle swarm optimization (Chen et al., 2007; Huang et al., 2010; Juang et al., 2011; Krohling & Coelho, 2006; l. Sun et al., 2011), and so on. In particular, in the field of ES, we can find many studies based on self-adaptive techniques (Beyer & Deb, 2001; Hansen & Ostermeier, 2001; Igel et al., 2007; 2006; Jägersküpper, 2007; Kita, 2001; Kramer, 2008a;b; Kramer et al., 2007; Meyer-Nieberg & Beyer, 2007; Wei et al., 2011).

Many researchers have also concentrated on using real-valued genes in genetic algorithms (GAs), as in (Ripon et al., 2007). It is reported that, for some problems, real-coded representation and associated techniques outperform conventional binary representation (Eshelman & Schaffer, 1993; Herrera et al., 1998; Janikow & Michalewicz, 1991; Lozano et al., 2004; Ono et al., 1999; Ono & Kobayashi, 1997; Surry & Radcliffe, 1996; Wright, 1991). Several theoretical studies of real-coded GAs have also been performed (Goldberg, 1991; Higuchi et al., 2000; Kita et al., 1998; Qi & Palmieri, 1994a;b). However, the role and behavior of genetic operators in real-coded GAs are fundamentally different from those in binary encodings although motivation of the operators and the framework of GAs are similar.

In this chapter, we try to verify different properties of crossover and mutation in real encodings from those in binary encodings through various experiments. We especially concentrate on the effect of genetic operators (the bias and functions of crossover and mutation) when they are used in real-coded GAs.

*Corresponding author: Yong-Hyuk Kim

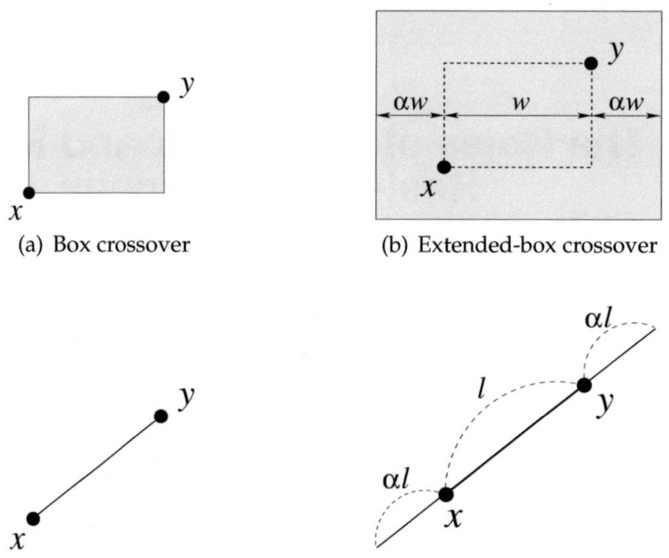

(a) Box crossover (b) Extended-box crossover

(c) Line crossover (d) Extended-line crossover

Fig. 1. The range of possible offspring in two-dimensional bounded real space

The remainder of this chapter is organized as follows. Traditional and recent genetic operators in real encoding are introduced in Section 2. Previous genetic operators are presented in Section 2.1 and ones we used in real encoding in this study are described in Section 2.2. In Section 3, we describe the concept of bias of genetic operators and analyze that in the case of crossover and mutation for GAs. In Section 4, experimental results for various combinations of crossover and mutation are provided and analyzed. Finally, we make conclusions in Section 5.

2. Genetic operators in real encoding

2.1 Previous operators

The roles of crossover and mutation may change according to the selection of the operators. We reviewed the most frequently used crossover and mutation operators for real-code representation. We are to analyze how the roles of crossover and mutation can change by studying various combinations of crossover and mutation operators.

In literature many crossover operators for real-code representation are found. Traditional crossover operators for the real-code representation are described in (Bäck et al., 2000). The two main families of traditional crossover operators (Mühlenbein & Schlierkamp-Voosen, 1993) are discrete crossovers[1] (Reed et al., 1967) and blend crossovers (Michalewicz, 1996). Blend crossover operators can be distinguished into line crossovers and box crossovers. Important variations of the last two crossover operators are the extended-line crossover and the extended-box crossover (Mühlenbein, 1994).

The discrete recombination family is the straightforward extension to real vectors of the family of mask-based crossover operators for binary strings including n-point and uniform crossover.

[1] It is also called *dominant crossover*.

```
box-crossover(x, y)
{
        for i ← 1 to n
            z_i ← a random real number in [min(x_i, y_i), max(x_i, y_i)];
        return z = (z_1, z_2, ..., z_n);
}
```

Fig. 2. Pseudo-code of box crossover

```
extended-box-crossover(x, y)
{
        for i ← 1 to n
            m ← min(x_i, y_i), M ← max(x_i, y_i);
            em ← m − α(M − m), eM ← M + α(M − m);
            z_i ← a random real number in [min(em, l_i), max(eM, u_i)];
        return z = (z_1, z_2, ..., z_n);
}
// α is extension rate.
```

Fig. 3. Pseudo-code of extended-box crossover

The mask is still a binary vector dictating for each position of the offspring vector from which parent the (real) value for that position is taken.

The blend recombination family does not exchange values between parents like discrete recombinations but it averages or blends them. Line recombination returns offspring on the (Euclidean) line segment connecting the two parents. Box recombination returns offspring in the box (hyper-rectangle) whose diagonally opposite corners are the parents. Extended-line recombination picks offspring on an extended segment passing through the parent vectors but extending beyond them and not only in the section between them. Analogously extended-box recombination picks offspring on an extended box whose main diagonal passes through the parents but extends beyond them.

Recently several new crossovers for the real-coded representation have been designed. Several non-traditional crossover operators for real-coded representation are found in the recent literature. They include SBX (simulated binary crossover) (Ballester & Carter, 2003; 2004b; Deb & Agrawal, 1995; Deb & Beyer, 1999; Deb & Kumar, 1995; Deb et al., 2007), UNDX (unimodal normal distribution crossover) (Kita et al., 1998; 1999; Ono et al., 1999; Ono & Kobayashi, 1997), SPX (simplex crossover) (Higuchi et al., 2000; Tsutsui & Goldberg, 2002; Tsutsui et al., 2001; 1999), PCX (parent-centric crossover) (Ballester & Carter, 2004a; Deb et al., 2002), etc (Herrera et al., 2003; 2005; Takahashi & Kita, 2001). Most of them are complex and based on the specific probability distribution of the offspring (SBX, UNDX, and PCX), self-adaptivity (SBX and UNDX), or multiple parents (UNDX and SPX). Some of them, e.g., include the function of mutation operators. In this study, we focus on traditional crossover that does not consider the specific probability distribution of the offspring but only what offspring can be generated with a probability greater than zero, given the two parents.

```
line-crossover(x, y)
{
        λ ← a random real number in [0,1];
        for i ← 1 to n
                z_i ← λx_i + (1 − λ)y_i;
        return z = (z_1, z_2, ..., z_n);
}
```

Fig. 4. Pseudo-code of line crossover

```
extended-line-crossover(x, y)
{
        m ← −∞, M ← ∞;
        for i ← 1 to n
                if x_i ≠ y_i
                        t_l ← (l_i − y_i)/(x_i − y_i), t_u ← (u_i − y_i)/(x_i − y_i);
                        t_m ← min(t_l, t_u), t_M ← max(t_l, t_u);
                        m ← max(m, t_m), M ← min(M, t_M);
        λ ← a random real number in [max(m, −α), min(M, 1 + α)];
        for i ← 1 to n
                z_i ← λx_i + (1 − λ)y_i;
        return z = (z_1, z_2, ..., z_n);
}
// α is extension rate.
```

Fig. 5. Pseudo-code of extended-line crossover

The most common form of mutation for real-code vectors generates an offspring vector by adding a vector M of random variables with expectation zero to the parent vector. There are two types of mutations bounded and unbounded depending on the fact that the range of the random variable is bounded or unbounded. The most frequently used bounded mutations are the creep mutation and the single-variable mutation and for the unbounded case is the Gaussian mutation. For the creep (or hyper-box) mutation $M \sim U([-a,a]^n)$ is a vector of uniform random variables, where a is a parameter defining the limits of the offspring area. This operator yields offspring within a hyper-box centered in the parent vector. For the single-variable mutation M is a vector in which all entries are set to zero except for a random entry which is a uniform random variable $\sim U([-a,a])$. Bounded mutation operators may get stuck in local optima. In contrast, unbounded mutation operators guarantee asymptotic global convergence. The primary unbounded mutation is the Gaussian mutation for which M is a multivariate Gaussian distribution.

2.2 Adopted operators for this study

As crossover operators for our analysis, we adopted four representative crossovers: box, extended-box, line, and extended-line crossovers. Their pseudo-codes are shown in Figures 2, 3, 4, and 5, respectively and the possible range for each crossover is represented in Figure 1.

```
mutation(z, p)
{
        for i ← 1 to n
                if a random number from [0,1] is less than mutation rate p
                   z_i ← z_i + N(0, (u_i − l_i)/10);
        return z = (z_1, z_2, ..., z_n);
}
```

Fig. 6. Pseudo-code of mutation

```
// x and y are parents.
fine-mutation(x, y, z, p)
{
        for i ← 1 to n
                if a random number from [0,1] is less than mutation rate p
                   z_i ← z_i + N(0, |x_i − y_i|);
        return z = (z_1, z_2, ..., z_n);
}
```

Fig. 7. Pseudo-code of fine mutation

And, as mutation operators for our analysis, we adopted two kinds of mutation: Gaussian mutation and fine mutation. Their pseudo-codes are shown in Figures 6 and 7, respectively. The Gaussian mutation is a simple static Gaussian mutation, the same as in Tsutsui & Goldberg (2001). The *i*-th parameter z_i of an individual is mutated by $z_i = z_i + N(0, \sigma_i)$ with a mutation rate p, where $N(0, \sigma_i)$ is an independent random Gaussian number with the mean of zero and the standard deviation of σ_i. In our study, σ_i is fixed to $(u_i - l_i)/10$ - the tenth of width of given area. The fine mutation is a simple dynamic Gaussian mutation inspired from Ballester & Carter (2004b). In different with Gaussian mutation, it depends on the distance between parents and, as population converges, the strength of the mutation approaches zero.

3. Bias of genetic operators

Pre-existing crossovers for the real-coded representation have an inherent bias toward the center of the space. Some boundary extension techniques to reduce crossover bias have been extensively studied (Someya & Yamamura, 2005; Tsutsui, 1998; Tsutsui & Goldberg, 2001). The concept of crossover *bias* first appeared in (Eshelman et al., 1997) and it has been extensively used in (Someya & Yamamura, 2005; Tsutsui & Goldberg, 2001), in which they tried to remove the bias of real-coded crossover heuristically (and theoretically incompletely).

Notice that the notion of bias of a crossover operator has different definitions depending upon the underlying representation considered. The bias toward the center of the space considered in real-coded crossovers conceptually differs from the crossover biases on binary strings, which focus on how many bits are passed to the offspring and from which positions, which, in turn conceptually differs from the bias considered in Genetic Programming focusing on bloat.

The notion of bias so defined can be understood as being the inherent preference of a search operator for specific areas of the search space. This is an important search property of a search

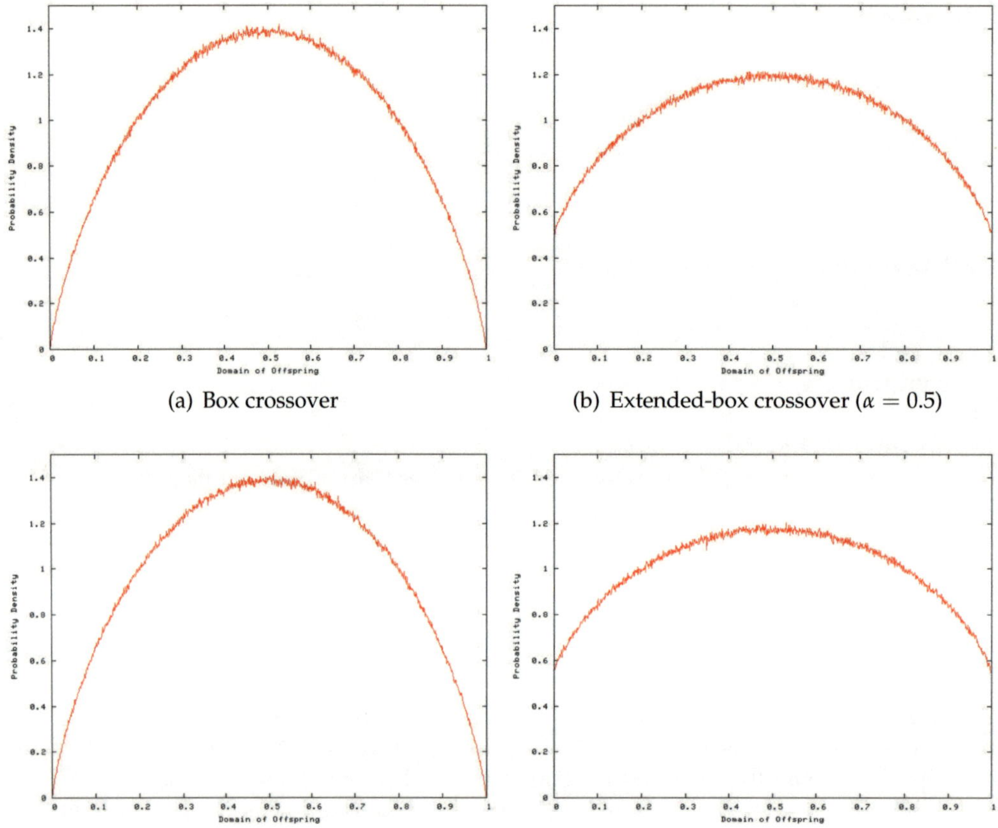

(a) Box crossover

(b) Extended-box crossover ($\alpha = 0.5$)

(c) Line crossover

(d) Extended-line crossover ($\alpha = 0.5$)

Fig. 8. Crossover bias in one-dimensional bounded real space

operator: an evolutionary algorithm using that operator, without selection, is attracted to the areas the search operator prefers. Arguably, also when selection is present, the operator bias acts as a background force that makes the search keener to go toward the areas preferred by the search operator. This is not necessarily bad if the bias is toward the optimum or an area with high-quality solutions. However, it may negatively affect performance if the bias is toward an area of poor-quality solutions. If we do not know the spatial distribution of the fitness of the problem, we may prefer not to have any *a priori* bias of the search operator, and instead use only the bias of selection, which is informed by the fitness of sampled solutions that constitute empirical knowledge about promising areas obtained in the search, and which is better understood.

In this chapter, we investigate the bias caused by crossover itself and crossover combined with mutation in real-coded GAs. Intuitively, box and line crossover are biased toward the center on the Euclidean space. This intuition is easy to verify experimentally by picking a large number of pairs (ideally infinitely many) of random parents and generating offspring uniformly at random in the boxes (or lines) identified by the pairs of parents.

Function	n	Range of x_i: $[l_i, u_i]$
Shifted sphere $\sum_{i=1}^{n}(x_i - o_i)^2 - 450$	30	$[-100, 100]$
Shifted Schwefel $\sum_{i=1}^{n}(\sum_{j=1}^{i}(x_j - o_j))^2 - 450$	30	$[-100, 100]$
Shifted Rosenbrock $\sum_{i=1}^{n-1}(100((x_i - o_i + 1)^2 - (x_{i+1} - o_{i+1} + 1))^2 + (x_i - o_i)^2) + 390$	30	$[-100, 100]$
Shifted Rastrigin $\sum_{i=1}^{n}((x_i - o_i)^2 - 10\cos(2\pi(x_i - o_i)) + 10) - 330$	30	$[-5, 5]$

Table 1. Test Functions
$\boldsymbol{o} = (o_1, o_2, \ldots, o_n)$ is the optimal solution, which is randomly located in the domain.

In the Hamming space, the distribution of the offspring of uniform crossover tends in the limit to be uniform on all space, whereas in the Euclidean space the distribution of the offspring tends to be unevenly distributed on the search space and concentrates toward the center of the space. One way to compensate, but not eliminate, such bias is using extended-line and extended-box crossovers. Figure 8 visualizes the crossover bias in the one-dimensional real space by plotting frequency rates of 10^7 offspring randomly generated by each type crossover. As we can see, box and line crossover are biased toward the center of the domain. We could also observe that extended-box and extended-line crossover largely reduce the bias but they are still biased toward the center.[2]

For analyzing the effect of mutation in relation with the bias, we also performed the same test using crossover combined with Gaussian mutation. We picked 10^7 pairs of random parents, generated offspring randomly using each type crossover, and then applied Gaussian mutation. The tests are performed for various mutation rates from 0.0 to 1.0. The results for box, extended-box, line, and extended-line crossover are shown in Figures 9, 10, 11, and 12, respectively. Interestingly, for all cases, we could observe that the higher mutation rate reduces the bias more largely. However, even high mutation rates cannot eliminate the bias completely.

4. Combination of crossover and mutation

In this section, we try to figure out the properties of crossover and mutation through experiments using their various combinations. For our experiments, four test functions are chosen from Suganthan et al. (2005). They are described in Table 1.

We mainly followed the genetic framework by Tsutsui & Goldberg (2001). Its basic evolutionary model is quite similar to that of CHC (Eshelman, 1991) and $(\mu + \lambda)$-ES (Beyer, 2001).

[2] We can find consistent results with this in Someya & Yamamura (2005); Yoon et al. (2012).

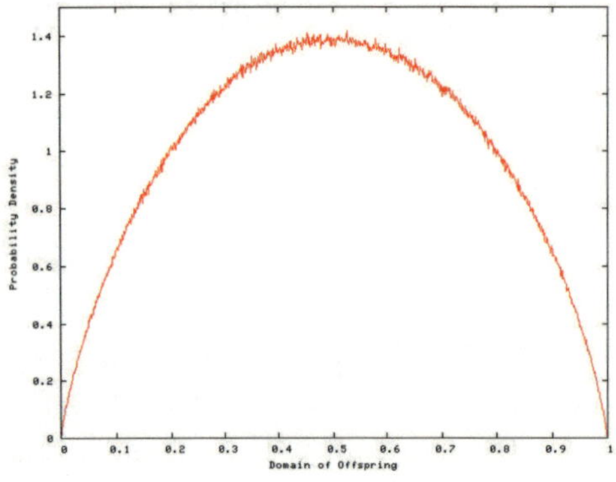

(a) Crossover without mutation

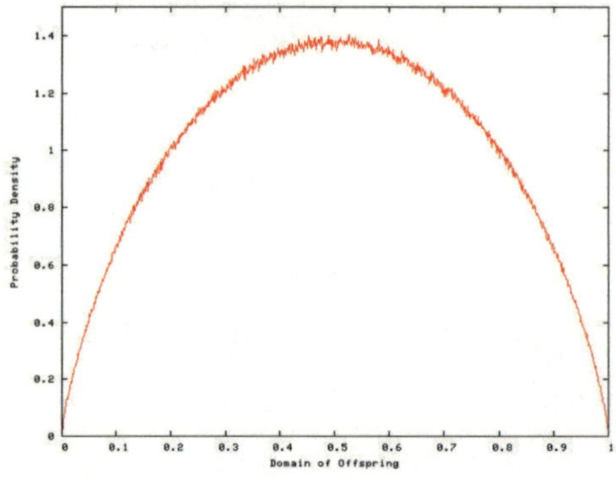

(b) Crossover with mutation ($p = 0.05$)

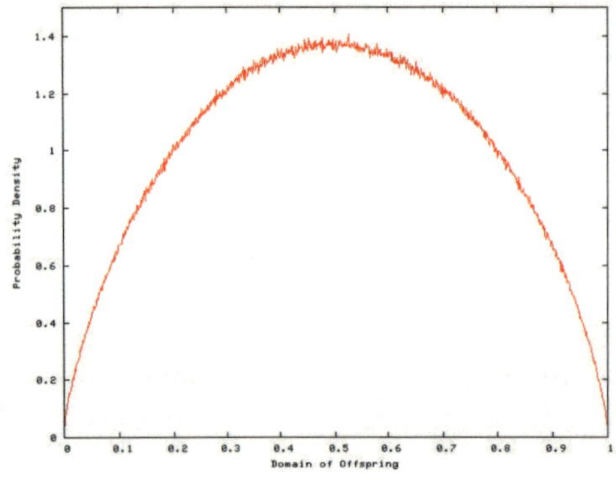

(c) Crossover with mutation ($p = 0.1$)

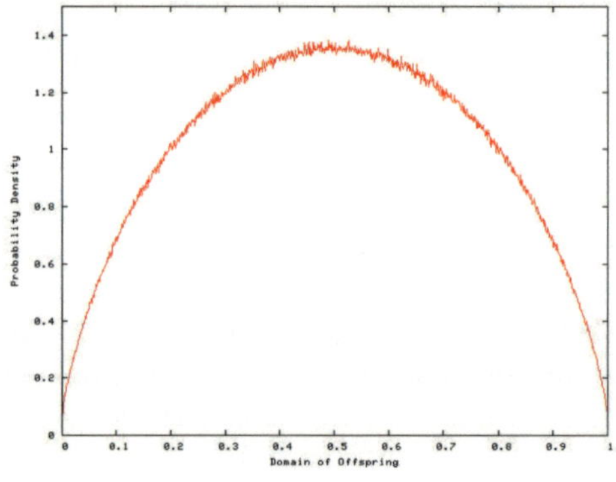

(d) Crossover with mutation ($p = 0.2$)

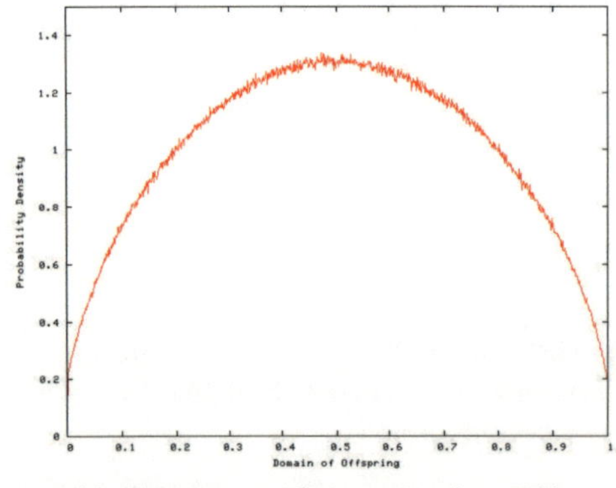

(e) Crossover with mutation ($p = 0.5$)

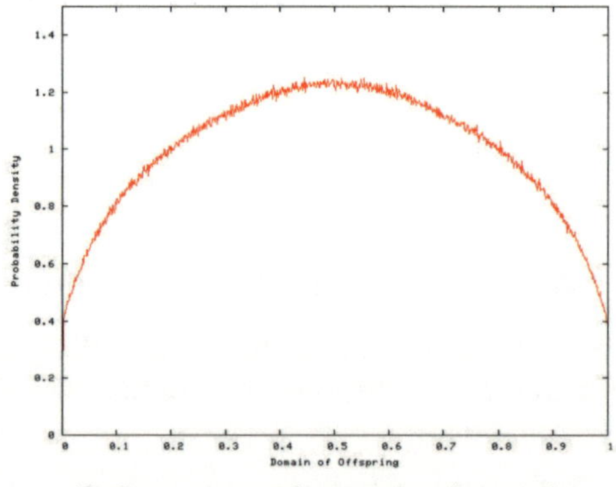

(f) Crossover with mutation ($p = 1.0$)

Fig. 9. Bias of box crossover with mutation

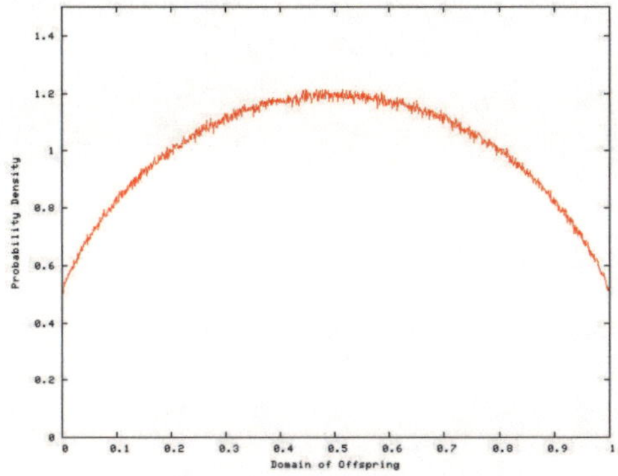

(a) Crossover without mutation

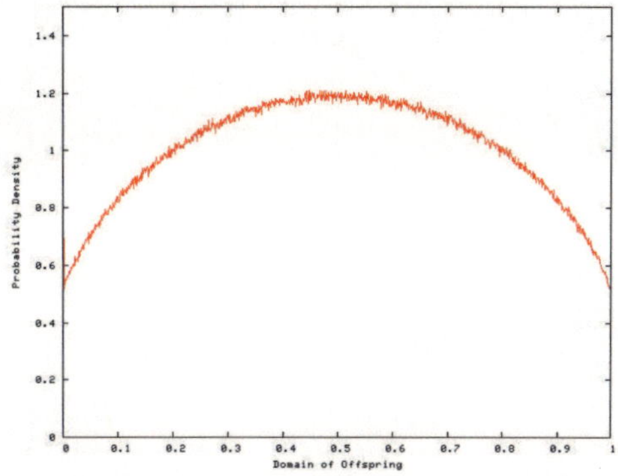

(b) Crossover with mutation ($p = 0.05$)

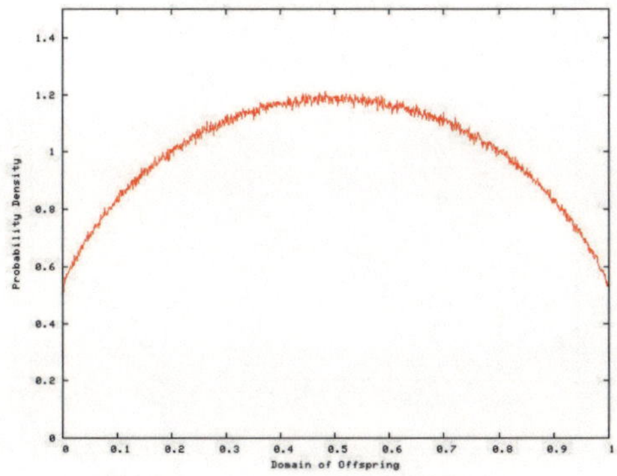

(c) Crossover with mutation ($p = 0.1$)

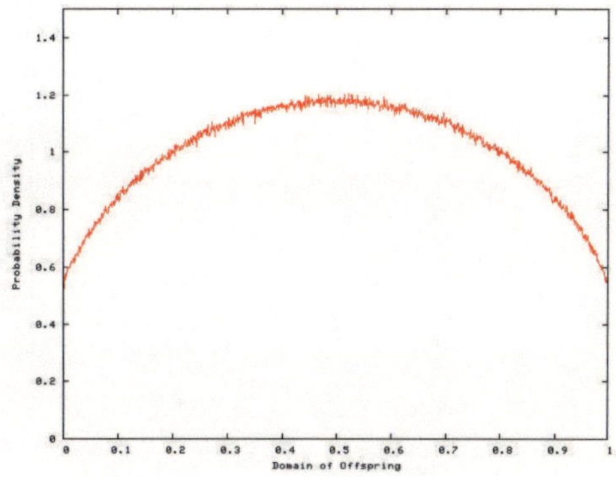

(d) Crossover with mutation ($p = 0.2$)

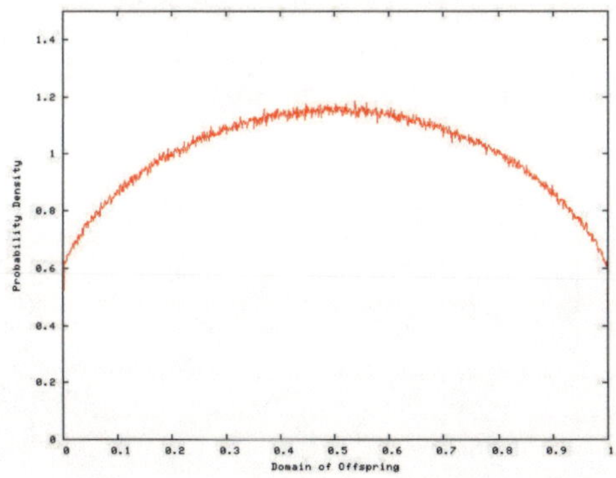

(e) Crossover with mutation ($p = 0.5$)

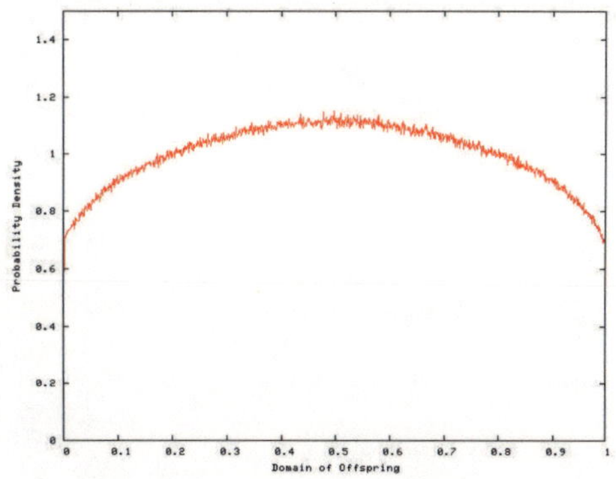

(f) Crossover with mutation ($p = 1.0$)

Fig. 10. Bias of extended-box crossover ($\alpha = 0.5$) with mutation

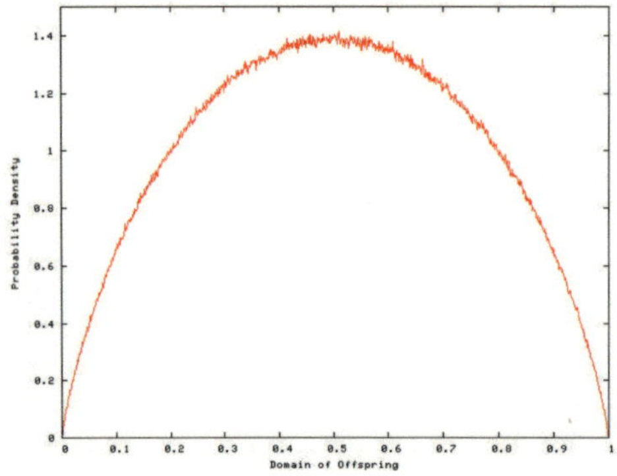

(a) Crossover without mutation

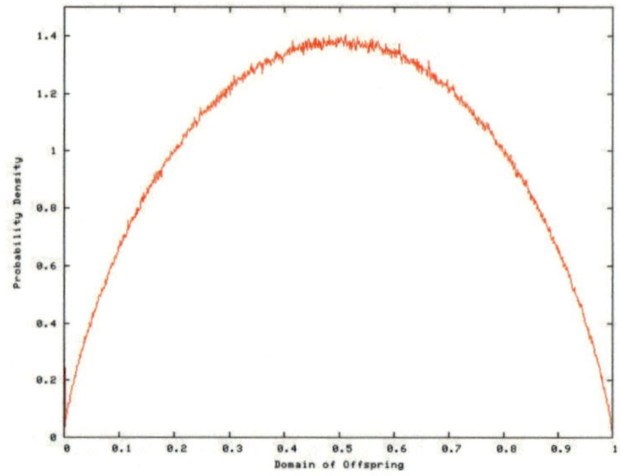

(b) Crossover with mutation ($p = 0.05$)

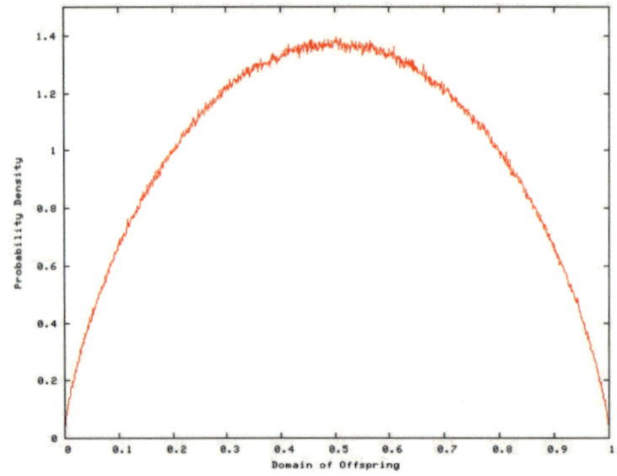

(c) Crossover with mutation ($p = 0.1$)

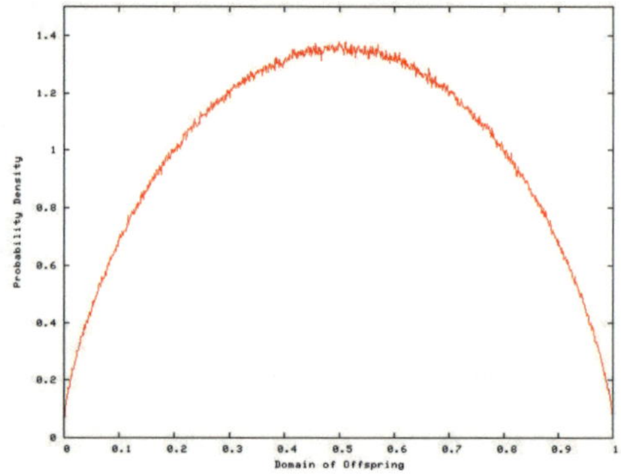

(d) Crossover with mutation ($p = 0.2$)

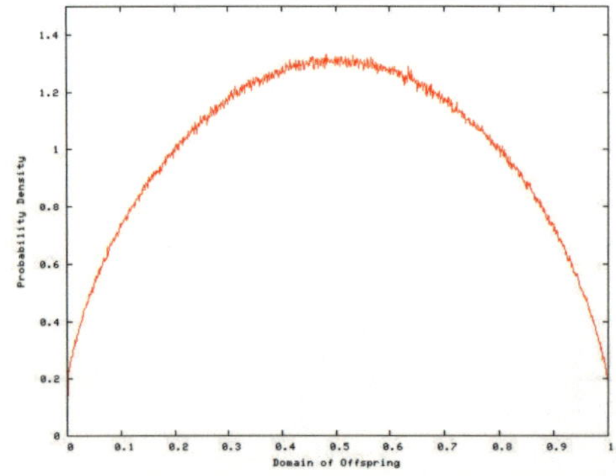

(e) Crossover with mutation ($p = 0.5$)

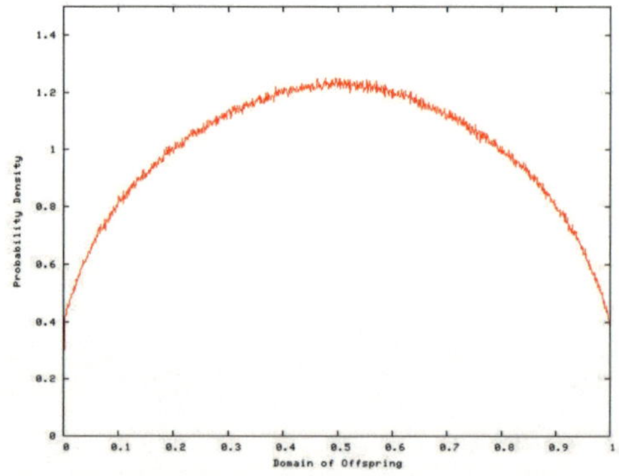

(f) Crossover with mutation ($p = 1.0$)

Fig. 11. Bias of line crossover with mutation

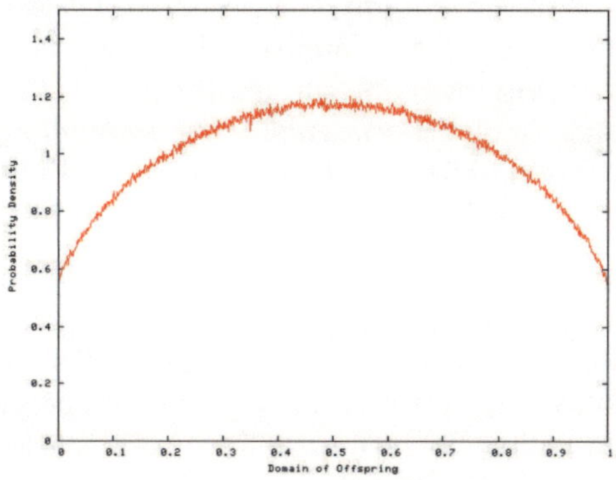

(a) Crossover without mutation

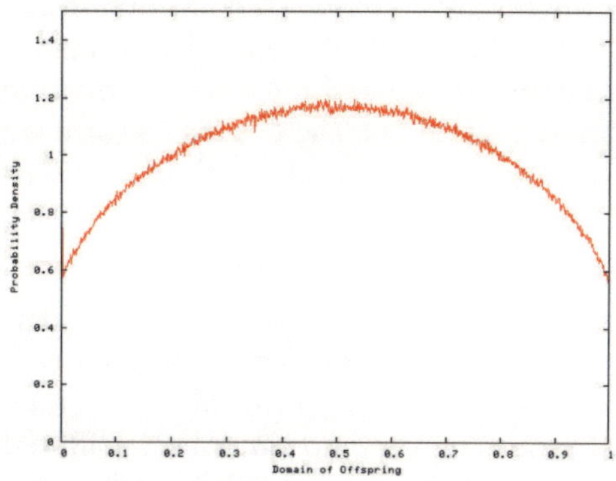

(b) Crossover with mutation ($p = 0.05$)

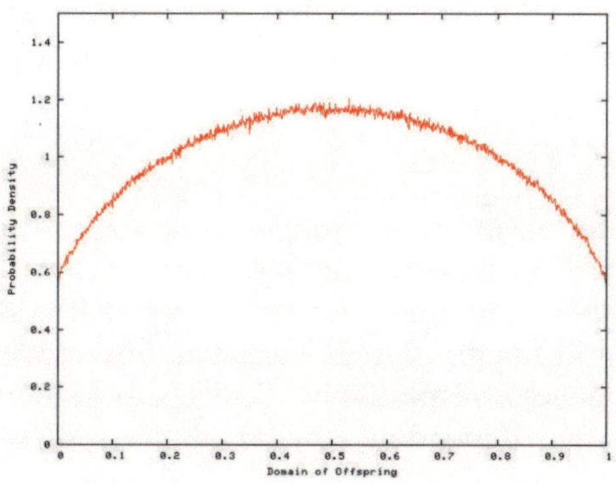

(c) Crossover with mutation ($p = 0.1$)

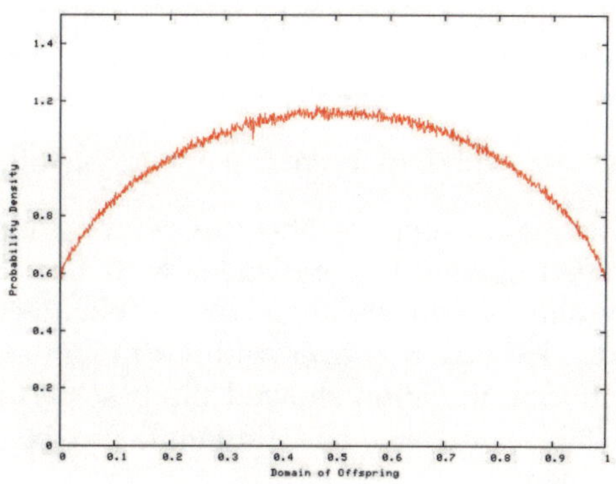

(d) Crossover with mutation ($p = 0.2$)

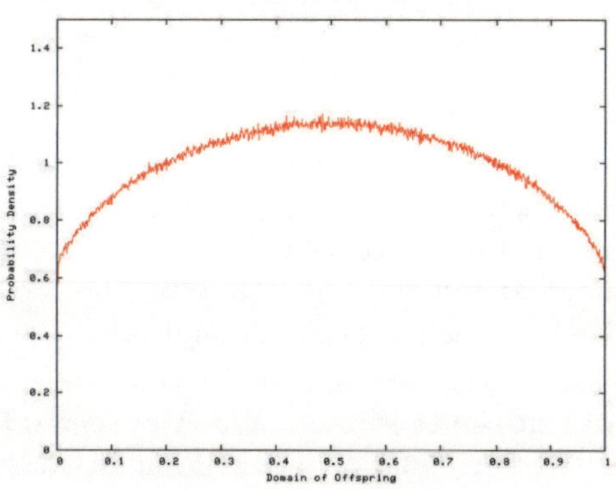

(e) Crossover with mutation ($p = 0.5$)

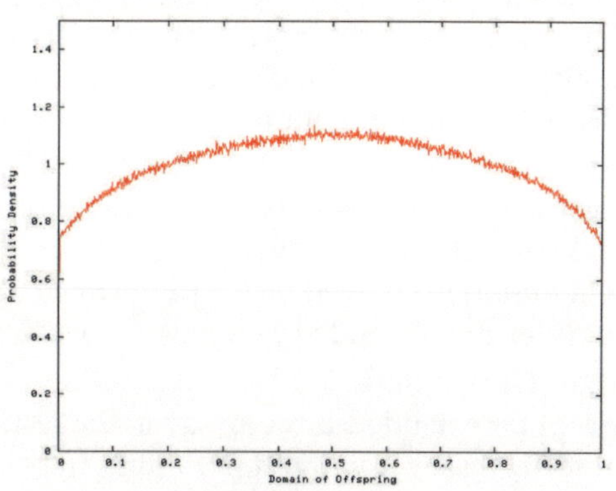

(f) Crossover with mutation ($p = 1.0$)

Fig. 12. Bias of extended-line crossover ($\alpha = 0.5$) with mutation

Let N the population size. A collection of $N/2$ pairs is randomly composed, and crossover and mutation are applied to each pair, generating $N/2$ offspring. Parents and newly generated offspring are ranked and the best N individuals among them are selected for the population in the next generation. The population size was 400 for all experiments. If the population has no change during $n \times r \times (1.0 - r)$ generations, it is reinitialized except for the best individual. Here, r is a divergence rate and we set it to 0.25 as in Eshelman (1991). The used GA terminates when it finds the global optimum.

For crossover, we used four crossover operators: box crossover, extended-box crossover (extension rate α: 0.5), line crossover, and extended-line crossover (extension rate α: 0.5). After crossover, we either mutate the offspring or do not. We used two different mutation operators; Gaussian mutation and fine mutation. Different mutation rates were applied to each crossover type and the rates decrease as the number of generations increases.

Table 2 shows the results from 30 runs. Each value in 'Ave' means the average function value from 30 runs. The smaller, the better. The limit of function evaluations is 50,000, i.e., the genetic algorithm terminates after 50,000 evaluations and outputs the best solution among evaluated ones so far over generations. In the table, $k = 1 + \lfloor numberOfGenerations/100 \rfloor$ and the rate of fine mutation is $0.5/k$.

From these experiments we can obtain the following properties.

- There is no superior operator combination for all over the problem instances. For the shifted sphere, box crossover with fine mutation showed the best performance. For the shifted Schwefel, line crossover with Gaussian mutation, for the shifted Rosenbrock, extended-box crossover without mutation, and for the shifted Rastrigin, box crossover with fine mutation showed the best performances, respectively. So we can know that suitable crossover and mutation can be varied depending on the property of given problem.
- Without mutation, extended-box crossover showed the best performance. That is, when we do not know the characteristic of given problem, it is a general choice that we use extended-box crossover as a crossover operator in real-coded genetic algorithms. It is convenient since parameter tuning with mutation is not required. However, it is possible to surpass the performance of extended-box crossover using well-designed combination of crossover and mutation.
- Unusually, for extended-box crossover, the results without mutation is the best and the performance becomes worse as mutation rate increases. However, for box crossover, moderate rate of mutation has a good effect to the performance. For all cases, box crossover with mutation showed better performance than that without mutation. From this fact, we can infer that extended-box crossover contains the function of mutation in itself but box crossover does not.
- Except for extended-box crossover, the results of crossover with mutation were better than those of crossover without mutation. In particular, fine mutation was better than Gaussian mutation. Fine mutation depends on the distance between parents so, as population converges, the strength of the mutation approaches zero. That is, the amount of mutation becomes very fine as population converges. In binary encodings, the main role of mutation is perturbation effect to prevent premature convergence. However, we can know that, in real encoding, the function of fine tuning by mutation is also important from this experiment.

	Function	Shifted Sphere	Shifted Schwefel	Shifted Rosenbrock	Shifted Rastrigin
Crossover	Mutation	Ave ($\sigma/\sqrt{n}$)	Ave ($\sigma/\sqrt{n}$)	Ave ($\sigma/\sqrt{n}$)	Ave ($\sigma/\sqrt{n}$)
None	0.05/k	5.46e+02 (4.59e+01)	1.68e+04 (9.05e+02)	1.87e+07 (1.70e+06)	-2.66e+02 (1.91e+00)
	0.10/k	**6.40e+01** (2.17e+01)	1.16e+04 (5.33e+02)	**4.64e+06** (3.86e+05)	**-2.68e+02** (1.65e+00)
	0.20/k	1.37e+02 (1.55e+01)	7.99e+03 (4.79e+02)	4.74e+06 (2.34e+05)	-2.64e+02 (1.58e+00)
	0.50/k	9.87e+02 (3.13e+01)	**7.87e+03** (3.18e+02)	1.89e+07 (8.19e+05)	-2.27e+02 (1.28e+00)
	1.00/k	2.38e+03 (6.45e+01)	1.24e+04 (3.76e+02)	7.12e+07 (2.45e+06)	-1.91e+02 (1.72e+00)
Box crossover	None	2.46e+04 (4.46e+02)	2.47e+04 (3.03e+02)	5.36e+09 (1.69e+08)	-1.83e+02 (1.64e+00)
	0.05/k	-3.61e+02 (1.81e+00)	1.44e+04 (1.96e+02)	2.66e+05 (8.26e+03)	-2.53e+02 (1.51e+00)
	0.10/k	-4.02e+02 (1.13e+00)	1.22e+04 (1.42e+02)	7.86e+04 (2.26e+03)	**-2.60e+02** (1.11e+00)
	0.20/k	**-4.25e+02** (6.96e-01)	9.98e+03 (1.40e+02)	**4.34e+04** (1.57e+03)	-2.48e+02 (2.37e+00)
	0.50/k	-3.40e+02 (3.04e+00)	**8.10e+03** (1.17e+02)	2.16e+05 (1.02e+04)	-1.94e+02 (1.90e+00)
	1.00/k	2.81e+02 (1.54e+01)	8.68e+03 (2.05e+02)	5.55e+06 (2.53e+05)	-1.71e+02 (1.48e+00)
	Fine	**-4.50e+02** (4.63e-03)	8.74e+03 (1.16e+02)	**1.40e+03** (7.16e+01)	**-3.03e+02** (1.60e+00)
	Fine + 0.05/k	**-4.50e+02** (2.54e-02)	8.43e+03 (1.36e+02)	1.99e+03 (8.59e+01)	-2.77e+02 (3.16e+00)
	Fine + 0.10/k	-4.48e+02 (8.07e-02)	8.10e+03 (1.42e+02)	3.33e+03 (1.59e+02)	-2.39e+02 (3.26e+00)
	Fine + 0.20/k	-4.37e+02 (5.19e-01)	**7.83e+03** (1.06e+02)	1.78e+04 (8.37e+02)	-2.07e+02 (1.87e+00)
	Fine + 0.50/k	-2.11e+02 (6.63e+00)	8.83e+03 (1.72e+02)	8.47e+05 (3.91e+04)	-1.82e+02 (1.64e+00)
	Fine + 1.00/k	6.67e+02 (2.51e+01)	1.20e+04 (2.27e+02)	1.08e+07 (5.26e+05)	-1.68e+02 (1.65e+00)
Extended box crossover ($\alpha = 0.5$)	None	**-4.50e+02** (2.72e-04)	**8.78e+03** (1.90e+02)	**7.45e+02** (3.21e+01)	**-2.21e+02** (2.33e+00)
	0.05/k	-4.49e+02 (3.17e-02)	9.63e+03 (2.20e+02)	3.14e+03 (1.67e+02)	-2.00e+02 (1.97e+00)
	0.10/k	-4.40e+02 (2.52e-01)	1.07e+04 (2.50e+02)	2.24e+04 (9.14e+02)	-1.95e+02 (1.75e+00)
	0.20/k	-3.59e+02 (2.22e+00)	1.25e+04 (2.45e+02)	3.35e+05 (1.86e+04)	-1.81e+02 (1.66e+00)
	0.50/k	2.54e+02 (1.91e+01)	1.60e+04 (3.92e+02)	6.93e+06 (3.35e+05)	-1.63e+02 (1.68e+00)
	1.00/k	1.60e+03 (5.17e+01)	2.10e+04 (4.98e+02)	4.65e+07 (1.85e+06)	-1.50e+02 (2.26e+00)
	Fine	**-4.23e+02** (7.81e-01)	**1.76e+04** (3.62e+02)	**2.07e+05** (1.21e+04)	**-1.75e+02** (1.71e+00)
	Fine + 0.05/k	-3.67e+02 (2.09e+00)	1.80e+04 (4.84e+02)	7.16e+05 (2.99e+04)	-1.68e+02 (1.56e+00)
	Fine + 0.10/k	-2.72e+02 (3.48e+00)	1.85e+04 (4.39e+02)	1.55e+06 (6.25e+04)	-1.68e+02 (1.83e+00)
	Fine + 0.20/k	-2.18e+01 (1.03e+01)	1.84e+04 (5.26e+02)	5.45e+06 (2.49e+05)	-1.63e+02 (2.22e+00)
	Fine + 0.50/k	9.07e+02 (3.03e+01)	2.24e+04 (5.74e+02)	2.69e+07 (1.32e+06)	-1.52e+02 (1.92e+00)
	Fine + 1.00/k	2.47e+03 (5.56e+01)	2.55e+04 (5.66e+02)	9.84e+07 (3.94e+06)	-1.37e+02 (2.26e+00)
Line crossover	None	4.29e+04 (6.09e+02)	3.44e+04 (8.72e+02)	1.22e+10 (4.00e+08)	-7.32e+01 (3.09e+00)
	0.05/k	-2.11e+02 (4.61e+00)	1.45e+04 (3.04e+02)	1.30e+06 (4.48e+04)	-2.24e+02 (2.19e+00)
	0.10/k	-3.55e+02 (2.03e+00)	1.26e+04 (2.19e+02)	2.12e+05 (7.95e+03)	**-2.32e+02** (1.56e+00)
	0.20/k	**-4.00e+02** (1.76e+00)	1.00e+04 (1.80e+02)	**9.66e+04** (3.77e+03)	-2.24e+02 (3.13e+00)
	0.50/k	-3.37e+02 (3.29e+00)	**7.26e+03** (1.59e+02)	2.33e+05 (1.30e+04)	-1.91e+02 (1.62e+00)
	1.00/k	2.37e+02 (2.04e+01)	6.93e+03 (1.46e+02)	4.34e+06 (2.80e+05)	-1.73e+02 (1.50e+00)
	Fine	**-4.48e+02** (1.22e-01)	9.38e+03 (1.38e+02)	1.07e+04 (8.87e+02)	**-2.87e+02** (2.31e+00)
	Fine + 0.05/k	-4.47e+02 (1.52e-01)	8.81e+03 (1.73e+02)	**8.13e+03** (4.91e+02)	-2.58e+02 (4.68e+00)
	Fine + 0.10/k	-4.43e+02 (4.00e-01)	8.16e+03 (1.54e+02)	1.10e+04 (6.89e+02)	-2.30e+02 (3.34e+00)
	Fine + 0.20/k	-4.32e+02 (5.20e-01)	7.79e+03 (1.37e+02)	2.95e+04 (1.63e+03)	-2.05e+02 (1.97e+00)
	Fine + 0.50/k	-2.27e+02 (7.78e+00)	**7.71e+03** (1.70e+02)	7.95e+05 (3.23e+04)	-1.82e+02 (1.50e+00)
	Fine + 1.00/k	5.76e+02 (2.37e+01)	9.91e+03 (1.62e+02)	9.54e+06 (5.55e+05)	-1.62e+02 (1.68e+00)
Extended line crossover ($\alpha = 0.5$)	None	3.85e+04 (9.05e+02)	3.11e+04 (6.79e+02)	9.81e+09 (5.11e+08)	-1.17e+02 (3.40e+00)
	0.05/k	-1.37e+02 (1.20e+01)	1.21e+04 (2.97e+02)	2.97e+06 (2.14e+05)	**-2.40e+02** (2.59e+00)
	0.10/k	-3.27e+02 (4.22e+00)	9.46e+03 (2.92e+02)	5.23e+05 (3.33e+04)	-2.37e+02 (2.16e+00)
	0.20/k	**-3.67e+02** (3.37e+00)	8.19e+03 (2.09e+02)	**2.02e+05** (1.00e+04)	-2.13e+02 (2.53e+00)
	0.50/k	-2.41e+02 (6.38e+00)	**7.03e+03** (1.43e+02)	6.22e+05 (3.95e+04)	-1.88e+02 (1.40e+00)
	1.00/k	4.60e+02 (2.41e+01)	8.00e+03 (1.61e+02)	7.43e+06 (3.58e+05)	-1.69e+02 (1.61e+00)
	Fine	**-4.46e+02** (2.66e-01)	7.67e+03 (1.98e+02)	**1.88e+04** (2.14e+03)	**-2.44e+02** (5.08e+00)
	Fine + 0.05/k	-4.39e+02 (4.12e-01)	7.69e+03 (1.76e+02)	2.28e+04 (1.56e+03)	-2.26e+02 (3.84e+00)
	Fine + 0.10/k	-4.29e+02 (1.03e+00)	7.52e+03 (1.90e+02)	3.51e+04 (2.50e+03)	-2.09e+02 (1.96e+00)
	Fine + 0.20/k	-3.92e+02 (2.23e+00)	**7.24e+03** (1.57e+02)	1.42e+05 (7.84e+03)	-1.92e+02 (1.67e+00)
	Fine + 0.50/k	-4.34e+01 (1.06e+01)	8.62e+03 (1.56e+02)	1.93e+06 (8.59e+04)	-1.73e+02 (1.65e+00)
	Fine + 1.00/k	8.69e+02 (3.33e+01)	1.10e+04 (2.63e+02)	1.51e+07 (9.43e+05)	-1.57e+02 (1.86e+00)

Table 2. Results

5. Conclusions

In this chapter, we tried to analyze distinct roles of crossover and mutation when using real encoding in genetic algorithms. We investigated the bias of crossover and mutation. From this investigation, we could know that extended crossover and mutation can reduce the inherent bias of traditional crossover in real-coded genetic algorithms.

We also studied the functions of crossover and mutation operators through experiments for various combinations of both operators. From these experiments, we could know that extended-box crossover is good in the case of using only crossover without mutation. However, it is possible to surpass the performance of extended-box crossover using well-designed combination of crossover and mutation. In the case of other crossover operators, not only the function of perturbation but also that of fine tuning by mutation is important, but extended-box crossover contains the fine tuning function in itself.

There are many other test functions defined on real domains. We conducted experiments with limited test functions. We may obtain more reliable conclusions through experiments with more other functions. So, more extended experiments on more various test functions are needed for future work. We may also find other useful properties from those empirical study.

6. Acknowledgments

The authors would like to thank Dr. Alberto Moraglio for his encouragement and valuable comments in improving this study. This work was supported by the Research and Development of Advanced Weather Technology of National Institute of Meteorological Research (NIMR) of Korea in 2011.

7. References

Akay, B. & Karaboga, D. (2010). A modified artificial bee colony algorithm for real-parameter optimization, *Information Sciences* . doi:10.1016/j.ins.2010.07.015.

Bäck, T., Fogel, D. B. & Michalewicz, T. (eds) (2000). *Evolutionary Computation 1: Basic Algorithms and Operators*, Institute of Physics Publishing.

Ballester, P. J. & Carter, J. N. (2003). Real-parameter genetic algorithms for finding multiple optimal solutions in multi-modal optimization, *Proceedings of the Genetic and Evolutionary Computation Conference*, pp. 706–717.

Ballester, P. J. & Carter, J. N. (2004a). An effective real-parameter genetic algorithm with parent centric normal crossover for multimodal optimisation, *Proceedings of the Genetic and Evolutionary Computation Conference*, pp. 901–913.

Ballester, P. J. & Carter, J. N. (2004b). An effective real-parameter genetic algorithms for multimodal optimization, *Proceedings of the Adaptive Computing in Design and Manufacture VI*, pp. 359–364.

Beyer, H.-G. (2001). *Theory of Evolution Strategies*, Springer.

Beyer, H.-G. & Deb, K. (2001). On self-adaptive features in real-parameter evolutionary algorithms, *IEEE Transactions on Evolutionary Computation* 5(3): 250–270.

Chen, Y.-P., Peng, W.-C. & Jian, M.-C. (2007). Particle swarm optimization with recombination and dynamic linkage discovery, *IEEE Transactions on Systems, Man, and Cybernetics, Part B* 37(6): 1460–1470.

Das, S. & Suganthan, P. N. (2011). Differential evolution - a survey of the state-of-the-art, *IEEE Transactions on Evolutionary Computation* 15(1): 4–31.

Dasgupta, S., Das, S., Biswas, A. & Abraham, A. (2009). On stability and convergence of the population-dynamics in differential evolution, *AI Commun.* 22(1): 1–20.

Deb, K. & Agrawal, R. B. (1995). Simulated binary crossover for continuous search space, *Complex Systems* 9(2): 115–148.

Deb, K., Anand, A. & Joshi, D. (2002). A computationally efficient evolutionary algorithm for real-parameter optimization, *Evolutionary Computation* 10(4): 371–395.

Deb, K. & Beyer, H.-G. (1999). Self-adaptation in real-parameter genetic algorithms with simulated binary crossover, *Proceedings of the Genetic and Evolutionary Computation Conference*, pp. 172–179.

Deb, K. & Kumar, A. (1995). Real-coded genetic algorithms with simulated binary crossover: Studies on multi-modal and multi-objective problems, *Complex Systems* 9: 431–454.

Deb, K., Sindhya, K. & Okabe, T. (2007). Self-adaptive simulated binary crossover for real-parameter optimization, *Proceedings of the Genetic and Evolutionary Computation Conference*, pp. 1187–1194.

Eshelman, L. J. (1991). The CHC adaptive search algorithm: How to have safe search when engaging in nontraditional genetic recombination, *Proceedings of the Workshop on Foundations of Genetic Algorithms*, pp. 265–283.

Eshelman, L. J., Mathias, K. E. & Schaffer, J. D. (1997). Crossover operator biases: Exploiting the population distribution, *Proceedings of the International Conference on Genetic Algorithms*, pp. 354–361.

Eshelman, L. J. & Schaffer, J. D. (1993). Real-coded genetic algorithms and interval-schemata, *Proceedings of the Workshop on Foundations of Genetic Algorithms*, pp. 187–202.

Goldberg, D. E. (1991). Real-coded genetic algorithms, virtual alphabets, and blocking, *Complex Systems* 5: 139–167.

Hansen, N. & Ostermeier, A. (2001). Completely derandomized self-adaptation in evolution strategies, *Evolutionary Computation* 9: 159–195.

Herrera, F., Lozano, M. & Sánchez, A. M. (2003). A taxonomy for the crossover operator for real-coded genetic algorithms: An experimental study, *International Journal of Intelligent Systems* 18(3): 309–338.

Herrera, F., Lozano, M. & Sánchez, A. M. (2005). Hybrid crossover operators for real-coded genetic algorithms: an experimental study, *Soft Computing* 9(4): 280–298.

Herrera, F., Lozano, M. & Verdegay, J. L. (1998). Tackling real-coded genetic algorithms: Operators and tools for behavioural analysis, *Artificial Intelligence Review* 12(4): 265–319.

Higuchi, T., Tsutsui, S. & Yamamura, M. (2000). Theoretical analysis of simplex crossover for real-coded genetic algorithms, *Proceedings of the Sixth International Conference on Parallel Problem Solving from Nature*, pp. 365–374.

Huang, H., Qin, H., Hao, Z. & Lim, A. (2010). Example-based learning particle swarm optimization for continuous optimization, *Information Sciences* . doi:10.1016/j.ins.2010. 10.018.

Igel, C., Hansen, N. & Roth, S. (2007). Covariance matrix adaptation for multi-objective optimization, *Evolutionary Computation* 15(1): 1–28.

Igel, C., Suttorp, T. & Hansen, N. (2006). A computational efficient covariance matrix update and a $(1+1)$-CMA for evolution strategies, *Proceedings of the Genetic and Evolutionary Computation Conference*, pp. 453–460.

Jägersküpper, J. (2007). Algorithmic analysis of a basic evolutionary algorithm for continuous optimization, *Theoretical Computer Science* 379(3): 329–347.

Janikow, C. Z. & Michalewicz, Z. (1991). An experimental comparison of binary and floating point representations in genetic algorithms, *Proceedings of the Fourth International Conference on Genetic Algorithms*, pp. 31–36.

Juang, Y.-T., Tung, S.-L. & Chiu, H.-C. (2011). Adaptive fuzzy particle swarm optimization for global optimization of multimodal functions, *Information Sciences* (20): 4539–4549.

Kang, F., Li, J. & Ma, Z. (2011). Rosenbrock artificial bee colony algorithm for accurate global optimization of numerical functions, *Information Sciences* (16): 3508–3531.

Kita, H. (2001). A comparison study of self-adaptation in evolution strategies and real-coded genetic algorithms, *Evolutionary Computation* 9(2): 223–241.

Kita, H., Ono, I. & Kobayashi, S. (1998). Theoretical analysis of the unimodal normal distribution crossover for real-coded genetic algorithms, *Proceedings of the International Conference on Evolutionary Computation*, pp. 529–534.

Kita, H., Ono, I. & Kobayashi, S. (1999). Multi-parental extension of the unimodal normal distribution crossover for real-coded genetic algorithms, *Proceedings of the Congress on Evolutionary Computation*, pp. 1581–1587.

Kramer, O. (2008a). Premature convergence in constrained continuous search spaces, *Proceedings of the Parallel Problem Solving from Nature*, pp. 62–71.

Kramer, O. (2008b). *Self-Adaptive Heuristics for Evolutionary Computation*, Springer.

Kramer, O., Gloger, B. & Goebels, A. (2007). An experimental analysis of evolution strategies and particle swarm optimisers using design of experiments, *Proceedings of the Genetic and Evolutionary Computation Conference*, pp. 674–681.

Krohling, R. A. & Coelho, L. S. (2006). Coevolutionary particle swarm optimization using gaussian distribution for solving constrained optimization problems, *IEEE Transactions on Systems, Man, and Cybernetics, Part B* 36(6): 1407–1416.

Kukkonen, S. & Lampinen, J. (2004). An extension of generalized differential evolution for multi-objective optimization with constraints, *Proceedings of the Parallel Problem Solving from Nature*, pp. 752–761.

Kukkonen, S. & Lampinen, J. (2005). GDE3: the third evolution step of generalized differential evolution, *Proceedings of the Congress on Evolutionary Computation*, pp. 443–450.

l. Sun, C., Zeng, J. & Pan, J. (2011). An improved vector particle swarm optimization for constrained optimization problems, *Information Sciences* 181(6): 1153–1163.

Lozano, M., Herrera, F., Krasnogor, N. & Molina, D. (2004). Real-coded memetic algorithms with crossover hill-climbing, *Evolutionary Computation* 12(3): 273–302.

Meyer-Nieberg, S. & Beyer, H.-G. (2007). Self-adaptation in evolutionary algorithms, *Proceedings of the Parameter Setting in Evolutionary Algorithms*, pp. 47–75.

Mezura-Montes, E., Miranda-Varela, M. E. & d. C. Gómez-Ramón, R. (2010). Differential evolution in constrained numerical optimization: An empirical study, *Information Sciences* 180(22): 4223–4262.

Michalewicz, Z. (1996). *Genetic Algorithms + Data Structures = Evolution Programs*, Springer.

Mühlenbein, H. (1994). The breeder genetic algorithm - a provable optimal search algorithm and its application, *IEE Colloquium on Applications of Genetic Algorithms*, pp. 5/1–5/3.

Mühlenbein, H. & Schlierkamp-Voosen, D. (1993). Predictive models for the breeder genetic algorithm I: Continuous parameter optimization, *Evolutionary Computation* 1(1): 25–49.

Noman, N. & Iba, H. (2005). Enhancing differential evolution performance with local search for high dimensional function optimization, *Proceedings of the Genetic and Evolutionary Computation Conference*, pp. 25–29.

Ono, I., Kita, H. & Kobayashi, S. (1999). A robust real-coded genetic algorithm using unimodal normal distribution crossover augmented by uniform crossover: Effects of self-adaptation of crossover probabilities, *Proceedings of the Genetic and Evolutionary Computation Conference*, pp. 496–503.

Ono, I. & Kobayashi, S. (1997). A real-coded genetic algorithm for function optimization using unimodal normal distribution crossover, *Proceedings of the Seventh International Conference on Genetic Algorithms*, pp. 246–253.

Qi, A. & Palmieri, F. (1994a). Theoretical analysis of evolutionary algorithms with an infinite population size in continuous space, Part I: Basic properties of selection and mutation, *IEEE Transactions on Neural Networks* 5(1): 102–119.

Qi, A. & Palmieri, F. (1994b). Theoretical analysis of evolutionary algorithms with an infinite population size in continuous space, Part II: Analysis of the diversification role of crossover, *IEEE Transactions on Neural Networks* 5(1): 120–129.

Reed, J., Toombs, R. & Barricelli, N. A. (1967). Simulation of biological evolution and machine learning, *Journal of Theoretical Biology* 17: 319–342.

Ripon, K. S. N., Kwong, S. & Man, K. F. (2007). A real-coding jumping gene genetic algorithm (RJGGA) for multiobjective optimization, *Information Sciences* 177(2): 632–654.

Rönkkönen, J., Kukkonen, S. & Price, K. (2005). Real-parameter optimization with differential evolution, *Proceedings of the Congress on Evolutionary Computation*, pp. 506–513.

Socha, K. & Dorigo, M. (2008). Ant colony optimization for continuous domains, *European Journal of Operational Research* 185(3): 1155–1173.

Someya, H. & Yamamura, M. (2005). A robust real-coded evolutionary algorithm with toroidal search space conversion, *Soft Computing* 9(4): 254–269.

Storn, R. & Price, K. (1997). Differential evolution - a simple and efficient heuristic for global optimization over continuous spaces, *Journal of Global Optimization* 11(4): 341–359.

Suganthan, P. N., Hansen, N., Liang, J. J., Deb, K., Chen, Y., Auger, A. & Tiwari, S. (2005). Problem definitions and evaluation criteria for the CEC 2005 special session on real-parameter optimization, *Technical Report NCL-TR-2005001*, Natural Computing Laboratory (NCLab), Department of Computer Science, National Chiao Tung University.

Surry, P. D. & Radcliffe, N. (1996). Real representations, *Proceedings of the Workshop on Foundations of Genetic Algorithms*, pp. 343–363.

Takahashi, M. & Kita, H. (2001). A crossover operator using independent component analysis for real-coded genetic algorithm, *Proceedings of the Congress on Evolutionary Computation*, pp. 643–649.

Tsutsui, S. (1998). Multi-parent recombination in genetic algorithms with search space boundary extension by mirroring, *Proceedings of the Fifth International Conference on Parallel Problem Solving from Nature*, pp. 428–437.

Tsutsui, S. & Goldberg, D. E. (2001). Search space boundary extension method in real-coded genetic algorithms, *Information Sciences* 133(3-4): 229–247.

Tsutsui, S. & Goldberg, D. E. (2002). Simplex crossover and linkage identification: Single-stage evolution vs. multi-stage evolution, *Proceedings of the IEEE International Conference on Evolutionary Computation*, pp. 974–979.

Tsutsui, S., Goldberg, D. E. & Sastry, K. (2001). Linkage learning in real-coded GAs with simplex crossover, *Proceedings of the Fifth International Conference on Artificial Evolution*, pp. 51–58.

Tsutsui, S., Yamamura, M. & Higuchi, T. (1999). Multi-parent recombination with simplex crossover in real coded genetic algorithms, *Proceedings of the Genetic and Evolutionary Computation Conference*, pp. 657–664.

Wei, L., Chen, Z. & Li, J. (2011). Evolution strategies based adaptive L_p LS-SVM, *Information Sciences* 181(14): 3000–3016.

Wright, A. H. (1991). Genetic algorithms for real parameter optimization, *Proceedings of the Workshop on Foundations of Genetic Algorithms*, pp. 205–218.

Yoon, Y., Kim, Y.-H., Moraglio, A. & Moon, B.-R. (2012). A theoretical and empirical study on unbiased boundary-extended crossover for real-valued representation, *Information Sciences* 183(1): 48–65.

Zhang, M., Luo, W. & Wang, X. (2008). Differential evolution with dynamic stochastic selection for constrained optimization, *Information Sciences* 178(15): 3043–3074.

5

A Splicing/Decomposable Binary Encoding and Its Novel Operators for Genetic and Evolutionary Algorithms

Yong Liang
Macau University of Science and Technology
China

1. Introduction

Most of the real-world problems could be encoded by different representations, but genetic and evolutionary algorithms (GEAs) may not be able to successfully solve the problems based on their phenotypic representations, unless we use some problem-specific genetic operators. Therefore, a proper genetic representation is necessary when using GEAs on the real-world problems (Goldberg, 1989; Liepins, 1990; Whitley, 2000; Liang, 2011).

A large number of theoretical and empirical investigations on genetic representations were made over the last decades. Earlier work (Goldberg, 1989c; Liepins & Vose, 1990) has shown that the behavior and performance of GEAs is strongly influenced by the representation used. As a result many genotypic representations were made for proper GEAs searching. Among of them, the binary, integer, real-valued, messy and tree structure representations are the most important and widely used by many GEAs.

To investigate the performance of the genetic representations, originally, the schema theorem proposed by Holland (1975) to model the performance of GEAs to process similarities between binary bitstrings. Using the definition of the building blocks (BBs) as being highly fit solutions to sub-problems, which are decomposed by the overall problem, the building block hypothesis (Goldberg, 1989c) states that GEAs mainly work due to their ability to propagate short, low order and highly fit BBs. During the last decade, (Thierens, 1995; Miller, 1996; Harik, 1997; Sendhoff, 1997; Rothlauf, 2002) developed three important elements towards a general theory of genetic representations. They identified that redundancy, the scaling of Building Blocks (BBs) and the distance distortion are major factors that influence the performance of GEAs with different genetic representations.

A genetic representation is denoted to be redundant if the number of genotypes is higher than the number of phenotypes. Investigating redundant representation reveals that give more copies to high quality solutions in the initial population result in a higher performance of GEAs, whereas encodings where high quality solutions are underrepresented make a problem more difficult to solve. Uniform redundancy, however, has no influence on the performance of GEAs.

The order of scaling of a representation describes the different contribution of the BBs to the individual's fitness. It is well known that if the BBs are uniformly scaled, GEAs solve all BBs implicitly in parallel. In contrast, for non-uniformly scaled BBs, domino convergence occurs and the BBs are solved sequentially starting with the most salient BB (Thierens, 1995). As a result, the convergence time increases and the performance is decreasing due to the noise from the competing BBs.

The distance distortion of a representation measures how much the distance between individuals are changed when mapping the phenotypes to the genotypes, and the locality of the representation means that whether similar genotypes correspond to similar phenotypes. The theoretical analysis shows that representation where the distance distortion and locality are equal to zero, that means the distances between the individuals are preserved, do not modify the difficulty of the problems they are used for, and guarantee to solve problems of bounded complexity reliably and predictably.

The importance of choosing proper representations for the performance of GAs is already recognized, but developing a general theory of representations is a formidable challenge. Up to now, there is no well set-up theory regarding the influence of representations on the performance of GAs. To help users with different tasks to search good representations, over the last few years, some researchers have made recommendations based on the existing theories. For example, Goldberg (Goldberg, 1989) proposed two basic design principles for encodings:

- Principle of minimal alphabets: The alphabet of the encoding should be as small as possible while still allowing a natural representation of solutions.
- Principle of meaningful building blocks: The schemata should be short, of low order, and relatively unrelated to schemata over other fixed positions.

The principle of minimal alphabets advises us to use bit string representation. Combining with the principle of meaningful building blocks (BBs), we construct uniform salient BBs, which include equal scaled and splicing/decomposable alleles.

The purpose of this chapter is to introduce our novel genetic representation — a splicing/decomposable (S/D) binary encoding, which was proposed based on some theoretical guidance and existing recommendations for designing efficient genetic representations. The S/D binary representation can be spliced and decomposed to describe potential solutions of the problem with different precisions by different number of uniform-salient BBs. According to the characteristics of the S/D binary representation, GEAs can be applied from the high scaled to the low scaled BBs sequentially to avoid the noise from the competing BBs and improve GEAs' performance. Our theoretical and empirical investigations reveal that the S/D binary representation is more proper than other existing binary encodings for GEAs searching. Moreover, a new genotypic distance d_g on the S/D binary space Φ_g is proposed, which is equivalent to the Euclidean distance d_p on the real-valued space Φ_p during GEAs convergence. Based on the new genotypic distance d_g, GEAs can reliably and predictably solve problems of bounded complexity and the methods depended on the phenotypic distance d_p for solving different kinds of optimization problems can be directly used on the S/D binary space Φ_g.

This chapter is organized as follows. Section 2 describes three most commonly used binary representations — binary, gray and unary encodings, and their theoretical analysis of the effect on the performance of GEAs. Section 3 introduces our proposed splicing/decomposable

(S/D) binary representation and its genotypic distance. Section 4 proposes the new genetic algorithm based on the S/D binary representation, the splicing/Decompocable genetic algorithm (SDGA). Section 5 discusses the performance of the SDGA and compares the S/D binary representation with other existing binary encodings from the empirical studies. The chapter conclusion are drawn in Section 6.

2. Background

Binary encodings are the most commonly used and nature-inspired representations for GEAs, especially for genetic algorithms (GAs) (Goldberg, 1989). When encoding real-valued problems by binary representations, different types of binary representations assign the real-value in different ways to the binary strings. The most common binary representations are the binary, gray and unary encodings. According to three aspects of representation theory (redundancy, scaled building block and distance distortion), Rothlauf (Rothlauf, 2002) studied the performance differences of GAs by different binary representations for real encoding.

2.1 The unary encoding and redundancy

In the unary encoding, a string of length $l = s - 1$ is necessary to represent s different phenotypic values. The ith phenotypic value is encoded by the number of ones $i - 1$ in the corresponding genotypic string. Thus, 2^{s-1} different genotypes only encode s different phenotypes. Analysis on the unary encoding by the representation theory reveals that encoding is redundant, and does not represent phenotypes uniformly. Therefore, the performance of GAs with the unary encoding depends on the structure of the optimal solution. Unary GAs fail to solve integer one-max, deceptive trap and BinInt (Rothlauf, 2002) problems, unless larger population sizes are used, because the optimal solutions are strongly underrepresented for these three types of problems. Thus, the unary GAs perform much worse than GAs using the non-redundant binary or gray encoding (Julstrom, 1999; Rothlauf, 2002).

2.2 The binary encoding, scaled building blocks and hamming cliff

The binary encoding uses exponentially scaled bits to represent phenotypes. Each phenotypic value $x_p \in \Phi_p = \{x_1, x_2, ..., x_s\}$ is represented by a binary string x_g of length $l = log_2(s)$. Therefore, the genotype-phenotype mapping of the binary encoding is one-to-one mapping and encodes phenotypes redundancy-free.

However, for non-uniformly binary strings and competing Building Blocks (BBs) for high dimensional phenotype space, there are a lot of noise from the competing BBs lead to a reduction on the performance of GAs. The performance of GAs using the binary encoding is not only affected by the non-uniformly scaling of BBs, but also by problems associated with the *Hamming cliff* (Schaffer, 1989b). The binary encoding has the effect that genotypes of some phenotypical neighbors are completely different. For example, when we choose the phenotypes $x_p = 7$ and $y_p = 8$, both individuals have a distance of one, but the resulting genotypes $x_g = 0111$ and $y_g = 1000$ have the largest possible genotypic distance $\|x - y\|_g = 4$. As a result, the locality of the binary representation is partially low. In the distance distortion theory, an encoding preserves the difficulty of a problem if it has perfect locality and if it does not modify the distance between individuals. The analysis reveals that the binary encoding changes the distance between the individuals and therefore changes the complexity of the optimization problem. Thus, easy problems can become difficult, and vice versa. The binary GAs are not able to reliably solve problems when mapping the phenotypes to the genotypes.

2.3 The gray encoding and modification of problem difficulty

The non-redundant gray encoding (Schaffer, 1989a) was designed to overcome the problems with the *Hamming cliff* of the binary encoding (Schaffer, 1989b). In the gray encoding, every neighbor of a phenotype is also a neighbor of the corresponding genotype. Therefore, the difficulty of a problem remains unchanged when using mutation-based search operators that only perform small step in the search space. As a result, easy problems and problems of bounded difficulty are easier to solve when using the mutation-based search with the gray coding than that with the binary encoding. Although the gray encoding has high locality, it still changes the distance correspondence between the individuals with bit difference of more than one. When focused on crossover-based search methods, the analysis of the average fitness of the schemata reveals that the gray encoding preserves building block complexity less than the binary encoding. Thus, a decrease in performance of gray-encoded GAs is unavoidable for some kind of problems (Whitley, 2000).

3. A novel splicing/decomposable binary genetic representation

The descriptions in above section show that the existing binary genetic representations are not proper for GAs searching and cannot guarantee that using GAs to solve problems of bounded complexity reliably and predictably. According to the theoretical analysis and recommendations for the design of an efficient representation, there are some important points that a genetic representation should try to respect. Common representations for GAs often encode the phenotypes by using a sequence of alleles. The alleles can separated (decomposed) into building blocks (BBs) which do not interact with each other and which determine one specific phenotypic property of the solution. The purpose of the genetic operators is to decompose the whole sequence of alleles by detecting which BBs influence each other. GAs perform well because they can identify best alleles of each BB and combine them to form high-quality over-all solution of the problem.

Based on above investigation results and recommendations, we have proposed a new genetic representation, which is proper for GAs searching. In this section, first we introduce a novel splicing/decomposable (S/D) binary encoding, then we define the new genotypic distance for the S/D encoding, finally we give the theoretical analysis for the S/D encoding based on the three elements of genetic representation theory (redundancy, scaled BBs and distance distortion).

3.1 A splicing/decomposable binary encoding

In (Leung, 2002; Xu, 2003a), we have proposed a novel S/D binary encoding for real-value encoding. Assuming the phenotypic domain Φ_p of the n dimensional problem can be specified by

$$\Phi_p = [\alpha_1, \beta_1] \times [\alpha_2, \beta_2] \times \cdots \times [\alpha_n, \beta_n].$$

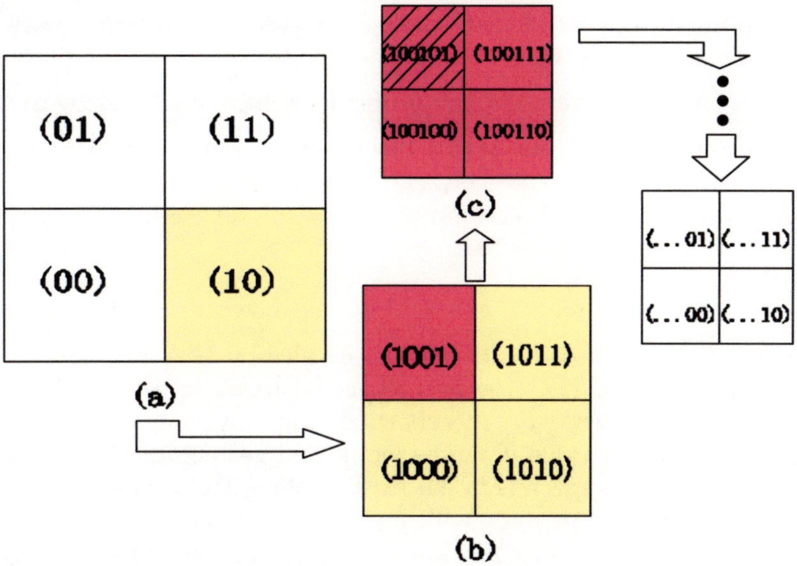

Fig. 1. A graphical illustration of the splicing/decomposable representation scheme, where (b) is the refined bisection of the gray cell (10) in (a) (with mesh size $O(1/2)$), (c) is the refined bisection of the dark cell (1001) in (b) (with mesh size $O(1/2^2)$), and so forth.

Given a length of a binary string l, the genotypic precision is $h_i(l) = \frac{(\beta_i - \alpha_i)}{2^{(\ell/n)}}$, $i = 1, 2, \cdots, n$. Any real-value variable $x = (x_1, x_2, ..., x_n) \in \Phi_p$ can be represented by a splicing/decomposable (S/D) binary string $b = (b_1, b_2, .., b_l)$, the genotype-phenotype mapping f_g is defined as

$$x = (x_1, x_2, \cdots, x_n) = f_g(b) = (\sum_{j=0}^{l/n} 2^{(l/n-j)} \times b_{j\times n+1},$$

$$\sum_{j=0}^{l/n} 2^{(l/n-j)} \times b_{j\times n+2}, \cdots, \sum_{j=0}^{l/n} 2^{(l/n-j)} \times b_{j\times(n+1)}),$$

where

$$\sum_{j=0}^{l/n} 2^{(l/n-j)} \times b_{j\times n+i} \leq \frac{x_i - \alpha_i}{h_i(l)} < \sum_{j=0}^{l/n} 2^{(l/n-j)} \times b_{j\times n+i} + 1.$$

That is, the significance of each bit of the encoding can be clearly and uniquely interpreted (hence, each BB of the encoded S/D binary string has a specific meaning). As shown in Figure 1, take $\Phi_p = [0,1] \times [0,1]$ and the S/D binary string $b = 100101$ as an example (in this case, $l = 6$, $n = 2$, and the genotypic precisions $h_1(l) = h_2(l) = \frac{1}{8}$). Let us look how to identify the S/D binary string b and see what each bit value of b means. In Figure 1-(a), the phenotypic domain Φ_p is bisected into four $\Phi_p^{\frac{1}{2}}$ (i.e., the subregions with uniform size $\frac{1}{2}$). According to the *left*-0 and *right*-1 correspondence rule in each coordinate direction, these four $\Phi_p^{\frac{1}{2}}$ then can be identified with $(00), (01), (10)$ and (11). As the phenotype x lies in the subregion (10) (the gray square), its first building block (BB) should be $BB_1 = 10$. This leads to the first two bits of the S/D binary string b. Likewise, in Figure 1-(b), Φ_p is partitioned into $2^{2\times 2}$ $\Phi_p^{\frac{1}{4}}$, which are obtained through further bisecting each $\Phi_p^{\frac{1}{2}}$ along each direction. Particularly this further divides $\Phi_p^{\frac{1}{2}} = (BB_1)$ into four $\Phi_p^{\frac{1}{4}}$ that can be respectively labelled by $(BB_1,00), (BB_1,01), (BB_1,10)$ and $(BB_1,11)$. The phenotype x is in $(BB_1,01)$-subregion (the dark square), so its second BB should be $BB_2 = 01$ and the first four positions of its corresponding S/D binary string b is 1001.

In the same way, Φ_p is partitioned into $2^{2\times 3}$ $\Phi_p^{\frac{1}{8}}$ as shown in Figure 1-(c), with $\Phi_p^{\frac{1}{4}} = (BB_1, BB_2)$ particularly partitioned into four $\Phi_p^{\frac{1}{8}}$ labelled by $(BB_1, BB_2, 00)$, $(BB_1, BB_2, 01)$, $(BB_1, BB_2, 10)$ and $(BB_1, BB_2, 11)$. The phenotype x is found to be $(BB_1, BB_2, 01)$, that is, identical with S/D binary string b. This shows that for any three region partitions, $b = (b_1, b_2, b_3, b_4, b_5, b_6)$, each bit value b_i can be interpreted geometrically as follows: $b_1 = 0$ ($b_2 = 0$) means the phenotype x is in the left half along the x-coordinate direction (the y-coordinate direction) in Φ_p partition with $\frac{1}{2}$-precision, and $b_1 = 1$ ($b_2 = 1$) means x is in the right half. Therefore, the first $BB_1 = (b_1, b_2)$ determine the $\frac{1}{2}$-precision location of x. If $b_3 = 0$ ($b_4 = 0$), it then further indicates that when $\Phi_p^{\frac{1}{2}}$ is refined into $\Phi_p^{\frac{1}{4}}$, the x lies in the left half of $\Phi_p^{\frac{1}{2}}$ in the x-direction (y-direction), and it lies in the right half if $b_3 = 1$ ($b_4 = 1$). Thus a more accurate geometric location (i.e., the $\frac{1}{4}$-precision location) and a more refined BB_2 of x is obtained. Similarly we can explain b_5 and b_6 and identify BB_3, which determine the $\frac{1}{8}$-precision location of x. This interpretation holds for any high-resolution l bits S/D binary encoding.

3.2 A new genotypic distance on the splicing/decomposable binary representation

For measuring the similarity of the binary strings, the Hamming distance (Hamming, 1980) is widely used on the binary space. Hamming distance describes how many bits are different in two binary strings, but cannot consider the scaled property in non-uniformly binary representations. Thus, the distance distortion between the genotypic and the phenotypic spaces make phenotypically easy problem more difficult. Therefore, to make sure that GAs are able to reliably solve easy problems and problems of bounded complexity, the use of equivalent distances is recommended. For this purpose, we have defined a new genotypic distance on the S/D binary space to measure the similarity of the S/D binary strings.

Definition 1: Suppose any binary strings a and b belong to the S/D binary space Φ_g, the genotypic distance $\|a - b\|_g$ is defined as

$$\|a - b\|_g = \sum_{i=1}^{n} \left| \sum_{j=0}^{l/n-1} \frac{a_{j\times n+i} - b_{j\times n+i}}{2^{j+1}} \right|,$$

where l and n denote the length of the S/D binary strings and the dimensions of the real-encoding phenotypic space Φ_p respectively.

genotypic distances

0101 (0.75)	0111 (1.0)	1101 (1.25)	1111 (1.5)
0100 (0.5)	0110 (0.75)	1100 (1.0)	1110 (1.25)
0001 (0.25)	0011 (0.5)	1001 (0.75)	1011 (1.0)
0000 (0.0)	0010 (0.25)	1000 (0.5)	1010 (0.75)

phenotypic distances

0101 (0.75)	0111 (0.79)	1101 (0.9)	1111 (1.1)
0100 (0.5)	0110 (0.56)	1100 (0.71)	1110 (0.9)
0001 (0.25)	0011 (0.35)	1001 (0.56)	1011 (0.79)
0000 (0.0)	0010 (0.25)	1000 (0.5)	1010 (0.75)

Fig. 2. The genotypic and phenotypic distances between $* * **$ and 0000 in the S/D binary representation.

For any two S/D binary strings $a, b \in \Phi_g$, we can define the Euclidean distance of their correspond phenotypes:

$$\|a-b\|_p = \sqrt{\sum_{i=1}^{n}\left(\sum_{j=0}^{l/n-1}\frac{a_{j\times n+i}}{2^{j+1}} - \sum_{j=0}^{l/n-1}\frac{b_{j\times n+i}}{2^{j+1}}\right)^2},$$

as the phenotypic distance between the S/D binary strings a and b. The phenotypic distance $\|\cdot\|_p$ and the genotypic distance $\|\cdot\|_g$ are equivalents in the S/D binary space Φ_g when we consider the convergence process of GAs. We state this as the following theorem.

Theorem 1: The phenotypic distance $\|\cdot\|_p$ and the genotypic distance $\|\cdot\|_g$ are equivalents in the S/D binary space Φ_g because the inequation:

$$\|\cdot\|_p \le \|\cdot\|_g \le \sqrt{n} \times \|\cdot\|_p$$

is satisfied in the the S/D binary space Φ_g, where n is the dimensions of the real-encoding phenotypic space Φ_p.

Proof: For $\forall a, b \in \Phi_g$:

$$\|a-b\|_g = \sum_{i=1}^{n}\left|\sum_{j=0}^{l/n-1}\frac{a_{j\times n+i}-b_{j\times n+i}}{2^{j+1}}\right|$$

$$= \sqrt{\left(\sum_{i=1}^{n}\left|\sum_{j=0}^{l/n-1}\frac{a_{j\times n+i}-b_{j\times n+i}}{2^{j+1}}\right|\right)^2}$$

$$= \sqrt{\begin{array}{l}\sum_{i=1}^{n}\left(\sum_{j=0}^{l/n-1}\frac{a_{j\times n+i}-b_{j\times n+i}}{2^{j+1}}\right)^2 \\ +\sum_{i_1\neq i_2}^{1\le i_1,i_2\le n}\left(2\times\left|\sum_{j=0}^{l/n-1}\frac{a_{j\times n+i}-b_{j\times n+i_1}}{2^{j+1}}\right|\right. \\ \left.\times\left|\sum_{j=0}^{l/n-1}\frac{a_{j\times n+i}-b_{j\times n+i_2}}{2^{j+1}}\right|\right)\end{array}}$$

because

$$0 \leq \begin{array}{l}\sum_{i_1 \neq i_2}^{1 \leq i_1, i_2 \leq n} (2 \times | \sum_{j=0}^{l/n-1} \frac{a_{j\times n+i} - b_{j\times n+i_1}}{2^{j+1}} | \\ \times | \sum_{j=0}^{l/n-1} \frac{a_{j\times n+i} - b_{j\times n+i_2}}{2^{j+1}} |)\end{array}$$

$$\leq (n-1) \sum_{i=1}^{n} (\sum_{j=0}^{l/n-1} \frac{a_{j\times n+i} - b_{j\times n+i}}{2^{j+1}})^2,$$

then

$$\|a-b\|_p \leq \|a-b\|_g \leq \sqrt{n} \times \|a-b\|_p.$$

Figure 2 shows the comparison of the genotypic distance $\|\cdot\|_g$ and phenotypic distance $\|\cdot\|_p$ between S/D binary strings and 0000 in 2 dimensional phenotypic space, where the length of the S/D binary string $l = 4$. For any two S/D binary strings a and b, if $\|a-0\|_p > \|b-0\|_p$, then $\|a-0\|_g > \|b-0\|_g$ is also satisfied. This means that $\|\cdot\|_p$ and $\|\cdot\|_g$ are equivalent for considering the points' sequence converge to 0. The searching process of GAs can be recognized to explore the points' sequence, which sequentially converge to optimum of the problem. So we can use the new genotypic distance to measure the similarity and convergence of the individuals on the S/D binary place.

The other advantage of the new genotypic distance $\|\cdot\|_g$ is that its computational complexity is $O(l)$ and much lower than the computational complexity $O(l^2)$ of the phenotypic distance $\|\cdot\|_p$. So using the new genotypic distance $\|\cdot\|_g$ can guarantee GA to reliably and predictably solve problems of bounded complexity and improve their performance when consider the similarity of the individuals.

3.3 Theoretical analysis of the splicing/decomposable binary encoding

The above interpretation reveals an important fact that in the new genetic representation the significance of the BB contribution to fitness of a whole S/D binary string varies as its position goes from front to back, and, in particular, the more in front the BB position lies, the more significantly it contributes to the fitness of the whole S/D binary string. We refer such delicate feature of the new representation to as the *BB-significance-variable property*. Actually, it is seen from the above interpretation that the first n bits of an encoding are responsible for the location of the n dimensional phenotype x in a global way (particularly, with $O(\frac{1}{2})$-precision); the next group of n bits is responsible for the location of phenotype x in a less global (might be called 'local') way, with $O(\frac{1}{4})$-precision, and so forth; the last group of n-bits then locates phenotype x in an extremely local (might be called 'microcosmic') way (particularly, with $O(\frac{1}{2^{\ell/n}})$-precision). Thus, we have seen that as the encoding length l increases, the representation

$$\begin{array}{l}(b_1, b_2, \cdots, b_n, b_{n+1}, b_{n+2}, \cdots, b_{2n}, \cdots, \\ \quad b_{(\ell-n)}, b_{(\ell-n+1)}, \cdots, b_l) \\ = (BB_1, BB_2, \cdots, BB_{l/n})\end{array}$$

can provide a successive refinement (from global, to local, and to microcosmic), and more and more accurate representation of the problem variables.

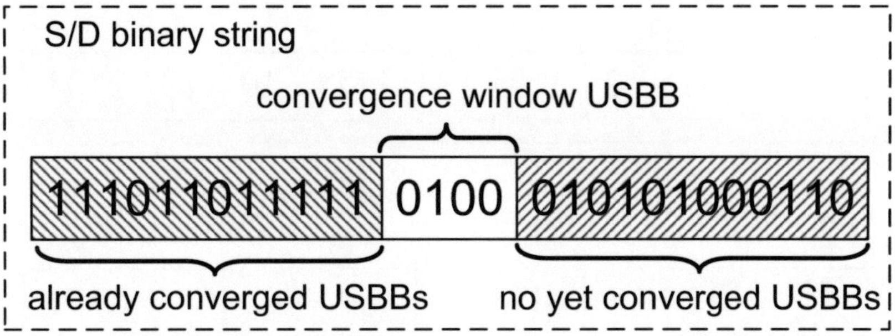

Fig. 3. Domino genotypic at the S/D encodings.

In each BB_i of the S/D binary string, which consists of the bits $(b_{i\times n+1}, b_{i\times n+2}, \cdots, b_{(i+1)\times n})$, $i = 0, \cdots, l/n - 1$, these bits are uniformly scaled and independent each other. We refer such delicate feature of BB_i to as the uniform-salient BB (USBB). Furthermore, the splicing different number of USBBs can describe the potential solutions of the problem with different precisions. So, the intra-BB difficulty (within building block) and inter-BB difficulty (between building blocks) (Goldberg, 2002) of USBB are low. The theoretical analysis reveals that GAs searching on USBB can explore the high-quality bits faster than GAs on non-uniformly scaled BB.

The S/D binary encoding is redundancy-free representation because using the S/D binary strings to represent the real values is one-to-one genotype-phenotype mapping. The whole S/D binary string is constructed by a non-uniformly scaled sequence of USBBs. The domino convergence of GAs occurs and USBBs are solved sequentially from high to low scaled.

The BB-significance-variable and uniform-salient BB properties of the S/D binary representation embody many important information useful to the GAs searching. We will explore this information to design new GA based on the S/D binary representation in the subsequent sections.

4. A new S/D binary Genetic Algorithm (SDGA)

The existing exponentially scaled representations including binary and gray encodings consist of non-uniformly scaled BBs. For non-uniformly and competing BBs in the high dimensional phenotype space, there are a lot of noise from the competing BBs lead to a reduction on the performance of GAs. Moreover, by increasing the string length, more and more lower salient BBs are randomly fixed due to the noise from the competing BBs, causing GAs performance to decline. Using large population size can reduce the influence of the noise from the competing BBs. However, in real-world problem, long binary string is necessary to encode a large search space with high precision, and hence we cannot use too large population size to solve the noise problem. Thus, GAs will be premature and cannon converge to the optimum of the problem.

To avoid the noise from the competing BBs of GAs, we have proposed a new splicing/decomposable GA (SDGA) based on the delicate properties of the S/D binary representation. The whole S/D binary string can be decomposed into a non-uniformly scaled sequence of USBBs. Thus, in the searching process of GAs on S/D binary encoding, the

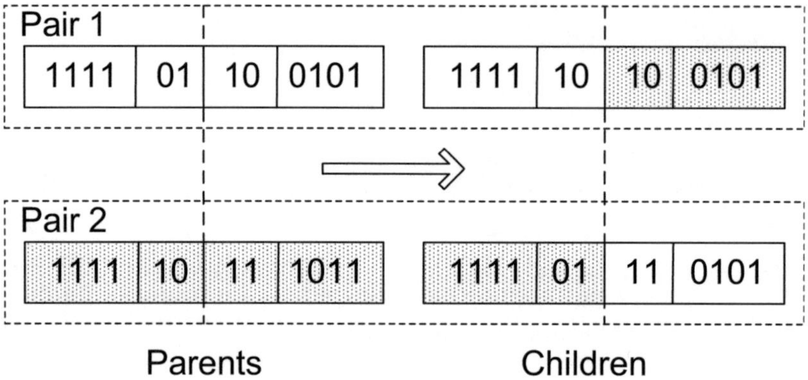

Fig. 4. The genetic crossover and selection in SDGA.

domino convergence occurs and the length of the convergence window is equal to n, the length of USBB. As shown in Figure 3 for 4 dimensional case, the high scaled USBBs are already fully converged while the low scaled USBBs did not start to converge yet, and length of the convergence window is 4.

In the SDGA, genetic operators apply from the high scaled to the low scaled USBBs sequentially. The process of the crossover and selection in SDGA is shown in Figure 4. For two individuals x_1 and x_2 randomly selected from current population, The crossover point randomly set in the convergence window USBB and the crossover operator two children c_1, c_2. The parents x_1, x_2 and their children c_1, c_2 can be divided into two pairs $\{x_1, c_1\}$ and $\{x_2, c_2\}$. In each pair $\{x_i, c_i\}(i = 1, 2)$, the parent and child have the same low scaled USBBs. The select operator will conserve the better one of each pair into next generation according to the fitness calculated by the whole S/D binary string for high accuracy. Thus, the bits contributed to high fitness in the convergence window USBB will be preserved, and the diversity at the low scaled USBBs' side will be maintain. The mutation will operate on the convergence window and not yet converged USBBs according to the mutation probability to increase the diversity in the population. These low salient USBBs will converge due to GAs searching to avoid the noise from the competing BBs. The implementation pseudocode for SDGA algorithm is shown in Figure 5.

Since identifying high-quality bits in the convergence window USBB of GAs is faster than that GAs on the non-uniform BB, while no noise from the competing BBs occurs. Thus, population can efficiently converge to the high-quality BB in the position of the convergence window USBB, which are a component of overrepresented optimum of the problem. According to theoretical results of Thierens (Thierens, 1995), the overall convergence time complexity of the new GA with the S/D binary representation is approximately of order $O(l/\sqrt{n})$, where l is the length of the S/D binary string and n is the dimensions of the problem. This is much faster than working on the binary strings as a whole where GAs have a approximate convergence time of order $O(l)$. The gain is especially significant for high dimension problems.

5. Empirical verification

In this section we present an empirical verification of the performance differences between the different genetic representations and operators we described in the previous sections.

Input: N—population size, m—number of USBBs,
  g—number of generations to run;
Termination condition: Population fully converged;
begin
  $g \longleftarrow 0$;
  $m \longleftarrow 1$;
  Initialize P_g;
  Evaluate P_g;
  while (not termination condition) **do**
   for $t \longleftarrow 1$ **to** $N/2$;
   randomly select two individuals x_t^1 and x_t^2 from P_g;
   crossover and selection x_t^1, x_t^2 into P_{g+1};
   end for
   mutation operation P_{g+1};
   Evaluate P_{g+1};
   if (USBB$_m$ fully converged) $m \longleftarrow m+1$;
  end while
end

Fig. 5. Pseudocode for SDGA algorithm.

5.1 Two integer benchmark optimization problems

In our experimentation, we use integer-specific variations of the one-max and the fully-deceptive trap problems for a comparison of different genetic representations defined on binary strings.

The integer one-max problem is defined as

$$f_1(x_1, x_2, \cdots, x_n) = \sum_{i=1}^{n} x_i,$$

and the integer deceptive trap is

$$f_2(x_1, x_2, \cdots, x_n) = \begin{cases} \sum_{i=1}^{n} x_i : \text{if each } i, x_i = x_{i,max} \\ \sum_{i=1}^{n} x_{i,max} - \sum_{i=1}^{n} x_i - 1 : \text{else.} \end{cases}$$

where $x \in \Phi_p$ and n is the dimension of the problems. In our implementation, we set $n = 30$. For the binary representation, the integer one-max problem is equal to the BinInt problem [Rudnick, 1992]. These two problems have an exponential salience or fitness structure for binary strings. The integer one-max problem is a fully easy problem, whereas the integer deceptive trap should be fully difficult to solve for GAs.

5.2 Comparison of the performance of GAs with different representations

In the first set of experiments we applied a standard GA (SGA) using binary, gray, unary, S/D encodings and SDGA on the integer one-max and deceptive trap problems to compare their performance. We performed 50 runs and each run was stopped after the population was fully converged. That means that all individuals in the population are the same. For fairness of

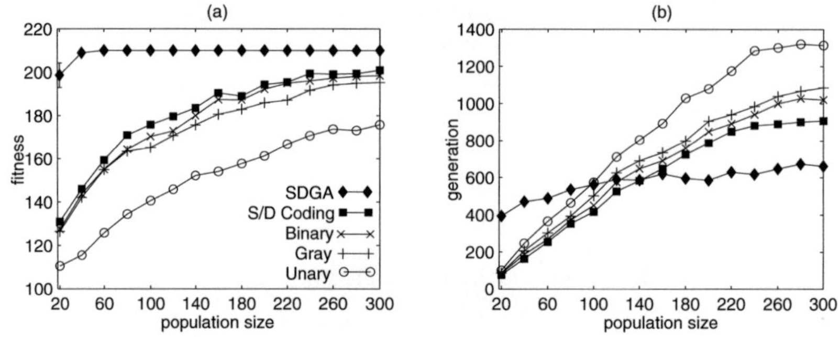

Fig. 6. Integer one-max problem of order 3.

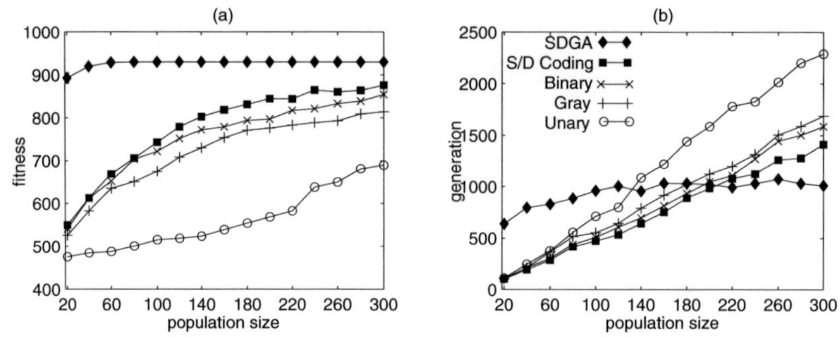

Fig. 7. Integer one-max problem of order 5.

comparison, we implemented SGA with different binary encodings and SDGA with the same parameter setting and the same initial population. For SGA, we used one-point crossover operator (crossover probability=1) and tournament selection operator without replacement of size two. We used no mutation as we wanted to focus on the influence of genetic representations on selectorecombinative GAs.

For the one-max problem, we used 30 dimensional problem for order 2 (in each dimension, the number of different phenotypes $s = 2^2 = 4$), 3 ($s = 2^3 = 8$), 4 ($s = 2^4 = 16$) and 5 ($s = 2^5 = 32$). Because in our implementation, the global optima of deceptive trap problems with low orders cannon be explored by all GAs we used. The deceptive trap problems with high orders are more difficult than those with low orders and are not solvable by GAs. Here, we only present results for the 30 dimensional deceptive trap problems of order 2 ($s = 2^2 = 4$) and 3 ($s = 2^3 = 8$). Using binary, gray and S/D encoding results for the order 2 problems in a string length $l = 60$, for order 3 in $l = 90$, for order 4 in $l = 120$, and for order 5 in $l = 150$. When using unary encoding we need $30 \times 3 = 90$ bits for order 2, $30 \times 7 = 210$ bits for order 3, $30 \times 15 = 450$ bits for order 4 and $30 \times 31 = 930$ bits for order 5 problems.

Figures 6-7 present the results for the integer one-max problem of orders 3 and 5 respectively, and Figures 8-9 show the results for integer deceptive trap problems of orders 2 and 3 respectively. The plots show for SGA with different representations and SDGA the best fitness at the end of the run (left) and the run duration — fully converged generation (right) with respect to the population size N.

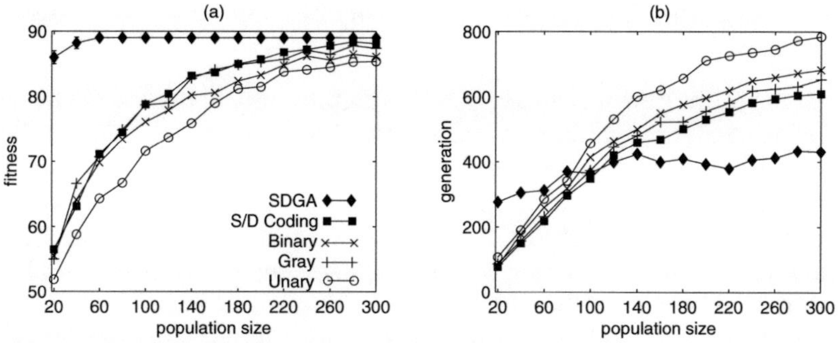

Fig. 8. Deceptive trap problem of order 2.

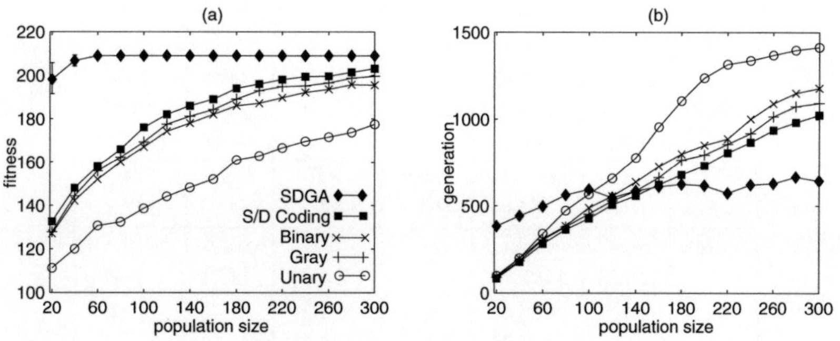

Fig. 9. Deceptive trap problem of order 3.

SGA with different scaled binary representations including binary, gray and S/D encodings complies the noise from the competing BBs. For small population sizes, the noise from the competing BBs strongly occurs and many bits in the binary strings are randomly fixed, so SGA fully converged faster but the best fitness is too bad. That means SGA is premature using small population sizes. For larger population sizes, SGA can explore better solutions, but its run duration is significantly increasing due to the noise from the competing BBs. Furthermore, for these high dimensional problems, the population size increases to 300 still not enough to avoid the noise from the competing BBs, so SGA cannot converge to the optima of the problems, which are overrepresented by BBs.

Due to the problems of the unary encoding with redundancy, which result in an underrepresentation of the optimal solution, SGA using unary encoding perform increasingly badly with increasing problem orders. Therefore, for one-max and deceptive trap problems of order more than three the performance of SGA using unary encoding performance is significantly worse than when using binary, gray and S/D encodings. SGA with gray encoding performs worse than the binary encoding for the one-max problems, and better for the deceptive trap problems.

As expected, SGA using S/D encoding performs better than that using binary and gray encodings for the one-max and the deceptive trap problems. Because in S/D encoding, more salient bits are continuous to construct short and high fit BBs, which are easily identified by SGA. This reveals that the S/D encoding is proper for GAs searching. However, lower salient bits in S/D binary string are randomly fixed by the noise from the competing BBs, the performance of SGA with S/D encoding cannot significantly better than those with binary and gray encodings.

As shown Figure 6-9, the performance of SDGA is significantly better than SGA with different encodings. Using small population size, the explored solutions when SDGA fully converged are much better than those of SGA because each bit is identified by the searching process of SDGA, and not randomly fixed by the noise from the competing BBs. According to the same reason, the run duration of SDGA is longer than that of SGA. That means there no premature and drift occur. For larger population sizes, the performance of SDGA is much better than that of SGA due to the high-quality solutions and short run duration, because GAs search on USBBs of S/D binary encoding faster than the non-uniformly scaled BBs and domino converge, which occurs only on the non-uniformly sequence of USBBs, is too weak.

P_m	one-max (order 2)		one-max (order 3)		one-max (order 4)	
	best fit. (St. Dev.)	run dur. (St. Dev.)	best fit. (St. Dev.)	run dur. (St. Dev.)	best fit. (St. Dev.)	run dur. (St. Dev.)
SDGA	89.6 (1.24)	383.1 (43.6)	209.2 (2.9)	577.3 (77.4)	448.1 (6.8)	768.7 (107.2)
S/D coding	81.1 (9.8)	446.1 (187.4)	180.9 (21.16)	597 (287)	375.9 (54.3)	694.9 (377.2)
Binary	80.1 (10.3)	473.7 (192.7)	177.7 (21.9)	651 (316.8)	370.5 (42.2)	748.8 (398)
Gray	78.3 (9.6)	496.9 (196.3)	173.1 (20.5)	691.2 (328.5)	365.2 (42.2)	803.6 (434.8)
Unary	76.1 (10.6)	536.8 (218.5)	150.5 (21.3)	844.2 (416.7)	281.5 (26.6)	1006 (558.4)

	one-max (order 5)		decep. (order 2)		decep. (order 3)	
SDGA	926.6 (9.8)	952.9 (118.2)	88.74 (0.78)	380 (48)	208.1 (2.8)	573.1 (75.6)
S/D coding	777.1 (101)	761.8 (422.4)	80.02 (9.7)	428 (173)	182.9 (21.6)	602.9 (285.4)
Binary	752.6 (91)	838.6 (481.6)	77.16 (9.1)	482 (192)	172.8 (21.1)	690.1 (334.8)
Gray	719.8 (87.9)	909.5 (502)	78.76 (9.4)	453 (183)	177.9 (21.8)	647 (309.5)
Unary	560.8 (72.4)	1216 (726.9)	74.18 (10.5)	549 (221)	150.7 (20.6)	882.7 (451.9)

Table 1. Comparison of results of SGA with different binary representations and SDGA for the one-max and deceptive problems.

Table 1 summarizes the experimental results for the one-max and the deceptive trip problems. The best fitness (run duration) of each problem is calculated as the average of the fitness (generations) GAs fully converged with different population sizes.

The average fitness of SDGA is much better than that of other SGA. The standard deviations of best fitness and run duration of SDGA for different problems are significantly smaller than other SGA. That reveals the population size is important parameter for SGA searching, but does not the significant parameter for SDGA searching. The run durations of SDGA for

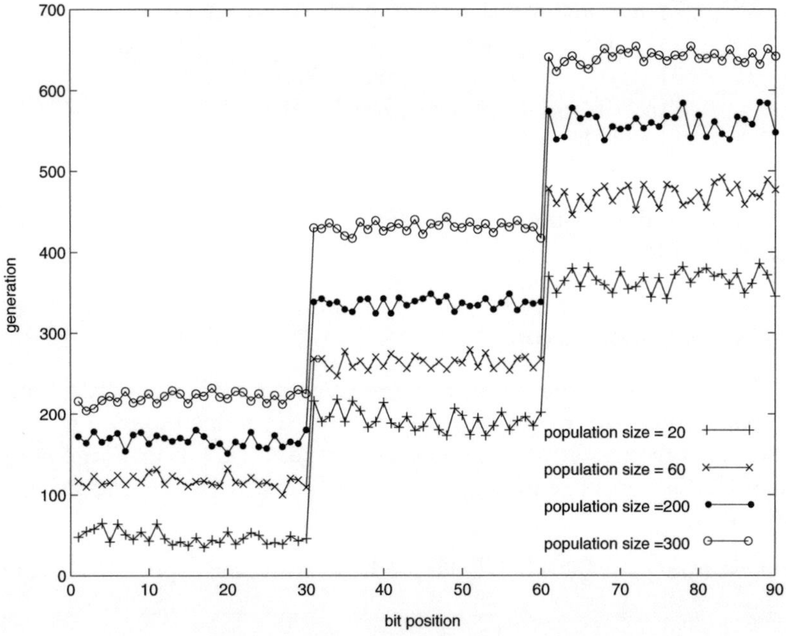

Fig. 10. Convergence process of SDGA without the noise from the competing BBs.

one-max problems with orders 4 and 5 are longer than those of SGA because SGA is strongly premature for the long binary string and small population sizes.

As in Table 1 described, for one-max and deceptive trap problems, all GAs converge to sidewise of the optima, which are overrepresented by BBs. But SGA with different binary representation cannot explore the optima of the problems. The ability of SDGA to explore optima, which are overrepresented by BBs, is significantly better than SGA. To explore the global optimum of the deceptive trap problems, we need use other niche methods to divide the whole population into some sub-populations. In each subpopulation, the global optimum is overrepresented by BBs, thus SDGA can efficiently explore this global optimum of the deceptive trap problems.

5.3 Avoid the noise from the competing BBs

To validate the predictions about avoiding the noise from the competing BBs, We have implemented our SDGA to solve 30 dimensional integer one-max problem of order 3. We have counted the number of generations it takes before each of bits fully converges. Results are averaged over 50 independent runs. Figure 10 shows the bits convergence for a string of length $l = 90$, and the population sizes are $20, 100, 200, 300$ respectively. The experimental results are summered in Table 2. The run duration of each USBB_i, $(i = 1, 2, 3)$ is an average of the fully converged generations of the bits, which belong to the USBB_i.

As shown in Figure 10 and Table 2, the whole S/D binary string includes three USBBs. In each USBB, the bits converge uniformly at almost same generations. For a non-uniform scaled sequence of USBBs, the domino converge occurs sequentially from high scaled to low scaled

population size	run duration of $USBB_1$	run duration of $USBB_2$	run duration of $USBB_3$
20	47.3(8.2)	193.7(12.7)	365.6(13.8)
100	116.6(6.8)	263.2(7.8)	470.8(12.1)
200	167.4(7.7)	366.5(6.7)	559.6(13.9)
300	220.3(7.0)	430.8(6.6)	633.6(7.8)

Table 2. Comparison of the run durations of USBBs fully converged with different population sizes.(Standard Deviation)

USBBs. Thus, no less salient bit converges with more salient bit at same generations and no noise from the competing BBs occurs.

On the other hand, we know the noise from the competing BBs strongly occurs when GAs using a small population size. In our implementations, when the population size of SDGA is small to 20, the convergence process of bits is as same as SDGA using large population size. The low scaled USBBs converge during long generations by SDGA and no noise from the competing BBs occurs.

It is clear form Figure 10 and Table 2 that the predictions and the experimental results coincide very well.

5.4 SDGA with the mutation operator

In this subsection we have consider the action of the mutation operator for SDGA searching. We have implemented our SDGA with different mutation probabilities to solve 30 dimensional integer one-max problem of order 3. Results are averaged over 50 independent runs. Figure 11 presents the experimental results where mutation probabilities are $0.001, 0.005, 0.01, 0.05$ and 0.1 respectively. The plots show for SDGA the run duration — fully converged generations with respect to the population size N.

As shown in Figure 11, when the mutation probabilities are smaller than 0.01, SDGA can fully converge with small and large population sizes and the run durations do not increase too long. When the mutation probabilities increase larger than 0.01, SDGA with large population sizes are difficult to fully converge, and only when using small population sizes, SDGA can fully converge, but the run durations increase significantly.

Table 3 summaries the experimental results with population sizes 20, 40 and 60. For small population sizes (20 and 40), the mutation operators can improve the performance of SDGA, because it can find some high-quality bits, which are not included in current population. For large population sizes ($\geq$ 60), all high-quality bits are included in the initial population, so mutation operator cannot improve the best fitness when SDGA fully converged. Furthermore, when the mutation probability is large than 0.01, SDGA cannot fully converge in a reasonable time (here we set the upper bound of the run duration equal to 10^6 generations).

5.5 Genotypic distance on the S/D binary representation

To validate the predictions about the methods depended on the distance of real-valued space, can be directly used on the S/D binary space based on our new defined genotypic distance, we have combined SGA with the S/D binary encoding and the dynamic niche sharing methods

P_m	$N = 20$		$N = 40$		$N = 60$	
	best fit. (St. Dev.)	run dur. (St. Dev.)	best fit. (St. Dev.)	run dur. (St. Dev.)	best fit. (St. Dev.)	run dur. (St. Dev.)
0	198.6 (5.7)	393 (72)	208.9 (1.2)	470 (55)	210 (0)	488 (54)
0.001	201.7 (100)	411 (49)	209.4 (1.2)	472 (43)	210 (0)	517 (54)
0.005	202.7 (2.9)	422 (55)	208.9 (1.3)	492 (82)	210 (0)	535 (89)
0.01	203.8 (2.2)	415 (59)	209.1 (1.2)	504 (76)	210 (0)	545 (80)
0.05	209.3 (1)	534 (158)	209.9 (0.3)	739 (202)	210 (0)	1202 (317)
0.1	209.8 (0.6)	688 (133)	210 (0)	5629 (1857)	210 (0)	66514 (21328)
0.2	209.8 (0.4)	10981 (7668)	– (–)	– (–)	– (–)	– (–)

Table 3. Comparison of results of SDGA with different mutation probabilities for one-max problem of order 3. ("-": cannot fully converged during 10^6 generations)

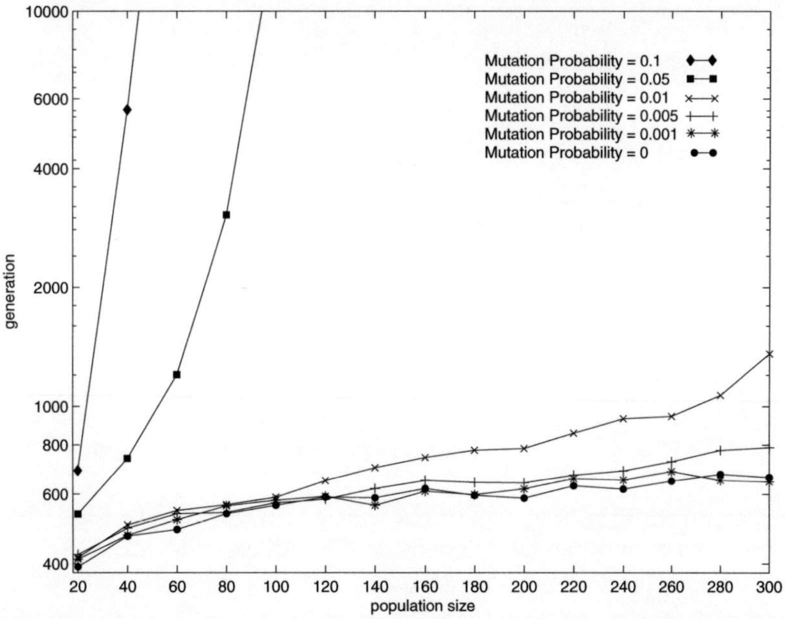

Fig. 11. SDGA with the mutation operator by different mutation probabilities for one-max problem of order 3.

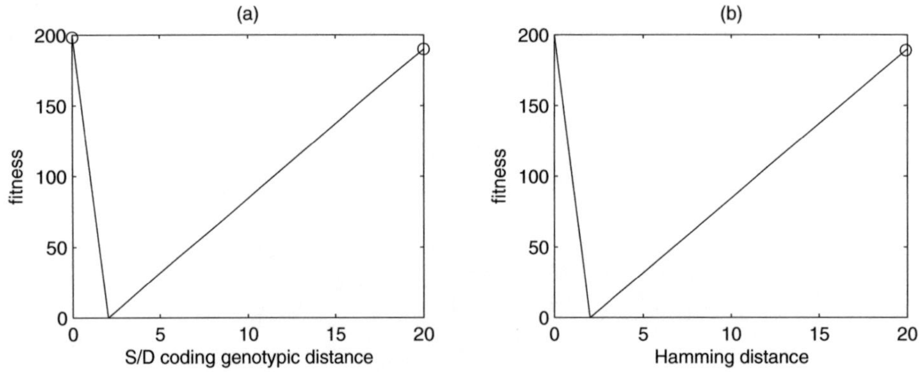

Fig. 12. Comparison of results of the dynamic niche sharing methods with S/D genotypic distance and Hamming distance for $f_3(x)$. (key: "o" — the optima in the final population)

[Miller] for multimodal function optimization to solve 4 benchmark multimodal optimization problems as listed in Table 4. To assess the effectiveness of the new genotypic distance on the S/D binary space, its performance is compared with the combination of SGA with S/D binary representation and the dynamic niche sharing methods based on Hamming distance. In applying SGA, we set the initial population size $N = 100$, the maximal generations $g_{mx} = 1000$, the length of S/D binary string for each dimension $l/n = 32$, the crossover probability $p_c = 0.8$ and the mutation probability $p_m = 0.005$.

Two-peak trap function (2 peaks):

$$f_3(x) = \begin{cases} \frac{200}{2}(2 - x), \text{ for } 0 \le x < 2; \\ \frac{190}{18}(x - 2), \text{ for } 2 \le x \le 20; \end{cases}$$

Deb's function (5 peaks):

$$f_4(x) = \sin^6(5\pi x), x \in [0, 1];$$

Deb's decreasing function (5 peaks):

$$f_5(x) = 2^{-2((x-0.1)/0.9)^2} \sin^6(5\pi x), x \in [0, 1];$$

Roots function (6 peaks):

$$f_6(x) = \frac{1}{1 + |x^6 - 1|}, \text{where } x \in C, x = x_1 + ix_2 \in [-2, 2];$$

Table 4. The test suite of multimodal functions used in our experiments.

Figures 12 - 15 show the comparison results of the dynamic niche sharing methods with the S/D genotypic distance and Hamming distance for $f_3(x) - f_6(x)$, respectively. Table 5 lists the solution quality comparison results in terms of the numbers of multiple optima maintained. We have run each algorithm 10 times. The dynamic niche sharing methods with the S/D

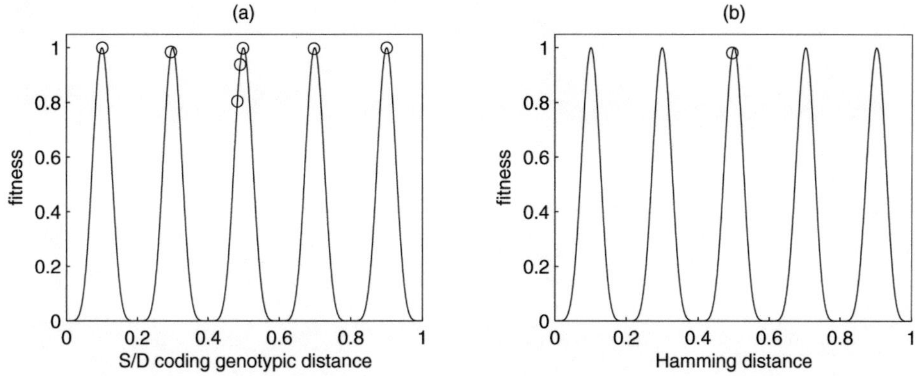

Fig. 13. Comparison of results of the dynamic niche sharing methods with S/D genotypic distance and Hamming distance for $f_4(x)$. (key: "o" — the optima in the final population)

genotypic distance can explore all optima in $f_3(x) - f_6(x)$ at each run. Contrary, for the niche methods with Hamming distance, the final population converged to a single optimum of the multimodal problem and cannot find multiply optima. That means the niche method cannon work due to the distance distortion between genotypic space (S/D binary space) and phenotypic space (real-valued space) when using Hamming distance.

The experimental investigations reveal that the methods depended on the Euclidean distance on the real-valued space can be directly used on the S/D binary space with our new defined genotypic distance.

	Distance	S/D genotypic distance		Hamming distance	
	threshold	Optima No.	Success rate	Optima No.	Success rate
f_3	2.0	2	100%	1	0%
f_4	0.16	5	100%	1	0%
f_5	0.16	5	100%	1	0%
f_6	0.8	6	100%	1	0%

Table 5. Comparison of results of the dynamic niche sharing methods with the S/D genotypic distance and Hamming distance.

6. Discussion

This paper has given for the first time a uniform-salient building block (USBB) in the S/D binary representation, which include uniformly scaled bits. This assumes that the phenotypic space Φ_p is uniformly scaled in each dimension. If the assumption is not be satisfied, we need to normalize the phenotypic space Φ_p first, then encoding the normalized phenotypic space Φ'_p into the S/D binary space Φ_g to guarantee that the bits in each USBB have same scaled.

SDGA applies on the S/D binary representation and converges from high scaled to low scaled USBBs sequentially. However, when the convergence window USBB cannon converge to single high-quality BB, there maybe are some high-quality BBs existing to describe different optima of the problem. At this time, we need to use some other methods (e.g. the niche methods) to divide the whole population into several sub-populations and each sub-population focus on each optimum. Thus, each optimum will be overrepresented by

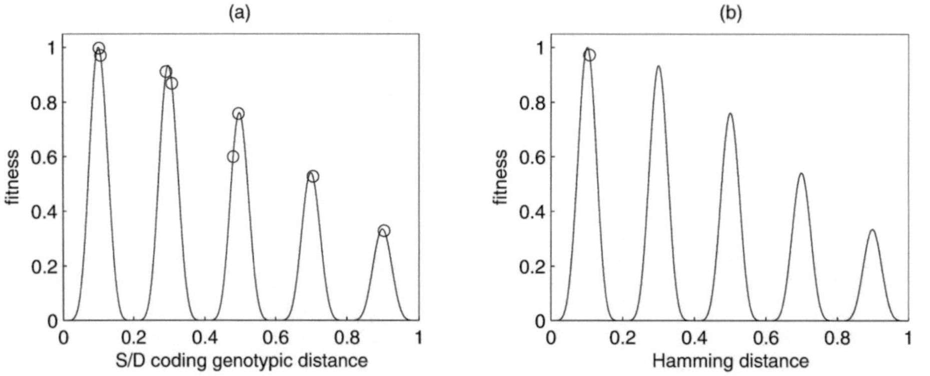

Fig. 14. Comparison of results of the dynamic niche sharing methods with S/D genotypic distance and Hamming distance for $f_5(x)$. (key: "o" — the optima in the final population)

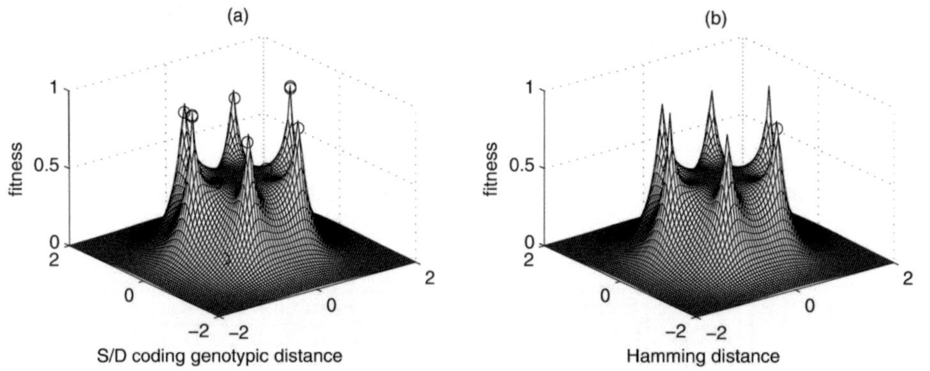

Fig. 15. Comparison of results of the dynamic niche sharing methods with S/D genotypic distance and Hamming distance for $f_6(x)$. (key: "o" — the optima in the final population)

BBs in its sub-population and SDGA can efficiently explore all the optima using these sub-populations.

7. Conclusions

In this paper, we introduce a new genetic representation — a splicing/decomposable (S/D) binary encoding, which was proposed based on some theoretical guidance and existing recommendations for designing efficient genetic representations. The S/D binary representation can be spliced and decomposed to describe potential solutions of the problem with different precisions by different number of uniform-salient building blocks (USBBs). According to the characteristics of the S/D binary representation, genetic and evolutionary algorithms (GEAs) can be applied from the high scaled to the low scaled BBs sequentially to avoid the noise from the competing BBs and improve GEAs' performance. Our theoretical and empirical investigations reveal that the S/D binary representation is more proper than other existing binary encodings for GEAs searching. Moreover, we define a new genotypic distance on the S/D binary space, which is equivalent to the Euclidean distance on the real-valued space during GEAs convergence. Based on the new genotypic distance, GEAs can reliably and predictably solve problems of bounded complexity and the methods depended on the Euclidean distance for solving different kinds of optimization problems can be directly used on the S/D binary space.

8. Acknowledgment

This research was supported by Macau Science and Technology Develop Funds (Grant No. 021/2008/A) and (Grant No. 017/2010/A2) of Macau Special Administrative Region of the People's Republic of China.

9. References

Goldberg, D. E. (1989). Genetic algorithms in search, optimization, and machine learning. Reading, MA: Addison-Wesley.

Hamming, R. (1980). Coding and information theory. Prentice-Hall. Han, K. H. & Kim, J. H. (2000). Genetic quantum algorithm and its application to combinatorial optimization problem, Proceeding of Congress on Evolutionary Computation 2000: Volume 1, pp. 1354-1360,

La Jolla, CA. Harik, G. R., Cantu-Paz, E., Goldberg, D. E. & Miller, B. L. (1997). The gambler's ruin problem, genetic algorithms and the size of populations. In Back, T. (Ed.), Proceedings of the Forth International Conference on Evolutionary Computation, pp. 7-12, New York.

Holland, J. H. (1975). Adaptation in natural and artificial systems. Ann Arbor, MI: University of Michigan Press. Julstrom, B. A. (1999). Redundant genetic encodings may not be harmful. Proceedings of the Genetic and Evolutionary Computation Conference 1999: Volume 1. San Francisco, CA: Morgan Kaufmann Publishers.

Leung, K. S., Sun, J. Y. & Xu, Z. B. (2002). Efficiency speed-up strategies for evolutionary computation: an adaptive implementation. Engineering Computations, 19 (3), pp. 272-304.

Leung, K. S. & Liang, Y. (2003). Adaptive elitist-population based genetic algorithm for multimodal function optimization. Proceeding of Genetic and Evolutionary Computation Conference 2003: Volume 1, pp. 1160-1171, Chicago, USA.

Liang, Y. & Leung, K. S. (2006). Evolution Strategies with Exclusion-based Selection Operators and a Fourier Series Auxiliary Function, Applied Mathematics and Computation, Volume 174, pp. 1080-1109.

Liepins, G. E. & Vose, M. D. (1990). Representational issues in genetic optimization. Journal of Experimental and Theoretical Artificial Intelligence, 2, pp.101-115.

Lobo, F. G., Goldberg. D. E. & Pelikan, M. (2000). Time complexity of genetic algorithms on exponentially scaled problems. Proceedings of the Genetic and Evolutionary Computation Conference 2000: Volume 1. San Francisco, CA: Morgan Kaufmann Publishers.

Mahfoud, S. W. (1996). Niching methods for genetic algorithms. Doctoral Thesis, University of Illinois at Urbana-Champaign.

Miller, B. L. & Goldberg, D. E. (1996). Optimal sampling for genetic algorithms (IlliGAL Report No. 96005). Urbana, IL: University of Illinois at Urbana-Champaign.

Rothlauf, F. (2002). Representations for genetic and evolutionary algorithms. Heidelberg; New York: Physica-Verl., 2002 Schaffer, J. D. (Ed.) (1989a). Proceedings of the

Third International Conference on Genetic Algorithms. San Francisco, CA: Morgan Kaufmann Publishers

Schaffer, J. D., Caruana, R. A., Eshelman, L. J. & Das, R. (1989b). A study of control parameters affecting online performance of genetic algorithms for function optimization. Proceedings of the Third International Conference on Genetic Algorithms. San Mateo, CA: Morgan Kaufmann.

Sendhoff, B., Kreutz, M. & von Seelen, W. (1997). A condition for the genotype-phenotype mapping: Causality. In Back, T. (ed.), Proceedings of the Seventh International Conference on Genetic Algorithms, pp. 73-80, San Francisco: Morgan Kaufmann.

Thierens, D. (1995). Analysis and design of genetic algorithms. Leuven, Belgium: Katholieke Universiteit Leuven.

Whitley, D. (2000). Local search and high precision gray codes: Convergence results and neighborhoods. In Martin, W., & Spears, W. (Eds.), Foundations of Genetic Algorithms 6. San Francisco, California: Morgan Kaufmann Publishers, Inc.

Wong, Y. Y., Lee, K. H., Leung, K. S. & C.W. Ho, C. W. (2003). A novel approach in parameter adaptation and diversity maintenance for genetic algorithm. Soft Computing, 7(8), pp. 506-515.

Wong, Z. Y., Leung, K. S., Wong, M. L. & Fang, J. (2000). A new type of nonlinear integrals and the computational algorithm. Fuzzy Sets and System, 112, pp. 223-231.

Xu, K. B., Wang, Z. Y., Heng, P. A. & Leung, K. S. (2003a). Classification by Nonlinear Integral Projections. IEEE Transactions on Fuzzy Systems, 11(2), pp. 187 - 201.

Xu, Z. B., Leung, K. S., Liang, Y. & Leung, Y. (2003b). Efficiency speed-up strategies for evolutionary computation: fundamentals and fast-GAs. Applied Mathematics and Computation 142, pp. 341-388.

Zhu, Z. Y. & Leung, K. S. (2002a). An enhanced annealing genetic algorithm for multi-objective optimization problems, Proceeding of Genetic and Evolutionary Computation Conference 2002, New York, USA.

Zhu, Z. Y. & Leung, K. S. (2002b). Asynchronous self-adjustable island genetic algorithm for multi-objective optimization problems, Proceeding of Congress on Evolutionary Computation 2002, Hawaii, USA.

Liang, Y. & Leung, K. S. (2011). Genetic Algorithm with Adaptive Elitist-population Strategies for Multimodal Function Optimization. Applied Soft Computing, 11(2), pp. 1160-1171.

6

Genetic Algorithms: An Overview with Applications in Evolvable Hardware

Popa Rustem
"Dunarea de Jos" University of Galati
Romania

1. Introduction

The genetic algorithm (GA) is an optimization and search technique based on the principles of genetics and natural selection. A GA allows a population composed of many individuals to evolve under specified selection rules to a state that maximizes the "fitness" (i.e., minimizes the cost function). The fundamental principle of natural selection as the main evolutionary principle has been formulated by Charles Darwin, without any knowledge about genetic mechanism. After many years of research, he assumed that parents qualities mix together in the offspring organism. Favorable variations are preserved, while the unfavorable are rejected. There are more individuals born than can survive, so there is a continuous struggle for life. Individuals with an advantage have a greater chance for survive i.e., the "survival of the fittest". This theory arose serious objections to its time, even after the discovering of the Mendel's laws, and only in 1920s "was it proved that Mendel's genetics and Darwin's theory of natural selection are in no way conflicting and that their happy marriage yields modern evolutionary theory" (Michalewicz, 1996).

The dynamical principles underlying Darwin's concept of evolution have been used to provide the basis for a new class of algorithms that are able to solve some difficult problems in computation. These "computational equivalents of natural selection, called evolutionary algorithms, act by successively improving a set or generation of candidate solutions to a given problem, using as a criterion how fit or adept they are at solving the problem." (Forbes, 2005). Evolutionary algorithms (EAs) are highly parallel, which makes solving these difficult problems more tractable, although usually the computation effort is huge.

In this chapter we focus on some applications of the GAs in Digital Electronic Design, using the concept of extrinsic Evolvable Hardware (EHW). But first of all, we present the genesis of the main research directions in Evolutionary Computation, the structure of a Simple Genetic Algorithm (SGA), and a classification of GAs, taking into account the state of the art in this field of research.

2. A brief history of evolutionary computation

In the 1950s and the 1960s several computer scientists independently studied evolutionary systems with the idea that evolution could be used as an optimization tool for engineering problems. The idea in all these systems was to evolve a population of candidate solutions to a given problem, using operators inspired by natural genetic variation and natural selection.

In the 1960s, two german scientists, Ingo Rechenberg and Hans-Paul Schwefel introduced "evolution strategies", a method they used to optimize real−valued parameters for the shape of airplane wings. The field of evolution strategies "has remained an active area of research, mostly developing independently from the field of genetic algorithms (although recently the two communities have begun to interact)" (Mitchell, 1997). Around the same time, completely independently, american scientist Lawrence Fogel developed a method of computational problem solving he termed "evolutionary programming", a technique in which candidate solutions to given tasks were represented as finite−state machines, which were evolved by randomly mutating their state−transition diagrams and selecting the fittest (Forbes, 2005).

Genetic algorithms (GAs) "were invented by John Holland in the 1960s and were developed by Holland and his students and colleagues at the University of Michigan in the 1960s and the 1970s. In contrast with evolution strategies and evolutionary programming, Holland's original goal was not to design algorithms to solve specific problems, but rather to formally study the phenomenon of adaptation as it occurs in nature and to develop ways in which the mechanisms of natural adaptation might be imported into computer systems. Holland's 1975 book *Adaptation in Natural and Artificial Systems* presented the genetic algorithm as an abstraction of biological evolution and gave a theoretical framework for adaptation under the GA. Holland's GA is a method for moving from one population of "chromosomes" (e.g., strings of ones and zeros, or "bits") to a new population by using a kind of "natural selection" together with the genetics−inspired operators of crossover, mutation, and inversion. (…) Holland's introduction of a population−based algorithm with crossover, inversion, and mutation was a major innovation" (Mitchell, 1997). Rechenberg's evolution strategies generate a single offspring, which is a mutated version of the parent.

"Holland was the first to attempt to put computational evolution on a firm theoretical footing. Until recently this theoretical foundation, based on the notion of "schemas," was the basis of almost all subsequent theoretical work on genetic algorithms. In the last several years there has been widespread interaction among researchers studying various evolutionary computation methods, and the boundaries between GAs, evolution strategies, evolutionary programming, and other evolutionary approaches have broken down to some extent. Today, researchers often use the term "genetic algorithm" to describe something very far from Holland's original conception" (Mitchell, 1997).

Current techniques are more sophisticated and combine the basic algorithms with other heuristics. Koza developed in 1992 "genetic programming", which applies a GA to writing computer programs. "The variables are various programming constructs, and the output is a measure of how well the program achieves its objectives. The GA operations of mutation, reproduction (crossover) and cost calculation require only minor modifications. GP is a more complicated procedure because it must work with the variable length structure of the program or function. A GP is a computer program that writes other computer programs" (Haupt & Haupt, 2004). "Genetic Programming uses evolution-inspired techniques to produce not just the fittest *solution* to a problem, but an *entire optimized computer program*." (Forbes, 2005).

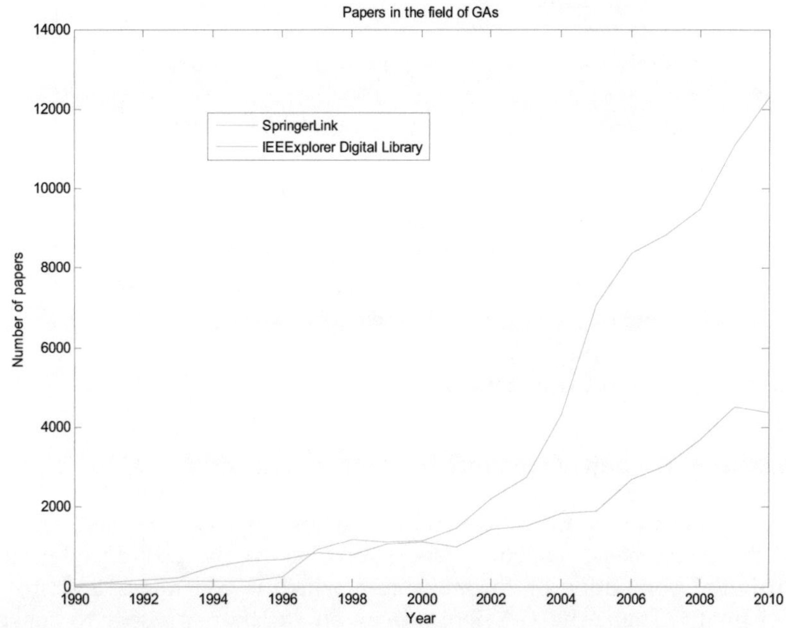

Fig. 1. Increasing the number of works in the field over the past 20 years

Figure 1 represents the number of papers in the field of GAs, in the last 20 years, in two of the most popular databases: SpringerLink from Springer, which contain 81187 papers on GAs, from a total amount of 5276591, and IEEExplore Digital Library from IEEE, which contain 32632 papers on GAs, from a total amount of 2926204.

3. A simple Genetic Algorithm

The set of all the solutions of an optimization problem constitutes the search space. The problem consists in finding out the solution that fits the best, from all the possible solutions. When the search space becomes huge, we need a specific technique to find the optimal solution. GAs provides one of these methods. Practically they all work in a similar way, adapting the simple genetics to algorithmic mechanisms. GA handles a population of possible solutions. Each solution is represented through a chromosome, which is just an abstract representation.

Coding all the possible solutions into a chromosome is the first part, but certainly not the most straightforward one of a GA. A set of reproduction operators has to be determined, too. Reproduction operators are applied directly on the chromosomes, and are used to perform selection of the parents, by using a fitness function (usually the most fitted, with some likelihood), recombinations (crossover) and mutations and over solutions of the problem. "Appropriate representation and reproduction operators are really something determinant, as the behavior of the GA is extremely dependant on it. Frequently, it can be extremely difficult to find a representation, which respects the structure of the search space and reproduction operators, which are coherent and relevant according to the properties of the problems" (Sivanandam & Deepa, 2008).

```
Procedure Genetic Algorithm
begin
    generate randomly the initial population of chromosomes;
    repeat
        calculate the fitness of chromosomes in population;
        repeat
            select 2 chromosomes as parents;
            apply crossover to the selected parents;
            apply mutation to the new chromosomes;
            calculate the fitness of new child chromosomes;
        until end of the number of new chromosomes
        update the population;
    until end of the number of generations
end
```

Fig. 2. Pseudocode description of the Procedure Genetic Algorithm

Once the reproduction and the fitness function have been properly defined, a GA is evolved according to the same basic structure (see source above in pseudocode). It starts by generating an initial population of chromosomes, which is generated randomly to ensure the genetic diversity. Then, the GA loops over an iteration process to make the next generation. Each iteration consists of fitness evaluation, selection, reproduction, new evaluation of the offsprings, and finally replacement in population. Stopping criterion may be the number of iterations (called here generations), or the convergence of the best chromosome toward the optimal solution.

4. Classification of Genetic Algorithms

Sometimes the cost function is extremely complicated and time-consuming to evaluate. As a result some care must be taken to minimize the number of cost function evaluations. An idea was to use parallel execution of various Simple GAs, and these algorithms are called Parallel Genetic Algorithms (PGAs). PGAs have been developed to reduce the large execution times that are associated with simple genetic algorithms for finding near-optimal solutions in large search spaces. They have also been used to solve larger problems and to find better solutions. PGAs have considerable gains in terms of performance and scalability. There are a lot of methods of PGAs (Independent PGA, Migration PGA, Partition PGA, Segmentation PGA) which are fully described in (Sivanandam & Deepa, 2008).

Hybrid Genetic Algorithms (HGAs) produce another important class of GAs. A hybrid GA combines the power of the GA with the speed of a local optimizer. The GA excels at gravitating toward the global minimum. It is not especially fast at finding the minimum when in a locally quadratic region. Thus the GA finds the region of the optimum, and then the local optimizer takes over to find the minimum. Some examples of HGAs used in Digital Electronics Design will be presented in the next section.

Adaptive genetic algorithms (AGAs) are GAs whose parameters, such as the population size, the crossing over probability, or the mutation probability are varied while the GA is running. "The mutation rate may be changed according to changes in the population; the longer the population does not improve, the higher the mutation rate is chosen. Vice versa, it is decreased again as soon as an improvement of the population occurs" (Sivanandam & Deepa, 2008).

Fast Messy Genetic Algorithm (FmGA) is a binary, stochastic, variable string length, population based approach to solving optimization problems. The main difference between the FmGA and other genetic approaches is the ability of the FmGA to explicitly manipulate building blocks (BBs) of genetic material in order to obtain good solutions and potentially the global optimum. Some works, like (Haupt & Haupt, 2004), use only the term of Messy Genetic Algorihms (mGAs).

Finally, Independent Sampling Genetic Algorithm (ISGA) are more robust GAs, which manipulate building blocks to avoid the premature convergence in a GA. Implicit parallelism and the efficacy of crossover are enhanced and the ISGAs have been shown to outperform several different GAs (Sivanandam & Deepa, 2008). Other classes of efficient GAs may be implemented for different specific applications.

5. Applications of Genetic Algorithms

"GAs have been applied in science, engineering, business and social sciences. Number of scientists has already solved many engineering problems using genetic algorithms. GA concepts can be applied to the engineering problem such as optimization of gas pipeline systems. Another important current area is structure optimization. The main objective in this problem is to minimize the weight of the structure subjected to maximum and minimum stress constrains on each member. GA is also used in medical imaging system. The GA is used to perform image registration as a part of larger digital subtraction angiographies. It can be found that GAs can be used over a wide range of applications" (Sivanandam & Deepa, 2008). GAs can also be applied to production planning, air traffic problems, automobile, signal processing, communication networks, environmental engineering and so on. In (Bentley & Corne, 2002), Evolutionary Creativity is discussed, using a lot of examples from music, art in general, architecture and engineering design. Evolutionary Electronics, both Analog and Digital, have been investigated in many publications (Bentley & Corne, 2002; Popa, 2004; Popa et al., 2005). (Higuchi et al., 2006) is a very good book on Evolvable Hardware.

Evolvable Hardware (EHW) is a hardware built on software reconfigurable Programmable Logic Devices (PLDs). In these circuits the logic design is compiled into a binary bit string and, by changing the bits, arbitrary hardware structures can be implemented instantly. The key idea is to regard such a bit string as a chromosome of a Genetic Algorithm (GA). Through genetic learning, EHW finds the best bit string and reconfigures itself according to rewards received from the environment (Iba et al., 1996).

In the rest of this section we present three applications in evolutionary design of digital circuits developed by the author, using GAs. First of them describes a method of synthesis of a Finite State Machine (FSM) in a Complex Programmable Logic Device (CPLD), using a standard GA. The other two applications use different techniques of hybridisation of a standard GA: first of them with two other optimisation techniques (inductive search and simulated annealing), to solve the Automatic Test Pattern Generation for digital circuits, a problem described in (Bilchev & Parmee, 1996), and the second one to improve the convergence of the standard GA in evolutionary design of digital circuits, using the new paradigm of Quantum Computation (Han & Kim, 2002).

5.1 Implementation of a FSM using a standard GA

This first example uses extrinsic hardware evolution, that is uses a model of the hardware and evaluates it by simulation in software. The FSM represented in the figure 3 is a computer interface for serial communication between two computers. A transition from one state to another depends from only one of the 4 inputs $x_i, i=\overline{1,4}$. The circuit has 4 outputs, each of them beeing in 1 logic only in a single state. The FSM has 6 states and has been presented in (Popa, 2004).

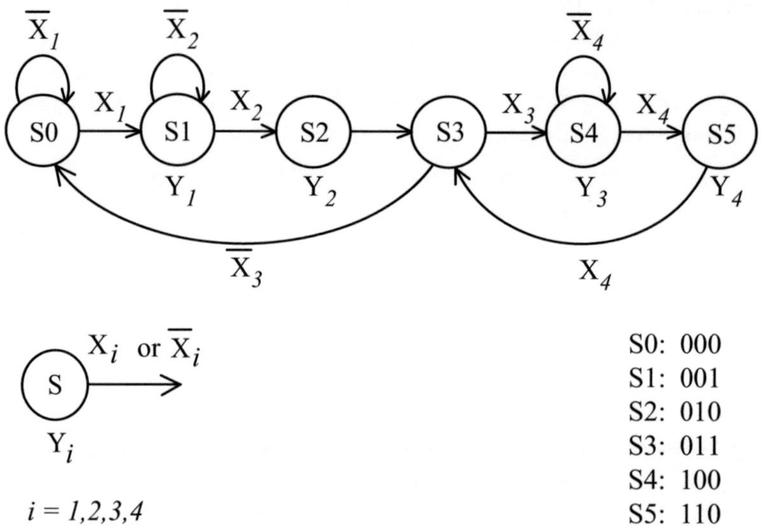

Fig. 3. A FSM described as state transition graph and manual state assignment

With the state assignment given in the figure 3, the traditional design with D flip-flops gives the following equations for the excitations functions:

$$D_2 = x_3 \cdot Q_1 \cdot Q_0 + Q_2 \cdot \bar{Q}_1 \quad (1)$$

$$D_1 = x_2 \cdot \bar{Q}_1 \cdot Q_0 + x_4 \cdot Q_2 + Q_1 \cdot \bar{Q}_0 \quad (2)$$

$$D_0 = x_1 \cdot \bar{Q}_2 \cdot \bar{Q}_0 + \bar{x}_2 \cdot \bar{Q}_1 \cdot Q_0 + Q_1 \cdot \bar{Q}_0 \quad (3)$$

The output functions, are given by the following equations:

$$y_1 = \bar{Q}_1 \cdot Q_0 \quad (4)$$

$$y_2 = \bar{Q}_2 \cdot Q_1 \cdot \bar{Q}_0 \quad (5)$$

$$y_3 = Q_2 \cdot \bar{Q}_1 \quad (6)$$

$$y_4 = Q_2 \cdot Q_1 \quad (7)$$

For the evolutionary design of this circuit we take into account that each boolean function has a maximum number of 5 inputs and a maximum number of 4 minterms. If we want to implement these functions in a PLD structure (an AND array and logic cells configurable as OR gate), then the number of fuse array links is $2 \cdot 5 \cdot 4 = 40$, and we may to consider this number as the total length of the chromosome (Iba et al., 1996).

Our GA is a standard one, with the population size of 30 chromosomes. One point crossover is executed with a probability of 80% and the mutation rate is 2%. Six worse chromosomes are replaced each generation. The stop criterion is the number of generations.

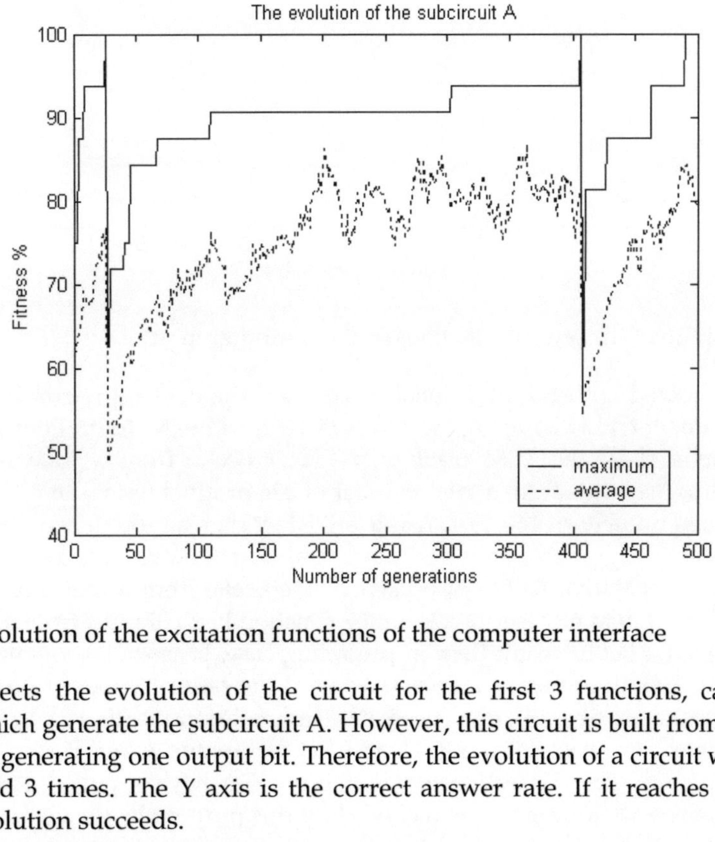

Fig. 4. The evolution of the excitation functions of the computer interface

Figure 4 reflects the evolution of the circuit for the first 3 functions, called excitation functions, which generate the subcircuit A. However, this circuit is built from 3 independent circuits, each generating one output bit. Therefore, the evolution of a circuit with one output bit is repeated 3 times. The Y axis is the correct answer rate. If it reaches 100%, then the hardware evolution succeeds.

In the same way, figure 5 reflects the evolution of the circuit for the output functions, which generate the subcircuit B. The evolution succeeds after a less number of generations because the total search space is in this case much lower than in previous case (all the output functions have only 3 variables).

Evolution may provide some non-minimal expressions for these boolean functions, but minimization is not necessary for PLD implementations. The length of the chromosomes is greater than the optimal one, and the evolved equations are much more complicated than the given equations (1-7). The complete cost of the whole combinational circuit is consisted of 15 gates and 37 inputs for traditional design, and 30 gates and 102 inputs for evolutionary design.

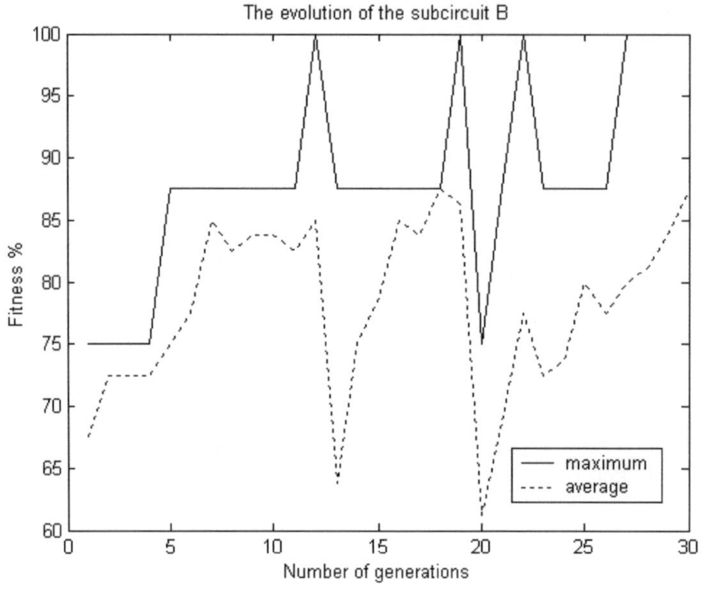

Fig. 5. The evolution of the output functions of the computer interface

We have implemented both the traditional design and the evolved circuit in a real Xilinx XCR3064 CoolRunner CPLD by using the Xilinx ISE 6.1i software. In traditional design, that is using equations (1-7), the FSM used only 7 macrocells from a total number of 64 macrocells, 11 product terms from a total number of 224 product terms, and 7 function block inputs, from a total number of 160. Surprising is the fact that, although evolutionary design, with the same state assignment, provides more complicated equations, the implementation of this circuit in XCR3064XL CPLD also used 7 macrocells from a total number of 64, 10 product terms from a total number of 224, and 7 function block inputs, from a total number of 160. This is even a better result than in preceding case, because the number of product terms is less with 1. Both implementations have used the same number of flip-flops (that is 3/64) and the same number of pins used like inputs/outputs (that is 9/32). We have preserved the state assignment of the FSM, and the subcircuits A and B are in fact as pure combinational circuits. The interesting fact is that our GA have supplied a better solution than the one given by the minimization tool used for this purpose by the CAD software.

5.2 Multiple hybridization of a GA

Hybrid Genetic Algorithms (HGAs) combine the power of the GA with the speed of a local optimizer. Usually the GA finds the region of the optimum, and then the local optimizer takes over to find the minimum. (Bilchev & Parmee, 1996) developed a search space reduction methodology, which was called the Inductive Search. The problem of global optimisation is partitioned into a sequence of subproblems, which are solved by searching of partial solutions in subspaces with smaller dimensions.

This method has been used to solve the Automatic Test Pattern Generation Problem in Programmable Logic Arrays (PLAs), that is to find an effective set of input test vectors, which are able to cover as many as possible faults in the circuit (we have taken into account two PLA structures with a total number of 50 and respective 200 stuck-at 0 possible faults).

(Wong & Wong, 1994) designed a HGA using the algorithm of Simulated Annealing as local optimizer. The optimisation process in Simulated Annealing is essentially a simulation of the annealing process of a molten particle. Starting from a high temperature, a molten particle is cooled slowly. As the temperature reduces, the energy level of the particle also reduces. When the temperature is sufficiently low, the molten particle becomes solidified. Analogous to the temperature level in the physical annealing process is the iteration number in Simulated Annealing. In each iteration, a candidate solution is generated. If this solution is a better one, it will be accepted and used to generate yet another candidate solution. If it is a deteriorated solution, the solution will be accepted with some probability.

Each of this two methods of hybridisation discussed above have some advantages. The inductive search effort at each inductive step controls the trade-off between the

Procedure MHGA
begin
    Initialize a partial solution for $N = 1$ and establish the initial temperature T_0;
    for $k = 2$ to N,
        Generate randomly the initial population of chromosomes;
        repeat
            append each chromosome to the partial solution, and evaluate it;
            repeat
                select, proportional with fitness, 2 parents;
                apply crossover to obtain 2 offsprings;
                apply mutation to the new chromosomes;
                calculate the fitness of new chromosomes;
                the new chromosomes are accepted or not accepted;
            until end of the number of chromosomes
            update the population, according with the fitness;
            the temperature is decreased;
        until end of the number of generations
        Update the partial solution;
    end
end

Fig. 6. The structure of the MHGA

computational complexity and the expected quality of results, while Simulated Annealing avoids the premature convergence and reduces the adverse effects of the mutation operation. In (Popa et al., 2002) we proposed a HGA that cumulates all these advantages in a single algorithm, through a double hybridisation of the Genetic Algorithm: with Inductive Search on the one hand, and with Simulated Annealing technique on the other hand. The structure of the Multiple Hybridated Genetic Algorithm is presented in figure 6.

We have conducted the experiments with all three HGAs described above, in the purpose to find the maximum fault coverage with a limited number of test vectors. We have tested first a PLA structure with 50 potential "stuck-at 0" faults, taking into account the maximum coverage with the faults with only 6 test vectors, and results may be seen in the figure 7. Then, we repeated the same algorithm for a more complicated PLA structure, with 200 potential "stuck-at 0" faults, and we tried to cover the maximum number of faults with 24 test vectors. The evolutions of these three algorithms may be seen in figure 8.

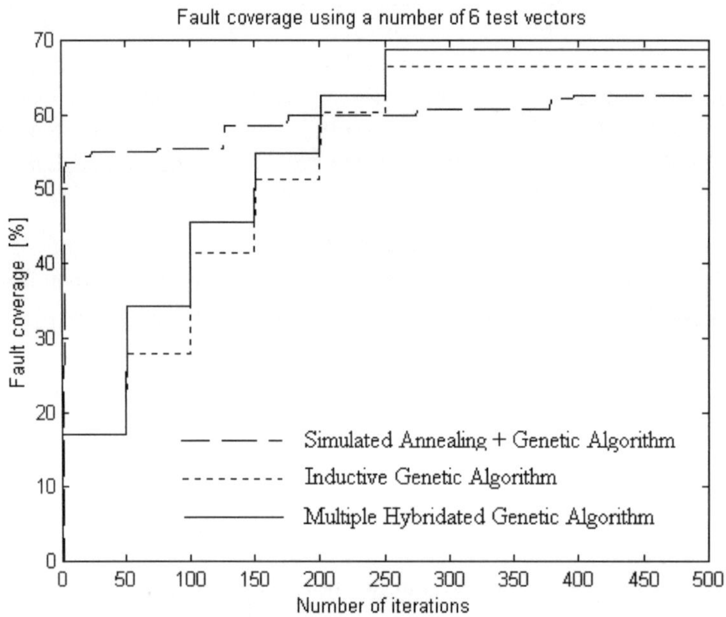

Fig. 7. Fault Coverage Problem of 50 possible faults solved with three HGAs in 500 iterations

If n is the number of covered faults and N is the number of all faults in the fault population, the associated fitness function is $f = \frac{n}{N} \cdot 100\%$. There may also be a number of constraints concerning the possible combinations of input signals. The designers of the circuit define the set of legal combinations in terms of the legal states of a number of channels. The set of all legal templates defines the feasible region. The main genetic parameters used in these algorithms are: a population size of 20 chromosomes, uniform crossover with 100% rate, uniform mutation with 1% rate. The maximum fault coverage achieved with the Multiple Hybridated Genetic Algorithm after 500 iterations was about 69%, while the maximum fault coverage achieved with the Inductive Genetic Algorithm, the best of the two single hybridated genetic algorithms, was about 66%. These results represent the average values of 5 succesive runnings. We have tried even with 10 or more number of runnings, but the results are basically the same.

Another set of experiments were made on a more complex digital structure of PLA type with 200 possible faults. Figure 8 shows the comparative performances of the three HGAs on this fault coverage problem. The number of input test vectors is 24. After 250 fitness function calls, that is 25 iterations, each with 10 generations per inductive step, the fault coverage of the Multiple Hybridated Genetic Algorithm is with about 1% better than the fault coverage of the Inductive Genetic Algorithm.

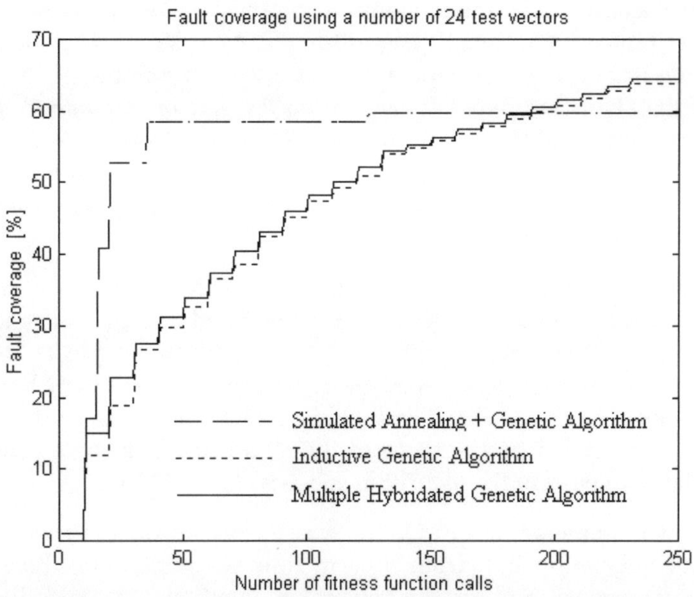

Fig. 8. Fault Coverage Problem of 200 possible faults solved with three HGAs

These experiments show that the proposed MHGA seems to offer a better performance than the two other HGAs: the Inductive Genetic Algorithm and the Genetic Algorithm hybridated by Simulated Annealing. We have proved on two different examples, with different complexities, that MHGA offers the greatest value of fault coverage in Automatic Test Pattern Generation Problem in digital circuits of PLA type.

5.3 A Quantum Inspired GA for EHW

Quantum Inspired Genetic Algorithm (QIGA) proposed in (Popa et al., 2010) uses a single chromosome, which is represented like a string of qubits, as is described in (Han & Kim, 2002; Zhou & Sun, 2005). A quantum chromosome which contains n qubits may be represented as:

$$q = \begin{bmatrix} \alpha_1 & \alpha_2 & \dots & \alpha_n \\ \beta_1 & \beta_2 & \dots & \beta_n \end{bmatrix}, \tag{8}$$

where each couple α_i, β_i, for $i = 1,...,n$, are the probability amplitudes associated with the $|0\rangle$ state and the $|1\rangle$ state such that $\alpha_i^2 + \beta_i^2 = 1$ and the values α_i^2 and β_i^2 represent the probability of seeing a conventional gene, 0 or 1, when the qubit is measured.

A quantum chromosome can be in all the 2^n states at the same time, that is:

$$|q\rangle = a_0|00...0\rangle + a_1|00...1\rangle + ...a_{2^n-1}|11...1\rangle, \tag{9}$$

where a_i represents the quantum probability amplitude, and a_i^2 is the probability of seeing the *i*-th chromosome from the all 2^n possible classic chromosomes (Zhou & Sun, 2005).

Due to this superposition of states in a quantum chromosome, we use a single chromosome in population. In Conventional Genetic Algorithm (CGA) or Simple Genetic Algorithm with the structure given in figure 2, the population has always a number of chromosomes, and the efficiency of the algorithm depends usually on the size of population. But a quantum chromosome can represent all the possible conventional chromosomes at the same time, and so, it may generates an arbitrary population of conventional chromosomes each generation. Quantum population will be transformed to conventional population when the fitness is evaluated.

Single Chromosome Quantum Genetic Algorithm (SCQGA) is described in (Zhou & Sun, 2005). In the first step, a quantum chromosome is generated using (8). A random number is compared with probabilities of each qubit, and it collapses to 0, or to 1. The conventional population of N chromosomes is obtained by repeating this process N times. In the next step, the fitness value is calculated for each conventional chromosome. It requires a lot of time, that involves the speed performance of the algorithm. The same problem of fitness evaluation and the low speed of the algorithm subsists also in CGAs.

Our idea, which was implemented in QIGA, was to initiate the collapse of the quantum chromosome each generation but, from time to time to generate a whole population of conventional chromosomes, and in the remaining iterations to generate only a single conventional chromosome. A new parameter, which we called the *probability of collapse*, establishes the rate of generating a conventional population during the evolution. The last important step of the algorithm is to establish a method of updating the quantum chromosome from the current generation to the next one. QIGA uses the same method described in (Han, 2003). The idea is to modify the probabilities of each quantum gene (or qubit) from the quantum chromosome using quantum rotation gate. This operator changes the probability amplitude by altering the quantum phase θ to $\theta + \Delta\theta$. The idea for the construction of the rotation gate is to make the changing of the entire population (quantum chromosome) to the direction of the best individual. Each bit from the best conventional chromosome is compared with the adequate bit from the average version of the quantum chromosome (this version is build using a probability of 0.5 for each qubit). If the two bits are equal with 0 or 1, then $\Delta\theta = 0$. If the bit of the best chromosome is 1 and the other one is 0, then $\Delta\theta = a$, otherwise $\Delta\theta = -a$. The angle parameter of the rotation gate $\Delta\theta$ may be 0, -a, or a, depending on the position of each qubit in chromosome. The parameter a is a positive small parameter, which decides the evolving rate (Zhou & Sun, 2005).

Basic structure of QIGA is given in figure 9. $q(t)$ is the quantum chromosome in the iteration t, and $P(t)$ is the population in the same iteration t. This population may contain a lot of chromosomes, or only one, depending on the probability of collapse in $q(t)$. These three algorithms, CGA, SCQGA and QIGA have been compared on the same problem, which consists on synthesis of a boolean function with 4 variables, using different logic gates. The chromosomes define the connection in the network between the primary inputs and primary outputs of the gates, and decide the logic operators of the gates. The population of CGA has 64 chromosomes, 20 of them being changed each generation, and genetic operators use a single point 100% crossover and 5% rate mutation.

Figure 10 illustrates the average of evolutions of the three algorithms after 10 successful runnings on 300 generations. A successful running presumes a fitness evaluation of 100%, that is the truth table of the evolved function must be identical with the truth table of the specified function. We can see some similarities in these evolutions, but significant differences may be seen in Table 1.

```
Procedure QIGA
begin
    t ← 0
    Initialize a quantum chromosome q(t);
    if the collaps of q(t) is likely
            generate multiple chromosomes in population P(t);
    else
            generate a single chromosome in population P(t);
    end
    evaluate all the chromosomes in population P(t);
    store the best solution b among P(t);
    while (not termination condition) do
            begin
                    t ← t + 1
                    if the collapse of q(t-1) is likely
                            generate multiple chromosomes in population P(t);
                    else
                            generate a single chromosome in population P(t);

                    end
                    evaluate all the chromosomes in population P(t);
                    update q(t) using quantum gates;
                    store the best result b among P(t);
            end
    end
end
```

Fig. 9. The structure of the QIGA

In CGA, global time of a successful run is about 74 seconds, and this value consists of both self time and the time spent for multiple evaluations of chromosomes in different populations. Self time is the time spent in an algorithm, excluding the time spent in its child functions. Self time also includes overhead resulting from the process of profiling, but this additional time is not important in our case. Evaluation time is almost 60 seconds, because the number of appeals to the evaluation function is elevated (25200 calls, that is evaluation of 64 plus 20 chromosomes in 300 generations).

In SCQGA, global time is less than 40 seconds, because the number of calls to the evaluation function is less than above (only 19200 calls, that is evaluation of 64 chromosomes in 300 generations), and this quantum algorithm doesn't use anymore genetic operators like crossover and mutation. Finally, our QIGA has a global time less than 20 seconds, as a consequence of the insignificant number of calls to the evaluation function (only 4836 calls, a random number given by the probability of collapse). Self time is comparable with SCQGA, and evaluation time is less than 12 seconds. Taking into account all these times, QIGA has the best ratio between evaluation and global time.

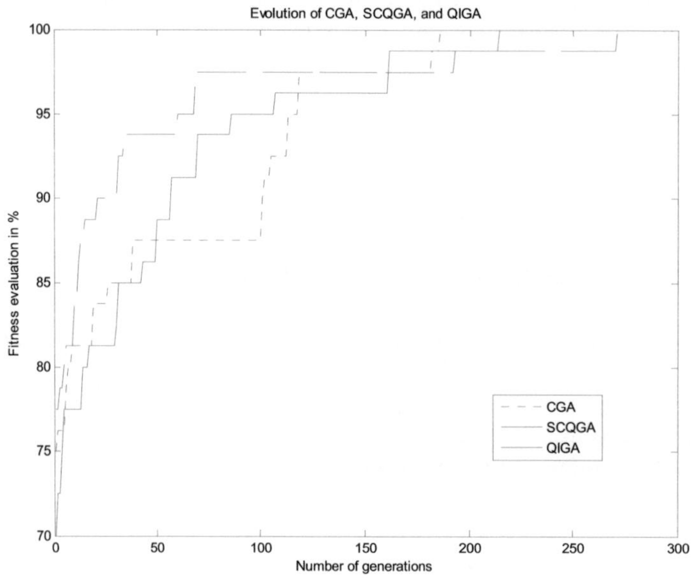

Fig. 10. The evolutions of CGA, SCQGA and QIGA

Parameter	CGA	SCQGA	QIGA
Global time	73.990 s	38.599 s	19.263 s
Self time	2.447 s	1.417 s	1.390 s
Evaluation time	59.561 s	31.536 s	11.750 s
Calls of evaluation function	25200	19200	4836
Ratio between evaluation and global time	80.5 %	81.7 %	60.9 %
Number of generations	300	300	300
Successful runnings in 10 attempts (with fitness of 100%)	7	6	6

Table 1. A comparison between CGA, SCQGA and IQGA

Unfortunately, the number of successful runs in 300 generations is only in the order of 70% for CGA, and 60% for the rest two algorithms. It occurs due to the constraint that only 100% in fitness evaluation is accepted. In other applications, this constraint may be not critical.

6. Conclusion

In this chapter we did a summary outline of GAs and discussed some possible applications. We presented three extrinsic evolutionary designs of digital circuits at gate level using GAs.

Future research must be done in this area. Firstly it is important to find a better representation of the circuit in chromosomes, because complex functions need a great number of architecture bits, which directly influences the GA search space. EHW successfully succeeds only when fitness reaches 100% and in huge search spaces this condition may be not always possible. This is the main reason that for the time being the complexity of evolved circuits is so far small. In our opinion, conclusion drawn in the paper (Yao & Higuchi, 1999) is still available: "EHW research needs to address issues, such as scalability, online adaptation, generalization, circuit correctness, and potential risk of evolving hardware in a real physical environment. It is argued that a theoretical foundation of EHW should be established before rushing to large-scale EHW implementations".

Recently appeared the idea of hybridization of a GA with elements of quantum computation (Han & Kim, 2002; Han, 2003). We have proposed a new quantum inspired genetic algorithm (QIGA) considerably faster than other similar algorithms, based on the idea of introducing a new parameter, which we called the probability of collapse, and to initiate the collapse of the quantum chromosome in order to generate a conventional population of chromosomes from time to time, and not each generation, as usually is done. We believe that some improvements in this method may be found in a future research, by establishing of a new method of updating the quantum chromosome from the current generation to the next one. Finally, some hybridization techniques may be useful for new quantum inspired evolutionary algorithms. (Rubinstein, 2001) used Genetic Programming to evolve quantum circuits with various properties, and (Moore & Venayagamoorthy, 2005) has developed an algorithm inspired from quantum evolution and Particle Swarm to evolve conventional combinational logic circuits.

7. References

Bentley, P. J. & Corne, D. W. (Ed(s).). (2002). *Creative Evolutionary Systems*, Academic Press, ISBN: 1-55860-673-4, San Francisco, USA

Bilchev, G. & Parmee, I. (1996). Constraint Handling for the Fault Coverage Code Generation Problem: An Inductive Evolutionary Approach, *Proceedings of 4-th Conference on Parallel Problem Solving from Nature (PPSN IV)*, pp. 880-889, Berlin, September 1996

Burda, I. (2005). *Introduction to Quantum Computation,* Universal Publishers, ISBN: 1-58112-466-X, Boca Raton, Florida, USA

Forbes, N. (2005). *Imitation of Life. How Biology Is Inspiring Computing,* MIT Press, ISBN: 0-262-06241-0, London, England

Han, K. H. & Kim, J. H. (2002). Quantum-Inspired Evolutionary Algorithm for a Class of Combinatorial Optimization, *IEEE Transactions on Evolutionary Computation,*vol.6, no.6, (December 2002), pp. 580-593, ISSN 1089-778X

Han, K. H. (2003). *Quantum-Inspired Evolutionary Algorithm,* Ph.D. dissertation, Department of Electrical Engineering and Computer Science, Korea Advanced Institute of Science and Technology, Korea, 2003

Haupt, R. L. & Haupt, S. E. (2004). *Practical Genetic Algorithms* (second edition), Wiley-Interscience, ISBN: 0-471-45565-2, New-Jersey, USA

Higuchi, T.; Liu, Y. & Yao, X. (Ed(s).). (2006). *Evolvable Hardware*, Spinger-Verlag, ISBN-13: 978-0387-24386-3, New-York, USA

Iba, H.; Iwata, M. And Higuchi, T. (1996). Machine Learning Approach to Gate-Level Evolvable Hardware. *Proceedings of the First International Conference on Evolvable Systems ICES'96,* pp.327-343, Tsukuba, Japan, October 1996

Mazumder, P. & Rudnick, E. M. (1999). *Genetic Algorithms for VLSI Design, Layout & Test Automation,* Prentice Hall PTR, ISBN: 0-13-011566-5, Upper Saddle River, New Jersey, USA

Michalewicz, Z. (1996). *Genetic Algorithms + Data Structures = Evolution Programs* (third edition), Springer-Verlag, ISBN: 3-540-58090-5, New-York, USA

Mitchell, M. (1997). *An Introduction to Genetic Algorithms* (third printing), MIT Press, ISBN: 0-262-13316-4, London, England

Moore, Ph. & Venayagamoorthy, G. K. (2005). Evolving Combinational Logic Circuits using a Hybrid Quantum Evolution and Particle Swarm Inspired Algorithm, *Proceedings of the 2005 NASA/DoD Conference of Evolution Hardware EH'05,* pp. 97–102, 2005

Popa, R.; Aiordachioaie, D. & Nicolau, V. (2002). Multiple Hybridization in Genetic Algorithms, *The 16-th European Meeting on Cybernetics and Systems Research EMCSR'2002*, pp.536-541, ISBN 3-85206-160-1, Vienna, Austria, April 2-5, 2002

Popa, R. (2004). Evolvable Hardware in Xilinx XCR3064 CPLD, *IFAC Workshop on Programmable Devices and Systems, PDS 2004,* pp. 232-237, ISBN: 83-908409-8-7, Cracow, Poland, November 18-19, 2004

Popa, R.; Aiordachioaie, D. & Sîrbu, G. (2005). Evolvable Hardware in Xilinx Spartan 3 - FPGA, *2005 WSEAS International Conference on Dynamical Systems and Control,* pp. 66-71, ISBN: 960-8457-37-8, Venice, Italy, November 2-4, 2005

Popa, R.; Nicolau, V. & Epure, S. (2010). A New Quantum Inspired Genetic Algorithm for Evolvable Hardware, *3rd International Symposium On Electrical and Electronics Engineering ISEEE 2010,* pp. 64-69, ISBN: 978-1-4244-8407-2, Galaţi, Romania, September 16-18, 2010 (in IEEExplore Digital Library, DOI 10.1109/ ISEEE.2010.5628539)

Rubinstein, B. I. P. (2001). Evolving Quantum Circuits using Genetic Programming, *Proceedings of the 2001 Congress on Evolutionary Computation, CEC2001,* pp. 114–121, IEEE Press, 2001

Schöneburg, E.; Heinzmann, F. & Feddersen, S. (1994). *Genetische Algorithmen und Evolutionsstrategien. Eine Einführung in Theorie und Praxis der simulierten Evolution,* Addison-Wesley, ISBN: 5-89319-493-2, München, Germany

Sivanandam, S. N. & Deepa, S. N. (2008). *Introduction to Genetic Algorithms,* Springer-Verlag, ISBN: 978-3-540-73189-4, India

Wong, K. P. & Wong, Y. W. (1994). Development of Hybrid Optimisation Techniques Based on Genetic Algorithms and Simulated Annealing, *Workshop on Evolutionary Computation (AI'94),* pp. 127-154, Armidale, Australia, November 1994

Yao, X. & Higuchi, T. (1999). Promises and Challenges of Evolvable Hardware, *IEEE Transactions on Systems, Man, and Cybernetics – Part C: Applications and Reviews, Evolutionary Computation,*vol.29, no.1, (February 1999), pp. 87-97, ISSN 1094-6977

Zhou, S. & Sun, Z. (2005). A New Approach Belonging to EDAs: Quantum-Inspired Genetic Algorithm with Only One Chromosome, *International Conference on Natural Computing, ICNC2005,* pp. 141–150, LNCS 3612, Springer-Verlag, 2005

Part 2

New Applications of Genetic Algorithm

7

Tune Up of a Genetic Algorithm to Group Documentary Collections

José Luis Castillo Sequera
University of Alcala, Department of Computer Science, Madrid Spain

1. Introduction

Both in industry and science there are some real problems regarding the optimization of difficult solution characterized by computational complexity, because the available exact algorithms are inefficient or simply impossible to implement. The metaheuristics (MHs) are a family of approximate methods of general purpose consisting in iterative procedures that guide heuristics, intelligently combining different concepts to explore and exploit properly the search space [12]. Therefore, there are two important factors when designing MHs : intensification and diversification. The diversification generally refers to the ability to visit many different regions of search space, while intensification refers to the ability to obtain high quality solutions in these regions. A search algorithm must achieve a balance between these two factors so as to successfully solve the problem addressed.

On the other hand, Information Retrieval (IR) can be defined as the problem of information selection through a storage mechanism in response to user queries [3]. The Information Retrieval Systems (IRS) are a class of information systems that deal with databases composed of documents, and process user's queries by allowing access to relevant information in an appropriate time interval. Theoreticly, a document is a set of textual data, but technological development has led to the proliferation of multimedia documents [4].

Genetic Algorithms (GAs) are inspired by MHs in the genetic processes of natural organisms and in the principles of natural evolution of populations [2]. The basic idea is to maintain a population of chromosomes, which represent candidate solutions to a specific problem , that evolve over time through a process of competition and controlled variation. One of the most important components of GAs is the crossover operator [7]. Considering all GA must have a balance between intensification and diversification that is capable of augmenting the search for the optimal, the crossover operator is often regarded as a key piece to improve the intensification of a local optimum. Besides, through the evolutionary process, every so often there are species that have undergone a change (mutation) of chromosome, due to certain evolution factors, as the mutation operator is a key factor in ensuring that diversification, and finding all the optimum feasible regions.

Efficiently assigning GA parameters optimizes both the quality of the solutions and the resources required by the algorithm [13]. This way, we can obtain a powerful search algorithm and domain independent, which may be applied to a wide range of learning tasks. One of the many possible applications to the field of IR might be solving a basic problem faced by an IRS: the need to find the groups that best describe the documents, and allow each other to place all documents by affinity. The problem that arises is in the difficulty of finding the group that best describes a document,since they do not address a single issue, and even if they did, the manner the topic is approached can also make it suitable for another group. Therefore, this task is complex and even subjective as two people could easily assign the same document to different groups using valid criteria.

Clustering is an important tool in data mining and knowdledge discovery because the ability to automatically group similar items together enables one to discover hidden similarity and key concepts [10]. This enables the users to comprehend a large amount of data. One example is searching the World Wide Web, because it is a large repository of many kinds of information, many search engines allow users to query the Web, usually via keyword search. However, a typical keyword search returns a large number of Web pages, making it hard for the user to comprehend the results and find the information that really needs. A challenge in document clustering is that many documents contain multiple subjects.

This paper presents a GA applied to the field of documentation, the algorithm improved itself by refining its parameters, offering a balance between intensification and diversity that ensures an acceptable optimal fitness along an unsupervised document cluster.

2. Documentary base

In this study we make use of two collections, the "Reuters 21578" collection and a Spanish documentary base that includes editorials of "El Mundo" from 2006 and 2007 in an open access format.

Reuters Documentary Base consists of real news wires that appeared in Reuters in 1987, this collection is becoming a standard within the domain of the automatic categorization of documents and is used by many authors in this area. The collection consists of 21578 documents distributed in 22 files. We developed a documentary process named NZIPF [6] [11] to generate documentary vectors that feed the system.

The documentary process consists of several stages of document processing, each of which represents a process that was developed on the base document to obtain documentary vectors more efficiently.

The first step is the called process of *Filter* whose main objective is to define the documents of the documental base with the purpose of having documents that belong to a single category, that which will allow to have a smaller complexity in the treatment of the documents. Then, the purpose of the process of *Zonning* on the documents is the one of obtaining the free text of each document. Next, we use a process of *Stop List*, we extract the terms of the text of the document where each one of the extracted words will be compared with a list of empty words that will eliminate the words that don't have interest or they lack own meaning. Then, the words will be able to suffer a process of cutting of their roots "*Stemming*", in our case, we have implemented and used an algorithm of Porter in English and another in Spanish. In this step, the *frequency* of the obtained terms is calculated, for all the documents of our documental base, with the purpose of being able to know that terms are more used in each one of the documents; and then with this information to be able to carry out a process of selection of those terms that are more representative. The following step will consist on selecting those terms with discriminatory bigger power to proceed to its normalization We apply the law of *Zipf*, we calculate the Point of Goffman [3] and the transition area that it allows us to obtain the terms of the documental base. Finally, we assign weight using a function *IDF* (Invert Document Frecuency) developed for Salton [4] that uses the frequency of a word in the document. After all these processes, we obtain the characteristic vectors of documents in the collection document.

The process is outlined in Figure 1.

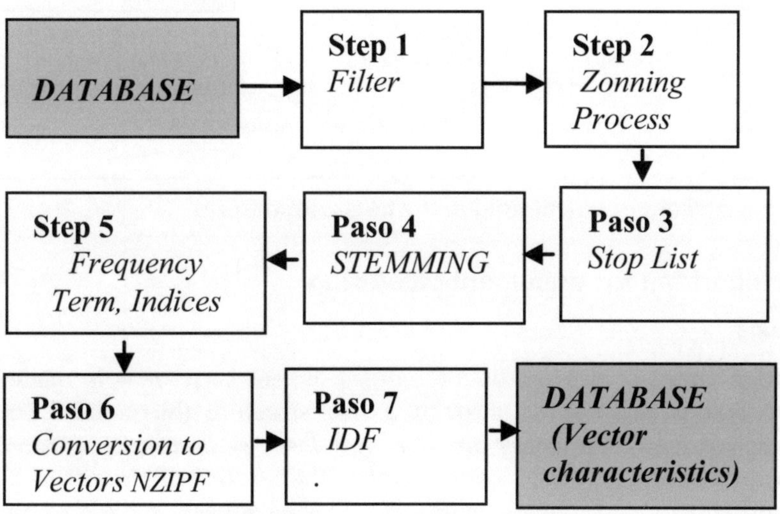

Fig. 1. Documentary process conducted

On the other hand, within the testing environment there should be a user to provide documents that are meant to be grouped. The role of the user who provides documents will be represented by the samples of "very few (20), few (50), many (80) and enough (150)" documents, with the requirement that belonged to only two categories of Reuters or distribution of Editorials in Spanish represented by their feature vectors stemmer. Figure 2 shows the documentary environment [10] that we used for the experiments, it is important to note that, unlike the algorithms of the type monitored, where the number obtained groups needs to be known, our algorithm will evolve to find the most appropriate structure, forming the groups by itself.

Due to the nature of simulation of GA, its evolution is pseudo-random, this translates into the need for multiple runs with different seeds to reach the optimal solution. The generation of the seed is carried out according to the time of the system. For this reason, the experiments with GA were made by carrying out five executions to each of the samples taken from experimental collections [1]. The result of the experiment will be the best fitness obtained and their convergence. To measure the quality of the algorithm, the best solution obtained and the average of five runs of the GA must be analized.

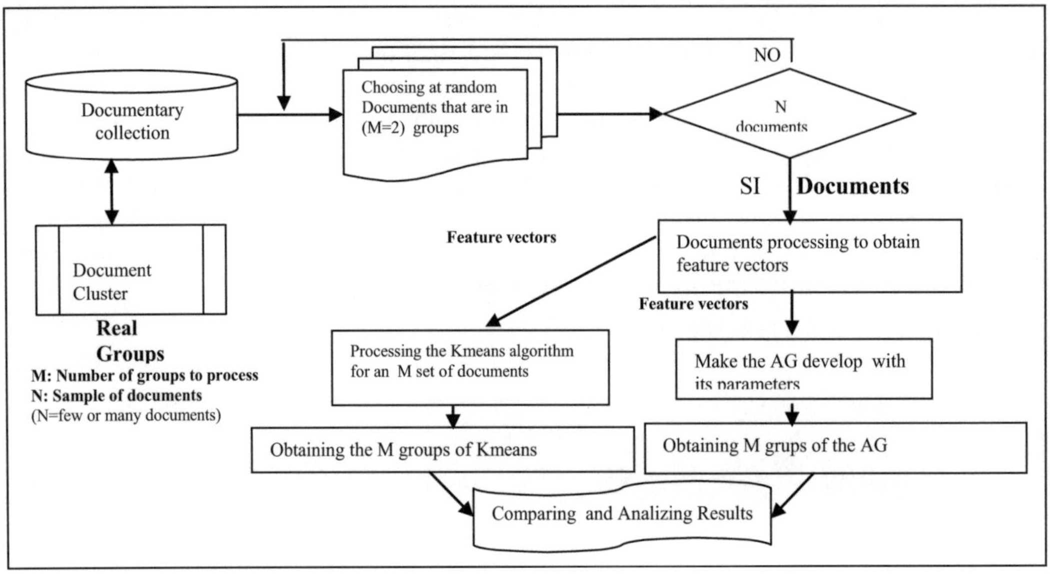

Fig. 2. Experimental environment used in the tests with the GA.

3. Genetic algorithm for document clustering

3.1 Individuals

The population consists of a set of individuals, where each of it is made of a linear chromosome that is represented through a tree structure (hierarchical structure). An individual shall formed on a binary tree structure *cluster all documents* prepared at the top, where each document consists of a *feature vector.* The vector will consist of the weighted values of the frequencies of the stemmer terms that have been selected to implement the document processing scheme [4]. This representation will be attempted to evolve so that the chromosome will undergo genetic changes and find the groups "Clusters" more appropriate for all documents of the IRS. Within the root node we will have our fitness function *(fitness)* that measure the quality of the resulting clustering. Depending on the number of documents that need to be processed and the depth (height) of the tree you want to create, chromosome may be of variable length.

The Figure 3 shows the initial generation (0), a scheme of tree-based representation is adopted in order to allow the encoding of sufficiently complex logical structures within a chromosome. The search area for the GA is the space of all possible trees that can be generated, resulting from the whole relevant functions and terminals. This way we can evolve individuals of various shapes and sizes [8], allowing evolution to decide what are the best settings.

Although the initial population is random, there is a defined set of parameters governing the establishment of such individuals. For example, *there should not be created in the initial set two equal individuals,* for this production rules are created to ensure the compliance with this condition. The above mentioned rules require that the building grammar of each individual nodes takes place in Preorder.

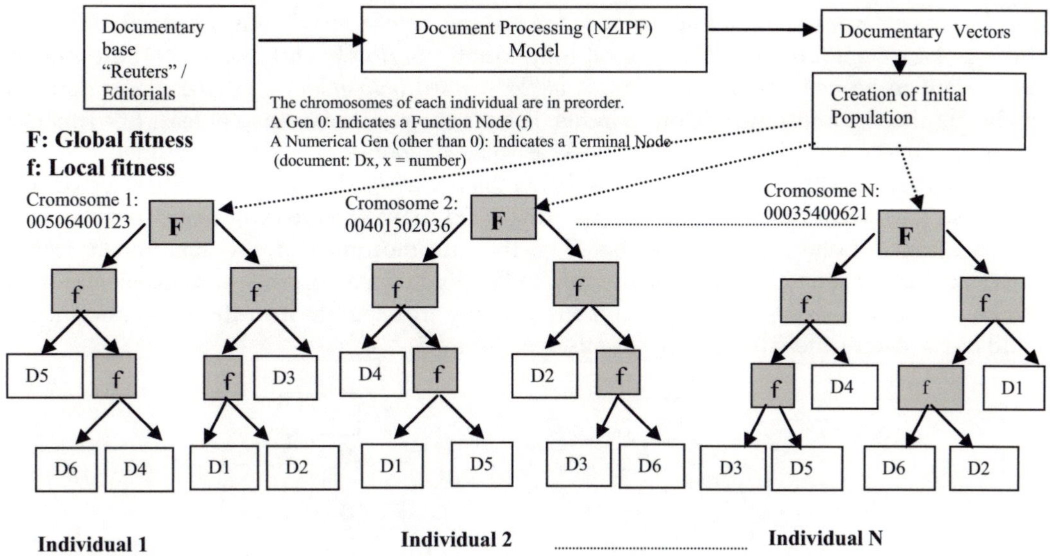

Fig. 3. Initial Population of Individuals GA (generation "0")

3.2 Production operators

The production operators are applied to each new generation. One or two individuals can be taken to produce new individuals for next generation by applying the transformations imposed by the operator. Both mutation operators and crossover will be implemented indistinctably. Both operators depend on a mutation probability and / or cross that is assigned to GA [7].

A *mutation operator* is applied on nodes (documents), selecting an individual from the population using the tournament method, and then randomly select a pair of terminal nodes of that individual to mutate its terminal nodes, generating a new individual transposing the nodes that have been chosen (see figure 4).

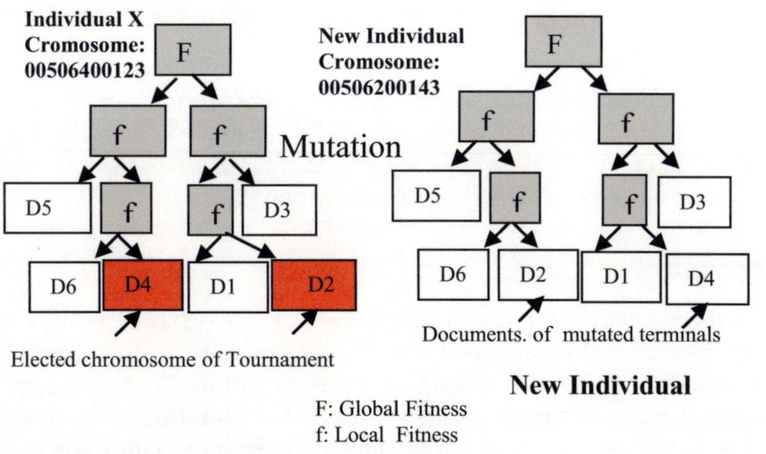

Fig. 4. Basic mutation operator applied to terminal

For the crossover operator, an operator based on *mask crossover* [9] is applied, which selects through tournament method two parent individuals, randomly chooses the chromosome of one parent to be used as "*crossover mask of the selected individual*". The crossing is done by analyzing the chromosome of both parents. If both chromosomes have at least one function node (node 0), the chosed father mask is placed, but if we find documents in the chromosomes of both parents, then, the father "*not elected*" document will be selected and we'll use it as pivot on the father "*elected*" (mask) to make the crossing that corresponds to the mentioned father, while interchanging the chromosomes of the mentioned father. This *creates a new individual,* and ensure that in the given chromosome set there are the same structural characteristics of the parents but we only incorporate it in the population if the child has a better fitness than their parents. (see figure 5).

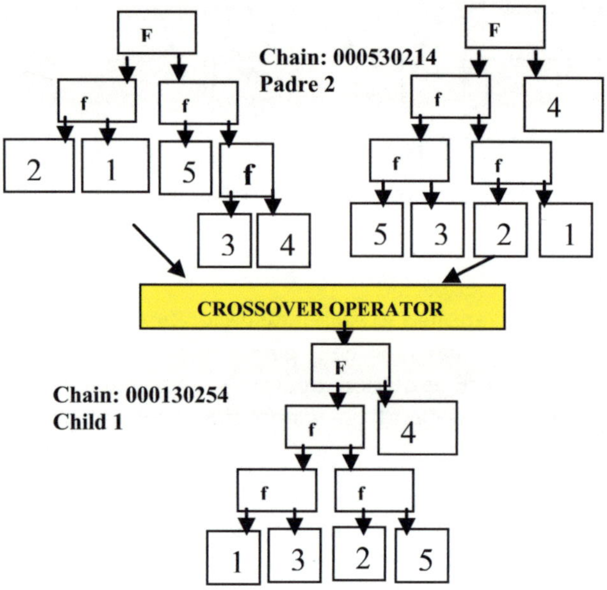

Fig. 5. Crossover operator (crossover mask)

3.3 Selection

After we evaluate population's fitness, the next step is chromosome selection. Selection embodies the principle of 'survival of the fittest' [5]. Satisfied fitness chromosomes are selected for reproduction, for it, we apply the method of selection of the tournament, using a tournament of 2, and we apply Elitism in each generation [2].

4. Parameter control

For its size, and the influence that small changes have on the behavior of the GA during the experiments [1], the choice of parameter values that are going to be used appears as a critical factor. For their election we paid attention to the variation of the GA performance indicators when it changed the value of any of these, specifically the evolution of the successes and the evolution of "*fitness*". Therefore, these parameters are very important parts as they directly influence the performance of the GA [13]. These parameters can be treated independently, but the overall performance of the algorithm does not depend exclusively on a single parameter but on a combination of all parameters. Many researchers pay more attention to some parameters than others, but most agree that the parameters that should be under controlare: selection schemes, population size, genetic variation operators and rates of their chances.

Because GA have several **parameters** that must be carefully chosen to obtain a good performance and avoid premature convergence, in our case and *after much testing,* we opted for the control of parameters, and some strategies such as:

To control the *population size* we use the strategy called GAVAPS (Genetic variation in population size) proposed by Michalewicz [9] using the concept of age and lifetime. When creating the first generation all individuals are assigned a zero age, referring to the birth of the individual, and every time a new generation is born the age of each individual increases by one. At the same time an individual is born it is assigned a lifetime, which represents how long it will live within. Therefore, the individual will die when it will reach the given age. The lifetime of each individual depends on the value of its fitness compared to the average of the entire population. Thus, if an individual has better fitness will have more time to live, giving it greater ability to generate new individuals with their features. In our case, we allow each generation to generate new individuals with similar characteristics with this strategy.

Therefore, we adopt this approach essentially the best individuals from each generation, and apply it to maintain *elitism* in the following generations, thus ensuring optimum intensification of available space, while keeping them during their lifetime [9]. However, to ensure diversity we *randomly* generate *the remaining individuals* in each generation. This way, we explore many different regions of the search space and allow for balance between intensification and diversity of feasible regions.

In all cases, the population size has been set at 50 individuals for the experiments conducted with samples following the suggestion of [1], which advises working with a population size between *l* and *2l* in most practical applications (the length of chromosome l) In our case, "l" the length of our chromosome is always equal to:

2 * number of documents to cluster -1.

On the hand, we use two measures of function fitness to calculate the distance and similarity between documents and to be able to form better cluster (see table 1).

Distance Euclidean	$d_{ij} = \sqrt{\sum_{k=1}^{t} (x_{ik} - x_{jk})^2}$
Coefficient of correlation of Pearson (Similarity)	$r = \frac{1}{n} \sum_{i=1}^{n} \left(\frac{x_i - \bar{x}_i}{\sigma x_i} \right) \left(\frac{x_j - \bar{x}_j}{\sigma x_j} \right)$
Fitness Global	Min (α Distance(Documents $_i$) + (1- α) (1/ Similarity(Documents $_i$)))

Table 1. Measures of the Function

with x_i and x_j the characteristic vectors of the documents that we are grouping, *"n"* the number of examples and σx_i , σx_j are the standard deviation of x_i and x_j and where: ***a:*** it will be the parameter that adjustment the distance and similarity. The fitness function is used to minimize the distance between the documents and maximize the similarity between them.

Therefore, for the experiments with our experimental environment, we used samples of documents "very few (20), few (50), many (80) and enough (150)" documents with the requirement that they belonged only to two categories of Reuters collections or Editorials. Each of the samples processed with five different seeds, and each of the results are compared with the method "*Kmeans.*" Then, each experiment was repeated by varying the rate of probability of genetic algorithm operators, using all the parameters shown in table 2 up to find that value of α that best fit the two metrics hat combine in our function fitness.

Parameters	**Values**
Population size (tree number)	50
Número de evaluaciones (Generaciones)	5000 maximum
Tournament size	2
Mutation Probability (Pm)	0.01, 0.03, 0.05, 0.07, 0.1, 0.3, 0, 5, 0.7
Crossover Probability (Pc)	0.70,0.75,0.80,0.85,0.90,0.95
Document cuantity	Very Few, Few, Many, enough
α coefficients	0.85 (best value found)
Depth Threshold	7 /10

Table 2. Parameters taken into consideration for the Genetic algorithm with composite function

4.1 Studies to determine the value of α in the GA

We use the distribution Reuters 21 of be that greater dispersion across your documents and apply the GA varying the value of α in each of the tests with the usual parameters, always trying to test the effectiveness of the GA. We analyzed the relationship between fitness and the value of α using the values in table 2. (the results are shown in table 3 and figure 6).

In figure 6, we can see that there is an increased dispersion of fitness values over 0.85, due to the increased contribution of Euclidean distance which makes it insensitive to fitness to find the clusters. The results, suggest that a value of α close to 0.85, provides better results because it gives us more effective in terms of number of hits, and a better fitness of the algorithm. This was corroborates with other distribution.

Documents	α	Generatión	Best *Fitness*	Average Middle *Fitness*	Hits	Effectiviness (%)
20	0,75	1436	0,25291551	0,46489675	15	75,0
20	0,80	1592	0,20298477	0,47026890	16	80,0
20	0,85	2050	0,15255487	0,24504483	17	85,0
20	0,90	3694	0,15266796	0,25909582	17	85,0
20	0,95	1520	0,15319261	0,24596829	17	85,0
50	0,75	3476	0,25290429	0,28744261	35	70,0
50	0,80	3492	0,20285265	0,27862528	36	72,0
50	0,85	3355	0,15312467	0,29128428	36	72,0
50	0,90	2256	0,15318358	0,28347470	36	72,0
50	0,95	2222	0,15345986	0,27863789	36	72,0
80	0,75	3049	0,25704660	0,36871676	61	76,2
80	0,80	1371	0,20782096	0,33303315	61	76,2
80	0,85	2131	0,15784449	0,34447947	62	77,5
80	0,90	1649	0,15815252	0,32398087	62	77,5
80	0,95	2986	0,17796620	0,36009861	61	76,2
150	0,75	2279	0,26194273	0,29866150	91	60,6
150	0,80	1273	0,20636391	0,22933754	93	62,0
150	0,85	3257	0,15468909	0,27518240	94	62,6
150	0,90	1136	0,25482251	0,28218144	94	62,6
150	0,95	2452	0,25456480	0,26788158	91	60,6
250	0,75	3617	0,25754282	0,31144435	120	48,0
250	0,80	3274	0,20844638	0,25112189	121	48,4
250	0,85	3066	0,15805103	0,19299910	121	48,4
250	0,90	2343	0,20634355	0,20432140	121	48,4
250	0,95	2047	0,25541276	0,27844937	120	48,0

Table 3. Results of tests with GA, takong different samples of documents with the distribution 21 of the Reuters collection, to determine the best value for α

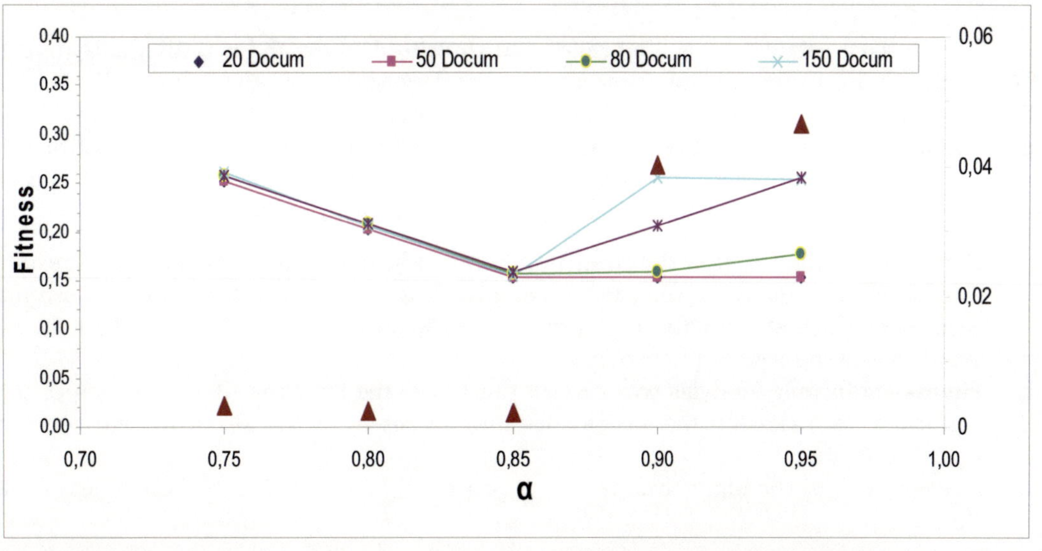

Fig. 6. Best Fitness versus α values for different samples of documents of the Reuters Collection: Distribution 21

4.2 Tests to determine the value of the rate of mutation operator and crossover operator rate

We began conducting an analysis of system behavior by varying the rate of mutation operator in a wide range of values to cover all possible situations. During experiments using different samples distribution Reuters. Thus, for the rate of mutation operator discussed a wide range of values in the range of: 0.01, 0.03, 0.05, 0.07, 0.1, 0.3, 0, 5, 0.7; that allowed us to apply the mutation operator of GA in different circumstances and study their behavior. For the study to determine the optimal value of the rate of crossover operator, is traced the interval from 0.70 to 0.95; value high, but oriented to frequently apply the operator we designed because that an optimum value for the *mutation probability* is much more important than the crossover probability, and choose to make a more detailed study of the odds ratio in our experiments. As a quality index value of the operator was given to the number of hits of the GA.

As for the *size of the tournament,* the value 2 has been chosen, because the binary tournament has shown a very good performance in a large number of applications of EAs. Although determining a optimal *fitness* function is not one of the fundamental objectives of this experiment, we have tried to add in a single value the measuring results as powerful and distinct as are the Euclidean distance and the Pearson correlation coefficient (based on cosine similarity).

Therefore, to find and the adjustment coefficient α that governs the weight that is to be given to both the distance as the inverse of similarity of the cluster documents, we've made many parameter controlled tests in order to obtain a value that allows an adequate contribution of both metrics with respect to fitness., finally finding a value for of 0.85.

The **number of maximum generations** the system has been set to is 5000, but this parameter may vary depending on the convergence of the algorithm. As for the **number of stemmer terms** to be used for representing the feature vectors of each of the documents we have used the terms, which have been selected through the NZIPF processing method [6][11].

Finally, we have established a limit called the **threshold of depth** for individuals (trees). Such a threshold, in the case of "*very few and few documents*" take the value of 7, and for the"*many and enough documents*" is set 10. To analyze the results, and to verify their effectiveness, we compared the results of the GA with the existing real groups of the document collection [6], and also compared the results with another supervised type of clustering algorithm in optimal conditions (Kmeans). We analized the following:

a. **Cluster efectiveness:** It is the most important indicator of the comparison of results considering the quality of the cluster. An analyzing process was carried out to see the successes achieved with the best fitness of GA, and also the average scores in all executions of the GA.
b. **Fitness evolution.** Analysis was carried out to see the evolving fitness in each of the performances, assessing their behaviour and successes of the GA when varying the probability rate.
c. **Convergence of the algorithm**: In which process the GA obtains the best fitness (best cluster).

Since, the GA parameters directly affect the fitness behavior, before the experiments, we performed a comprehensive analysis of all GA performances, in order to determine its robustness and adjusting each of its parameters. Finally, we experimentally used the parameters discussed in Table 1 and analyzed the behavior of the algorithm. We show in Figure 7 the average number of hits returned by the GA for samples of 20, 80 and 150 documents, changing the mutation rate, and show the hit factor of the GA against the mutation rate. We appreciate that we got the best performance with a rate of 0.03, this result shows that the best medium fitness could also be obtained by using this rate. We corroborated that conduct with another collection.

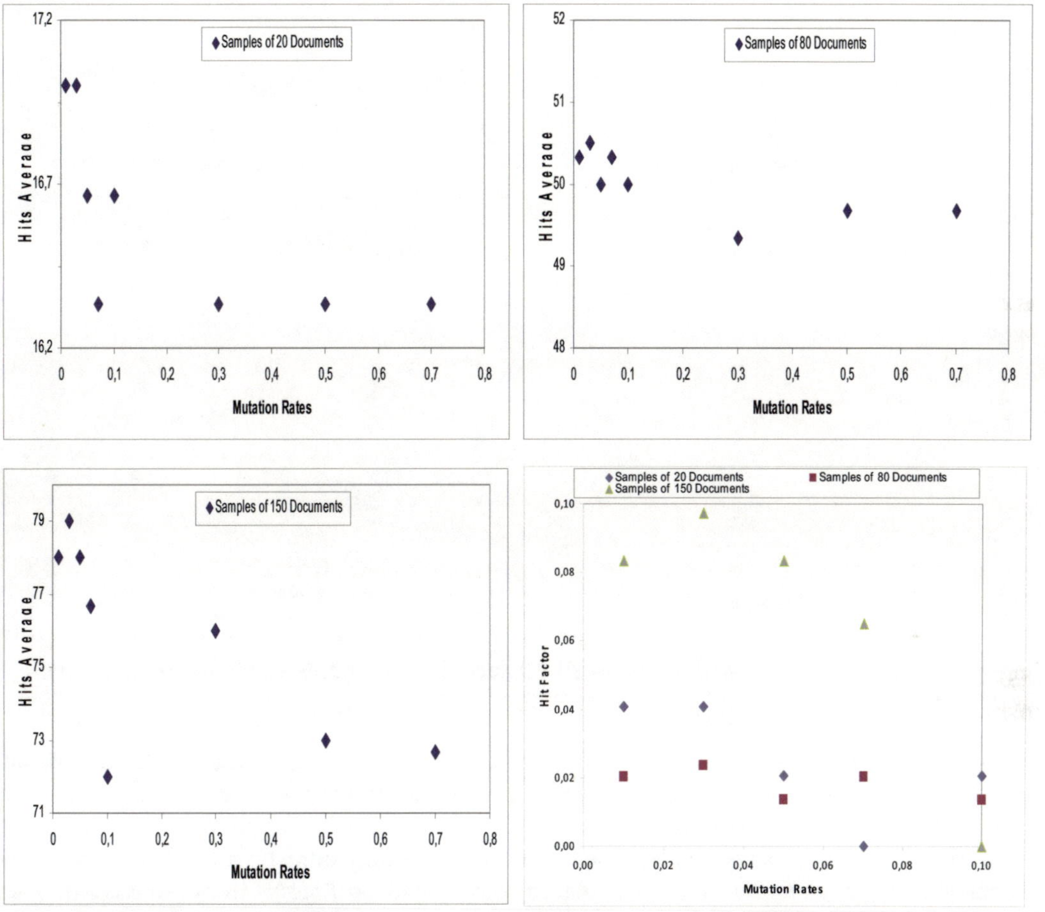

Fig. 7. Hits average of GA with samples 20, 80 and 150 documents varying mutation rate and hit the GA.

In addition, we analyzed the incidence of crossover operator on the final results. The figures 8 show the behavior of the crossover rate versus hits average with very few samples (20), many (80) and many documents (150) respectively. Besides a comparative analysis is the success factor of GA varying the crossover rate. It makes clear, the GA performed better when using a rate of 0.80 for the crossover operator, regardless of the sample. Therefore, this value appears to be ideal if we maximize the efficiency of the algorithm, which is why we conclude that is the rate that gives us better results.

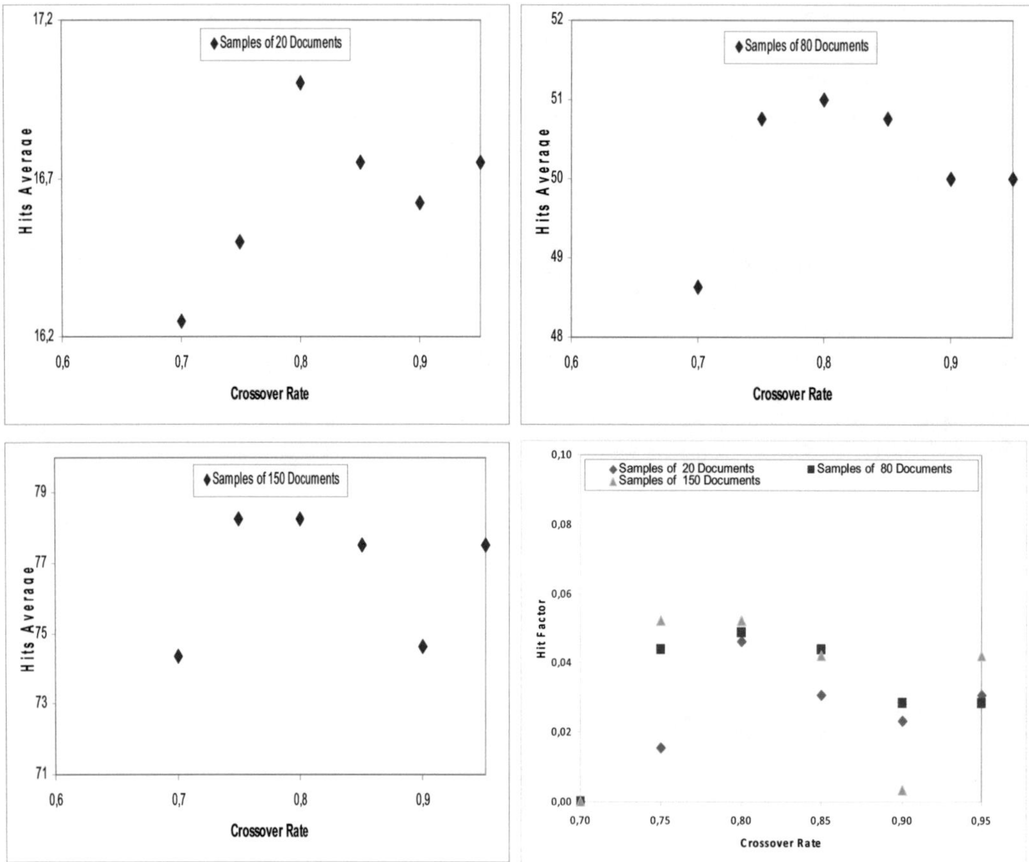

Fig. 8. Hits average of GA with samples 20, 80 and 150 documents varying crossover rate and hit the GA.

To corroborate the results of the GA, we compare their results with the *Kmeans* algorithm, which was processed with *the same samples,* passing as input the number of groups that needed to be obtained. This algorithm used exclusively as a function of the Euclidean distance measure and being a supervised algorithm, the only adjustment of parameters was the *number of groups to process*, and is therefore executed on *Kmeans* in optimal conditions. We proved that *the medium effectiveness* of the GA is very acceptable, being in most cases better than *Kmeans* supervised algorithm [10] when using these parameters of mutation and crossover, but with the added advantage that we processed the documents in an unsupervised way, allowing evolution perform clustering with our adjustment. So, details of such behavior, we show graphically in figure 7 and 8, even showing a comparison of the same for each type of operator used in our experiments the evolutionary algorithm processed proposed for this work.

Then, in the table 4, 5, 6 and 7 show comparative results obtained with our algorithm using the optimal parameters of mutation and crossover with major documentary collection distribution Reuters 21578.

Distribution 2 Reuters Collection 1	*Documents Categories: Acq y Earn Best Result*			*Best Average*			
Samples of documents	*Fitness*	*Effectiveness*	*Convergence*	*Average Fitness*	*Deviation Fitness*	*Average Convergence*	*Kmeans*
Very Few documents (20 documents)	0,155447570	*85% (18 hits)*	886	0,15545476	0,00000828	*1086*	*16,6*
Few Documents (50 documents)	0,156223280	*94% (47 hits)*	*3051*	0,15624280	0,00002329	*2641*	*45,8*
Many Documents (80 documents)	0,159009400	*89% (71 hits)*	*2500*	0,15921181	0,00020587	*2246*	*67,8*
Enough Documents (150 documents)	0,165013920	*77% (115 hits)*	*2342*	0,16508519	0,00007452	*2480*	*121,6*
More Documents (246 documents)	0,174112100	*69% (170 hits)*	*2203*	0,17430502	0,00033602	*2059*	*202,8*

Table 4. Comparative results Evolutionary System with various samples of documents showing the best results and the average results of evaluations with the "Distribution 2" of the Reuters 21578 collection.

Distributión 8 Reuters Collection 2	*Documents Categories: Acq y Earn Best Result*			*Best Average*			
Samples of documents	*Fitness*	*Effectiveness*	*Convergence*	*Average Fitness*	*Deviation Fitness*	*Average Convergence*	*Kmeans*
Very Few documents (20 documents)	0,151163560	*85% (17 hits)*	555	0,15116356	0,00000000	*679*	*15,8*
Few Documents (50 documents)	0,154856500	*96% (48 hits)*	*1615*	0,15485650	0,00000000	*1334*	*43,8*
Many Documents (80 documents)	0,157073880	*85% (68 hits)*	*746*	0,15708362	0,00000898	*1360*	*66,2*
Enough Documents (150 documents)	0,162035070	*69,3% (104 hits)*	*1989*	0,16242664	0,00033091	*2283*	*117,6*
More Documents (188 documents)	0,163014600	*68,63% (129 hits)*	*2293*	0,16334198	0,00027325	*1773*	*140,6*

Table 5. Comparative results Evolutionary System with various samples of documents showing the best results and the average results of evaluations with the "Distribution 8" of the Reuters 21578 collection.

Distribution 20 Reuters Collection 3	*Documents Categories: Acq y Earn Best Result*			*Best Average*			
Samples of documents	*Fitness*	*Effectiveness*	*Convergence*	*Average Fitness*	*Deviation Fitness*	*Average Convergence*	*Kmeans*
Very Few documents (20 documents)	0,153027060	*85% (17 hits)*	1092	0,15321980	0,00018398	*1108*	*16,8*
Few Documents (50 documents)	0,156198620	*92% (46 hits)*	*2173*	0,15666137	0,00030077	*2635*	*44,8*
Many Documents (80 documents)	0,158069980	*81,25% (65 hits)*	*2196*	0,15810383	0,00001884	*1739*	*66,8*
Enough Documents (108 documents)	0,159031080	*69.4% (75 hits)*	*1437*	0,15927630	0,00026701	*2636*	*82,2*

Table 6. Comparative results Evolutionary System with various samples of documents showing the best results and the average results of evaluations with the "Distribution 20" of the Reuters 21578 collection.

Distribution 21 Reuters Collection 4	*Documents Categoríes: Acq y Earn Best Result*			*Best Average*			
Samples of documents	*Fitness*	*Effectiveness*	*Convergence.*	*Average Fitness*	*Deviation Fitness*	*Average Convergence*	*Kmeans*
Very Few documents (20 documents)	0,152048900	*90% (18 hits)*	1163	0,15206069	0,00001601	*1165*	*17,8*
Few Documents (50 documents)	0,153006650	*92% (46 hits)*	*2079*	0,15304887	0,00004569	*2736*	*45,6*
Many Documents (80 documents)	0,156029510	*81% (65 hits)*	*2787*	0,15637693	0,00025014	*2810*	*66,4*
Enough Documents (132 documents)	0,157012180	*70,4% (93 hits)*	*3359*	0,15720766	0,00024132	*1980*	*98,6*

Table 7. Comparative results Evolutionary System with various samples of documents showing the best results and the average results of evaluations with the "Distribution 21" of the Reuters 21578 collection

To then display the results graphically in figure 9.

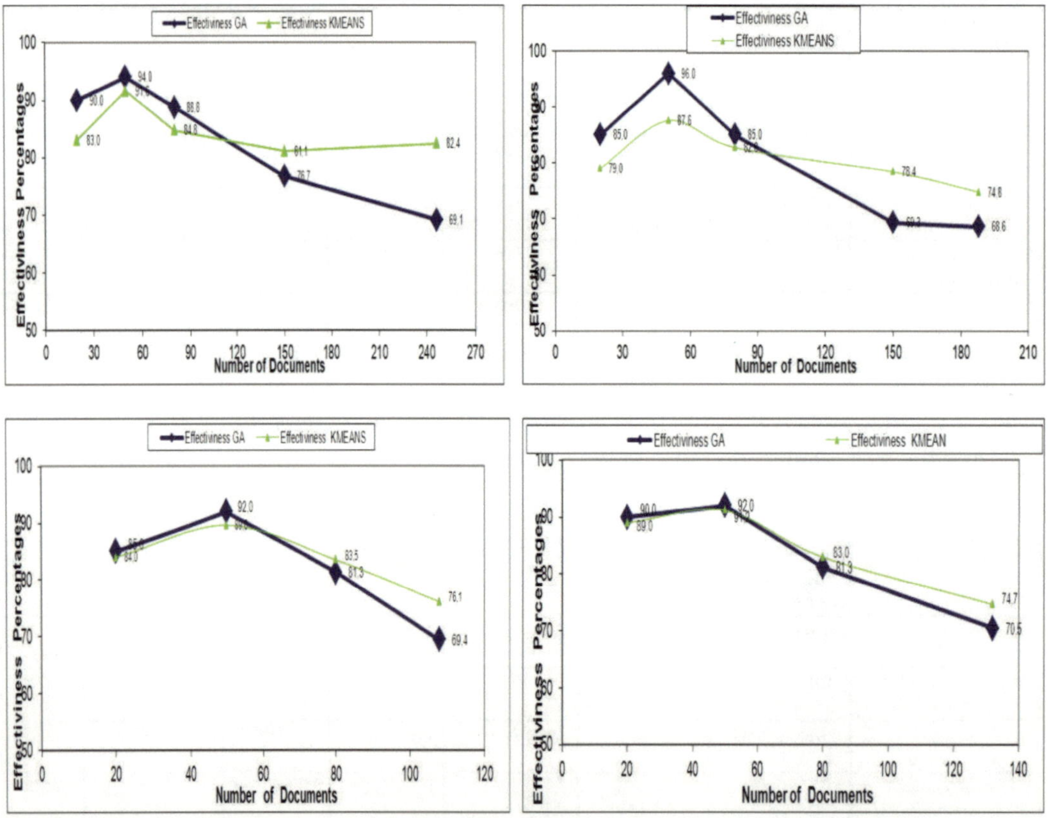

Fig. 9. Graphs compare the results obtained with the composite function against Kmeans (four collection Reuters)

Finally, to corroborate the results,we compare their results with the other collection in Spanish, which was processed in the same way, using all values of table 2. (see figure 10).

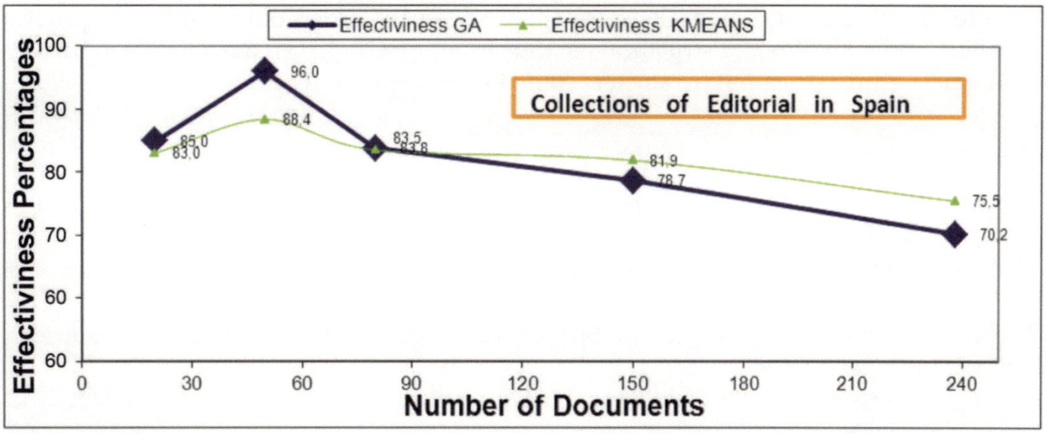

Fig. 10. Graphs compare the results obtained with the composite function against Kmeans (Spain collection)

5. Conclusion

In this study, we have proposed a new taxonomy of parameters of GA numerical and structural, and examine the effects of numerical parameters of the performance of the algorithm in GA based simulation optimization application by the use of a test clustering problem. We start with the characteristics of the problem domain.

The main characteristic features of our problem domain are:

- There is a dominance of a set of decision variables with respect to the objective function value of the optimization problem: The objective function value is directly related with the combination of this dominant set of variables equal a value of α close to 0.85.
- The good solutions are highly dominant over other solutions with respect to the objective function value, but not significantly diverse among each other.

These properties of the problem domain generate a rapid convergent behavior of GA. According to our computational results lower mutation rates give better performance. GA mechanism creates a lock-n effect in the search space, hence lower mutation rates decreases the risk of premature convergence and provides diversification in the search space in this particular problem domain. Due to the dominance crossover operator does not have significant impact on the performance of GA. Moreover, starting with a seeded population generates more efficient results.

We can conclude that the GA had a favourable evolution, offering optimal document cluster in an acceptable and robust manner, based on a proper adjust of the parameters. We proved that *the medium effectiveness* of the GA is very acceptable, being in most cases better than Kmeans supervised algorithm, but with the added advantage that we processed the documents in an unsupervised way, allowing evolution perform clustering with our adjustment. As a result of our experiments, we appreciate that we got the best performance with a rate of 0.03 for the mutation operator and using a rate of 0.80 for the crossover operator, this values appears to be ideal if we maximize the efficiency of the genetic algorithm.

As a future research direction, the same analyses can be carried out for different problem domains, and with different structural parameter settings, and even the interaction between the numerical and structural parameters could be investigated.

6. References

[1] [Alander, 1992] Alander. J*"On optimal populations size of genetic algorithms"* Proc CompEuro 1992.

[2] [Bäck, 1996] Bäck T, *"Evolutionary Algorithms in theory and Practice"*, Oxford University Press, 1996.

[3] [Berry Michael, 2004] M. Berry , Survey of Text Mining - Clustering and Retrieval, Springer 2004.

[4] [Berry Michael, et al,2008] M. Berry, Malu Castellano Editors:*"Survey of Text Mining II"*, Springer,2008.

[5] [Castillo,Fernandéz,León,2008] *"Information Retrieval with Cluter Genetic"* IADIS Data Mining, 2008.

[6] [Castillo,Fernandéz,León,2009] *"Feature Reduction for Clustering with NZIPF"* IADIS e-Society 2009.

[7] [Goldberd D,1989] *Genetic algorithms in search, optimization and machine learning*. Addison Wesley M.A. 1989.

[8] [Holland J.H, 1975] *Adaptation in Natural and Artificial Systems* University of Michigan Press, Ann Arbor 1975.

[9] [Michalewicz, 1999] Michalewicz Z.*"Genetic Algorithms + Data Structures = Evolution"*. Springer-1999.

[10] [Olson David, 2008] Olson D. *"Advanced Data Mining Techniques"*, Springer 2008 ISBN:978-3-540-76916-3

[11] [Pao M.L, 1976] Pao M.*"Automatic indexing based on Goffman transition of word occurrences"*. In American society for Information Science. Meeting (40th: 1977:ChicagoIl). Information Management in the 1980's: proceedings of the ASIS annual meeting 1977, volume 14:40th annual meeting, Chicago.

[12] [Reeves CR, 1993] *Modern Heuristic Techniques for Combitational* Problems, Wiley, New York, 1993.

[13] [Schaffer et al,1989] Shaffer, et al, *"A study of control parameters performance on GA for function optimization", 1989.*

8

Public Portfolio Selection Combining Genetic Algorithms and Mathematical Decision Analysis

Eduardo Fernández-González, Inés Vega-López and Jorge Navarro-Castillo
Autonomous University of Sinaloa
México

1. Introduction

A central and frequently contentious issue in public policy analysis is the allocation of funds to competing projects. Public resources for financing social projects are particularly scarce. Very often, the cumulative budget being requested ostensibly overwhelms what can be granted. Moreover, strategic, political and ideological criteria pervade the administrative decisions on such assignments (Peterson, 2005). To satisfy these normative criteria, that underlie either prevalent public policies or governmental ideology, it is obviously convenient both to prioritize projects and to construct project-portfolios according to rational principles (e.g., maximizing social benefits). Fernandez et al. (2009a) assert that public projects may be characterized as follows.

- They may be undoubtedly profitable, but their benefits are indirect, perhaps only long-term visible, and hard to quantify.
- Aside from their potential economic contributions to social welfare, there are intangible benefits that should be considered to achieve an integral view of their social impact.
- Equity, regarding the magnitude of the projects' impact, as well as the social conditions of the benefited individuals, must also be considered.

Admittedly, the main difficulty for characterizing the "best public project portfolio" is finding a mechanism to appropriately define, evaluate, and compare social returns. Regardless of the varying definitions of the concept of social return, we can assert the tautological value of the following proposition.

Proposition 1: *Given two social projects, A and B, with similar costs and budgets, A should be preferred to B if A has a better social return.*

Ignoring, for a moment, the difficulties for defining the social return of a project portfolio, given two portfolios, C and D, with equivalent budgets, C should be preferred to D if and only if C has a better social return. Thus, the problem of searching for the best project-portfolio can be reduced to finding a method for assessing social-project returns, or at least a comparative way to analyze alternative portfolio proposals.

The most commonly used method to examine the efficiency impacts of public policies is "cost-benefit" analysis (e.g. Boardman, 1996). Under this approach, the assumed consequences of a project are "translated" into equivalent monetary units where positive consequences are considered "benefits" and negative consequences are considered "loses" or "costs". The temporal distribution of costs and benefits, modeled as net-cash-flows and adjusted by applying a "social discount rate", allows computing the net present-value of individual projects. A positive net present-value indicates that a project should be approved whenever enough resources are available (Fernandez et al., 2009a). Therefore, the net present-value of a particular project can be used to estimate its social return. As a consequence, the social impact of a project portfolio can be computed as the sum of the net-present-value of all the projects in the portfolio. The best portfolio can then be found by maximizing the aggregated social return (portfolio net-present-social benefit) using 0-1 mathematical programming (e.g. Davis and Mc Keoun, 1986).

This cost-benefit approach is inadequate for managing the complex multidimensionality of the combined outcome of many projects, especially when it is necessary to assess intangibles that have no well-defined market values. In extreme cases, this approach favors unacceptable practices (either socially or morally) such as pricing irreversible ecological damages, or even human life. Aside from ethical concerns, setting a price to intangibles for which a market value is highly controversial can hardly be considered a good practice. For a detailed analysis on this issue, the reader is referred to the works by French (1993), Dorfman (1996), and Bouyssou et al. (2000).

Despite this drawback, cost-benefit analysis is the preferred method for evaluating social projects (Abdullah and Chandra, 1999). Besides, not using this approach for modeling the multi-attribute impacts of projects leave us with no other method for solving portfolio problems with single objective 0-1 programming. A contending approach to cost-benefit is multi-criteria analysis. This approach encompasses a variety of techniques for exploring the preferences of the Decision Makers (DM), as well as models for analyzing the complexity inherent to real decisions (Fernandez et al., 2009a). Some of the most broadly known multi-criteria approaches are MAUT (cf. Keeney and Raiffa, 1976), AHP (cf. Saaty, 2000, 2005), and outranking methods (Roy, 1990; Figueira et al., 2005; Brans and Mareschal, 2005).

Multi-criteria analysis represents a good alternative to overcome the limitations of cost-benefit analysis as it can handle intangibles, ambiguous preferences, and veto conditions. Different multi-criteria methods have been proposed for addressing project evaluation and portfolio selection (e.g. Santhanam and Kyparisis, 1995 ; Badri et al., 2001 ; Fandel and Gal, 2001 ; Lee and Kim, 2001 ; Gabriel et al., 2006; Duarte and Reis, 2006; Bertolini et al., 2006; Mavrotas et al., 2006; Sugrue et al., 2006; Liesio et al., 2007 ; Mavrotas et al., 2008; Fernandez et al., 2009a,b). The advantages of these methods are well documented in the research literature and the reader is referred to Kaplan y Ranjithan (2007) and to Liesio et al. (2007) for an in-depth study on the topic.

Multi-criteria analysis offers techniques for selecting the best project or a small set of equivalent "best" projects (this is known as the P_α problem, according to the known classification by Roy (1996)), classifying projects into several predefined categories (e.g. "good", "bad", "acceptable"), known as the P_β problem, and ranking projects according to the preferences or priorities given by the decision maker (the P_γ problem).

Given a set of ranked projects, funding resources may be allocated following the priorities implicit in the ranking until no resources are left (e.g. Martino, 1995). This is a simple but rigid process that has been questioned by several authors (e.g. Gabriel et al., 2006, Fernandez et al., 2009 a,b). According to our perspective, the decision on which projects should receive financing must be made based on the best portfolio, rather than on the best individual projects. Therefore, it is insufficient to compare projects to one another. Instead, it is essential to compare portfolios. Selecting a portfolio based on individual projects' ranking guarantees that the set of the best projects will be supported. However, this set of projects does not necessarily equals the best portfolio. In fact, these two sets might be disjoint. Under this scenario, it is reasonable to reject a relatively good (in terms of its social impact) but expensive project if it requires disproportionate funding (Fernandez et al. 2009 a,b). Therefore, obtaining the best portfolio is, we argue, equivalent to solving the P_α problem defined over the set of all feasible portfolios.

Mavrotas et al. (2008) argue that, when the portfolio is optimized, good projects can be outranked by combinations of low-cost projects with negligible impact. However, this is not a real shortcoming whenever the following conditions are satisfied.

- Each project is individually acceptable
- The decision maker can define his/her preferences over the set of feasible portfolios (by using some quality measure, or even by intuition)
- The decision maker prefers the portfolio composed of more projects with lower costs.

In order to solve the selection problem over the set of feasible portfolios, the following issues should be addressed.

- The nature of the decision maker should be defined. It must be clear that this entity can address social interest problems in a legit way. In addition, the following questions should be answered. Is the decision-maker a single person? Or is it a collective with homogeneous preferences such that these can be captured by a decision model? Or is it, instead, a heterogeneous group with conflicting preferences? How is social interest reflected on the decision model?
- A computable model of the DM's preferences on the social impacts of portfolios is required.
- Portfolio selection is an optimization problem with exponential complexity. The set of possible portfolios is the power set of the projects applying for funding. The cardinality of the set of portfolios is 2^N, where N is the number of projects. The complexity of this problem increases significantly if we consider that each project can be assigned a support level. That is, projects can be partially supported. Under these conditions, the optimization problem is not only about identifying which projects constitute the best portfolio but also about defining the level of support for each of these projects.
- If effects of synergetic projects or temporal dependencies between them are considered, the complexity of the resulting optimization model increases significantly.

The first issue is related to the concepts of social preferences, collective decision, democracy, and equity. The second issue, on the other hand, constitutes mathematical decision analysis' main area of influence. These capabilities for building preference models that incorporate different criteria and perspectives is what makes these techniques useful (albeit with some limitations) for constructing multidimensional models of conflicting preferences.

The DM´s preferences on portfolios (or their social impacts) can be modeled from different perspectives, using different methods, and to achieve different goals. Selecting one of these options depends on who the DM is (e.g., a single person or a heterogeneous group), as well as on how much effort this DM is willing to invest in searching for the solution to the problem. Therefore, the information about the impact and quality of the projects that constitute a portfolio can be obtained from the DM using one of several available alternatives. This requires us to consider different modeling strategies and, in consequence, different approaches for finding the solution to this problem. We should note that the DM's preferences can be modelled using different and varying perspectives; ranging from the normative approach that requires consistency, rationality, and cardinal information, to a totally relaxed approach requiring only ordinal information. The chosen model will depend on the amount of time and effort the decision maker is willing to invest during the modelling process, and on the available information on the preferences. Here, we are interested in constructing a functional-normative model of the DM's preferences on the set of portfolios.

Evolutionary algorithms are powerful tools for handling the complexity of the problem (third and fourth issues listed above). Compared with conventional mathematical programming, evolutionary algorithms are less sensitive to the shape of the feasible region, the number of decision variables, and the mathematical properties of the objective function (e.g., continuity, convexity, differentiability, and local extremes). Besides, all these issues are not easily addressed using mathematical programming techniques (Coello, 1999). While evolutionary algorithms are not more time-efficient than mathematical programming, they are often more effective, generally achieving satisfactory solutions to problems that cannot be addressed by conventional methods (Coello et al., 2002).

Evolutionary algorithms provide the necessary instruments for handling both the mathematical complexity of the model and the exponential complexity of the problem. In addition, mathematical decision analysis methods are the main tools for modelling the DM´s preferences on projects and portfolios, as well as for constructing the optimization model that will be used to find the best portfolio.

The rest of this chapter is organized as follows. An overview of the functional-normative approach to decision making, as well as its use as support for solving selection, ranking and evaluation problems is considered in Section 2. In Section 3, we study the public portfolio selection problem where a project's impact is characterized by a project evaluation, and the DM uses a normative approach to find the optimal portfolio (i.e., the case where maximal preferential information is provided). In the same section we also describe an evolutionary algorithm for solving the optimization problem. An illustrative example is provided in Section 4. Finally, some conclusions are presented in Section 5.

2. An outline of the functional approach for constructing a global preference model

Mathematical decision analysis provides two main approaches for constructing a global preference model using the information provided by an actor involved in a decision-making process. The first of these approaches is a functional model based on the normative axiom of perfect and transitive comparability. The second approach is a relational model better known for its representation of preferences as a fuzzy outranking relation. In this work, however, we will focus on the functional approach only.

When using the functional model, also known as the functional-normative approach (e.g. French, 1993), the Decision Maker must establish a weak preference relation, known as the *at least as good as* relation and represented by the symbol $\succsim$.This relation is a weak order (a complete and transitive relation) on the decision set A. The statement "a is at least as good as b" ($a \succsim b$) is considered a logical predicate with truth values in the set {*False*, *True*}. If $a \succsim b$ is false then $b \succsim a$ must be true, implying a strict preference in favor of b over a. Given the transitivity of this relation, if the DM simultaneously considers that predicates $a \succsim b$ and $b \succsim c$ are true, then, the predicate $a \succsim c$ is also set to true. This approach does not consider the situation where both predicates, $a \succsim b$ and $b \succsim a$, are false, a condition known as incomparability. Because of this, the functional model requires the DM to have an unlimited power of discrimination.

The relation $\succsim$ can be defined over any set whose elements may be compared to each other and, as a result of such comparison, be subject to preferences. Of particular interest is the situation where the decision maker considers risky events and where the consequences of the actions are not deterministic but rather probabilistic. To formally describe this situation, let us introduce the concept of lottery at this point.

Definition 1. A lottery is a 2N-tuple of the form $(p_1, x_1; p_2, x_2;\ldots p_N, x_N)$, where $x_i \in \Re$ represents the consequence of a decision, p_i is the probability of such consequence , and the sum of all probabilities equals 1.

Given that the relation $\succsim$ is complete and transitive, it can be proven that a real-valued function V can be defined over the decision set A ($V: A \rightarrow \Re$), such that for all $a, b \in A$, $V(a) \geq V(b) \Leftrightarrow a \succsim b$. This function is known as a value or utility function in risky cases (French, 1993). If the decision is being made over a set of lotteries, the existence of a utility function U can be proven such that $\bar{U}(L_1) \geq \bar{U}(L_2) \Leftrightarrow L_1 \succsim L_2$, where L_1 and L_2 are two lotteries from the decision set and $\bar{U}$ is the expected value of the utility function (French, 1993).

The value, or utility, function represents a well formed aggregation model of preferences. This model is constructed around the set of axioms that define the rational behavior of the decision maker. In consequence, it constitutes a formal construct of an ideal behavior. The task of the analyst is to conciliate the real versus the ideal behavior of the decision maker when constructing this model. Once the model has been created, we have a formal problem definition. This is a selection problem that is solved by maximizing either V or $\bar{U}$ over the set of feasible alternatives. From this, a ranking can be obtained by simply sorting the values of these functions. By dividing the range of these values into M contiguous intervals, discrete ordered categories can be defined for labeling the objects in the decision set A (for instance, Excellent, Very Good, Good, Fair, and Poor). These categories are considered as equivalence classes to which the objects are assigned to.

When building a functional model, compatibility with the DM's preferences must be guaranteed. The usual approach is to start with a mathematical formulation that captures the essential characteristics of the problem. Parameters are later added to the model in a way that they reflect the known preferences of the decision maker. Hence, every time the

DM indicates a preference for object *a* over object *b*, the model (i.e., the value function V) must satisfy condition V(*a*) > V(*b*). Otherwise, the model should satisfy condition V(*a*) = V(*b*), indicating that the DM has no preference of *a* over *b*, nor has the DM a preference of *b* over *a*. This situation is known as indifference on the pair (*a*, *b*). If V is an elemental function, these preference/indifference statements on the objects become mathematical expressions that yield the values of V's parameters. To achieve this, usually the DM provides the truth values of several statements between pairs of decision alternatives (a_i, b_i). Then, the model's parameter values are obtained from the set of conditions V(a_i) = V(b_i). Finally, the value and utility functions are generally expressed in either additive or product forms, and, in the most simple cases, as weighted-sum functions.

The expected gain in a lottery is the average of the observed gains in the lottery's history. If the DM plays this lottery a sufficiently large number of times, the resulting gain should be close the lottery's expected gain. However, it is not realistic to assume that a DM will face (play) the same decision problem several times as decision problems are, most of the times, unique and unrepeatable. Therefore it is essential to model the DM's behavior towards risk. Persons react differently when facing risky situations. In real life, a DM could be risk prone, risk averse, or even risk neutral. Personal behavior for confronting risk is obviously a subjective characteristic depending on all of the following.

- The DM's personality
- The specific situation of the DM as this determines the impact of failing or succeeding.
- The amount of the gain or loses that will result from making a decision.
- The relationship of the DM with these gains and loses.

All these aspects are closely related. While the first of them is completely subjective, the remaining three have evident objective features.

The ability for modeling the decision maker's behavior when facing risk is one of the most interesting properties of the functional approach. At this point, it is necessary to introduce the concept of certainty equivalence in a lottery.

Definition 2. Certainty equivalence is the "prize" that makes an individual indifferent between choosing to participate in a lottery or to receive the prize with certainty.

A risk averse DM will assign a lottery a certainty equivalence value lower than the expected value of the lottery. A risk prone DM, on the other hand, will assign the lottery a certainty equivalence value larger than the lottery's expected gain. We say a DM is risk neutral when the certainty equivalence value assigned to a lottery matches the lottery's expected gain. This behavior of the DM yields quite interesting properties on the utility function. For instance, it can be proven that a risk averse utility function is concave, a risk prone utility function is convex, and a risk neutral function is linear.

Let us conclude this section by summarizing both the advantages and disadvantages of the functional approach. We start by listing the main advantages of the functional approach.

- It is a formal and elegant model of rational decision making.
- Once the model exists, obtaining its prescription is a straight forward process.
- It can model the DM's behavior towards risk.

Now, we provide a list of drawbacks we have identified on the functional approach.

- It cannot incorporate ordinal or qualitative information.
- In real life, DM's do not exactly follow a rational behavior.
- When decisions are made by a collective, the transitivity of the preference relation cannot be guaranteed.
- It cannot precisely model threshold effects, nor can it use imprecise information.
- In most cases, the DM does not have the time to refine the model until a precise utility function is obtained.

3. A functional model for public portfolio optimization using genetic algorithms

Let us consider a set P_r of public projects whose consequences can be estimated by the DM. These projects have been considered acceptable after some prior evaluation. That is, the DM would support all of them, given that enough funds are available and that no mutually exclusive projects are members of the set. However, projects are not, in general, mutually independent. In fact, they can be redundant or synergetic. Furthermore, they may establish conflicting priorities, or compete for material or human resources, which are indivisible, unique, or scarce.

For the sake of generality, let us consider a planning horizon partitioned in T adjacent time intervals. When T=1, this problem is known as the stationary budgeting problem (one budgeting cycle) (Chan et al., 2005). In non-stationary cases, there could be different levels of available funds for each period.

In its more general form, a portfolio is a finite set of pairs of projects and periods $\{(p_i, t(p_i))\}$, where $p_i \in P_r$ and $t(p_i) \in T$ denotes the period when p_i starts. A portfolio is feasible whenever it satisfies financial and scheduling restrictions, including precedence, and it does not contain redundant or mutually exclusive projects. These restrictions may also be influenced by equity, efficiency, geographical distribution, and the priorities imposed by the DM. In particular, if only one budgeting cycle is considered, the portfolios are subsets of P_r.

The set of projects is partitioned in different areas, according to their knowledge domain, their social role, or their geographic zone of action. One project can only be assigned to one area. Such partition is usually due to the DM's interest for obtaining a balanced portfolio. Given a set of areas $A = \{A_1, A_2, \ldots, A_n\}$, the DM can set the minimum and maximum amounts of funding that will be assigned to projects belonging to area $A_i \in A$.

The general problem is to determine which projects should be supported, in what period should the support start, and the amount of funds that each project should receive, provided that the overall social benefit from the portfolio is maximised.

In order to have a formal problem statement, we should answer the following questions.

- How can the return of a public project-portfolio be formally defined?
- How can objective and subjective criteria be incorporated for optimizing project-portfolio returns?
- Under what conditions can the return of a portfolio be effectively maximized?
- What methods can be used to select the best portfolio?

To achieve the goal of maximizing social return we need to formally define a real-valued function, V_{social}, that does not contravene the relation $\succsim_{social}$. The construction of such function is, however, problematical due to the following reasons.

i. A set of well defined social preferences must exist.
ii. This set of preferences must be revealed.

The preference-indifference social relation is required to be transitive and complete over social states (premise *i*). However, due to the known limitations for constructing collective rational-preferences (e.g., Condorcet's Paradox, Arrow's Impossibility Theorem, and context-dependent preferences), (Bouyssou et. al., 2000; Tversky and Simonson, 1993; French, 1993), and to the difficulty in obtaining valid information about social preferences from the decision maker, premises *i* and *ii* are rarely fulfilled in real-world cases (Sen, 2000, 2008).

The success of public policies is measured in terms of their contribution to social equity and social "efficiency". A project's social impact should be an integrated assessment of such criteria. In the research literature, it is possible to find several methods that have been proposed for estimating a project contribution to social well-fare. Unfortunately, they all show serious limitations for handling intangible attributes. Furthermore, these methods' objectivity for measuring the contribution of each project or public policy is questionable. In any society, a wide variety of interests and ideologies can coexist. This human condition makes it complicated to reach a consensus on what an effective measure of social benefit should be. In turn, the absence of consensus leads to a lack of objectivity on any defined measure. This lack of objectivity is closely related to a nonexistent function of social preference and to the ambiguity of collective preferences as reported by Condorcet, Arrow, and Sen (Bouyssou et al., 2000; Sen, 2000, 2008).

While the social impact is objective, its assessment is highly subjective as it depends on the ideology, preferences and values of the person measuring the impact. This subjectivity, however, does not necessarily constitute a drawback as it is not arbitrary. In the end, decision making does not lack of subjective elements. The set of criteria upon which the decision making is based should strive to be objective. However, the assessment of the combined effect of such criteria, some of them in conflict with each other, is subjective in nature as it depends on the perception of the decision maker. The objectivity of decision making theory is not based on eliminating all subjective elements. Instead, it is based on creating a model that reflects the system of values of the decision maker.

In every decision problem it is necessary to identify the main actor whose values, priorities, and preferences, are to be satisfied. In this context (the problem of efficiently and effectively allocating public resources), we will call "supra-decision-maker" (SDM) to this single or collective actor. For the rest of the discussion, we drop the idea of modeling public returns from a social perspective in favor of modeling the SDM's preferences.

Focusing exclusively on the SDM's preferences is a pragmatic representation of the problem that raises ethical concerns. This is particularly true when the SDM is elected democratically and, as such, his/her decisions formally represent the preferences of the society. In real life, an SDM may possibly have a very personal interpretation of social welfare and subjective parameters to evaluate project returns that do not necessarily represent the generalized social values but rather the ambition of a certain group. Thus, even under the premise of ethical behavior, the SDM —who is supposed to distribute resources according to social preferences— can only act in response to his/her own preferences. The reasons for this are that either the SDM hardly knows the actual social preferences, or he/she pursues his/her own satisfaction —according to his/her preferences— in an honest attempt to achieve what he/she thinks is socially better. Unethical behavior or lack of information can cause the SDM's preferences to significantly deviate from the predominant social interests. In turn, this situation might trigger events such as social protests claiming to reduce the distance between the SDM's preferences and social interests. Therefore, solving a public project-portfolio selection problem is about finding the best solution from the SDM's perspective. This solution (under the premise of ethical behavior) should be close to the portfolio with the highest social return.

3.1 A Functional model of the subjective return

In order to maximize the portfolio's subjective return (that is, the return from the SDM perspective), we must build a value function that satisfies relation $\succsim_{\text{portfolios}}$. For a starting analogy, let us accept that each project's return can be expressed by a monetary value, in a similar way as cost-benefit analysis. If no synergy and no redundancy exist (or they can be neglected) among the projects, the overall portfolio's return can be calculated as follows.

$$R_t = x_1 c_1 + x_2 c_2 + \ldots + x_N c_N \quad (1)$$

In Equation 1, N is the cardinality of P_r. The value of x_i is set to 1 whenever the i-th project is supported, otherwise $x_i = 0$. Finally, c_i is the return value of the i-th project.

Let M_i denote the funding requirements for the i-th project. Let $\boldsymbol{d}$ be an N-dimensional vector of real values. Each value, d_i, of vector $\boldsymbol{d}$ is associated to the funding given to the i-th project. If a project is not supported, then the corresponding value in $\boldsymbol{d}$ associated to such project will be set to zero. With this, we can now formally define the problem of portfolio selection.

Problem definition 1. Portfolio selection optimization can be obtained after maximizing R_t, subject to $\boldsymbol{d} \in R_F$, where R_F is a feasible region determined by the available budget, constraints for the kind of projects allowed in the portfolio, social roles, and geographic zones.

Problem 1 is a variant of the knapsack problem, which can be efficiently solved using 0-1 programming. Unfortunately, this definition is an unrealistic model for most social portfolio selection problems due to the following issues.

1. For Equation 1 to be valid, the monetary value associated to each project's social impact must be known. Monetary values can be added to produce a meaningful figure. However, due to the existence of indirect as well as intangible effects on such projects, it is unrealistic to assume that such monetary equivalence can be defined for all projects. If we cannot guarantee that every c_i in Equation 1 is a monetary value, then the expression becomes meaningless.
2. Most of the times, the decision is not about accepting or rejecting a project but rather about the feasibility of assigning sufficient funds to it.

3. The effects of synergy between projects can be significant on the portfolio social return. Therefore, they must be modeled. For instance consider the following two projects, one for building a hospital and the other for building a road that will enhance access to such hospital. Both of such projects have, individually, an undeniable positive impact. However their combined social impact is superior.
4. Time dependences between projects are not considered by Problem definition 1.
5. It is possible that for a pair of projects (i and j) $c_i >> c_j$ and $M_i >> M_j$, the solution to this problem indicates that project i should not be supported ($x_i = 0$) whereas project j is supported ($x_j = 1$). The SDM might not agree to this solution, as it fails to support a high-impact project while it provides funds to a much less important project. Furthermore, such situation will be difficult to explain to the public opinion.

The functional normative approach presented in Section 2 is used to address the first issue on this list. Here, we present a new approach based on the work of Fernandez and Navarro (2002), Navarro (2005), Fernandez and Navarro (2005), and Fernandez et al. (2009). Addressing issues 2 to 5 on the list above requires using a heuristic search and optimization methods.

This new approach is constructed upon the following assumptions.

Assumption 1: Every project has an associated value subjectively assigned by the SDM. This value increases along with the project's impact.

Assumption 2: This subjective value reflects the priority that the SDM assigns to the project. Each project is assigned to a category from a set of classes sorted in increasing order of preference. These categories can be expressed qualitatively (e.g., {poor, fair, good, very good, excellent}) or numerically in a monotonically increasing scale of preferences.

Assumption 3: Projects assigned to the same category have about the same subjective value to the SDM. Therefore, the granularity of the discrete scale must be sufficiently fine so that no two projects are assigned to the same class if the SMD can establish a strict preference between them.

Assumption 4 (Additivity): The sum of the subjective values of the projects belonging to a portfolio is an ordinal-valued function that satisfies relation $\succsim_{portfolios}$.

Fernandez et al. (2009) rationalize this last assumption by considering that each project is a lottery. A portfolio is, in consequence, a "giant" lottery being played by a risk-neutral SDM. Under this scenario, the subjective value of projects and portfolios corresponds to their certainty equivalent value.

Under Assumption 4, the interaction between projects cannot be modeled. Synergy and redundancy in the set of projects are characteristics that require special consideration that will be introduced later.

Under Assumptions 1 and 4, the SDM assess a subjective value to portfolio given by the following equation.

$$V = x_1 c_1 + x_2 c_2 + \ldots + x_N c_N \quad (2)$$

In Equation 2, c_i represents the subjective value of the *i*-th project. Equations 1 and 2 are formally equivalent. However, the resulting value of *V* only makes sense if there is a process to assign meaningful values to c_i.

Before we proceed to the description of the rest of the assumptions, we need to introduce the concept of elementary portfolio.

Definition 3: An elementary portfolio is a portfolio that contains only projects of the same category. It will be expressed in the form of a C-dimensional vector, where C is the number of discrete categories. Each dimension is associated to one particular category. The value in each dimension corresponds to the number of projects in the associated category. Consequently, the C-dimensional vector of an elementary portfolio with n projects will have the form (0, 0, …, n, 0, …, 0).

Assumption 5: The SDM can define a complete relation $\gtrsim$ on the set of elementary portfolios. That is, for any pair of elementary portfolios, P and Q, one and only one of the following propositions is true.

- Portfolio P is preferred to portfolio Q
- Portfolio Q is preferred to portfolio P
- Portfolios P and Q are indifferent.

Assumption 6 (Essentiality): Given two elementary portfolios, P and Q, defined over the same category. Let P = (0, 0, …, n, 0, …, 0) and Q = (0, 0,…, m, 0, …, 0). P is preferred to Q if an only if n > m.

From the set of discrete categories, let C_1 be the lowest category, C_L be the highest, and C_j a category preferred to C_1.

Assumption 7 (Archimedean): For any category C_j, there is always an integer value *n* such that the SDM would prefer a portfolio composed of *n* projects in the C_1 category to any portfolio composed of a single project in the C_j category.

Assumption 8 (Continuity): If an elementary portfolio P = (x, 0, …, 0,…, 0) is preferred to an elementary portfolio Q = (0,…, 1, 0,…, 0), defined over category j for $1 < j \leq L$, there is always a pair of integers values n and m (n > m) such that an elementary portfolio with n projects of the lowest category is indifferent to another elementary portfolio with m projects of the *j*-th category.

Assumption 5 characterizes the normative claim of the functional approach for decision-making. Assumption 6 is a consequence of Assumption 4 (additivity) combined with the premise that all projects satisfy minimal acceptability requirements. Assumption 7 is a consequence of both essentiality and the non-bounded character of the set of natural numbers. Assumption 8 simulates the way in which a person balances a scale using a set of two types of weights whose values are relative primes.

Let us say that c_1 is a number representing the subjective value of the projects belonging to the lower category C_1. Similarly, let us use c_j to represent the value of projects in category C_j. Now, suppose that the elementary portfolios P (containing n projects in C_1) and Q (integrated by m projects in C_j) are indifferent. That is, P and Q have the same V value. If we combine Assumption 8 with Equation 2, we obtain the following expression.

$$n\, c_1 = m\, c_j \Leftrightarrow c_j = (n/m) c_1$$

If V is a value function, then every proportional function is also a value function satisfying the same preferences. Therefore, we can arbitrarily set $c_1=1$ to obtain Equation 3 below.

$$c_j = n/m \tag{3}$$

In consequence, Equation 2 can now be re-stated as follows.

$$U = \Sigma_{i,k}\, w_{ik} x_{ik} \tag{4}$$

In Equation 4, the variable *j* is used to index categories, whereas variable *k* indexes projects. The value of w_{1k} is set to 1, and $w_{jk} = n/m_j$, where m_j denotes the cardinality of an elementary portfolio defined over category C_j. Additionally, factors w_{ik} might be interpreted as importance factors. These weights express the importance given by the SDM to projects within certain category. Therefore, they should be calculated from the SDM's preferences, expressed while solving the indifference equations between elementary portfolios, as stated by Assumption 8 and according to Equation 3. A weight must be calculated for every category. If the cardinality of the set of categories is too large, the resolution of such categories can be reduced to simplify the model. A temporary set of weights is obtained using these coarse categories. By interpolation on such set, the values of the original (finer resolution) set can be obtained.

3.2 Fuzziness of requirements

Another important issue is the imprecise estimation of the monetary resources required by each project. If d_k are the funds assigned to the k-th project, then there is an interval $[m_k, M_k]$ for d_k where the SDM is uncertain about whether or not the project is being adequately supported. Therefore, the proposition "the k-th project is adequately supported" may be seen as a fuzzy statement. If we consider that the set of projects with adequate funds is fuzzy, then the SDM can define a membership function $\mu_k(d_k)$ representing the degree of truth of the previous proposition. This is a monotonically increasing function on the interval $[m_k, M_k]$, such that $\mu_k(M_k) = 1$, $\mu_k(m_k) > 0$, and $\mu_k(d_k) = 0$ when $d_k < m_k$.

The subjective value assigned by the SDM to the k-th project is based on the belief that the project receives the necessary funding for its operation. When $d_k < m_k$ the SDM is certain that the project is not sufficiently funded. When $m_k \le d_k < M_k$, the SDM hesitates about the truth of that statement. This uncertainty affects the subjective value of the project, because it reduces the feasible impact of the project, which had been subjectively estimated under the premise that funding was sufficient. The reduction of the project's subjective value can be modeled by the product of the original value and a feasibility factor f. This factor is a monotonically increasing function with μ_k as an argument such that $f(0) = 0$ and $f(1) = 1$. Equation 5 below, is generated by introducing this factor into Equation 4, and assuming that $f(\mu_{ik}) > 0 \Leftrightarrow x_{ik} = 1$.

$$U = \Sigma_{ik}\, f(\mu_{ik})\, w_{ik} \tag{5}$$

The simplest definition of the feasibility factor is to make $f(\mu_{ik}) = \mu_{ik}$. This is equivalent to a fuzzy generalization of Equation 4. In such case, x_{ik} can be considered as the indicator function of the set of supported projects. When a non-fuzzy model includes the binary indicator function of a crisp set, the fuzzy generalization provided by classical "fuzzy technology" is made substituting this function with a membership function expressing "the degree of membership" to the more general fuzzy set. In this way, Equation 5 becomes Equation 6 shown below.

$$U = \Sigma_{ik}\, w_{ik}\, \mu_{ik} \quad (6)$$

Equation 6 was proposed by Fernandez and Navarro (2002) as a measure of a portfolio's subjective value.

3.3 Synergy and redundancy

Redundancy between projects can be addressed using constraints. For every pair of redundant projects, (p_i, p_j), $i < j$, condition $\mu_i(d_i) \times \mu_j(d_j) = 0$ should be enforced.

Let $S = \{S_1, S_2, \ldots, S_k\}$ be the set of coalitions of synergetic projects. In a model like the one represented by Equation 5, each of these coalitions should be treated as an (additional) individual project. As a result, each coalition has an associated cost (i.e., the sum of the costs of the individual projects in the coalition), and an evaluation. This evaluation should be better than the evaluation of any of the projects in the coalition. Let us assume that coalitions S_i and S_j become projects P_{N+i} and P_{N+j}, respectively. If S_i is a subset of S_j, then it does not make sense to include them both in a portfolio. Therefore, P_{N+i} and P_{N+j} must be considered redundant projects. Furthermore, if project p_n is a member of S_i, then the pair (p_n, p_{N+i}) is also redundant (since the value of p_n is included in the value of p_{N+i}).

3.4 A Genetic algorithm for optimizing public portfolio subjective value

Suppose that a feasible region of portfolios, R_F, is defined by constraints on the total budget and on the distribution of projects by area. In addition, the SDM could include further constraints on the portfolios due to following reasons.

- The particular budget distribution of the portfolio could be very difficult to justify. Let us suppose that the SDM asserts that "project p_j is much better than project p_i". In consequence, any portfolio in which μ_i is greater than μ_j could be unacceptable. This implies the existence of some veto situations that can be modeled with the following constraint. For every project p_i and p_j, being s_i, and s_j their corresponding evaluations, if $(s_i - s_j) \geq v_s$, then $(\mu_i(d_i) - \mu_j(d_j))$ must be greater than (or equal to) 0, where v_s is a veto threshold. In the following they will be called veto constraints.
- A possible redundancy exists between projects.

Let us use R'_F, $R'_F \subset R_F$, to denote the set of values for the decision variables that make every portfolio acceptable. All the veto constraints are satisfied in R'_F and there are no redundant projects in the portfolios belonging to this region. The optimization problem can now be defined as follows.

Problem definition 2. An optimal portfolio can be selected by maximizing $U = \Sigma_{ik} f(\mu_{ik}(d_{ik}))\, w_{ik}$, subject to $\boldsymbol{d} \in R'_F$, where d_{ik} indicates the financial support assigned to the k-th project belonging to the i-th category.

Solving this problem requires a complex non linear programming algorithm. The number of decision variables involved can be in the order of thousands. Due to the discontinuity of μ_i, the objective function is discontinuous on the hyper planes defined by $d_{ik} = m_{ik}$. Therefore, its continuity domain is not connected. The shape of the feasible region R'_F is too convoluted, even more if synergy and redundancy need to be addressed. R'_F hardly has the mathematical properties generally required by non linear programming methods. Note that veto constraints on the pairs of projects (p_i, p_k) and (p_j, $p_{k'}$) are discontinuous on the hyper planes defined by $d_{ik} = m_{ik}$ and $d_{jk'} = m_{jk'}$. In a real world scenario, where hundreds or even thousands of projects are considered, non-linear programming solutions cannot handle these situations. Using Equation 6, a simplified form of Problem definition 2, was efficiently solved by Fernandez et al. (2009) and later by Litvinchev et al. (2010) using an integer-mixed programming model. Unfortunately, this approach cannot handle synergy, redundancy, veto constraints, nor can it handle the non-linear forms of function f in Problem definition 2.

Evolutionary algorithms are less sensitive to the shape of the feasible region, the number of decision variables, and the mathematical properties of the objective function (e.g., continuity, convexity, differentiability, and local extremes). In contrast, all of these issues are a real concern for mathematical non linear programming techniques (Coello, 1999). While evolutionary algorithms are not time-efficient, they often find solutions that closely approximate the optimal. Problem definition 2 represents a relatively rough model. However, the main interest is not on fine tuning the optimization process but rather on the generality of the model and on the ability to reach the optimal solution or a close approximation.

In Figure 1, we illustrate the genetic algorithm used for solving the optimization problem stated in Problem definition 2. This algorithm is based on the work of Fernandez and Navarro (2005). As in any genetic algorithm, a fundamental issue is defining a codification for the set of feasible solutions to the optimization problem. In this case, each individual represents a portfolio and each chromosome contains N genes, where N is the number of projects. For the chromosome, we use a floating point encoding representing the distribution of funding among the set of projects in the portfolio. The financial support for each project is represented by its membership function, $\mu_j(d_j)$, which is real-valued with range in [0, 1]. That is, a floating point number represents each project's membership value. This membership value is a gene in our definition of chromosomes. As discussed earlier, the number of genes can be increased in order to address the effects of synergetic projects.

The fitness value of each individual is calculated based on function U given by Equation 5. Remember that this is a subjective value that captures the SDM's certainty that the project receives the necessary funding for its operation. The SDM's idea that a project has been assigned sufficient funds is modeled using two parameters, α and β. The domain for both parameters is the continuous interval [0, 1].The first parameter, α, can be interpreted as the degree of truth of the assertion "the project has sufficient financial support if it receives m monetary units of funding". When this financial support reaches the value βM, the predicate "the project has sufficient funding" is considered true. The value of these two parameters is needed to establish models for function μ_j in order to calculate the value of U. To generate these models, we propose to choose parameters α and β ($0< \alpha <1$, $m/M < \beta \leq 1$) for modelling μ as shown in Figure 2. For the experiments presented here, the values of $\alpha = 0.5$ and $\beta = 1$ have been used. The most promising values for these parameters are reasonably found in the intervals [0.5, 0.7] and [0.9, 1], respectively.

Algorithm 1. A Genetic Algorithm for Project Portfolio Selection.

Input: `cycles`, the number of iterations before the algorithm converges
`generations`
`c_r`, the Crossover rate
`m_r`, the Mutation rate

Output: `best_solution`, the best solution found

```
Set best_solution ← any feasible portfolio. // this is the best so far
Set N ← the number of projects (chromosomes)

Set Population ← {best_solution}

for (i = 1 to cycles) do
    for (j = 1 to N - 1) do
        set new_solution ← best_solution
        randomly select a gene in new_solution and mutate it
        set Population ← Population ∪ {new_solution}
    end

    evaluate every individual ∈ Population
    set best_solution ← the fittest individual ∈ Population

    for (k = 1 to generations) do
        perform crossover on (N × c_r) individuals ∈ Population
        perform mutation on (N × m_r) individuals ∈ Population

        set Population ← Population ∪ {best_solution}
        evaluate every individual ∈ Population
        set best_solution ← the fittest individual ∈ Population
    end
end

return best_solution
```

Fig. 1. A Genetic Algorithm for Project Portfolio Selection

For the selection stage, the roulette wheel technique was used. That is, the probability that a particular individual is selected for reproduction is proportional to its fitness value. For the experiments, the crossover rate was set to 0.2. Therefore twenty percent of the population is selected for crossover in any given reproductive trial. The crossover operator takes genes from each parent string and combines them to produce the offspring of the next generation. The main reason for doing this is that by creating new strings from fit parent strings, new and promising zones of the search space will be explored. While many crossover techniques have been reported, in this algorithm the classic crossover technique based on a random cut point was used. The number of offspring resulting from this process is one fifth the size of the population.

The replacing process dictates how to update the current population with the individuals obtained by crossover. A random replacement approach (every individual has the same probability to be replaced) is used for reducing selective pressure. A similar approach is used for implementing an elitist policy. That is, an individual is randomly chosen from the current population and is replaced by the individual with the highest evaluation. Consequently, the presence of the best individual (`best_solution` in Algorithm 1) in the updated population is guaranteed.

Algorithm 1 uses a constant mutation rate that is set a priori. Each individual in the population is considered for mutation, and all the individuals have the same probability of mutating, which is defined by the mutation rate. Once an individual has been selected for mutation, one of its genes is randomly chosen. This gene will change by adding to it a random value in the [-0.2, 0.2] interval, excluding zero. The resulting gene value, however is limited to the [0, 1] interval.

Redundancy is addressed in a very simple way. If, as the result of some genetic operator an individual (i.e., a portfolio) containing redundant projects is generated, this individual is immediately "killed". That is, its incorporation to the current population is denied.

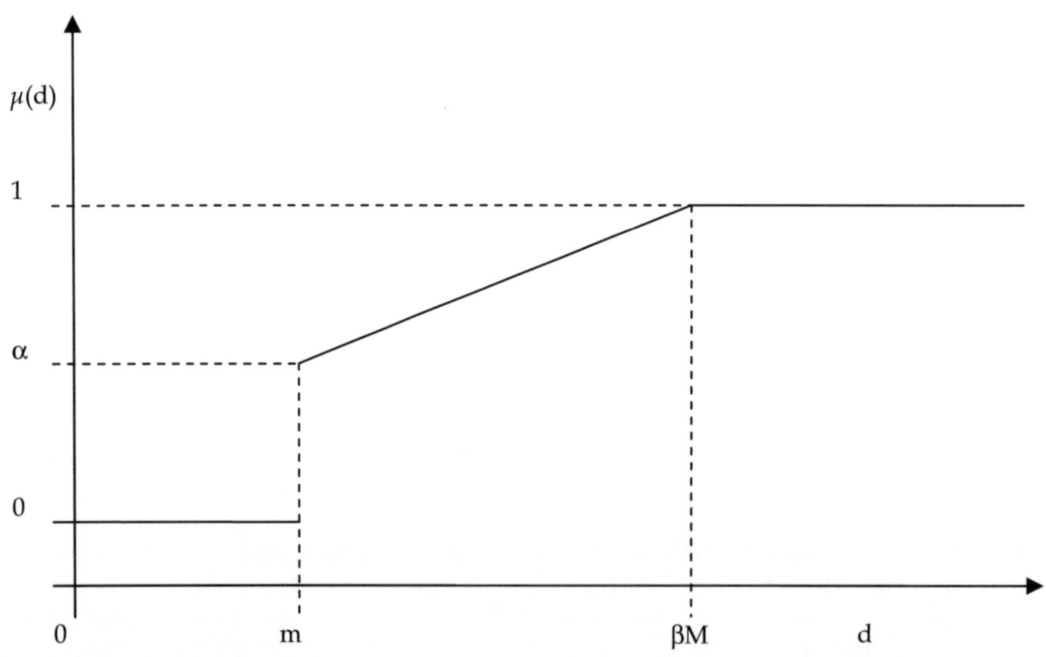

Fig. 2. The Membership Function

3.5 An illustrative example

Let us now consider the following example taken from (Fernandez and Navarro, 2005). The goal is to distribute a budget of 50 million dollars among of 400 R&D projects. These projects are distributed in four areas, namely engineering, life sciences, formal sciences, and social sciences. There are 140 projects in the first area (engineering), 80 projects in the second one (life sciences), 100 projects in the third area (formal sciences), and 80 project in the last area (social sciences). No synergetic effects are considered.

The classification of the projects, according to their evaluations and areas, is described in Table 1. The projects subjective values corresponding to each category and area are shown in Table 2. These values were obtained taking a social sciences project evaluated as Below Average as baseline (w = 1). These values define a ranking on the set of projects that can be used to allocate funds according to the conventional heuristic described in Section 1 (with all its known limitations).

	Area 1	Area 2	Area 3	Area 4
Very Good	54	28	13	12
Good	23	9	18	24
Above Average	62	32	36	28
Average	1	9	17	11
Below Average	0	2	16	5
Total	**140**	**80**	**100**	**80**

Table 1. Distribution of Projects by Area.

	Area 1	Area 2	Area 3	Area 4
Very Good	5.838	4.3785	3.892	2.9190
Good	4.540	3.4055	3.027	2.2700
Above Average	3.027	2.2700	2.018	1.5135
Average	2.108	1.5810	1.405	1.0540
Below Average	2.000	1.5000	1.333	1.0000

Table 2. Projects Subjective Values.

Four different instances of the problem were generated by assigning random budget ranges to each area. For each project, random values of m_{ik}, and M_{ik} were defined, representing its minimum and maximum funding requirements. The proposed evolutionary algorithm was run 30 times to optimize the expression given by Problem definition 2. For simplicity $f(\mu_{ik})$ was taken to be identical to μ_{ik} .

The algorithm was coded using Visual C++. Its execution time was about 25 minutes for one million generations running on a Pentium-4 processor with a, 2.1 GHz clock cycle. This architecture was complemented with 256 MB of physical memory and a 74.5-GB hard disk drive. The experimental results shown in Table 3 indicate a significant improvement in the value of the optimized portfolio with respect to conventional approaches.

These results represent an average saving of 6.514 million dollars, equivalent to 13.02% of the total budget. This improvement has a positive impact on the number of supported projects, as Table 4 reveals. The average number of supported projects is 12.5 % higher than when conventional methods were used.

Instance	Value of the portfolio funding following the ranking given by project evaluations	Value of the optimized portfolio	Improvement
1	1406.80	1533.95	9%
2	1282.36	1496.16	16.67%
3	1279.58	1458.48	14%
4	1393.58	1566.97	12.44%

Table 3. Traditional Funding versus our Approach.

Instance	Number of supported projects funding following the ranking given by project evaluations	Number of supported projects in the optimized portfolio	Increment
1	237	267	12.76%
2	257	285	10.89%
3	265	299	12.83%
4	246	279	13.41%

Table 4. Traditional Funding versus our Approach (portfolio's cardinality).

3.6 Modeling temporal dependencies

The model described in Problem definition 2 can be generalized to incorporate temporal restrictions.

Problem definition 3. An optimal portfolio of projects with temporal dependencies can be selected by maximizing $U = \Sigma_{ik} f(\mu_{ik}(d_{ik})) w_{ik}$, subject to $(\mathbf{d}, \mathbf{t}) \in R''_F$, where vector $\mathbf{t} = (t(p_1), t(p_2), \ldots)$ denotes the decision variables valid during the period of time when each project starts. R''_F contemplates time-precedence restrictions, restrictions on the time projects can start, and the available funds for each time interval.

This problem can be solved using a genetic algorithm similar to the one previously presented. However, a different encoding for individuals must be devised. Our proposal is to encode individuals as a 2N-dimensional vector of the form (μ_1, t_1, μ_2, t_2, ..., μ_N, t_N). As before, genes corresponding to μ_i have domain defined by the continuous interval [0, 1]. Genes corresponding to t_i have a domain defined by the set {1, 2, 3, ..., T}, where T is the maximum number of time periods. Crossover can only occur between genes of the same kind. However, mutations may occur at any gene. Restrictions such as time precedence and the earliest time a project can start are controlled by constraints as described by Carazo et al. (2010).

4. Concluding remarks

Given a set of premises, it is possible to create a value model for selecting optimal portfolios from an SDM perspective. While this problem is Turing-decidable, finding its exact solution requires exponential time. However, the use of genetic algorithms for solving this problem can closely approximate the optimal portfolio selection.

Inspired by a normative approach, the set of premises presented here is based on the following assumptions.

- To the SMD, every project and every portfolio has a subjective value that depends on its social impact. This value exists even if it cannot be initially quantified.
- The SDM either has already defined a consistent system of preferences, or has the aspiration of doing so.
- The SDM is willing to invest a considerable amount of mental effort in order to define this consistent set of preferences and produce the aforementioned value model.

As for the algorithmic solution to the portfolio problem, its computational complexity can increase considerably when synergic effects and temporal dependencies are considered. However strategic planning requires a high quality model. The problems defined in this scenario are so important that they justify the use of computational intensive solutions.

5. Acknowledgements

This work was sponsored in part by the Mexican Council for Science and Technology (CONACyT) under grants 57255 and 106098.

6. References

Abdullah, A. & Chandra, C.K. (1999). *Sustainable Transport: Priorities for Policy Sector Reform*, World Bank, Retrieved from <http://www.worldbank.org/html/extpb/sustain/sustain.htm>

Badri, M.A. & Davis, D. (2001). A Comprehensive 0-1 Goal Programming Model for Project Selection. *International Journal of Project Management*, No. 19, pp. 243-252.

Bertolini, M., Braglia, M., & Carmignani, G. (2006). Application of the AHP Methodology in Making a Proposal for a Public Work Contract. *International Journal of Project Management* No. 24, pp. 422-430.

Boardman, A. (1996). *Cost-benefit Analysis: Concepts and Practices*, Prentice Hall.

Boyssou, D., Marchant, Th., Perny, P., Tsoukias, A., & Vincke, Ph. (2000). *Evaluations and Decision Models: A Critical Perspective*, Kluwer Academic Publishers, Dordrecht.

Brans, J.P. & Mareschal, B. (2005). PROMETHEE Methods, In: *Multiple Criteria Decision Analysis: State of the Art Surveys*, Figueira, J., Greco, S., & Erghott, M., pp. 163-190, Springer Science + Business Media, New York.

Carazo, A.F., Gomez, T., Molina, J., Hernandez-Diaz, A.G., Guerrero, F.M., & Caballero, R. (2010). Solving a Comprehensive Model for Multiobjective Portfolio Selection. *Computers & Operations Research* No. 37, pp. 630-639.

Chan, Y., DiSalvo, J., & Garrambone, M., A. (2005). Goal-seeking Approach to Capital Budgeting. *Socio-Economic Planning Sciences*, No.39, pp. 165-182.

Coello, C. (1999). A Comprehensive Survey of Evolutionary-based Multiobjective Optimization Techniques. *Knowledge and Information Systems*, No. 1, pp. 269-308

Coello, C., Van Veldhuizen, D., & Lamont, G. (2002). *Evolutionary Algorithms for Solving Multi-objective Problems*, Kluwer Academic Publishers, New York-Boston-Dordrecht-London-Moscow.

Davis, K. & Mc Kewon, P. (1986). Quantitative Models for Management (in Spanish), Grupo Editorial Iberoamérica, Mexico.

Dorfman, R. (1996). Why Cost-benefit Analysis is Widely Disregarded and what to do About It?, *Interface*, Vol. 26, No. 1, pp. 1-6.

Duarte, B. & Reis, A. (2006). Developing a Projects Evaluation System Based on Multiple Attribute Value Theory. *Computers & Operations Research*, No. 33, pp. 1488-1504.

Fandel, G. & Gal, T. (2001). Redistribution of Funds for Teaching and Research among Universities: The Case of North Rhine Westphalia. *European Journal of Operational Research*, No. 130, pp. 111-120.

Fernandez, E. & Navarro J. (2002). A Genetic Search for Exploiting a Fuzzy Preference Model of Portfolio Problems with Public Projects, *Annals of Operations Research*, No. 117, pp. 191-213.

Fernandez, E. & Navarro J. (2005). Computer–based Decision Models for R&D Project Selection in Public Organizations. *Foundations of Computing and Decision Sciences*, Vol. 30, No.2, pp. 103-131.

Fernandez, E., Felix, F., & Mazcorro, G. (2009). Multiobjective Optimization of an Outranking Model for Public Resources Allocation on Competing Projects. *International Journal of Operational Research*, No. 5, pp. 190-210.

Fernandez, E., Lopez, F., Navarro, J., Litvinchev, I., & Vega, I. (2009). An Integrated Mathematical-computer Approach for R&D Project Selection in Large Public Organizations. *International Journal of Mathematics in Operational Research*, No. 1, pp. 372-396.

Figueira, J., Greco, S., Roy, B., & Słowiński, R. (2010). ELECTRE Methods: Main Features and Recent Developments, In: *Handbook of Multicriteria Analysis, Applied Optimization*, Zopounidis, C., & Pardalos, M.., pp. 51-89, Springer, Heidelberger-Dordrecht-London-New York.

French, S. (1993). *Decision Theory: An Introduction to the Mathematics of Rationality*, Ellis Horwood, London.

Gabriel, S., Kumar, S., Ordoñez, J., & Nasserian, A. (2006). A Multiobjective Optimization Model for Project Selection with Probabilistic Consideration. *Socio-Economic Planning Sciences*, No. 40, pp. 297-313.

Kaplan, P. & Ranjithan, S.R., (2007). A new MCDM Approach to Solve Public Sector Planning Problems, *Proceedings of the 2007 IEEE Symposium on Computational Intelligence in Multi Criteria Decision Making*, pp. 153-159.

Keeney, R.L. & Raiffa, H. (1976). *Decisions with Multiple Objectives. Preferences and Value Trade-offs*, Wiley and Sons, New York.

Lee, J. & Kim, S. (2001). An Integrated Approach for Interdependent Information System Project Selection. *International Journal of Project Management*, No. 19, pp. 111-118.

Liesio, J., Mild, P., & Salo, A. (2007). Preference Programming for Robust Portfolio Modeling and Project Selection. *European Journal of Operational Research*, No. 181, pp. 1488-1505.

Litvinchev, I., Lopez, F., Alvarez, A., & Fernandez, E. (2010). Large Scale Public R&D Portfolio Selection by Maximizing a Biobjective Impact Measure, *IEEE Transactions on Systems, Man and Cybernetics* , No. 40, pp. 572-582.

Martino, J. (1995). *Research and Development Project Selection,* Wiley, NY- Chichester-Brisbane-Toronto-Singapore.

Mavrotas, G., Diakoulaki, D., & Caloghirou, Y. (2006). Project Prioritization under Policy Restrictions. A combination of MCDA with 0-1 Programming. *European Journal of Operational Research*, No.171, pp. 296-308.

Mavrotas, G., Diakoulaki, & D., Koutentsis, A. (2008). Selection among Ranked Projects under Segmentation, Policy and Logical Constraints. *European Journal of Operational Research*, No. 187, pp. 177-192.

Navarro, J. (2005). *Intelligent Techniques for R&D Project Selection in Public Organizations* (in Spanish), PhD. Dissertation, Autonomous University of Sinaloa, Mexico.

Peterson, S. (2005). *Interview on Financial Reforms in Developing Countries*, Kennedy School Insight, John Kennedy School of Government, Harvard University, Retrieved from: <www.ksg.harvard.edu/ksgnews/KSGInsight/speterson.htm>

Roy, B. (1990). The Outranking Approach and the Foundations of ELECTRE Methods, In: *Reading in Multiple Criteria Decision Aid,* Bana and Costa, C.A., pp. 155-183, Springer-Verlag, Berlin,.

Roy, B. (1996). *Multicriteria Methodology for Decision Aiding*, Kluwer.

Saaty, T. L. (2000). *Fundamentals of the Analytic Hierarchy Process*, RWS Publications, Pittsburg.

Saaty, T. L. (2005). The Analytic Hierarchy and Analytic Network Processes for the Measurement of Intangible Criteria for Decision-making, In: *Multiple Criteria Decision Analysis: State of the Art Surveys*, Figueira, J., Greco, S. and Erghott, M., pp. 345-407, Springer Science + Business Media, New York.

Santhanam, R. & Kyparisis, J. (1995). A Multiple Criteria Decision Model for Information System Project Selection. *Computers and Operations Research*, No. 22, pp.807-818.

Sen, A. (2000). *Development as Freedom*, Anchor Books, New York.

Sen, A. (2008). *On Ethics and Economics* (18th Edition), Blackwell Publishing, Malden-Oxford-Carlton.

Sugrue, P., Mehrotra, A., & Orehovec, P.M. (2006). Financial Aid Management: An Optimization Approach. *International Journal of Operational Research*, No. 1 pp. 267-282.

Tversky A. & Simonson I. (1993). Context Dependent Preferences. *Management Science*, No. 39, pp. 1179-1189.

9

The Search for Parameters and Solutions: Applying Genetic Algorithms on Astronomy and Engineering

Annibal Hetem Jr.
Universidade Federal do ABC
Brasil

1. Introduction

Genetic Algorithms (GAs) can help solving a great variety of complex problems, and the characterization of these problems as possible subject for GA is the first step in applying this technique. After some years, we have used this strong tool to solve problems from astronomy and engineering, and both fields demand complex models and simulations.

With the aim of improving previous models and test new ones, we have developed a methodology generate solutions based on GAs. From a first analysis, one must establish the model input and output parameters, and then workout on the inversion of the problem, what we called the inverted model. This concept leads to the final formalism that can be subject to the GA implementation.

After a brief presentation of the main concerns and ideas, it will be described some applications and their results and discussions. Some details on implementation are also given together with the particularities of each model/solution. A special section regarding error bars estimates is also provided. The GA method gives a good quality of fit, but the range of input parameters must be chosen with caution, as unrealistic parameters can be derived.

GAs can also be used to verify if a given model is better than another for solving a problem. Even considering the limitation of the derived parameters, the automatic fitting process provides an interesting tool for the statistical analysis large samples of data and the models considered.

2. Characterization of NP-Complete problems

In this section, the NP-Complete problems are presented as the main targets of GAs. Before starting to project a GA, it is of greatest importance to study and characterize the problem to justify the technique to use.

The early first notion of NP-completeness was proposed by Stephen Cook (1971), in his famous paper *The complexity of theorem proving procedures*. The main ideas presented in this section have their origins in the excelent works of Garey & Johnson (1979) and Papadimitriu (1995).

Deep inside any GA code there is a model of the inverted problem to be solved. This routine works like I don't know what the correct answer is, but I kwon if a candidate to an answer is good or bad. So, the problem to be solved by a GA must have the property that any proposed solution to an instance must be quickly checked for correctness. For one thing, the solution must be concise, with length polynomially bounded by that of the instance.

To formalize the notion of quick checking, we will say that there is a polynomial-time algorithm that takes as input instance and the solution and decides whether or not it is a solution. If a problem demands a nondeterministic polynomial time to be solved, it is said a NP-problem, as defined by complexity theory researchers. It means that a solution to any search problem can be found and verified in polynomial time by nondeterministic algorithm.

2.1 Inverting the problem

The most remarkable characteristic of a NP-complete problem is the lack known algorithms to find its solution. In a P-Problem, any given candidate to solution can be verified quickly for its accuracy or validity. On the other hand, the time required to solve a NP-problem using any currently known search algorithm increases exponentially with the size of the problem grows. As a consequence, one of the principal unsolved problems in computer science today is determining whether or not it is possible to solve these problems quickly, called the P versus NP problem.

Then, suppose one has a problem M to be solved and asks if a GA based program could solve it. The steps to be followed are:

1. To write down formally the set of parameters to be found, something like $S=\{p_1, p_2, p_3, \dots, p_n\}$, where the p_i set is a representation of the input parameters. Each p_i must be a single number (float or integer), so the S set could be interpreted as a chromosome and each p_i as a gene.
2. To express the problem as a function of the set of parameters: $M=f(S)$, with $M=\{q_1, q_2, q_3, \dots, q_m\}$, where the q_i set is the representation of the output (desired) parameters.
3. Obtain the inverse problem, or the formalities need to compute $S= g(M) =f^{1}(M)$.

If the $g(M)$ function can be translated to a writable algorithm, and this algorithm is computable in a finite time, then the $g(M)$ is a P-problem. If the $f(S)$ function cannot be translated to a writable algorithm, or this algorithm is computable only with by verifying all possibilities in the S space, then the $f(S)$ is a NP-problem.

With both answers: the $f(S)$ function is a NP-problem, and its inverse, $g(M)$ is a P-problem, then the problem can be solved by a GA.

3. Applications on astrophysics

Astrophysics is a field of research very rich in NP-complete problems. Many of actual astrophysicists deal with non-linear systems and unstable conditions. In some cases, the comparative data, or the environment in GA jargon, is an image originated in telescopes or instruments placed in deep space. It is common the need for fit models with multi-spectral data, like radio, infrared, visible and gamma-rays. All these solution constraints lead to an incredible variety of possibilities for using GA tools.

In this section, it will be presented how GAs were used to model protoplanetary discs, an application that involves non-linear radiative-density profile relations. The model combines spectral energy distribution, observed in a wide range of the electromagnetic spectrum, and emissivity behaviour of different dust grain species.

Another interesting application is the use of GAs together with and spectral synthesis in the calculation of abundances and metallicities of T Tauri stars. In this problem, the model is outside the GA code, as one of the conditions imposed is to use a standard, well tested, spectral generator. It is presented how to deal with the challenge of changing a ready to use tool into a NP-complete problem and invert it.

3.1 Using GA to model protoplanetary discs

This subsection is based on the published work *The use of genetic algorithms to model protoplanetary discs* (Hetem & Gregorio-Hetem 2007).

During its formation process, a young star object (YSO) can be surrounded by gas, dust grains and debris, that shall be gravitationally (and also electrostatically) agglomerate in the future solar system bodies. This material receives the energy brought from the star surface and re-irradiates it in other wavelengths. The contribution of this circumstellar matter to the spectral energy distribution (SED) slope is often used to recognize different categories of young YSOs by following an observational classification based on the near-infrared spectral index (Lada & Wilking 1984; Wilking, Lada & Young 1989; André, Ward-Thompson & Barsony 1993). Actually, this classification suggests a scenario for the evolution of YSOs, from Class 0 to Class III, which is well established for TTs.

Here, the adopted model is a flared configuration, according to Dullemond et al. (2001) modelling of a passively irradiated circumstellar disc with an inner hole. We used this model as the P-problem core of a GA based optimization method to estimate the circumstellar parameters.

3.1.1 Presenting the problem

In this subsection we describe the implementation of the GA method for the flared-disc model.

The SED for a given set of parameters is evaluated according to Dullemond et al. (2001) model equations. The disc is composed by three components: the inner rim, the shadowed region, and the flared region with two layers: an illuminated hot layer and an inner cold layer. The disc parameters are: radius, R_D; mass, M_D; inclination, θ; density power law index, p; and inner rim temperature, $T_{\rm rim}$. The stellar parameters are: distance, d; mass, $M_\star$; luminosity, $L_\star$; and temperature, $T_\star$.

The model starts by establishing a vertical boundary irradiated directly by the star, which considers the effect arising from shadowing from the rim, and the variations in scale height as a function of the radius. Figure 1 presents the obtained SED for the star AB Aurigae, as presented in Hetem & Gregorio-Hetem (2007).

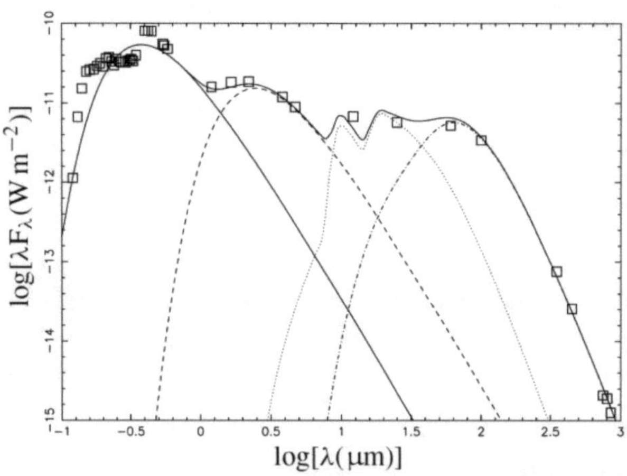

Fig. 1. Results from Dullemond et al. (2001) model applied to the star AB Aurigae. The Synthetic SED is the sum of its components: star emission (continuous thin line); rim emission (dashed line); disc cold layer emission (dot–dashed line); and the disc hot layer emission (dotted line). The observational data in various wavelengths is represented by squares (Hetem & Gregorio-Hetem 2007).

3.1.2 Implementation

The GA code was designed and built to find the best disk parameters, namely S= {R_D; M_D; θ; p; $T_{\rm rim}$, d; $M_\star$; $L_\star$; $T_\star$}, as discussed in subsection 2.1. However, some of these parameters are already known: the stellar parameters d, $L_\star$; and $T_\star$ are adopted from observations and easily found in literature. Essentially, the GA method used implements a χ^2 minimization of the SED fitting provided by the Dullemond et al. (2001) model. The main structures used to manipulate the data are linked lists containing the solutions (parameter set, adaptation level, χ^2_i, and the genetic operator, Φ_i), expressed by

$$M_i = \{(R_{Di}, \theta_i, M_{Di}, p_i, T_i), (\chi_i^2, \Phi_i)\} \tag{1}$$

where S_i denotes the ith solution, and T_i is the ith Trim. Following Goldberg (1989), the code starts with the construction of the first generation, where all parameters are randomly chosen within an allowed range (for example, 50 ≤ RD ≤ 1000 AU). We chose as the number of individuals (parameter sets) in all the generations to be 100. In the following interactions loops, the evaluation function runs the Dullemond et al. (2001) model for each individual, and compares the synthetic SED with the observed data through a χ^2 measure, using the modified expression (Press et al. 1995):

$$\chi_i^2 = \frac{1}{N}\sum_j^N (F_j - \varphi_{ij})^2 \tag{2}$$

where F_j is the observed flux at wavelength λ_j, N is the number of observed data points, and $\varphi_{i\,j}$ is the calculated flux for the solution S_i. The smallest χ^2 is assumed to be the *gof*, the goodness-of-fit measure for that generation. The evaluation function is applied to all individuals, and then the judgement procedure sorts the list by increasing χ^2. It also sets one of the genetic operators to the field Φ_i: copy, crossover, mutation or termination. Each Φ is attributed to a fraction of the number of individuals following the values suggested by Koza (1994), Bentley & Corne (2002) and references therein.

With the genetic operators chosen, the next generation is evaluated by applying specific rules according to the genetic operators. The copy operator uses an elitist selection, as the solutions with the smallest χ^2_i are copied to the next generation. For the crossover operator, a random mix of two distinct individuals' genes is built. The mutation operator copies the original individual, except for one of the genes, which is randomly changed. The process loop continues to build new generations until the end condition is reached, as illustrated by the schematic view in figure. 2.

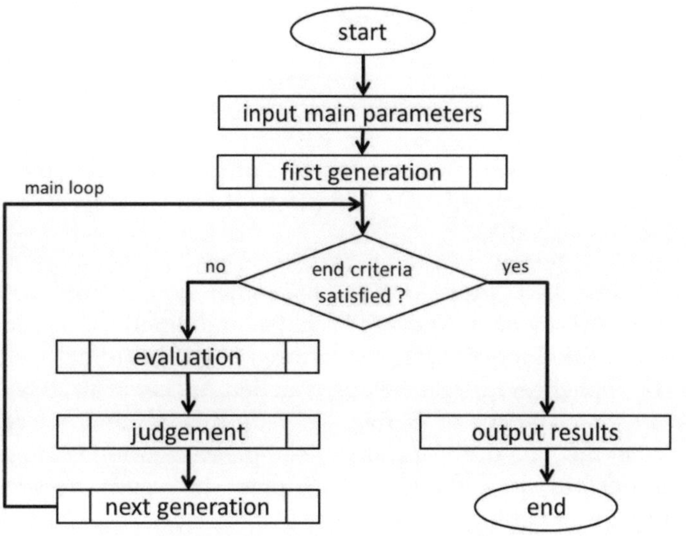

Fig. 2. Main steps of a generic GA (adapted from Hetem & Gregorio-Hetem 2007).

We also can estimate the error bars in the final results by analysing the χ^2 behaviour as a function of the parameter variation. Then one can determine the confidence levels of a given parameter, as suggested by Press et al. (1995). Once the GA end condition has been reached, one can evaluate the inverse of the Hessian matrix $[C] \equiv [\alpha]^{-1}$ whose components are given by

$$\alpha_{ij} = \sum_{k=1}^{N} \left(\frac{\partial y(\lambda_k)}{\partial a_i} \frac{\partial y(\lambda_k)}{\partial a_j} \right) \tag{3}$$

where $\partial y(\lambda_k)/\partial a_i$ is the partial derivative of the SED with respect to parameter a_i at $\lambda = \lambda_k$, and N is the number of observed data points. The main diagonal of C can be used to estimate the error bars on each parameter by $\sigma_i \cong C^{1/2}/N$. We estimated the error bars for the 1σ confidence level and the respective disc parameters for AB Aurigae, resulting in $M_D = 0.1 \pm 0.004 M_\odot$, $R_D = 400 \pm 44$ AU, $\theta = 65 \pm 3^o$, and $T_{rim} = 1500 \pm 26$ K, and these results are in agreement with the error-bar estimation provided by the surface contour levels described below. Fig. 3 presents the contour levels of the $gof(M_D, R_D)$ surface calculated for a set of 400 random pairs of disc mass and radius around the parameters for the AB Aurigae model taken from Dominik et al. (2003). The result at the minimum is *gof* ~ 0.046, what means that the error bar estimation converged to a narrow range around the parameter set.

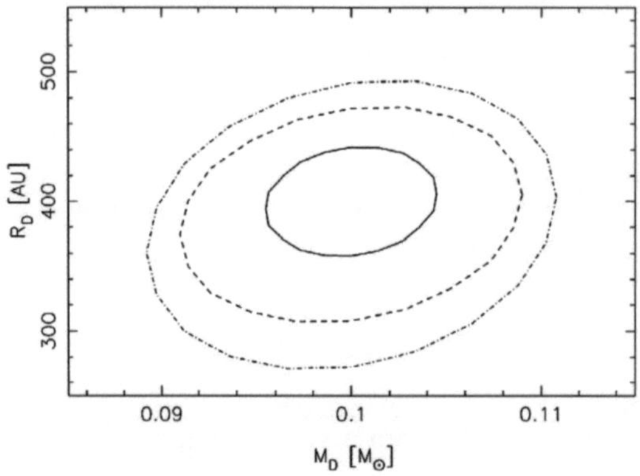

Fig. 3. Contour levels $gof(M_D, R_D)$ estimated for AB Aurigae presenting the confidence levels $\chi^2(68\%)= 0.082$ (continuous line), $\chi^2(90\%)= 0.15$ (dashed) and $\chi^2(99\%)= 0.21$ (dot–dashed) (Hetem & Gregorio-Hetem 2007).

We also applied the described GA method to a four other stars, in order to verify the quality of the fitting for objects showing different SED shapes and different levels of infrared excess. Our set was chosen by the slope of their near-infrared SED. The infrared excess in Herbig Be stars is the result of a spherical dusty envelope (van den Ancker et al. 2001), whereas a thick-edge flared disc are characteristic of Herbig Ae. With this in mind, we selected A-type or late-B-type stars from the Pico dos Dias Survey sample (Gregorio-Hetem et al. 1992; Torres et al. 1995; Torres 1998) to apply the GA SED fitting. The results are presented in table 1 together with their corresponding *gofs* (see figure 4).

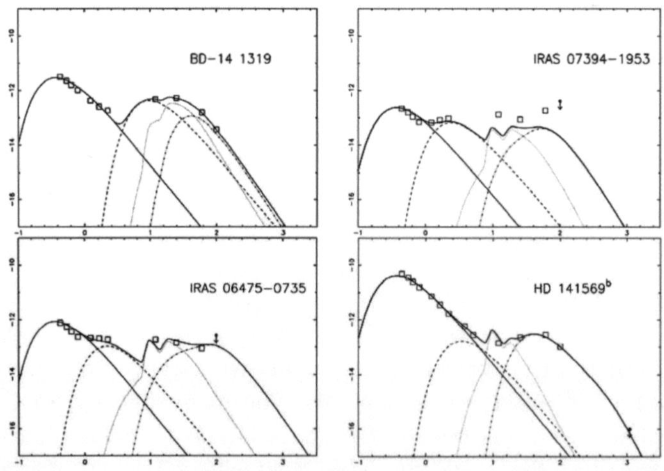

Fig. 4. GA SEDs obtained the stars BD-14 1319, IRAS 07394-1953, IRAS 06475-0735 and HD 141569. The plots are given as $log[\lambda F_\lambda(Wm^{-2})]$ versus $log[\lambda(\mu m)]$ (Hetem & Gregorio-Hetem 2007).

PDS	Name	$M_\star$ ($M_\odot$)	R_D (AU)	M_D ($M_\odot$)	T_{rim} (K)	θ (°)	p	gof
398	HD 141569	2.4	13	0.06	1085	0.6	-2.0	0.006
022	BD−14 1319	2.8	690	0.003	380	40	-10.	0.006
130	IRAS 06475−0735	2.0	309	0.20	1705	53	-1.5	0.016
257	IRAS 07394−1953	2.0	859	0.64	1838	47	-2.0	0.098

Table 1. Obtained parameters for the chosen stars (Hetem & Gregorio-Hetem 2007).

3.2 Abundances and Metallicities of young stars via Spectral Synthesis

This subsection is based on the published work The use of Genetic Algorithms and Spectral Synthesis in the Calculation of Abundances and Metallicities of T Tauri stars (Hetem & Gregorio-Hetem 2009).

In the previous subsection, we presented a method that uses a calculation technique based on GA aiming to optimize the parameters estimation of protoplanetary disks of T Tauri stars. Inspired by the success of that application, which gives accurate and efficient calculations, we decided to develop a similar method to determine atomic stellar abundances.

3.2.1 Artificial spectra as a measurement tool

In astrophysics, the absorption spectra are obtained and employed as an analytical chemistry tool to determine the presence of atoms and ions in stellar atmospheres and, if possible, to quantify the amount of the atoms present. In stellar atmospheres, each element produces a number of spectrum absorption lines, at wavelengths which can be measured with extreme accuracy when compared to spectra emission tables provided by laboratory experiments.

The presence of a given element in the star atmosphere can be verified (and measured) by looking for its absorption lines at the correct wavelength. The hydrogen is present in all stars by its Balmer absorption lines, and is often used to calibrate the measurements. An example of a high-resolution spectrum is presented in figure 5.

The way astrophysics use to calculate the abundances of atoms in stars follows the steps:

1. Obtain the star spectrum in a given range (or ranges) of wavelength, where the lines of the elements in study should be;
2. Generate an artificial spectrum, considering the lines whose origin are the desired elements and the known physics of absorption line production;
3. Compare the artificial and observed spectra. Here a simple χ^2 test is enough to compute a general comparison index;
4. Use a GA methodology to optimize the artificial spectrum in order to minimize the differences with the observed spectrum (the inverted problem, subsection 2.1);
5. Once the optimization methodology reaches its goals, consider the elemental parameters (density, temperature, ionization, etc) as the measures of the elements in the stellar atmospheres.

3.2.2 Inverting the problem

From our discussion on section 2, one can see that generating a synthetic spectrum is a P-problem, as the result is obtained from a set of parameters, and no more computing is need. The generation time is obviously finite, and there are a number of very efficient software tools that do that. The only care to be taken is to assure that the artificial spectrum has the same wavelength resolution of the observed spectrum, in order to simplify the future comparison.

The above mentioned step 4, a methodology to optimize the artificial spectrum, is the trick point. If one wants to use GA so solve the abundances problem, it is necessary to invert the P-problem, that is, it is necessary to use the artificial spectrum generation tool as an external routine of a bigger and more complex algorithm. The algorithm used to this task is presented in figure 6.

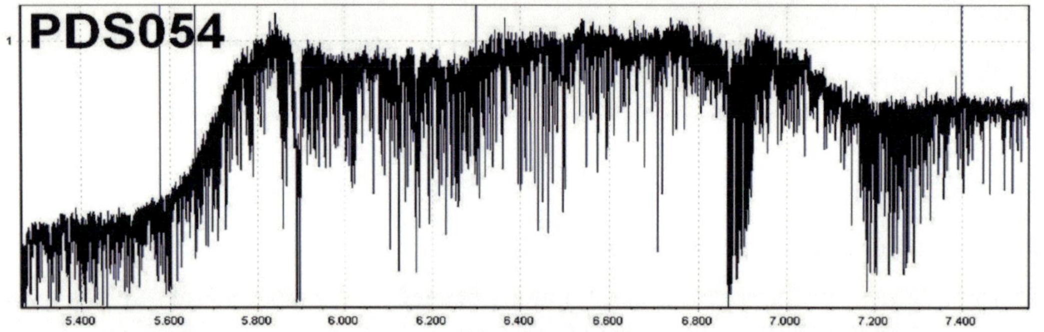

Fig. 5. FEROS spectrum for star PDS054 (Rojas et al. 2008).

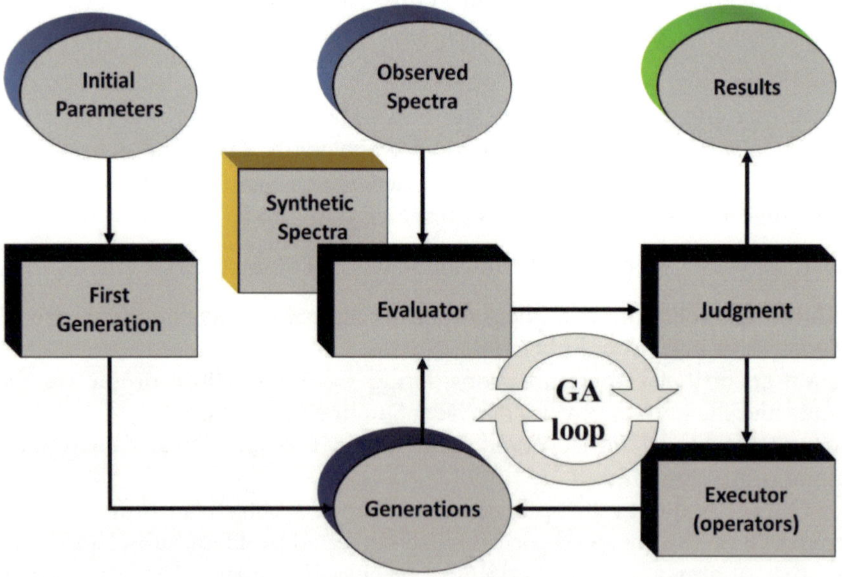

Fig. 6. Main blocks of a GA code to fit multi-band spectra of T Tauri stars (adapted from Hetem & Gregorio-Hetem 2009).

Establishing the abundances of each element as the parameters to be found, one individual in the GA terminology is the set of all elemental abundances added to some atmospheric parameters. The initial parameter set is used to build the first generation with 100 individuals. The evaluator routine creates a synthetic spectrum whose entries are the genetic data in each chromosome. This task is performed by calling the elected spectral tool.

There are a number of very efficient software tools that can be chosen. In our application, the abundances of chemical species are determined by using the spectral synthesis software SPECTRUM provided by Corbally (Gray & Corbally 1994) and the atmosphere model software ATLAS9 from Kurucz (1993).

3.2.3 Results

In this section we present the results of the GA method for three stars, whose high-resolution spectra were obtained at *European Southern Observatory* (ESO) in La Silla, Chile, with the *Fibber Extended Range Optical Spectrograph* (FEROS) at the 1.52m telescope. The stellar parameters (effective temperature and gravity) were calculated by excitation and ionization equilibrium of iron absorption lines (Rojas et al. 2008). The atomic and molecular line data were mainly from the National Institute of Standards and Technology[1] and the Kurucz site[2]. The solar atomic abundances are from Grevesse & Sauval (1998), and the hyperfine structure constants were taken from Dembczyński et al. (1979) and Luc & Gerstenkorn (1972). The atmosphere models where obtained from the Kurucz library. Specific atmosphere models were calculated through a GNU-Linux porting of the ATLAS9 program (Kurucz 1993).

The method performs a multi-range fitting of specific regions of the observed spectrum, looking for best fit. The demands and commands to SPECTRUM are only those for generating the specific regions of interest, but the χ^2 comparing index is evaluated over all wavelength ranges. Figures 7 and 8 present the results for some stars on chosen lines.

The metallicities and abundances found for the stars are compatible with those previously obtained for this particular sample. These preliminary results, achieved by using the GA technique, indicate the efficiency of the method. In the future, we intend to use the method in a larger sample of T Tauri stars.

4. Applications on Rocket Engine engineering

This section presents two solutions in applying GAs in the aerospace area, both concerning the fuel pumping in liquid propellant rocket engines. There are many choices to be done in the design of a high performance fuel pump, being one of them the type of pump.

Two different types of pumps were modelled: the Harrington pumps and the turbo pumps. Both present a complex design methodology, which includes: tabled functions interpolations, numerical integrals and constructive material choices.

---

[1] http://physics.nist.gov/PhysRefData/ASD/index.html
[2] http://kurucz.harvard.edu 4 and http://wwwuser.oat.ts.astro.it/castelli/

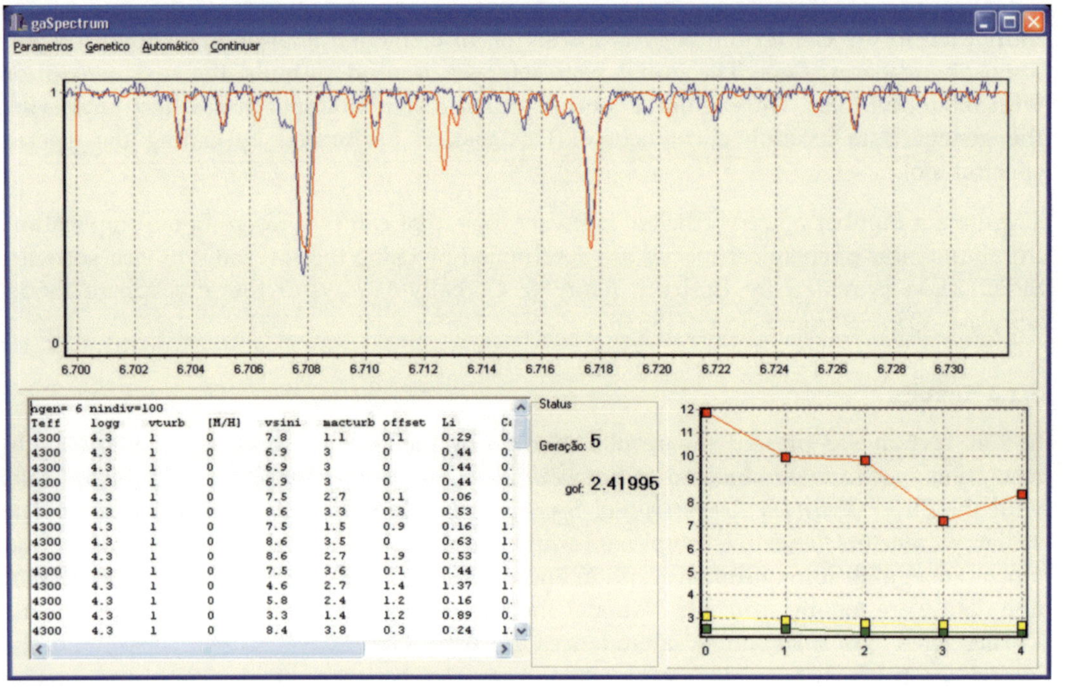

Fig. 7. Main screen of the program GASpectrum after five generations. The upper panel presents the spectra: the blue line represents the observed spectrum and the red line represents the best individual spectrum (adapted from Hetem & Gregorio-Hetem 2009).

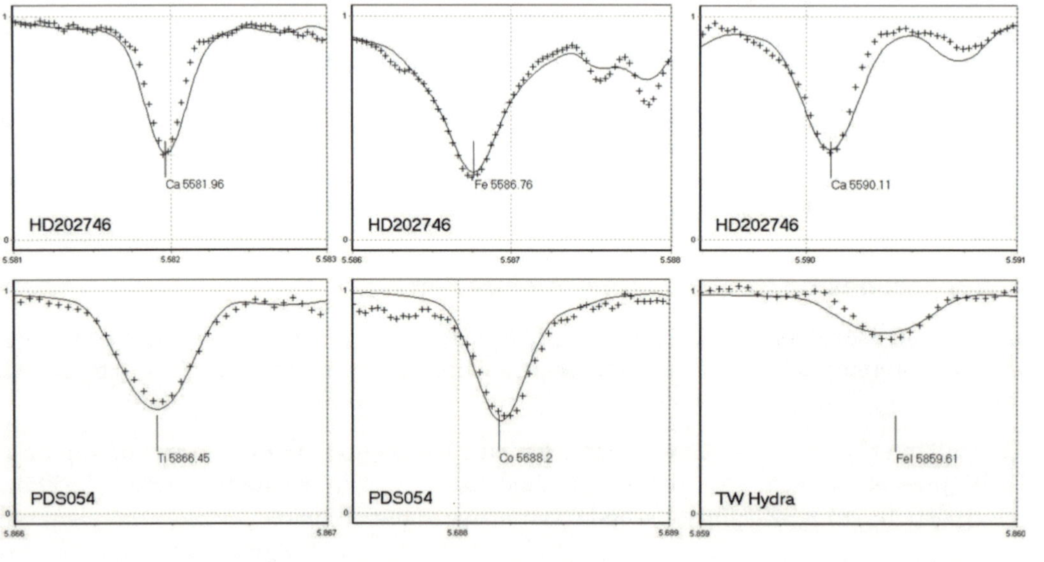

Fig. 8. Main results for stars HD202746, PDS054 and TW Hydra, on calcium, iron, titanium and cobalt lines (adapted from Hetem & Gregorio-Hetem 2009).

4.1 Using GA to parameterize the design of Harrington pumps

This subsection is based on the published work *Artificial Intelligence Parametrization of Harrington Pumps* (Caetano & Hetem 2011).

Since the beginning of liquid engine spacecraft history, the choices on pumping were the turbo pumps (Neufeld 1995). However, turbo pumps present many difficulties to design and to achieve their optimum performance. Good and experienced designers can project specialized turbo pumps that can deliver 70-90% efficiency, but figures less than half that are not uncommon. Low efficiency may be acceptable in some applications, but in rocketry this is a severe problem. Common problems include: 1) excessive flow from the high pressure rim back to the low pressure inlet along the gap between the casing of the pump and the rotor; 2) excessive recirculation of the fluid at inlet; 3) excessive vortexing of the fluid as it leaves the casing of the pump; 4) damaging cavitation to impeller blade surfaces in low pressure zones; and 5) critical shaping of the rotor itself is hardly precise (see the many examples and demonstrations presented by Dixon & Hall (2010) for a better understanding of these concerns).

On the other end, the options are the pressurized tanks. In this choice, the fuel and oxidizer reservoir are filled charged with a high pressure gas (helium or nitrogen) that pushes the fluid to the thrust chamber. So, it is easy to see that the tank output fuel pressure drops as the rocket engine consumes its content. As an option, the designer can increase the inside pressure, but this came also with a high cost in material (due to tank thickness) and instability. Actually, pressurized propellant tanks are used on small rockets like the last stages on space missions.

As an elegant intermediate solution between these two extremes, Harrington (2003) presented a design fills the gap between the pressure fed and the turbo pumps. This solution also has the advantage of lowering the costs of a rocket project, keeping low weight and without the high complexity of a turbo pump, whose operation, theoretical concerns and constructive details are explained in next section.

4.1.1 Pump description and operation

The construction consists of two chambers (B1 and B2 on figure 9) and a set of 8 valves. The chambers are connected to the main tank (Mt) through valves k3 and k4. These chambers also deliver propellant to the combustion chamber (CB) through valves k5 and k6. There is a high pressure gas generator (Hp) that is connected to the chambers through valves k1 and k2. Valves k7 and k8 serve as ventilation for the chambers.

The pumps work alternating two states. In state 1, B1 is being filled by Mt and B2 is feeding the combustion chamber; and in state 2 their role is inverted, say B2 is being filled by Mt and B1 is feeding the combustion chamber. The state change is done by opening and closing the valves, as presented in figure 9 and table 2. The opening and closing of the valves is controlled by a small processor.

4.1.2 The model: Pump constructive details

Designing a Harrington pump is simple, but the optimization process is not (as expected: a P-problem and a NP-problem respectively). A pump with a small chamber must be filled and vented quickly, with minimal head loss through the gas and liquid valves and plumbing. Making the pump cycle as fast as possible would make it lightweight, but higher flow velocities cause problems (Harrington 2003).

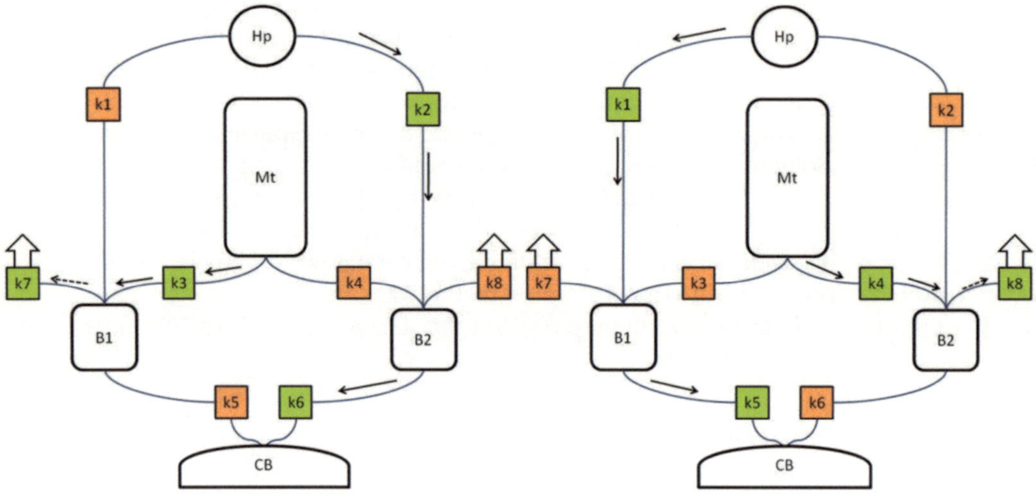

Fig. 9. Schematic view and operation of a Harrington pump, with its chambers (B1 and B2) and valves (k1-8). The main rocket fuel tank is represented by Mt whereas Hp represents a high pressure gas generator. The two states are presented. Left: B1 is being filled by Mt while B2 is feeding the combustion chamber. Right: B1 is feeding the combustion chamber while B2 is being filled by Mt. the arrows indicate the flow. (Caetano & Hetem 2011).

valve	state 1	state 2
k1	closed	open
k2	open	closed
k3	open	closed
k4	closed	open
k5	closed	open
k6	open	closed
k7	open	closed
k8	closed	open

Table 2. Derived model parameters for the sample (Caetano & Hetem 2011).

The choice of pump tanks material plays an important role, as its mass density and stress coefficients are the main keys in the pump design. The main tank pressure (about 300 kPa) and the area of the inlet valves set up the limits for the maximum inflow rate. If the inflow velocity is increased this can cause the propellant to be aerated, what is not desirable for the proper working of the engine. The extra volume of pressurized gas in the pump chamber should be small to minimize gas usage, but if it is too small, there will be a loss of propellant through the vent.

The primary parameters for the calculations are the state changing cycle, t_{cy}, the volume flow determined by the rocket engine needs, Q, the specific impulse of the propellants, I_{sp}, at the fuel pressure, P_f, the fuel mass density, ρ_f, the thrust, T, and the material properties: the mass density, ρ_c, and stress coefficient, σ_c. From these parameters, considering the pump chambers are spherical, one can instantly obtain the diameter of one chamber:

$$D_c = \sqrt[3]{6\frac{\int_0^{t_{cy}} Q dt}{\pi}}, \quad (4)$$

where the integral results in the chamber volume, and for the simplest case of steady flow, it resumes to $V_c=Q.t_{cy}$. Knowing the diameter and applying the stress formulae from Young (1989), the chamber walls thickness can be obtained by

$$t_w = \frac{P_f D_c}{\sigma_c}, \quad (5)$$

and the total chamber mass by

$$M_c = \pi t_w D_c^2 \rho_c . \quad (6)$$

To obtain the thrust, one can apply the momentum equation for the case of ideal expansion, and:

$$T = gQI_{sp}\rho_f , \quad (7)$$

where g represents the gravity acceleration.

Manipulation of these expressions and an estimative of the relative weight of the valves and other accessories lead to expression 7 from Harrington (2003), the pump thrust to weight ratio:

$$\frac{T}{W} = 0.43\frac{gI_{sp}\rho_f}{P_f T_{cy}}\frac{\sigma_c}{\rho_c}, \quad (8)$$

that is to be optimized. The total pump mass is M_p=1.56 M_c, and the mass flow can be easily obtained by $\dot{m} = Q\rho_f$. The expressions (4)-(8) were coded in a program to test the feasibility of this set of equations as a model. Table 3 presents the results obtained for typical parameter values. These results are in agreement with rocket engine pump literature (Griffinand & French 1991; Sutton 1986).

Entry parameters			Model results		
t_{cy}	5	s	V_c	0,016667	m^3
Q	200	l/min	D_c	31,69203	cm
I_{sp}	285	s	t_w	0,090549	cm
ρ_f[1]	935	kg/m^3	M_c	0,8	kg
P_f	4	Mpa	M_p	1,248	kg
T	8800	N	T	8704,85	N
σ_c[2]	350	MPa	T/W	8718,8	
ρ_c[2]	2,8	g/cm^3	$\dot{m}$	3,116667	kg/s

[1] Propellant mixture: LOX/RP-1
[2] 2219 Aluminum alloy

Table 3. Test values for the pump model and results.

4.1.3 GA optimization method

Here we describe de Genetic Algorithm (GA) optimization method and the formalism applied to code the problem to its needs.

The pump parameters we want to find are a subset of those described as primary parameters: the state changing cycle, t_{cy}, the fuel pressure, P_f, the fuel mass density, ρ_f, and the material properties: the mass density, ρ_c, and stress coefficient, σ_c. These are the GA free parameters, formally

$$\Lambda = \{t_{cy}, P_f, \rho_c, \sigma_c\} , \tag{9}$$

known as the parameter set. The technique used to work with the material parameters, ρ_c and σ_c, are explained in sub-section 4.1.4.

The obtained pump must deliver a desired mass rate, , of a given propellant, ρ_f, and must be made of a given material, ρ_c and σ_c. Some variables are project dependent, like the volume flow, Q, the specific impulse of the propellants, I_{sp}, at the fuel pressure, and the thrust, T. These three parameters are those the rocket engine designer should define to specify the pump he needs. Differently from the first parameters described on the above paragraph, these values cannot be altered by the algorithm, and can be included in another group, the constant set:

$$\Psi = \{Q, I_{sp}, T\} . \tag{10}$$

Another group of variables is need: the result set. These are the values that are obtained by running the model code:

$$\Gamma = \{V_c, D_c, t_w, M_c, M_p, T, T / W, \dot{m}\} . \tag{11}$$

To satisfy the GA formalism, one must write down the model that describes the necessary transformations to obtain Γ from Ψ and Λ, or $\Lambda = f(\Psi, \Gamma)$.

Now we explain how the GA method was implemented in the Harrington pump model described above. We first clarify the GA nomenclature in the field of pump design. A *parameter* (e.g. volume flow) corresponds to the concept of a 'gene', and a change in a parameter is a 'mutation'. A parameter set that yields a possible solution corresponds to a 'chromosome', our Λ. An 'individual' is a solution that is composed of one parameter set and two additional GA control variables. One of these variables is χ^2, which refers to the 'adaptation' level. The other control variable is Φ, the genetic operator. The term 'generation' means 'all the individuals' (or all the solutions) present in a given iteration.

The code uses the parameters described in (9), namely $\Lambda = \{t_{cy}, P_f, \rho_c, \sigma_c\}$. Essentially, the GA method presented herein implements a χ^2 minimization of the comparison between the desired results $\Gamma_0 = \{V_c, D_c, t_w, M_c, M_p, T, T/W, \dot{m}\}$, and the results obtained by the application of expressions (4) to (8), the model results. There are three main advantages of using a GA for this task: (i) the GA method potentially browses the whole permitted parameter space, better avoiding the 'traps' of local minima; (ii) the method is not affected by changes in the model; (iii) the GA implementation does not need to compute the derivatives of χ^2 (such as $\partial\chi^2/\partial P_f$, for example) required by the usual methods. This fact simplifies the code and minimizes computer errors caused by gradient calculations.

The main structures used to manipulate the data are linked lists containing the solutions (parameter set, adaptation level, χ_i^2, and the genetic operator, Φ_i, expressed by $S_i = \{\Psi, \Lambda_i, \Gamma_i, (\chi_i^2, \Phi_i)\}$, where S_i denotes the *i*th solution. Following Goldberg (1989) and Hetem & Gregorio-Hetem (2007), the code starts with the construction of the first generation, where all parameters are randomly chosen within an allowed range (for example, 15 cm < D_c < 30 cm). Here, the number of parameter sets in the first generation is assumed to be 100. In the next step, the evaluation function runs the model for each solution, and compares the synthetic Γ_i with the desired data, Γ_0, to find χ^2, using a modified expression given by Press et al. (1995):

$$\chi_i^2 = \frac{1}{n_p}\sum_{j=1}^{n_p}\left(\frac{\Gamma_{0j} - \Gamma_{ij}}{\Gamma_{0j}}\right)^2, \tag{12}$$

where n_p is the number of values in the result set, Γ_{0j}, is the desired value on position *j* (e.g. $\Gamma_{01}=V_c$), and Γ_{ij} is the calculated value for the solution S_i. The smallest χ^2 corresponds to the goodness-of-fit, or simply *gof.* The *gof* values express how each individual is adapted, or how close each solution is, to the best solution (Bentley & Corne 2002). For the value of *T/W*, which we want to optimize, it is enough to establish a corresponding to Γ_{0j} very high.

A judgment function then determines the genetic operator Φ to be applied to a solution. Its values can be 'copy': the individual remains the same in the next generation; 'crossover': the individual is elected to change a number of genes (parameters) with another individual, creating a new one; 'mutation': one of its genes is randomly changed; or 'termination': none of the genes continue to subsequent generations. The chosen action is expressed by the Φ_i variable, associated with each individual. The next step is to evolve the current generation (*k*) to the next (*k* + 1) one, which is done through a multi-dimensional function β that considers the solutions and the genetic operators. Formally,

$$[S_1,S_2,\ldots,S_N]_{k+1} = \beta[(S_1,\Phi_1),(S_2,\Phi_2),\ldots,(S_N,\Phi_N)]_k \,. \quad (13)$$

As soon as a new generation is ready, the evaluation function is reapplied, and the algorithm repeats the described actions until an end-of-loop condition is reached. The end condition can be based on the number of iterations or the quality (a low level for the χ_i^2 values).

4.1.4 The choice of chamber constructive material

The main material properties, the mass density, ρ_c, and stress coefficient, σ_c, can also be chosen by the GA. Instead of working directly with these parameters, it was created a material parameter, K_c, an integer that points to a density-stress database. So, our new parameter set becomes

$$\Lambda = \{t_{cy}, P_f, \rho_c(K_c), \sigma_c(K_c)\}\,, \quad (14)$$

or simply

$$\Lambda = \{t_{cy}, P_f, K_c\}\,. \quad (15)$$

As K_c is a discrete value, it was needed to build special routines to manipulate the genes in the first generation and in mutation events.

4.1.5 Results and conclusion

Table 4 presents the main results for a GA run of 20 generations. The values are in agreement with the expected for the pump. The material chosen for the chambers was cooper 99.9%. A typical running with about 100 generation is achieved in ~5 seconds in a simple laptop computer.

t_{cy}	8.2	s	Vc	0.00393786	m^3
Q	200	l/min	Dc	0.195924	cm
I_{sp}	285	s	tw	0,089	cm
ρ_f[1]	935	kg/m^3	Mc	0.957973	kg
P_f	4	Mpa	Mp	1.49444	kg
σ_c[2]	350	MPa	T/W	843.227	
ρ_c[2]	2,8	g/cm^3	$\dot{m}$	0.448098	kg/s

[1] Propellant mixture: LOX/RP-1
2 Copper 99.9% Cu

Table 4. GA result values for the pump model.

The GA proved to be efficient, and due to the method itself being independent of model complexity, it certainly can be used in future implementations of pump design. Future evolutions and increasing complexity of the model, like thermal transfer and realistic valves, can benefit of GA robustness and reliability.

The next step in this work is to enhance the model with more realistic and specific trends. It is expected to incorporate non-linear functions, differential equations and integrals. Also tabled functions are not far from what can be found in a pump project, with its intrinsic interpolations. The overall problem of finding parameters for a pump design can easily turn to a NP-Problem, that is a problem that is very difficult to find a solution, but, once one has a candidate to solution it is easy to verify if it is a good solution.

4.2 Using GA to parameterize the design of turbo pumps to be used in rocket engines

This subsection is based on the published work Parametric Design of Rocket Engine Turbo pumps with Genetic Algorithms (Burian et al. 2011).

Turbo pumping in high-thrust, long-duration liquid propellant rocket engine applications, generally results in lower weights and higher performance when compared to pressurized gas feed systems. Turbo pump feed systems require only relatively low pump-inlet pressures, and thus propellant-tank pressures, while the major portion of the pressure required at the thrust chamber inlets is supplied by the pumps, saving considerable vehicle weight. As stated by Huzel & Huang (1967) the best performing turbo pump system is defined as that which affords the heaviest payload for a vehicle with a given thrust level, range or velocity increment: gross stage take-off weight; and thrust chamber specific impulse (based on propellant combination, mixture ratio, and chamber operating efficiency).

The particular arrangement or geometry of the major turbo pump components is related to their selection process (Logan & Roy 2003). Some complex designs, like the SSME-Space Shuttle Main Engine, have a multiple stage pump, but most propellant pumps have a single-stage main impeller. Eventually, one or more design limits are reached which requires more iteration, each with a new changed parameter or approach. For a better example, see table 5 which presents some data from the V2 (II world war German missile) alcohol pump.

Parameter	value
impeller diameter	34 cm
rotation	5000 rpm
performance	265 kW
delivery	50 kg/s
delivery pressure	25 atm

Table 5. Parameters from the alcohol V2 pump, adapted from Sutton & Biblarz (2001).

This subsection considers the development of a software tool based on GA to assist the determination of the excellent parameters for the configuration of turbo pumps in engines for liquid propellant rockets. We present the first version, which considers the calculation of the main parameters of a compressor stage.

4.2.1 The model

The pump compressor model used in this work is based on chapter 10 of Sutton & Biblarz (2001). This model provides a coherent basis for the modeling, and is sufficiently complex to be used as a valid test on the further parameter optimizing step.

The pump parameters we want to find are: the inlet compressor diameter, d1, the compressor outlet diameter, d_2, the fluid input velocity, v_1, the suction specific speed, S, the shaft cross section, A_{S1}, the pressure in the main tank, P_t, the total fluid friction (viscosity included) due to flow through the pipes, valves, etc, P_f, the pressure due to the tank elevation from the pump inlet, P_e. In particular, this last parameter leads to project insights concerning the pump position inside the rocket. These are the GA free parameters, formally $\Lambda = \{d_1, d_2, v_1, S, d_{S1}, P_t, P_f, P_e\}$, known as the parameter set. The obtained compressor must deliver a desired mass rate, $\dot{m}$, and, from an input pressure P_1, generate a flow with an output pressure P_2. Some constants shall be considered, like the fluid mass density, ρ, and the external gravity, g_0. We assumed as fluid the ethanol (C_2H_6OH) due to its green properties and green results. These three parameters are those the rocket engine designer should define to specify the compressor he needs. Differently from the first eight parameters described on the above paragraph, these values cannot be altered by the algorithm, and can be included in another group, the result set $\Gamma = \{\dot{m}, P_1, P_2\}$.

To satisfy the GA formalism, one must write down the model, or the formalism that describes the necessary transformations to obtain Γ from Λ, or $\Gamma = f(\Lambda)$. One can obtain these expressions following Sutton & Biblarz (2001) model and converting their expressions. First, the pressures should be converted to heads, or the height necessary to the fluid to cause a given pressure, so we define H_t, H_e and H_f, the tank head, the elevation head and the friction head, respectively, that can be obtained by

$$P_t = \int_{H_t} g_0 \rho dh , \tag{16}$$

$$P_e = \int_{H_e} g_0 \rho dh , \tag{17}$$

and

$$P_f = \int_{H_f} g_0 \rho dh . \tag{18}$$

The effective area of the inlet is given by

$$A_{1eff} = \frac{1}{4}\frac{d_1^2}{\pi} - A_{S1} , \tag{19}$$

which determines the volume flow

$$Q = \iint_{A_{1eff}} v_1 dA \,. \tag{20}$$

Then, the absolute positive head can be obtained by

$$H_1 = H_t + H_e - H_f \tag{21}$$

and the net positive suction head or available suction head above vapor pressure can be obtained by

$$H_s = H_t + H_e - H_f - H_v \,, \tag{22}$$

where H_v is the combustible vapor pressure. The required suction head will be taken as 80% of the available suction head in order to provide a margin of safety for cavitation, or H_{SR}=0.8H_1. To avoid pump cavitation, H_s has to be higher than H_{SR}. If additional head is required by the pump, the propellant may have to be pressurized by external means, such as by the addition of another pump in series (a booster pump) or by gas pressurization of the propellant tanks. A small value of H_{SR} is desirable because it may permit a reduction of the requirements for tank pressurization and, therefore, a lower inert tank mass.

The shaft speed is given by

$$N_{rpm} = \frac{SH_{SR}^{\phi}}{u_{SI}\sqrt{Q}} \,, \tag{22}$$

where φ=3/4 and u_{SI}=17.827459 are constants. u_{SI} is necessary due to SI convertions (see Sutton & Biblarz 2001, eq. 10-7). This last expression allows us to obtain $N_{rad/s}$, the shaft speed in radians per second. The impeller vane tip speed is given by

$$u = \frac{1}{2} d_2 N_{rad/s} \,. \tag{23}$$

With u, we can evaluate the head delivered by the pump

$$\Delta H = \frac{u^2}{\psi g_0} \,, \tag{24}$$

where ψ has values between 0.90 and 1.10 for different designs. As for many pumps, ψ = 1.0, we adopt this value.

At this point, we are able to obtain all the final results, $\Gamma = \{\dot{m}, P_1, P_2\}$:

$$P_1 = H_1 g_0 \rho \,, \tag{25}$$

$$P_2 = (\Delta H + H_1) g_0 \rho \,, \tag{26}$$

and

$$\dot{m} = \rho Q \,. \tag{27}$$

It is also interesting to evaluate the shaft specific speed

$$N_s = \frac{u_{SI}\sqrt{Q}}{H_{SR}^{\phi}}, \tag{28}$$

which, with the aid of table 10-2 of Sutton & Biblarz (2001), defines the pump and impeller type.

4.2.2 Results and conclusion

We built a computer code to optimize equations in the same way it was done to the Harrington pumps (see subsection 4.1). The resulting parameters obtained from the GA code where in good agreement with what is expected for this kind of project. Some comparisons between GA results and correct results are presented in table 6.

		$\dot{m}$ (kg/s)	P_1 (Pa)	P_2 (Pa)	mean error (%)
Correct answer		226,8	342669	6816870	
generations	10	228,1	342345	6816450	0,22
	20	227,5	342360	6816440	0,13
	50	227,1	342601	6816890	0,05
	100	226,9	342670	6816880	0,01

Table 6. Comparison between obtained results (GA) and correct answer (Γ_0) for an ethanol compressor.

Evidently, for the simple definitions presented for this model, one does not need a sophisticated method as described to obtain a good result. But, as all designers know very well, there are no simple projects, especially concerning rocket engine pumps. The next step in this work is to enhance the model with more realistic and specific trends. It is expected to incorporate non-linear functions, differential equations and integrals. Also tabled functions are not far from what can be found in a pump project, with its intrinsic interpolations. The overall problem of finding parameters for a pump design can easily turn to a NP-Problem, that is a problem that is very difficult to find a solution, but, once one has a candidate to solution it is easy to verify if it is a good solution. Again, the GA proved to be efficient, and due to the method itself being independent of model complexity, it certainly can be used in future implementations. Future evolutions and increasing complexity of the model can benefit of GA robustness and reliability.

5. Applications on energy distribution

The application described in this section solves the problem of allocation of protective devices in electric power distribution plants. For a given power plant distribution, it is necessary to choose in which points one must place equipment for the net protection, or not.

This problem is entirely based on discrete elements - there are no floating point parameters. So, the main discussion here is how to build a chromosome syntax that can be used under the GA rules, and still be meaningful for the model. Besides, as the problem is fully discretized, there are high probabilities of finding different solutions that are equally evaluated in their adaptation function. This leads to new enhancements in the model to better evaluate the solutions, enhancing the separation between different individuals.

5.1 Using GA in the allocation of electric power protective devices

This subsection is based on the published work Automatic Allocation of Electric Power Distribution Protective Devices (Burian et al. 2010).

The measurement of how well the electric power distribution system can provide a secure and adequate supply of power to satisfy the customer's requirements is called "reliability". Regarding electric power distribution systems, the electric utilities companies are responsible for the most reliable service as possible, reflecting the most advanced state of technology with reasonable cost to the end product that is the electric power[3]. Most utilities record outage information such as the number of outages, elapse time, and the number of customers interrupted. These data and statistics may be reported for each circuit or operating division, for comparison purposes, using the standard performance indices.

The performance indices provide historical *datum* which can be used to determine increasing or decreasing trends and to measure whether system improvement plans have yielded expected results.

The quality model we consider in this subsection uses the following indices, based on the sustained outage data: the SAIDI and SAIFI indexes, explained as follows:

1. SAIDI (System Average Interruption Duration Index): defined by the rate of average interruption duration per customer served per year. This index is commonly referred to as minutes of interruption per customer.

$$\text{SAIDI} = \frac{\text{Sum of Customer Interruption Durations}}{\text{Total Number of Customers Served}} \tag{29}$$

2. SAIFI (System Average Interruption Frequency Index): that defined by the rate of average number of times that a customer's service is interrupted during a reporting period per customer served in a given period (usually one year). A customer interruption is defined as one sustained interruption to one customer:

$$\text{SAIFI} = \frac{\text{Total Number of Customer Interruptions}}{\text{Total Number of Customers Served}} \tag{30}$$

It is easy to see that what is desired is a circuit with minimal SAIDI and SAIFI with the smaller cost in protective installed devices. The resulting circuit with these characteristics will the optimized circuit.

---

[3] instead of guarantying continuous service to their customers…

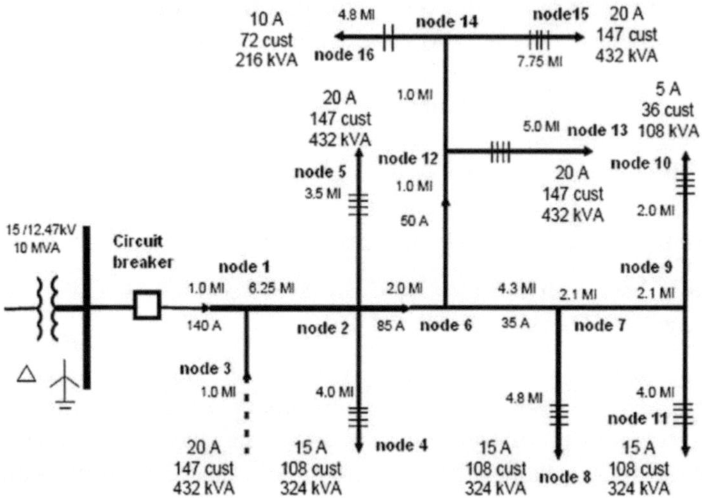

Fig. 10. Circuit with Circuit Breaker in the Electric Power Substation without Reclosing Capability, based on Bishop (1997).

5.1.1 The model

The chosen model was based in the work developed by Bishop (1997) whose circuit has multiple laterals with customer's numbers and load KVA values seen on the figure 10. To perform the analysis one needs some statistics, like: number of customers; placement of protective devices on the electric power utility; good possibilities to implement protective devices; distribution circuit response to the quality indices; and traditional values of repair and recover in accordance with Bishop's indices.

The initial circuit used to the analysis is presented by figure 10, where it was considered the values of Bishop (1997) to the indices in circuits of electric power distribution with similar features in North American solutions. The used general statistical parameters are presented in table 7. As a base case analysis, the system was modelled with no reclosing of substation device. This is intended only to yield values for relative comparison with other circuits, with protective devices like recloses and fuses placed on the circuit, achieving the comparison landscape with the SAIDI and SAIFI indices.

Faults per circuit mile per year	0.22
Percent of permanent faults	20%
Percent of temporary faults	80%
Manual restoration time	2.0 hours
Repair time for 30 lines	3.0 hours
Repair time for 10 lines	2.5 hours

Table 7. General statistical parameters used in the model.

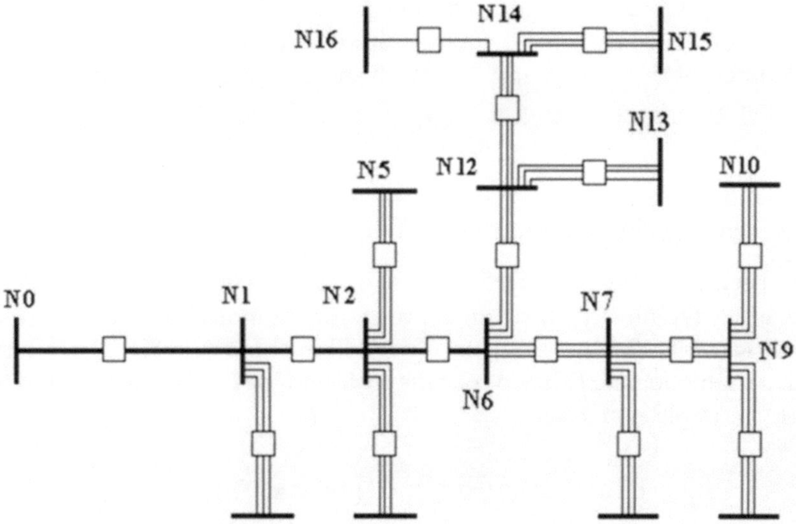

Fig. 11. Representation of the circuit of figure 10 with the nodes with all the possible locations for protective devices (adapted from Burian et al. 2010).

5.1.2 The methodology: Converting to a GA application

The first step is to provide formalism in such a way that the protective devices net could be represented by a set of genes in a chromosome Λ, and that the Bishop (1997) model could be expressed as a P-problem whose parameters are given by Λ.

The solution chosen was to code the circuit as a series of nodes, designed by N*i*, with *i* being an integer number, and to build a list of links between the nodes (see figure 11). The special node N0 is the main protective switch in the substation (which is present in all solutions). Each link between nodes can have a protective device, and its location is designed as $P_{i,j}$, with *i* and *j* being the two nodes that define the link. Special data structure is provided to the nodes to storage information about the number of phases, number of consumers, distance to neighbours nodes, etc.

The adopted solution considers *S* as a ordered list of tokens, and the position in the ordered list corresponds to a location as $P_{i,j}$. Then, for the circuit of figure 11, one has

$$\Lambda = \begin{Bmatrix} P_{0,1}, P_{1,2}, P_{1,3}, P_{2,4}, P_{2,5}, P_{2,6}, P_{6,7}, P_{6,12}, P_{7,8}, \\ P_{7,9}, P_{9,10}, P_{9,11}, P_{12,13}, P_{12,14}, P_{14,15}, P_{14,16} \end{Bmatrix}. \quad (31)$$

So, Λ is a finite set of tokens, and its number of elements is much smaller than the number of nodes squared[4], that assumes the role of parameter set in the P-problem. These tokens can represent a protective device to be placed in its respective circuit position. The possible devices are: main substation switch, only possible in location $P_{0,1}$ (S); fuse (F), automatic reclose switch (R) and nothing (no device).

[4] Of course! When representing an electric circuit one does not link one node to all the other nodes…

The kind of device defines the algorithm to be used to obtain the overall cost of protective devices, and the SAIDI and SAIFI indexes according to Bishop (1997). So, each set Λ_i represents a different circuit, and applying the Bishop's algorithms one obtains a result set

$$\Gamma_i(\Lambda_i) = \{\text{SAIDI}_i, \text{SAIFI}_i, c_{Si}, c_{Ri}, c_{fi}\}. \tag{32}$$

where c_S, c_R and c_f are the costs of the main switch reclose switch and fuses, which are expressed in monetary "units", being one unit the cost of the a monophasic fuse.

As the set Γ_i itself cannot express the degree of adaptation the individual Λ_i to the problem we want to solve, we must provide an expression to summarize Γ_i in a more convenient, single valued variable, like the *gof* value, described in subsection 3.1. The definition of this *gof* should have a monotonic behaviour as the costs and the SAIDI and SAIFI index increase. We adopted the simple expression

$$gof = \kappa_a(\text{SAIDI} + \text{SAIFI}) + \kappa_b\left(c_S + c_R + c_f\right). \tag{33}$$

where κ_a and κ_b are constant scale converters. Then, one can say that optimized circuit will be that one that offers the smaller *gof*. With this, our inverted NP-problem can be solved by looking for the individual Λ_i that presents the smaller *gof*. As all the parameters are limited range integer numbers (tokens), some special care must be taken in the GA routines that deal with new individuals and mutation. So, these routines where rebuild taking into account the discrete character of the chromosomes. The overall behaviour of the GA optimization code follows the algorithm proposed in figure 2.

5.1.3 Results and conclusion

The resulting optimized circuit is shown in figure 12, and its corresponding indexes are presented in table 8. The GA code performed the ranging of large number of solutions and configurations, within the universe of about 50 generations of configurations. This demonstrates the GA potential in this kind of analysis and application to discrete allocation equipment's. GA optimization techniques has been showed to be an effective technique to optimize the allocation of protective devices inside the electrical distribution systems.

Index	value
SAIDI	2.7694
SAIFI	1.04385
Cost S	60 units
Number S	1
Cost R	280 units
Number R	3
Cost F	25 units
Number F	9
Total Cost	365 units

Table 8. Indexes values for optimized circuit.

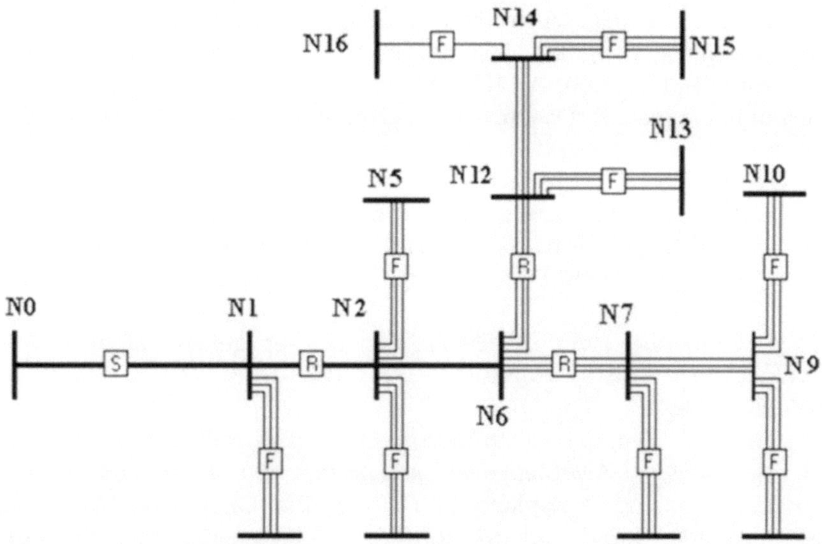

Fig. 12. Optimized circuit obtained with the GA method (adapted from Burian et al. 2010).

6. Acknowledgments

The author wants to thank UFABC/CECS - Engineering, Modeling and Social Sciences Center of Federal University do ABC; AEB – Brazilian Space Agency / UNIESPAÇO Program; FAPESP and CNPq.

7. References

André P., Ward-Thompson D., Barsony M., (1993), ApJ, 406, 122

Bentley, P.J., & Corne D.W. (2002) *Creative Evolutionary Systems*. Morgan-Kaufmann, San Francisco.

Bishop, M.T. (March 1997) *Establishing Realistic Reliability Goals*. The Tech Advantage 97 Conference & Electric Expo.

Burian, R.; Hetem, A., Caetano, C. A. C. *Automatic Allocation of Electric Power Distribution Protective Devices* (2010) Opatija. 33rd International Convention on Information and Communication Technology, Electronics and Microelectronics. Opatija / Abbazia : IEEE, 2010. v. 1. p. 22-22.

Caetano, C.A.C., & Hetem, A. (2011) *Artificial Intelligence Parametrization of Harrington Pumps*, to be submitted to International Journal of Heat and Fluid (in preparation).

Cook, Stephen (1971) *The complexity of theorem proving procedures*. Proceedings of the Third Annual ACM Symposium on Theory of Computing. pp. 151–158.Dembczyński, J., Ertmer, W., Johann, U., Penselin, S., & Stinner, P. 1979, Z. Phys. A, 291, 207

Dixon, S. L.,Hall,C. A. (2010) *Fluid mechanics and thermodynamics of turbomachinery* 6th ed. ISBN 978-1-85617-793-1.

Dominik C., Dullemond C. P., Waters L. B. F. M., Walch S. (2003) A&A, 398, 607

Dullemond C. P., Dominik C., Natta A. (2001) ApJ, 560, 957

Garey, M. R., & Johnson, D. S. (1979) *Computers and Intractability: A Guide to the Theory of NP-completeness*. W. H. Freeman.

Goldberg D. E. (1989) *Genetic Algorithms in Search, Optimization and Machine Learning*. Addison-Wesley Longman, Boston, MA

Gray, R.O., & Corbally, C.J. (1994) AJ, 107, 742.

Gregorio-Hetem J., Lépine J. R. D., Quast G. R., Torres C. A. O., de la Reza R. (1992) AJ, 103, 549

Grevesse, N. & Sauval, A.J. (1998) Space Science Reviews 85, 161

Griffinand, M.D., & French, J.R. (1991) *Space Vehicle Design*, AIAA.

Harrington, S. (2003) *Pistonless Dual Chamber Rocket Fuel Pump*, 39th AIAA/ASME/SAE/ASEE Hoint Propulsion Conference and Exhibit. AIAA 2003-4479.

Hetem, A., & Gregorio-Hetem, J. (2007) The use of genetic algorithms to model protoplanetary discs, MNRAS 382, 1707–1718 (2007) doi:10.1111/j.1365-2966.2007.12442.x

Hetem Jr, A. ; Gregorio-Hetem, J. (2009) *The use of Genetic Algorithms and Spectral Synthesis in the Calculantion of Abundances and Metallicities of T Tauri stars*. In: Young stars, Brown Dwarfs and Protoplanetary Disks Special Session 7 - IAU XXVII General Assembly, 2009, Rio de Janeiro - RJ. IAU XXVII General Assembly Abstract Book. Paris - France : International Astronomical Union, 2009. v. 1. p. 481-481.

Huzel, D.K. & Huang, D.H. (1967) *Design of Liquid Propellant Rocket Engines*, Rocketdyne Division, North American Aviation, Inc.

Koza J. R. (1994) *Genetic Programming II: Automatic Discovery of Reusable Programs*. MIT Press.

Kurucz, R. L. (1993) CD-ROM 13, *Atlas9 Stellar Atmosphere Programs and 2 km/s Grid* (Cambridge: Smithsonian Astrophys. Obs.)

Lada C. J., Wilking B. A. (1984) ApJ, 287, 610

Logan, E., Jr., & Roy, R, (eds) (2003) H*andbook of Turbomachinery (Second Edition Revised and Expanded)*, Marcel Dekker, Inc.

Luc, P. & Gerstenkorn, S. (1972) AA, 18, 209

Neufeld, M. J. (1995) *The Rocket and the Reich*. The Smithsonian Institution. pp. 80–1, 156, 172. ISBN 0-674-77650-X.

Papadimitriou, C. H. (1995) *Computational Complexity*. Addison-Wesley, Reading Massachusetts.

Press W. H., Teukolsky S. A., Vetterling W. T., Flannery B. P. (1995) *Numerical Recipes in C*, 2nd edn. Cambridge Univ. Press, New York

Rojas, G., Gregorio-Hetem, J., Hetem, A. (2008) MNRAS, 387, Issue 3, pp. 1335-1343.

Sutton, G.P., & Biblarz, O. (2001) *Rocket Propulsion Elements* 7th editon, JOHN WILEY & SONS, INC.

Sutton, G.P. (1986) *Rocket Propulsion Elements an Introduction to Engineering of Rockets*, John Wiley & Sons.

Torres C. A. O. (1998) *Publicação Especial do Observatório Nacional*, No. 10/99. Observatório Nacional, Rio de Janeiro

Torres C. A. O., Quast G. R., de la Reza R., Gregorio-Hetem J., Lépine J. R. D. (1995) AJ, 109, 2146

van den Ancker M. E., Meeus G., Cami J., Waters L. B. F. M.,Waelkens C. (2001) A&A, 369, 217

Wilking B. A., Lada C. J., Young E. T. (1989) ApJ, 340, 823

Young, W. C. (1989) *Roark's formulas for stress and strain*, McGraw-Hill

10

Fusion of Visual and Thermal Images Using Genetic Algorithms

Sertan Erkanli[1,2], Jiang Li[2] and Ender Oguslu[1,2]
[1]*Turkish Air Force Academy,*
[2]*Old Dominion University,*
[1]*Turkey*
[2]*USA*

1. Introduction

Biometric technologies such as fingerprint, hand geometry, face and iris recognition are widely used to identify a person's identity. The face recognition system is currently one of the most important biometric technologies, which identifies a person by comparing individually acquired face images with a set of pre-stored face templates in a database.

Though the human perception system can identify faces relatively easily, face reorganization using computer techniques is challenging and remains an active research field. Illumination and pose variations are currently the two obstacles limiting performances of face recognition systems. Various techniques have been proposed to overcome those limitations in recent years. For instance, a three dimensional face recognition system has been investigated to solve the illumination and pose variations simultaneously [Bowyer et al., 2004; S. Mdhani et al., 2006]. The illumination variation problem can also be mitigated by additional sources such as infrared (IR) images [D. A. Socolinsky & A. Selinger, 2002].

Thermal face recognition systems have received little attention in comparison with recognition in visible spectra partially due to the high cost associated with IR cameras. Recent technological advances of IR cameras make it practical for face recognition. While thermal face recognition systems are advantageous for detecting disguised faces or when there is no control over illumination, it is challenging to recognize faces in IR images because 1) it is difficult to segment faces from background in low resolution IR images and 2) intensity values in IR images are not consistent due to the fact that different body temperatures result in different intensity values in IR images.

The overall goal of this research is to develop computational methods for obtaining efficiently improved images. The research objective will be accomplished by integrating enhanced visual images with IR Images through the following steps: 1) Enhance optical images, 2) Register the enhanced optical images with IR images, and 3) Fuse the optical and IR images with the help of Genetic Algorithm.

Section 2 surveys related work for IR imaging, image enhancement, image registration and image fusion. Section 3 discusses the proposed nonlinear image enhancement methods.

Section 4 presents the proposed image fusion algorithm. Section 5 reports the experimental results of the proposed algorithm. Section 6 concludes this research.

2. Literature survey

In this section, we will present related work in IR Image technology, nonlinear image enhancement algorithms, image registration and image fusion.

2.1 IR tecnology

One type of electromagnetic radiation that has received a lot of attention recently is Infrared (IR) radiation. IR refers to the region beyond the red end of the visible color spectrum, a region located between the visible and the microwave regions of the electromagnetic spectrum.

Today, infrared technology has many exciting and useful applications. In the field of infrared astronomy, new and fascinating discoveries are being made about the Universe and medical imaging as a diagnostic tool.

Humans, at normal body temperature, radiate most strongly in the infrared, at a wavelength of about 10 microns. The area of the skin that is directly above a blood vessel is, on average, 0.1 degrees Celsius warmer than the adjacent skin. Moreover, the temperature variation for a typical human face is in the range of about 8 degrees Celsius [F. Prokoski, 2000].

In fact, variations among images from the same face due to changes in illumination, viewing direction, facial expressions, and pose are typically larger than variations introduced when different faces are considered. Thermal IR imagery is invariant to variations introduced by illumination facial expressions since it captures the anatomical information. However, thermal imaging has limitations in identifying a person wearing glasses because glass is a material of low emissivity, or when the thermal characteristics of a face have changed due to increased body temperature (e.g., physical exercise) [G. S. Kong et al., 2005]. Combining the IR and visual techniques will benefit face detection and recognition.

2.2 Nonlinear image enhancement techniques

2.2.1 The nonlinear log transform

The non-linear log transform converts an original image g into an adjusted image g' by applying the log function to each pixel $g[m, n]$ in the image,

$$g'[m, n] = k\log(g[m, n]) \tag{1}$$

where $k=L/log(L)$ is a scaling factor that preserve the dynamic range and L is intensity. The log transformis typically applied either to dark images where the overall contrast is low, or to images that contain specular reflections or glints. In the former case, the brightening of the dark pixels leads to an overall increase in brightness. In the latter case, the glints are suppressed thus increasing the effective dynamic range of the image.

The log function as defined in equation 1 is not parameterized, i.e. it is a single input/output transfer function. A modified parameterized function was proposed by Schreiber in [W. F. Schreiber, 1978] as: image,

$$g'(l) = (L-1)\left[\frac{\log(1+\alpha g(l)) - \log(\alpha+1)}{\log(1+\alpha L) - \log(\alpha+1)}\right] + 1 \tag{2}$$

where α parameterizes the non-linear transfer function.

2.3 Registration

Image registration is a basic task in image processing to align two or more images, usually refereed as a reference, and a sensed image [R. C. Gonzalez et al., 2004]. Registration is typically a required process in remote sensing [L. M. G. Fonseca & B. S. Manjunath, 1996], medicine and computer vision. Registration can be classified into four main categories according to the manner how the image is obtained [B. Zitova & J. Flusser, 2003]:

- Different viewpoints : Images of the same scene taken from different viewpoints.
- Different times : Images of the same scene taken at different times.
- Different sensors : Images of the same scene taken by different sensors.
- Scene to model registration : Images of a scene taken by sensors and images of the same scene but from a model (digital elevation model).

It is impossible to implement a comprehensive method useable to all registration tasks and there are many different registration algorithms. The focus is on the feature based registration techniques in this research and they usually consist of the following three steps [B. Zitova & J. Flusser, 2003].

- Feature detection: The step tries to locate a set of control points such as edges, line intersections and corners in the image. They could be manually or automatically detected.
- Feature matching: The second step is to establish the correspondence between the features detected in the sensed image and those detected in the reference image.
- Transform model estimation, Image resampling and Geometric transformation: The sensed image is transformed and resampled to match the reference image by proper interpolation techniques [B. Zitova & J. Flusser, 2003].

Each registration step has its specific problems. In the first step, features that can be used for registration must spread over the images and be easily detectable. The determined feature sets in the reference and sensed images must have enough common elements, even though the both images do not cover exactly the same scene. Ideally, the algorithm should be able to detect the same features [B. Zitova & J. Flusser, 2003].

In the second step, known as feature matching, physically corresponded features can be dissimilar because of the different imaging conditions and/or the different spectral sensitivities of the sensors. The choice of the feature description and measuring of similarity has to take into account of these factors. The feature descriptors should be efficient and invariant to the assumed degradations. The matching algorithm should be robust and efficient. Single features without corresponding counterparts in the other image should not affect its performance [B. Zitova & J. Flusser, 2003].

In the last step, the selection of an appropriate resampling technique is restricted by the trade-off between the interpolation accuracy and the computational complexity. In the literature, there are popular techniques such as the nearest-neighbor and bilinear interpolation [B. Zitova & J. Flusser, 2003].

2.4 Genetic Algorithm

2.4.1 Introduction

Optimization can be distinguished by either discrete or continuous variables. Discrete variables have only a finite number of possible values, whereas continuous variables have an infinite number of possible ones. Discrete variable optimization is also known as combinatorial optimization, because the optimum solution consists of a certain combination of variables from the finite pool of all possible variables. However, when trying to find the minimum value of $f(x)$ on a number line, it is more appropriate to view the problem as continuous [J. H. Holland, 1975; S. K. Mitra et al., 1998].

Genetic algorithms manipulate a population of potential solutions for the problem to be solved. Usually, each solution is coded as a binary string, equivalent to the genetic material of individuals in nature. Each solution is associated with a *fitness value* that reflects how good it is, compared with other solutions in the population. The higher the fitness value of an individual, the higher its chances of survival and reproduction in the subsequent generation. Recombination of genetic material in genetic algorithms is simulated through a crossover mechanism that exchanges portions between strings.

Another operation, called mutation, causes sporadic and random alteration of the bits in strings. Mutation has a direct analogy in nature and plays the role of regenerating lost genetic material [M. Srinivas & L. M. Patnaik, 1994]. GAs have found applications in many fields including image processing [J. Zhang , 2008; L. Yu et al., 2008].

2.4.2 Continuous Genetic Algorithm (CGA)

GAs typically represent solution as binary strings. For many applications, it is more convenient to denote solutions as real numbers known as continuous Genetic algorithms (CGA). CGAs have the advantage of requiring less storage and are faster than the binary counterparts. Figure 1 shows the flowchart of simple CGA [Randy L. Haupt & Sue Ellen Haupt, 2004].

2.4.2.1 Components of a Continuous Genetic Algorithm

The various elements in the flowchart are described below [D.Patnaik, 2006].

2.4.2.1.1 Cost function

The goal of GAs is to solve an optimization problem defined as a cost function with a set of parameters involved. In CCA, the parameters are organized as a vector known as a chromosome. If the chromosome has N_{var} variables (an N-dimensional optimization problem) given by $p_1, p_2, p_3, ..., p_{N_{var}}$, then the chromosome is written as an array with 1x N_{var} elements as [Randy L. Haupt & Sue Ellen Haupt, 2004]:

$$\text{chromosome} = [p_1, p_2, p_3, ..., p_{N_{var}}] \quad (3)$$

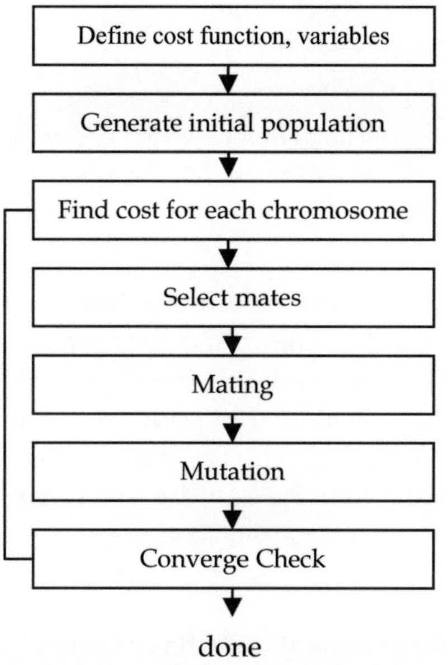

Fig. 1. Flowchart of CGA

In this case, the variable values are represented as floating-point numbers. Each chromosome has a cost found by evaluating the cost function f at the variables $p_1, p_2, p_3, \ldots, p_{N_{var}}$,

$$\text{cost} = f(\text{chromosome}) = f(p_1, p_2, p_3, \ldots, p_{N_{var}}) \quad (4)$$

Equations (3) and (4) along with applicable constraints constitute the problem to be solved. Since the GA is a search technique, it must be limited to exploring a reasonable region of variable space. Sometimes this is done by imposing a constraint on the problem. If one does not know the initial search region, there must be enough diversity in the initial population to explore a reasonably sized variable space before focusing on the most promising regions.

2.4.2.1.2 Initial population

To begin the CGA process, an initial population of N_{pop} must be defined, a matrix represents the population, with each row being a 1x N_{var} chromosome of continuous values [D.Patnaik, 2006]. Given an initial population of N_{pop} chromosomes, the full matrix of N_{pop} x N_{var} random values is generated by:

$$pop = rand(N_{pop}, N_{var}) \quad (5)$$

All variables are normalized to have values between 0 and 1. If the range of values is between p_{lo} and p_{hi}, then the normalized values are given by:

$$p = (p_{hi} - p_{lo})p_{norm} + p_{lo} \quad (6)$$

where

p_{lo} = highest number in the variable range
p_{hi} = lowest number in the variable range
p_{norm} = normalized value of variable

This society of chromosomes is not a democracy: the individual chromosomes are not all created equal. Each one's worth is assessed by the cost function. So at this point, the chromosomes are passed to the cost function for evaluation [Randy L. Haupt & Sue Ellen Haupt, 2004].

Now is the time to decide which chromosomes in the initial population are good enough to survive and possibly reproduce offspring in the next generation. As done for the binary version of the algorithm, the N_{pop} costs and associated chromosomes are ranked from lowest cost to highest cost. This process of natural selection occurs in each iteration to allow the population of chromosomes to evolve. Of the N_{pop} chromosomes in a given generation, only the top N_{keep} are kept for mating and the rest are discarded to make room for the new offspring [Randy L. Haupt & Sue Ellen Haupt, 2004].

2.4.2.1.3 Pairing

A set of eligible chromosomes is randomly selected as parents to generate next generation. Each pair produces two offspring that contain traits from each parent. The more similar the two parents, the more likely are the offspring to carry the traits of the parents.

2.4.2.1.4 Mating

As for the binary algorithm, two parents are chosen to produce offsprings. Many different approaches have been tried for crossing over in continuous GAs. The simplest method is to mark a crossover points first, then parents exchange their elements between the marked crossover points in the chromosomes. Consider two parents:

$$\begin{aligned} parent_1 &= [p_{m1}, \ldots\ldots, p_{mN_{var}}] \\ parent_2 &= [p_{d1}, \ldots\ldots, p_{dN_{var}}] \end{aligned} \tag{7}$$

two offspring's might be produced as:

$$\begin{aligned} offspring_1 &= [p_{m1}, p_{m2}, p_{d3}, p_{d4}, p_{m5}, p_{m6}, \ldots\ldots, P_{mN_{var}}] \\ offspring_2 &= [p_{d1}, p_{d2}, p_{m3}, p_{m4}, p_{d5}, p_{d6}, \ldots\ldots, P_{dN_{var}}] \end{aligned} \tag{8}$$

2.4.2.1.5 Natural selection

The extreme case is selecting N_{var} points and randomly choosing which of the two parents will contribute its variable at each position. Thus one goes down the line of the chromosomes and, at each variable, randomly chooses whether or not to swap information between the two parents. This method is called uniform crossover [Randy L. Haupt & Sue Ellen Haupt, 2004]:

$$\begin{aligned} offspring_1 &= [p_{m1}, p_{d2}, p_{d3}, p_{d4}, p_{d5}, p_{m6}, \ldots\ldots, P_{dN_{var}}] \\ offspring_2 &= [p_{d1}, p_{m2}, p_{m3}, p_{m4}, p_{m5}, p_{d6}, \ldots\ldots, P_{mN_{var}}] \end{aligned} \tag{9}$$

The problem with these point crossover methods is that no new information is introduced: each continuous value that was randomly initiated in the initial population is propagated to the next generation, only in different combinations. Although this strategy worked fine for binary representations, in case of continuous variables, we are merely interchanging two data points. These approaches totally rely on mutation to introduce new genetic material. The blending methods remedy this problem by finding ways to combine variable values from the two parents into new variable values in the offspring [Randy L. Haupt & Sue Ellen Haupt, 2004]. A single offspring variable value, *pnew*, comes from a combination of the two corresponding offspring variable values:

$$pnew = \beta p_{mn} + (1-\beta)p_{dn} \tag{10}$$

where

β = random number in the interval [0, 1]
p_{mn} = the *n*th variable in the mother chromosome
p_{dn} = the *n*th variable in the father chromosome

The same variable of the second offspring is merely the complement of the first (i.e., replacing β by 1 - β). If β = 1, then p_{mn} propagates in its entirety and p_{dn} dies. In contrast, if β = 0, then p_{dn} propagates in its entirety and p_{mn} dies. When β = 0.5, the result is an average of the variables of the two parents. This method is demonstrated to work well on several interesting problems in [Randy L. Haupt & Sue Ellen Haupt, 2004].

Choosing which variables to blend is the next issue to be solved. Sometimes, this linear combination process is done for all variables to the right or to the left of some crossover point. Any number of points can be chosen to blend, up to N_{var} values where all variables are linear combinations of those of the two parents. The variables can be blended by using the same β for each variable or by choosing different β's for each variable. These blending methods effectively combine the information from the two parents and choose values of the variables between the values bracketed by the parents; however, they do not allow introduction of values beyond the extremes already represented in the population. The simplest way is the linear crossover [Randy L. Haupt & Sue Ellen Haupt, 2004], where three offspring are generated from two parents by

$$\begin{aligned} pnew_1 &= 0.5p_{mn} + 0.5p_{dn} \\ pnew_2 &= 1.5p_{mn} - 0.5p_{dn} \\ pnew_3 &= -0.5p_{mn} + 1.5p_{dn} \end{aligned} \tag{11}$$

Any variable outside the bounds is discarded. Then the best two offspring are chosen to propagate. Of course, the factor 0.5 is not the only one that can be used in such a method. Heuristic crossover [Randy L. Haupt & Sue Ellen Haupt, 2004] is a variation where some random number, β, is chosen on the interval [0, 1] and the variables of the offspring are formed by:

$$pnew = \beta(p_{mn} - p_{dn}) + p_{mn} \tag{12}$$

Variations on this theme include choosing any number of variables to modify and generate different β for each variable. This method also allows generations of offspring outside the value ranges of the two parent variables. If this happens, the offspring is discarded and the algorithm tries to use another *b*. The blend crossover (BLX-α) method [Randy L. Haupt & Sue Ellen Haupt, 2004] begins by choosing some parameters that determine the distance outside the bounds of the two parent variables that the offspring variable may lay. This method allows new values outside of the range of the parents without letting the algorithm stray too far.

The algorithm is a combination of an extrapolation method with a crossover method. The goal was to find a way to closely mimic the advantages of the binary GA mating scheme. It begins by randomly selecting a variable in the first pair of parents to be the crossover point:

$$\alpha = roundup\{random * N_{\text{var}}\} \tag{13}$$

Let

$$\begin{aligned} parent_1 &= [p_{m1}, \ldots, p_{m\alpha}, \ldots, p_{mN_{\text{var}}}] \\ parent_2 &= [p_{d1}, \ldots, p_{d\alpha}, \ldots, p_{dN_{\text{var}}}] \end{aligned} \tag{14}$$

where the *m* and *d* subscripts discriminate between the *mom* and the *dad* parent. Then the selected variables are combined to form new variables that will appear in the children:

$$\begin{aligned} pnew_1 &= p_{m\alpha} - \beta[P_{m\alpha} - P_{d\alpha}] \\ pnew_2 &= p_{d\alpha} + \beta[P_{m\alpha} - P_{d\alpha}] \end{aligned} \tag{15}$$

where β is a random value between 0 and 1. The final step is to complete the crossover with the rest of chromosome:

$$\begin{aligned} offspring_1 &= [p_{m1}, p_{m2}, .p_{new1} \ldots, P_{dN_{\text{var}}}] \\ offspring_2 &= [p_{d1}, p_{d2}, .p_{new2} \ldots, P_{mN_{\text{var}}}] \end{aligned} \tag{16}$$

where β is also a random value between 0 and 1. The final is to complete the crossover with the rest of the chromosome as before:

If the first variable of the chromosomes is selected, then only the variables to the right of the selected variable are swapped. If the last variable of the chromosomes is selected, then only the variables to the left of the selected variable are swapped. This method does not allow offspring variables outside the bounds set by the parent unless $\beta > 1$.

2.4.2.1.6 Mutation

If care is not taken, the GA can converge too quickly into one region on the cost surface. If this area is in the region of the global minimum, there is no problem. However, some functions have many local minima. To avoid overly fast convergence, other areas on the cost surface must be explored by randomly introducing changes, or mutations, in some of the variables. Random numbers are used to select the row and columns of the variables that are to be mutated [Randy L. Haupt & Sue Ellen Haupt, 2004].

2.4.2.1.7 Next generation

After all these steps, the chromosomes in the starting population are ranked and the bottom ranked chromosomes are replaced by offspring from the top ranked parents to produce the next generation. Some random variables are selected for mutation from the bottom ranked chromosomes. The chromosomes are then ranked from lowest cost to highest cost. The process is iterated until a global solution is achieved.

2.5 Image fusion

In last decades, the rapid developments of image sensing technologies make multisensory systems popular in many applications. Researchers have begun to work on the fields of these systems such as medical imaging, remote sensing and the military applications [D.Patnaik, 2006]. The outcome of using these techniques is a great increase of the amount of diversity data available. Multi-sensor image data often present complementary information about the region surveyed so that image fusion provides an effective method to enable comparison and analysis of such data [H. Wang, 2004]. Image fusion is defined as the process of combining information in two or more images of a scene to enhance viewing or understanding of the scene. The fusion process must preserve all relevant information in the fused image [A. Mumtaz & A. Majid, 2008; S. Erkanli & Zia-Ur Rahman, 2010].

Image fusion can be done at pixel, feature and decision levels. Out of these, the pixel level fusion method is the simplest technique, where average/weighted averages of individual pixel intensities are taken to construct a fused image [K. Kannan & S. Perumal, 2007]. Despite their simplicity, these methods are not used nowadays because of some serious disadvantages they possess. For instance, the contrast of the fused information is reduced and also redundant information is introduced in the fused image, which may mask the useful information. These disadvantages are overcomed by feature level and decision level fusion methods. Feature and decision level fusion methods are based on human vision system. Decision level fusion combines the results from multiple algorithms to yield a final fused image. Several pyramid transform methods for feature level fusion have been suggested [A. Wang et al., 2006]. Recently, developed methods based on the wavelet transform become popular [A. Wang et al., 2006]. In the method source images are decomposed into subimages of different resolutions and in each subimage different features become prominent. To fuse the original source images, the corresponding subimages of different source images are combined based some criteria to form composite subimages. Inverse pyramid transform of composite transform gives the final fused image.

3. Enhancing poor visibility images

3.1 Introduction

The human visual system (HVS) allows individuals to assimilate information from their environment [S. Erkanli & Zia-Ur Rahman, 2010b; H. Kolb, 2003]. The HVS perceives colors and detail across a wide range of photometric intensity levels much better than electronic cameras. The perceived color of an object, additionally, is almost independent of the type of illumination, i.e., the HVS is color constant. Electronic cameras suffer, by comparison, from limited dynamic range and the lack of color constancy and current imaging and display devices such as CRT monitors and printers have limited dynamic range of about two orders of magnitude, while the best photographic prints can provide contrast up to $10^3:1$. However; real world scenes can have a dynamic range of six orders of magnitude [S. Erkanli & Zia-Ur Rahman, 2010b; L. Tao et al., 2005]. This can result in overexposure that causes saturation in high contrast images, or underexposure in dark images [Z. Rahman, 1996]. The idea behind enhancement techniques are to bring out details in images that are otherwise too dim to be perceived either due to insufficient brightness or insufficient contrast [Z. Rahman, 1997]. A large number of image enhancement methods have been developed, like log transformations, power law transformations, piecewise-linear transformations and histogram equalization. However these enhancement techniques are based on global processing which results in a single mapping between the input and the output intensity space. These techniques are thus not sufficiently powerful to handle images that have both very bright and very dark regions. Other image enhancement techniques are local in nature, i.e., the output value depends not only on the input pixel value but also on pixel values in the neighborhood of the pixel. These techniques are able to improve local contrast under various illumination conditions.

Single-Scale Retinex (SSR), is a modification of the Retinex algorithm introduced by Edwin Land [G. D. Hines et al., 2004; E. Land, 1986]. It provides dynamic range compression (DRC), color constancy, and tonal rendition. SSR gives good results for DRC or tonal rendition but does not provide both simultaneously. Therefore, the Multi-Scale Retinex (MSR) was developed by Rahman et al. The MSR combines several SSR outputs with different scale constants to produce a single output image, which has good DRC, color constancy and good tonal rendition. The outputs of MSR display most of the detail in the dark pixels but at the cost of enhancing the noise in these pixels and the tonal rendition is poor in large regions of slowly changing intensity. As a result, Multi-Scale Retinex with Color Restoration (MSRCR) was developed by Jobson et al., for synthesizing local contrast improvement, color constancy and lightness/color rendition. Other non-linear enhancement models include the Illuminance Reflectance Model for Enhancement (IRME) proposed by Tao et al. [L. Tao et al., 2005], and the Adaptive and Integrated Neighborhood-Dependent Approach for Nonlinear Enhancement (AINDANE) described by Tao [L.Tao, 2005]. Both use a nonlinear function for luminance enhancement and tune the intensity of each pixel based on its relative magnitude with respect to the neighboring pixels.

In this section, a new image enhancement approach is described: Enhancement Technique for Nonuniform and Uniform-Dark Images (ETNUD). The details of the new algorithm are given in Section 3.2, respectively. Sections 3.3 describe experimental results and compare our results with other techniques for image enhancement. Finally in Section 3.4, conclusions are presented.

3.2 Enhancement Technique for Nonuniform and Uniform-Dark Images (ETNUD)

The major innovation in ETNUD is in the selection of the transformation parameters for DRC, and the surround scale and color restoration parameters. The following sections describe the selection mechanisms.

3.2.1 Selection of transformation parameters for DRC

The intensity I of the color image I_c can be determined by:

$$I(m,n) = 0.2989r(m,n) + 0.587g(m,n) + 0.114b(m,n) \quad (17)$$

where *r, g, b* are the red, green, and blue components of I_c respectively, and *m* and *n* are the row and column pixel locations respectively. Assuming I to be 8-bits per pixel, I_n is the normalized version of I, such that:

$$I_n(m,n) = I(m,n) / 255 \quad (18)$$

Using linear input-output intensity relationships typically does not produce a good visual representation compared with direct viewing of the scene. Therefore, nonlinear transformation for DRC is used, which is based on some information extracted from the image histogram. To do this, the histogram of the intensity images is subdivided into four ranges:

r_1 =0–63, r_2 = 64–127, r_3 = 128–191 and r_4 = 192–255. I_n is mapped to I_n^{drc} using the following:

$$I_n^{drc} = \begin{cases} (I_n)^x + \alpha & 0 < x < 1 \\ (0.5 + (0.5I_n)^x) + \alpha & x \geq 1 \end{cases} \quad (19)$$

The first mapping pulls out the details in the dark regions, and the second suppresses the bright overshoots. The value of *x* is given by

$$x = \begin{cases} 0.2, & if \ (f(r_1 + r_2) \geq f(r_3 + r_4)) \ \Lambda \ (f(r_1) \geq f(r_2)) \\ 0.5, & if \ (f(r_1 + r_2) \geq f(r_3 + r_4)) \ \Lambda \ (f(r_1) < f(r_2)) \\ 3.0, & if \ (f(r_1 + r_2) < f(r_3 + r_4)) \ \Lambda \ (f(r_3) \geq f(r_4)) \\ 5.0, & if \ (f(r_1 + r_2) < f(r_3 + r_4)) \ \Lambda \ (f(r_3) < f(r_4)) \end{cases} \quad (20)$$

where $f(a)$ refers to number of pixels between the range *(a)*, $f(a_1 + a_2) = f(a_1) + f(a_2)$, and Λ is the logical AND operator. α is the offset parameter, helping to adjust the brightness of image. The determination of the *x* values and their association with the range-relationships as given in Equation 20 was done experimentally using a large number of non-uniform and uniform dark images and *x* value can be also determined manually. The DRC mapping of the intensity image performs a visually dramatic transformation. However, it tends to have poor contrast, so a local, pixel dependent contrast enhancement method is used to improve the contrast.

3.2.2 Selection of surround parameter and color restoration

Many local enhancement methods rely on center/surround ratios [L. Tao, 2005]. Hurlbert [A. C. Hulbert, 1989] investigated the Gaussian as the optimal surround function. Other surround functions proposed by [E. Land, 1986] were compared with the performance of the Gaussian proposed by [D. J. Jobson, et al., 1997]. Both investigations determined that the Gaussian form produced good dynamic range compression over a range of space constants. Therefore, the luminance information of surrounding pixels is obtained by using 2D discrete spatial convolution with a Gaussian kernel, *G(m, n)* defined as:

$$G(m,n) = K\exp\left(-\frac{m^2+n^2}{\sigma_s^2}\right) \tag{21}$$

where σ_s is the surround space constant equal to the standard deviation of *G(m, n)*, and *K* is determined under the constraint that $\sum_{m,n} G(m,n) = 1$.

The center-surround contrast enhancement is defined as:

$$I_{enh}(m,n) = 255(I_n^{drc}(m,n))^{E(m,n)} \tag{22}$$

where, *E(m, n)* is given by:

$$E(m,n) = \left[\frac{I_{filt}(m,n)}{I(m,n)}\right]^S \tag{23}$$

where
$$I_{filt}(m,n) = I(m,n) * G(m,n) \tag{24}$$

S is an adaptive contrast enhancement parameter related to the global standard deviation of the input intensity image, *I(m, n),* and '*' is the convolution operator, *I(m, n)* is defined by:

$$S = \begin{cases} 3 & for \quad \sigma \le 7 \\ 1.5 & for \quad 7 < \sigma \le 20 \\ 1 & for \quad \sigma \ge 20 \end{cases} \tag{25}$$

σ is the contrast—standard deviation—of the original intensity image. If σ < 7, the image has poor contrast and the contrast of the image will be increased. If $\sigma \ge 20$, the image has sufficient contrast and the contrast will not be changed. Finally, the enhanced image can be obtained by linear color restoration based on chromatic information contained in the original image as:

$$S_j(x,y) = I_{enh}(x,y)\frac{I_j(x,y)}{I(x,y)}\lambda_j \tag{26}$$

where $j \in \{r,g,b\}$ represents the RGB spectral band and λ_j is a parameter which adjusts the color hue.

3.2.3 Evaluation citeria

In this work, following evaluation criteria was used.

3.2.3.1 A new metric

There are some metrics such as brightness and contrast to characterize an image. Another such metric is sharpness. Sharpness is directly proportional to the high-frequency content of an image. So the new metric is defined as [Z. Rahman, 2009]:

$$S = \sqrt{\|h \otimes I\|^2} = \sqrt{\sum_{v_1=0}^{M_1-1} \sum_{v_2=0}^{M_2-1} \left| \hat{h}[v_1, v_2] \hat{I}[v_1, v_2] \right|} \tag{27}$$

where h is a high-pass filter, periodic with period $M_1 x M_2$ and $\hat{h}$ is its direct Discrete Fourier Transform (DFT). I is also DFT of Image I. The role of $\hat{h}$ (or h) is to weight the energy at the high frequencies relative to the low frequencies, thereby emphasizing the contribution of the high frequencies to S. The larger the value of S, the greater the sharpness of I and conversely.

Equation 27 defines how the sharpness should be computed and defined as:

$$\hat{h}[v_1, v_2] = 1 - \exp\left(-\frac{v_1^2 + v_2^2}{\sigma^2} \right) \tag{28}$$

where σ is the parameter at which the attenuation coefficient $= 1.0 - e^{-1} \approx 2/3$. A smaller value of σ implies that fewer frequencies are attenuated and vice versa. For this research σ =0.15.

3.2.3.2 Image qality asessment

The overall quality of images can be measured by using the brightness μ, contrast σ and sharpness S, where brightness and contrast are assumed to be the mean and the standard deviation. However, instead of using global statistics, it is used regional statistics. In order to do this [Z. Rahman, 2009]:

1. Divide the $M_1 x M_2$ image I into $(M_1/10)x(M_2/10)$ non-overlapping blocks, I_i, i=1,…,100, such that $I \approx \cup_{i=1}^{N} I_i$, (Total Number of Regions are 100).
2. For each block compute the measures, μ, σ and S,
3. Classify the block as either GOOD or POOR based on the computed measure (will be discussed with the following).
4. Classify the image as a whole as GOOD or POOR based upon the classification of regions (will be discussed with the following).

The following criteria are used for brightness, contrast and sharpness [Z. Rahman, 2009]:

1. Let μ_n be normalized brightness parameter, such that:

$$\mu_n = \begin{cases} \mu/255 & \mu < 154 \\ 1 - \mu/255 & otherwise \end{cases} \tag{29}$$

A region is considered to have sufficient brightness when $0.4 \le \mu_n \le 0.6$.

2. Let σ_n be normalized contrast parameter, such that:

$$\sigma_n = \begin{cases} \sigma / 128 & \mu \le 64 \\ 1 - \sigma / 128 & \textit{otherwise} \end{cases} \tag{30}$$

A region is considered to have sufficient contrast when $0.25 \le \sigma_n \le 0.5$. When $\sigma_n < 0.25$, the region has poor contrast, and when $\sigma_n > 0.5$, the region has too much contrast.

3. Let S_n be normalized sharpness parameter, such that $S_n = min(2.0, S/100)$. When $S_n > 0.8$, the region has sufficient sharpness. Image Quality is evaluated using by:

$$Q = 0.5\mu_n + \sigma_n + 0.1S_n \tag{31}$$

where $0 < Q < 1.0$ is the quality factor. A region is classified as good when $Q > 0.55$, and poor when $\sigma_n \le 0.5$. An image is classified as GOOD when the total number of regions classified as GOOD, $N_G > 0.6N$.

3.3 Experimental result

The image samples for ETNUD were selected to be as diverse as possible so that the result would be as general as possible. MATLAB was used for AINDANE and IRME algorithms and their codes were developed by the author and research team. MSRCR enhancement was done with commercial software, Photo Flair. From visual experience, the following statements are made about the proposed algorithm:

1. In the Luminance enhancement part it has been shown that ETNUD works well for darker images and the technique adjusts itself to the image (Figure 2).
2. In the contrast enhancement part it is clear that unseen or barely seen features of low contrast images are made visible.
3. In Figure 2 Gamma Correction with γ = 1.4 does not provide good visual enhancement. IRME and MSRCR bring out the details in the dark but have some enhancement of noise in the dark regions, which can be considered objectionable. AINDANE does not bring out the finer details of the image. The ETNUD algorithm gives good result and outperforms the other algorithms if the results are compared (in Table 1) due to the Evaluation Criteria. The ETNUD provides better visibility enhancement the best sharpness can be adjusted by the α parameter in Equation 19.

Figure 2	Original Image	Gamma	Irme	Aindane	Msr	Etnud
Number of Good Regions	32	52	95	90	90	99
Number of Poor Regions	68	48	5	10	10	1

Table 1. The Results of Evaluation Criteria for Figure 2.

3.4 Conclusion

The ETNUD image enhancement algorithms provide high color accuracy and better balance between the luminance and contrast in images.

4. Entropy-based image fusion with Continuous Genetic Algorithm

4.1 Introduction

Image fusion is defined as the process of combining information from two or more images of a scene to enhance the viewing or understanding of that scene. The images that are to be fused can come from different sensors, or have been acquired at different times, or from different locations. Hence, the first step in any image fusion process is the accurate registration of the image data. This is relatively straightforward if parameters such as the instantaneous field-of-view (IFOV), and locations and orientations from which the images are acquired are known, especially when the sensor modalities produce images that use the same coordinate space. This is more of a challenge when sensor modalities differ significantly and registration can only be accomplished at the information level. Hence, the goal of the fusion process is to preserve all relevant information in the component images and place it in the fused image (FI). This requires that the process minimize the noise and other artifacts in the FI. Because of this, the fusion process can be also regarded as an optimization problem [K. Kannan and S. Perumal, 2002]. In recent years, image fusion has been applied to a number of diverse areas such as remote sensing [T. A.Wilson, and S. K. Rogers,1997], medical imaging [C. S. Pattichis and M. S. Pattichis, 2001], and military applications [B. V. Dasarathy, 2002].

Fig. 2. Comparisons of Enhancement Techniques: (top-left) Original; (top-right) IRME; (middle-left) Gamma correction, g = 1.4; (middle-right) MSR; (bottom-left) AINDANE;(bottom-right) ETNUD.

Image fusion can be divided into three processing levels: pixel, feature and decision. These methods increase in abstraction from pixel to feature to decision levels. In the pixel-level approach, simple arithmetic rules like average of individual pixel intensities or more sophisticated combination schemes are used to construct the fused image. At the feature-level, the image is classified into regions with known labels, and these labeled regions from different sensor modalities are used to combine the data. At the decision level, a combination of rules can be used to include part of the data or not.

Genetic algorithms (GA) are an optimization technique that seeks the optimum solution of a function based on the Darwinian principles of biological evolution. Even though there are several methods of performing and evaluating image fusion, there are still many open questions. In this section, a new measure of image fusion quality is provided and compared with many existing ones. The focus is on pixel-level image fusion (PLIF) and a new image fusion technique that uses GA is proposed.

The GA is used to optimize the parameters of the fusion process to produce an FI that contains more information than either of the individual images. The main purpose of this section is in finding the optimum weights that are used to fuse images with the help of CGA. The techniques for GA and image fusion are given in Section 4.2. Section 4.3 describes the evaluation criteria. Section 4.4 describes the experimental results, and compares our results with other image fusion techniques. In Section 4.5, conclusion is provided.

4.2 The techniques of GA and image fusion

4.2.1 Genetic Algorithm

As stated earlier, GA is a non-linear optimization technique that seeks the optimum solution of a function via a non-exhaustive search among randomly generated solutions. GAs use multiple search points instead of searching one point at a time and attempt to find global, near-optimal solutions without getting stuck at local optima. Because of these significant advantages, GAs reduce the search time and space. However, there are disadvantages of using GAs as well: they are not generally suitable for real-time applications since the time to converge to an optimal solution cannot be predicted. The convergence time depends on the population size, and the GA crossover and mutation operators. In this fusion process, a continuous genetic algorithm has been selected.

4.2.2 Continuous Genetic Algorithm (CGA)

GAs typically operates on binary data. For many applications, it is more convenient to work in the analog, or continuous, data space rather than in the binary space of most GAs. Hence, CGA is used because they have the advantage of requiring less storage and are faster than binary. CGA inputs are represented by floating-point numbers over whatever range is deemed appropriate. Figure 6 shows the flowchart of a simple CGA [Randy L. Haupt & Sue Ellen Haupt, 2004]. The various elements in the flowchart are described below:

i. *Definition of the cost function and the variables:* The variable values are represented as floating point numbers (p_1). In each chromosome, the basic GA processing vector, there are number of value depending on the parameters $(p_1,...,p_{N\,var})$. Each chromosome has a cost determined by evaluating the cost function [Randy L. Haupt & Sue Ellen Haupt, 2004].
ii. *Initial Population:* To begin the CGA process, an initial population must be defined. A matrix represents the population, with each row being a $1 \times N_{var}$ chromosome of continuous values. The chromosomes are passed to the cost function for evaluation [Randy L. Haupt & Sue Ellen Haupt, 2004].

iii. *Natural Selection:* The chromosomes are ranked from the lowest to highest cost. Of the total of chromosomes in a given generation, only the top N_{Keep} are kept for mating and the rest are discarded to make room for the new offspring .

iv. *Mating:* Many different approaches have been tried for crossover in continuous GAs. In crossover, all the genes to the right of the crossover point are swapped. Variables are randomly selected in the first pair of parents to be the crossover point: $\alpha = (U(0,1)N_{\text{var}})$, where *U(0,1)* is the uniform distribution. The parents are given by [Randy L. Haupt & Sue Ellen Haupt, 2004]:

$$\begin{aligned} parent_1 &= [P_{m1}, \ldots\ldots, P_{mN_{\text{var}}}] \\ parent_2 &= [P_{d1}, \ldots\ldots, P_{dN_{\text{var}}}] \end{aligned} \tag{32}$$

where subscripts *m* and *d* represent the mom and dad parent. Then the selected variables are combined to form new variables that will appear in the children.

$$\begin{aligned} pnew_1 &= p_{m\alpha} - \beta[P_{m\alpha} - P_{d\alpha}] \\ pnew_2 &= p_{d\alpha} + \beta[P_{m\alpha} - P_{d\alpha}] \end{aligned} \tag{33}$$

where β is a random value between 0 and 1. The final step is to complete the crossover with the rest of chromosome:

$$\begin{aligned} offspring_1 &= \left[P_{m1}, P_{m2}, \ldots, pnew_1, \ldots, P_{dN_{\text{var}}}\right] \\ offspring_2 &= \left[P_{d1}, P_{d2}, \ldots, pnew_2, \ldots, P_{mN_{\text{var}}}\right] \end{aligned} \tag{34}$$

v. *Mutation:* If care is not taken, the GA can converge too quickly into one region of the cost surface. If this area is in the region of the global minimum, there is no problem. However, some functions have many local minima. To avoid overly fast convergence, other areas of the cost surface must be explored by randomly introducing changes, or mutations, in some of the variables. Multiplying the mutation rate by the total number of variables that can be mutated in the population gives the amount of mutation. Random numbers are used to select the row and columns of the variables that are to be mutated.

vi. *Next Generation:* After all these steps, the starting population for the next generation is ranked. The bottom ranked chromosomes are discarded and replaced by offspring from the top ranked parents. Some random variables are selected for mutation from the bottom ranked chromosomes. The chromosomes are then ranked from lowest cost to highest cost. The process is iterated until a global solution is achieved [Randy L. Haupt & Sue Ellen Haupt, 2004].

4.2.3 Image fusion

A set of input images of a scene, captured at a different time or captured by different kinds of sensors at the same time, reveals different information about the scene. The process of extracting and combining data from a set of input images to form a new composite image with extended information content is called image fusion.

4.3 Evaluation criteria

In this section, the following criteria were defined to evaluate the performance of the image fusion algorithm.

4.3.1 Image quality assessment

This evaluation criterion was discussed in Section 3.2.3.

4.3.2 Entropy

Entropy is often defined as the amount of information contained in an image. Mathematically, entropy is usually given as:

$$E = -\sum_{i=0}^{L-1} p_i \log_2 p_i \tag{35}$$

where L is the total number of grey levels, and $p = \{p_0, ..., p_{L-1}\}$ is the probability of occurrence of each level. An increase in entropy after fusion can be interpreted as an overall increase in the information content. Hence, one can assess the quality of fusion by assessing entropy of the original data, and the entropy of the fused data.

4.3.3 Mutual information indices

Mutual Information Indices are used to evaluate the correlative performances of the fused image and the source images. Let A and B be random variables with marginal probability distributions $p_A(a)$ and $p_B(b)$ and the joint probability distribution $p_{AB}(a,b)$. The mutual information is then defined as:

$$I_{AB} = \sum p_{AB}(a,b)\log[p_{AB}(a,b) / (p_A(a)p_B(b))] \tag{36}$$

A higher value of Mutual Information (MI) indicates that the fused image, *F*, contains fairly good quantity of information present in both the source images, *A* and *B*. The MI can be defined as $MI = I_{AF} + I_{BF}$.

A high value of MI does not imply that the information from the both images is symmetrically fused. Therefore, information symmetry (IS) is introduced. IS is the indication of how symmetrically distributed is the information in the fused image, with respect to input images. The higher the value of IS, the better the fusion result. IS is given by :

$$IS = 2 - abs[I_{AF} / (I_{AF} + I_{BF}) - 0.5] \tag{37}$$

4.4 Experimental results

The goal of this experiment is to fuse visual and IR images. To minimize registration issues, it is important that the visual and the thermal images are captured at the same time. Pinnacle software was used to capture the visual and the thermal images simultaneously. Although radiometric calibration is important, the thermal camera can not always be calibrated in field conditions because of constraints on time. Figure 3 shows an example where the IR and visual image were captured at the same time. It is obvious from the figure that the images need to be registered before they can be fused since the field-of-view and the pixel resolution are obviously different.

The performance of the proposed algorithm was tested and compared with different PLIF methods. The IR and visual images were not previously registered as shown in Figure 3. The registered image, base image (IR Image) and fused image with CGA are shown in Figure 4. The cost function is very simple and defined as:

$$Entropy(F = w_a V + w_b IR) \quad (38)$$

where V and IR are the visual and IR images, w_a and w_b are the respective associated weights, and F is the fused image. The initial population size is 100×3. The first and second columns in population matrix represent $w_a V$, and $w_b IR$ and the last column represents the cost function which is the entropy of F. Then initial population has been ranked based on the cost. In each iteration of the GA, 20 of the 100 rows are kept for mating and the rest are discarded. The crossover has been applied based on the Equation 35. The mutation rate was set to 0.20, hence the total number of mutated variables is 40. The value of a mutated variable is replaced by a new random value in the same range.

Fig. 3. Visual and IR Images: Left: Visual Image, Right: IR Image.

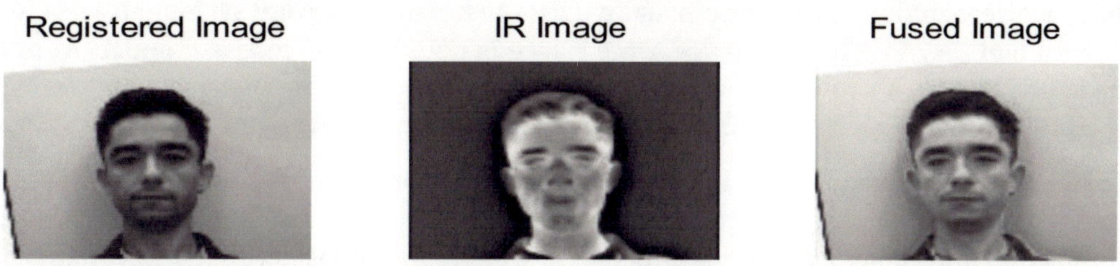

Fig. 4. The Result of Fusion: Left: Registered Images, Middle: IR Image Right: Fused Image with GA.

The CGA results after 50 iterations of the GA such that the CGA maximize the cost and find optimum weights of images. In the 2nd, 8th, and 25th iterations, the cost increased but was not associated with the global solution. The optimum solution was determined in 45th iteration and remained unchanged because it is optimum solution. Figure 4 shows the fusion results of point-rules based PLIF. After registering IR and visual data, we determined that w_a = 0.9931 and w_b = 0.0940 provide the optimum values for maximizing the entropy cost function for the F specified in Equation 38. The evaluation of these weights results is shown in Table 2. Table 2 shows that CGA based fusion method gives better results (optimum weights for maximizing the entropy of *F*) for entropy and IS from which it can concluded that CGA performs better than other PLIFs.

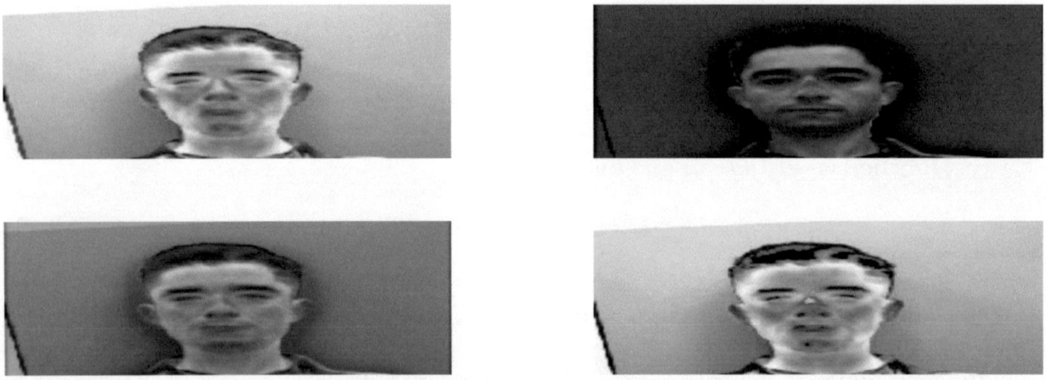

Fig. 5. Fusion Results: (top-left) highest value from IR or Visual Images; (top-right) lowest value form IR or Visual Images; (bottom-left) average of IR and Visual Images; (bottom-right) threshold value.

4.5 Conclusion

In this section, CGA based image fusion algorithm was introduced and compared with other classical PLIFs. The results show that CGA based image fusion gives better result than other PLIFs.

5. Experimental results

5.1 Introduction

With face recognition, a database usually exists that stores a group of human faces with known identities. In a testing image, once a face is detected, the face is cropped from the image or video as a probe to check with the database for possible matches. The matching algorithm produces a similarity measure for each of the comparing pairs.

Variations among images from the same face due to changes in illumination are typically larger than variations rose from a change of face identity. In an effort to address the illumination and camera variations, a database was created, considering these variations to evaluate the proposed techniques.

Besides the regular room lights, four additional spot lights are located in the front of the person that can be turned off and on in sequence to obtain face images under different illumination conditions. Note that it is important to capture visual and thermal images at the same time in order to see the variations in the facial images. Visual and thermal images are captured almost at the same time. Although radiometric calibration is important, the thermal camera can not be calibrated because of current IR camera characteristics.The Pinnacle (Pinnacle Systems Ltd.) software has been implemented to capture 16 visual and thermal images at the same time. Figure 6 (a) and (e) shows an example of visual and thermal images taken at the same time.

	Highest (Fig 5)	Lowest (Fig 5)	Average (Fig 5)	Threshold (Fig 5)	GA_based (Fig 4)
Entropy	6.91	3.14	6.56	6.93	7.28
Image Quality	100	70	100	100	100
IS	1.90	1.63	1.96	1.91	1.96

Table 2. Performance Comparision of Image Fusion Methods for Figure 4 and Figure 5.

In this chapter, the focus is on visual image enhancement. Then the visual images will be registered with the IR images based landmark registration algorithm. Finally, the registered IR and visual images are fused for face recognition.

5.2 Enhancement of visual images

The ETNUD algorithm was applied to 16 visual images as shown in Figure 6 under different illumination conditions. In all figures besides the regular room lights, the four extra spot lights located in the front of the person were turned off and on for creating different illumination conditions. To enhance those visual images, the luminance is first balanced, then image contrast is enhanced and finally, the enhanced image is obtained by a linear color restoration based on chromatic information contained in the original image. The results in the luminance enhancement part showed that the algorithms work well for dark images. All the details, which cannot be seen in the original image, become evident. The experiment results have shown that for all color images, the proposed algorithms work sufficiently well.

5.3 IR and visual images registration

First, the IR and visual images taken from different sensors, viewpoints, times and resolution were resized for the same size. The correspondence between the features detected in the IR image and those detected in the visual image were then established. Control points were picked manually from those corners detected by the Harris corner detection algorithm from both images, where the corners were in the same positions in the two images.

In the second step, a spatial transformation was computed to map the selected corners in one image to those in another image. Once the transformation was established, the image to be registered was resampled and interpolated to match the reference image. For RGB and intensity images, the bilinear or bicubic interpolation method is recommended since they lead to better results. In the experiments, the bicubic interpolation method was used.

5.4 Discussion

Experimental results have been applied on the database, which is created by the research team. This algorithm is categorized into four steps, which are described respectively. In the first step, there is enhancement of visual images, as described in Section 3. The fused image should be more suitable for human visual perception and computer-processing tasks. The experience of image processing has prompted the research to consider fundamental aspects for good visual presentation of images, requiring nonlinear image enhancement techniques of visual recorded images to get a better image, which has more information from the original images. In the second step, the corners of visual and IR images were determined with the help of Harris Detection algorithm for registration purpose to use as control points. In the third step, because the source images are obtained from different sensors, they present different resolution, size and spectral characteristic, the source images have to be correctly registered. In the last step, an image fusion process is performed, which was described in Section 4.

The registered images were overlapped at an appropriate transparency. The pixel value in the fused image was a weighted submission of the corresponding pixels in the IR and visual images. In the next section, results from advanced image fusion approaches are presented.

5.5 Fusion of visual and IR images

The Image fusion algorithm was applied with the help of Genetic Algorithm to the database. One of the issues is the determination of the quality of image fusion results. As part of the general theme of fusion evaluation there is a growing interest to develop methods that address the scored performance of image fusion algorithms as described in Section 4. Given the diversity of applications and various methods of evaluation metrics, there are still open questions concerning when to perform image fusion. There is an interest in exploring mean, standard deviation, entropy, mutual information, peak signal to noise ratio and image quality as described in Section 4. Because source images have different spectrum, they show quite distinct characters and have complementary information. It can be seen in Figure 6 (a and c) that the visual image does not have enough information to see the faces and is very dark. Figure 6 (b) shows that the luminance enhancement part works well for dark images and the technique adjusts itself to the image. In the contrast enhancement part it is clear that unseen or barely seen features of low contrast images were made visible. Enhancement algorithms were developed to improve the images before the fusion process. After enhancement it was found that the corners of the enhanced image and the IR image then registered the enhanced image as shown in Figure 6 (d). Then, the enhanced image was fused with the IR image in Figure 6 (f).

Figures 6 show the result of CGA after 100 iterations. The optimum solution was determined with a population size of 100x3 after 76 iterations. It was determined that $w_a = 0.99$ and $w_b = 0.47$ are the optimum values for maximizing the entropy cost function which is 7.58 for the F specified in Equation 38. The evaluation of these weights results is shown in Table 3. By inspection, the faces and the details in the fused image are clearer as compared to either the original IR image or the visual image.

Table 3 shows the detailed comparison results of the fused images. A is the fused image by averaging the visual and IR images. B is the fused image by the proposed approach. The total images used in this experiment were from the created database. The results show that this approach is better than the averaging fusion result.

	MEAN		ENTROPY		PSNR		IQ	
Database Images	A	B	A	B	A	B	A	B
1(Fig.19)	101.61	153.50	7.03	7.58	14.16	35.73	85	94
2	111.78	144.92	7.26	7.68	13.64	35.73	90	95
3	105.35	124.06	7.25	7.42	13.84	28.13	87	96
4	118.91	140.72	7.33	7.53	13.21	28.33	97	96
5	104.2	117.17	7.41	7.82	14.12	29.40	91	94
6	106.82	117.41	7.46	7.78	14.10	29.15	97	94
7	115.76	137.67	7.37	7.68	14.12	29.26	98	98
8	116.18	137.02	7.56	7.83	14.50	29.64	97	96
9	93.22	134.03	7.29	7.63	15.22	33.41	87	83
10	114.05	143.26	7.23	7.60	14.64	36.17	99	98
11	111.50	131.12	7.34	7.51	13.92	28.25	93	99
12	117.51	142.50	7.37	7.66	13.60	30.10	96	95
13	114.65	139.16	7.34	7.51	14.18	30.05	94	96
14	116.47	141.82	7.29	7.54	15.08	30.94	99	99
15	115.81	132.06	7.53	7.60	14.39	28.75	98	97
16	118.57	137.00	7.34	7.68	14.93	28.90	99	99

Table 3. The Statistics of Database.

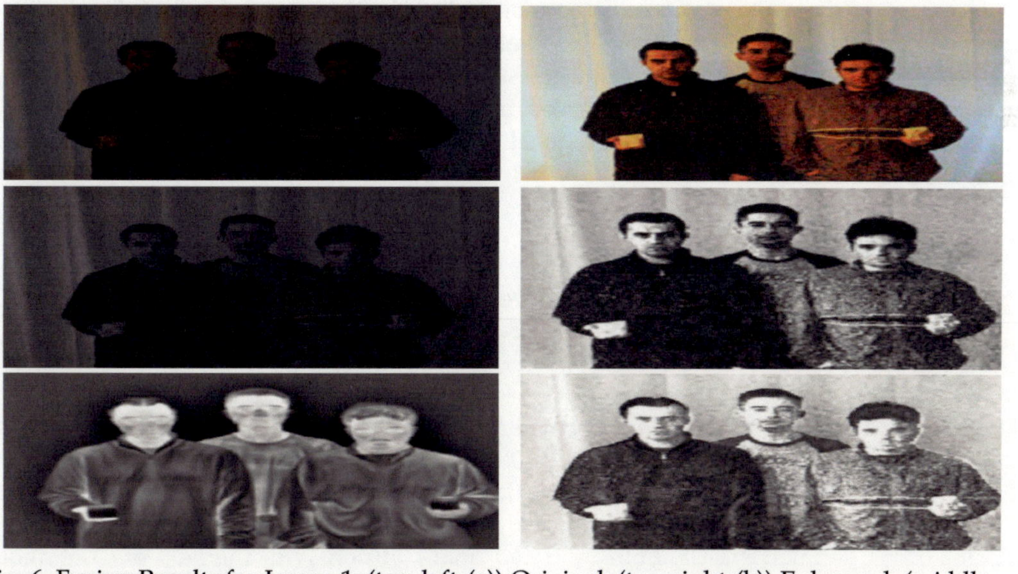

Fig. 6. Fusion Results for Image 1: (top-left-(a)) Original; (top-right-(b)) Enhanced; (middle-left-(c)) Original; (middle-right-(d)) Enhanced; (bottom-left-(e)) IR;(bottom-right-(f)) Fused Images; Graph-Genetic Algorithm result after 100 iterations.

6. Conclusions

In this chapter, a database for visual and thermal images was created and several techniques were developed to improve image quality as an effort to address the illumination challenge in face recognition.

Firstly, one image enhancement algorithm was designed to improve the images' visual quality. Experimental results showed that the enhancement algorithm performed well and provided good results in terms of both luminance and contrast enhancement. In the luminance enhancement part, it has been shown that the proposed algorithm worked well for both dark and bright images. In the contrast enhancement part, it was proven that the proposed nonlinear transfer functions could make unseen or barely seen features in low contrast images clearly visible.

Secondly, the IR and enhanced visual images taken from different sensors, viewpoints, times and resolution were registered. A correspondence between an IR and a visual image was established based on a set of image features detected by the Harris Corner detection algorithm in both images. A spatial transformation matrix was determined based on some manually chosen corners and the transformation matrix was utilized for the registration.

Finally, a continuous genetic algorithm was developed for image fusion. The continuous GA has the advantage of less storage requirements than the binary GA and is inherently faster than the binary GA because the chromosomes do not have to be decoded prior to the evaluation of the cost function.

Data fusion provides an integrated image from a pair of registered and enhanced visual and thermal IR images. The fused image is invariant to illumination directions and is robust under low lighting conditions. They have potentials to significantly boost the performances of face recognition systems. One of the major obstacles in face recognition using visual images is the illumination variation. This challenge can be mitigated by using infrared (IR) images. On the other hand, using IR images alone for face recognition is usually not feasible because they do not carry enough detailed information. As a remedy, a hybrid system is presented that may benefit from both visual and IR images and improve face recognition under various lighting conditions.

7. References

Bowyer W., Chang K. and Flynn P., A Survey of Approaches To Three-Dimensional Face Recognition, *ICPR*, Vol. 1, pp. 358 - 361, 2004.

Dasarathy B. V., Image Fusion in the Context Of Aerospace Applications, *Inform. Fusion*, Vol. 3, 2002.

Erkanli S. and Rahman Zia-Ur., Enhancement Technique for Uniformly and Non-Uniformly Illuminated Dark Images, *ISDA 2010, Cairo, Egypt*, 2010b.

Erkanli S. and Rahman Zia-Ur., Wavelet Based Enhancement for Uniformly and Non-Uniformly Illuminated Dark Images, *ISDA 2010, Cairo, Egypt*, 2010c.

Erkanli S.and Rahman Zia-Ur, Entropy Based Image Fusion With the help of Continuous Genetic Algorithm, *IEEE ISDA Conference, December* 2010.

Fonseca L. M. G. and Manjunath B. S., Registration Techniques for Multisensor Remotely Sensed Imagery, *Photogrammetric Engineering & Remote Sensing*, Vol. 62, pp. 1049-1056, 1996.

Gonzalez R. C., Woods R. E. and Eddins S. L., Digital Image Processing, *Pearson Education, Inc. Prentice Hall*, 2004.

Haupt Randy L. and Haupt Sue Ellen, *Practical Genetic Algorithms, Second Edition*, ISBN 0-471-45565-2 Copyright © 2004 John Wiley & Sons, Inc.

Hines G. D., Rahman Z., Jobson D. J., and Wodell G. A., Single-Scale Retinex Using Digital Signal Processors *In Proceedings Of The GSPX*, 2004.

Holland J. H., Adaptation In Natural and Artificial Systems, *University of Michigan Press*, 1975.

Hulbert A. C., The Computation of Color, *Ph.D. Dissertaion, Mass. Inst. Tech., Cambridge, MA*, Sept. 1989.

Jobson D. J., Rahman Z. and Woodell G. A., Properties and Performance of a Center/Surround Retinex, *IEEE Trans.Image Processing*, Vol.6, pp. 451-462, 1997.

Kannan K. and Perumal S., Optimal Decomposition Level of Discrete Wavelet Transform for Pixel Based Fusion of Multi-Focused Images, *International Conference On Computational Intelligence And Multimedia Applications*, 2007.

Kolb H., How the Retina works, *American Scientist*, Vol. 91, 2003.

Kong G. S., Heo J., Abidi B. R., Paik J. and Abidi M. A., Recent Advances in Visual and Infrared Face recognition—a Review, *Computer Vision and Image Understanding*, Vol. 1, pp. 103-135, 2005.

Land E., An Alternative Technique For The Computation of The Designator in The Retinex Theory of Color Vision, *Proc. Of The National Academy Of Science USA*, Vol. 83, pp. 2078-3080, 1986.

Mdhani S., Ho J., Vetter T. and Kriegman D. J., Face Recognition Using 3-D Models: Pose and Illumination, *Proceedings of the IEEE*, Vol. 94, pp. 1977 –1999, 2006.

Mitra S. K., Murthy C. A. and Kundu M. K., Technique for Fractal Image Compression using Genetic Algorithm, *IEEE Trans Image Process*. pp. 586-93, 1998.

Mumtaz A. and Majid A., Genetic Algorithms and its application to Image Fusion, *International Conference On Emerging Technologies ICET*, 2008.

Patnaik D., Biomedical Image Fusion using Wavelet Transforms and Neural Network, *IEEE International Conference on Industrial Technology*, pp. 1189 - 1194, 2006.

Pattichis C. S. and Pattichis M. S., Medical Imaging Fusion Applications— An Overview, *In Conf. Rec. Asilomar Conf. Signals, Systems Computers*, Vol. 2, pp. 1263–1267, 2001.

Prokoski F., History, Current Status, and Future of Infrared Identification, *Computer Vision Beyond the Visible Spectrum: Methods and Applications, Proceedings IEEE Workshop*, pp. 5-14, 2000.

Rahman Z., Jobson D. and Woodell G. A., Multiscale Retinex For Color Image Enhancement, *In Proceedings of the IEEE International Conference On Image Processing*, 1996.

Rahman Z., The Lectures Notes of Image Processing, *Old Dominion University*, 2009.

Rahman Z., Woodell G. A. and Jobson D., A Comparison of The Multiscale Retinex with other Image Enhancement Techniques, *In Proceedings Of The IS&T 50th Anniversary Conference*, pp. 426-431, 1997b.

Schreiber W. F., Image processing for quality improvement, *Proceedings of the IEEE*, Vol. 66, pp. 1640–1651, 1978.

Socolinsky D. A. and Selinger A., A Comparative Analysis of Face Recognition Performance with Visible and Thermal Infrared Imagery, *IEEE International Conference of Pattern Recognition*, Vol. 4, pp. 217 –222, 2002.

Srinivas M. and Patnaik L. M., Genetic Algorithms: a Survey, pp. 17 – 26, Vol. 27, Jun 1994.

Tao L., An Adaptive And Integrated Neighborhood Dependent Approach For Nonlinear Enhancement Of Color Images, *SPIE Journal of Electronic Imaging*, pp. 1.1-1.14, 2005.

Tao L., Tompkins R. C., and Asari K. V., An Illuminance Reflectance Model For Nonlinear Enhancement Of Video Stream For Homeland Security Applications, *IEEE International Workshop on Applied Imagery and Pattern Recognition, AIPR*, October 19 - 21, 2005.

Wang A., Sun H. and Guan Y., The Application of Wavelet Transform to Multi-Modality Medical Image Fusion, *Networking, Sensing and Control, ICNSC Proceedings Of The 2006 IEEE International Conference*, pp. 270-274, 2006.

Wang H., Multisensory Image Fusion by using Discrete Multiwavelet Transform, *The Third International Conference on Machine Learning and Cybernetics, Shanghai*, 26-29 August 2004.

Wilson T. A., and Rogers S. K., Perceptual-Based Image Fusion for Hyperspectral Data, *IEEE Trans. Ge. Remote Sensing*, Vol. 35, pp. 1007–1017, July 1997.

Yu L., Yung T., Chan K., Ho Y. and Ping Chu Y., Image Hiding with an improved Genetic Algorithm and an Optimal Pixel Adjustment Process, *Eighth International Conference On Intelligent Systems Design And Applications*, 2008.

Zhang J., Feng X., Song B., Li M. and Lu Y., Multi-Focus Image Fusion using Quality Assessment of Spatial Domain And Genetic Algorithm, *Human System Interactions*, pp. 71 – 75, 25-27 May 2008.

Zitova B. and Flusser J., Image Registration Methods: A Survey, *Image and Vision Computing 21*, pp. 977–1000, 2003.

11

Self Adaptive Genetic Algorithms for Automated Linear Modelling of Time Series

Pedro Flores[1], Larysa Burtseva[2] and Luis B. Morales[3]
[1]*Universidad de Sonora*
[2]*Universidad Autónoma de Baja California*
[3]*Universidad Nacional Autónoma de México*
México

1. Introduction

In this work it is developed a methodological proposal to build linear models of Time Series (TS) from setting out the problem of obtaining a good linear model, such as solving a problem of nonlinear optimization with bounded variables. It is worth to mention that to build these problems are taken some ideas of the traditional statistical approach.

As product of the methodology here presented, it will be developed two heuristic algorithms for the treatment of TS, which allow building several models for the same problem, where the accuracy of these can be increased by increasing the number of terms of the model, situation that does not happen with the traditional statistical approach. Thus, with this algorithms it can be obtained several proposals of solution for the same problem, of which it can be selected the one that presents the best results in the forecasting. In addition, the algorithms proposed in this work allow building different linear versions, but equivalent to the Autoregressive (AR) and the classic Autoregressive with Moving Average (ARMS) models, with the added advantage of the possibility of obtaining models for not stationary TS, and with non stationary variance, in cases where the traditional methodology does not work.

Since optimization problems set out here may present multiple local minimums, it is needed to use a special technique to solve them. With this end it was developed a version of the Self Adaptive Genetic Algorithms (SAGA), encoded on real numbers that allows, without intervention of the user, to find satisfactory solutions for different problems without making changes in the parameters of the code.

On the other hand, among the principal points of this methodology it is the fact that in many cases, these linear versions present a phenomenon that has been named 'forecasting delay', which allows to modify the linear model obtained to find a more accurate forecasting.

It is important to notice that the first AR version of the algorithms developed for the TS were tested in the examples of the international competition:

"NN3 Artificial Networks & Computational Intelligence Forecasting Competition"

that from now on it will be called NN3, which was realized in 2006-2007 (http://www.neural-forecasting-competition.com/NN3/results.htm). This competition is held annually to evaluate the accuracy of methods in the area of Computational Intelligence in diverse problems of TS. In this edition the problem at hand was to forecast with the same methodology 18 future values of a set of series where the majority are measurements of real phenomena. The competition has two categories: the NN3-Complete has 111 problems and the NN3-Reduced consists of 11 problems. In this competition using only models with four terms it was obtained the third place in the category NN3-Complete from 29 competitors, and the sixth in the category NN3-Reduced from 53 competitors. This work will be referenced in various sections in relation to the examples of this competition. An analysis of the results of NN3 can be found in (Crone & Hibon & Nikolopoulos, 2011)

2. Methodology

The forecasting process consists in calculating or predicting the value of some event that is going to happen in the future. To realize adequately this process it is needed to analyze the event data in question and build a model that allows the incorporation of the behavior patterns that have occurred in the past under the assumption that they can happen again in the future. It is important to note that there is not interest in explaining how the mechanism that produces the events works, but to predict their behavior.

The TS models are used for studying the behavior of data that varies with time. The data can be interpreted as measurements of some value (observable variable) of a phenomenon, realized at time intervals equal and consecutive. There are several methods to construct TS models and an overview of the most important can be found in (Weigend & Gershenfeld, 1994). In (Palit & Popovic, 2005) it is shown an overview of the methodologies most used in the area of computational intelligence. One of the most used methods is based on considering the TS as a realization of a stochastic process. This approach is the basis of statistical treatment of TS that can be found in (Box & Jenkins, 1976) and (Guerrero, 2003). Nowadays the construction of model for TS is an area of great development as evidenced by the articles of the Journal of Time Series Analysis (http://www.wiley.com/bw/journal.asp?ref=0143-9782&site=1) in addition to the papers presented in international competitions on time series modelling such as NN3. Nevertheless the existence of GA papers in which are used the TS (Alberto et all, 2010; Battaglia & Protopapas, 2011; Chiogna & Gaetan & Masarotto, 2008; Hansen et all, 1999; Mateo & Sovilj & Gadea, 2010; Szpiro, 1997; Yadavalli et all, 1999), it is important to note that it was not found any reference to the use of SAGA for this purpose.

The data will be represented by $\{Z_t\}$ with the implicit assumption that t takes the values $1, 2, ..., N$ where the parameter N indicates up to what moment the information is had. When it is had a model for the data set, then it can be estimated values for the TS, which are denoted by $\{F_t\}$. In addition in order to consider a model as a good one, it is required that the values of $\{F_t\}$ be "similar" to those of $\{Z_t\}$. The main purpose of this work is to build linear models for the data set to have good estimates of the K unknown values of the phenomenon being studied in the moments $N+1, N+2, ..., N+K$.

In the forecasting subject, when it is had a TS with these $N+K$ data, the set of the first N is called training set, and is used to construct the model of the series and realize the estimation of its parameters. The set of the last K terms in the series is called training set, and is used for the comparison of different models to choose the most suitable. Especially, it is been interested in building automated Autoregressive models of order p (AR (p)). For the TS are expressions of the form:

$$Z_t = \delta + \phi_1 Z_{t-1} + \phi_2 Z_{t-2} + ... + \phi_p Z_{t-p} + a_t \quad (1)$$

Where Z_t is the observable variable in question,δ and ϕ_i are the parameters to be determined and the variable a_t represents a random variable of noise called *residual*. The expression (1) means that to predict what will happen at the time t are required the p values previous to t, these values are called *delays* or *lags*.

In the classic theory of linear models is set the restriction that a_t represents a white noise, but in this work it was not included this boundary, which will allow to find AR expressions for the residuals with which it will be possible to increase the accuracy of the models.

The interest in this type of models is originated in the fact that they represent the most important information about the behavior of the series eliminating the noise that may appear. It should also be added that, for these models, it is important that in the expression (1) only appears a number of terms set in advance. This will allow finding models for a TS, controlling the accuracy of the approximation of the same series according to the number of terms utilized.

Problem 1: If $\{Z_t\}$ is the original TS and $\{F_t\}$ is the forecasting obtained of the form

$$F_t = \delta + \phi_1 Z_{t-1} + \phi_2 Z_{t-2} + ... + \phi_p Z_{t-p} \quad (2)$$

with $t > p$.

It is necessary to find the values for δ and ϕ_i that minimize the function:

$$\sqrt{\sum_{i=p}^{N} (Z_i - F_i)^2} \quad (3)$$

This function will be called *Root of the Sum of Squares* (RSS). It is necessary to add that for rapidity in calculation it is preferable to use the square of this function obtaining the same results.

In this initial setting out the construction of the model is presented as if a linear interpolation problem was solved, and given that the values for δ and ϕ_i will not be arbitrary but will be looked at certain intervals are necessary methods to solve the Problem 1 working in addition with bounded variables.

The RSS function can have multiple local optima, and to solve this problem it was developed an original version of SAGA algorithms, which allows to solve real nonlinear optimization problems and with bounded variables. The selection of a self Adaptive version was carried out by the fact that it is wanted to automate as much as possible the process of building these models.

3. Self adaptive genetic algorithms

The SAGA algorithms were developed by Thomas Bäck (Bäck, 1992a, 1992b) and have the characteristic that they alone look for the best parameters for their operation. In them, the parameters that will be self Adaptive are encoded in the representation of the individual, for which they are altered by the actions of the genetic operators. With this, the best values of these parameters will produce better individuals, which have major probability of surviving, and in consequence, will spread towards the whole population the best values of the parameters. There are several versions of SAGA that differ especially in the parameters that will be adjusted automatically (Eiben at all, 1999). In the case of this work four self Adaptive parameters are used: *individual probability of crossing* p_c, *repetition of crossing* r_c, *individual probability of mutation* p_m and *repetition of mutation* r_m as presented in (4). The selection of these parameters and its values is based on the idea that genetic operations of crossing and mutation can be multiple, but they cannot have very large values. A binary version of this algorithm already had been used by one of the authors of this work in other problems (Flores, 1999; Garduño, 2000; Garduño, 2001; Sanchez, 2004), and this, as well as the presented one here (with the representation of real numbers) according to the literature reviewed, are original of himself.

The individuals for these problems will be proposed as solutions to them, and in addition will have four more components, where it will be represented the values of: *individual probability of crossing* p_c, *repetition of crossing* r_c, *individual probability of mutation* p_m and *repetition of mutation* r_m. To this section of the individual it is called section of the self Adaptive parameters, and with this, our entire individual is represented by:

$$(\delta, \phi_1, \phi_2, ..., \phi_p, p_c, r_c, p_m, r_m) \tag{4}$$

The above mentioned is necessary, so in this model, the probability of crossing and mutation will be characteristic of each individual (not of the population as is traditional in the GA), and in addition it is considered that the crossing and the mutation can be multiple, that is to say, to operate several times in the same time. The multiple crossing and mutation are repetitions of the crossing and mutation that are used in the GA, when are used individuals represented by vectors of real components. The way of operating with these parameters is similar to that presented in (Bäck, 1992a, 1992b).

The limits that were used in the code of this work for the self Adaptive parameters are: *individual probability of crossing* p_c that changes in the interval (0.5, 0.95), *repetition of crossing* r_c in (1.0, 4.0) what means that only can be crossed from one to three times, *individual probability of mutation* p_m that varies in (0.5, 0.85) and *repetition of mutation* r_m in (1.0, 5.0) what means that just it is possible to mutated from one to four times. The limits of these self Adaptive parameters were chosen on the basis of the experience of other works (Flores, 1999; Garduño, 2000; Garduño, 2001; Sanchez, 2004) , where they proved to give good results.

Later there are detailed the procedures of crossing and mutation.

3.1 Crossing and mutation

Given two individual, the crossing is realized taking as probability of crossing the average of the values of the individual crossings. Once it has been decided if the individuals cross, it is taken the integer part of the average individual crossing, and that is the number of times they cross. The crossing of two individuals consists of exchanging the coordinates of both vectors from a certain coordinate chosen at random. The multiple crossing is the result of applying this procedure several times to the same vectors.

For the mutation it is taken the individual probability of mutation of the individual, and accordingly to this it is decided whether mutated or not. As soon as has been decided that an individual mutates, this is mutated as many times as the value of the integer part that has in the repetition of mutation of himself. To apply the mutation to an individual a coordinate of the vector is chosen at random, and it is changed its value for another (chosen also at random) between the limits established for the above mentioned coordinate. The multiple mutation is the application of this procedure to the same individual several times.

3.2 Use of the self adaptive genetic algorithms

Since SAGA are random, it is common to realize several runs on the same problem and choose the best result from them. These algorithms are applied in three stages to solve our problems. In the first two stages are defined which are the important variables to solve the problem, and in the third stage, it is where the solution is calculated properly. It is important to note that the individuals have two parts, but in this section only there is born in mind the first part of the individual, which corresponds to the Autoregressive components. Here is the procedure based on SAGA, which is performed to obtain a solution to the problem.

In the first stage are used SAGA to explore the space of solutions and later to define which variables among $\delta, \phi_1, \phi_2, ..., \phi_p$, are the most important for the problem in question. For this were done 10 repetitions of 1000 iterations each, and with the solutions of each repetition, a vector is constructed by the sum of the absolute values of $\delta, \phi_1, \phi_2, ..., \phi_p$. (see Figure 1)

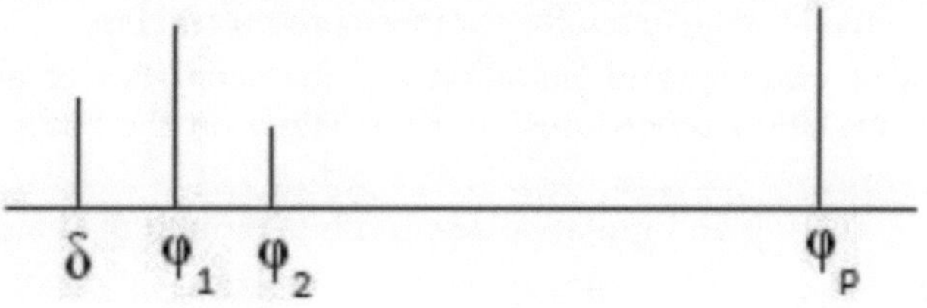

Fig. 1. Solution using all variables.

In this first stage, the aim is to realize an exploration of the space of solutions, and for that are performed 10 iterations with all variables to consider. Then, with the 10 solutions obtained, a vector is built by adding the 10 solutions with all its positive components, and it is assumed that the largest values of these components are the most important.

In the second stage the SAGA are applied to find solutions by considering only the important variables of the problem. For this is defined in advance how many variables are required (this will be seen to detail below), and are chosen those which correspond to larger values of the first stage. In this stage 5 repetitions are realized, where each one is finished until the optimum is not modified in the last 200 iterations. Of these 5 repetitions the best result obtained is chosen (see Figure 2).

In this second stage, only are considered the variables that had greatest values in the part of the autoregressive components of the individual, and for them are kept the original intervals of its values: For all the other variables in this part of the individual, it is stated that the upper and lower limits are zero. In this stage 5 repetitions are realized and from them is chosen the one that has lower value of RSS.

In the third stage it will be found the solution in which only are taken into account the important variables obtained in the previous stage. For this are extended the boundaries

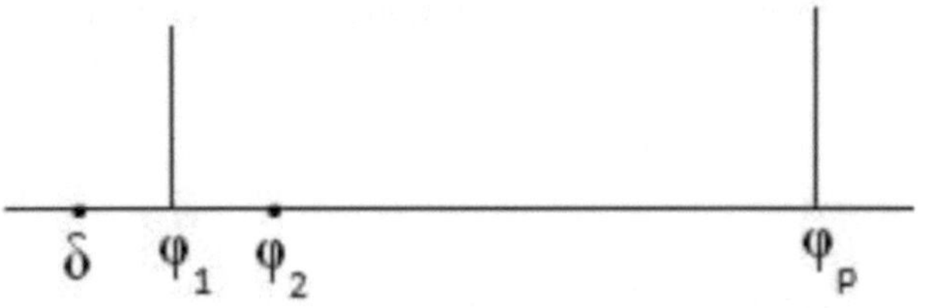

Fig. 2. Solution using the most important values.

of the variables of the solution obtained in the previous stage, which absolute value is grater than 0.01. The upper limits of the variables considered are the nonzero values obtained in the previous best solution of more than 1.0 and the lower with less than 1.0. The upper and lower limits of the other variables of the autoregressive components of the individual will be zero. With these limits is solved once until the optimum is not improved in 250 iterations. Since the GA are random for each problem were performed 5 iterations, and of them it was chosen the best.

The main characteristics of the SAGA version used in this work that make them original are:

- Real coding is used for the variables of the problem. This allows a more simple code that can easily pass from one stage to another of those presented here.
- The probabilities of crossing and mutation are characteristics of each individual and the crossing and mutation procedures are established on the basis of these individual characteristics.
- The repetitions of crossing and mutation are multiple though the values that take are not very big.
- It was introduced a control mechanism that prevents the proliferation within the population of the best individual copies, thus eliminating the risk of premature convergence.

Above all, the last three features are inspired by the fact that the nature behavior is more flexible than rigid, and therefore should be allowed more variability within the SAGA.

The main disadvantage that has the use of SAGA, is the major computational cost compared with traditional versions, but the advantage that is obtained is that with the same code it is possible to solve automatically all the problems of nonlinear modelling of TS.

4. Autoregressive models

The TS linear models are important because there are many applications where linear estimations are sufficient, besides they have a wide use in industrial situations. On the other hand, are also important because there are other methodologies that use forecasting (Medeiros & Veiga, 2000,2005). The classic reference for the treatment of linear models is (Box & Jenkins, 1976).

In the specific case of the AR that we care for TS, the value at a certain time should be calculated as a linear expression of the values of a certain number of previous measurements, as described in (Box & Jenkins, 1976). The AR models developed here fulfill the stochastic process of the residuals $\{a_t\}$ associated with them; it is not a white noise. The latter will allow that once it is built a good AR model of TS, it can be build for it another AR model for residuals $\{a_t\}$, which together with the original one allow obtaining the equivalent of an ARMA model, but with major forecasting possibilities.

On the other hand, to solve the problem 1 it is first necessary to address the following questions, taking into account that is necessary to find an AR model with K terms, where K is established beforehand:

1. How many p terms must be considered?
2. At what intervals are the coefficients of the linear expression?
3. What K terms are most appropriate to solve this problem?
4. What are the values of this K terms that minimize the function (3)?

The following summarizes the results of the BJ methodology that is used in our proposal.

4.1 Main results of the Box Jenkins methodology

Univarieted TS were analyzed by the Box-Jenkins (BJ) methodology from the formulation of equations in differences with a random additive component denominated white noise. For these BJ models the conditions in which is presented the stationarity property of the series and the scheme that has to be follow to determine the parameters of the particular model were studied.

The most general model is denominated ARMA(p,q) (Autoregressive Moving Average) and indicates the presence of autoregressive components both in the observable variable $\{Z_t\}$ as well as in the white noise $\{a_t\}$. A particular class of model for stationary series corresponds to the Autoregressive models AR(p) (that are denoted as AR), which is represented by the expression:

$$Z_t = \delta + \phi_1 Z_{t-1} + \phi_2 Z_{t-2} + ... + \phi_p Z_{t-p} + a_t \tag{5}$$

When the series is stationary δ and ϕ_i are constants that satisfy the following relations:

$$|\phi_1| < 1, \tag{6}$$

$$\mu = \frac{\delta}{1 - \sum \phi_i}$$

and

$$\sum \phi_i < 1$$

Where μ represents the average of the series $\{ F_t \}$. The relations in (6) are a consequence of the stationarity property and can be consulted in (Box & Jenkins, 1976).

The correlation structure presented by a TS related to an AR model for separate observations k time units is given by the autocorrelation function:

$$p_k = \phi_1 p_{k-1} + \phi_2 p_{k-2} + ... + \phi_p p_{k-p}$$

where p_k is the autocorrelation for data of series separated k time units. From the initial conditions that satisfy this equation in differences are presented the following possible behaviors: exponential or sinusoidal decay. This permits to determine if a series is stationary or not.

The most general model is the model ARIMA (p, d, q) (AutoRegressive Integrated Moving Average processes) that includes not stationary series for which apply differences of order d to stationarize it:

$$\phi_p(B)\nabla^d z_t = \delta + \theta_q(B)a_t$$

Where $\phi_p(B), \theta_q(B)$ and B are operators that satisfy the following relations:

$$\phi_p(B)z_t = (1 - \phi_1 B - \phi_2 B^2 - ... - \phi_p B^p) = z_t - \phi_1 z_{t-1} - ... - \phi_p z_{t-p}$$

and

$$\theta_q(B)a_t = (1 - \theta_1 B - \theta_2 B^2 - ... - \theta_q B^q)a_t = a_t - \theta_1 a_{t-1} - ... - \theta_q a_{t-q}$$

$$B^k z_t = z_{t-k}$$

$$\nabla^d z_t = (1 - B)^d z_t$$

Similarly, there is a general model that considers the presence of stationarity or cyclic movement of short term of longitude s modeled by the expression:

$$\phi_P(B^s)\phi_p(B)\nabla^d z_t = \delta + \theta_Q(B^s)\theta_q(B)a_t$$

Where $\phi_P(B^s)$ y $\theta_Q(B^s)$ are polynomial operators similar to the above mention, but its powers are multiples of s, $\{a_t\}$ are residuals in the moment t and θ_t are its components in the part of moving averages.

BJ methodology satisfies the following stages:

(a). Identification of a possible model among the ARIMA type models. To accomplish this first is necessary to determine if the series is stationary or not. When an observed series is not stationary the difference operator is applied:

$$\nabla z_t = z_t - z_{t-1}$$

as many times as it will be necessary up to stationarity. To avoid overdifferentiation it is calculated the variances of the new obtained series choosing the one with the smallest value.

When a series is stationary in its mean, but its variance is increasing or decreasing according to BJ methodology it should be applied a transformation (generally logarithmic) for the stability of the variance. It is important to notice that this is not necessary in our proposal.

Given a stationary series the behavior pattern of the autocorrelation function and the partial autocorrelation indicate the possible number of parameters i and j that the model should have.

Besides the presence of stationarity in a temporal series there is other property that is required in the ARIMA models denominated invertibility, which permits to represent the series as an autoregressive model of infinite extension that satisfy the condition:

$$\lim_{i \to \infty} \phi_i = 0$$

The above mention allows that with a finite number of terms could be obtained an expression that satisfies the form (1) for the series. This means that only the ARIMA models that have the invertibility property can be approximated by an AR model of the form (1).

(b). Estimation of the model parameters by means of non linear estimation techniques.

(c). Checking that the model provides an adequate fitting and that the basic assumptions implied in the model are satisfied through the analysis of the residuals behavior. Is important to mention that our proposal does not need such analysis because the residuals do not correspond, in general, to the white noise.

(d). Use of the model.

Next are presented the characteristics of the heuristic proposed algorithms. Note that these algorithms are used to build models AR of TS since the ARMA models are built from these.

4.2 Proposed algorithms

The heuristic algorithms built in this work are based in the following assumptions:

(a). Regardless the original series type (stationary or non stationary) the model looked will always be of the form AR presented in (1).

(b). To determine how many delays p are required, first is necessary to choose the differences series that will be used to estimate these, afterwards it is defined the number of delays according to the behavior of the autocorrelation sample function of the difference series chosen. This implies a difference with the BJ methodology, which applies the number of delays under the terms of the information that provides both the autocorrelation function as well as the partial autocorrelation function and the hypothesis of the random component as white noise. This choice has as consequence in the models developed here that at will not be white noise.

(c). The conditions of (6) become more relax, since in spite of be satisfied it in the stationary series, in this work these will be applied to series that could not be stationary.

It is necessary to add that the heuristic algorithms presented here allow the treatment of series with trend and variance time-dependant, since they do not require the conditions that traditionally are asked to the TS, as is the fact that they are stationary or of stationary variance or that they result from applying a logarithmic transformation or moving averages.

The first algorithm that we propose builds a linear approximation for the series of differences (of first, second or third order) that could be stationary. Then, from this linear approximation and using the result 1, it is built another linear model of the original series.

4.2.1 First algorithm

In this stage, first it is decided which series will be used to work with among the original, the first differences, the second differences and in our case it is included the possibility of working with third differences series. In order to decide this it is chosen the series that have the lowest variance, which we consider as an indication of having a stationary series (Box & Jenkins, 1976).

Once that was chosen the series to work with it will be estimated how many terms are necessary for the linear approximation of the series with base in the autocorrelation function. In this work were calculated 30 values for the autocorrelation function and for selecting how many terms are required two cases were utilized. If the function is decreasing a value of 4 is taken, on the contrary a value equal to the value in which the first maximum of this function is observed it will be chosen (see Figure 3). With this procedure if the series presents stationarity and the period is smaller than 30 the models that are built here can represent appropriately such stationarity.

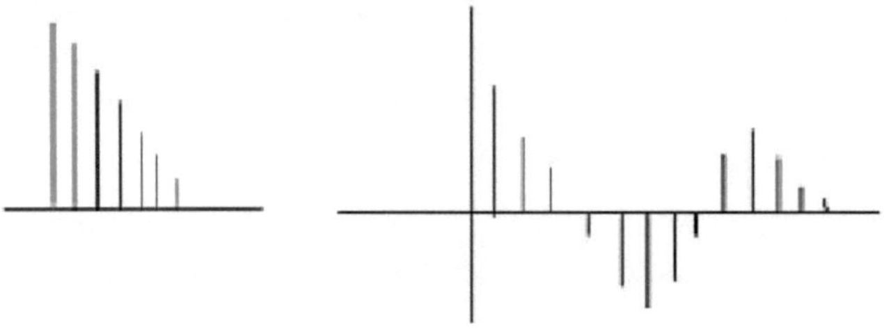

Fig. 3. Possible autocorrelation function graphs.

With this information are built the limits for the coefficients intervals of the chosen series, for that are taken all the ϕ_i in $[-1,1]$ except the independent term δ which limits are calculated between zero an the average value of the series. The reason why these limits are established is obtained from the equations presented in (6) With all the previous information it is complete the proposal of the p number of terms required and that are the limits of its coefficients. From this information is solved the **problem 1** applying the SAGA in the first two stages depicted in section 3.2 with base on the following:

Result 1. If $\{y_t\}$ is a difference series for $\{x_t\}$ with a model

$$y_t = h_0 + h_1 y_{t-1} + h_2 y_{t-2} + ... + +h_k y_{t-k}$$

then, for the difference series with terms $y_t = x_t - x_{t-1}$ must be

$$x_t = h_0 + (1 + h_1)x_{t-1} + (h_2 - h_1)x_{t-2} + ... + (h_k - h_{k-1})y_{t-k} - h_k y_{t-k-1} \tag{7}$$

is a model for the series $\{x_t\}$.

From this result two important consequences are obtained:

- The model for the series $\{x_t\}$ has one term more than the series $\{y_t\}$
- If y_t has a coefficient value between -1.0 and 1.0, the coefficient of x_t may not be in this range.

Applying the **result 1** as many times as necessary, it can be obtained a model for the original series, and to this model it is applied the stage three of section 3.2 to obtain a linear model for the TS. Note that if it is had a model AR for some series of differences, the model built for the original series has more terms than the series of differences, so if K terms are needed for the original series, then must be found models for the series of differences of less terms that K.

4.2.2 Second algorithm

The second algorithm only utilizes of the BJ methodology the estimation of how many terms are necessary in the linear approximation of the series of differences, which could be stationary, thus, from this is determined the numbers of terms that will be used in the original series.

From now on, are applied the stages presented in section 3.2, taking the limits of all the coefficients in $[-1, 1]$, but always working with the original series. There is not a result that justifies the use of these limits, and only it has been found a reference (Cortez at all, 2004) where it is used. On the other hand is a fact that a high percentage of cases in the NN3 presented better results with this algorithm than with the first. As an example of this the second algorithm outperformed the first in 46 of the 111 examples of NN3-Complete.

5. NN3 results

The international competition *NN3 Artificial Neural Network & Computational Intelligence Forecasting Competition 2007* aims at assessing the latest methodologies for the forecasting of TS. This competition is open to use methods based on Neural Networks, Fuzzy Logic, Genetic Algorithms and others in the area of artificial intelligence. The problems in question are presented in two groups called NN3-Complete (with 111 examples of TS) and NN3-Reduced (with 11 examples), and the purpose of the competition is to obtain the best models for each example of the two sets using the same methodology. The notation of this section is similar to that used in NN3.

To evaluate the performance of a model in some example s, it is estimated the forecasting F and it is measured the performance with the average of the indicator *Symmteric Mean Absolute Percent Error* SMAPE in all the values of the series. The SMAPE measures the absolute symmetric error in percentage between the real values of the original series Z and the forecasting F for all observations t of the test set of size n for each series s with SMAPE equal to:

$$\frac{1}{n}\sum_{t=1}^{n}\frac{|z_t - f_t|}{(z_t + f_t)/2} * 100 \tag{8}$$

and finally it is averaged over all examples in the same set of data. Other measures of forecasting accuracy of a model can be found in (Hyndman & Koehler, 2006).

This indicator can evaluate the performance of applying different methodologies on the same set of data and the methodology that produces the lowest value is considered the best. In the set NN3-Complete the best result was of 14.84% and applying the algorithms developed in this work was of 16.31%. In the NN3-Reduced the results were 13.07% and 15.00% respectively. However, it is possible to build linear models with the methodology presented in this work to improve these results because:

- Although the competition was intended to determine the best model for each example in this work was found an AR model with 4 terms for each example. It is expected that if it is divided the series in a training set and in other set of test it can be found models with higher forecasting capacity that improve the results obtained.
- It were not used ARMA models that include the behavior of the residuals or the advancement of forecasting that substantially improve the results.

To build the NN3 competition models were conducted several activities. First it was worked the NN3-Reduced problems where, with the two algorithms developed, were realized 50 runs of every algorithm in each example looking for linear models with 4 terms. Table 1 presents the results of linear expressions and calculation of RSS.

After reviewing the behavior of the 50 solutions of these examples it was concluded that five runs were enough to obtain satisfactory results. For this reason only five runs were realized for the examples of the NN3-Complete using each algorithm and it was chosen the best of these. The results of the NN3-Complete examples are not presented.

Problem	Linear Model	RSS
101	$F_t = 1269.3358 + 0.3467Z_{t-1} + 0.6978Z_{t-12} - 0.2921Z_{t-13}$	1713.55
102	$F_t = 1.9987 + 0.9218Z_{t-1} + 0.9574Z_{t-12} - 0.8792Z_{t-13}$	5440.262
103	$F_t = 1.9989 + 0.9218Z_{t-1} + 0.8124Z_{t-12} - 0.3734Z_{t-13}$	80019.738
104	$F_t = 9.113 + 0.7252Z_{t-1} + 0.8316Z_{t-12} - 0.5592Z_{t-13}$	7321.538
105	$F_t = 1.998 + 0.9099Z_{t-1} + 0.3104Z_{t-11} - 0.2225Z_{t-13}$	1513.984
106	$F_t = 2821.9541 + 0.2673Z_{t-2} - 0.1699Z_{t-7} + 0.3422Z_{t-12}$	4464.87
107	$F_t = 0.9978 + 0.7937Z_{t-1} + 0.3152Z_{t-12} - 0.1125Z_{t-13}$	1387.011
108	$F_t = 2000.5819 + 0.2885Z_{t-2} - 0.1456Z_{t-4} + 0.2379Z_{t-5}$	10417.433
109	$F_t = 1.9988 + 0.9951Z_{t-1}$	2297.306
110	$F_t = 1863.0699 + 0.2520Z_{t-1} - 0.1058Z_{t-5} + 0.2359Z_{t-11}$	18593.279
111	$F_t = 474.1106 + 0.2420Z_{t-11} - 0.3319Z_{t-12} + 0.2688Z_{t-13}$	7248.281

Table 1. Linear models for the NN3-REDUCED.

5.1 NN3 graphs

In this section are showed some of the graphs of the series obtained with the best result of some heuristic algorithms here presented. The values correspondent to the last 18 points on the graph are the result of the forecasting obtained on having evaluated the expressions of the linear models that appear in Table 1.

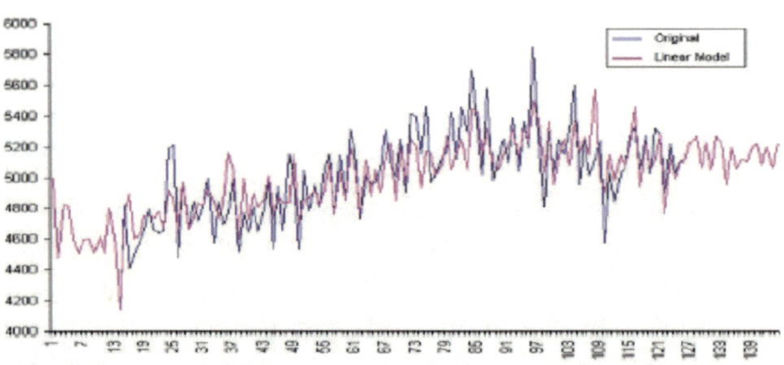

Fig. 4. Example 101.

6. ARMA models for time series

In this section the methodology already developed is applied to obtain AR components of the error series obtained by subtracting from the original series the values that are assigned by the AR model. With this is obtained a new model by adding these two components, thus it is obtained the equivalent in our methodology of the traditional ARMA models.

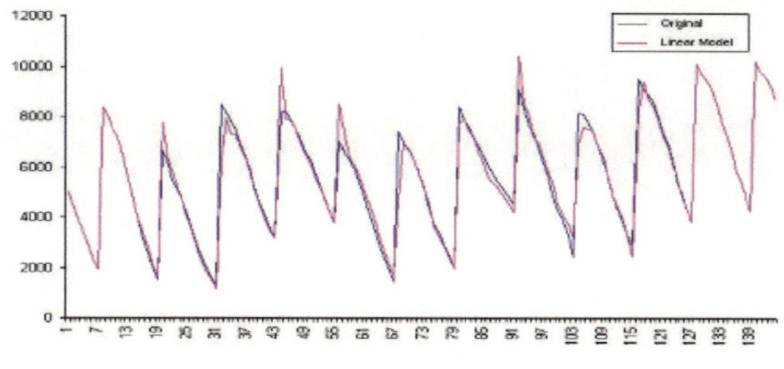

Fig. 5. Example 102.

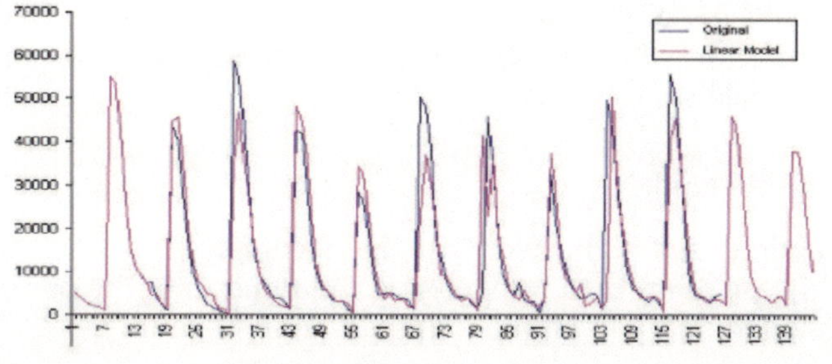

Fig. 6. Example 103.

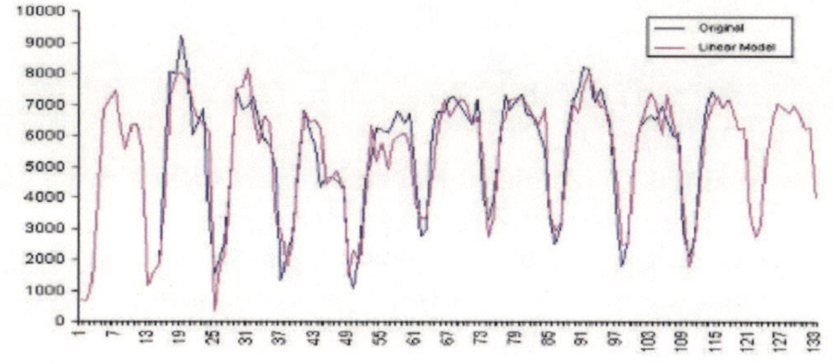

Fig. 7. Example 104.

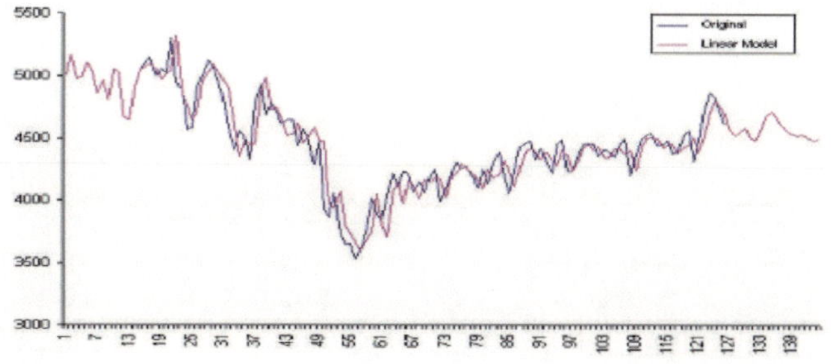

Fig. 8. Example 105.

In the first part of this section is presented, as an example, the Fig. 10 of the error obtained with our methodology for a certain series for a particular series that for its behavior it can be concluded that is not a white noise. Note that when are realized tests of white noise to the errors obtained with this methodology it was not observed that this was a white noise.

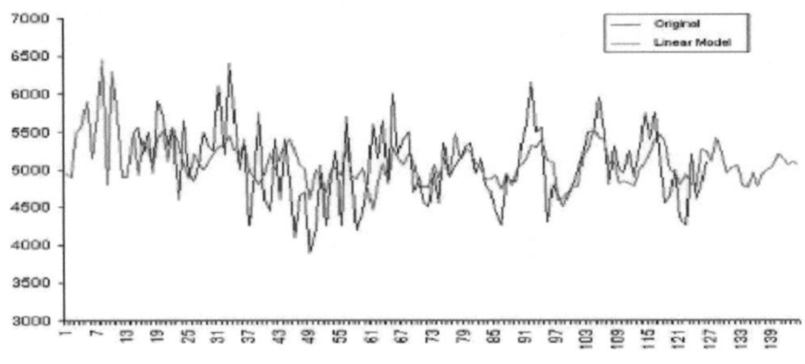

Fig. 9. Example 106.

Therefore it can be built AR models for these error series, which will have the capability to adequately model the error, which allows, when considering these two models, to obtain a bigger forecasting capability.

6.1 Building of the ARMA models

The most general models used in this work are the Autoregressive Moving Averages ARMA (p, q) that contain the presence of autoregressive components in the observable variable Z_t and in the error a_t, where:

$$a_t = Z_t - (\delta + \sum_{i=1}^{p} \phi_i Z_{t-i})$$

and

$$F_t = \delta + \sum_{i=1}^{p} \phi_i Z_{t-i} + \sum_{j=1}^{q} \gamma_j a_{t-j}$$

Once the AR model is obtained for a series it can be built an ARMA model from the acquiring other AR model for the series obtained when considering the a_t errors between the original series and its AR model. When is added to the AR model an additional component that considers the autoregressive terms corresponding to the error is obtained the complete ARMA model. Figure. 10 shows an example of the error for the series.

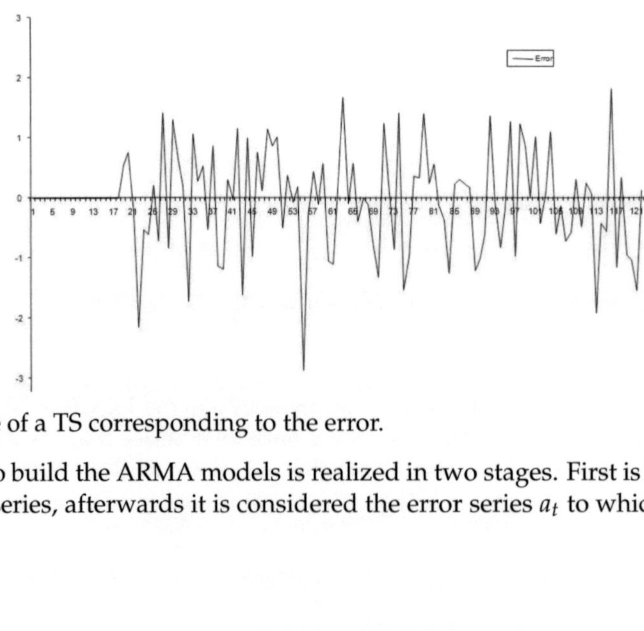

Fig. 10. Example of a TS corresponding to the error.

The procedure to build the ARMA models is realized in two stages. First is built an AR model for the original series, afterwards it is considered the error series a_t to which it is found other

AR model. In both procedures the most important stage is to define how many terms are required for each model.

From know on the ARMA notation for a series changes, for this it will be indicated to which part of the expression of AR or MA corresponds, and the constants ϕ_i and γ_j will represent the terms of the corresponding expression, in other words the terms F_{t-i} and a_{t-j} it will not be written.

7. The forcasting delay phenomenon

Analyzing the graphs of the built models with this methodology for the examples of the NN3-complete it was detected a phenomenon that visually appears as if the graph of the model were almost the same that the original series, but with a displacement of one unit to the right. This phenomenon was observed in the NN3-Complete in 20 examples: 51, 64, 66, 74, 80, 82, 83, 84, 85, 86, 88, 89, 90, 91, 92, 95, 100, 105, 107 and 109.

Given that the first 50 examples of the competition corresponded to series of 50 values (apparently built by experts) and the last 61 examples were series of 150 terms (seemingly of real phenomenon) it was supposed that the 34% of the real examples of the NN3 present this behavior. From this information we can assume that this phenomenon appears in a large percentage of the models built with this metodology and, for this reason the model built with this methodology will give better results when applying to these series. Following is showed in Fig. 11 an example of this phenomenon corresponding to the AR model of the example 74 obtained with the methodology of this work.

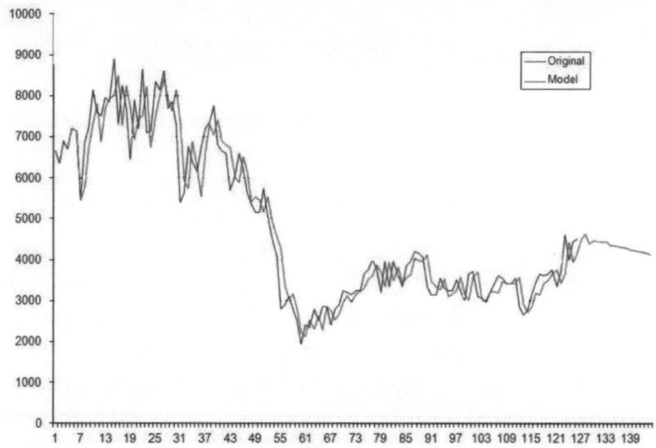

Fig. 11. Example 74 of the NN3-Complete.

This phenomenon was called in this work as *forecasting delay* (FD), since is equivalent to forecast in a certain moment what happen in the previous moment.

8. The procedure of advancement of forecasting

The FD phenomenon can be used by modifying the graph of the linear models obtained by applying a displacement of one unit to the left of its graph. This procedure was defined as *advancement of forecasting* (AF) and it is formalized next.

Definition: Be a time series with model AR or ARMA

$$F_t = \delta + \sum_{i=1}^{p} \phi_i Z_{t-i} + \sum_{j=1}^{q} \gamma_j a_{t-j}$$

The advancement of the forecasting was denominated as the following operation:

$$F_t = F_{t-1}, for, t > \max(p, q) \tag{9}$$

When is applied to an AR or ARMA this operation it is said that is a linear model AR or linear ARMA with AF respectively. In figure 12 is shown the linear model of the example 74 with AF.

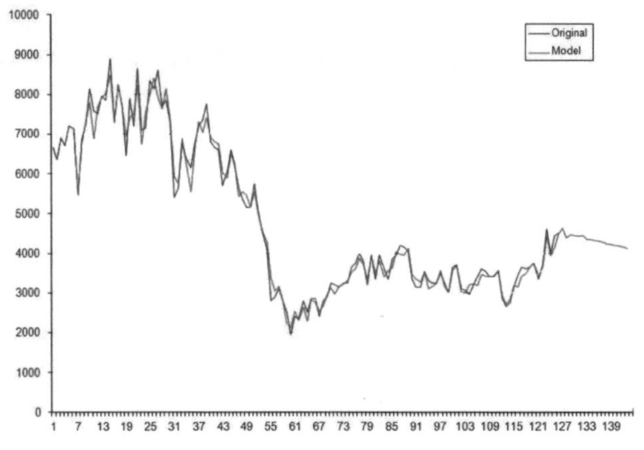

Fig. 12. Example 74 of NN3-Complete to which it was applied the advancement of forecasting.

A first result obtained is that if a series that presents FD it is applied the AF, then the value of RSS for these models is smaller than the error of the original ARMA models. This is caused because when is displaced the graph of a model one unit to the left, which is what means the operation (9), almost it is superimposed to the graph of the original series. Extrapolating this behavior to the region of forecasting it is expected that the same effect occurs and that the values of the linear model with AF be a better approximation than those of the linear models. Due to the above it is supposed that the linear models with AF will have a better forecasting capacity. As an example, in Table 2 is showed the improvement of the linear models with AF for 10 examples of NN3 that present DF.

The improvement (imp) in the models here presented ranges from 10.28% to 97.27% with an average of 48.48%, and it is expected that as the percentage is greater the ability of the forecasting model increases by a similar proportion. It should be noted that when it is had an AR model with four terms it is very difficult to improve substantially the value of RSS by incrementing the terms of the AR model or including terms of the part of the moving averages.

Example	AR	RSS	RSS AF	imp %
51	$0.9968 + 0.8129_1 + 0.6594_{12} - 0.4799_{13}$	3767.009	3379.4502	10.28
64	$0.3894 + 0.9199_1 + 0.6778_{12} - 0.5999_{13}$	3899.114	3495.0649	10.36
66	$0.9984 + 0.9202_1 + 0.5858_{12} - 0.5103_{13}$	3893.0544	2803.1406	27.99
74	$0.9993 + 0.9448_1 + 0.5226_{12} - 0.4800_{13}$	4894.1655	3340.5911	31.74
86	$-0.9991 + 0.6235_1 + 0.2161_2 + 0.1907_{17}$	4114.1499	1917.1523	53.40
88	$0.9979 + 0.7001_1 + 0.1531_{11} + 0.1438_{18}$	2449.5383	1265.7606	48.32
89	$0.9995 + 0.8914_1 + 0.2169_{12} - 0.1079_{13}$	1247.8290	339.8757	97.27
105	$1.9980 + 0.9099_1 + 0.3104_{11} - 0.2225_{13}$	1513.984	664.8109	56.08

Table 2. Comparison of RSS for linear and linear with AF models.

9. Comparisons with other methodologies

To evaluate the performance of a model on a TS data is divided into two sets called training set and test set. The training set has the first values of the series (approximately 90% of the total) and the test set the last 10%. The information of the training set model is used to choose the model and evaluate the parameters. Once chosen the corresponding model is evaluated its ability to forecast the test set, and when it is had different model proposals it is common to choose the best result of the test set. For this assessment can be used several measures of performance (Hyndman & Koehler, 2006). In this work preferably is used RSS.

To build the models with the methodology of this wok it is proceeded as follows:

(a). In this first stage is calculated the AR part of the model. For this, from $K = 2$ are built the models AR with K terms and is tested the performance on the test set. As soon as the first K value is obtained where the RSS of the model is less than the values obtained for the $K - 1$ and $K + 1$ is considered that the AR part of the model has the already found K terms and passes to the second stage.

(b). It is calculated the error series obtained from the original series and the ones calculated by the model obtained in the previous stage. On this new series it is applied the same procedure above mention and it is obtained the part corresponding to the component of the MA moving average of the ARMA model. It may be the case that by including the MA components of the model it will be had the worst approximations in the test set than those obtained with the AR part. In this case the model would only have the AR component.

(c). It is checked if the model AR obtained in the stage 1 presents the FD phenomenon occurs, and if so to realize the displacement of the graph one unit to the left according to (9) as long as with this procedure the result is improved.

To test the performance of our models of (8) we used the series A, B, C, D, E and F appearing in (Box & Jenkins, 1976), used and presented in chapter 3.

In (Hansen at all, 1999) are shown the results of building several linear models for these series. The first is the classic BJ, and others apply when BJ model do not satisfy the postulate that the error is a white noise. In (McDonald & Yexiao, 1994) it is indicated that the use of these latest models improved from 8% to 13% the capability of prediction of the model when the error is not white noise. Immediately it is presented the relationship of these models for the linear models.

- Standard ARIMA model. Here applies the traditional methodology of BJ where the main components are the autoregressive models with moving averages that are linear in the time series $\{Z_t\}$ and white noise $\{a_t\}$ (Box & Jenkins, 1976).
- Ordinary least squares (OLS). These are used when the distribution of the error presents the leptokurtosis problem and allows diminishing the error in the forecasting (Huber, 2004).
- Least Absolute Deviation (LAD). It is used to minimize the sum of the absolute values rather the sum of squares. This is done to reduce the influence of the extreme errors (Huber, 2004).
- Generalized t-distribution (GT). Here is minimized the objective function in relation to the parameters but assuming that the error has a t-distribution (McDonald & Newey, 1988).
- Exponential Generalized beta distribution of the second kind (EGB2). Here it is supposed that the errors have a distribution of this kind (McDonald & Newey, 1988).

Additionally in (Hansen at all, 1999) are presented the results of two models of neural networks, one heuristic (Heuristic NN), and another based on genetic algorithms (GANN), which are included in the commercial software BioComp Systemt's NeuroGenetic Optimizer ®.

To make comparisons with the models described above, it will be used the same size of training set and test sets shown in (Hansen at all, 1999), where if the number of elements of the series is greater than 100 the sizes of test sets are set to 10. In the event that they are less than or equal to 100 the test sets will have size five. The size of the training sets is the original size of the series minus the number of elements of the test set.

With the methodology of this work were obtained the models of the Table 3, where for each example is presented the component AR and if necessary the MA. Note that when it is shown "AF" in the last column of the table it was applied the displacement presented in (9).

Series	AR	MA	AF
A	$1.1035 + 0.5648_1 + 0.1919_6 + 0.1245_9$ $+0.0544_{13}$	$-0.2271_1 + 0.1046_2 + 0.051_{43}$	No
B	$0.8302 + 1.1274_1 - 0.1685_2 + 0.0644_4$ -0.0258_6	$0.0460_2 - 0.0576_5 + 0.1381_6$ $+0.0587_7$	Yes
C	$0.8425_1 - 0.8488_2$		No
D	$0.7609 + 0.8997_1 + 0.0511_{12} - 0.0335_{16}$		Yes
E	$1.9993 + 1.0051_1 - 0.2590_3 + 0.1538_{10}$		Yes
F	$1.9996 + 0.6555_2 + 0.2938_3$		No

Table 3. Solution to the Box Jenkins problems.

In Table 4 are shown the results of the different methodologies presented in (Hansen at all, 1999) and those obtained with the algorithm proposed in this work. Table 4 is used as a criterion of comparison of the sum of absolute values of errors. The results of our model are presented in the line called "Linear AF" and the place obtained when confronted with other models is in the line called "Place." It should be noted that each group of comparisons, except in one instance", the results obtained with our methodology are better than those obtained with the confronted statistical methods and also have good results when compared with those obtained by neural networks.

Table 5 presents the results of comparing the method proposed in this work with those reported in (Cortez at all, 2004). In this paper are confronted the methodologies:

- Holt-Winters Methodology. This methodology is widely used due to its simplicity and accuracy of its forecasting's especially with periodic time series. It is based on four basic equations that represent the regularity, trend, periodicity and forecasting of the series (Chatfield, 2000).
- Box-Jenkins Methodology that already was widely commented in previous sections (Box & Jenkins, 1976).
- Evolutionary forecasting method. It is a methodology based on evolutionary programming (Cortez at all, 2004).
- Evolutionary meta algorithms. It is a metaheuristic that uses two architecture levels, in the first is chosen the ARMA model in question, and in the second the corresponding parameters are estimated (Cortez at all, 2004).

To test the performance of the models, were used some of the series in (Hyndman, 2003). which are known as: Passengers, which is a series (144 data) that represents the number of monthly passengers on an airline; Paper, this series (120 data) represents the paper monthly sales in France; Deaths, which is a series (169 data) that represents the death and injury on roads of Germany; Maxtemp represents the maximum temperatures (240 data) in Melbourne, Australia; and Chemical, which is a series (198 data) of readings of the concentrations of a chemical reactor. The training sets of these series contain 90% of the data and remaining 10% are in the test set.

	Series A	Series B	Series C	Series D	Series E	Series F	Series G
Linear AF	3.9	75	5.9	2.87	87	46	173
Heuristic NN	4.519	88.312	9.138	2.942	98.873	43.966	
GA NN	3.705	72.398	6.684	2.952	69.536	36.4	
ARIMA ML	4.005	78.855	11.247	3.114	3.114	49.161	
OLS	3.937	83.17	10.74	3.08	114.8	45.5	
LAD	3.96	79.47	10.3	3.066	117.6	44.46	
GT	3.937	80.68	10.25	3.064	106.5	44.59	
EBG2	4.017	81.01	10.3	3.066	111.8	44.5	
PLACE	1	2	1	1	2	6	

Table 4. Comparison of the models with regard to a sum of values of absolute errors.

Using the method proposed in this work it were obtained the models that are shown in table 5. Note that form this examples none presents DF.

In Table 6 were confronted the results for these TS. The results of our models are shown in the column called "Linear AF" and the place gotten when comparing with the other models is shown in the column "Place".

From the results presented in the tables of this section it can be concluded that the model built with our methodology outperform all the models obtained with statistical methods and are competitive with non-linear methods presented here. In addition, it must be added that this methodology is fully automated and allows modelling TS than other traditional methodologies can not.

Series	AR	MA
Passengers	$1.3400 + 0.9087_1 + 1.0612_{12} - 0.9633_{13}$	
Paper	$6.2323 + 0.9583_{12}$	
Deaths	$1.9941 + 0.9053_{12} + 0.0832_{14}$	$4.3636 + 0.405_2$
Maxtemp	$0.7046 + 0.3362_1 - 0.0668_7 + 0.4060_{11}$ $+0.2910_{12}$	$18.662 + 0.1045_5 - 0.1857_{11}$ -0.1930_{12}
Chemical	$0.5419 + 0.6081_1 + 0.3753_7 - 0.0144_{15}$	

Table 5. Solutions with the methodology proposed in this work.

Series	Holt Winter	Box Jenkings	Heuristic Evolutionay	Meta Evolutionay	Linear AF	Place
Passengers	16.5	17.8	21.9+ -1.2	17.2+ - 0.2	16.3	1
Paper	49.2	61	60.2+ - 2.2	52.5+ - 0.1	5.59	1
Deaths	135	144	135.9+ - 1.7	137+ - 2	140	3
Maxtemp	0.72	1.07	0.95+ - 0.02	0.93+ - 0.4	0.94	2
Chemical	0.35	0.36	0.36+ - 0.0	0.34+ -0.0	0.34	1

Table 6. Comparison with other methodologies.

10. Conclusions

From the above it can be obtained several conclusions. The first is that the methodology developed here based on setting out the building of linear models as an optimization problem, where the construction of the problem is guided by the classical TS theory, is correct because allows to build better models than those obtained by the traditional methods.

Another conclusion is that the fact of choosing the SAGA as an alternative to solve the problems set out here is very important since allows exploring the solution space of our problem and finding the most significant variables to solve it. In addition, the SAGA version developed has proved to be very robust in solving many different problems with out adjustment of parameters.

As a result not contemplated it was found that the phenomenon of FD, which allowed us to construct new linear models for TS, which in some cases are better alternatives compared to other linear and nonlinear models. In addition, these new models have great potential for application in areas such as industrial control, economics, finance, etc. In particular, we think that the FD is a characteristic of the phenomenon in question, but that is only detected if the model is built with an appropriate methodology, particularly in the selection and setting limits of variables.

Finally, it should be noted that having a fully automated methodology with the ability to model phenomena that other methodologies can not open a whole world of possibilities in the development of computer systems for modelling and process control.

11. References

Alberto I. & Beamonte A. & Gargallo P. & Mateo P. & Salvador M.(2010). Variable selection in STAR models with neighbourhood effects using genetic algorithms. *Journal of Forecasting*, Vol 29, Issue 8, page numbers (728-750), ISSN 0277-6693.

Bäck T. (1992).The interaction of mutation rate, selection, and self-adaptation within genetic algorithm. *Proc. 2nd Conf. on Parallel Problem Solving from Nature*, (Brussels,1992), ISBN 0444897305, Elsevier Amsterdam.

Bäck T. (1992). Self-adaptation in genetic algorithms. *Proc. 1st Eur. Conf. on Artificial Life*. MIT Press. Cambridge, MA.

Battaglia F. & Protopapas M.(2011). Time-varying multi-regime models fitting by genetic algorithms. *Journal of Time Series Analysis*, Vol 32, Issue 3. page numbers (237-252), ISSN 1467-9892.

Box G. & Jenkins G. (1976). *Time Series Analysis: Forecasting and Control*.Holden-Day, INC. ISBN 0-13-060774-6, Oakland, California USA 1976.

Chatfield C. (2000). *The Series Forecasting*. CRC Press. ISBN 1584880635, USA.

Chiogna M. & Gaetan C. & Masarotto G.(2008). Automatic identification of seasonal transfer function models by means of iterative stepwise and genetic algorithms. *Journal of Time Series Analysis*, Vol 29, Issue 1, page numbers (37-50), ISSN 1467-9892.

Cortez P. & Rocha M. & Neves J. (1996). Evolving Time Series Forecasting ARMA Models. *Journal of Heuristics*, Vol 10., No 4., page numbers (415-429), ISSN 1381-1231.

Eiben Á. E. & Hinterding R. & Michalewicz Z. (1999). Parameter Control in Evolutionary Algorithms. *IEEE Transactions on Evolutionary Computation*, Vol 3., No 2., page numbers (124-141), ISSN 1089-778X.

Flores P. & Garduño R. & Morales L. & Valdez M. (1999). Prediction of Met-enkephalin Conformation using a Sieve Self Adaptive Genetic Algorithm. *Proceedings of the Second International Symposium on Artificial Intelligence: Adaptive Systems ISSAS'99.*, page numbers (186-190)

Garduño R. & Morales L. & Flores P. (2000). Dinámica de Procesos Biológicos no Covalentes a Nivel Molecular. *Revista Mexicana de Física*, Vol 46., Suplemento 2., page numbers (135-141), ISSN 0035-001X.

Garduño R. & Morales L. B. & Flores P. (2001). About Singularities at the Global Minimum of Empiric Force Fields for Peptides. *Journal at Molecular Structure (Theochem)*, page numbers (277-284), ISSN 0166-1280.

Guerrero V. (2003). *Análisis Estadístico de Series de Tiempo Económicas*,Thomson Editores, ISBN 9706863265, México DF.

Hansen J. & McDonald J. & Nelson R. (1999). Time Series Prediction with Genetic Algorithms designed neural networks, an empirical comparison with modern statistical models. *Computational Intelligence*, Vol 15., No 3., page numbers (171-184), ISSN 0824-7935.

Huber P. (2004). *Robust Statistics*. Wiley-IEEE. ISBN 978-0-521-88068-8, USA.

Hyndman R.& Koehler A. (2006). Another look at measures of forecast accuracy. *International Journal of Forecasting*, Vol 22, Issue 4, page numbers (679-688), ISSN 0169-2070.

Hyndman R. (2003). Time Series Data Library.*Available in http;//www.robjhyndman.com/TSDL*

Mateo F. & Sovilj D. & Gadea R.(2010). Approximate k -NN delta test minimization method using genetic algorithms; Application to time series. *Neurocomputing*, Vol 73, Issue 10-12. page numbers (2017-2029), ISSN 0925-2312.

McDonald J. & Newey W. (1988). Partially adaptive estimation of regression models via the generalized t distribution.*Econometric Theory*, Vol 4., page numbers (428-457), ISSN 0266-4666.

McDonald J. & Yexiao X. (1994). Some forecasting applications of partially adaptive estimators of ARIMA models. *Economics Letters*, Vol 45., Issue 4., page numbers (155-160), ISSN 0165-1765.

Medeiros C. & Veiga Á. (2000). A Hybrid Linear-Model for Time Series Forecasting. *IEEE Transactions on Neural Networks*, Vol 11., No 6., page numbers (1402-1412), ISSN 1045-9227.

Medeiros C. & Veiga Á. (2005). A Flexible Coefficient Smooth Transition Time Series Model. *IEEE Transactions on Neural Networks*, Vol 16., No 1., page numbers (97-113), ISSN 1045-9227.

Miller B. & Goldberg D. (1995). Genetic Algorithms, Tournament Selection, and the Effects of Noise. *Complex Systems*, Vol 9., page numbers (193-212), ISSN 0891-2513.

Journal of Time Series Analysis. *available in http;//www.blackwellpublishing.com/journal.asp?ref=0143-9782*

Palit A. & Popovic D. (2005). *Computational Intelligence in Time Series Forecasting, theory and engineering applications.* Springe-Verlag. ISBN 1852339489, London.

Sánchez V. & Flores P. & Valera J. & Pérez M. (2004). Mass Balance Calculations in Copper Flash Smelting by Means of Genetic Algorithms. *Journal of Metals*, Vol 56., No 12., page numbers (29-32), ISSN 1047-4838.

Szpiro G. (1997). Forecasting chaotic time series with genetic algorithms. *Physical Review E*, Vol 5., No 3., page numbers (2557-2568), ISSN 1539-3755.

Weigend A. & Gershenfeld N. (1994). *Time Series Prediction, Forecasting the future and Undestanding the Past.* Addison-Wesley Publishing Company. ISBN 9780201626025, USA.

Yadavalli V. & Dahule R. & Tambee S. & Kulkarni B. (1999). Obtaining functional form for chaotic time series using genetic algorithm. *CHAOS*, Vol 9., No 3., page numbers (789-794), ISSN 1054-1500.

12

Optimal Feature Generation with Genetic Algorithms and FLDR in a Restricted-Vocabulary Speech Recognition System

Julio César Martínez-Romo[1], Francisco Javier Luna-Rosas[2], Miguel Mora-González[3], Carlos Alejandro de Luna-Ortega[4] and Valentín López-Rivas[5]

[1,2,5]*Instituto Tecnológico de Aguascalientes*
[3]*Universidad de Guadalajara, Centro Universitario de los Lagos*
[4]*Universidad Politécnica de Aguascalientes*
Mexico

1. Introduction

In every pattern recognition problem there exist the need for variable and feature selection and, in many cases, feature generation. In pattern recognition, the term variable is usually understood as the raw measurements or raw values taken from the subjects to be classified, while the term feature is used to refer to the result of the transformations applied to the variables in order to transform them into another domain or space, in which a bigger discriminant capability of the new calculated features is expected; a very popular cases of feature generation are the use of principal component analysis (PCA), in which the variables are projected into a lower dimensional space in which the new features can be used to visualize the underlying class distributions in the original data [1], or the Fourier Transform, in which a few of its coefficients can represent new features [2], [3]. Sometimes, the literature does not make any distinction between variables and features, using them indistinctly [4], [5].

Although many variables and features can be obtained for classification, not all of them posse discriminant capabilities; moreover, some of them could cause confusion to a classifier. That is the reason why the designer of the classification system will require to refine his choice of variables and features. Several specific techniques for such a purpose are available [1], and some of them will be reviewed later on in this chapter.

Optimal feature generation is the generation of the features under some optimality criterion, usually embodied by a cost function to search the solutions' space of the problem at hand and providing the best option to the classification problem. Examples of techniques like these are the genetic algorithms [6] and the simulated annealing [1]. In particular, genetic algorithms are used in this work.

Speech recognition has been a topic of high interest in the research arena of the pattern recognition community since the beginnings of the current computation age [7], [8]; it is due, partly, to the fact that it is capable of enabling many practical applications in artificial intelligence, such as natural language understanding [9], man-machine interfaces, help for the impaired, and others; on the other hand, it is an intriguing intellectual challenge in which new mathematical methods for feature generation and new and more sophisticated classifiers appear nearly every year [10], [11]. Practical problems that arise in the implementation of speech recognition algorithms include real-time requirements, to lower the computational complexity of the algorithms, and noise cancelation in general or specific environments [12]. Speech recognition can be user or not-user dependant.

A specific case of speech recognition is word recognition, aimed at recognizing isolated words from a continuous speech signal; it find applications in system commanding as in wheelchairs, TV sets, industrial machinery, computers, cell phones, toys, and many others. A particularity of this specific speech processing niche is that usually the vocabulary is comprised of a relatively low amount of words; for instance, see [13] and [14].

In this chapter we present an innovative method for the restricted-vocabulary speech recognition problem in which a genetic algorithm is used to optimally generate the design parameters of a set of bank filters by searching in the frequency domain for a specific set of sub-bands and using the Fisher's linear discriminant ratio as the class separability criterion in the features space. In this way we use genetic algorithms to create optimum feature spaces in which the patterns from **N** classes will be distributed in distant and compact clusters. In our context, each class $\{\omega_0, \omega_1, \omega_2,\ldots, \omega_{N-1}\}$ represents one word of the lexicon. Another important part of this work is that the algorithm is required to run in real time on dedicated hardware, not necessarily a personal computer or similar platform, so the algorithm developed should has low computational requirements.

This chapter is organized as follows: the section 2 will present the main ideas behind the concepts of variable and feature selection; section 3 presents an overview of the most representative speech recognition methods. The section 4 is devoted to explain some of the mathematical foundations of our method, including the Fourier Transform, the Fisher's linear discriminant ratio and the Parseval's theorem. Section 5 shows our algorithmic foundations, namely the genetic algorithms and the backpropagation neural networks, a powerful classifier used here for performance comparison purposes. The implementation of our speech recognition approach is depicted in section 6 and, finally, the conclusions and the future work are drawn in section 7.

2. Optimal variable and feature selection

Feature selection refers to the problem of selecting features that are most predictive of a given outcome. Optimal feature generation, however, refers to the derivation of features from input variables that are optimal in terms of class separability in the feature space. Optimal feature generation is of particular relevance to pattern recognition problems because it is the basis for achieving high correct classification rates: the better the discriminant features are represented, the better the classifier will categorize new incoming patterns. Feature generation is responsible for the way the patterns lay in the features space, therefore, shaping the decision boundary of every pattern recognition problem; linear as well as non-linear classifiers can be beneficiaries of well-shaped feature spaces.

The recent apparition of new and robust classifiers such as support vector machines (SVM), optimum margin classifiers and relevance vector machines [4], and other robust kernel classifiers seems to demonstrate that the new developments are directed towards classifiers which, although powerful, must be preceded by reliable feature generation techniques. In some cases, the classifiers use a filter that consists of a stage of feature selection, like in the Recursive Feature Elimination Support Vector Machine [15], which eliminates features in a recursive manner, similar to the backward/forward variable selection methods [1].

2.1 Methods for variable and feature selection and generation

The methods for variable and feature selection are based on two approaches: the first is to consider the features as scalars *-scalar feature selection-*, and the other is to consider the features as vectors *-feature vector selection-*. In both approaches a class separability measurement criteria must be adopted; some criteria include the receiver operating curve (ROC), the Fisher Discriminant Ratio (FDR) or the one-dimensional divergence [1]. The goal is to select a subset of k from a total of K variables or features. In the sequel, the term features is used to represent variables and features.

2.1.1 Scalar feature selection

The first step is to choose a class separability measuring criterion, C(K). The value of the criterion C(K) is computed for each of the available features, then the features are ranked in descending order of the values of C(K). The k features corresponding to the k best C(K) values are selected to form the feature vector. This approach is simple but it does not take into consideration existing correlations between features.

2.1.2 Vector feature selection

The scalar feature selection may not be effective with features with high mutual correlation; another disadvantage is that if one wishes to verify all possible combinations of the features –in the spirit of optimality- then it is evident that the computational burden is a major limitating factor. In order to reduce the complexity some suboptimal procedures have been suggested [1]:

Sequential Backward Selection. The following steps comprise this method:

a. Select a class separability criterion, and compute its value for the feature vector of all the features.
b. Eliminate one feature and for each possible combination of the remaining features recalculate the corresponding criterion value. Select the combination with the best value.
c. From the selected *K-1* feature vector eliminate one feature and for each of the resulting combinations compute the criterion value and select the one with the best value.
d. Continue until the feature vector consists of only the k features, where k is the predefined size.

The number of computations can be calculated from: $1+1/2\ ((K+1)K - k(k+1))$.

Sequential Forward Selection. The reverse of the previous method is as follows:

a. Compute the criterion value for each individual feature; select the feature with the "best" value,
b. From all possible two-dimensional vectors that contains the winner from the previous step. Compute the criterion value for each of them and select the best one.

2.1.3 Floating search methods

The methods explained suffer from the *nesting* effect, which means that once a feature (or variable) has been discarded it can't be reconsidered again. Or, on the other hand, once a feature (or variable) was chosen, it can't be discarded. To overcome these problems, a technique known as *floating search method,* was introduced by Pudin and others in 1994 [1], allowing the features to enter and leave the set of the k chosen features. There are two ways to implement this technique: one springs from the forward selection and the other from de backward selection rationale. A three steps procedure is used, namely *inclusion, test,* and *exclusion.* Details of the implementation can be found in [1], [16].

2.1.4 Some trends in feature selection

Recent work in feature selection are, for instance, the one of Somol *et al.*, [17], where besides of optimally selecting a subset of features, the size of the subset is also optimally selected. Sun and others [18] faced the problem of feature selection in conditions of a huge number or irrelevant features, using machine learning and numerical analysis methods without making any assumptions about the underlying data distributions. In other works, the a feature selection technique is accompanied by instance selection; instance selection refers to the "orthogonal version of the problem of feature selection" [19], involving the discovery of a subset of instances that will provide the classifier with a better predictive accuracy than using the entire set of instances in each class.

2.2 Optimal feature generation

As can be seen from section 2.1, the class separability measuring criterion in feature selection is used just to measure the effectiveness of the k features chosen out of a total of K features, with independence of how the features were generated. The topic of optimal feature generation refers to involving the class separability criterion as an integral part of the feature generation process itself. The task can be expressed as: If x is an m-dimensional vector of measurement samples, transform it into another l-dimensional vector andso that some class separability criterion is optimized. Consider, to this end, the linear transformation $y=A^Tx$.

By now, it will suffice to note the difference between *feature selection* and *feature generation.*

3. Speech recognition

For speech processing, the electrical signal obtained from an electromechanoacoustic transducer is digitized and quantized at a fixed rate (the sampling frequency, F_s), and subsequently segmented into small frames of a typical duration of 10 milliseconds. Regarding to section 2, the raw digitized values of the voice signal will be considered here as the input variable; the mathematical transformations that will be applied to this variable will produce the *features*.

Two important and widely used techniques for speech recognition will be presented in this section due to its relevance to this field. *Linear Predictive Coding*, or *LPC*, is a predictive technique in which a linear combination of some K coefficients and the last K samples from the signal will predict the value of the next one; the K coefficients will represent the distinctive features. The following section will explain the LPC method in detail.

3.1 Linear Predictive Coding (LPC)

LPC is one of the most advanced analytical techniques used in the estimation of patterns, based on the idea that the present sample can be predicted from a linear combination of some past samples, generating a spectral description based on short segments of signal considering a signal $s[n]$ to be a response of an all-pole filter excitation $u[n]$.

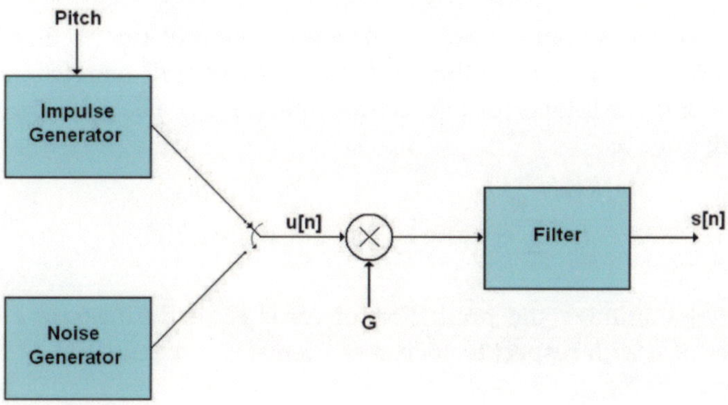

Fig. 1. LPC model of speech.

Figure 1 shows the model the LPC is based on, considering that the excitation $u[n]$ is the pattern waiting to be recognized. The transfer function of the filter is described as [3]:

$$H(z) = \frac{S(z)}{U(Z)} = \frac{G}{1 - \sum_{k=1}^{p} a_k z^{-k}} = \frac{G}{A(z)}, \tag{1}$$

where G is a gain parameter, $\boldsymbol{a_k}$ are the coefficients of filter and $\boldsymbol{p}$ determines the order of the filter. In Figure 1, the samples $s[n]$ are related to the excitation $u[n]$ by the equation:

$$s[n] = \sum_{k=1}^{p} a_k s[n-k] + Gu[n], \tag{2}$$

Considering that the linear combination of past samples is calculated by using an estimator $\tilde{s}[n]$ which is denoted by:

$$\tilde{s}[n] = \sum_{k=1}^{p} a_k s[n-k], \tag{3}$$

the error in the prediction is determined by the lack of accuracy with respect to $s[n]$, which is defined as [20]:

$$e[n] = s[n] - \tilde{s}[n] = s[n] - \sum_{k=1}^{p} a_k s[n-k], \tag{4}$$

$$e[z] = s[z]\left(1 - \sum_{k=1}^{p} a_k z^{-k}\right). \tag{5}$$

from equation (5), it is possible to recognize that the sequence of prediction of the error has in its components a FIR-type filter system which is defined by:

$$A(z) = 1 - \sum_{k=1}^{p} a_k z^{-k} = \frac{E(z)}{S(z)}, \tag{6}$$

equations (2) and (4) show that $e[n]=Gu[n]$. The estimation of the prediction coefficients is obtained by minimizing the error in the prediction. Where $e[n]^2$ denotes the square error of the prediction and E is the total error over a time interval (m). The prediction error in a short time segment is defined as:

$$E = \sum_{m} e[m]^2 = \sum_{m} (s[m] - \sum_{k=1}^{p} a_k s[m-k])^2, \tag{7}$$

the coefficients $\{a_k\}$ minimize the prediction of error E on the fragment obtained by the partial derivatives of E with respect to such coefficients; this means that:

$$\frac{\partial E}{\partial a_i} = 0, \quad 1 \le i \le p. \tag{8}$$

Through equations (7) and (8) the final equation is obtained:

$$\sum_{k=1}^{p} a_k \sum_{n} s[n-k]s[n-i] = -\sum_{n} s[n]s[n-i], \qquad 1 \le i \le p, \tag{9}$$

this equation is written in terms of least squares and is known as a normal equation. For any definitions of the signal $s[n]$, equation (9) forms a set of $\boldsymbol{p}$ equations with $\boldsymbol{p}$ unknowns that must be solved for coefficients $\{a_k\}$, trying to reduce the error E of equation (7). The minimum total squared error, denoted by Ep, is obtained by expanding equation (7) and substituting the result in equation (9), this is:

$$Ep = \sum_{n} s^2[n] + \sum_{k=1}^{p} a_k \sum_{n} s[n]s[n-k], \tag{10}$$

using the autocorrelation method to solve it [8].

For application, it is assumed that the error of equation (7) is minimized for infinite duration defined as $-\infty<n<\infty$, thus equations (9) and (10) are simplified as:

$$\sum_{k=1}^{p} a_k R(i-k) = -R(i), \qquad 1 \le i \le p, \tag{11}$$

$$Ep = R(0) + \sum_{k=1}^{p} a_k R(k), \tag{12}$$

where:

$$R(i) = \sum_{n=-\infty}^{\infty} s[n]s[n+i], \tag{13}$$

which is the autocorrelation function of the signal $s[n]$, with $R(i)$ as an even function. The coefficients $R(i\text{-}k)$ generate auto-correlation matrix, which is a symmetric Toeplitz matrix; ie, all elements in each diagonal are equal. For practical purposes, the signal $s[n]$ is analyzed in a finite interval. One popular method of approach this is by multiplying the signal $s[n]$ times a window function $w[n]$ in order to obtain an $s'[n]$ signal:

$$s'[n] = \begin{cases} s[n]w[n], \ 0 \le n \le N-1 \\ 0, \qquad \text{otherwise}' \end{cases} \tag{14}$$

Using equation 14, the auto-correlation function is given by:

$$R(i) = \sum_{n=0}^{N-1-i} s'[n]s'[n+i], \qquad i \ge 0. \tag{15}$$

One of the most common ways to find the coefficients $\{a_k\}$, is by computational methods, where the equation (11) is expanded to a matrix with the form:

$$\begin{bmatrix} R_0 & R_1 & R_2 & \cdots & R_{p-1} \\ R_1 & R_0 & R_1 & \cdots & R_{p-2} \\ R_2 & R_1 & R_0 & \cdots & R_{p-3} \\ \vdots & \vdots & \vdots & & \vdots \\ R_{p-1} & R_{p-2} & R_{p-3} & \cdots & R_0 \end{bmatrix} \begin{bmatrix} a_1 \\ a_2 \\ a_3 \\ \vdots \\ a_p \end{bmatrix} = \begin{bmatrix} R_1 \\ R_2 \\ R_3 \\ \vdots \\ R_p \end{bmatrix}, \tag{16}$$

and it is necessary to use an algorithm to find these coefficients; one of the most commonly used, is the Levinson-Durbin one, which is described below [21]:

$$E^0 = R(0)$$
$$a_0 = 1$$
$$\text{for } i = 1, 2, \ldots, p$$
$$k_i = \frac{\left(R(i) - \sum_{j=1}^{i-1} a_j^{(i-1)} R(i-j) \right)}{E^{(i-1)}}$$
$$a_i^{(i)} = k_i$$

if $i > 1$ then for $j = 1,2,...,i-1$

$$a_j^{(i)} = a_j^{(i-1)} - k_i a_{i-j}^{(i-1)}$$

end

$$E^{(i)} = (1 - k_i^2) E^{(i-1)}$$

end

$$a_j = a_j^{(p)} \quad j = 1,2,...,p.$$

An important feature of this algorithm is that, when making the recursion, an estimation of the half-quadratic prediction error must be made. This prediction satisfies the system function given in equation (17), which corresponds to the term A (z) of equation (1); namely:

$$A^{(i)}(z) = A^{(i-1)}(z) - k_i z^{-i} A^{(i-1)} z^{-1}, \tag{17}$$

where the fundamental part for the characterization of the signal in coefficients of prediction, is met by establishing an adequate number of coefficients $\boldsymbol{p}$, according to the sampling frequency (fs) and based on the resonance in kHz [3] which is:

$$p = 4 + \frac{f_s}{1000} \tag{18}$$

where the optimal number of LPC coefficients is the one that represents the lowest mean square error possible. Figure 2 shows the calculation of LPC in a voice signal with 8 kHz sampling rate and the effect of varying the number of coefficients in a segment (frame).

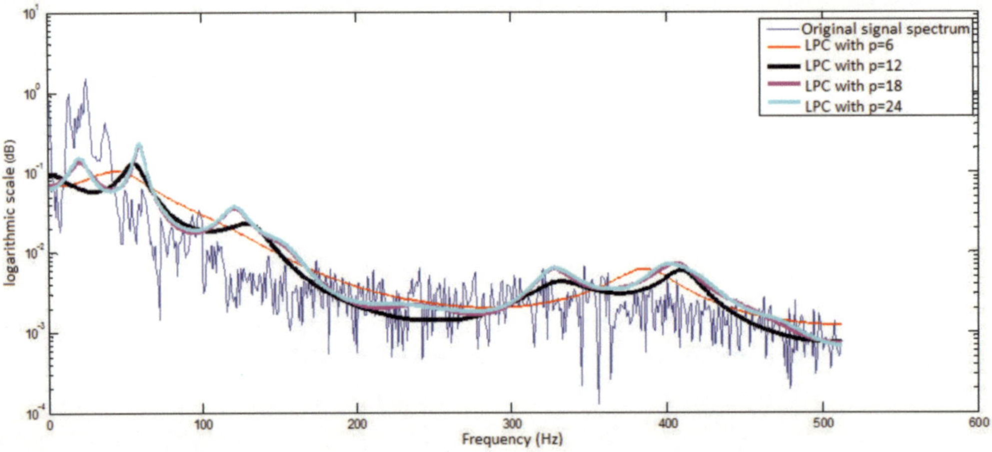

Fig. 2. Comparison of the original signal spectrum and LPC envelope with different numbers of coefficients.

3.2 Dynamic Time Warping (DTW)

Another commonly used technique used in speech recognition is the dynamic time warping. Is presented here, again, for it relevance to the this field. Dynamic time warping is a technique widely used in pattern recognition, particularly oriented to temporal distortions between vectors, such as the time of writing, speed of video camera, the omission of a letter, etc. These temporal variations are not proportional and vary accordingly to each person, object or event, and those situations are not repetitive in any aspects. DTW uses *dynamic programming* to find similarities and differences between two or more vectors.

This method considers two sequences representing feature vectors defined by $a(i)$, i=1,2,…,I and $b(j)$, j=1,2,…,J, where, in general, the number of elements differs in each vector ($I \neq J$). The aim of DTW is to find an appropriate distance between the two sequences and in a two-dimensional plane, where each sequence represents one axis, and each point corresponds to the local relationship between two sequences. The nodes (i,j) of the plane are associated with a cost that is defined by the function $d(c)=d(i,j)=|a(i)-b(j)|$, which represents the distance between the elements $a(i)$ and $b(j)$.

The collection of points begins in the starting point (i_0,j_0) and finishes in the (i_k,j_k) nodes, and it being an ordered pair of size k, where k is the number of nodes along the way. Every path established with the points is associated with a total cost D and defined by

$$D = \sum_{k=0}^{K-1} d(i_k, j_k), \tag{19}$$

and the distance between the two sequences is defined as the minimum value D of all the possible paths

$$D(a,b) = \min_k(D). \tag{20}$$

There are normalization and temporary limitations in the search for the minimum distance between patterns to compare [22], [1]. These limitations are: endpoint, monotonicity conditions, local continuity, global path and slope weight.

The final point is bounded by the size of windowing and performed in each pattern, at most cases is empirical and defined to extremes, that is:

$$\begin{aligned} i(1) = 1, j(1) = 1 \\ i(K) = I, j(K) = J. \end{aligned} \tag{21}$$

Figure 3 shows an example in which it is only partially considered one of the sequences, a situation that is not allowed to search the minimum cost.

The monotonicity conditions try to maintain the temporal order of the normalization of the time, and avoid negative slopes, by

$$i_{k+1} \geq i_k \tag{22}$$

and

$$j_{k+1} \geq j_k. \tag{23}$$

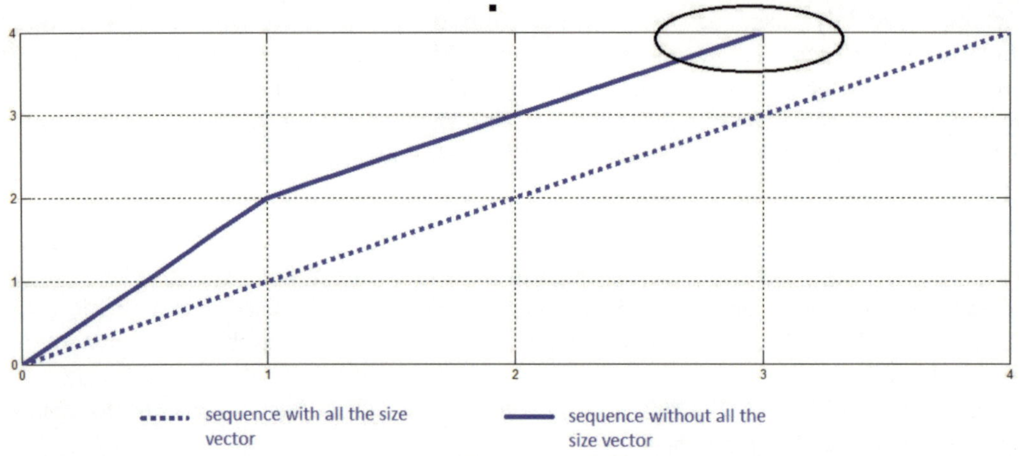

Fig. 3. Example of a sequence that violates the rule of the endpoint.

Figure 4 shows an example without monotonicity paths, which are not allowed to find the optimal path.

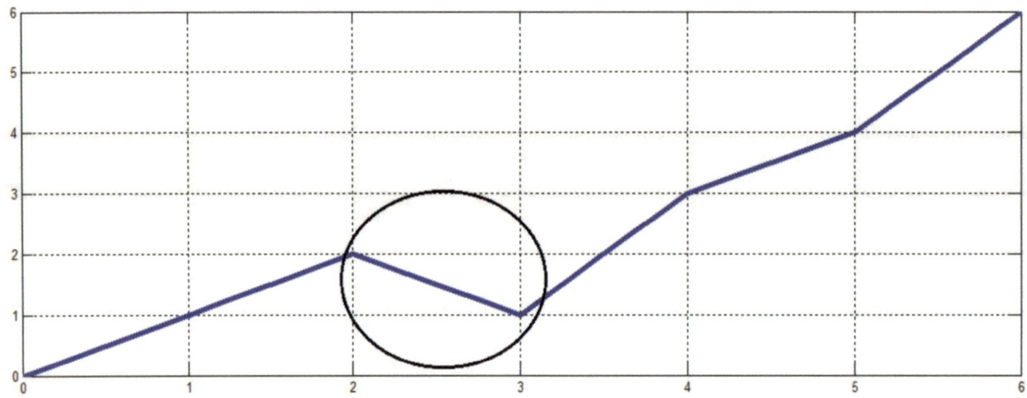

Fig. 4. Without monotonicity path example.

The continuity conditions

$$i(K) - i(k-1) \leq 1 \quad \text{And} \quad j(K) - j(K-1) \leq 1, \tag{24}$$

are defined by maintaining the relationship between two consecutive points of the form:

$$c(K-1) = \begin{cases} (i(k), j(k)-1), \\ (i(k)-1, j(k)-1), \\ (i(k)-1, j(k)), \end{cases} \tag{25}$$

Global limitations define a region of nodes where the optimal path is found, and is based on a parallelogram that offers a feasible region [7], thereby avoiding unnecessary regions involved in processing. Figure 5 shows the values of the key points of the parallelogram.

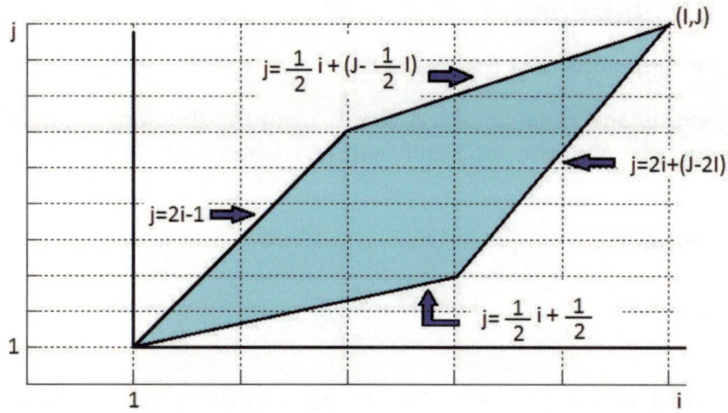

Fig. 5. Global region and determination of slopes.

The optimal path layout defined a measure of dissimilarity between the two sequences of features, whose general form is

$$D(a,b) = \min_{F} \left[\frac{\sum_{k=1}^{K} d(c(k)) \cdot w(k)}{\sum_{k=1}^{K} w(k)} \right], \tag{26}$$

where $d(c(k))$ and $w(k)$ are the local distance between the windows $i(k)$ of the reference vector and $j(k)$ of the recognize vector, and a weighting function in k to maintain a flexible way and improve alignment, respectively. The simplified computational algorithm for calculating the distance of DTW is shown below [1] :

$$
\begin{aligned}
& D(0,0) = 0 \\
& \text{for } i = 1:I \\
& \quad D(i,0) = D(i-1,0) + 1 \\
& \text{end} \\
& \text{for j} = 1:\text{J} \\
& \quad D(0,j) = D(0,j-1) + 1 \\
& \text{end} \\
& \text{for } i = 1:I \\
& \quad \text{for } j = 1:J \\
& \quad\quad c1 = D(i-1,j-1) + d(i,j \mid i-1,j-1) \\
& \quad\quad c2 = D(i-1,j) + 1 \\
& \quad\quad c3 = D(i,j-1) + 1 \\
& \quad\quad D(i,j) = \min(c1,c2,c3) \\
& \quad \text{end} \\
& \text{end} \\
& D(a,b) = D(I,J)
\end{aligned}
$$

4. Mathematical foundations

4.1 Fisher's Linear Discriminant Ratio FLDR

Fisher's Linear Discriminant Ratio, is used as an optimization criterion in several research fields, including speech recognition, handwriting recognition, and others [1]. Consider the following definitions:

Within-class scatter matrix.

$$S_w = \sum_{i=1}^{M} P_i S_i \tag{27}$$

where S_i is the covariance matrix for class ω_i, and P_i the a priori probability of class ω_i. Trace$\{S_w\}$ is a measure of the average variance of the features, or descriptive elements of the class.

Between-class scatter matrix

$$S_b = \sum_{i=1}^{M} P_i (\mu_i - \mu_0)(\mu_i - \mu_0)^T \tag{28}$$

where μ_0 is the global mean vector

$$\mu_0 = \sum_{i}^{M} P_i \mu_i \tag{29}$$

Trace$\{S_b\}$ is a measure of the average distance of the mean of each individual class from the respective global value.

Mixture scatter matrix

$$S_m = E\left[(\mu_i - \mu_0)(\mu_i - \mu_0)^T\right] \tag{30}$$

S_m is the covariance matrix of the feature vector with respect to the global mean, and E[.] is the mathematical operator of the expected mean value. Based on the just given definitions, the following criteria can be expressed:

$$J_1 = \frac{trace\{S_m\}}{trace\{S_w\}}$$
$$J_2 = \frac{|S_b|}{|S_w|} = |S_w^{-1} S_b| \tag{31}$$

It can be shown that J_1 and J_2 take large values when the samples in the *l*-dimensional are well clustered around their mean, within each class, and the clusters of different classes are well separated. Criteria in equation (31) can be used to guide an optimization process, since they measure the goodness of data clustered; the data to be clustered could be the set of features representative of the items of a class. Trace$\{S_b\}$ is a measure of the average distance of the mean of each individual class from the respective global value.

Figure 6 shows an example in which the FLDR is evaluated using equation (31); FLDR and the respective values are displayed. Notice that the more the blue clusters are separated from the red cluster, the bigger FLDR value is.

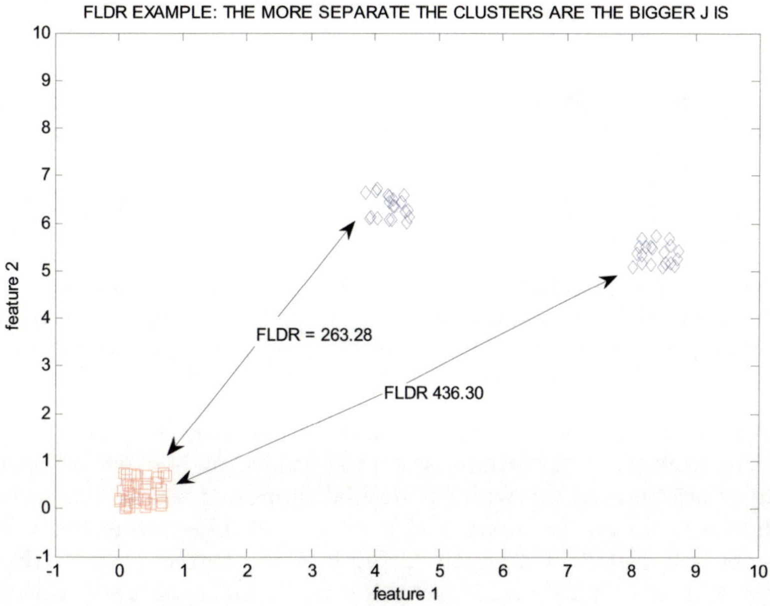

Fig. 6. Example of the FLDR values for two clusters.

4.2 Parseval's theorem and the Fourier Transform

Parseval's theorem states, in an elegant manner, that the energy of a discrete signal in the time domain can be calculated in the frequency domain by a simple relation [2], [3]:

$$\sum_{i=0}^{N-1} x[i]^2 = \frac{2}{N} \sum_{k=0}^{N/2} |X[k]|^2 \tag{32}$$

where

N is the number of samples of the discrete signal,
x[i] is the *i*-th sample of the discrete signal,
X[k] is the *k*-th sample of the Fourier transform of x[i].

For a discrete signal x[i], the Fourier transform can be computed using the well known *Discrete* Fourier Transform via the efficient algorithm for its implementation, the FFT [2], [3]:

$$X[k] = \sum_{n=0}^{N-1} x[n] e^{-2i\pi k \frac{n}{N}} \quad k=0, 1, \ldots, N-1 \tag{33}$$

The implication of the Parseval's theorem is that an algorithm can search for specific energetic properties of a signal in the frequency domain off-line, and then use the information obtained off-line to configure a bank of digital filters to look for the same energetic properties in the time domain on-line, in real time. The *link* between both domains is the energetic content of the signal.

5. Algorithmic foundations

This section is devoted to describe two important figures in pattern recognition: *backpropagation neural networks* BPNN and *genetic algorithms* GA. The BPNN is used as a reference classifier to compare the performance of the approach presented here to the word recognition problem. The GA is an integral part of the generation of the features in the proposed technique.

5.1 Learning paradigms

There are several major paradigms, or approaches, to machine learning. These include supervised, unsupervised, and reinforcement learning. In addition, many researchers and application developers combine two o more of these learning approaches into one system [23].

Supervised learning is the most common form of learning and is sometimes called programming by example. The learning system is trained by showing it examples of the problem state or attributes along with the desired output or action. The learning system make a prediction based on the inputs and if the output differs from the desired output, then the system is adjusted or adapted to produce the correct output. This process is repeated over and over until the system learns to make accurate classifications or predictions. Historical data from databases, sensor logs, or trace logs is often used as the training or example data.

Unsupervised learning is used when the learning system needs to recognize similarities between inputs or to identify features in the input data. The data is presented to the system, and it adapts so that it partitions the data into groups. The clustering or segmenting process continues until the system places the same data into the same group on successive passes over the data. An unsupervised learning algorithm performs a type of feature detection where important common attributes in the data are extracted.

Reinforcement learning is a type of supervised learning used when explicit input/output pairs of training data are not available. It can be used in cases where there is a sequence of inputs and the desired output is only known after the specific sequence occurs. This process of identifying the relationship between a series of input values and a later output value is called temporal credit assignment. Because we provide less specific error information, reinforcement learning usually takes longer than supervised learning and is less efficient. However, in many situations, having exact prior information about the desired outcome is not possible. In many ways, reinforcement learning is the most realistic form of learning.

Another important distinction in learning systems is whether the learning is done on-line or off-line. On-line learning means that the system is sent out to perform its tasks and that it can learn or adapt after each transaction is processed. On-line learning is like on the job training and places severe requirements on the learning algorithms. It must be very fast and very stable. Off-line learning, on the other hand, is more like a business seminar. You take your salespeople off the floor and place them in an environment where they can focus on improving their skills without distractions. After a suitable training period, they are sent out to apply their new found knowledge and skills. In an intelligent system context, this means that we would gather data from situations that the systems have experienced. We could then augment this data with information about the desired system response to build a training data set. Once we have this database we can use it to modify the behavior of our system.

5.2 Backpropagation Neural Networks

Backpropagation is the most popular neural network architecture for *supervised learning*. It features a *feed-forward* connection topology, meaning that data flow through the network in a single direction, and uses a technique called the *backward propagation* of errors to adjust the connection weights Rumelhart, Hinton, and Williams 1986 in [23]. In addition to a layer of input and output units, a back-propagation network can have one or more layers of hidden units, which receive inputs only from other units, and not from the external environment. A backpropagation network with a single hidden layer or processing units can learn to model any continuous function when given enough units in the hidden layer. The primary applications of backpropagation networks are for prediction and classification.

Figure 7 shows the diagram of a backpropagation neural network and illustrates the three major steps in the training process.

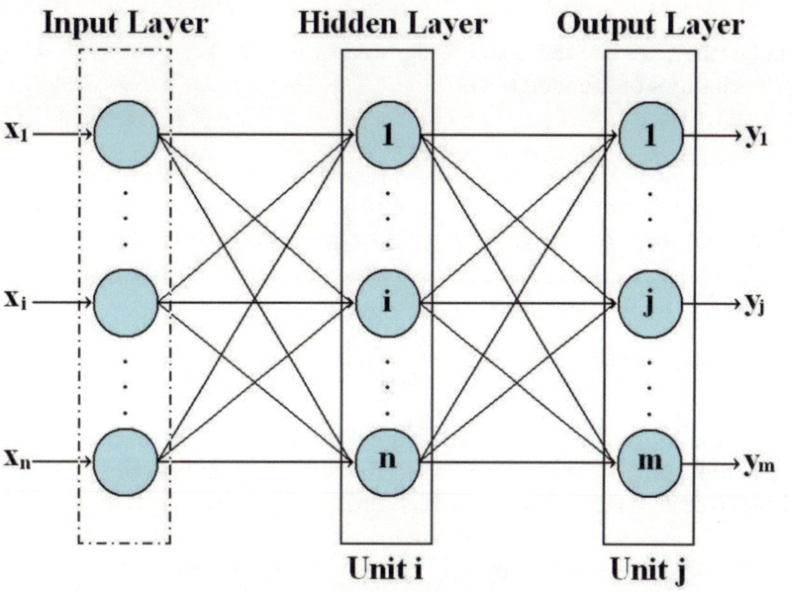

Fig. 7. Topology of a backpropagation neural network.

First, input data is presented to the units of the input layer on the left, and it flows through the network until it reaches the network output units on the right. This is called the forward pass.

Second, the activations or values of the output units represent the actual or predicted output of the network, because this is supervised learning.

Third, the difference between the desired and the actual output is computed, producing the network error. This error term is then passed backwards through the network to adjust the connection weights.

Each network input unit takes a single numeric value, x_i, which is usually scaled or normalized to a value between 0.0 and 1.0. This value becomes the input unit activation. Next, we need to propagate the data forward, through the neural network. For each unit in the hidden layer, we compute the sum of the products of the input unit activations and the weights connecting those input layer units to the hidden layer. This sum is the inner product (also called the dot or scalar product) of the input vector and the weights in the hidden unit. Once this sum is computed, we add a threshold value and then pass this sum through a nonlinear activation function, f, producing the unit activation y_i. The formula for computing the activation of any unit in a hidden or output layer in the network is

$$y_i = f\left(sum_j = \sum x_i w_{ij} + \theta_i\right) \tag{34}$$

where *i* ranges over all the units leading into the *j*-th unit, and the activation function is

$$f\left(sum_j\right) = \frac{1}{1+e^{-sum_j}} \tag{35}$$

As mentioned earlier, we use the *S*-shape sigmoid or logistic function for *f*. The formula for calculating the changes of the weights is

$$\Delta w_{ij} = \eta \delta_j y_i \tag{36}$$

where w_{ij} is the weight connecting unit i to unit j, η is the learn rate parameter, δ_j is the error signal for that unit, and y_i is the output or activation value of unit i. For units in the output layer, the error signal is the difference between the target output t_j and the actual output y_i multiplied by the derivative of the logistic activation function.

$$\delta_j = \left(t_j - y_j\right) f_j'\left(sum_j\right) = \left(t_j - y_j\right) y_j \left(1 - y_j\right) \tag{37}$$

For each unit in the hidden layer, the error signal is the derivative of the activation function multiplied by the sum of the products of the outgoing connection weights and their corresponding error signals. So for the hidden unit j.

$$\delta_j = f_j'\left(sum_j\right) \sum \delta_k w_{jk} \tag{38}$$

where k ranges over the indices of the units receiving *j*-th unit´s output signal.

A common modification of the weight update rule is the use of a momentum term α, to cut down on oscillation of the weight change becomes a combination of the current weight change, computed as before, plus some fraction (α ranges from 0 to 1) of the previous weight change. This complicates the implementation because we now have to store the weight changes from the prior step.

$$\Delta w_{ij}(n+1) = \eta \delta_j y_i + \alpha \Delta w_{ij}(n) \quad (39)$$

The mathematical basis for backward propagation is described in detail in [23]. When the weight changes are summed up (or batched) over an entire presentation of the training set, the error minimization function performed is called gradient descent.

5.3 Genetic Algorithms

In this section a brief description of a simple genetic algorithm is given. Genetic algorithms are based on concepts and methods observed in nature for the evolution of the species. Genetic algorithms were brought to the artificial intelligence arena by Goldberg [6], [24]. They apply certain operators to a population of solutions of the problem to be solved, in a such a way that the new population is improved compared to the previous one according to a certain criterion function J [5], [1], [6], [24]. Repetition of this procedure for a preselected number of iterations will produce a last generation whose best solution is the optimal solution to the problem.

The solutions of the problem to be solved are coded in the *chromosome* and the following operations are applied to the coded versions of the solutions, in this order:

Reproduction. Ensures that, in probability, the better a solution in the current population is, the more replicates it has in the next population,

Crossover. Selects pair of solutions randomly, splits them in a random position, and exchanges their second parts.

Mutation. Selects randomly an element of a solution and alters it with some probability. It helps to move away from local minima.

Besides the coding of the solutions, some parameters must be set up:

N, number of solutions in a population. Fixed or varied.
p, probability with which two solutions are selected for crossover.
m, probability with which an element of a solution is mutated.

The performance of the GA depends greatly on these parameters, as well as on the coding of the solutions in the chromosome. The solutions can be coded in some of the following formats:

Binary. Bit strings represent the solution(s) of the problem. For instance, a chromosome could represent a series of integer indexes to address a database, or the value of a variable(s) that must be integer, or each bit could represent the state (present-absent) of a part of an architecture that is being optimized, and so on.

Real valued. The bit strings represent the value of a real valued variable, in fixed of floating point.

The aspect of one chromosome could be like this: C = {100101010101010101}; the interpretation will vary in accordance with the coding scheme selected to represent the knowledge domain of the problem. For instance, it might represent a set of six indices of three bits each one; or it could have a meaning with all the bits together, representing an 18 bit code.

The primary reason of the success of genetic algorithms is its wide applicability, easy use and global perspective [6], [24], [25]. The next is the listing of a simple genetic algorithm.

```
Procedure (Genetic_Algorithm)
   M = Population size. (*# Of possible solutions at any instance.*)
   Ng = Number of generations. (*# Of iterations.*)
   No = Number of offsprings. (*# To be generated by crossover.*)
   Pμ = Mutation probability. (*# Also called mutation rate Mr.*)
   P ← Ξ (M)
   For j = 1 to M
       Evaluate f(p[i])
   EndFor
   For i = 1 to Ng
      For (j=1 to No)
         (x,y) ←Ø(p) (*Select two parents x and andfrom current population*)
         Offspring[j] ← X(x,y)  (*Generate offsprings by crossover of parents x and y*)
         Evaluate f(offspring[j]) (*Evaluate  fitness of each offsprings*)
      EndFor
     For j = 1 to N0  (*With probability pμ apply mutation*)
        Mutated[j] ← μ(y)
        Evaluate f(mutated[j])
     EndFor
     p ← Selected(p, iffsprings) (*Select best M solutions from parents & offsprings. *)
   EndFor
   Return highest scoring configuration in p.
End
```

The genetic algorithms find application in the field of speech processing via the solution to the problem of variable and feature selection [11], [14], [26], [27], [28], [29], [30].

6. Restricted-vocabulary speech recognition system

The expression restricted-vocabulary speech recognition refers to the recognition of repetitions of spoken words that belongs to a limited set of words within a semantic field. This means that the words have connected meanings, for instance, the digits = {0,1,2,…, 9} or the days of the week={Saturday, Monday,…, Friday}. The applications of the recognition of limited size word-sets include voice-commanded systems, spoken entry and search for computer databases in warehouse systems, voice-assisted telephone dialing, man-machine interfaces, and others. The advantage of a system developed for a specific semantic field is that it can be built to be much more accurate than those constructed for the general speech recognition, also requiring less extensive training sets.

Restricted-vocabulary speech recognition is also an important research topic because of the intricacies involved in the underlying pattern recognition problem: variable selection, feature generation/selection and classifier selection. Variable selection is mostly restricted to select the raw digitized voice signal as the variable; alternatively, the surrounding environmental noise could be used as another variable for noise cancelation purposes. Feature generation has been carried out by obtaining linear predictive coefficients (LPC),

AR/ARMA coefficients, Fourier coefficients, Cepstral coefficients, Mel Spectral Coefficients, and others [31]. In many the cases, the coefficients are computed over a short-time window (typically 10 ms) and over the voiced segments of the speech signal. As well as for the feature generation, for the classifier several options are available: Hidden Markov Models HHM (perhaps the most popular), neural networks (backpropagation, self-organizing maps, radial basis, etc.), support vector and other kernel machines, Gaussian mixtures, Bayesian type classifiers, LVQ, and others. It should be noted that this list of choices of each element in the pattern recognition chain is by no means extensive. Please note that by simply considering all the combinations of variables, features and classifiers mentioned here, it is easily seen that there exist too many ways to implement a restricted-vocabulary speech recognition system.

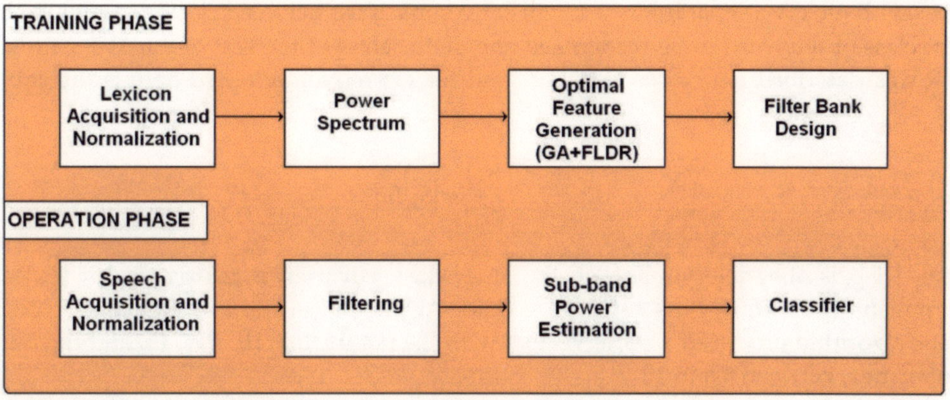

Fig. 8. Block diagram showing the optimal feature generation with the GA and FLDR.

6.1 Methodology

Figure 8 shows a block diagram of the whole speech recognition system. The system works in two phases: training and operation. The blocks of the training-phase are described below.

Lexicon Acquisition and Normalization. In this stage, the set $\mathbf{L} = \{\mathbf{w_0}, \mathbf{w_1}, \mathbf{w_2}, \ldots, \mathbf{w_{M\text{-}1}}\}$ of $\mathbf{M}$ words that will comprise the lexicon to be recognized is acquired from the speaker(s) that will use the system; vectors containing the digitized versions of the voice signals will be at the disposal of the next stage.

Power Spectrum. The power spectrum has been traditionally the source of features for speech recognition; here, the power spectrum of the voice signals will be used by the genetic algorithm to determinate discriminant frequency bands.

Optimal Feature Generation. The features selected here are a) the energy $\mathbf{E}$ of eight to twelve frequency regions (sub-bands) of the spectrum, b) the bandwidth (BW) of each sub-band, and c) the central frequency (F_C) of the sub-bands. See Figure 9. Sub-band processing in speech have been previously used, but in different manners [32], [33], [34]. A genetic algorithm with elitism is used here to select each bandwidth (*BW*) its central frequency (F_c) and a number of sub-bands. The main parameters of the genetic algorithm are listed in table 1. The cost function of the GA is an expression aimed at maximizing the Fisher's linear discriminant ratio (FLDR). The use of the FLDR in the cost function ensures

Parameter	***Value***
Population	20-120
Mutation	Gaussian (1-2 , 1-2) (scale,shrink)
Selection	Elitism
Crossover	Scattered, one-point and two-points

Table 1. Parameters of the Genetic Algorithm.

increasing both, class separability and cluster compactness between classes ω_0 and ω_1, being ω_0 the class of the word to be recognized and ω_1 the class of the rest of the M-1 words. The FLDR was described here in section 4.1, and the expression adopted here is the equation (31):

$$J_2 = \frac{|S_b|}{|S_w|} = |S_w^{-1} S_b|$$

where $|S_b|$ is the determinant of the inter-class covariance matrix and $|S_b|$ is the determinant of the intra-class covariance class. At the end of the evolutionary process the genetic algorithm produced a set of vectors with the parameters [***E***, ***BW***, ***F***$_c$] and the number of sub-bands, between 8 and 12.

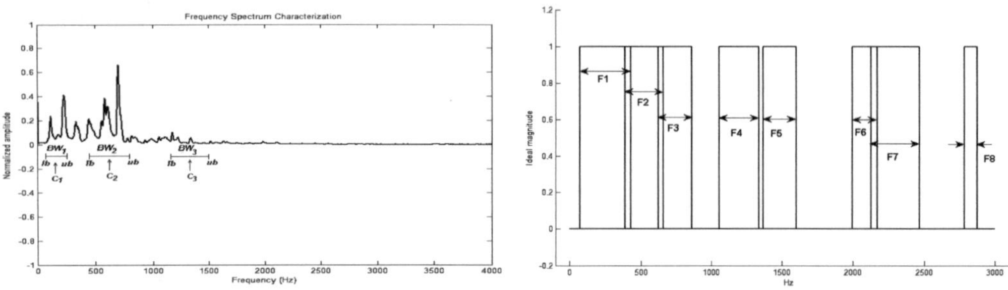

Fig. 9. Sub-band spectrum division to separate the power spectra in discriminant regions.

Bank-filter Design. During the operation phase, the calculation of the power espectrum of the incoming voice signals is not practical for real-time response because the discrete Fourier transform (DFT [2], [3]) requires too much time to be calculated, and the fast Fourier Transform (FFT [2], [3]) requires that the number of samples to be a power of 2, requiring zero padding most of the times. Instead of using the power spectrum, in this application it is used the Parseval's theorem, described in section 4.2, which states that the energy in time and frequency is equal. In discrete form, we recall equation (32):

$$\sum_{i=0}^{N-1} x[i]^2 = \frac{2}{N} \sum_{k=0}^{N/2} |X[k]|^2$$

where *x[i]* is the time domain signal with and *X[k]* is its modified frequency espectrum, which is found by taking the DFT of the signal and dividing the first and last frequencies by the square rooth of two. Therefore, all that have to be done is to filter the sub-bands out of the time signals and then to calculate the energy in each sub-band. This can be perfectly accomplished by a bank of digital band-pass filters whose parameters match the parameters found by the genetic algorithm, and the advantage is that at the end of the last sample of voice in real-time a word can be immediately recognized.

In the Operation Phase, the three first stages operate simultaneously at each time a sample of the voice is acquired, and occur between two successive sampling intervals; in the first stage the voice signal is acquired and a normalization coefficient N_c is updated with the maximum value of the signal; the block labeled filtering represent the action of the filter bank and the outgoing signal is squared and added sample by sample. At the end of a voiced segment of sound, the third block provides to a classifier with the set of features for word classification.

6.2 System design

In this section the details of the system design will be presented.

6.2.1 Characterization of the frequency spectrum using sub-bands

Consider the Fourier Transform of a signal:

$$S(\omega) = F(s(t)) \tag{40}$$

Now consider the frequency spectrum split in sub-bands, as shown in Figure 9. Please notice in Figure 9 that *S(w)* has been normalized to unitary amplitude. For each sub-band, the energy can be calculated as:

$$E_i = k_0 \sum_{lb}^{ub} \left(S(\omega)^2 \right) \tag{41}$$

where E_i, is the energy of the *i*-th sub-band, k_0 is a constant proportional to the bandwidth (BW_i) of the *i*-th sub-band, *lb* and *ub* are the lower and upper bounds of the *i*-th sub-band. The feature vector of the *n-th* utterance of *s(t)* in the frequency domain becomes:

$$Sr_n(\omega) = [E_1\ E_2\ E_3\ E_4 \cdots E_M] \tag{42}$$

In which *M* is the number of sub-bands, and Sr_n is the reduced version of the *n*-th *S(ω)*. In order to characterize a word in the vocabulary, *N* samples of *s(t)* must be entered. From the example in Figure 9 and without loss of generality, the set of parameters of the respective filter bank that will operate in the time domain is:

$$BF = [C_1\ BW_1\ C_2\ BW_2\ C_3\ BW_3 \cdots C_L\ BW_L] \tag{43}$$

The number of filters to be applied in the time-domain signal in this case is L. For a vocabulary of *K* words (*K* small), the spectra in which the solution must be searched is given by *K* matrices of *N* rows and 2000 columns.

6.2.2 Genetic algorithm set up

6.2.2.1 Coding the chromosome

The chromosome is comprised of the parameters of the filter bank described in equation 43. The number of sub-bands is fixed, and each one of the centers and bandwidths are subject to the genetic algorithm. Real numbers are used.

6.2.2.2 The cost function

The cost function is given by equation (32), criterion J_2. The goal is to maximize J_2 as a function of the centers and bandwidths.

6.2.2.3 Restrictions

The following restrictions apply:

R1. Sub-bands overlapping < = 50Hz,

R2. Bandwidth is limited to range from 40 to 400 Hz, varying according to the performance of the genetic algorithm.

6.2.2.4 Operating parameters of the genetic algorithm

The main parameters of the genetic algorithm are summarized in the Table 1. The values of the parameters are given according to the best results obtained by experimentation. The genetic algorithm was ran in Matlab®, using the genetic algorithms toolbox and the *gatool* guide. The nomenclature of the parameters in Table 1 is the one used by Matlab®.

6.2.2.5 Application's algorithm

To make operational de methodology described so far, the following steps apply:

1. *Vocabulary definition*. 2 to K words. In many real life applications, K in 8 to 15 words do the job.
2. *Database acquisition*. 15 to 20 utterances of each word from the vocabulary, for learning purposes. The sampling frequency can be set from 6000 to 8000 Hz. Human voice accommodates easily here.
3. *s(t)* to *S*(w) transformation. Apply Fourier transform to the data, normalize to unitary amplitude and to a fixed length of 2000.
4. *Data preparation for the GA*. Set-up the size (eq. 43) and restrictions (subsection 6.2.2.3) of the filter bank (chromosome).
5. *Running the GA*. Run the GA to find the sub-bands whose J_2 (eq. (32)) is the maximum.
6. *Filters realization*. For each sub-band, compute the coefficients of the respective bandpass filters. For real-time implementation, order from 4 to 8 is recommended, type IIR, elliptic. Elliptic filters achieve great discrimination and selectivity. Implementation details can be found in [2].
7. *Modeling the commands*. To make comparisons and therefore classification, a Gaussian statistical model of each word is to be constructed for each command in the vocabulary. Proceed as follows for each command:
   a. Construct a matrix *C* of 15-20 rows of $Sr_n(w)$ and *M* columns (one row per sample of the command, one column per sub-band selected by the AG),
   b. Compute the mean value overall the samples, to find the average energy per sub-band, this is the feature vector of the command (μ_i)

c. Compute the covariance matrix, $S_i = cov(C_i)$.

d. At any time, the Mahalanobis distance between the model of the *i*-th command and the feature vector *x* of an incoming command is:

$$dM(x,\mu_i) = (x-\mu_i)^{*}\Sigma_i^{-1}{}^{*}(x-\mu_i)^{-1} \qquad (44)$$

To make the real-time implementation, a digital system must sample the input microphone continuously. Each sample of a command must be filtered by each filter (sub-band extraction). The integral of the energy of the signal leaving each filter over the period of the command is used to create the feature vector of that command, that is, *x* in equation 44. The feature vector is compared to each model in the vocabulary, and the command is recognized as the one with the minimum *dM* score. This is the so-called "minimum distance classifier" [5].

7. Results

To test the system, the following lexicons were used: L_0={faster, slower, left, right, stop, forward, reverse, brake}, L_1={zero, one, two, three, four, five, six, seven, eigth, nine}, L_2={rápido, lento, izquierda, derecha, alto, adelante, reversa, freno}, L_3 = {uno, dos, tres, cuatro, cinco}. In all the lexicons, 3 male and 3 female volunteers were enrolled. They donated 116 samples of each word, 16 for training and 100 for testing. To demostrate the power of our approach we used the minimum distance classifier with the Mahalanobis distance. In all the cases, the genetic algorithm was ran 30 times to find the best response in the training set. During the training phase, the leave-one-out method was used to exploit the limited size of the training set [1]. Table 2 summarizes the results. In columns 5 and 7 are shown the comparison against a backpropagation neural network using as features Cepstral coefficients. The experiments were done using Matlab(R) and its associated toolboxes of genetic algorithms, neural networks and digital signal processing. The real-time implementation was done with a TMS320LF2407 Texas Instruments(R) Digital Signal Processor mounted on an experimentation card.

			Simulations		Real-time on DSP	
			MDC[3]	BPNN[4]	MDC[3]	BPNN[4]
G[1]	**L[2]**	**Training Set**	**Testing Set**	**Testing Set**	**Real scenario**	**Real scenario**
Female	0	100	97	92	94	90
	1	100	98	90	95	90
	2	100	100	97	94	89
	3	100	100	91	95	88
Male	0	100	100	94	96	89
	1	100	100	90	95	90
	2	100	99	92	94	90
	3	100	98	92	93	88

[1]Gender, [2] Lexicon, [3]Minimum distance classifier, [4]Backpropagation neural network [1] 8-32-K neurons per layer, K according to the experiment, one neuron for each word in L.

Table 2. Percentage (%) of correct classification with 4 lexicons, 2 languages, 6 persons, male and female voices, 2 classifiers. Simulations and real time implementation.

7.1 Results and discussion

7.1.1 Results in the L_3 Spanish vocabulary

The genetic algorithm was executed 30 times, and the maximum Fisher's ratio obtained was 62. The resulting best chromosome was:

BF = [254 180 526 132 744 118 1196 141 1483 115 2082 86 2295 171 2828 46]

From which the corresponding center and bandwidth were:

$$C = [254\ 526\ 744\ 1196\ 1483\ 2082\ 2295\ 2828]$$
$$BW = [180\ 132\ 118\ 141\ 115\ 86\ 171\ 46]$$

The recognition rates in the training and testing sets were 100% and 99%, respectively. In real conditions the correct classification rate was 93.5% in 40 repetitions of each word to the microphone.

7.1.2 The genetic algorithm in L_3

Consecutive executions of the GA produced variable Fisher's ratios. It was observed here that the population size is critical, since a population of 20 chromosomes produced Fisher's ratios between 35 and 42, while a population of 120 individuals easily produced Fisher's ratios above 58. It was noticed during experimentation that specific values for restrictions R1 and R2 also have a strong influence in the outcome.

Comparing the results over a traditional approach with neural networks and cepstral coefficients it is evident a higher performance and, more important, the system exhibits real-time operation and very low computational effort compared to neural networks and real-time computation of the Cepstral coefficients.

7.1.3 Results in the L_0 English vocabulary

The genetic algorithm was executed 30 times, varying population size, probability of mutation, restrictions, number of sub-bands, and other parameters. The initial number of sub-bands was 8, then it was scaled to 9 and 12; in this scenario, the Fisher's ratio varied from 23 (8 sub-bands, population size = 20) to 48 (12 sub-bands, population size = 200). The resulting centers and bandwidths were:

$$C = [250\ 446\ 648\ 1283\ 1483\ 1776\ 2018\ 2506\ 2737\ 3197\ 3383\ 3833]$$
$$BW = [\ 5\ 138\ 187\ 157\ 139\ 43\ 207\ 106\ 105\ 98\ 148\ 224]$$

Intra-class repeatability and inter-class differences

The performance in the training set was 100%; the performance in the testing set was 99%. The correct classification per word was {100% 100% 98% 100% 97% 100% 98% 99%} for the respective words {*'faster','slower','left','right','stop','forward','reverse','brake'*}, respectively. Figure 10 shows the normalized espectra of two utterances of the word 'faster' and the word 'slower'. In both cases notice the repeatability in the frequency domain, as well as the difference between both sets of spectra.

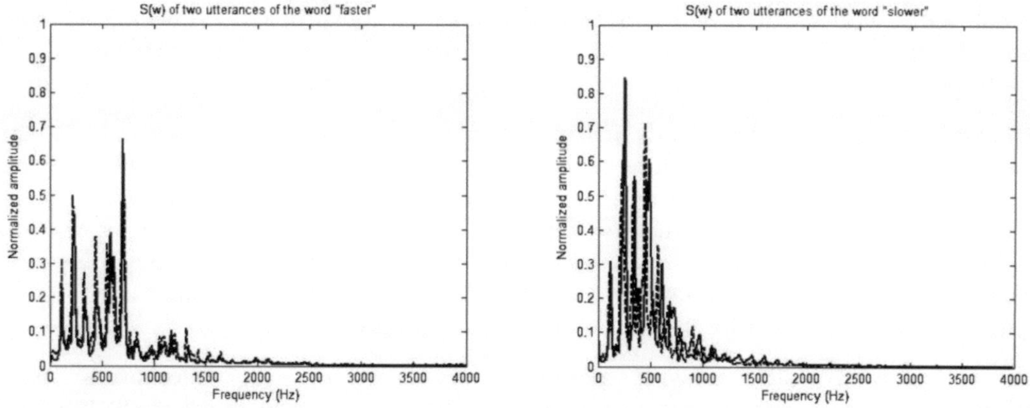

Fig. 10. Normalized spectra of the words "faster" and "slower".

7.1.4 Results of the real-time implementation

A minimum distance classifier was implemented in a digital signal processor TMS320LF2407 for each of the four lexicons **L**={L_0, L_1, L_2, L_3} from Texas Instruments, in order to verify the performance using in a nearly real-life application. The voiced/no-voiced segmentation was performed using a push-button to start and finish capturing the voice. The DSP has a built-in 10-bit analog to digital converter facilitating the interfacing task. The digital filters used were IIR topology, elliptic type, 8th order. The filter coefficients (*A*, *B*) were calculate using the Matlab® Software. The analog-to-digital conversion was set-up to acquire one sample every T seconds, (T=1/6000); each time a sample came into de device, the filters actuated and the respective output was squared and accumulated to calculate the energy of the signal. Scaling issues had to be solved since the model was created in a real valued [-1 , 1] scale, while the DSP just "see" integer values. Once a whole command was processed, it was just a matter of a few miliseconds to apply the minimum distance classifier and provide the classification. The correct classification rate was in this case of the order of 94.5%, in a total of 1200 repetitions of the words in **L**.

8. Conclusions and future work

In this chapter was presented a method to implement a high performance, real-time, restricted-vocabulary speech recognition system, combining a genetic algorithm and the Fisher's Linear Discriminant Ratio (FLDR) in its matrix formulation. A review of the concepts of variable and feature selection as well as feature generation was made; also were presented some concepts related with speech processing, like the LPC formulation and the DTW method for template matching.

One of the conceptual tools used here was the energy of the signal in certain sub-bands in the frequency domain; thanks to the Parseval's theorem, the same amounts of energy can be calculated in the time domain via a bank of digital filters, enabling thus a very fast way to apply the recognizer, since the process goes on at the same time as the occurrence of the word is exerted. Mainly, two experiments were shown, in Spanish and English, with male and female participants; in both cases high performance was attained, beyond 94% at the worst case. Compared to a typical implementation with backpropagation neural networks and cepstral coefficients, this approach was at least 10% more effective in near real-life application.

The genetic algorithm consistently maximized the criteria of inter-class separability and intra-class compactness, under different conditions of population, probability of mutation, etc., and also varying the restriction set. It is remarkable and worth to mention that the genetic algorithm didn't gave the best result in its first execution, which means that the execution must be repeated to achieve good results; increasing the population and manipulating the restriction set demonstrated that it is possible to obtain a variety of different outcomes, so it is important to experiment carefully.

The future work will consist of developing the voice/unvoiced detection in noisy environments, investigate an adapt more features that can be easily computed in time and with a dual in frequency, start working on the non-dependant speaker approach, making use of more robust classifiers, and finally, increase the vocabulary size, although still restricted to a specific semantic field, like in [35]. Another interesting venue is the one in which the user aging process is taken into account by the speech recognition system [36].

9. Acknowledgment

The authors wish to express their gratitude for financial support of this project to *Universidad Politécnica de Aguascalientes*.

10. References

[1] K. Koutroumbas and S. Theodoridis, *Pattern Recognition*, 1st ed. California, E. U. A.: Academic Press, 1999.

[2] John G. Proakis and Dimitris G. Manolakis, *Digital Signal Processing. Principles, Algorithms, and Applications.*, 3rd ed. New Jersey, U.S.A.: Prentice Hall, 1996.

[3] L. R. Rabiner and R. W. Schafer, *Introduction to Digital Signal Processing*, 1st ed. Hannover, U.S.A.: Now Publishers Inc., 2007.

[4] Isabelle Guyon and André Elisseeff, An Introduction to Variable and Fature Selection, *Journal of Machine Learning Research*, vol. 3, pp. 1157-1182, 2003.

[5] R. O. Duda, P. E. Hart, and D. G. Stork, *Pattern Classification*, 1st ed. New York, U.S.A.: John Wiley & Sons, Inc., 2001.

[6] D. E. Goldberg, *Genetic Algorithms in Search, Optimization and Machine Learning*. U. S. A.: Addison-Wesley Professional, 1989.

[7] F. Itakura, Minimum Prediction Residual Principle applied to Speech Recognition, *IEEE Transactions on Acoustics, Speech, and Signal Processing*, vol. 23, no. 2, pp. 67-72, 1975.

[8] J. Makhoul, Linear Prediction: A Tutorial Review, *Proceedings of IEEE*, vol. 63, no. 4, pp. 561-580, 1975.

[9] C. D. Manning, *Foundations of Statistical Natural Language Processing*, 6th ed. Cambridge, Massachussets, U.S.A.: MIT Press, 2003.

[10] J. Ramírez, J. M. Górriz, and J. C. Segura, Voice Activity Detection. Fundamentals and Speech Recognition System Robustness, in *Robust Speech Recognitin and Understanding*, M. Grimm and K. Kroschel, Eds. Vienna, Austria: In-Tech, 2007, cap. 1, pp. 1-22.

[11] L. D. Vignolo, H. L. Rufiner, D. H. Milone, and J. C. Goddard, Evolutionary Splines for Cepstral Filterbank Optimization in Phoneme Classsification, in *EURASIP Journal on Advances in Signal Processing*, vol. 2011, 2011, pp. 1-15.

[12] T. Takiguchi, N. Miyake, H. Matsuda, and Y. Ariki, Voice and Noise Detection with AdaBoost, in *Robust Speech Recognition and Understanding*, M. Grimm and K. Kroschel, Eds. Vienna, Austria: In-Tech, 2007, cap. 4, pp. 67-74.

[13] S. Y. Suk and H. Kojima, Voice Activated Appliances for Severely Disabled Persons, in *Speech Recognition, Technologies and Applications*, F. Mihelic and J. Zibert, Eds. Vienna, Austria: In-Tech, 2008, cap. 29, pp. 527-538.

[14] R. Cardin, Improved Learning Strategies for Small Vocabulary Automatic Speech Recognition, McGill University, Montreal, Quebec, Canadá, Doctor of Philosophy Thesis 1993.

[15] Isabelle Guyon. (2011, june) Isabelle Guyon's home page. [on-line]. Hyperlink http://www.clopinet.com/ isabelle/.

[16] I. S. Oh, J. S. Lee, and B. R. Moon, Hybrid Genetic Algorithms for Feature Selection, *IEEE Transactions on Pattern Analysis and Machine Intelligence*, vol. 26, no. 11, pp. 1424-1437, November 2004.

[17] P. R. Somol, J. Novovicova, and P. Pudil, Efficient Feature Subset Selection and Subset Size Optimization, in *Pattern Recognition Recent Advances*, A. Herout, Ed. Vienna, Austria: InTech, 2010, cap. 4, pp. 75-98.

[18] Y. Sun, S. Todorovic, and S. Goodison, Local-Learning-Based Feature Selection for High-Dimensional Data Analysis, *IEEE Transactions of Pattern Analysis and Machine Intelligence*, vol. 32, no. 9, pp. 1610-1626, September 2010.

[19] J. Teixeria de Souza, R. A. Ferreira do Carmo, and G. Campos de Lima, On the Combination of Feature Selection and Instance Selection, in *Machine Learning*, Y. Zhang, Ed. Vienna, Austria: In-Tech, 2010, cap. 9, pp. 158-171.

[20] X. Huang, A. Acero, and H. W. Hon, *Spoken Language Processing. A guide to Theory, Algorithm, and System Development*, 1st ed. New Jersey, U.S.A.: Prentice Hall PTR, 2001.

[21] A. Zacknich, *Principles of Adaptive Filters and Self-Learning Systems*, 1st ed. London, England: Springer, 2005.

[22] H. Sakoe and S. Chiba, Dynamic Programming Algorithm Optimization for Spoken Word Recognition , *IEEE Transactions on Acoustics, Speech, and Signal Processing*, vol. 26, no. 1, pp. 43-49, 1978.

[23] P. J. Bigus and J. Bigus, *Constructing Intelligent Agents with Java. A Programmer´s Guide to Smarter Applications.*, 1st ed.: John Wiley & Sons, Inc., 2001.

[24] K. S. Tang, K. F. Man, S. Kwong, and Q. He, Genetic Algorithms and their Applications, *IEEE Signal Processing Magazine*, pp. 22-37, November 1996.

[25] S. M. Sait and A. Youssef, *Iterative Computer Algorithms with Applications in Engineering.*, 1st ed. Los Alamitos, Cal., U.S.A.: IEEE Computer Society, 1999.

[26] S. M. Ahadi, H. Sheikhzadeh, R. L. Brennan, and G. H. Freeman, An Effective Front-End for Automatic Speech Recognition, in *2003 International Conference on Electronics, Circuits and Systems*, Sharah, United Arab Emirates, 2003, pp. 1-4, Sub-band speech recognition.

[27] M. P. G. Saon, G. Zweig, J. Huang, B. Kingsbury, and L. Mangu, Evolution of the Performance of Automatic Speech Recogntion Algorithms in Transcribing

Conversational Telephone Speech, in *IEEE Instrumentation and Measurement Technology Conference*, Budapest, Hungary, 2001, pp. 1926-1931.

[28] S. Kwong, Q. H. He, K. F. Man, K. S. Tang, and C. W. Chau, Parallel Genetic-based Hybrid Pattern Matching Algorithm for Isolated Word Recognition, *International Journal of Pattern Recognition and Artificial Intelligence*, vol. 12, no. 4, pp. 573-594, 1998.

[29] V. V. Ngoc, J. Whittington, and J. Devlin, Real-time Hardware Feature Extraction with Embedded Signal Enhancement for Automatic Speech Recognition, in *Speech Technologies*. Vienna, Austria: In-tech, 2011, cap. 2, pp. 29-54.

[30] S. A. Selouani and D. O'Shaughnessy, Robustness of Speech Recognition using Genetic Algorithms and Mel-cepstral Subspace Approach, in *IEEE International Conference on Acoustics, Speech, and Singal Processing 2004 ICASSP '04*, Montreal, Quebec, Canada, 2004, pp. I-201-4.

[31] L. R. Rabiner, Tutorial on Hidden Markov Models and Selected Applications in Speech Recognition, *Proceedings of the IEEE*, vol. 77, no. 2, pp. 257-286, 1989.

[32] S. Okawa, E. Bocchieri, and A. Potamianos, Multi-Band Speech Recognition in Noisy Environments, in *International Conference on Acoustics, Speech and Signal Processing ICASSP 1998*, Prague, Czech Republic, 1998, pp. 1-4.

[33] A. de la Torre et al., Speech Recognition Under Noise Conditions: Compensation Methods, in *Speech Recognition and Understanding*, M. Grimm and K. Kroschel, Eds. Vienna, Austria: In-Tech, 2007, cap. 25, pp. 440-460.

[34] A. Álvarez et al., Application of Feature Subset Selection Based on Evolutionary Algorithms for Automatic Emotion Recognition in Speech, *Lecture Notes in Computer Science. Advances in Nonlinear Speech Processing*, vol. 4885, pp. 273-281, May 2007.

[35] G. E. Dahl, D. Yu, L. Deng, and A. Acero, Large Vocabulary Continuous Speech Recognition with Context Dependent DBN-HMMS, in *International Conference on Acoustics, Speech and Signal Processing ICASSP 2011*, Prague, Czech Republic, 2011, pp. 1-4.

[36] B. M. Ben-David et al., Effects of Agging and Noise on Real-Time Spoken Word Recognition: Evidence from Eye Movements, *Journal of Speech, Language, and Hearing Research*, vol. 54, pp. 243-262, February 2011.

13

Performance of Varying Genetic Algorithm Techniques in Online Auction

Kim Soon Gan, Patricia Anthony, Jason Teo and Kim On Chin
Universiti Malaysia Sabah, School of Engineering and Information Technology, Sabah Malaysia

1. Introduction

Genetic algorithm is one of the successful optimization algorithm used in computing to find exact or approximate solutions for certain complex problems. This novel algorithm was first introduced by John Holland in 1975 (Holland, 1975). Besides Holland, many other researchers have also contributed to genetic algorithm (Davis, 1987; Davis, 1991; Grefenstte, 1986; Goldberg, 1989; Michalewicz, 1992). This is an algorithm that imitates the evolutionary process concept based on the Darwinian Theory which emphasizes on the law of "the survival of the fittest". This algorithm used techniques which are inspired from evolution biology such as inheritance, selection, crossover and mutation (Engelbrecht, 2002).

There are several important components in genetic algorithm which includes representation, fitness function, and selection operators (parent selection and survivor selection, crossover operator and mutation operator). Genetic algorithm starts by generating an initial population of individuals randomly. The individuals are represented as a set of parameter which is the solution to the problem domain. Normally, individuals are fixed length binary string. The individuals are then evaluated using fitness functions. The evaluation will give a fitness score to individuals indicating how well the solutions perform in the problem domain. The individuals that have been evaluated using the fitness function will be selected to be parents to produce offspring through the crossover and mutation operators. The genetic algorithms will repeat the above process except for the population initialization until the termination criteria is met. Fig. 1 shows the structure of a genetic algorithm.

GAs have been applied successfully in many applications including job shop scheduling (Uckun *et al.* 1993), the automated design of fuzzy logic controllers and systems (Karr 1991; Lee & Takagi, 1993), hardware-software co-design and VLSI design (Catania *et al.* 1997; Chandrasekharam *et al.* 1993). In this chapter, variations of genetic algorithms are applied in optimizing the bidding strategies for a dynamic online auctions environment.

Auction is defined as a bidding mechanism and is expressed by a set of auction rules that specify how the winner is determined and how much he or she has to pay (Wolfstetter, 2002). Jansen defines an online auction as an Internet-based version of a traditional auction (Jansen, 2003). In today's e-commerce market, online auction has acted as an important tool in the services for procuring goods and items either for commercialize purposed or for personal used. Online auctions have been reported as one of the most popular and effective ways of trading goods over the Internet (Bapna *et al.* 2001). Electronic devices, books, computer software, and hardware are among the thousands items sold in the online auctions every day. To date, there are 2557 auction houses that conduct online auctions as listed on the Internet (Internet Auction List, 2011). These auction houses conduct different types of auctions according to a variety of rules and protocols. eBay, as one of the largest auction house alone has more than 94 million registered users and had transacted more than USD 92 billion worth of goods during 2010 (eBay, 2010). These figures clearly show the importance of online auctions as an essential method for procuring goods in today's e-commerce market.

```
Begin
Generation = 0
Randomly Initialize Population
While termination criteria are not met
     Evaluate Population Fitness
     Crossover Process
     Mutation Process
     Select new population
     Generation = Generation + 1
End
```

Fig. 1. The structure of a Genetic Algorithm

The auction environment is highly dynamic in nature. Since there are a large number of online auction sites that can be readily accessed, bidders are not constrained to participate in only one auction; they can bid across several alternative auctions for the same good simultaneously. As the number of auction increases, difficulties such as monitoring the process of auction, tracking bid and bidding in multiple auctions arise when the number of auctions increases. The user needs to monitor many auctions sites, pick the right auction to participate, and make the right bid in order to have the desired item. All of these tasks are somewhat complex and time consuming. The task gets even more complicated when there are different start and end times and when the auctions employ different protocols. For this reasons, a variety of software support tools are provided either by the online auction hosts or by third parties that can be used to assist consumers when bidding in online auctions.

The software tools include automated bidding software, bid sniping software, and auction search engines. Automated bidding software or proxy bidders act on the bidder's behalf and place bids according to a strict set of rules and predefined parameters. Bid sniping software, on the other hand, is a practice of placing of bid a few minutes or seconds before an auction closes. These kinds of software, however, have some shortcomings. Firstly, they are only available for an auction with a particular protocol. Secondly, they can only remain in the same auction site and will not move to other auction sites. Lastly, they still need the intervention of the user, that is, the user still needs to make decision on the starting bid (initially) and the bid increments.

To address the shortcomings mentioned above, an autonomous agent was developed that can participate in multiple heterogeneous auctions. It is empowered with trading capabilities and it is able to make purchases autonomously (Anthony, 2003; Anthony & Jennings, 2003b). Two primary values that heavily influenced the bidding strategies of this agent are the k and β. These two values correspond to the polynomial function of the four bidding constraints, namely the remaining time left, the remaining auction left, the user's desire for bargain and the user's level of desperateness. Further details on the strategies will be discussed in Section 3. The k value ranges from 0 to 1 while the β value is from 0.005 to 1000. The possible combinations between these two values are endless and thus, the search space for the solution strategies is very large. Hence, genetic algorithms were used to find the nearly optimal bidding strategy for a given auction environment.

This work is an extension of the solution above, which has been successfully employed to evolve effective bidding strategies for particular classes of environment. This work is to improve the existing bidding strategy through the optimization techniques. Three different variations of genetic algorithm techniques are used to evolve the bidding strategies in order to search for the nearly optimal bidding solution. The three techniques are parameter tuning, deterministic dynamic adaptation, and self-adaptation. Each of this method will be detailed in Section 4, 5 and 6. The remainder of the chapter is organized as follow. Section 2 discusses related work. The bidding strategy framework is discussed in Section 3. The parameter tuning experiment is discussed in Section 4. Section 5 and 6 discussed the deterministic adaptive experiment and self-adaptive experiment. A comparison between all the schemes is discussed in Section 7. Finally, the conclusion is discussed in Section 8.

2. Related work

Genetic algorithm has shown to perform well in the complex system by which the old search algorithm has been solved. This is due to the nature of the algorithms that is able to discover optimal areas in a large search space with little priori information. Many researches in auctions have used genetic algorithm to design or enhance the auction's bidding strategies. The following section discusses works related to evolving bidding strategies.

An evolutionary approach was proposed by Babanov (2003) to study the interaction of strategic agents with the electronic marketplace. This work describes the agents' strategies based on different methodologies that employ incompatible rules in collecting information and reproduction. This work used the information collected from the evolutionary framework for economic studies as many researches have attempted to use evolutionary frameworks for economics studies (Nelson, 1995; Epstein & Axtell, 1996; Roth, 2002; Tesfatsion, 2002). This evolutionary approach allows the strategies to be heterogeneous rather than homogenous since only a particular evolutionary approach is applied. This work has shown that the heterogeneous strategies evolved from this framework can be used as a useful research data.

ZIP, introduced by Cliff, is an artificial trading agent that uses simple machine learning to adapt and operate as buyers or sellers in online open-outcry auction market environments (Cliff, 1997). The market environments are similar to those used in Smith's (Smith, 1962) experimental economics studies of the CDA and other auction mechanisms. The aim of each zip agent is to maximize the profit generated by trading in the market. A standard genetic algorithm is then applied to optimize the values of the eight parameters governing the behavior of the ZIP traders which previously must be set manually. The result showed that GA-optimized traders performed better than those populated by ZIP traders with manually set parameter values (Cliff, 1998a; Cliff, 1998b). This work is then extended to 60 parameters to be set correctly. The experiment showed promising result when compared to the ZIP traders with eight parameters (Cliff, 2006). Genetic algorithm is also used to optimize the auction market parameters setting. Many tests have been conducted on ZIP to improve the agent traders and the auction market mechanism using genetic algorithm (Cliff, 2002a; Cliff, 2002b). Thus, ZIP was able to demonstrate that genetic algorithm can perform well in evolving the parameters of bidding agents and the strategies.

In another investigation, a UDA (utility-based double auction) mechanism is presented (Choi et, al. 2008). In UDA, a flexible synchronous double auction is implemented where the auctioneer maximizes all traders' diverse and complex utility functions through optimization modeling based on genetic algorithm. It is a double auction mechanism based on dynamic utility function integrating the notion of utility function and genetic algorithm. The GA-optimizer is used to maximize total utility function, composed of all participants' dynamic utility functions, and matches the buyers and sellers. Based on the experimental result, it performance is better than a conventional double auction.

3. The bidding strategy framework

As mentioned, this work is an extension of Anthony's work (Anthony, 2003) to tackle the problem of bidding in multiple auctions that employ varying auctions protocols. This section details the electronic marketplace simulation, the bidding strategies and the genetic algorithm implemented in the previous work.

3.1 The electronic market place simulation

The market simulation employed three different auction protocols, English, Vickrey and Dutch that run simultaneously in order to simulate the real auction environment. The market simulation is used in this work to evaluate the performance of the evolved bidding strategies. The following section explains how the market simulation works.

The marketplace simulator shown in Fig. 2 consists of concurrent running auctions that employ different protocols. These protocols are English, Dutch and Vickrey. All of these auctions have a known starting time and only English and Vickrey auctions have a known ending time. The bidding agent is given a deadline (t_{max}) by when it must obtain the desired item and it is told about the consumer's private valuation (p_r) for this item. The agent must only buy an instance of the desired item.

The marketplace announces the current bid values and the current highest bids for English auctions and the current offers for Dutch auctions at each time step. At the end of a given auction, it determines the winning bid and announces the winner. This set of information is used by the agent when deciding in which auction to participate, at what value to bid and in which time to bid.

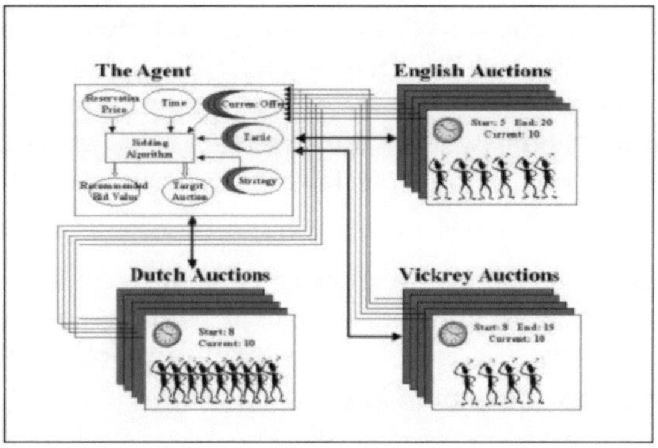

Fig. 2. The Marketplace Simulator

3.2 Bidding strategy

The bidding algorithm for this framework is shown in Fig. 3. Let *Item_NA* be a boolean flag to indicate whether the target item has already been purchased by the agent. Assume that the value of p_r is based on the current reliable market prices observed from past auctions and that the marketplace is offering the item which the agent is interested in. While the bidder agent has not obtained the desired item, the bidder agent needs to build an active auctions list in order to keep track of the current active auction. Active auction is defined as auction that is ongoing or just started but has not reach the ending time yet.

while (t ≤ tmax) and (Item_NA = true)
    Build active auction list;
    Calculate current maximum bid using the agent's strategy;
    Select potential auctions to bid in, from active auction list;
    Select target auction as one that maximizes agent's expected utility;
    Bid in the target auction using current maximum bid as reservation price at this time;
Endwhile

Fig. 3. The bidding agent's algorithm

for all $i \in A$
    if $((t \geq \sigma_i)$ *and* $(t \leq \eta_i)$ *or* $(S_i(t) = ongoing)$
        add i *to* $L(t)$
    endif
endfor

Fig. 4. Building active auction list algorithms

In order to build the active auction list, the bidder agent follows the algorithm as shown in Fig. 4. $S_i(t)$ is a boolean flag representing the status of auction i at time t, such that $i \in A$ and $S_i(t) \in$ *(ongoing; completed)*. Each auction $i \in A$, has a starting time σ_i, and its own ending time η_i. The active auction list is built by taking all the auctions that are currently running at time t. In English and Vickrey auctions, any auction that has started but has not reached its ending time is considered as active. $S_i(t)$ is used in Dutch auctions since the ending time of this type of auction is not fixed.

After the bidder agent builds the active auctions list, the bidder agent will start calculating the current maximum bid based on the agent strategy. The current maximum bid is defined as the amount of the agent willing to bid at the current time that is lesser than or equal to the agent's private valuation. Four bidding constraints are used to determine the current maximum bid namely the remaining time left, the remaining auction left, the desire for bargain and the level of desperateness.

The remaining time tactic considers the amount of bidding time the bidder agent has to obtain the desire item. This tactic determines the bid value based on the bidding time left. Assuming that the bidding time t is between 0 and t_{max} ($0 \le t \le t_{max}$), the current bid value is calculated based on the following expression:

$$f_{rt} = \alpha_{rt}(t) P_r \tag{1}$$

where $\alpha_{rt}(t)$ is a polynomial function of the form:

$$\alpha_{rt}(t) = k_{rt} + (1 - k_{rt}) \left(\frac{t}{t_{\max}} \right)^{\frac{1}{\beta}} \tag{2}$$

This function is a time dependent polynomial function where the main consideration is the time left from the maximum time allocated. k_{rt} is a constant that determines the value of the starting bid of the agent in any auction multiplied by the size of the interval. This time dependent functions can be defined as those that start bidding near p_r rapidly to those only bid near p_r right at the end along with all the possibilities in between with variation of the value $\alpha_{rt}(t)$. Different shapes of curve can be obtained by varying the values of β by using the equation defined above. There are unlimited numbers of possible tactics for each value of β. In this tactic, β value is defined between $0.005 \le \beta \le 1000$. It is possible to have two different behaviors for β. When $\beta < 1$, the tactic will bid with a low value until the deadline is almost reached, whereby this tactic concedes by suggesting the private valuation as the recommended bid value. When $\beta > 1$, the tactic starts with a bid value close to the private valuation and quickly reaches the private valuation long before the deadline is reached. Fig. 5 shows the different shape of the curves with varying β values.

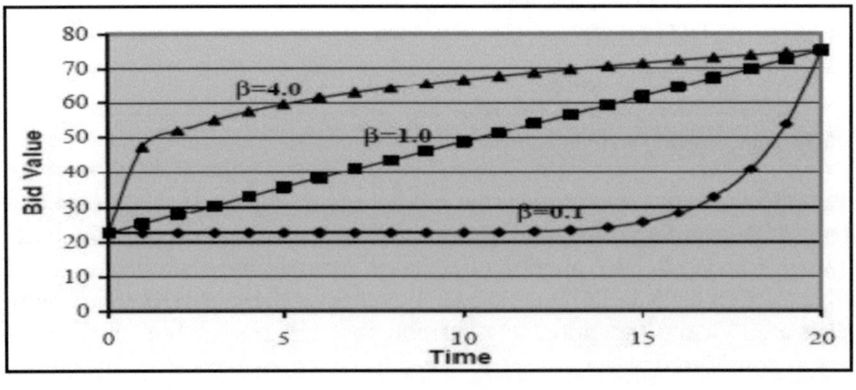

Fig. 5. The curve with varying β value. (Anthony, 2003)

The remaining auction left tactic, on the other hand, considers the number of remaining auctions that the bidder agent is able to participate in order to obtain the item. This tactic bids closer to p_r as the number of the remaining auctions decreases when the bidder agent is running out of opportunities to obtain the desired item. The current bid value is calculated based on the following expression:

$$f_{ra} = \alpha_{ra}(t) p_r \tag{3}$$

where $\alpha_{ra}(t)$ is a polynomial function of form:

$$\alpha_{ra} = k_{ra} + (1 - k_{ra}) \left(\frac{c(t)}{|A|} \right)^{\frac{1}{\beta}} \tag{4}$$

The polynomial function α_{ra} is quite similar to the terms use in α_{rt}, whereby the only difference between the two function is the *c(t)*. *c(t)* is a list of auctions that have been completed between time 0 and t. The β value for this tactic is identical to the remaining time tactic between $0.005 \leq \beta \leq 1000$.

The desire for a bargain tactic is the bidder agent that is interested in getting a bargain for obtaining the desired item. In this scenario, the bidder agent needs to take into account all the ongoing auctions and the time left to obtain the item. The current bid value is calculated based on the following expression:

$$f_{ba} = \omega(t) + \alpha_{ba}(t)(p_r - \omega(t)) \tag{5}$$

In the expression above, the variable $\omega(t)$ takes into account all the ongoing auctions along with the current bid value. The Dutch and English are considered solely in this expression as only these two auctions have current bid value. As a consequence, the minimum bid value is calculated based on the current bid value and also the proportion of the time left in the auction. These values are summed and averaged with respect to the number of active auctions at that particular time. The expression for $\omega(t)$ is calculated based on the formula as below:

$$\omega(t) = \frac{1}{|L(t)|} \left(\sum_{1 \leq i \leq L(t)} \frac{t - \sigma_i}{\eta_i - \sigma_i} v_i(t) \right) \tag{6}$$

where v_i is the current highest bid value in an auction *I* at time *t*, and $I \in L(t)$;

σ_i, and η_i is the start and end time of auction *i*

The expression for $\alpha_{ba}(t)$ is defined as:

$$\alpha_{ba}(t) = k_{ba} + (1 - k_{ba}) \left(\frac{t}{t_{\max}} \right)^{\frac{1}{\beta}} \tag{7}$$

The valid range for the constant k_{ba} is $0.1 \leq k_{ba} \leq 0.3$ and the β value is $0.005 \leq \beta \leq 0.5$. The β value is lower than 1 as bidder agent that is looking for bargain will never bid with the behavior of $\beta > 1$. The β value is, therefore, constantly lower than 1 in order to maintain a low bid until the closes to the end time. Hence, the value of $\beta < 0.5$ is used.

The level of desperateness tactic is the bidder agent's desperateness to obtain the target item within a given period and thus, the bidder agent who possesses this behavior tend to bid aggressively. This tactic utilizes the same minimum bid value and the polynomial function as the desire for bargain tactic but with a minor variation to the β and k_{de} value. The valid range for the constant k_{de} for this tactic is $0.7 \leq k_{de} \leq 0.9$ while the β value is $1.67 \leq \beta \leq 1000$. The β value is higher than 1 in this case as the bidder agent that is looking for bargain will never bid with the behavior of $\beta < 1$. As a result, the β value is always higher than 0.7 since the bidder agent will bid close to the private valuation.

There is a weight associated to each of this tactic and this weight is to emphasize which combination of tactics that will be used to bid in the online auction. The final current maximum bid is based on the combination of the four tactics by making use of the weight. Fig. 6 shows various combinations of the bidding constraints based on the different weight associated to the bidding tactics. It can also be seen that different bidding patterns are generated by varying the value of weights of the bidding constraints.

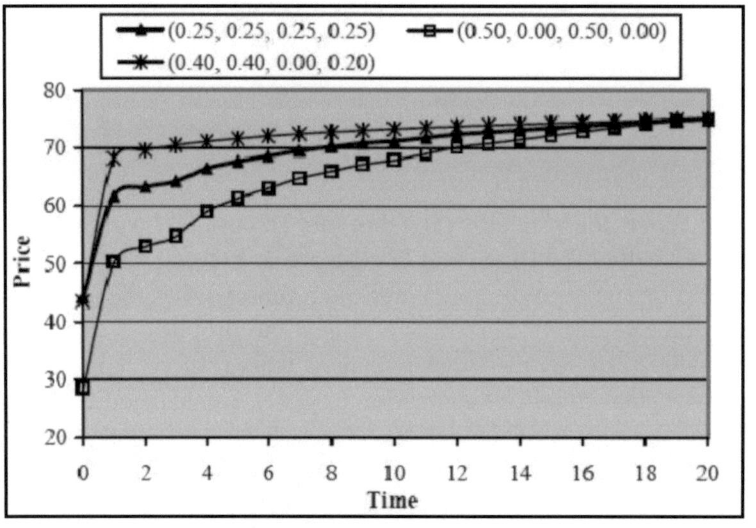

Fig. 6. Various combinations of the bidding constraints

3.3 Genetic algorithm

3.3.1 Representation

Floating point encoding is applied in this particular work as floating point encoding has shown to produce faster, more consistent and more accurate results (Janikow & Michalewicz, 1991). The floating encoding is, therefore, represented using an array of structure. The individuals that are represented in a floating point array structure are shown in Table 1.

p_r	Agent's private valuation
t_{max}	Deadline given to the agent to obtain the desired item
k_{rt}	k for the remaining time tactic
β_{rt}	β for the remaining time tactic
k_{ra}	k for the remaining auction tactic
β_{ra}	β for the remaining auction tactic
k_{ba}	k for the desire for a bargain tactic
β_{ba}	β for the desire for a bargain tactic
k_{de}	k for the desperateness tactic
β_{de}	β for the desperateness tactic
w_{rt}	Relative weight for the remaining time tactic
w_{ra}	Relative weight for the remaining auction tactic
w_{ba}	Relative weight for the desire for a bargain tactic
w_{de}	Relative weight for the desperateness tactic
fitness	Fitness score for the individual

Table 1. Bidding strategies representation

3.3.2 Representation

Fitness function is an objective function that quantifies the optimality of a solution in a genetic algorithm so that the particular chromosome may be ranked against all the other chromosomes. The main focus of the strategies evaluation in this work is the success rate and average utility of the strategies. Three fitness equations are used to evaluate the performance of the strategies namely the success rate, the agent's utility function and agent's utility with penalty. The success rate is the rate in obtaining the desired item and the second fitness function is the agent's utility

$$U_i(v) = \left(\frac{p_r - v}{p_r} \right) + c \tag{8}$$

where v represents the winning bid and c is an arbitrary constant 0.001 to ensure that the agent receives some value when the winning bid is equivalent to its private valuation. The third fitness equation involves a variation of the agent utility. If the agent fails to get the item, a penalty that ranges from 0.01 to 0.05 is incurred. Basically, Fitness Equation 1 is used if the delivery of the item is of utmost importance to the user. Fitness Equation 2 is used when the agent is looking for a bargain. Fitness Equation 3 is used when both the delivery of the item and looking for a bargain are equally important. The fitness score is then computed by taking the average utility from a total of 2000 runs.

3.3.3 Selection operators

Elitism is an operator used to retain some number of the best individuals in each generation to the next generation in order to ensure that the fittest individual is not lost during the evolution process (Obitko, 1998). Elitism is applied in this work to retain ten percent of the best individuals to the new population and to ensure that a significant number of the fitter individuals will make it to the next generation. Tournament selection is applied in the genetic algorithm for selecting the individuals to the mating pools for the remaining ninety percent of the population (Blickle & Thiele, 2001). Tournament selection technique was chosen because it is known to perform well in allowing a diverse range of fitter individuals to populate the mating pool (Blickle & Thiele, 1995). By implementing the tournament selection, fitter individuals can contribute to the next generation genetic construction and the best individual will not dominate in the reproduction process compared to the proportional selection.

3.3.4 Crossover process

The extension operator floating point crossover operator is used this work (Beasley *et al.* 1993b). This operator works by taking the differences between the two values, adding it to the higher value (giving the maximum range), and subtracting it from the lower value (giving the minimum range). The new values for the genes are then generated between the minimum and the maximum range that were derived using this operator (Anthony & Jennings, 2002).

3.3.5 Mutation process

Since the encoding is a floating point, the mutation operator used in this work must be a non-binary mutation operator. Beasley has suggested a few non-binary mutation operators such as random replacement, creep operator and geometric creep (Beasley *et al.* 1993b) that can be used. The *creep* operator which adds or subtracts a small randomly generated amount from selected gene is used to allow a small constant of 0.05 to be added or subtracted from the selected gene depending on the range limitation of the parameter (Anthony & Jennings, 2002).

3.3.6 Stopping criteria

The genetic algorithm will repeat the process until the termination criteria are met. In this work, the evolution stops after 50 iterations. An extensive experiment was conducted to determine the point at which the population converges. It was decided to choose 50 as the stopping criterion since it is was observed that the population will always converge before or at the end of the 50 iterations.

Anthony's work has some shortcoming where the crossover and mutation rate used in the work is based on literature review recommended values. However, researches have shown that the crossover rate and mutation rate applied in the application are application dependent, thus, simulation need to be conducted in order to find the suitable crossover and mutation rate. Besides that, other variations of genetic algorithm have proven to perform better that traditional genetic algorithm which is worthwhile to be investigated.

4. Parameter tuning

Many researchers such De Jong, Grefenstte, Schaffer and others have contributed considerable efforts into finding the parameters values which are good for a number of numerical test problems. The evolution of the bidding strategies by Anthony and Jennings (Anthony & Jennings, 2002) employed a fixed crossover and mutation probability based on the literatures. However, these recommended values may not perform at its best in the genetic algorithm as it has been proven that the parameter values are dependent on the nature of problems to be solved (Engelbrecht, 2002). In this experiment, the crossover and mutation rates are fine tuned with different combination of probabilities in order to discover the best combination of genetic operators' probabilities. Thus, the main objective of this experiment is to improve the effectiveness of the bidding strategies by "hand tuning" the values of the crossover rate and mutation rate to allow a new combination of static crossover and mutation rates to be discovered. By improving the algorithm, more effective bidding strategies can be found during the exploration of the solution.

The experiment is subdivided to two parts. The first one varies the crossover rate and the second one varies the mutation rate. At the end of this experiment, the combination rate discovered is compared and empirically evaluated with the bidding strategies evolved in Anthony's work (Anthony, 2003).

4.1 Experimental setup

Table 2 and 3 show the evolutionary and parameter setting for the genetic algorithm. The parameters setting in the simulated environment for the empirical evaluations are shown in Table 4. These parameters include the agent's reservation price; the agent's bidding time and the number of active auctions. The agent's reservation price is the maximum amount that the agent is willing to pay for the item while the bidding time is the time allocated for the agent to obtain the user's required item. The active auctions are the list of auctions that is ongoing before time $t_{max.}$ Fig. 7 shows the pseudocode of the genetic algorithm.

Representation	Real Values Number
Crossover	Extension Combination Operator
Mutation	Creep Operator
Selection	Tournament Selection

Table 2. Genetic algorithm evolutionary setting

Number of Generations	50
Number of Individuals	50
Elitism	10%
Crossover Probability	0.2, 0.4, 0.6, 0.8
Mutation Probability	0.2, 0.02, 0.002
Termination Criteria	After 50 Generation
Number of Run	10

Table 3. Genetic algorithm parameter setting

Agent reservation price	$73 \leq p_r \leq 79$
Bidding time for each auction	$21 \leq t_{max} \leq 50$
Number of active auction	$20 \leq L(t) \leq 45$

Table 4. Configurable parameters for the simulated marketplace

```
Begin
   Randomly create initial bidder populations;
   While not (Stopping Criterion) do
     Calculate fitness of each individual by running the
     marketplace 2000 times;
     Create new population
       Select the fittest individuals (HP);
       Create mating pool for the remaining population;
       Perform crossover and mutation in the mating
       pool to create new generation(SF);
       New generation is HP + SF;
   Gen = Gen + 1
   End while
End
```

Fig. 7. Genetic algorithm

4.2 Experimental evaluation

The performance of the evolved strategies is evaluated based on three measurements. Firstly, the average fitness is the fitness of the population at each generation over 50 generations. The average fitness shows how well the strategy converges over time to find the best solution.

Secondly, success rate is the percentage of time that an agent succeeds in acquiring the item by the given time at any price less than or equal to its private valuation. This measure will determine the efficiency of the agent in terms of guaranteeing the delivery of the requested item. Individual will be selected from each of the data set to compete in the simulated marketplace for 200 times. The success is calculated based on the number of time the agent is able to win the item over 200 runs. The formula below is used to calculate the success rate.

$$\text{Success Rate=} \frac{(\text{Number of winning}) \text{ x } 200}{100} \tag{9}$$

Finally, the third measurement is the average payoff which is defined as

$$\frac{\sum_{1 \leq x \leq 100} \left(\frac{p_r - v_i}{p_r} \right)}{n} \tag{10}$$

where p_r is the agent's private valuation, n is the number of runs, v_i is the winning bid value for auction i. This value is then divided by the agent's private valuation, summed and average over the number of runs. The agent's payoff is 0 if it is not successful in obtaining the item.

A series of experiments was conducted using the set of crossover and mutation rate described in Table 2. It was found that 0.4 crossover rate and 0.02 mutation rate performed better than the other combinations (Gan *et al*, 2008a, Gan *et al*, 2008b). An experiment was conducted with the newly discovered crossover rate $p_c = 0.4$ and mutation rate $p_m = 0.02$. The result was then compared with the original combination of the genetic operators' ($p_c = 0.6$ and $p_m = 0.02$). Figures 8, 9 and 10 shows the comparison between the strategies evolved using a combination of crossover rate 0.4 and a mutation rate of 0.02 and the combination of crossover rate 0.6 with a mutation rate of 0.02. The new strategies evolved from the combination of the crossover rate of 0.4 and mutation rate of 0.02 produced better result in terms of the average fitness, the success rate and the average payoff. It can be observed that the mutation rate of 0.02 evolved better strategies when compared to other mutation rates as well (0.2 and 0.002). This rate is similar to the research outcome by Cervantes (Cervantes & Stephen, 2006) in which a mutation rate below the 1/N and error threshold is recommended. Besides, the results of the comparison showed that the combination of 0.4 crossover rate and 0.02 mutation rate can achieve better balance in the exploration and exploitation in evolving the bidding strategies as well. T-test is performed to show the significant improvement of this newly discovered combination of genetic operator probabilities. The symbol of ⊕ in Table 5 indicates that the P-value is less than 0.05 and has significant improvement.

	P Value
Average Fitness	⊕
Success Rate	⊕
Average Payoff	⊕

Table 5. P value of the t-test statistical analysis for comparison between newly discovered genetic operator probabilities with the old set of genetic operator probabilities

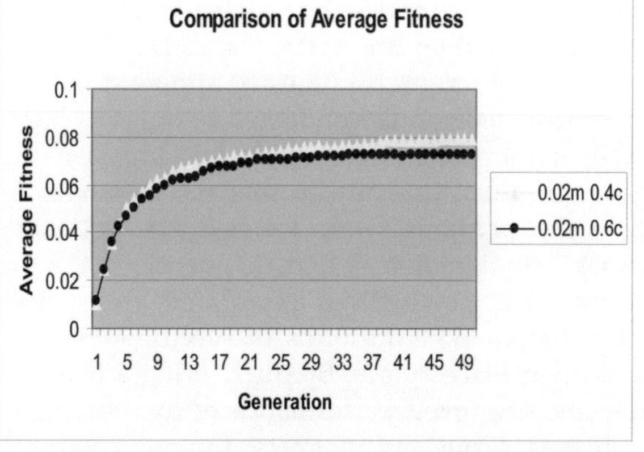

Fig. 8. Comparison of Average Fitness between the benchmark and the newly discovered rate.

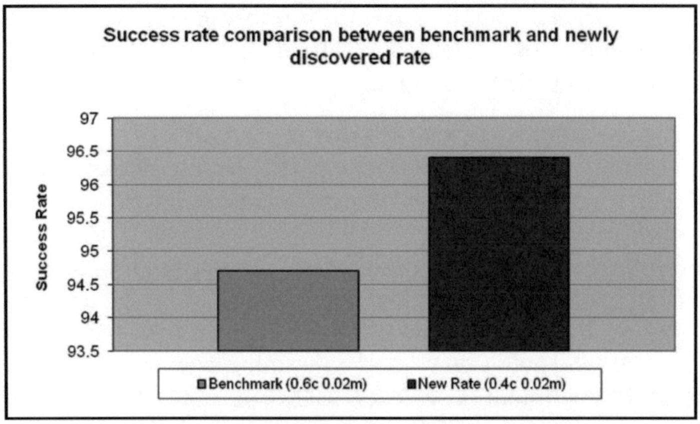

Fig. 9. Success rate for strategies evolved with the benchmark and the newly discovered rate

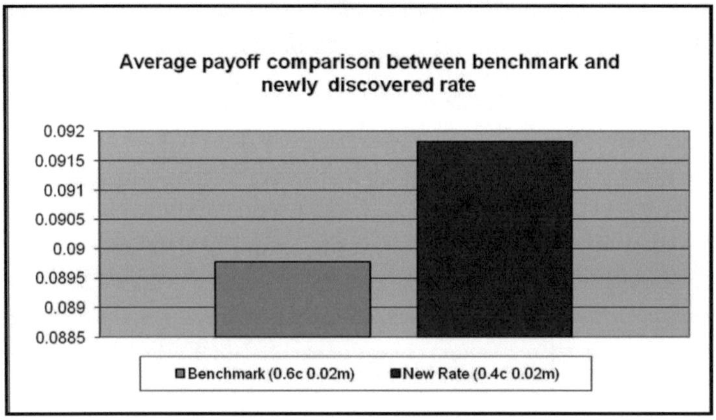

Fig. 10. Average payoff for strategies evolved with the benchmark and the newly discovered rate

This section investigated the performance of various combinations of predetermined sets of genetic operators' rates in genetic algorithm on a flexible and configurable heuristic decision making framework that is capable to tackle the problem of bidding across multiple auctions that applied different protocols (English, Vickrey and Dutch). As mentioned earlier, the optimal combinations of operators' probabilities of applying these operators are problem dependent. Thus, experiments have to be conducted in order to discover a new operator of combinations genetic operator probability which can improve the effectiveness of the bidding strategy. This experiment has proven that the crossover rate and mutation rate which were applied in the previous work are not the best value to be used in this framework. With this new combination of genetic operators, the experimental evaluation has also shown that the strategies evolved performed better than the other strategies evolved from the other combinations in terms of success rate and average payoff when bidding in the online auction marketplace. By discovering a better combination of genetic operator's probabilities, the improved performance of the bidding strategies as shown in Fig. 8, 9, and 10 are achieved. From this parameter tuning experiment, it can be confirmed that the parameters are problem dependent. However, trying out all of the different combinations systematically is practically impossible as hand tuning the parameter is very time consuming. Therefore, in the second stage of the experiment, deterministic dynamic adaptation is applied to genetic algorithm to evolve the bidding strategies in order to overcome the manual tuning problem.

5. Deterministic dynamic adaptation

Many researchers have applied deterministic dynamic adaptation in evolutionary algorithms as a method to improve the limitation in the performance of evolutionary algorithms. This type of adaptation alters the value of strategy parameter by using some deterministic rule (Fogarty, 1989; Hinterding *et al.* 1997). The value of the strategy parameter is modified by the deterministic rule which is normally a time-varying schedule. It is different from the standard genetic algorithm since GA applies a fixed mutation rate over the evolutionary process. Most of the practical applications often favor larger or non-constant settings of the genetic operators' probabilities. (Back & Schutz, 1996). Some of the studies have proved the usefulness and effectiveness of larger, varying mutation rates (Back, 1992; Muhlenbein, 1992).

In this work, a time-variant dependent control rule is applied to change the control parameters over time without taking into account any present information by the evolutionary process itself (Eiben *et al.* 1999; Hinterding *et al.* 1997). Several studies have shown that a time dependent schedule is able to perform better than a fixed constant control parameter (Fogarty, 1989; Hesser & Manner, 1990; Hesser & Manner, 1992; Back & Schutz, 1996). The control rule is used to change the control parameter over the generation of the evolutionary process. The newly discovered crossover and mutation rates from the first experiment will be used in this particular schedule to serve as the midpoint in the time schedule. The parameter step size will change equally over the generation of the evolutionary process as well. This experiment is intended to discover the best deterministic dynamic adaptation by varying the genetic operators' probability scheme in exploring the bidding strategies.

The deterministic increasing and decreasing schemes for the crossover and mutation are different due to the changing scale of the values. The newly discovered crossover rates obtained from Section 3 is used as the midpoint for the time variant schedule because the convergence period of the evolution occur around the 25th generation. Consequently, the deterministic increasing scheme for the crossover rate will change progressively from p_c = 0.2 to p_c = 0.6 over the generation whereas the decrease scheme for the crossover rate is vice versa. The mutation rate obtained from the previous experiment is used as the midpoint of the time variant schedule for the increasing and decreasing schemes. The deterministic increasing scheme for the mutation rate, in contrast, will change progressively from p_m = 0.002 to p_m = 0.2 over the generation and vice versa for the deterministic decreasing schemes. The changing scale during each generation is decided by taking the difference between ranges of the rate divided by the total number of generation.

5.1 Experimental setup

Table 6 shows the parameter setting for the deterministic dynamic adaptation genetic algorithm. The evolutionary setting and parameter setting in the simulated environment is the same as Tables 2 and 4. Fig. 11 shows the pseudocode of the deterministic dynamic adaptive genetic algorithm.

Representation	Floating Points Number
Number of Generations	50
Number of Individuals	50
Elitism	10%
Selection Operator	Tournament Selection
Crossover Operator	Extension Combination Operator
Crossover Probability	Change(Range from 0.4 to 0.6) / Fixed (0.4)
Mutation Operator	Creep Operator
Mutation Probability	Change (Range from 0.2 to 0.002) / Fixed (0.02)
Termination Criteria	After 50 Generation
Numbers of Repeat Run	30

Table 6. Deterministic dynamic adaptation parameter setting

```
Begin
   Randomly create initial bidder populations;
   While not (Stopping Criterion) do
     Calculate fitness of each individual by running the
     marketplace 2000 times;
     Create new population
       Select the fittest individuals (HP);
       Create mating pool for the remaining population;
       Perform crossover and mutation in the mating
       pool to create new generation(SF);
       New generation is HP + SF;
   Change the control parameter value (Crossover / Mutation)
   Gen = Gen + 1
   End while
End
```

Fig. 11. The Deterministic Dynamic Adaptation Genetic Algorithm

Crossover Rate	Mutation Rate	Abbreviation
Fixed	Increase	CFMI
Fixed	Decrease	CFMD
Increase	Fixed	CIMF
Decrease	Fixed	CDMF
Increase	Increase	CIMI
Decrease	Decrease	CDMD
Increase	Decrease	CIMD
Decrease	Increase	CDMI

Table 7. The Deterministic Dynamic Adaptation testing sets

5.2 Experimental evaluation

The performance of the evolved bidding strategies is evaluated based on three measurements discussed in Section 4.2. As before, the average fitness of the each population is calculated over 50 generations. The success rate of the agent's strategy and the average payoff is observed over 200 runs in the market simulation.

A series of experiments were conducted with the deterministic dynamic adaptation using the testing sets in Table 7. From the experiments, CFMD and CDMI performed better than the other combinations (Gan *et al*, 2008a, Gan *et al*, 2008b). Fig. 12 shows that the population evolved with deterministic dynamic adaptation is able to perform a lot better than the fixed constant crossover and mutation rates. This result is similar to the ones observed by other researches where non-constant control parameter performed better than fixed constant control parameter (Back 1992; Back 1993; Back & Schutz 1996; Fogarty 1989; Hesser & Manner, 1991; Hesser & Manner, 1992). Even though, the point of convergence for the different dynamic deterministic scheme is similar, the population with CDMI achieved a higher average fitness when compared to the populations with CFMD. The CDMI scheme with the increase mutation rate is able to maintain exploration velocity in the search space till the end of the run with the decreasing crossover rate achieving a balance between exploitation with the exploration in the search space and also to achieve a balance between exploration and exploitation in this setting.

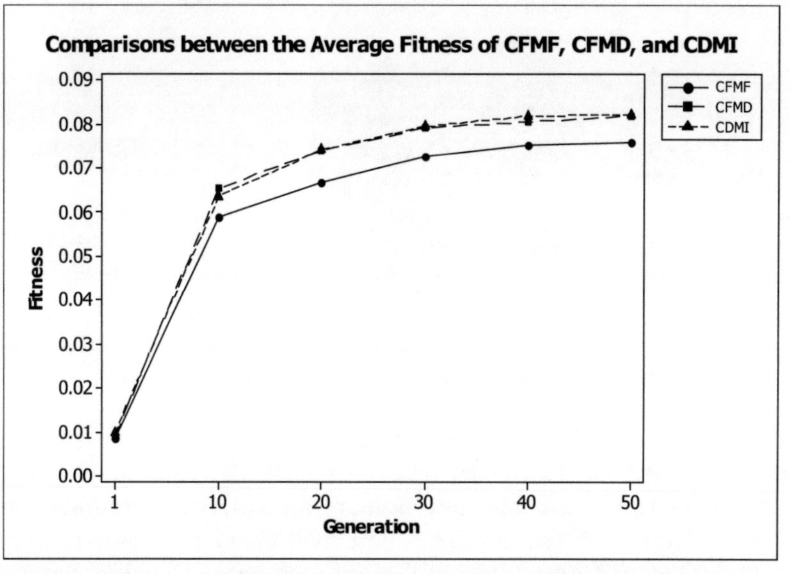

Fig. 12. Comparisons between the average fitness of CFMF, CFMD, and CDMI

Based on Fig. 13 and Fig. 14 CDMI outperformed CFMF and CFMD in both the success rate and the average payoff. This shows that the strategy evolved by using the CDMI does not only generate a better average fitness but also evolves better effective strategies compared to the strategy evolved for the other deterministic schemes and they are able to gain a higher profit when procuring the item at the end of the auction. It achieved a higher average fitness function during the evolution process as well.

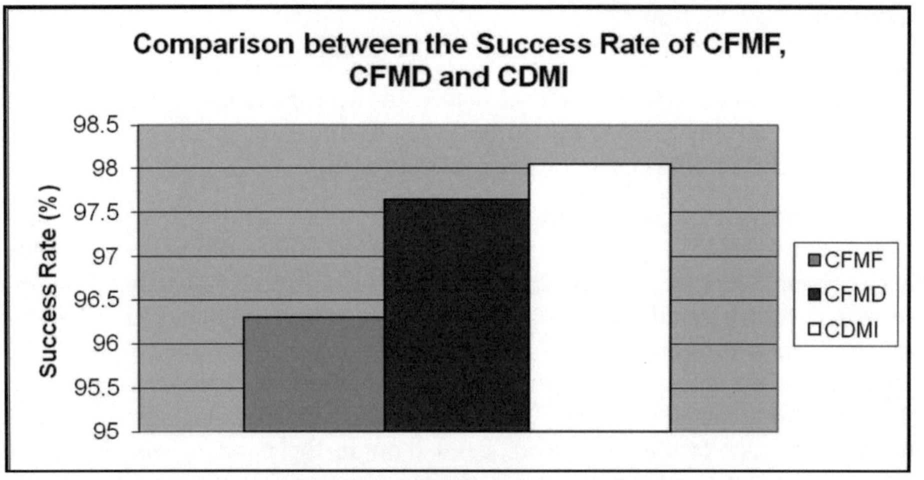

Fig. 13. Success rate comparison between CFMF, CFMD and CDMI

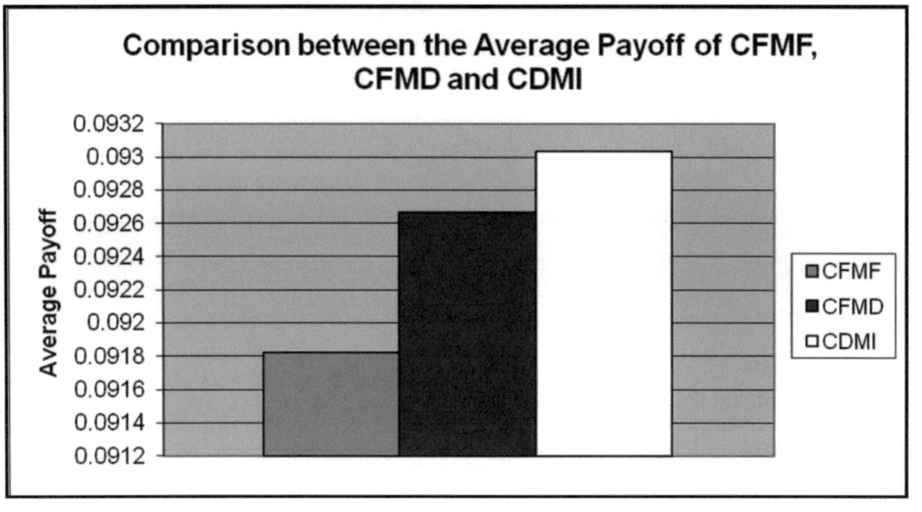

Fig. 14. Average payoff comparison between CFMF, CFMD and CDMI

This experiment has proven that non-constant genetic probabilities are more favorable than constant genetic probabilities. However, the deterministic dynamic adaptation may change the control parameter without taking into account the current evolutionary process as it does not take feedback from the current state evolutionary process whether the genetic operators' probabilities performed best at that current state of evolutionary process. The third stage of the experiment applies another adaptation method known as self-adaptation. The self-adaptation method is different from the deterministic dynamic adaptation where the self-adaptation evolves the parameter based on the current status of the evolutionary process. The self-adaptation method incorporates the control parameters into the chromosomes, thereby, subjecting them to evolution. In the last stage of the experiment, the self-adaptation is applied to genetic algorithm in order to evolve the bidding strategies.

6. Self-adaptation

The idea of self-adaptation is based upon the evolving of evolution. Self-adaptation has been used as one of the method to regulate the control parameter. As the name implies, the algorithm controls the adjustment of the parameters itself. This is done by encoding the parameter into the individual genomes by undergoing mutation and recombination. The control parameters can be any of the strategy parameters in evolutionary algorithm such as mutation rate, crossover rate, population size, selection operators and others (Back et al. 1997). However, the encoded parameters do not affect the fitness of the individuals directly, but rather, "better" values will lead to "better" individuals and these individuals will be more likely to survive and produce offspring and hence, proliferating these "better" parameter values. The goal of the self-adaptation is not only to find the suitable adjustment but also to execute it efficiently. The task is further complicated when the optimizer faced by a dynamic problem is taken into account since a parameter setting that was optimal at the beginning of an EA-run might become unsuitable during the evolution process. This scenario has been shown in some of the researches that different values of parameters might be optimal at different stages of the evolutionary process (Back, 1992a; Back, 1992b; Back, 1993; Davis, 1987; Hesser & Manner, 1991). Self-adaptation aims at biasing the distribution towards appropriate regions of search space and maintains sufficient diversity among individuals in order to enable further evolvability (Angeline, 1995; Meyer-Nieberg & Beyer, 2006).

The self-adaptation method has been commonly used in evolutionary programming (Fogel, 1962; Fogel, 1966) and evolutionary strategies (Rechenberg, 1973; Schwefel, 1977) but it is rarely used in genetic algorithms (Holland, 1975). This work applies self-adaptation in genetic algorithm which aims to adjust the crossover rate and mutation rate. The optimal rate for different phases of the evolution is obtained when different self-adaptation is capable in improving the algorithm by adjusting the crossover rate and mutation rate based on the current phase of the algorithm. Researchers have shown that the self-adaptation is able to improve the crossover in genetic algorithm (Schaffer & Morishima, 1987; Spears, 1995). In addition, studies also showed that the self-adaptive mutation rate does perform better than fixed constant mutation rate by incorporating the mutation rate into the individual genomes (Back, 1992a; Back, 1992b). In this section, three different self-adaptation schemes will be tested to discover the best self-adaptation scheme from this testing set. The self-adaptation requires the crossover and mutation rates to be encoded into the individual's genomes. Thus, some modification the encoding representation needs to be performed. The crossover and mutation rate become part of the genomes which will go through the crossover and mutation processes similar to the other alleles.

6.1 Experimental setup

Table 8 shows the parameter setting for the self-adaptive genetic algorithm. The evolutionary setting and parameter setting in the simulated environment is same as Table 2 and 4. Fig. 15 shows the pseudocode of the deterministic dynamic adaptive genetic algorithm. Fig. 16 shows the different encoding representation of the individual genome that will be used in the experiment. The crossover and mutation rate are encoded into the representation in order to go through the evolution process.

Representation	Floating Points Number
Number of Generations	50
Number of Individuals	50
Elitism	10%
Selection Operator	Tournament Selection
Crossover Operator	Extension Combination Operator
Crossover Probability	Self-Adapted / Fixed (0.4)
Mutation Operator	Creep Operator
Mutation Probability	Self-Adapted / Fixed (0.02)
Termination Criteria	After 50 Generation
Numbers of Repeat Run	30

Table 8. Self-adaptation genetic algorithm parameter setting

```
Generation = 0
Random initialize population
While generation not equal 50
    Evaluate population fitness
    Select the top 10% to next generation
    Tournament Selection Parents to Mating Pool
    Check Parents Crossover Rate
    Generating offspring through crossover process
    Check Individual Mutation Rate
    Mutate the offspring
    Select offspring to the next generation
    Generation = Generation + 1
```

Fig. 15. The self adaptation algorithm both genetic operators

k_{rt}	β_{rt}	k_{ra}	β_{ra}	k_{ba}	β_{ba}	k_{de}	β_{de}	w_{rt}	w_{ra}	w_{ba}	w_{de}	p_c	p_m

Fig. 16. Encoding of a bidding strategy for self-adaptation crossover and mutation rate

Crossover Rate	Mutation Rate	Abbreviation
Fixed	Self-Adapted	SAM
Self-Adapted	Fixed	SAF
Self-Adapted	Self-Adapted	SACM

Table 9. Self-adaptation testing sets

6.2 Experimental evaluation

The performance of the evolved bidding strategies is also evaluated based on the three measurements discussed in Section 4.2. As before, the average fitness of the each population is calculated over 50 generations. The success rate of the agent's strategy and the average payoff is observed over 200 runs in the market simulation.

A series of experiments were conducted with the self-adaptive testing sets described in Table 10. From the experiments, self-adapting both crossover and mutation rates performed better than the other combinations (Gan *et al*, 2009). The population with self adaptive crossover and mutation (SACM) achieved a higher average fitness compared to the population of self-adaptive crossover (SAC) and self –adaptive mutation schemes (SAM) as shown in Fig. 17. This scenario implies that the population with self adaptive crossover and mutation perform at its best among other populations and this is due to the self-adaptation crossover and mutation scheme which has combined the advantageous of the self-adaptive crossover and self-adaptive mutation scheme together. By having the two parameters to self-adapt, the control parameter can be adjusted to find the solution in different stages with the best control parameter which have been shown in the previous study indicating that different evolution stages will possess different optimal parameter values (Eiben *et al.* 1999).

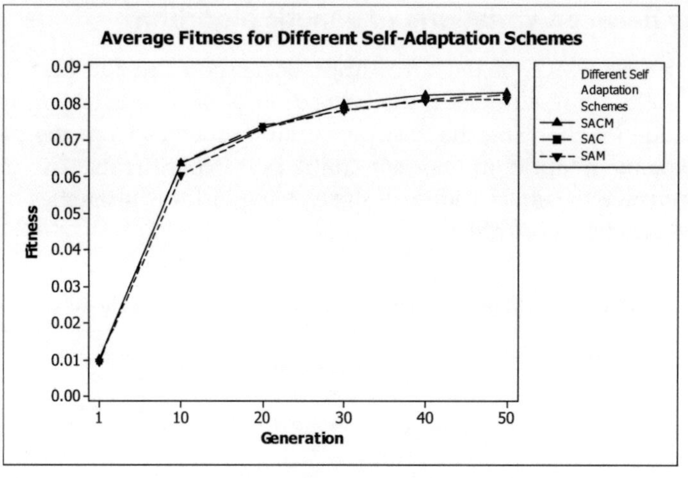

Fig. 17. Average fitness for different self-adaptation schemes

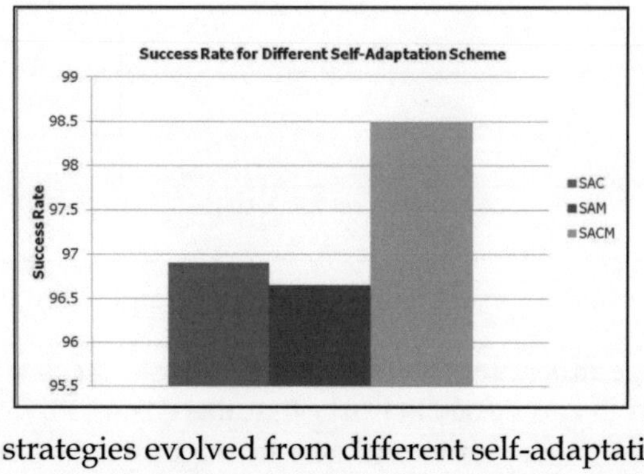

Fig. 18. Success rate for strategies evolved from different self-adaptation schemes

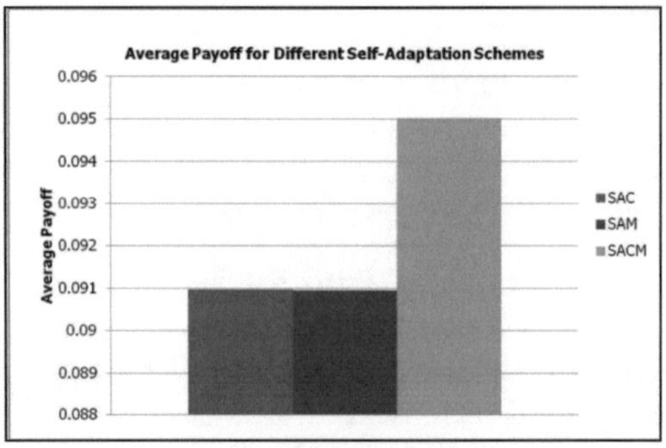

Fig. 19. Average payoff for strategies evolved from different self-adaptation schemes

All of the individuals generated a 4% increase in success rate and average payoff after employing the self adaptive crossover and mutation schemes as shown in Fig. 18 and Fig. 19 This has proven that the strategy evolved by using the self adaptive crossover and mutation does not only generate a better average fitness and success rate but also evolves better effective strategies compared to the strategy evolved for other self adaptive schemes.

7. Comparison between variations of genetic algorithm

In order to determine which of the three approaches perform the best in improving the effectiveness of the bidding strategies, the best result of each experiment is compared. The comparison is made by choosing the best performing schemes from the parameter tuning, deterministic dynamic adaptation and self-adaptation experiments. The main objective of this work is to improve the effectiveness of the existing bidding strategies by using different disciplines of the genetic algorithm.

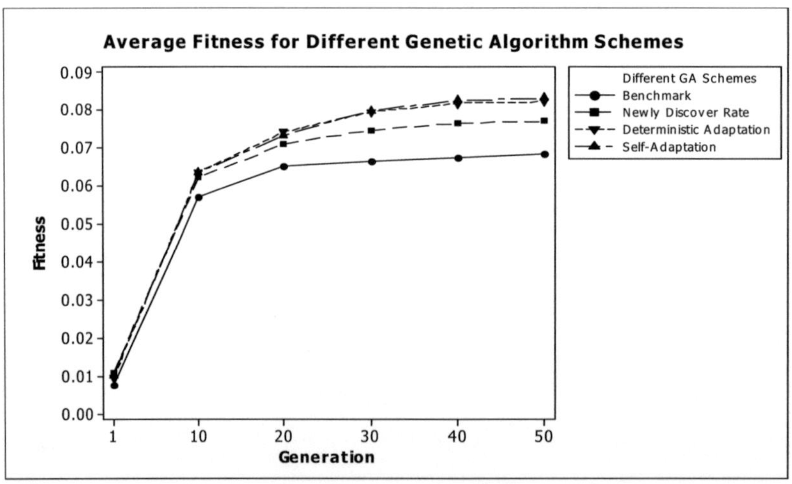

Fig. 20. Average fitness population with different genetic algorithm disciplines

Fig. 20 shows the average fitness for the evolving bidding strategy with different disciplines of the genetic algorithm. It can be seen clearly that there is an obvious differences between the convergence points in the different genetic algorithm disciplines. Self-adaptation achieves a higher average fitness compared to benchmark, the newly discovered static rate and deterministic dynamic adaptation. Although average fitness of the self-adaptation and deterministic dynamic adaption is similar, self-adaptation achieves a higher average fitness when compared to deterministic dynamic adaptation.

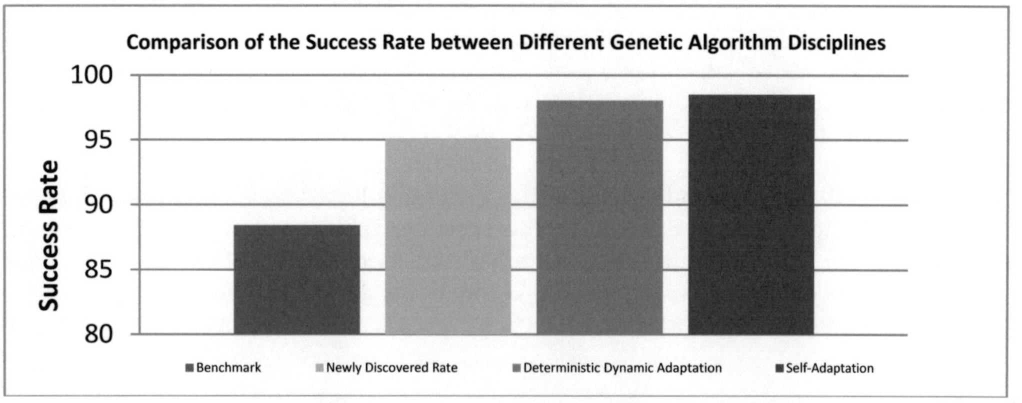

Fig. 21. Success rate for strategies evolved from different genetic algorithm disciplines

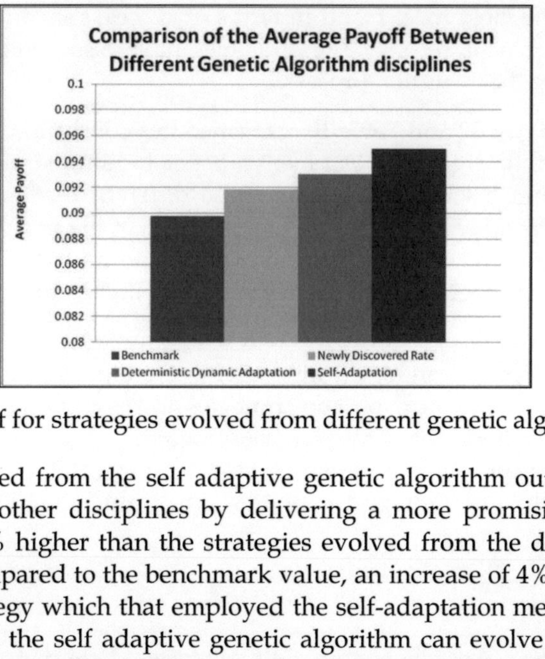

Fig. 22. Average payoff for strategies evolved from different genetic algorithm disciplines

The individuals evolved from the self adaptive genetic algorithm outperformed the other individuals from the other disciplines by delivering a more promising success rate. The strategy evolved is 1% higher than the strategies evolved from the deterministic dynamic adaptation. When compared to the benchmark value, an increase of 4% in the success rate is generated by the strategy which that employed the self-adaptation method. As a result, the strategy evolved from the self adaptive genetic algorithm can evolve better strategies and deliver higher success rate when bidding in online auctions which will eventually, improve the GA in searching for better bidding strategies.

All of the strategies evolved from the self adaptive genetic algorithm outperformed the rest with 2% higher average payoff when compared to the strategies which applied deterministic dynamic adaptation and 4% higher when compared to the strategies from the benchmark. This result obtained indicates that the strategy evolved by using the self adaptive genetic algorithm does not only produce a better average fitness and success rate but also evolves better effective strategies compared to the other strategies evolved for other disciplines and they have gained higher profit when procuring the item.

SA	Benchmark	Newly Discovered Static Rate	DDA
Success Rate	⊕	⊕	⊕
Average Payoff	⊕	⊕	⊕

Table 10. P value for the comparison between different disciplines in term of success rate and average payoff

The symbol ⊕ in Table 10 indicates that the P-value is less than 0.05 and has significant improvement. The result of P value in the t-test in Table 10 shows the improvement generated by the self-adaptation is more significant compared to the other disciplines. Hence, it can be confirmed that self-adaptation is the best discipline in improving the effectiveness of the bidding strategies.

8. Conclusion

Based on the results of the experiments, the strategies evolved with self adaptive genetic algorithm achieved the most ideal result in terms of success rate and average payoff in an online auction environment setting. The strategies have also achieved a higher average fitness function during the evolution process.

The result in Figure 20, 21, 22 and Table 10 confirmed this conclusion by empirically proving that self adaptive genetic algorithm can evolve better bidding strategies compared to the other genetic algorithm disciplines. Among these different methods, the self-adaptation outperformed all of the other methods due to the nature of the method. In order to achieve better bidding strategies, the self-adaptation crossover and mutation scheme can be used to ensure better bidding strategies which in turn produces higher success rate, average fitness and average payoff.

Further investigation can be conducted by evolving the bidding strategies with two other evolution methods which are the evolution strategies and evolution programming. Evolving the bidding strategies with the evolution programming and evolution strategies may generate interesting result which different from genetic algorithm. A comparison between performances the evolutions strategies, evolution programming and genetic algorithm may produce interesting results.

9. References

Angeline, P. J. 1995. Adaptive and Self-Adaptive Evolutionary Computation. *In* Palaniswami, M., Attikiouzel, Y., Marks, R. J., Fogel, D., & Fukuda, T. (eds.). *A Dynamic System Perspective*, pp. 264-270. New York: IEEE Press.

Anthony, P. 2003. *Bidding Agents for Multiple Heterogeneous Online Auctions.* PhD's Thesis. University of Southampton.

Anthony, P. and Jennings, N. R. 2002. Evolving Bidding Strategies for Multiple Auctions. Amsterdam: *Proceedings of the 15th European Conference on Artificial Intelligence*, pp. 178-182. IOS Press.

Anthony, P. and N. R. Jennings. 2003a. Agents in Online Auctions. *In* Yaacob, S. Nagarajan, R., Chekima, A. and Sainarayanan, G. (Eds.). *Current Trends in Artificial Intelligence and Applications*, pp. 42-50. Kota Kinabalu: Universiti Malaysia Sabah.

Anthony, P. and N. R. Jennings. 2003b. Developing a Bidding Agent for Multiple Heterogeneous Auctions. *ACM Transactions on Internet Technology*, 3(3): 185-217.

Anthony, P. and N. R. Jennings. 2003c. A Heuristic Bidding Strategy for Multiple Heteregenous Auctions. *Proceedings of the Fifth International Conference on Electronic Commerce*, pp. 9-16. New York: ACM.

Babanov, A., Ketter, W. and Gini, M. L. 2003. An Evolutionary Approach for Studying Heterogeneous Strategies in Electronic Markets. *Engineering Self-Organising Systems 2003*. pp. 157-168.

Back T. and Schutz M. 1996. Intelligent Mutation Rate Control in Canonical Genetic Algorithms. *Proceedings of the International Symposium on Methodologies for Intelligent Systems. In* Ras, Z. W. and Michalewicz, Z. (Eds.) *Lecture Notes In Computer Science*, 1079: 158-167. London: Springer-Verlag.

Back, T. 1992a. The Interaction of Mutation Rate, Selection, and Self-Adaptation within a Genetic Algorithm. In Manner, R. and Manderick, B. (Eds). *Proceeding 2nd Conferences of Parallel Problem Solving from Nature*, pp. 85-94. Belgium: Elsevier.

Back, T. 1992b. Self-Adaptation in Genetic Algorithms. *In* Varela, F. J. and Bourgine, P. (Eds.) *Toward a Practice of Autonomous Systems: Proceeding 1st European Conference of Artificial Life*, pp. 263-271. Cambridge: MIT Press.

Back, T. 1993. Optimal Mutation Rates in Genetic Search. *Proceedings of the 5th International Conferences of Genetic Algorithms*, pp. 2-8. San Francisco: Morgan Kaufmann.

Back, T. Fogel, David. and Michalewicz, Z. Eds. 1997. *Handbook of Evolutionary Computation*. New York: Oxford University Press.

Bapna, R., P. Goes, and A. Gupta (2001). Insights and Analyses of Online Auctions. *Communications of the ACM*, 44 (11): 43-50.

Beasley, D., Bull, D. R. and Martin R. R. 1993. An Overview of Genetic Algorithms: Part 2, Research Topics. *University Computing* 15(4): 170 - 181.

Blickle, T. and Thiele, L. 1995. A Comparison of Selection Schemes Used in Genetic Algorithms. *Technical Report 11*. Zurich: Swiss Federal Institute of Technology.

Blickle, T. and Thiele, L. 2001. A Mathematical Analysis of Tournament Selection. *Proceedings of the Sixth International Conference on Genetic Algorithms*, pp. 9-16. San Francisco: Morgan Kaufmann.

Catania, V., Malgeri, M. and Russo, M. 1997. Applying Fuzzy Logic to Codesign Partitioning. *IEEE Micro* 17(3): 62-70.

Cervantes, J. and Stephens, C. R. 2006. "Optimal" mutation rates for genetic search. *Proceedings of the 8th Annual Conference on Genetic and Evolutionary Computation Conference*, pp.1313 – 1320. New York: ACM Press.

Chandrasekharam, R., Subhramanian, S. and Chaudhury, S. 1993. Genetic Algorithm for Node Partitioning Problem and Application in VLSI Design. *IEE Proceedings Series E: Computers and Digital Techniques*, 140(5): 255–260.

Choi, J. H., Ahn, H., and Han, I. 2008. Utility-based double auction mechanism using genetic algorithms. Expert System Applicationl. 2008, pp. 150-158.

Cliff, D. 1997. Minimal Intelligence Agents for Bargaining Behaviours in Market Environment. *Technical Report HPL-97-91*. Hewlett Packard Laboratories.

Cliff, D. 1998a. Genetic optimization of adaptive trading agents for double-auction markets. *Proceedings Computing Intelligent Financial Engineering (CIFEr)*. pp. 252–258.

Cliff, D. 1998b. Evolutionary optimization of parameter sets for adaptive software-agent traders in continuous double-auction markets. *Artificial Society Computing Markets (ASCMA98) Workshop at the 2nd Int. Conference. Autonomous Agents*. (unpublished)

Cliff, D. 2002a. Evolution of market mechanism through a continuous space of auction types. *Proceeding Congress Evolutionary Computation*. pp. 2029–2034.

Cliff, D. 2002b. Visualizing search-spaces for evolved hybrid auction mechanisms. *Presented at the 8th Int. Conference. Simulation and Synthesis of Living Systems (ALifeVIII) Conference. Beyond Fitness: Visualizing Evolution Workshop, Sydney*.

Cliff, D. 2006. ZIP60: Further Explorations in the Evolutionary Design of Trader Agents and Online Auction-Market Mechanisms. *IEEE Transactions on Evolutionary Computation*.

Davis, L. 1987. *Genetic Algorithm and Simulated Annealling*. San Francisco: Morgan Kaufmann.

Davis, L. 1991a. *Handbook of Genetic Algorithms*. New York: Van Nostrand Reinhold.

Davis, L. 1991b. Hybridization and Numerical Representation, *In* Davis, L. (ed), *The handbook of Genetic Algorithm*, pp. 61-71. New York: Van Nostrand Reinhold.

eBay. 2008. "eBay Inc. Annual Report 2010," (19 October 2010). http://investor.ebayinc.com/annuals.cfm ..

Eiben, A. G., Hinterding, R., and Michalewicz, Z. 1999. Parameter Control in Evolutionary Algorithms. *IEEE Transactions on Evolutionary Computation, 3*(2). pp. 124 - 141.

Engelbrecht, A.P. 2002. *Computational Intelligence an Introduction*. New Jersey: John Wiley & Sons.

Epstein, J. M. and Axtell, R. 1996. *Growing Artificial Societies: Social Science from the Bottom Up*. Cambridge: MIT Press.

Fogarty, T. 1989. Varying the probability of mutation in genetic algorithm. *In* Schaffer, J. D. (Ed.) *Proceedings of the Third International Conference on Genetic Algorithms*, pp. 104-109. San Francisco: Morgan Kaufmann.

Fogel, D. B. 1992. *Evolving Artificial Intelligence*. PhD Thesis. Berkeley: University of California.

Fogel, L. J. 1962. Autonomous Automata. *Industrial Research,* 4: 14-19.

Gan K.S., Anthony P. and Teo J. 2008a. The Effect of Varying the Crossover Rate in the Evolution of Bidding Strategies. *4th International IASTED Conference on Advances in Computer Science and Technology (ACST-2008),* Langkawi, Malaysia, April 2008.

Gan K.S., Anthony P., Teo J. and Chin K.O. 2008b, Mutation Rate in The Evolution of Bidding Strategies, *The 3rd International Symposium on Information Technology 2008 (ITSim2008)*, Kuala Lumpur, Malaysia, August 2008

Gan K.S., Anthony P., Teo J. and Chin K.O. 2008c, Dynamic strategic parameter control in evolving bidding strategies. *Curtin University of Technology Science and Engineering (CUTSE) International Conference 2008*, Sarawak, Malaysia, November 2008.

Gan K.S., Anthony P., Teo J. and Chin K.O. 2008d, Evolving Bidding Strategies Using Deterministic dynamic adaptation. *The 4th International Conferences on Information Technology and Multimedia (ICIMU2008)*, Bangi, Malaysia, November 2008.

Gan K.S., Anthony P., Teo J. and Chin K.O. 2009, Evolving Bidding Strategies Using Self-Adaptation Genetic Algorithm, International Symposium on Intelligent Ubiquitous Computing and Education, Chengdu, China.

Goldberg, D. E. 1989. *Genetic Algorithms in Search, Optimization and Machine Learning*. New York: Addison-Wesley.

Hesser, J. and Manner, R. 1990. Towards an optimal mutation probability for genetic algorithms. *In* Schewefel, H. P. and Manner, R. (Eds.) *Proceedings for eh 1st Conferences on Parallel Problem Solving from Nature, Lecture Notes in Computer Science*, 496, pp 23-32. London: Springer-Verlag.

Hesser, J. and Manner, R. 1992. Investigation of the m-heuristic for optimal mutation probabilities, *Proceedinng of the 2nd Parallel Problem Solving from Nature*. pp. 115-124. Belgium: Elsevier.

Hinterding, R., Michalewicz, Z., and Eiben, A. E. 1997. Adaptation in Evolutionary Computation: A survey. *Proceeding 4th IEEE Conference of Evolutionary Computation*. pp. 65-69.

Hinterding, R., Michalewicz, Z., and Eiben, A. E. 1997. Adaptation in Evolutionary Computation: A survey. *Proceeding 4th IEEE Conference of Evolutionary Computation*. pp. 65-69.

Holland, J. H. 1975. *Adaption in Natural and Artificial System*. Michigan: MIT Press.

Internet Auction List. 2008. Listing Search in USAWeb.com, http://internetauctionlist.com/Search.asp. 19 October 2011.

Janikow, C. Z. and Michalewiz, Z. 1991. An experimental comparison of Binary and Floating Point Representations in Genetic Algorithms, *In* Belew, R. K. and Booker, L. B. (eds), *Proceedings of the 4th International Conferences in Genetic Algorithms*. pp 31-36. San Francisco: Morgan Kaufmann.

Jansen, E. 2003. Netlingo the Internet Dictionary. http://www.netlingo.com/. 10 November 2008.

Karr, C. 1991. Genetic Algorithms for Fuzzy Controllers. *AI Expert*. 6(2): 26-33.

Lee, M. A. and Takagi, H. 1993. Integrating Design Stages of Fuzzy Systems Using Genetic Algorithms. *Proceedings of the IEEE International Conference on Fuzzy Systems*. pp. 612–617.

Meyer-Nieberg, S. and Beyer, H-G. 2006. Self-Adaptation in Evolutionary Algorithms. *In* Lobo, F., Lima, C., and Michalewicz, Z. (Eds.) *Parameter Setting in Evolutionary Algorithm*. London: Springer-Verlag.

Michalewicz, Z. 1992. *Genetic Algorithms + Data Structure = Evolution Programs*. London: Springer-Verlag.

Muhlenbein, H. 1992. How Genetic Algorithm Really Work: I. Mutation and HillClimbing. *In* Manner, R. & Manderick, B. (Eds) *Parellel Problem Solving from Nature 2*. pp. 15-25. Belgium: Elsevier.

Nelson. R. R. 1995. Recent evolutionary theorizing about economic change. *Journal of Economic Literature*. 33(1): 48-90.

Obitko, M. 1998. Introduction to Genetic Algorithms. http://cs.felk.cvut.cz/ xobitko/ga/. 12 November 2008.

Rechenberg, I. 1973. *Evolutionsstrategie: Optimierung technischer Systeme nach Prinzipien der biologischen Evolution (Evolution Strategy: Optimization of Technical Systems by Means of Biological Evolution)*. Stuttgart: Fromman-Holzboog.

Roth, A. E. 2002. The economist as engineer: Game theory, experimentation, and computation as tools for design economics. *Econometrica*, 70(4): 1341-1378.

Schaffer, J. D. and Morishima, A. 1987. An Adaptive crossover distribution mechanism for Genetic Algorithms. *In* Grefensttete, J. J. (Ed) *Genetic Algorithms and their Applications: Proceedings of the Second International Conference on Genetic Algorithms.* pp. 36-40.

Schwefel, H. P. 1977. Numerishce Optimierung von Computer-Modellen mittels der Evolutionsstrategic. *Interdisciplinary System Research.* 26.

Smith, V. 1962. Experimental study of competitive market behavior. *Journal Political Economy*, 70: 111–137.

Spears, W. M. 1995. Adapting Crossover in Evolutionary Algorithm. *Proceedings of the Fourth Annual Conference on Evolutionary Programming.* pp. 367-384. Cambridge: MIT Press.

Tesfatsion, L. 2002. Agent-based computational economics: Growing economies from the bottom up. *Artificial Life*, 8(1): 55-82.

Uckun, S., Bagchi, S. and Kawamura, K. 1993. Managing Genetic Search in Job Shop Scheduling. *IEEE Expert: Intelligent Systems and Their Applications*, 8(5): 15-24.

Wolfstetter, E. 2002. Auctions: An Introduction. *Journal of Economic Surveys*, 10: 367-420.

14

Mining Frequent Itemsets over Recent Data Stream Based on Genetic Algorithm

Zhou Yong*, Han Jun and Guo He
School of Software of Dalian University of Technology, Dalian
China

1. Introduction

Data stream is massive sequence of data elements generated at a rapid rate which is characterized by continuously flowing, high arrival rate, unbounded size of data and real-time query requests. The knowledge embedded in a data stream is more likely to be changed as time goes by. Identifying the recent change of a data stream, especially for an online data stream, can provide valuable information for the analysis of the data stream. Frequent patterns on a data stream can provide an important basis for decision making and applications. Because of the data stream's fluidity and continuity, the information of frequent patterns changes with the new data coming.

Mining over data streams is one of the most interesting issues of data mining in recent years. Online mining of data streams is an important technique to handle real-world applications, such as traffic flow management, stock tickers monitoring and analysis, wireless communication management, etc. In most of the data stream applications, users tend to pay more attention to the mode information of the recent data stream. Therefore, mining frequent patterns in recent data stream is a challenging work. The mining process should have one-pass algorithm, high efficiency of updating, limited space cost and online response of queries. However, most of mining algorithms or frequency approximation algorithms over a data stream could not have high efficiency to differentiate the information of recently generated data elements from the obsolete information of old data elements which may be no longer useful or possibly invalid at present.

Many previous studies contributed to efficient mining of the frequent itemsets over the streams. Generally, three processing models are used which are the landmark model, the sliding window model and the damped model[1]. The landmark model analyzes the stream in a particular window, which starts from a fixed timestamp called landmark and ends up with the current timestamp. For the sliding window model case, the mining process is performed over a sliding window of a fixed length. Based on the sliding window model, the oldest data is pruned immediately when a new data arrives. The damped model uses the entire stream to compute the frequency with a decay factor *d*, which makes the recent data more important than the previous ones.

* Supported by Fundamental Research Funds for the Central Universities No. DUT10JR15

Mining frequent patterns on a data stream has been studied in many ways and the mining methods include Dstree[2,3,4], FP-tree[5,6,7]as well as estDec[11] algorithm.

FP-Tree structure is generated by reading data from the transaction database. Each tree node contains an item marker and a count. The count shows transaction numbers which is mapped in the path. Initially FP-Tree contains only one root node, marked with the symbol null. First of all it scans the data set to determine the support count of each item to discard non-frequent items, and list the frequent items in descending order according to their support count. Then, it scans data set secondly to construct FP-Tree. After reading the first transaction data, it can create a node and the path of the first transaction and give the transaction a code. We design the frequency count as 1 to all of the nodes on the path. Then, it should read each of the other transaction data in order to form different paths and nodes. The frequency count will be adjusted until each transaction is mapped to a path on FP-Tree. After reading all the transaction formation to construct the FP-Tree, the FP-Stream algorithm could be used on FP-Tree to mine its frequent itemsets.

DStree algorithm is a relatively new algorithm for mining frequent itemsets which have the concept of nested sub windows in sliding window. DStree algorithm separates the current transaction database data into blocks, then statistic frequent itemsets in the current window. When a next block of data comes to the moment, the prior block data becomes the historical data. The second block of data replace the first one. Some of the information are available in current DStree and prepare for the next generation of a DStree

estDec algorithm is a effective way to mine frequent itemsets of current on-line data stream. Each node of estDec algorithm model tree contains a triple (*count, error, Id*). For the relevant item *e*, its number is shown by *count*. The maximum error count of *e* is shown with *error* and *Id* is the determined factor of *e* wich contains the most recent transactions. estDec algorithm is divided into four parts: update parameter, update count, the delay difference and choose frequent items.

As using model tree in FP-Tree , DStree and estDec algorithm, it is difficult to make the algorithm computing parallel and the algorithm run time is also difficult to reduce.

With the development of the card, GPU (Graphic Process Unit) become more and more powerful. It has transcended the CPU computation not only on graphic but also on scientific computing. CUDA is a parallel computation framework which is introduced by NVIDIA. The schema makes GPU be able to solve complex calculations. It contains the schema CUDA instruction set and internal computation engine. GPU is characterized by processing parallel computation and dense data, so CUDA suites large-scale parallel computation field very well[12].

This work proposes a NSWGA (Nested Sliding Window Genetic Algorithm) algorithm. Firstly, NSWGA gets the current data stream through the sliding window and uses a nested sub-window dividing up the data stream in current window into sub-blocks; then, the parallel idea of genetic algorithm and parallel computation ability of GPU are used to seek frequent itemsets in the nested sub-window; at last, NSWGA gets the frequent patterns in the current window through the frequent patterns of the nested sub-windows.

This chapter is organized as follows. Theoretical foundation is described in Section 2. The algorithm is designed for Nested Sliding Window Genetic Algorithm of mining frequent itemsets in data streams in Section3. In Section 4, comprehensive experiments for the algorithm are implemented in built environment and give the comparison with other methods. Moreover, algorithm analysis is also proposed for mining time-sensitive sliding windows in this section.. Finally, we summarize the work in Section 5.

2. Theoretical foundation

The study combines the sliding window techniques, frequent itemsets, genetic algorithm and parallel processing technology.

Sliding window has been used in the network communication, time-series data mining, data stream mining and so on. This algorithm uses the sliding window [9,10] to obtain the current data stream.

Definition 1 sliding window: For a positive number ω1, a certain time T, data sets D = (d_0, d_1 ,..., d_n) fall into the window SW(the size of window SW is ω1), the window SW is called the sliding window.

Definition 2 nested sub-window: For a positive number ω2, a certain time T, the newest data set dn in sliding window SW falls into the nested window NSW (the size of NSW is ω2), the nested window NSW is called the nested sub-window.

As shown in Figure 1, the application of sliding window for dynamic updating of data sets is explained.

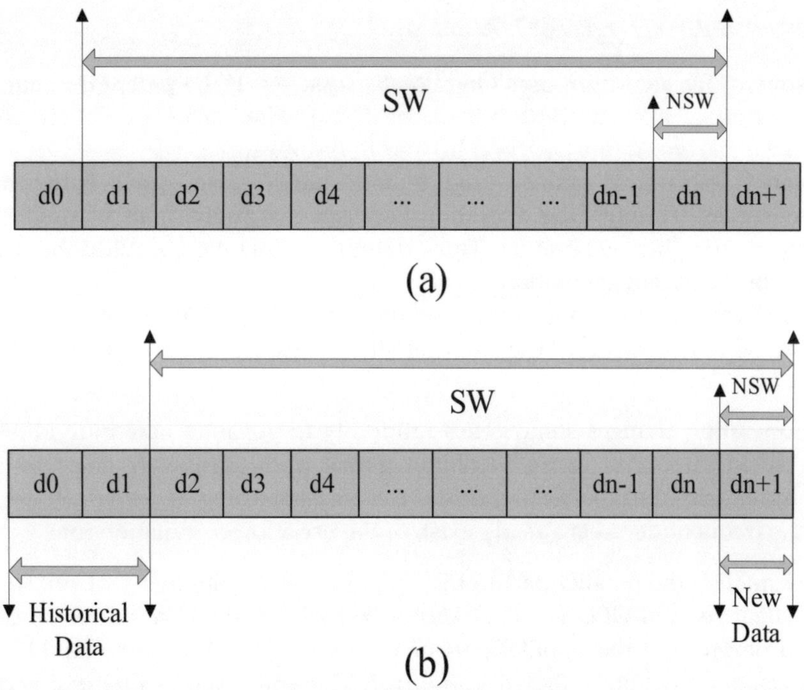

Fig. 1. Dynamic updating of the data in sliding window

Definition 3 frequent itemsets in sliding window: For the current data in sliding window, a collection of items I = {i_1, i_2, ..., i_n} , transaction iterm data set S = {s_1, s_2 ,..., s_n}, each transaction iterm is a collection of items, s⊆I。If X⊆S, then X is an itemset. If there are k elements in X, we call X the k-itemsets. With respect to an itemset X, if its support degree is greater than or equal to the minimum support threshold given by the user, then X is called the frequent itemsets.

Genetic algorithm starts the search process from an initial population. Each individual in the population is a possible frequent pattern. We use the genetic algorithm to achieve the result mainly through crossover, mutation and selection [8]. After several generations of selection, we achieve a final frequent itemsets. The major rules and operators in genetic algorithm are as follows:

1. Coding rule: this work codes with the integer. For example, each transaction item has ABCDE five attributes in a data stream, the transaction item which is coded 21530 expresses that we take the second value of A attribute, take the first value of B attribute, and analogizes in turn, we use 0 to express that we do not consider the value of E attribute.
2. The fitness function: $F_i=W_i/W_Z$, F_i is the support degree of transaction item i, W_i is the number of the transaction items which have the same value for each attribute, W_Z is the total number of transaction items in the window.
3. The selection operator: This algorithm uses the Roulette Wheel Selection. For individual i, its fitness degree F_i, the population size M, then its probability of being selected is expressed as $p_i = F_i / \sum_{i=1}^{M} F_i$, (i=1, 2, … , M).
4. Crossover: This algorithm uses One Point Crossover. If the parent chromosomes are A ($a_1a_2a_3$ ... a_i ... a_n) and B ($b_1b_2b_3$ ... b_i ... b_n), after cross operation, the daughter chromosomes are A_1 ($a_1a_2a_3$ ... b_i ... b_n) and B_1 ($b_1b_2b_3$ ... a_i ... a_n).
   Crossover operator is mainly used to interchange some genes between the parent chromosomes. Through the operation between two individuals of parent generation, we get the daughter generation. Thus, daughter generation would inherit the effective models of the parent generation.
5. Mutation Operator: The algorithm uses the Simple Mutation. If the parent chromosome is A ($a_1a_2a_3$ ... a_i ... a_n), after the variation, the daughter chromosome becomes A_1 ($a_1a_2a_3$ ... b_i ... a_n).

Mutation operation changes some genes randomly to generate new individuals. Mutation operation is an important cause to obtain global optimization. It helps to increase the population diversity, but in this algorithm, the corresponding genes which are required to generate the frequent itemsets already exist, so we use a lower mutation rate.

When we establish the parallel part in the program, we can let this part run into GPU. The function which runs in GPU is called kernel (kernel function). A kernel function is not a complete program, but the parallel part of the entire CUDA program[13,14]. A complete CUDA program execution is shown in figure 2. The graph shows that in a kernel function there are two parallel levels, the parallel blocks in the grid and the parallel threads in the block.

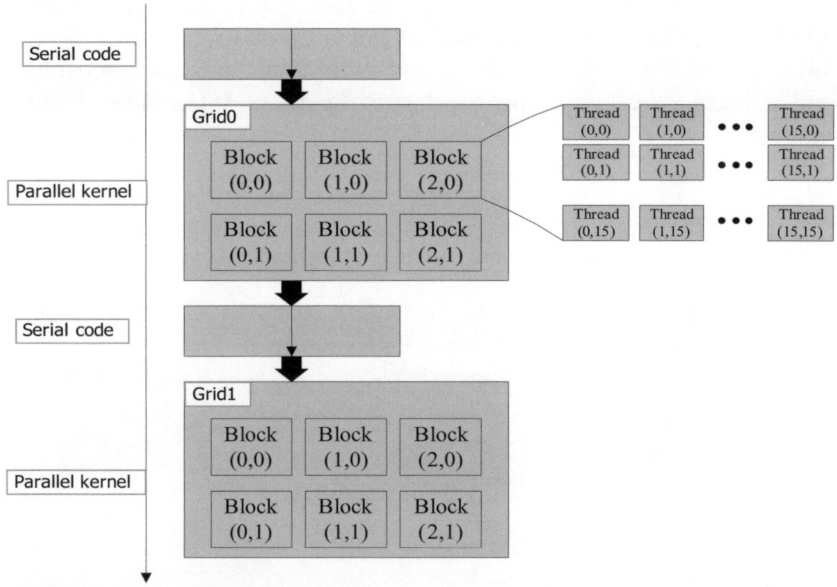

Fig. 2. CUDA programme model

3. Algorithm design

NSWGA uses the sliding window to get the recent data and uses genetic algorithms to mine frequent itemsets of the data in the current window.

3.1 Algorithm description

Input data streams to be mined

Output frequent itemsets of recent data stream

NSWGA algorithm is divided into three parts: (1) NSWGA uses the parallelism of genetic algorithm to search for the frequent itemsets of the latest data in the nested sub-window. (2)The final frequent itemsets of the sliding window are obtained by the integrated treatment of this series of frequent itemsets in nested sub-windows. (3)With the new data coming, the expired data is deleted periodically. Repeat the above two operations.

In the first part, the current frequent itemsets in NSW is obtained. The process is shown as figure 3.

Step 1. Set the size of sliding window SW ω1. Set the size of nested sub-window NSW ω2.Window sizes are determined by the properties of the data stream. ω1 depends on how many current affairs whose frequent itemsets we are interested in. ω2 depends on the processing capability of the algorithm and our statistical frequency. Given the support threshold S, fitness function $F_i=W_i/W_Z$, when $F_i \geq S$, transaction iterm i is a frequent pattern of the data set in sliding window.
The iteration times T depends on the number of attributes that a transaction iterm includs and the scope of the attribute values and the original population size. The

role of nested sub-window is to avoid repeatedly processing the data which is still in the sliding window after the old data out of the sliding window.

Let the crossover probability is P, the individual mutation probability is Q. To implement parallel computing, the data in the nested sub-window is divided into Z segments.

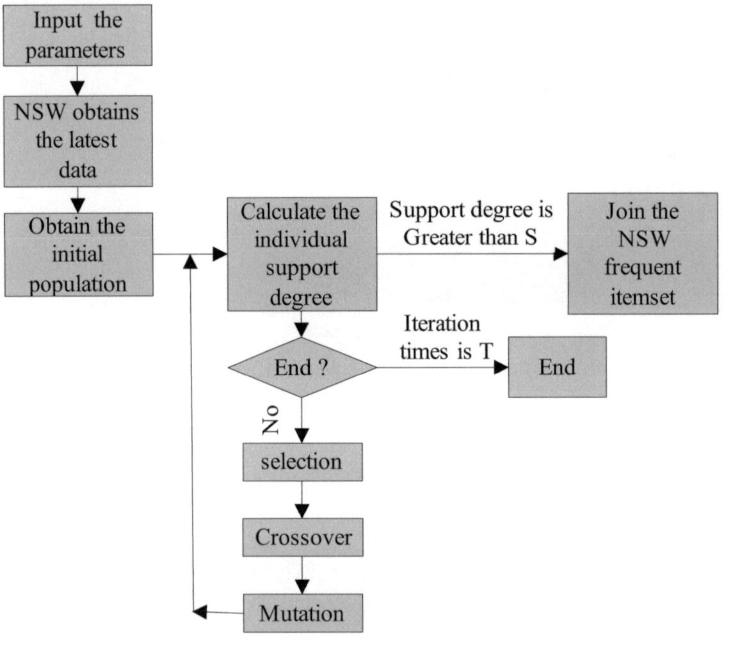

Fig. 3. The generation of initial population.

Step 2. Use the nested sub-window to achieve the latest data, get frequent 1-itemsets of the data, encode the frequent 1 - itemsets to integer strings, and combine the frequent 1 - itemsets randomly to constitute the initial population in the nested sub-window. The individuals of this population are possible frequent patterns.

1 Statistics the number of I_1, I_2, I_3 in A attribute;
2 Statistics the number of I_1, I_2, I_3 in B attribute;
3 Statistics the number of I_1, I_2, I_3 in C attribute;
4 Reserve the value which is greater than or equal to the threshold S, let others are 0 (in this case, S takes 3);
5 Remove the all zero -line, set non- zero values according to their original row;
6 Line up every non-zero value and keep its original location in the line, fill in the rest position with 0;
7 Combine non-zero iterms according to their original location.Constitute the initial population with frequent 1 –itemsets and the combination iterms.

The process is shown in Figure 4.

Step 3. Calculating the individual fitness degree is the process that individuals in the initial population match with the actual transaction iterms. In order to realize parallel matching, we divide the data into Z sections. Although this operation increases the memory expenses, it reduces the running time. It is important in mining frequent

patterns of data stream. Make Roulette Wheel Selection according to the fitness degree. Make crossover with the Crossover probability P. Carry on the variation with the variation probability Q. Ascertain the individual fitness degree after scanning the data. Join the individual which satisfies the condition into the frequent itemsets.
Relying on the powerful parallel computing capability of GPU, parallel matching with Z sections, that will reduce a lot of running time, the process is shown in Figure 5.

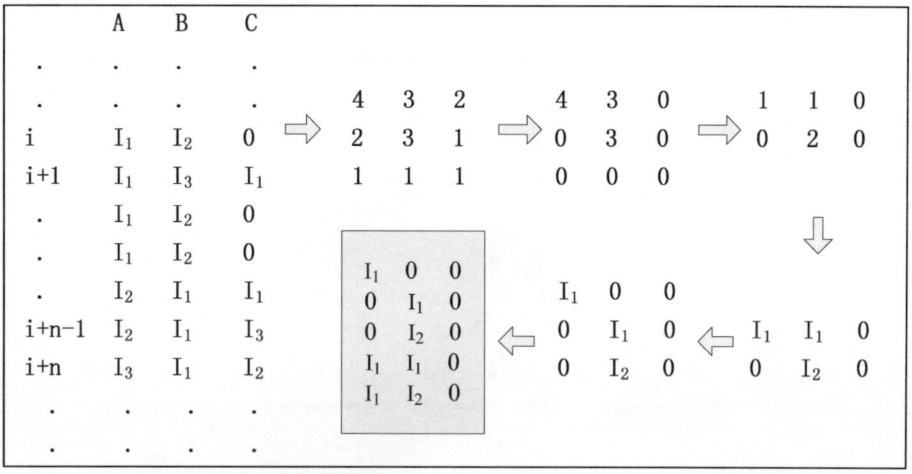

Fig. 4. The generation of initial population

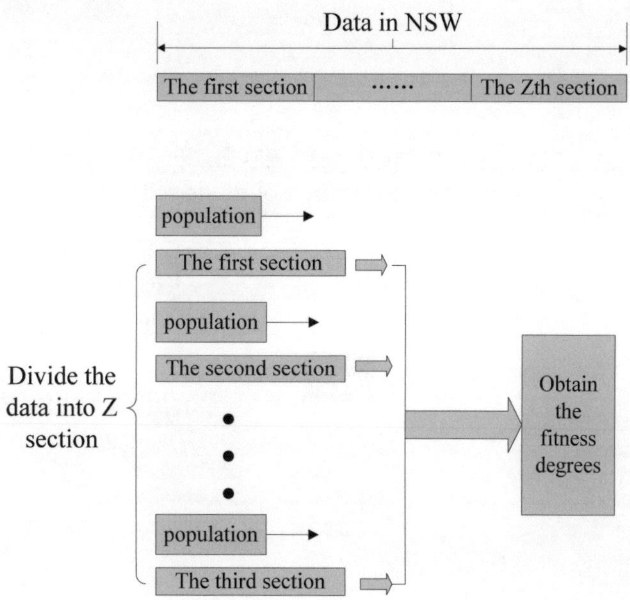

Fig. 5. Parallel computing fitness degree

Step 4. If the number of iterative times is smaller than T, the algorithm jumps to the step 3. After T times of iterative computation, finish iterative and obtain the frequent itemsets in current nested sub-window;

In the second part, the final frequent itemsets in sliding window is obtained. The process is shown as step5.

Step 5. Constitute the mode sets with the frequent itemsets that we obtained this time and the previous frequent itemsets obtained in the last M (M = ω1/ω2-1) times. Carry on a search to determine the final frequent itemsets in the sliding window.

```
For i = 1: M+1
Constitute the mode sets;
End
Make a parallel search in the sliding window SW;
When a mode's support degree is greater than or equal to S, identify it as a final
frequent mode;
```

The process is shown in Figure 6 (a) (b).

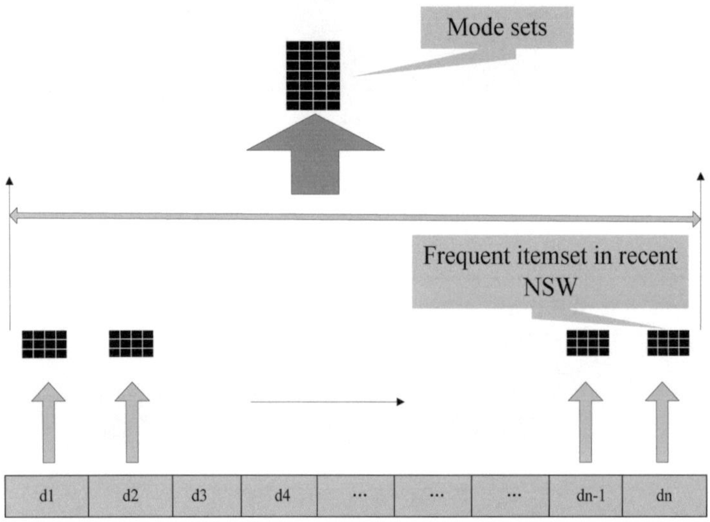

(a) The generation of mode sets

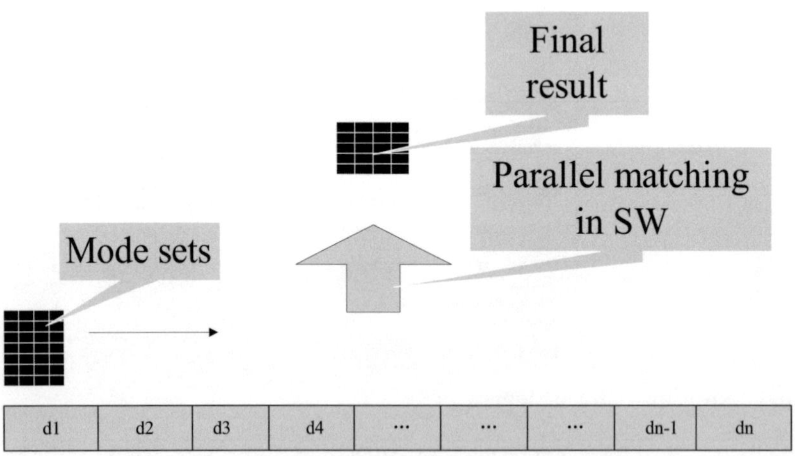

(b) The generation of final frequent patterns

Fig. 6. The process of obtaining frequent patterns

In the third part, repeat the above two operations dynamically. The process is shown as step6.

Step 6. With the data stream flowing, this algorithm continues to deal with the new incoming data and discard the old data, transfer to step 2 and continue the above operations until the data stream coming to the end.

3.2 NSWGA algorithm analysis

Comparing with other algorithms which use pattern tree to maintain the historical information of data stream, NSWGA processes a quantity of data parallelly at one time, while the pattern tree algorithms process a single transaction item at one time, each transaction item needs match repeatedly. Mining the frequent itemsets of the data in the current window, the time of whole process is not only dependent on the times of scanning the data in the window, but also dependent on the internal basic operation - the number of matching.

Suppose a data stream has N transaction items, each transaction item has V attributes; each attribute has K possible values. The pattern tree algorithms may have K^V frequent pattern search paths. Let the window size is N. When the entire data stream in the window flow over, the necessary calculated amount to get frequent itemsets is N * K * V.

For fp-tree algorithm, when the fp-tree has L paths, the calculated amount is 2 * N * V + V * L, the number L will increase with the threshold of support degree reducing.

When the support degree is S, iteration times of genetic algorithms is T, the number of parallel computing is Z (Z according to the amount of data, in this case set Z 200),the sliding window size is N, the necessary calculated amount to get frequent itemsets is P = P1 + P2 + P3. Thereinto:

P1 = N * V the calculated amount to get 1 - frequent itemsets;

P2 = V * T * N / S * Z the calculated amount to get the frequent itermsets in the nested sub-window;

P3= α *V*N/S*Z*M (1<= α <=1/S) the calculated amount to get the final frequent itemsets.

When the property value K is large, this algorithm has obvious advantage in time complexity. When the number of Z is larger, the runtime will become shorter.

4. Experiment and analysis

4.1 Experiment

In this experiment, we use artificial data sets and the MATLAB and CUDA C language to implement NSWGA algorithm. We use the computer with 2.61GHZ CPU, 2GMB memory, Nvidia GPU C1060, windows XP operating system to test the performance of the algorithm.

The size of the sliding window is 100k. The size of the data set is 200K.With the data flowing, we make statistic every 10K of the data.

1. The analog data stream has three attributes. Each attribute has 10 possible values. The running results of the algorithms are shown in Table 1.

algorithm	suport degree	average runtime
fp-tree	10%	0.156
fp-tree	20%	0.087
fp-tree	30%	0.029
NSWGA	10%	0.087
NSWGA	20%	0.032
NSWGA	30%	0.015

Table 1. The comparison of fp-tree **algorithm** and NSWGA algorithm

2. The analog data stream is the same as above. The running results of the algorithms are shown in Table 2.

algorithm	suport degree	average runtime
Dstree	10%	0.138
Dstree	20%	0.139
Dstree	30%	0.141
NSWGA	10%	0.087
NSWGA	20%	0.032
NSWGA	30%	0.015

Table 2. The comparison 1 of Dstree algorithm and NSWGA algorithm

3. The analog data stream has three attributes. Each attribute has 20 possible values. The running results of the algorithms are shown in Table 3.

algorithm	suport degree	average runtime
Dstree	10%	0.406
Dstree	20%	0.397
Dstree	30%	0.402
NSWGA	10%	0.090
NSWGA	20%	0.041
NSWGA	30%	0.017

Table 3. The comparison 2 of Dstree algorithm and NSWGA algorithm

4.2 Analysis of the experimental results

As shown in Table 1, with the support degree increasing, the frequent patterns of these two algorithms are rapidly reducing, the number of matching is reduced and eventually the runtime will be reduced. However, fp-tree algorithm not only needs to maintain the global frequent pattern tree, but also requires additional time to build a sub-pattern tree for each data segment. Then this algorithm saves the information of the sub-pattern tree to the global frequent pattern tree. With the times of process increasing，the runtime of fp-tree algorithm is becoming longer than NSWGA.

Table 2 shows that, with the support degree increasing, the algorithms which use pattern tree to maintain the information of the frequent patterns such as Dstree algorithm can not reduce the runtime, but NSWGA algorithm is able to save a lot of runtime.

In Table 2, the attribute of analog data has 10 possible property values, and in Table 3 there are 20. With the number of possible property values increasing, the runtime of Dstree algorithm will be greatly increased, while the runtime of NSWGA algorithm almost has no change.

5. Summary

It is important for prediction and decision-making to find frequent items among huge data stream. This chapter presents an approach, namely NSWGA (Nested Sliding Window Genetic Algorithm), about mining frequent itemsets on data stream within the current window. NSWGA uses the parallelism of genetic algorithm to search for the frequent itemset of the latest data in the nested sub-window. The final frequent itemsets of the sliding window is obtained by the integrated treatment of this series of frequent itemsets in nested sub-window. NSWGA captures the latest frequent itemsets accurately and timely on data stream. At the same time the expired data is deleted periodically. As the use of nested windows and the parallel processing capability of genetic algorithm, this method reduced the time complexity.

In this chapter, an algorithm about mining frequent patterns of data stream- NSWGA algorithm is proposed. The main contributions of this algorithm: (1) The parallelism of genetic algorithm is used to mine the frequent patterns of data stream , which reduces the runtime; (2) The algorithm combines the sliding window with genetic algorithm to propose an improved method to obtain initial population; (3) This algorithm gurantees the speed of implementation and query precision.

6. References

[1] Lichao Guon, HongyeSu,YuQu. Approximate mining of global closed frequent itemsets over data streams. Journal of the Franklin Institute 348 (2011) 1052–1081.

[2] Chao-Wei Li, Kuen-Fang Jea. An adaptive approximation method to discover frequent itemsets over sliding-window-based data streams. Expert Systems with Applications 38 (2011) 13386 - 13404.

[3] Syed Khairuzzaman Tanbeer, Chowdhury Farhan Ahmed, Byeong-Soo Jeong *, Young-Koo Lee. Sliding window-based frequent pattern mining over data streams. Information Sciences 179 (2009) 3843 - 3865.

[4] Carson Kai-Sang Leung Quamrul I. Khan.DSTree: A Tree Structure for the Mining of Frequent Sets from Data Streams[C].Hong Kong: Proceedings of the Sixth International Conference on Data Mining. (2006)928–932.

[5] Tzung Pei Hong, Chun Wei Lin, Yu Lung Wu. Maintenance of fast updated frequent pattern trees for record deletion. Computational Statistics & Data Analysis,Vol.53,(2009)2485-2499.

[6] Han J, Jian P.Miningfrequent patterns without candidate generation[C].Dallas,TX: Proceedings of ACM SIGMOD International Conference on Management of Data, (2000)1-12.

[7] Zhi-Xin Feng, Zhong Cheng. An algorithm for mining maximal frequent patterns based on FP-tree. Computer Engineering, Vol.30, (2004) 123-124.

[8] Wang Xiaoping, Cao Liming. Genetic algorithm - theory, application and software implementation [M]. Xi'an：Xi'an Jiaotong University Press,(2002).

[9] Syed Khairuzzaman Tanbeer, Chowdhury Farhan Ahmed, Byeong-Soo Jeong. Sliding window-based frequent pattern mining over data streams. Information Sciences: an International Journal, Vol.179,(2009) 3843 - 3865.

[10] Joong Hyuk Chang, Won Suk Lee. A sliding window method for finding recently frequent itemsets over online data streams. Journal of Information Science and Engineering ,Vol.20,(2004)753 - 762.

[11] Joong Hyuk Chang, Won Suk Lee.Finding Recent Frequent Itemsets Adaptively over Online Data Streams[C]. Washington: Proceedings of the ninth ACM SIGKDD international conference on Knowledge discovery and data mining.(2003) 487 – 492.

[12] F.Molnar Jr.,T.Szakaly,R.Meszaros,I.Lagzi..Air pollution modelling using a Graphics Processing Unit with CUDA[J]. Computer Physics Communications, 2010,181(1):105-112.

[13] NVIDIA Corporation.CUDA programming guide[Z].2008.

[14] Harish P, Narayanan PJ. Accelerating large graph algorithms on the GPU using CUDA[C].Springer Heidelberg,2007:367-390.

15

Optimal Design of Power System Controller Using Breeder Genetic Algorithm

K. A. Folly and S. P. Sheetekela
University of Cape Town Private Bag., Rondebosch 7701
South Africa

1. Introduction

Genetic Algorithms (GAs) have recently found extensive applications in solving global optimization problems (Mitchell, 1996). GAs are search algorithms that use models based on natural biological evolution (Goldberg, 1989). They are intrinsically robust search and optimization mechanisms and offer several advantages over traditional optimization techniques, including the ability to effectively search large space without being caught in local optimum. GAs do not require the objective function to have properties such as continuity or smoothness and make no use of hessians or gradient estimates.

In the last few years, Genetic Algorithms (GAs) have shown their potentials in many fields, including in the field of electrical power systems. Although GAs provide robust and powerful adaptive search mechanism, they have several drawbacks (Mitchell, 1996). Some of these drawbacks include the problem of "genetic drift" which prevents GAs from maintaining diversity in its population. Once the population has converged, the crossover operator becomes ineffective in exploring new portions of the search space. Another drawback is the difficulty to optimize the GAs' operators (such as population size, crossover and mutation rates) one at a time. These operators (or parameters) interact with one another in a nonlinear manner. In particular, optimal population size, crossover rate, and mutation rate are likely to change over the course of a single run (Baluja, 1994). From the user's point of view, the selection of GAs' parameters is not a trivial task. Since the 'classical' GA was first proposed by Holland in 1975 as an efficient, easy to use tool which can be applicable to a wide range of problems (Holland, 1975), many variant forms of GAs have been suggested often tailored to specific problems (Michalewicz, 1996). However, it is not always easy for the user to select the appropriate GAs parameters for a particular problem at hand because of the huge number of choices available. At present, there is a little theoretical guidance on how to select the suitable GAs parameters for a particular problem (Michalewicz, 1996). Still another problem is that the natural selection strategy used by GAs is not immune from failure. To cope with the above limitations, an extremely versatile and effective function optimizer called Breeder Genetic Algorithm (BGA) was recently proposed (Muhlenbein, 1994). BGA is inspired by the science of breeding animals. The main idea is to use a selection strategy based on the concept of animal breeding instead of "natural selection" (Irhamah & Ismail, 2009). The assumption behind this strategy is as follows: "*mating two individuals with high fitness is more likely to produces an offspring of high fitness than mating two randomly selected individuals*".

Some of the features of BGA are:

- BGA uses real-valued representation as opposed to binary representation used in classical GAs.
- BGA only requires a few parameters to be chosen by the user.
- The selection technique used is (always) truncation, whereby a selected top *T*% of the fittest individuals are chosen from the current generation and goes through recombination and mutation to form the next generation. The rest of the individuals are discarded.

The main advantage of using BGA is its simplicity with regard to the selection method (Irhamah & Ismail, 2009) and the fewer parameters to be chosen by the user. However, there is a price to pay for this simplicity. Since only the best individuals are selected in each generation to produce the children for the next generation, there is a likelihood of premature convergence. As a result, BGA may converge to local optimum rather than the desired global one. It should be mentioned that most of the Evolutionary Algorithms including GA have problems with premature convergence to a certain degree. The general way to deal with this problem is to apply mutation to a few randomly selected individuals in the population. In this work, instead of a fixed mutation rate, we have used adaptive mutation strategy (Green, 2005), (Sheetekela & Folly, 2010). This means that the mutation rate is not fixed but varies according to the convergence and performance of the population. In general, even with fixed mutation rate, BGA may still perform better than GA as discussed in (Irhamah & Ismail, 2009).

The application of Evolutionary Algorithm to design power system stabilizer for damping low frequency oscillations in power systems has received increasing attention in recent years, see for example, (Wang, *et al* 2008), (Chuang, & Wu, 2006), (Chuang, & Wu, 2007), (Eslami, *et al* 2010), (Hongesombut, *et al* 2005), (Folly, 2006), and (Hemmati, *et al* 2010).

Low frequency oscillations in power systems arise due to several causes. One of these is the heavy transfer of power over long distance. In the last few years, the problems of low frequency oscillations are becoming more and more important. Some of the reasons for this are:

a. Modern power systems are required to operate close to their stability margins. A small disturbance can easily reduce the damping of the system and drive the system to instability.
b. The deregulation and open access of the power industry has led to more power transfer across different regions. This has the effect of reducing the stability margins.

For several years, traditional control methods such as phase compensation technique (Hemmati *et al*, 2010), root locus (Kundur, 1994), pole placement technique (Shahgholian & Faiz, 2010), etc. have been used to design Conventional PSSs (CPSSs). These (CPSSs) are widely accepted in the industry because of their simplicity. However, conventional controllers cannot provide adequate damping to the system over a wide range of operating conditions. To cover a wide range of operating conditions when designing the PSSs several authors have proposed to use multi-power conditions, whereby the PSS parameters are optimized over a set of specified operating conditions using various optimization techniques such as sensitivity technique (Tiako & Folly, 2009), (Yoshimura& Uchida, 2000),

Differential Evolutionary (Wang, *et al* 2008), hybrid Differential Evolutionary (Chuang, & Wu, 2006), (Chuang, & Wu, 2007), Particle Swarm Optimization (Eslami, *et al* 2010), Population-Based Incremental Learning (Folly,2006), (Sheetekela, 2010), etc.

In this chapter, Breeder Genetic Algorithm (BGA) with adaptive mutation is used for the optimization of the parameters of the Power System Stabilizer (PSSs). An eigenvalue based objective function is employed in the design such that the algorithm maximizes the lowest damping ratio over specified operating conditions. A single machine infinite bus system is used to show the effectiveness of the proposed method. For comparison purposes, Genetic Algorithms (GAs) based PSS and the Conventional PSS (CPSS) are included. Frequency and time domain simulations show that BGA-PSS performs better than GA-PSS and CPSS under both small and large disturbances for all operating conditions considered in this work. GA-PSS in turn gives a better performance than the Conventional PSS (CPSS).

2. Background theory to breeder genetic algorithm

BGA is a relatively new evolution algorithm. It is similar to GAs with the exception that it uses artificial selection and has fewer parameters. Also, BGA uses real-valued representation as opposed to GAs which mainly uses binary and sometimes floating or integer representation. In this work, a modified version of BGA called Adaptive Mutation BGA is used (Green, 2005), (Sheetekela & Folly, 2010). Truncation selection method is adopted whereby a top T% of the fittest individuals are chosen from the current population of N individuals and goes through recombination and mutation to form the next generation. The rest of the individuals are discarded. In truncation method, the fittest individual in the population called an *ellist* is guaranteed a place in the next generation. The other top (T-1) % goes through recombination and mutation to form up the rest of the individuals in the next generation. The process is repeated until an optimal solution is obtained or the maximum number of iteration is reached.

2.1 Recombination

Recombination is similar to crossover in GAs (Michalewicz, 1996). The Breeder Genetic Algorithm proposed in this work allows various possible recombination methods to be used, each of them searching the space with a particular bias. Since there is no prior knowledge as to which bias is likely to suit the task at hand, it is better to include several recombination methods and allow selection to do the elimination. Two recombination methods were used in this work: volume and line recombination (Sheetekela, 2010).

In volume recombination, a random vector r of the same length as the parent is generated and the child z_i is produced by the following expression.

$$z_i = r_i x_i + (1 - r_i) y_i \tag{1}$$

where x_i and y_i are the two parents.

In other words, the child can be said to be located at a point inside the hyper box defined by the parents as shown in Fig. 1.

In line recombination, a single uniformly random number r is generated between 0 and 1, and the child is obtained by the following expression (Green, 2005).

$$z_i = rx_i + (1-r)y_i \quad (2)$$

where x_i and y_i are the two parents.

In light of this, a child can be said to be located at a randomly chosen point on a line connecting the two parents as shown in Fig.2.

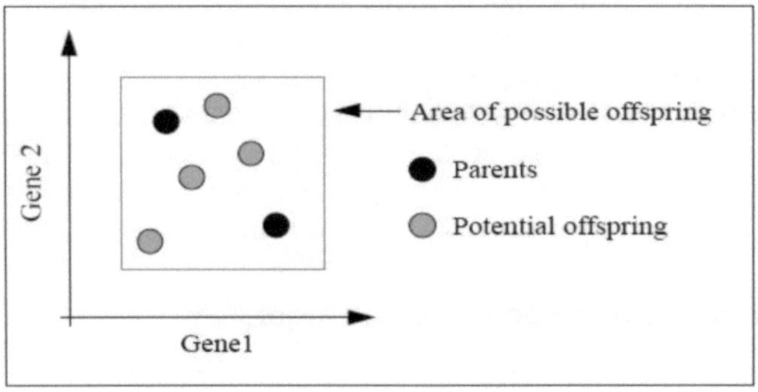

Fig. 1. Volume recombination

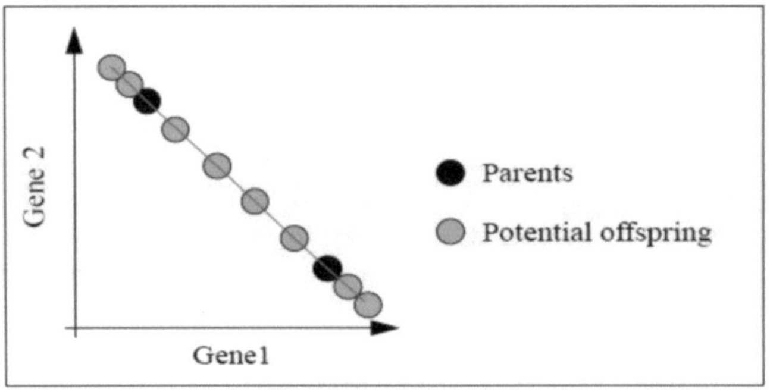

Fig. 2. Line recombination

2.2 Mutation

One problem that has been of concern in GAs is premature convergence, whereby a good but not optimal solution will come to dominate the population. In other words, the search may well converge to local optimum than the desired global one. This problem can be eliminated by adding a small vector of normally-distributed zero-mean random numbers (say with a standard deviation *R)* to each child before inserting it into the population. The magnitude of the standard deviation **R** of the vector is very critical, as small *R* might lead to premature converge and large *R* might impair the search and reduce its ability to converge optimally. Therefore, it's better to use an adaptive approach whereby the rate of mutation is modified during the course of the search. We set *R* to the nominal rate R_{nom}. The population is divided into two halves *X* and *Y*. A mutation rate of $2R_{nom}$ is applied to *X* whereas a mutation of $R_{nom}/2$ is applied to Y. The mutation rate R_{nom} is adjusted depending on the population (*X* or *Y*) that is producing better and fitter solutions on average. If *X* individuals are fitter, then the mutation rate R_{nom} is increased slightly by say 10%. If *Y* is fitter then the mutation rate, R_{nom} is reduced by a similar amount.

3. Test model

The power system considered is a single machine infinite bus (SMIB) system as shown in Fig. A. 1 of Appendix 8.2.1. The generator is connected to the infinite bus through a double-circuit transmission line. The generator is modeled using a 6th order machine model, and is equipped with an automatic voltage regulator (AVR) which is represented by a simple exciter of first order differential equation as given in the Appendix 8.1.4. The block diagram of the AVR is shown in Fig. A. 2 of Appendix 8.2.2. A supplementary controller also known as power system stabilizer (PSS) is to be designed to damp the system's oscillations. The block diagram of the PSS is shown in Fig. A.3 of Appendix 8.2.3.

The non-linear differential equations of the system are linearized around the nominal operating condition to form a set of linear equations as follows:

$$\begin{cases} \dfrac{d}{dt}x = Ax + Bu \\ y = Cx + Du \end{cases} \tag{3}$$

where:

A is the system state matrix, B is the system input matrix, C is the system output matrix and D is the feed-forward matrix
x is the vector of the system states, u is the vector of the system inputs and y is the vector of the system outputs.

In this work, $x = [\Delta\delta\ \Delta\omega\ \Delta\psi_{fd}\ \Delta\psi_{1d}\ \Delta\psi_{1q}\ \Delta\psi_{2q}\ \Delta E_{fd}\ ]$; $u = [\Delta T_m\ \Delta V_{ref}]$; $y = \Delta\omega$; where, $\Delta\delta$ is the rotor angle deviation, $\Delta\omega$ is the speed deviation, $\Delta\psi_{fd}$ is the field flux linkage deviation, $\Delta\psi_{1d}$ is d-axis amortisseur flux linkage deviation, $\Delta\psi_{1q}$ is the 1st q-axis amortisseur flux linkage deviation, $\Delta\psi_{2q}$ is the 2nd q-axis amortisseur flux linkage deviation, ΔE_{fd} is the exciter output voltage deviation. ΔT_m is the mechanical torque deviation and ΔV_{ref} is the voltage reference deviation.

Several operating conditions were considered for the design of the controllers. These operating conditions were obtained by varying the active power output, P_e and the reactive power Q_e of the generator as well as the line reactance, X_e. However, for simplicity, only three operating conditions will be presented in this paper. These operating conditions are listed in the Table 1 together with the open loop eigenvalues and their respective damping ratios in % in brackets.

case	Active Power Pe [p.u]	Reacctive Power Qe [p.u]	Line reactance Xe [p.u]	Eigenvalues (Damping ratio)
1	1.1000	0.4070	0.7000	-0.2894 ± j5.2785 (0.0547)
2	0.5000	0.1839	1.1000	-0.3472 ± j4.3271 (0.0800)
3	0.9000	0.3372	0.9000	-0.2704 + j4.7212 (0.0572)

Table 1. Selected operating conditions with open-loop eigenvalues

4. Fitness function

The fitness function is used to provide the measure of how individuals performed. In this instance, the problem domain was that the PSS parameters should stabilize the system simultaneously over a certain range of specified operating conditions. The PSS which parameters are to be optimized has a structure similar to the conventional PSS (CPSS) as shown in Fig. A. 3. of Appendix 8.2.3. There are three parameters K_S, T_1 and T_2 that are to be optimized, where K_s is the PSS gain and T_1 and T_2 are lead-lag time constants. T_w is the washout time constant which is not critical and therefore has not been optimized.

The fitness function that was used is to maximize the lowest damping ratio. Mathematically the objective function is formulated as follows:

$$val = \max(\min(\varsigma_{ij})) \tag{4}$$

where

$i = 1,2, \ldots n$, $j = 1, 2, \ldots .m$

$$\varsigma_{ij} = \frac{-\sigma_{ij}}{\sqrt{\sigma_{ij}^2 + \omega_{ij}^2}}$$

ζ_{ij} is the damping ratio of the ith eigenvalue of the jth operating conditions. The number of the eigenvalues is n, and m is the number of operating conditions.

σ_{ij} and ω_{ij} are the real part and the imaginary part (frequency) of the eigenvalue, respectively.

5. PSS design

The following parameter domain constraints were considered when designing the PSS.

$$0 < K_s \leq 20$$

$$0.001 \leq T_i \leq 5$$

where K_s and T_i denote the controller gain and the lead lag time constants, respectively .

5.1 BGA-PSS

The following BGA parameters have been used during the design

- Population: 100
- Generation: 100
- Selection: Truncation selection (i.e., selected the best 15% of the population)
- Recombination: Line and volume
- Mutation initial R_{nom}: 0.01

The parameters of the BGA-PSS are given in *Table A*.1 of Appendix 8.2.3.

5.2 GA-P15 Folly_secondSS

The following GA parameters have been used during the design

- Population: 100
- Generation: 100
- Selection: Normalized geometric
- Crossover: Arithmetic
- Mutation: Non-uniform

More information on the selection, crossover and mutation can be found in (Michalewicz, 1996), (Sheetekela & Folly, 2010).

The parameters of the GA-PSS are given in *Table A*.1 of Appendix 8.2.3.

5.3 Conventional-PSS

The Conventional PSS (CPSS) was designed at the nominal operating condition using the phase compensation method. The phase lag of the system was first obtained, which was found to be 20°, thus only a single lead-lag block was used for the PSS. After obtaining the phase lag, a PSS with a phase lead was designed using the phase compensation technique. The final phase lead obtained was approximately 18°, thus giving the system a slight phase lag of 2°. Once the phase lag is improved, then the damping needed to be improved as well by varying the gain K_S. The parameters of the CPSS are given in *Table A*.1 of Appendix 8.2.3.

6. Simulation results

6.1 Eigenvalue analysis

Under the assumption of small-signal disturbance (i.e, small change in V_{ref} or T_m), the eigenvalues of the system are obtained and the stability of the system investigated. Table 2 shows the eigenvalues of the system for the different PSSs. The damping ratios are shown in brackets. For all of the cases, it can be seen that on average, BGA-PSS provides more damping to the system than GA-PSS. On the other hand, GA-PSS performs better than CPSS. For example for case 1, BGA-PSS provides a damping ratio of 50% as compared to 48.85% for GA-PSS and 44.93% for CPSS. This means that, BGA gives the best performance. Likewise, BGA provides better damping ratios for cases 2 and 3.

case	BGA-PSS	GA-PSS	CPSS
1	-3.0664 ±j 5.3117 (0.5000)	-2.9208 ± j5.2172 (0.4885)	-1.9876 ± j3.9516 (0.4493)
2	-1.2793 ± j4.3024 (0.2850)	-1.2305± j4.2616 (0.2774)	-0.9529 ± j3.9443 (0.2348)
3	-2.1245 + j4.6503 (0.4155)	-2.0268 + j4.5784 (0.4048)	-1.3865 + j3.8881 (0.3359)

Table 2. Closed-loop eigenvalues

It should be mentioned that a maximum damping ratio of 50% was imposed on the BGA and GA, otherwise, their damping ratios could have been higher. If the damping of the electromechanical mode is too high this could negatively affect other modes in the system.

6.2 Large disturbance

A large disturbance was considered by applying a three-phase fault to the system at 0.1 seconds. The fault was applied at the sending-end of the system (near bus 1 on line 2) for 200ms. The fault was cleared by disconnecting line 2. Fig. 3 to Fig. 5 show the speed responses of the system.

Figure 3 shows the speed responses of the generator for case 1. When the system is equipped with GA-PSS and BGA-PSS it settles around 3 seconds. On the other hand, the settling time of the system equipped with the CPSS is more than doubled (6 seconds). In addition, the subsequent oscillations are larger than those of BGA and GA PSSs.

Figure 4 shows the speed responses for case 2. The system equipped with CPSS is seen to have bigger oscillations as compared to the system equipped with BGA-PSS and GA-PSS. With both BGA and GA PSSs, the system settled in approximately 3.5 sec., whereas CPSS takes more than 6 sec. to settle down. The performances of the BGA-PSS and GA-PSS are quite similar, even though the BGA-PSS performs slightly better than the GA- PSS.

Figure 5 shows the speed responses of the system for case 3. It can be seen that the system equipped with BGA and GA PSS settled in less than 4 sec compared to more than 6 sec. for the CPSS. With CPSS, the system has large overshoots and undershoots.

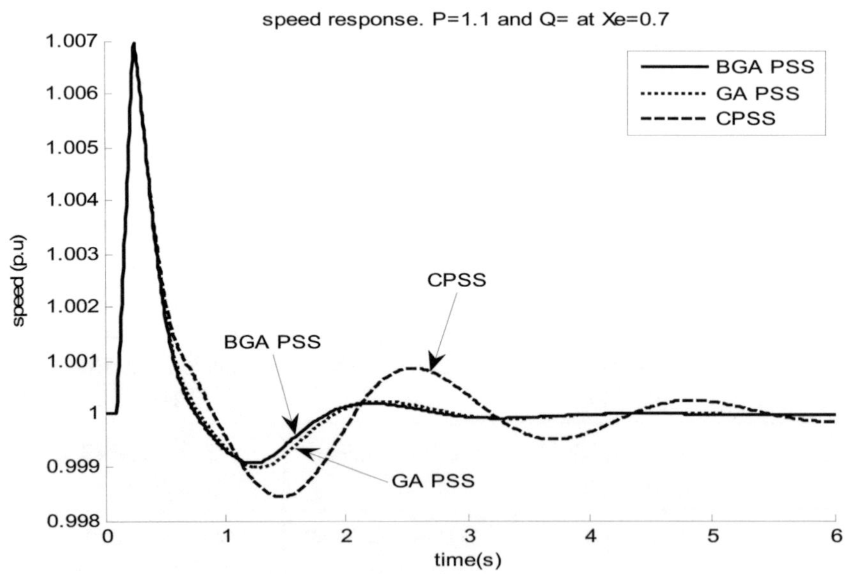

Fig. 3. Speed response of case 1 under three-phase fault

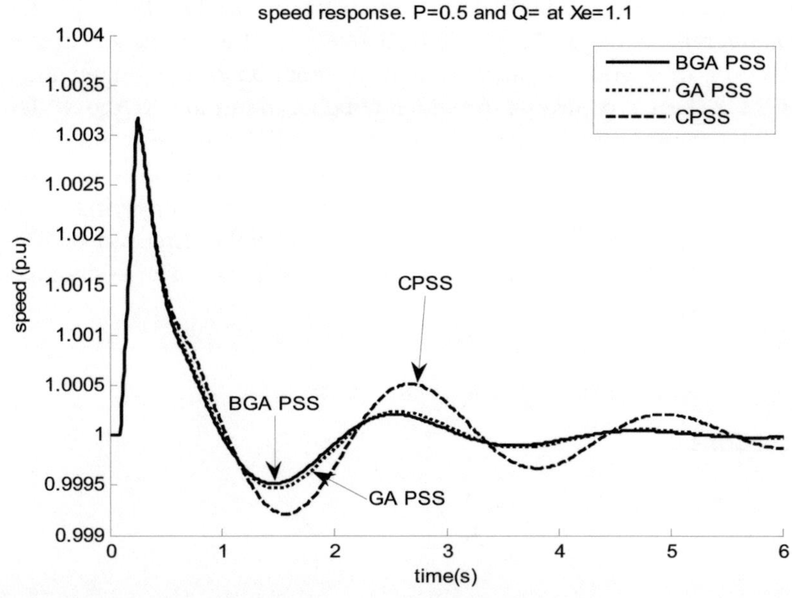

Fig. 4. Speed responses of case 2 under three-phase fault

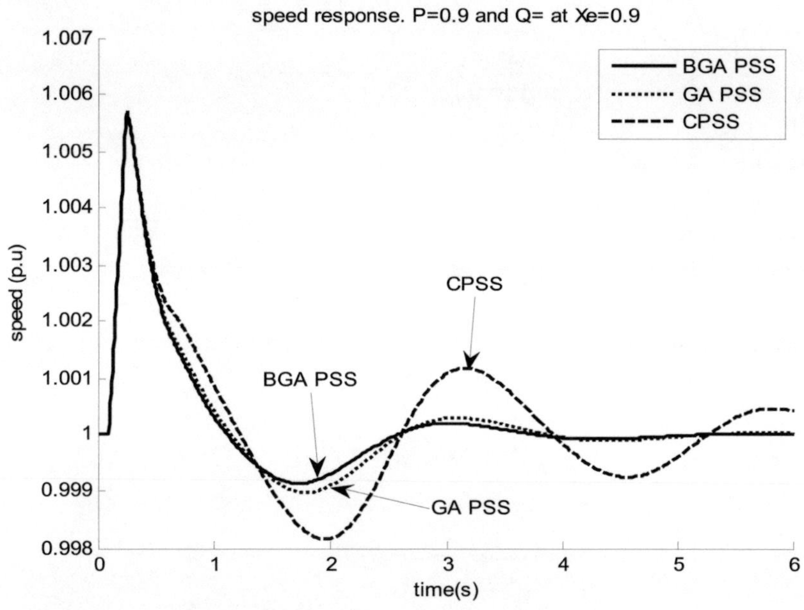

Fig. 5. Speed responses of case 3 under three-phase fault

7. Conclusion

Breeder Genetic Algorithms is an extremely versatile and effective function optimizer. The main advantage of BGA over GA is the simplicity of the selection method and the fewer genetic parameters. In this work, adaptive mutation has been used to deal with the problem of premature convergence in BGA. The effectiveness of the proposed approach was demonstrated by the time and frequency domain simulation results. Eigenvalue analysis shows that the BGA based controller provides a better damping to the system for all operating conditions considered than a GA based controller. The conventional controller provides the least damping to all the operating conditions considered. The robustness of the BGA controller under large disturbance was also investigated by applying a three-phase fault to the system. Further research will be carried out in the direction of using multi-objective functions in the optimization and using a more complex power system model.

8. Appendix

8.1 Generator and Automatic Voltage Regulator (AVR) equations

8.1.1 Swing equations

$$\frac{d}{dt}\Delta\omega = \frac{1}{2H}(T_m - T_e - K_D\Delta\omega)$$

$$\frac{d}{dt}\Delta\delta = \omega_0\Delta\omega$$

where

$\delta$is the rotor angle in rad
ω is the synchronous speed in per-unit (p.u.)
ω_0 is the synchronous speed in rad/sec
H is the inertia constant in sec.
T_m is the mechanical torque in p.u.
T_e is the mechanical torque in p.u.
K_D is the damping coefficient in torque/ p.u.

8.1.2 Rotor circuit equations

$$\frac{d}{dt}\psi_{fd} = \omega_0(E_{fd} - \frac{R_{fd}}{L_{fd}}i_{fd})$$

$$\frac{d}{dt}\psi_{1d} = -\omega_0 R_{1d} i_{1d}$$

$$\frac{d}{dt}\psi_{1q} = -\omega_0 R_{1q} i_{1q}$$

$$\frac{d}{dt}\psi_{2q} = -\omega_0 R_{2q} i_{2q}$$

where

ψ_{fd}, ψ_{1d}, ψ_{1q}, ψ_{2q}, E_{fd} are the same as defined in section 3.
R_{fd},, L_{fd}, are the field winding resistance and inductance, respectively.
R_{1d}, *is* the d-axix amortisseur resistance.
R_{1q},, *is* the 1st q-axix amortisseur resistance.
R_{2q} is the 2nd q-axix amortisseur resistance.

The rotor currents are expressed a follows:

$$i_{fd} = \frac{1}{L_{fd}}(\psi_{fd} - \psi_{ad})$$

$$i_{1d} = \frac{1}{L_{1d}}(\psi_{1d} - \psi_{ad})$$

$$i_{1q} = \frac{1}{L_{1q}}(\psi_{1q} - \psi_{aq})$$

$$i_{2q} = \frac{1}{L_{2q}}(\psi_{2q} - \psi_{aq})$$

where

ψ_{fd}, ψ_{1d}, ψ_{1q}, ψ_{2q} are defined as before
ψ_{ad}, ψ_{aq}, are the mutual flux linkages in the d and q axis, respectively.
L_{1d} is the d-axix amortisseur inductance.
L_{1q} is the 1st q-axix amortisseur inductance.
L_{2q} is the 2nd q-axix amortisseur inductance.

8.1.3 Electrical torque

The electrical torque is expressed by the following:

$$T_e = \psi_d i_q - \psi_q i_d$$

where ψ_d, and ψ_q are the d and q axis flux linkages, respectively.

8.1.4 AVR equations

$$\frac{d}{dt}E_{fd} = \frac{K_A}{T_A}(V_{ref} - V_t) - \frac{E_{fd}}{T_A}$$

where K_A and T_A are the gain and time constant of the AVR. V_t is the terminal voltage of the generator.

In this work K_A=200 and T_A = 0.05 sec.

8.2 Power system model, AVR parameters and PSS block diagram and parameters

8.2.1 Power system model diagram

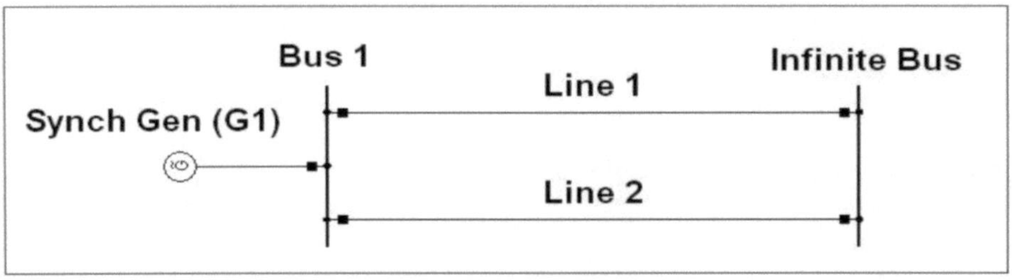

Fig. A1. System model- Single-Machine Infinite Bus (SMIB)

8.2.2 Block diagram of the Automatic Voltage Regulator (AVR)

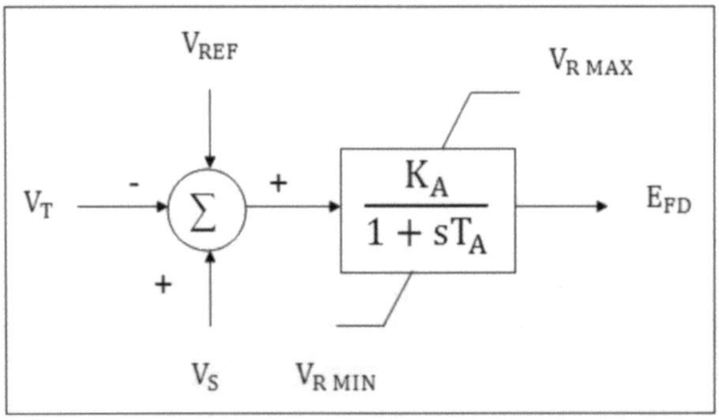

Fig. A2. Automatic voltage regulatore structure

8.2.3 Block diagram and parameters of the PSSs

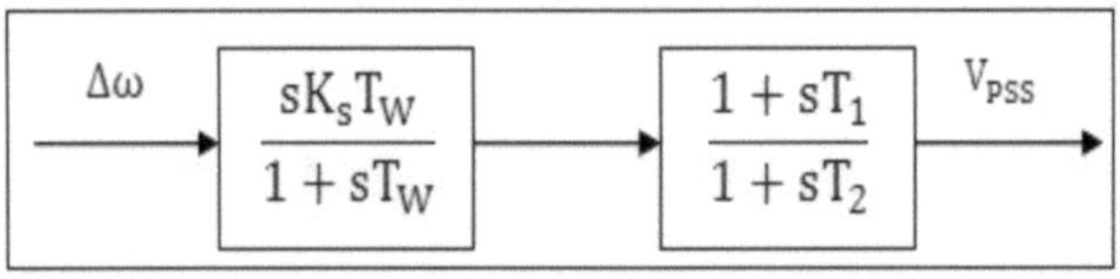

Fig. A3. Power system stabilizer structure

In Fig. A3, V_{PSS} is the output signal of the PSS, while $\Delta\omega(s)$ is the input signal, which in this case is the speed deviation.

PSSs	*Ks*	T_1	T_2	T_w
CPSS	9.7928	1.1686	0.2846	2.5000
GA-PSS	13.7358	3.5811	1.2654	2.5000
BGA-PSS	18.8838	3.7604	1.7390	2.5000

Table A1. PSS parameters.

8.3 Generator's parameters

X_l =0.0742 p.u, , X_d=1.72 p.u,, X'_d=0.45 p.u,, X''_d=0.33 p.u,T'_{d0}=6.3sec., T''_{d0} = 0.033 p.u,, X_q =1.68 p.u,, X'_q =0.59 p.u,, X''_q =0.33 p.u, T'_{q0} =0.43 sec

T''_{q0} = 0.033sec., H = 4.0sec

8.4 Pseudo code for BGA generator's parameters

```
Begin
    Randomly initialize a population of N individuals;
    Initialize mutation rate R_nom
    While termination criterion not met
        evaluate goodness of each individuals
        save the best individual in the new population
        select the best T%  individuals and discarding the rest;
        for I =1 to N-1 do
            randomly select two individuals among the T% best individual
            recombine the two parents to obtain one offspring
        end
        divide the new population into two halves (X and Y)
        apply mutation rate r_nom/2 to X and  2 R_nom to Y
        evaluate the average fitness value for the two half population (X and Y)
        If X performs better than Y; assign r= R_nom -0.1 r_nom;
        If Y performs better than X; assign r= R_nom + 0.1 r_nom;
    end
end
```

9. Acknowledgment

The authors would like to acknowledge the financial support of THRIP and TESP.

10. References

Baluja, S. (1994). Population-Based Incremental Learning: A method for Integrating Genetic Search Based Function Optimization and Competitive Learning. *Technical Report CMU-CS-94-163*, Carnegie Mellon University.

Chuang, Y.S . & Wu, C. J. (2006). A Damping Constant Limitation Design of Power System Stabilizer using Hybrid Differential Evolution. *Journal of Marine Science and Technology*. Vol..14, No. 2, pp. 84-92.

Chuang, Y.S . & Wu, C. J. (2007). Novel Decentralized Pole Placement Design of Power System Stabilizers using Hybrid Differential Evolution. *International Journal of Mathematics and Computer in Simulation*. Vol..1, No. 4, pp. 410-418.

Eslami, M., Shareef, H., Mohamed, A., & Ghohal, S. P. (2010). Tuning of Power System Stabilizer using Particle Swarm Optimization with Passive Congregation. *International Journal of Physical Sciences*. Vol..5, No. 17, pp. 2574-2589.

Goldberg, D. E. (1989). *Genetic Algorithms in Search, Optimization & Machine Learning*. Addison-Wesley; 1989.

Green, J. (2005). The Idea Behind Breeder Genetic Algorithm, *Department of Electrical Eng., University of Cape Town*

Folly KA (2006). Design of Power System Stabilizer: A Comparison Between Genetic Algorithms and Population Based Incremental Learning, *2006 IEEE Power Engineering Society General Meeting*, ISSN: 19325517.

Hemmati, R. , Mojtaba, S, Boroujeni, S & Abdollahi, M. (2010). Comparison of Robust and Intelligent Based Power System Stabilizers. *International Journal of the Pysical Science.* Vol. 5, No. 17, pp. 2564-2573.

Holland, J. H. (1975). *Adaptation in Nature and Artificial Systems*, University of Michigan Press, Ann Arbor.

Hongesombut, K., Dechanupaprittha S., Mitani, Y. & Ngamroo, I (2005). Robust Power System Stabilizer Tuning based on Multiobjective Design Using Hirerarchical & Parallel Micro Genetic Algorithm. *Proc. of the 15th Power Syst. Comp. Conf.*, Liege.

Irhamah & Ismail, Z. (2009). A Breeder Genetic Algorithm for Vehicle Routing Probelm with Stochastic Demands. *Journal of Applied Research,* Vol.5, No.11, pp. 1998-2005

Kundur, P. (1994). *Power System Stability and Control* Mc Graw Hill; 1994.

Michalewicz, Z. (1996) *Genetic Algorithms+Data Structure =Evolution Programs.* 3rd Ed. Springer-Velag

Mitchell, M. (1996), *An introduction to genetic algorithms*, The MIT Press.

Muhlenbein, H. (1994), The Breeder Genetic Algorithm-A Provable Optimal Search Algorithm and its Application, Available from http://*ieeexplore*.ieee.org

Sheetekela, S & Folly KA (2010). Breeder Genetic Algorithm for Power System Stabilizer Design. *2010 IEEE Congress on Evolutionary Computation (CEC)*, Barcelona, Spain.

Sheetekela (2010). *Design of Power System Stabilizer using Evolutionary Algorithms,* MSc. Thesis Department of Electrical Eng., University of Cape Town

Shahgholian, G. & Faiz, J. (2010). The effect of Power System Stabilizer on Small Signal Stability in Single Machine Infinite-Bus. *Internatonal Journal of Electrical and Power Engineering.*Vol.14, No. 2, pp. 45-53.

Sundareswara, K. & Begum, S. R. (2004). Genetic Tuning of a Power System Stabilizer. *Euro. Trans. Electr.* Vol..14, pp. 151-160.

Tiako, R. & Folly, K A. (2009). Investigation of Power System Stabilizer Parameters Optimisation using multi-power flow conditions. *Australian Journal of Electrical & Electronics Engineering.* Vol..5, No. 3, pp. 237-244.

Yoshimura, K. & Uchida, N. (2000). Optimization of P+w Parameters for Stability and Robustness Enhancement in a Multimachine Power System. *Electrical Engineeringin Japan.* Vol..131, No. 1, pp. 19-31 (Translated from Denki Gakkai Ronbunshi, Vol. 11, Nov. 1198, pp. 1312-1320).

Wang, Z. Chung, C.Y., & Wong, C.T. (2008). Robust Power System Stabilizer Design under multi-operating conditions using Differential Evolution. *IET Generation, Transmission & Distribution.* Vol..2, No. 5, pp. 690-700.

16

On the Application of Optimal PWM of Induction Motor in Synchronous Machines at High Power Ratings

Arash Sayyah[1] and Alireza Rezazadeh[2]
[1]ECE Department, Boston University, Boston, MA
[2]ECE Department, Shahid Beheshti University, Tehran
[1]USA
[2]Iran

1. Introduction

Distinctive features of synchronous machines like constant operation-speed, producing substantial savings by supplying reactive power to counteract lagging power factor caused by inductive loads, low inrush currents, and capabilities of designing the torque characteristics to meet the requirements of the driven load, have made them optimal options for a multitude of industries. Economical utilization of these machines and also increasing their efficiencies are issues that should receive significant attention.

At high power rating operations, where high switching efficiency in the drive circuits is of utmost importance, optimal pulsewidth modulation (PWM) is the logical feeding scheme (Holtz, 1992). Application of optimal PWM decreases overheating in machine and therefore results in diminution of torque pulsation. Overheating, resulted from internal losses, is a major factor in rating a machine. Moreover, setting up an appropriate cooling method is a particularly serious issue, increasing in intricacy with machine size. Among various approaches for achieving optimal PWM, *harmonic elimination method* is predominant ((Mohan et al., 1995), (Enjeti et al., 1990), (Sun et al., 1996), (Chiasson et al., 2004), (Czarkowski et al., 2002), (Sayyah et al., 2006c)). Since copper losses are fundamentally determined by current harmonics, defining a performance index related to undesirable effects of the harmonics is of the essence in lieu of focusing on specific harmonics (Bose, 2002). Herein, the total harmonic current distortion (THCD) is the objective function for minimization of machine losses.

Possessing asymmetrical structure in direct (d) and quadrature (q) axes makes a great difference in modeling of synchronous machines relative to induction ones. Particularly, it will be shown that the THCD in high-power synchronous machines is dependent upon some internal parameters of the machine; particularly l_q and l_d, the inductances of q and d axes, respectively. Based on gathered input and output data at a specific operating point, these parameters are determined using online identification methods (Ljung & Söderström, 1983). In light of the identified parameters, the problem is redrafted as an optimization task, and the optimal pulse patterns are sought through genetic algorithm (GA). Indeed, the complexity and nonlinearity of the proposed objective function increases the probability of trapping the conventional optimization methods in suboptimal solutions. The GA provided with salient features [3]-[5], can cope effectively with shortcomings of the deterministic optimization methods.

The mentioned parameters are affected by several factors like modification in operating point, aging and temperature rise. Variations in these parameters invalidate the pre-calculated optimal pulse patterns and therefore impose excessive computational and processing burden; to carry out identification procedure, and subsequently optimization process to determine new optimal pulse patterns. Notwithstanding of accepting this computational burden and storing the accomplished optimal pulse patterns in read-only memories (ROMs) to serve as look-up tables (LUTs), substitution in LUTs provokes an adverse transient condition, which make it a formidable task (Rezazadeh et al., 2006).

In this study, optimal pulse patterns of induction machine (Sayyah et al., 2006b), whose total harmonic current distortion is independent of its parameters, as established in (Sun, 1995), are applied to current harmonic model of synchronous machines with different values of $\frac{l_q}{l_d}$. The results are compared with corresponding minimum power losses. Based on the demonstrated comparisons, if deviation from the minimum power losses is acceptable, application of optimal pulse patterns of induction machine (the so-called suboptimal solutions), is an appropriate alternative to preceding methods considering their excessive processing burdens.

2. Preliminaries and problem formulation

In this section, we examine the prerequisites for developing the approach of this study. Since the content has been set forth in preceding works (Rezazadeh et al., 2006), (Sayyah et al., 2006a), (Sayyah et al., 2006b), (Sayyah et al., 2006c), the discussions are provided for the sake of reproducibility.

2.1 Waveform representation

For the scope of this paper, a PWM waveform is a 2π-periodic function $f(\theta)$ with two distinct normalized levels of $-1, +1$ for $0 \leq t \leq \pi/2$ and has the symmetries $f(\theta) = f(\pi - \theta)$ and $f(\theta) = -f(2\pi - \theta)$.

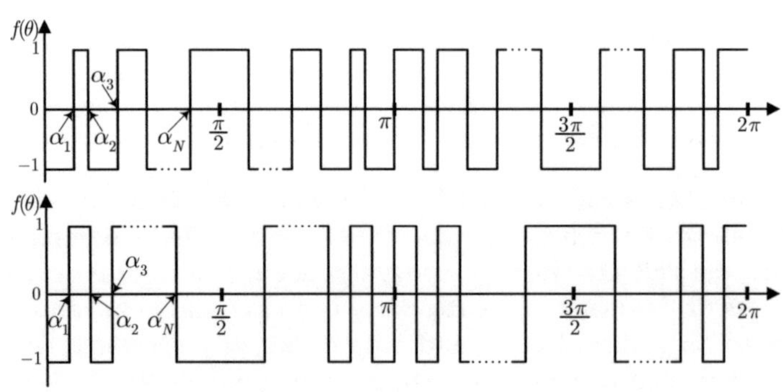

Fig. 1. A typical normalized PWM structure.

Owing to the symmetries in normalized PWM waveform of Fig. 1, only the odd harmonics exist. As such, $f(\theta)$ can be written with the Fourier series as

$$f(\theta) = \sum_{k=1,3,5,\ldots} u_k \sin(k\theta) \tag{1}$$

with

$$\begin{aligned} u_k &= \frac{4}{\pi} \int_0^{\frac{\pi}{2}} f(\theta) \sin(k\theta) \\ &= \frac{4}{k\pi}\Big(-1 + 2\sum_{i=1}^{N} (-1)^{i-1} \cos(k\alpha_i)\Big). \end{aligned} \tag{2}$$

2.2 THCD formulation in induction machine

The harmonic equivalent circuit and its approximation of an induction motor operating in steady-state conditions is illustrated in Fig. 2 (Sun, 1995).

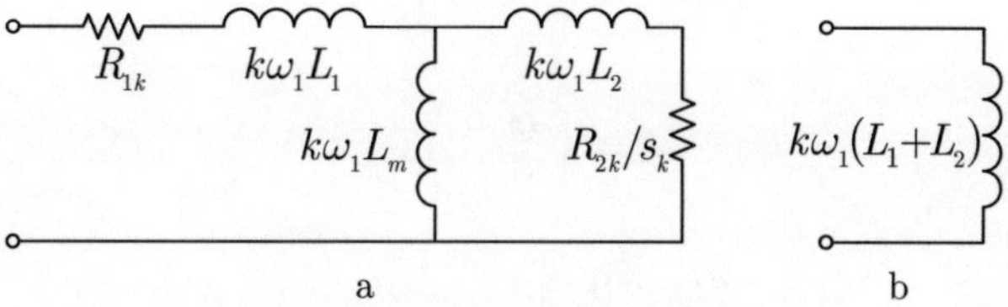

Fig. 2. Equivalent circuit of an induction motor operating in steady-state conditions: (a) The kth order harmonic equivalent circuit, (b) Approximation of (a), $(k > 1)$.

The approximation of the equivalent circuit is deduced regarding the fact that inductive reactances increase linearly with frequency, while the stator and rotor resistances are almost constant. Since s_k is approximately unity, circuit resistance is negligible in comparison with reactance at the harmonic frequency. In addition, the magnetizing inductance L_m is much larger than the rotor leakage inductance L_2 and may be omitted. Hence, the motor impedance presented to the kth-order harmonic input voltage is $k\omega_1(L_1 + L_2)$ and the kth-order current harmonic would be:

$$I_k = \frac{u_k}{k\omega_1(L_1 + L_2)} \propto \frac{u_k}{k}. \tag{3}$$

Thus, the objective function of this optimization can be stated as:

$$\sigma_i^{\text{ind}} = \sqrt{\sum_{k\in S_3} (u_k/k)^2}, \tag{4}$$

where $S_3 = \{5, 7, \ldots, 6l - 1, 6l + 1, \ldots\}$ stands for the set of triple harmonics in consideration.

Throughout the optimization procedure, it is desired to maintain the fundamental output voltage at a constant level: $V_1 = M$. M so-called the modulation index may be assumed to have any value between 0 and $\frac{4}{\pi}$. It can be shown that α_N is dependent on modulation index and the rest of $N - 1$ switching angles. As such, one decision variable can be eliminated explicitly (Sayyah et al., 2006b).

2.3 THCD formulation in synchronous machine

In this section, we formulate the THCD in high-power synchronous machines. Some simplifications and assumptions are considered in modeling of these machines; space harmonics of the flux linkage distribution are neglected, linear magnetics due to operation in linear portion of magnetization curve prior to experiencing saturation knee is assumed, iron losses are neglected, and slot harmonics and deep bar effects are not considered.

Synchronous machine model equations can be written as follows (Holtz, 1995):

$$\boldsymbol{u}_S^R = \boldsymbol{r}_S \boldsymbol{i}_R^S + \jmath\omega \boldsymbol{\Psi}_S^R + \frac{d\boldsymbol{\Psi}_S^R}{d\tau}, \tag{5}$$

$$\boldsymbol{0} = \boldsymbol{R}_D \boldsymbol{i}_D + \frac{d\boldsymbol{\Psi}_D}{d\tau}, \tag{6}$$

$$\boldsymbol{\Psi}_S^R = \boldsymbol{l}_S \boldsymbol{i}_S^R + \boldsymbol{\Psi}_m^R, \tag{7}$$

$$\boldsymbol{\Psi}_m^R = \boldsymbol{l}_m(\boldsymbol{i}_D + \boldsymbol{i}_F), \tag{8}$$

$$\boldsymbol{\Psi}_D = \boldsymbol{l}_D \boldsymbol{i}_D + \boldsymbol{l}_m(\boldsymbol{i}_S + \boldsymbol{i}_F), \tag{9}$$

where:

$$\boldsymbol{l}_S = \boldsymbol{l}_{lS} + \boldsymbol{l}_m = \begin{pmatrix} l_d & 0 \\ 0 & l_q \end{pmatrix}, \quad \boldsymbol{i}_F = \begin{pmatrix} 1 \\ 0 \end{pmatrix} i_F, \tag{10}$$

and

$$\boldsymbol{l}_m = \begin{pmatrix} l_{md} & 0 \\ 0 & l_{mq} \end{pmatrix}, \quad \boldsymbol{l}_D = \begin{pmatrix} l_{Dd} & 0 \\ 0 & l_{Dq} \end{pmatrix}, \tag{11}$$

where l_d and l_q are inductances of the motor in d and q axes; $\boldsymbol{i}_D$ is damper winding current; $\boldsymbol{u}_S^R$ and $\boldsymbol{i}_S^R$ are stator voltage and current space vectors, respectively; $\boldsymbol{l}_D$ is the damper inductance; l_{md} is the d-axis magnetization inductance; l_{mq} is the q-axis magnetization inductance; l_{Dd} is the d-axis damper inductance; l_{Dq} is the q-axis damper inductance; $\boldsymbol{\Psi}_m$ is the magnetization flux; $\boldsymbol{\Psi}_D$ is the damper flux; i_F is the field excitation current and $\jmath \triangleq \sqrt{-1}$. Time is also normalized $\tau = \omega t$, where ω is the angular frequency. The total harmonic current distortion is defined as follows:

$$\sigma_i^{\text{synch}} = \sqrt{\frac{1}{T}\int_T [\boldsymbol{i}_S(t) - \boldsymbol{i}_{S1}(t)]^2 dt}, \tag{12}$$

in which $\boldsymbol{i}_{S1}$ is the fundamental component of stator current.

Assuming that the steady state operation of machine makes a constant exciting current, the dampers current in the system can be neglected. Therefore, we have the machine model in rotor coordinates as:

$$\boldsymbol{u}_S^R = \boldsymbol{r}_S \boldsymbol{i}_S^R + \jmath\omega \boldsymbol{l}_S \boldsymbol{i}_S^R + \jmath\omega \boldsymbol{l}_m \boldsymbol{i}_F + \boldsymbol{l}_S \frac{d\boldsymbol{i}_S^R}{d\tau}. \tag{13}$$

With the *Park* transformation, we have the machine model in stator coordinates (the so-called $\alpha - \beta$ coordinates) as:

$$\begin{aligned} \boldsymbol{u}_{\alpha\beta} &= R_S \boldsymbol{i}_{\alpha\beta} + \omega(l_d - l_q)\begin{pmatrix} -\sin 2\theta & \cos 2\theta \\ \cos 2\theta & \sin 2\theta \end{pmatrix} \boldsymbol{i}_{\alpha\beta} + \frac{l_d - l_q}{2}\begin{pmatrix} \cos 2\theta & \sin 2\theta \\ \sin 2\theta & -\cos 2\theta \end{pmatrix} \frac{d\boldsymbol{i}_{\alpha\beta}}{d\tau} \\ &+ \frac{l_d + l_q}{2}\frac{d\boldsymbol{i}_{\alpha\beta}}{d\tau} + \omega l_{md}\begin{pmatrix} -\sin\theta \\ \cos\theta \end{pmatrix} i_F, \end{aligned} \tag{14}$$

in which θ is the rotor angle. Neglecting the ohmic terms in (14), we have:

$$\boldsymbol{u}_{\alpha\beta} = \frac{d}{d\tau}(\boldsymbol{l}_S(\theta)\boldsymbol{i}_{\alpha\beta}) + l_{md}\frac{d}{d\tau}\left(\begin{pmatrix}\cos\theta\\ \sin\theta\end{pmatrix} i_F\right), \tag{15}$$

in which:

$$\boldsymbol{l}_S(\theta) = \frac{l_d + l_q}{2}\mathbf{I}_2 + \frac{l_d - l_q}{2}\begin{pmatrix}\cos 2\theta & \sin 2\theta\\ \sin 2\theta & -\cos 2\theta\end{pmatrix}. \tag{16}$$

$\mathbf{I}_2$ is the 2×2 identity matrix. Hence:

$$\begin{aligned}
\boldsymbol{i}_{\alpha\beta} &= \boldsymbol{l}_S^{-1}(\theta)\cdot\left(\int \boldsymbol{u}_{\alpha\beta}d\tau - l_{md}\begin{pmatrix}\cos\theta\\ \sin\theta\end{pmatrix} i_F\right)\\
&= \begin{pmatrix}\frac{l_d+l_q}{2l_dl_q} - \frac{l_d-l_q}{2l_dl_q}\cos 2\theta & -\frac{l_d-l_q}{2l_dl_q}\sin 2\theta\\ -\frac{l_d-l_q}{2l_dl_q}\sin 2\theta & \frac{l_d+l_q}{2l_dl_q} + \frac{l_d-l_q}{2l_dl_q}\cos 2\theta\end{pmatrix}\cdot\left\{\int \boldsymbol{u}_{\alpha\beta}d\tau - l_{md}\begin{pmatrix}\cos\theta\\ \sin\theta\end{pmatrix} i_F\right\}\\
&= \left(\frac{l_d+l_q}{2l_dl_q}\mathbf{I}_2 - \frac{l_d-l_q}{2l_dl_q}\begin{pmatrix}\cos 2\theta & \sin 2\theta\\ \sin 2\theta & -\cos 2\theta\end{pmatrix}\right)\cdot\left(\int \boldsymbol{u}_{\alpha\beta}d\tau - l_{md}\begin{pmatrix}\cos\theta\\ \sin\theta\end{pmatrix} i_F\right).
\end{aligned} \tag{17}$$

With further simplification, we have $\boldsymbol{i}_{\alpha\beta}$ as:

$$\boldsymbol{i}_{\alpha\beta} = \frac{l_d + l_q}{2l_dl_q}\int \boldsymbol{u}_{\alpha\beta}d\tau + J_1 - \frac{l_d - l_q}{2l_dl_q}J_2, \tag{18}$$

in which:

$$J_1 = -l_{md}\frac{l_d + l_q}{2l_dl_q}\begin{pmatrix}\cos\theta\\ \sin\theta\end{pmatrix} i_F + l_{md}\frac{l_d - l_q}{2l_dl_q}\begin{pmatrix}\cos 2\theta & \sin 2\theta\\ \sin 2\theta & -\cos 2\theta\end{pmatrix}\cdot\begin{pmatrix}\cos\theta\\ \sin\theta\end{pmatrix}, \tag{19}$$

and

$$J_2 = \begin{pmatrix}\cos 2\theta & \sin 2\theta\\ \sin 2\theta & -\cos 2\theta\end{pmatrix}\cdot\int \boldsymbol{u}_{\alpha\beta}d\tau. \tag{20}$$

Using the trigonometric identities, $\cos(\theta_1 - \theta_2) = \cos\theta_1\cos\theta_2 + \sin\theta_1\sin\theta_2$ and $\sin(\theta_1 - \theta_2) = \sin\theta_1\cos\theta_2 - \cos\theta_1\sin\theta_2$, the term J_1 in Equation 18 can be simplified as:

$$\begin{aligned}
J_1 &= -l_{md}\frac{l_d + l_q}{2l_dl_q}\begin{pmatrix}\cos\theta\\ \sin\theta\end{pmatrix} i_F + l_{md}\frac{l_d - l_q}{2l_dl_q}\begin{pmatrix}\cos 2\theta\cdot\cos\theta + \sin 2\theta\cdot\sin\theta\\ \sin 2\theta\cdot\cos\theta - \cos 2\theta\cdot\cos\theta\end{pmatrix} i_F\\
&= -l_{md}\frac{l_d + l_q}{2l_dl_q}\begin{pmatrix}\cos\theta\\ \sin\theta\end{pmatrix} i_F + l_{md}\frac{l_d - l_q}{2l_dl_q}\begin{pmatrix}\cos\theta\\ \sin\theta\end{pmatrix} i_F\\
&= \frac{l_{md}}{l_d}\begin{pmatrix}\cos\theta\\ \sin\theta\end{pmatrix} i_F.
\end{aligned} \tag{21}$$

On the other hand, writing the phase voltages in Fourier series:

$$u_A = \sum_{s \in S_3} u_{2s+1} \sin((2s+1)\theta),$$
$$u_B = \sum_{s \in S_3} u_{2s+1} \sin((2s+1)(\theta - \frac{2\pi}{3})),$$
$$u_C = \sum_{s \in S_3} u_{2s+1} \sin((2s+1)(\theta - \frac{4\pi}{3})),$$

and using 3-phase to 2-phase transformation, we have:

$$\begin{pmatrix} u_\alpha \\ u_\beta \end{pmatrix} = \begin{pmatrix} u_A \\ \frac{1}{\sqrt{3}}(u_B - u_C) \end{pmatrix} = \begin{pmatrix} \sum_{s \in S_3} u_s \sin(s\theta) \\ \sum_{s \in S_3} u_s \sin(s(\theta - \frac{2\pi}{3}) + \varphi_s) \end{pmatrix} \tag{22}$$

in which:

$$\varphi_s = \begin{cases} \frac{\pi}{6} & \text{for } s = 1, 7, 13, \cdots \\ -\frac{\pi}{6} & \text{for } s = 5, 11, 17, \cdots \end{cases}.$$

As such, we have:

$$\boldsymbol{u}_{\alpha\beta} = \begin{pmatrix} \sum_{l=0}^{\infty} u_{6l+1} \sin((6l+1)\theta) \\ \sum_{l=0}^{\infty} u_{6l+1} \sin((6l+1)(\theta - \frac{2\pi}{3}) + \frac{\pi}{6}) \end{pmatrix} + \begin{pmatrix} \sum_{l=0}^{\infty} u_{6l+5} \sin((6l+5)\theta) \\ \sum_{l=0}^{\infty} u_{6l+5} \sin((6l+5)(\theta - \frac{2\pi}{3}) - \frac{\pi}{6}) \end{pmatrix}. \tag{23}$$

Integration of $\boldsymbol{u}_{\alpha\beta}$ yields:

$$\begin{aligned} \int \boldsymbol{u}_{\alpha\beta} d\tau = & -\frac{1}{\omega} \times \\ & \left\{ \begin{pmatrix} \sum_{l=0}^{\infty} \frac{u_{6l+1}}{6l+1} \cos((6l+1)\theta) \\ \sum_{l=0}^{\infty} \frac{u_{6l+1}}{6l+1} \cos((6l+1)\theta - 4\pi l - \frac{\pi}{2}) \end{pmatrix} \right. \\ & \left. + \begin{pmatrix} \sum_{l=0}^{\infty} \frac{u_{6l+5}}{6l+5} \cos((6l+5)\theta) \\ \sum_{l=0}^{\infty} \frac{u_{6l+5}}{6l+5} \cos((6l+5)\theta - 4\pi l - \frac{3\pi}{2}) \end{pmatrix} \right\} \\ = & -\frac{1}{\omega} \times \begin{pmatrix} \sum_{l=0}^{\infty} [\frac{u_{6l+1}}{6l+1} \cos((6l+1)\theta) + \frac{u_{6l+5}}{6l+5} \cos((6l+5)\theta)] \\ \sum_{l=0}^{\infty} [\frac{u_{6l+1}}{6l+1} \sin((6l+1)\theta) - \frac{u_{6l+5}}{6l+5} \sin((6l+5)\theta)] \end{pmatrix} \end{aligned} \tag{24}$$

By substitution of $\int \boldsymbol{u}_{\alpha\beta} d\tau$ in Equation 18, the term J_2 can be written as:

$$\begin{aligned} J_2 = & \begin{pmatrix} \cos 2\theta & \sin 2\theta \\ \sin 2\theta & -\cos 2\theta \end{pmatrix} \cdot \int \boldsymbol{u}_{\alpha\beta} d\tau = -\frac{1}{\omega} \times \\ & \left\{ \begin{pmatrix} \sum_{l=0}^{\infty} \frac{u_{6l+1}}{6l+1} \cos((6l+1)\theta) \cdot \cos 2\theta \\ \sum_{l=0}^{\infty} \frac{u_{6l+1}}{6l+1} \cos((6l+1)\theta) \cdot \sin 2\theta \end{pmatrix} + \begin{pmatrix} \sum_{l=0}^{\infty} \frac{u_{6l+1}}{6l+1} \sin((6l+1)\theta) \cdot \sin 2\theta \\ -\sum_{l=0}^{\infty} \frac{u_{6l+1}}{6l+1} \sin((6l+1)\theta) \cdot \cos 2\theta \end{pmatrix} \right. \\ & \left. + \begin{pmatrix} \sum_{l=0}^{\infty} \frac{u_{6l+5}}{6l+5} \cos((6l+5)\theta) \cdot \cos 2\theta \\ \sum_{l=0}^{\infty} \frac{u_{6l+5}}{6l+5} \cos((6l+5)\theta) \cdot \sin 2\theta \end{pmatrix} + \begin{pmatrix} -\sum_{l=0}^{\infty} \frac{u_{6l+5}}{6l+5} \sin((6l+5)\theta) \cdot \sin 2\theta \\ \sum_{l=0}^{\infty} \frac{u_{6l+5}}{6l+5} \sin((6l+5)\theta) \cdot \cos 2\theta \end{pmatrix} \right\} \\ = & -\frac{1}{\omega} \begin{pmatrix} \sum_{l=0}^{\infty} [\frac{u_{6l+1}}{6l+1} \cos((6l-1)\theta) + \frac{u_{6l+5}}{6l+5} \cos((6l+7)\theta)] \\ \sum_{l=0}^{\infty} [-\frac{u_{6l+1}}{6l+1} \sin((6l-1)\theta) + \frac{u_{6l+5}}{6l+5} \sin((6l+7)\theta)] \end{pmatrix}. \end{aligned} \tag{25}$$

Considering the derived results, we can rewrite $i_A = i_\alpha$ as:

$$i_A = \Big(-\frac{l_d+l_q}{2l_d l_q \omega}\Big)\cdot \sum_{l=0}^{\infty}[\frac{u_{6l+1}}{6l+1}\cos((6l+1)\theta)+\frac{u_{6l+5}}{6l+5}\cos((6l+5)\theta)]$$
$$+\Big(\frac{l_d-l_q}{2l_d l_q \omega}\Big)\cdot \sum_{l=0}^{\infty}[\frac{u_{6l+1}}{6l+1}\cos((6l-1)\theta)+\frac{u_{6l+5}}{6l+5}\cos((6l+7)\theta)] - \frac{l_{md}}{l_d} i_F\cos\theta. \quad (26)$$

Using the appropriate dummy variables $l = l' + 1$ and $l = l'' - 1$, we have:

$$i_A = \Big(-\frac{l_d+l_q}{2l_d l_q \omega}\Big)\cdot \Big\{\sum_{l=0}^{\infty}\frac{u_{6l+1}}{6l+1}\cos((6l+1)\theta)+\sum_{l=0}^{\infty}\frac{u_{6l+5}}{6l+5}\cos((6l+5)\theta)\Big\}+$$
$$\Big(\frac{l_d-l_q}{2l_d l_q \omega}\Big)\cdot \Big\{\sum_{l'=-1}^{\infty}\frac{u_{6l'+7}}{6l'+7}\cos((6l'+5)\theta)+\sum_{l''=1}^{\infty}\frac{u_{6l''-1}}{6l''-1}\cos((6l''+1)\theta)\Big\}$$
$$-\frac{l_{md}}{l_d} i_F\cos\theta$$
$$= \Big(-\frac{l_d+l_q}{2l_d l_q \omega}\Big)\cdot \Big\{\sum_{l=0}^{\infty}\frac{u_{6l+1}}{6l+1}\cos((6l+1)\theta)+\sum_{l=0}^{\infty}\frac{u_{6l+5}}{6l+5}\cos((6l+5)\theta)\Big\}$$
$$+\Big(\frac{l_d-l_q}{2l_d l_q \omega}\Big)\cdot \Big\{\sum_{l=0}^{\infty}\frac{u_{6l+7}}{6l+7}\cos((6l+5)\theta)+\sum_{l=0}^{\infty}\frac{u_{6l-1}}{6l-1}\cos((6l+1)\theta)+u_1\cos\theta\Big\}$$
$$-\frac{l_{md}}{l_d} i_F\cos\theta. \quad (27)$$

Thus, we have i_A as:

$$i_A = \Big(-\frac{1}{2l_d l_q \omega}\Big)\cdot \Big\{\sum_{l=0}^{\infty}[(l_d+l_q)\frac{u_{6l+1}}{6l+1}-(l_d-l_q)\frac{u_{6l-1}}{6l-1}]\cdot\cos((6l+1)\theta)+$$
$$\sum_{l=0}^{\infty}[(l_d+l_q)\frac{u_{6l+5}}{6l+5}-(l_d-l_q)\frac{u_{6l+7}}{6l+7}]\cdot\cos((6l+1)\theta)-(l_d-l_q)u_1\cos\theta\Big\}$$
$$-\frac{l_{md}}{l_d} i_F\cos\theta. \quad (28)$$

Removing the fundamental components from Equation 28, we have:

$$i_{Ah} = \Big(-\frac{1}{2l_d l_q \omega}\Big)\cdot \Big\{\sum_{l=1}^{\infty}[\{(l_d+l_q)\frac{u_{6l+1}}{6l+1}-(l_d-l_q)\frac{u_{6l-1}}{6l-1}\}\cdot\cos((6l+1)\theta)]+$$
$$\sum_{l=0}^{\infty}[\{(l_d+l_q)\frac{u_{6l+5}}{6l+5}-(l_d-l_q)\frac{u_{6l+7}}{6l+7}\}\cdot\cos((6l+5)\theta)]\Big\}$$
$$= \Big(-\frac{1}{2l_d l_q \omega}\Big)\cdot \Big\{\sum_{l=0}^{\infty}\{(l_d+l_q)\frac{u_{6l+7}}{6l+7}-(l_d-l_q)\frac{u_{6l+5}}{6l+5}\}\cdot\cos((6l+7)\theta)+$$
$$\sum_{l=0}^{\infty}\{(l_d+l_q)\frac{u_{6l+5}}{6l+5}-(l_d-l_q)\frac{u_{6l+7}}{6l+7}\}\cdot\cos((6l+5)\theta)\Big\}. \quad (29)$$

On the other hand, σ_l^2 can be written as:

$$\begin{aligned}\sigma_l^2 &= \Big((l_d+l_q)\frac{u_{6l+7}}{6l+7}-(l_d-l_q)\frac{u_{6l+5}}{6l+5}\Big)^2+\Big((l_d+l_q)\frac{u_{6l+5}}{6l+5}-(l_d-l_q)\frac{u_{6l+7}}{6l+7}\Big)^2\\ &= 2(l_d^2+l_q^2)\Big(\frac{u_{6l+7}}{6l+7}\Big)^2+2(l_d^2+l_q^2)\Big(\frac{u_{6l+5}}{6l+5}\Big)^2-4(l_d^2-l_q^2)\frac{u_{6l+5}u_{6l+7}}{(6l+5)(6l+7)}.\end{aligned} \tag{30}$$

With normalization of σ_l^2; i.e. $\tilde{\sigma}_l^2 = \frac{\sigma_l^2}{l_d^2+l_q^2}$ and also the definition of the total harmonic current distortion as $\sigma_i^2 = \sum_{l=0}^{\infty}\tilde{\sigma}_l^2$, we have:

$$\sigma_i^2 = \sum_{l=0}^{\infty}\Big\{\Big(\frac{u_{6l+5}}{6l+5}\Big)^2+\Big(\frac{u_{6l+7}}{6l+7}\Big)^2-2\frac{l_d^2-l_q^2}{l_d^2+l_q^2}\Big(\frac{u_{6l+5}}{6l+5}\Big)\Big(\frac{u_{6l+7}}{6l+7}\Big)\Big\}.$$

Considering the set $S_3 = \{5, 7, 11, 13, \cdots\}$ and with more simplification, σ_i in high-power synchronous machines can be explicitly expressed as:

$$\sigma_i = \sqrt{\sum_{k\in S_3}\Big(\frac{u_k}{k}\Big)^2-2\frac{l_d^2-l_q^2}{l_d^2+l_q^2}\sum_{l=1}^{\infty}\Big(\frac{u_{6l-1}}{6l-1}\Big)\cdot\Big(\frac{u_{6l+1}}{6l+1}\Big)}. \tag{31}$$

As mentioned earlier, THCD in high-power synchronous machines depends on l_d and l_q, the inductances of d and q axes, respectively.

3. Switching scheme

Switching frequency in high-power systems, due to the use of gate turn-off thyristor (GTO) in the inverter is limited to several hundred hertz. In this work, the switching frequency has been set to $f_s = 200$ Hz. Considering the frequency of the fundamental component of PWM waveform to be variable with maximum value of 50 Hz (i.e. $f_{1\max} = 50$ Hz), we have: $\frac{f_s}{f_{1\max}} = 4$. This condition forces a constraint on the number of switches, since we have:

$$\frac{f_s}{f_1} = N. \tag{32}$$

On the other hand, in electrical machines with rotating magnetic field, in order to maintain the torque at a constant level, the fundamental frequency of the PWM should be proportional to its amplitude (modulation index is also proportional to the amplitude) (Leonhard, 2001). That is:

$$M = kf_1 = \frac{k}{N}\cdot f_s = k\cdot\frac{f_{1\max}}{N}\cdot\frac{f_s}{f_{1\max}}. \tag{33}$$

Also, we have:

$$M = kf_1|_{f_1=f_{1\max}} = 1 \Rightarrow k = \frac{1}{f_{1\max}}. \tag{34}$$

Considering Equations (33) and (34), the following equation is resulted:

$$\frac{f_s}{f_{1\max}} = M\cdot N. \tag{35}$$

The value of $\frac{f_s}{f_{1\max}}$ is plotted versus modulation index in Figure 3.

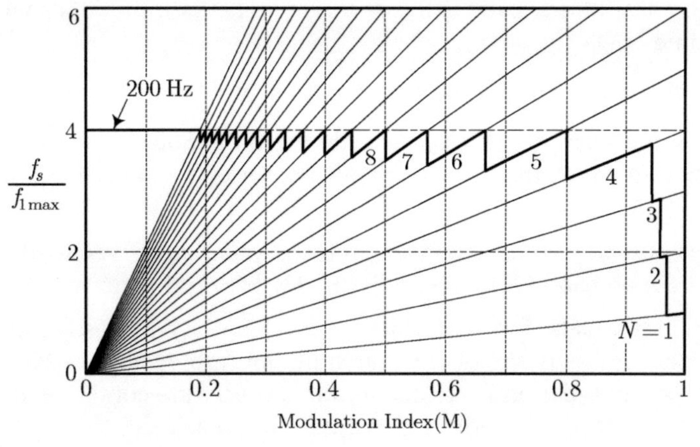

Fig. 3. Switching scheme

Figure 3 shows that as the number of switching angles increases and M declines from unity, the curve moves towards the upper limit $\frac{f_s}{f_{1\max}}$. The curve, however, always remains under the upper limit. When N increases and reaches a large amount, optimization procedure and its accomplished results are not effective. Additionally, it does not show a significant advantage in comparison with space vector PWM (SVPWM). Based on this fact, in high power machines, the feeding scheme is a combination of optimized PWM and SVPWM.

At this juncture, feedforward structure of PWM fed inverter is emphasized. Presence of current feedback path means that the switching frequency is dictated by the current which is the follow-on of system dynamics and load conditions. This may give rise to uncontrollable high switching frequencies that indubitably denote colossal losses. Furthermore, utilization of current feedback for PWM generation intensifies system instability and results in chaos.

4. Optimization procedure

A numerical optimization algorithm is expected to perform the task of global optimization of an objective function. However, as objective function may possess numerous local optima, algorithms are prone to get trapped in local solutions. The genetic algorithms (GAs) among the numerical algorithms, have been extensively used as search and optimization tools in dealing with global optimization problems, due to their capability of avoiding local solutions from terminating the optimization process. There are certain other advantages to GAs such as their indifference to system specific information, especially the derivative information, the versatility of application, the ease with which heuristics can be incorporated in optimization, the capability of learning and adapting to changes over time, the implicitly parallel directed random exploration of the search space, and the ability to accommodate discrete variables in the search process, to name a few (Bäck et al., 1997).

GAs operate on a population of potential solutions to generate close approximations to the optimal solution through evolution. The population is a set of chromosomes, and the basic GA operators are selection, crossover and mutation. At each generation, a new set of approximations is created by the process of selecting individuals and breeding them together using crossover and mutation operators which are conceptually borrowed from natural genetics. This process leads to the evolution of better individuals with near-optimum solutions over time.

The GA methodology structure for the problem considered herein is as follows:

1. Feasible individuals are generated randomly for initial population. That is a $n \times (N-1)$ random matrix, in which the rows' elements are sorted in ascending order, lying in $[0, \frac{\pi}{2}]$ interval.
2. Objective-function-value of all members of the population is evaluated by σ_i. This allows estimation of the probability of each individual to be selected for reproduction.
3. Selection of individuals for reproduction is done. When selection of individuals for reproduction is done, crossover and mutation are applied, based on forthcoming arguments. New population is created and this procedure continues from step (2). This procedure is repeated until a termination criterion is reached.

Whether the algorithm will find a near-optimum solution and whether it will find such a solution efficiently is determined through proper choosing of GA parameters. In the sequel, some arguments for strategies in setting the components of GA can be found.

Population size plays a pivotal role in the performance of the algorithm. Large sizes of population decrease the speed of convergence, but help maintain the population diversity and therefore reduce the probability for the algorithm to trap into local optima. Small population sizes, on the contrary, may lead to premature convergences. With choosing the population size as $\lfloor (10 \cdot N)^{1.2} \rfloor$, in which the bracket $\lfloor \cdot \rfloor$ marks that the integer part is taken, satisfying results are yielded.

Gaussian mutation step size (Eiben et al., 1999) is used with arithmetical crossover to produce offspring for the next generation. Mutations are realized by replacing components of the vector $\boldsymbol{\alpha}$ by

$$\alpha_i' = \alpha_i + \mathcal{N}(0, \sigma) \tag{36}$$

where $\mathcal{N}(0, \sigma)$ is a random Gaussian number with mean zero and standard deviation σ. We replaced the static parameter σ by a dynamic parameter, a function $\sigma(t)$ defined as

$$\sigma(t) = 1 - \frac{t}{T} \tag{37}$$

where t is the current generation number varying from zero to T, which is the maximum generation number.

Here, the mutation step size $\sigma(t)$ will decrease slowly from one at the beginning of the run $(t = 0)$ to 0 as the number of generations t approaches T. We set the mutation probability (P_m) to a fixed value of 0.2 throughout all stages of optimization process. One purpose of having a relatively high mutation rate is to maintain the population diversity, explore the search space effectively and prevent premature convergence. Arithmetical crossover (Michalewicz, 1996) is considered herein, and probability of this operator is set to 0.8. When two parent individuals are denoted as $\boldsymbol{\alpha}^k = (\alpha_1^k, \ldots, \alpha_M^k), k \in \{1, 2\}$, two offspring $\boldsymbol{\alpha}'^k = (\alpha_1'^k, \ldots, \alpha_M'^k)$ are reproduced as interpolations of both parents' genes:

$$\alpha'^1_m = \lambda\alpha^1_m + (1-\lambda)\alpha^2_m$$
$$\alpha'^2_m = (1-\lambda)\alpha^1_m + \lambda\alpha^2_m \qquad (38)$$

where the parameter λ, is a randomly chosen number in the interval [0,1].

There are different selection methods that can be used in the GAs algorithm. Tournament selection (Goldberg, 1989) with size 2 is one of these methods which is used as the selection mechanism in this study. An elitist strategy is also enabled during the replacement operation. Elitism usually brings about a more rapid convergence of the population and also improves the chances of locating the optimal individual. Elite count considered in this study is 5% of population size. In this study the termination criteria is reaching 500th generation, which stated that the algorithm is repeated until a predetermined number of generations is reached. It should be noted that to increase the precision of the optimal solutions accomplished by the algorithm, we used a local search function which finds the minimum of a scalar function of several variables, starting at initial estimate which is the outcome of the GA.

5. Optimal pulse patterns for synchronous machines

The characteristics of electric machines depend decisively upon the use of magnetic materials. These materials are required to form the magnetic circuit and are used by the machine designers to obtain specific desired characteristics. Striving to attain optimal usage of magnetic material, and consequently reduce its dimensions, volume and cost, has concentrated endeavors in the design of electric machines on locating machine's rated operating point near the saturation knee of magnetization curve. Furthermore, modifications in operating point, probably caused by various factors, results in substantial changes in machine's inductances. Considering the disproportion between the air gaps in d- and q-axis (q-axis air gap is larger), d-axis inductance experiences saturation region more quickly. This appreciably influences the value of $\frac{l_q}{l_d}$. Other factors, namely aging and temperature rise should also be taken into account in studying the variations of machine's inductances.

Based on discussion above, online identification of machine's inductances seems indispensable. Either an optimization procedure is to be performed or pre-determined $\frac{l_q}{l_d}$s are to be used for addressing the corresponding LUT and switching patterns to control the inverter. The latter is possible only in case various LUTs are available for different values of $\frac{l_q}{l_d}$.

Regarding identification algorithms for synchronous machines, unavailability of numerous machine variables, like dampers current, leads to negligence of such dynamics. As a result, bias in identified parameters, and deviation from their real values are quite possible. Considering the sensitivity of the problem to $\frac{l_q}{l_d}$, presence of bias in these parameters leads to arriving at switching patterns that are different from optimal ones. As observed, online identification procedure and offline calculation of optimal pulse patterns, both, require immoderate processing burden. Substitution in LUTs, causes transient conditions. The drawbacks associated with transient conditions can briefly be stated as follows:

1. Power losses increase during transition and reduction in THCD is not realized.

2. Intensification of transient conditions may reach an unacceptable level and cause system to trip.

Hence, considerable efforts to compensate transient conditions, while keeping system's operating point fixed, enhance system's cost.

6. Comparison results

Accomplished optimal pulse patterns for induction motor, which are the fundamental components for the performed comparison, are shown in Fig. 4.

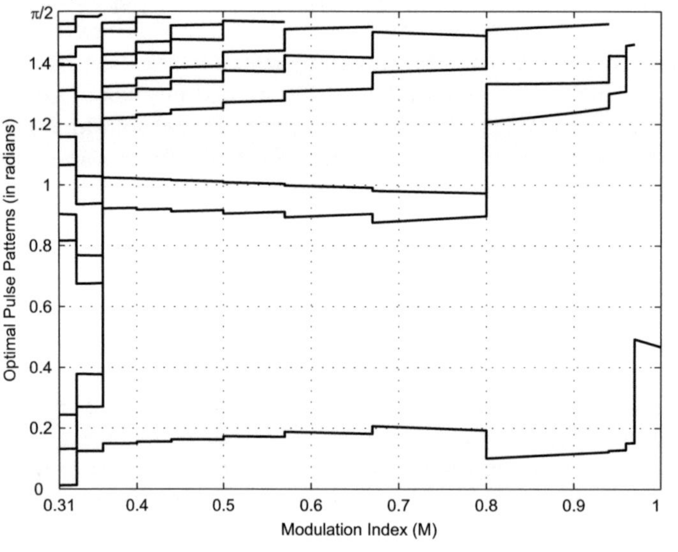

Fig. 4. Optimal pulse patterns of induction motor.

To distinguish between suboptimal and global solutions, the insight on the distribution scheme of switching angles over the considered interval (i.e. $[0, \frac{\pi}{2}]$), along with tracing the increase in the number of switching angles, were of significant assistances. Also, optimal pulse patterns in synchronous machines for $\frac{l_q}{l_d} = 0.3$ are shown in Fig. 5.

Minimized THCD and resulted THCD using optimal pulse patterns of induction motor (suboptimal solutions) are illustrated in Fig. 6 for $\frac{l_q}{l_d} = 0.3$.

For comparison, an index is defined:

$$\text{Error Percentage} = \frac{\sigma_i^{\text{synch}*} - \sigma_i^{\text{synch}}}{\sigma_i^{\text{synch}}} \times 100\%, \qquad (39)$$

in which $\sigma_i^{\text{synch}*}$ denotes the resulted THCD of synchronous machines using optimal switches of induction motor. For $\frac{l_q}{l_d} = 0.3$ to 0.8 with increments of 0.1, the Error Percentages are illustrated in Fig. 7. Since the resulted system is intended for use in high modulation indices, the proposed approach is quite justifiable, considering these comparison results.

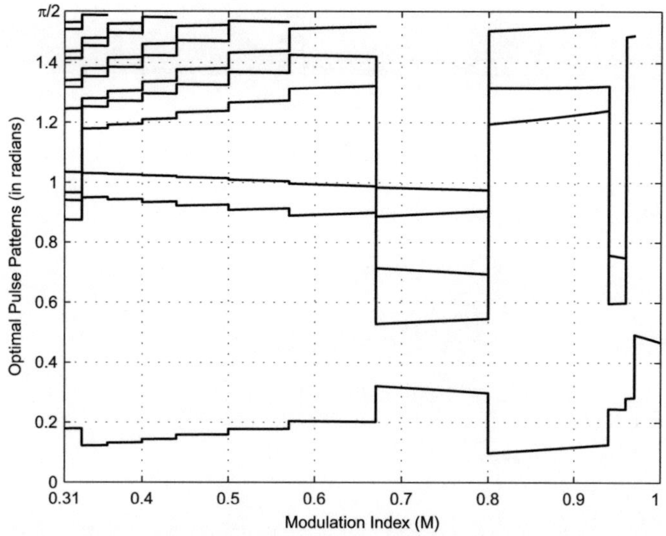

Fig. 5. Optimal pulse patterns of synchronous machine for $\frac{l_q}{l_d} = 0.3$.

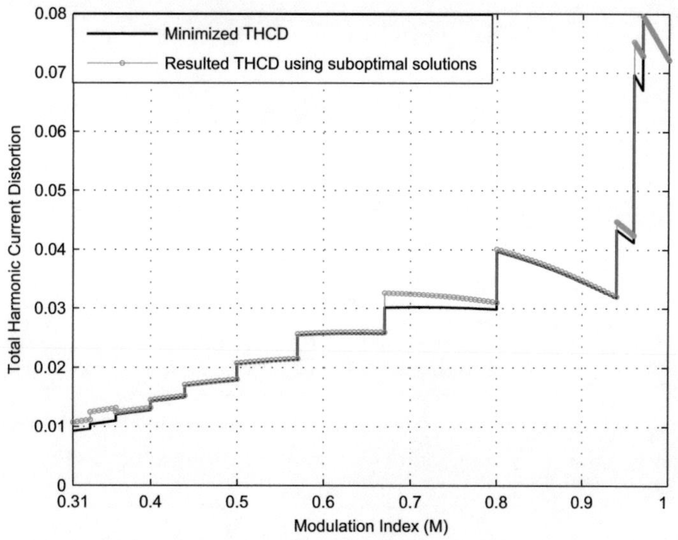

Fig. 6. Comparison between minimized THCD and resulted THCD in synchronous machine using suboptimal solutions for $\frac{l_q}{l_d} = 0.3$.

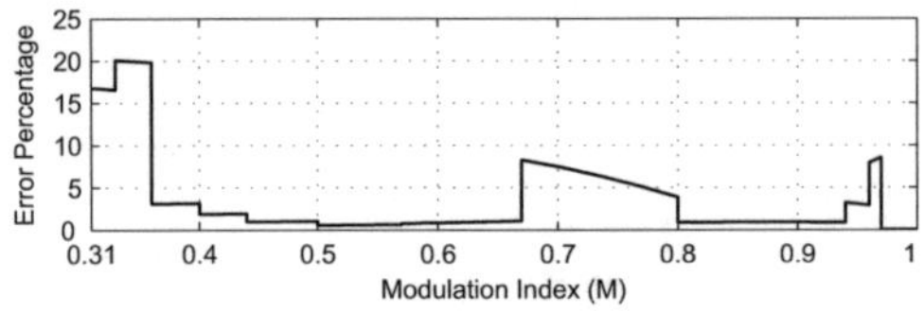

(a) $\frac{l_q}{l_d} = 0.3$

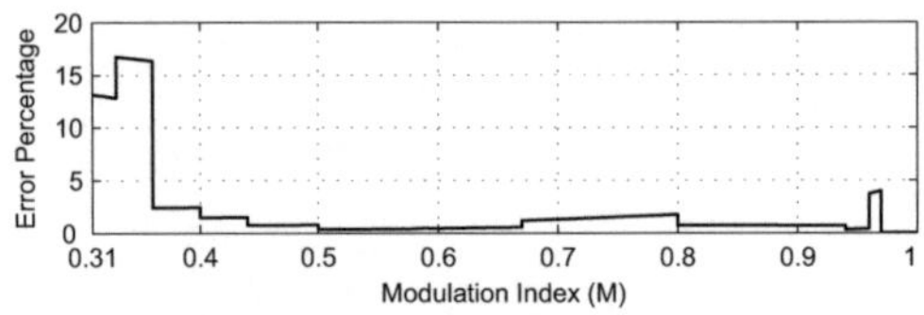

(b) $\frac{l_q}{l_d} = 0.4$

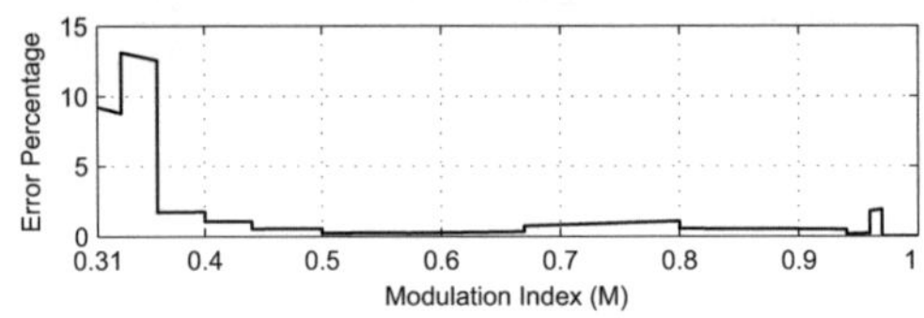

(c) $\frac{l_q}{l_d} = 0.5$

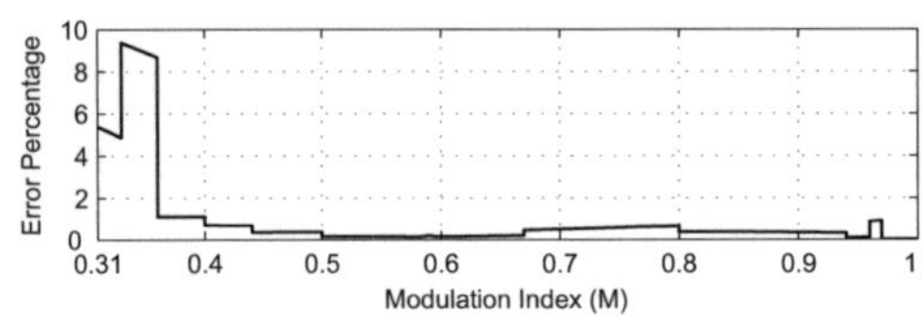

(d) $\frac{l_q}{l_d} = 0.6$

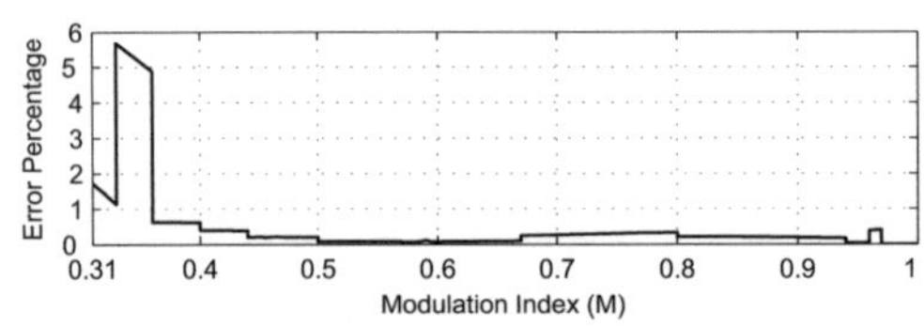

(e) $\frac{l_q}{l_d} = 0.7$

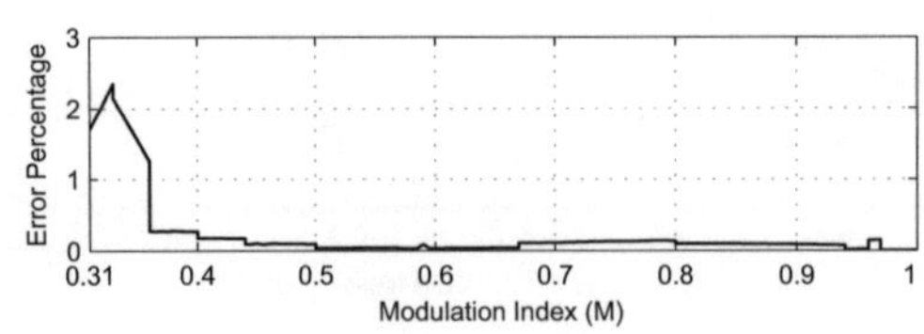

(f) $\frac{l_q}{l_d} = 0.8$

Fig. 7. Comparison results for distinct values of $\frac{l_q}{l_d}$.

7. Conclusions

This paper presents an efficient alternative approach for minimization of harmonic losses in high-power synchronous machines. The proposed current harmonic model in these machines is dependent on the inductances of d and q axes, the inductances in direct and quadrature axes, respectively. As high power application is of concern, finding the global optimum solution to have minimum losses in every specific operating point is of great consequence. For an identified typical machine, with specified characteristics, the problem is redrafted as an optimization task, and the optimal pulse patterns are sought through genetic algorithm (GA) in order to minimize the total harmonic current distortion (THCD). Optimal pulsewidth modulation (PWM) waveforms are accomplished up to 12 switches (per quarter period of PWM waveform), in which for more than this number of switching angles, space vector PWM (SVPWM) method, is preferred to optimal PWM approach. Selection of GA as the optimization method seems completely defensible considering its salient features which can cope with shortcomings of the deterministic optimization methods, particularly when decision variables increase, more probability of finding the global optimum solution, and also nonlinearity and complexity of the proposed objective function.

The aforementioned inductances are appreciably influenced by modifications in operating point, aging, and temperature rise. As such, in-progress switching patterns are no longer global optimum patterns, therefore performing optimization process to determine new optimal pulse patterns from among prior identification procedure results, is indispensable. Substitution in switching patterns provokes an unfavorable transient condition. Optimal pulse patterns of induction motor, whose current harmonic model is independent of its parameters, are applied to harmonic model of synchronous machine with distinct values of $\frac{l_q}{l_d}$. Effectiveness of the proposed approach is noteworthy, particularly in large values of $\frac{l_q}{l_d}$ and high modulation indices.

8. Acknowledgments

The authors would like to thank Professor Joachim Holtz of the University of Wuppertal for apposite suggestion of the approach developed in this study.

9. References

Bäck, T.; Hammel, U. & Schwefel, H. P. (1997). Evolutionary computation: comments on the history and current state. *IEEE Transactions on Evolutionary Computation*, Vol. 1, No. 1, April 1997, 3-17.

Boldea, I. & Nasar, S. A. (1992). *Vector Control of AC Drives*, CRC Press, Boca Raton, FL.

Bose, B. K. (2002). *Modern Power Electronics and AC Drives*, Prentice Hall, Upper Saddle River, NJ.

Chiasson, J.; Tolbert, L. M.; McKenzie, K. & Du, Z.: (2004). A complete solution to the harmonic elimination problem. *IEEE Transactions on Power Electronics*, Vol. 19, No. 2, March 2004, 491-499.

Czarkowski, D.; Chudnovsky, D. V.; Chudnovsky, G. V. & Selesnick, I. W. (2002). Solving the optimal PWM problem for single-phase inverters. *IEEE Transactions on Circuits and Systems–I*, Vol. 49, No. 4, April 2002, 465-475.

Davis, L. (1991). *Handbook of genetic algorithms*, Van Nostrand Reinhold, New York.

Eiben, Á. E.; Hinterding, R. & Michalewicz, Z. (1999). Parameter control in evolutionary algorithms. *IEEE Transactions on Evolutionary Computation*, Vol. 3, No. 2, July 1999, 124-141.

Enjeti, P. N. ; Ziogas, P. D. & Lindsay J. F. (1990). Programmed PWM techniques to eliminate harmonics: a critical evaluation. *IEEE Transactions on Industrial Applications*, Vol. 26, No. 2, Mar./Apr. 1990, 302âĂŞ316.

Goldberg, D. E. (1989). *Genetic algorithms in search, optimization and machine learning*, Addison-Wesley, Reading, MA.

Holtz, J. (1992). Pulsewidth modulation–a survey. *IEEE Transactions on Industrial Electronics*, Vol. 39, No. 5, December 1992, 410-419.

Holtz, J. (1995). The representation of ac machine dynamics by complex signal flow graphs. *IEEE Transactions on Industrial Electronics*, Vol. 42, No. 3, June 1995, 263-271

Leonhard, W. (2001). *Control of Electrical Erives*, 3rd ed., Springer-Verlag, New York.

Ljung, L. & Söderström, T. (1983). *Theory and Practice of Recursive Identification*, MIT Press, Cambridge, MA.

Michalewicz, Z. (1996). *Genetic algorithms + data structures=evolution programs*, Springer-Verlag, New York.

Mohan, N.; Undeland, T. M. & Robbins, W. P. (1995). *Power electronics: converters, applications, and design*, Wiley, New York.

Rezazadeh, A. R.; Sayyah, A. & Aflaki, M. (2006). Modulation error observation and regulation for use in off-line optimal PWM fed high power synchronous motors, *Proceedings of 1st IEEE conference on industrial electronics and applications*, pp. 1300-1307, May 2006, Singapore

Sayyah, A.; Aflaki, M. & Rezazadeh, A. R. (2006). GA-based optimization of total harmonic current distortion and suppression of chosen harmonics in induction motors, *Proceedings of international symposium on power electronics, electrical drives, automation and motion*, pp. 1361-1366, Italy, May 2006, Taormina (Sicily)

Sayyah, A.; Aflaki, M. & Rezazadeh, A. R. (2006). Optimal PWM for minimization of total harmonic current distortion in high-power induction motors using genetic algorithms, *Proceedings of SICE-ICASE international joint conference*, Korea, pp. 5494-5499, October 2006, Busan.

Sayyah, A.; Aflaki, M. & Rezazadeh, A. R. (2006). Optimization of THD and suppressing certain order harmonics in PWM inverters using genetic algorithms, *Proceedings of IEEE international symposium on intelligent control*, pp. 874-879, Germany, October 2006, Munich.

Sun, J. (1995). *Optimal Pulsewidth Modulation Techniques for High Power Voltage-source Inverters*, Thesis, University of Paderborn, Germany.

Sun, J.; Beineke, S. & Grotstollen, H.: (1996). Optimal PWM based on real-time solution of harmonic elimination equations. it IEEE Transactions on Power Electronics, Vol. 11, No. 4, July 1996, 612-621.

Part 3

Artificial Immune Systems and Swarm Intelligence

17

Artificial Immune Systems, Dynamic Fitness Landscapes, and the Change Detection Problem

Hendrik Richter
HTWK Leipzig University of Applied Sciences
Germany

1. Introduction

To let biological processes, behaviors and structures inspire the design of problem solving algorithms and devices has been a prominent and persistent theme in engineering and applied sciences in the last few decades. Within this context, bio–inspired computing has taken a pioneering role. Fields such as evolutionary computing (1; 8; 25), artificial immune systems (4; 6; 43), membrane computing (29) or swarm systems (9; 22) have outgrown their infancy and found theoretical ground as well as important applications. The fact that and the way how these fields advanced into its current form is due to three major developments: (i) the upcoming of cheap, fast and reliable computational power in form of digital computers, (ii) the understanding that computational power in connection with implementing an algorithmic approach creates potent problem solvers, and (iii) the insight that biological systems can be fruitfully understood as information–processing units and can hence frequently be employed for computational and/or algorithmic proposes. This trend is of course not to be confused with computational biology, but it is highly related and probably unthinkable without the fundamental progress towards algorithmization and mathematization in biology, see e.g. (5; 16; 21; 38) for some recent discussion. Among the mentioned fields of bio–inspired computing, evolutionary algorithms and artificial immune systems play a unique role as their history is particularly long and the maturity reached is notably high. In this paper we will use both schemes in connection to solve the intertwined problem of maximum tracking and change detection in dynamic optimization.

For successfully solving dynamic optimization problems by evolutionary computation, there is a need for additions to the standard algorithmic structure, namely by operators maintaining and enhancing population diversity. Dynamic optimization here means that the topology of the associated fitness landscape changes with time. A considerable number of these operators for diversity management (for instance memory schemes, random immigrants or hyper–mutation (24; 26; 30; 33; 35; 39; 45)) can only be provoked and hence made to work properly if the points in time are known where the changes in the fitness landscape occur. So, the problem of change detection is of high practical relevance in solving dynamic optimization problems (3; 19; 27).

In principle, change detection is based on using information about the fitness values of points in the search space extracted from the fitness landscape. This extraction of information can be done in two ways. One is to use the fitness evaluations of the evolutionary algorithm's population, which is called population–based detection, the other is to use additional measurement of the landscape's fitness on prescribed points (26), which is called sensor–based detection. Recently, a study (34) compared both types of methods. It has been shown that in populations–based detection there is no need for additional fitness function evaluation, but elaborate statistical tests have to be carried out. On the other hand, sensor–based detection can forgo these tests but at the cost of redoing measurements in the fitness landscape. Irrespective of the quality of the change detection, using statistical tests on population–based fitness data is sometimes generally objectionable. Although using non–parametric statistical tests fits the non-Gaussian nature of the fitness distribution, the tests require independent samples to be accurately employed. This independence might not be given for fitness distributions from sequential generations. The fitness values of next generation's population have their origin in the current generation and are only partly affected by the stochastic influence driving the evolutionary algorithm. This situation might be different if a (randomly induced) change in the fitness landscape has occurred, but again there is no guarantee that the resulting fitness distributions are statistically independent. Because of these reasons, it would be desirable to have alternative methods. A promising option is the use of methods from artificial immune systems, particularly negative selection (4; 7; 13; 18; 44). These algorithms have been successfully employed to solve similar problems, for instance network security, computer virus detection, network intrusion detection and fault diagnosis, see e.g. (13; 18; 43). In this paper, we present an immunological approach to change detection in dynamic fitness landscapes.

The paper is organized like this. In the next two sections, dynamic fitness landscapes are introduced and the change detection problem is defined. Then, in section 4, the immunological change detection scheme is given and its main components, shape space, affinity function, detector generation and detection processing, are described. In section 5, we present numerical experiments with the scheme and use receiver–operating characteristics (ROC) as well as the area under the ROC curve (AUC) as an analyzing tool. We end with summarizing the findings and pointing at future work.

2. Dynamics and fitness landscapes

The concept of fitness landscapes is an important approach to foster theoretical understanding in evolutionary computation (20; 40; 41). Such landscapes are traditionally considered to be static and can be obtained from either a genotype–to–fitness mapping or more generally by encoding all possible solutions of the optimization problem and giving a fitness value to each solution. All the possible solutions span a search space S , while a fitness function $f(s) : S \rightarrow \mathbb{R}$ provides every point $s \in S$ with a fitness value. In case of a genotype–to–fitness mapping, S coincides with the genotypical space. If the search space S is not metric, we must explain which solutions we would obtain if we were to slightly modify a possible solution $s \in S$ (and hence were to move it locally in the search space). This is done by a neighborhood structure $n(s)$ which gives every point in the search space a set of direct and possibly also more distant neighbors.

If the fitness landscape is dynamic all of its three defining ingredients – search space S, fitness function $f(s)$, neighborhood structure $n(s)$ – can, in principle, be changing with time. So, we additionally need for description a time set and mappings that tell how S, $f(s)$ and/or $n(s)$

evolve with time (31; 32; 37). Dynamic optimization problems considered in the literature so far address all these possibilities of change to some extend. Whereas a real alteration of the fundamental components of a search space such as dimensionality or representation (binary, integer, discrete, real, etc.) is really rare, a change in the feasibility of individuals is another and less substantial kind of a dynamic search space and is discussed within the problem setting of dynamic constraints (28; 36). The works on dynamic routing can partially be interpreted as a changing neighborhood structures (2; 15), while most of the work so far has been devoted to time–dependent fitness function (24; 26; 30; 33; 35; 39; 45), which will also be the focus of this paper.

In dynamic optimization problems (DOPs), the fitness landscape

$$f(x,k), k \geq 0 \tag{1}$$

defined over a fixed bounded search space $M \subset \mathbb{R}^n$ with $x \in M$, changes with discrete time $k \in \mathbb{N}_0$. The DOP is solved by an evolutionary algorithm (EA) with population $P \in \mathbb{R}^n$ and generational time $t \in \mathbb{N}_0$. Its population dynamics can be described by the generation transition function

$$P(t+1) = \psi\left(P(t)\right), t \geq 0, \tag{2}$$

which explains how a population $P(t+1)$ at generation $t+1$ originates from the population $P(t)$ at generation t. Both the time scales t and k work as a measuring and ordering tool for changes (t for changes in the population from one generation to the next, k for changes in the dynamic fitness landscape). As μ individuals $p_i(t) \in P(t), i = 1, 2, \ldots, \mu$, populate the fitness landscape (1), they can be labeled with a fitness value $f(p_i(t), k)$. Both time scales are related in the solving process of the DOP by the change frequency $\gamma \in \mathbb{N}$ with

$$t = \gamma k. \tag{3}$$

Usually, γ is considered to be constant for all generations t, but it might also be a function of k and even be different (for instance a positive integer realization of a random process) for every k. Note that we require more than one generation in between landscape changes, $\gamma > 1$, and hence $k = \lfloor \gamma^{-1} t \rfloor$.

3. The change detection problem

From (3), we see that the fitness landscape changes every γ generations. As the temporal patterns of these changes are assumed to be not explicitly known, our interest is now to infer from the fitness values

$$f_i(k) = f(p_i, k) \tag{4}$$

of the individuals $p_i(t) \in P(t)|_{t=\gamma k}$ if a change in the fitness landscape has occurred or not. This we call the change detection problem in dynamic fitness landscapes using fitness data from the population. More explicitly, we want to detect the change point t_{cp} with the property $\exists x \in M$ for which

$$f(x, \lfloor \gamma^{-1}(t_{cp} - 1) \rfloor) \neq f(x, \lfloor \gamma^{-1} t_{cp} \rfloor). \tag{5}$$

Our convention is to define the change point t_{cp} in the generational time scale t as we base the detection solely on the fitness values $f(x, \lfloor \gamma^{-1} t \rfloor)$ of the population $P(t)$. From (3) follows

$\lfloor \gamma^{-1}(t_{cp} - 1) \rfloor = k - 1$ and $\lfloor \gamma^{-1} t_{cp} \rfloor = k$, that is for every integer $\gamma^{-1}t$ there is a change in the fitness landscape (1).

The change point definition (5) says that a change in the fitness landscape has happened no matter how small and insignificant the alteration in the landscape's topology actually is. From a computational point of view this raises some problems regarding practical detectability. Change detection based on population data assumes that a change in the fitness landscape affects a substantial number of its points and makes them to increase or decrease their fitness values. Moreover, generally there is $P(t) \neq P(t-1)$ so that we cannot check if $f(p_i, \lfloor \gamma^{-1}(t-1) \rfloor) \neq f(p_i, \lfloor \gamma^{-1} t \rfloor)$ as $p_i(t-1) \neq p_i(t)$.

Another aspect is that the given framework is unsuitable for discriminating between small but gradual changes and larger but abrupt changes. Such a distinction can only be made in terms of the fitness landscape considered. The treatment and discussion presented here is intended to apply for fitness landscapes that undergo abrupt and substantial changes in their topology. Hence, it can reasonably be assumed that these changes are practically detectable. We exclude small but gradual changes in the fitness landscape (for instance those resulting from the presence of noise and/or other perturbations in the fitness evaluation process). This is in line with the application context of the change detection scheme considered here. It should help to trigger and control the diversity enhancement and maintenance of the EA. For fitness landscapes with small but gradual changes an additional change–activated diversity management does not play a prominent role anyway; other types of EAs (particularly those emphasizing robustness such as self–adaption) are found to be more apt here.

As shown above it is generally not possible to verify condition (5) directly. The basic idea behind using the fitness values $f(p_i, k)|_{k=\lfloor \gamma^{-1} t \rfloor}$ of the population's individuals $p_i(t) \in P(t)$ is that these quantities form a fitness distribution

$$F(t) = (f_1(t), f_2(t), \ldots, f_\mu(t)) \tag{6}$$

that can be analyzed by itself or compared to the ℓ preceding ones, that is creating a time window of width ℓ, $(F(t-1), F(t-2), \ldots, F(t-\ell))$. The fitness distributions can be regarded as a data stream and monitoring this data stream should make visible the normal optimum finding mode of the EA but also reflect that this normal mode is disrupted if a change in the fitness landscape has occurred (and hence results in a different pattern when evaluating $F(t)$ and $F(t-1)$, respectively). Statistically speaking, the considered data set $F(t)$ can be regarded as coming from an unknown distribution $\mathcal{D}(t)$. This transforms the problem of change detection into the problem of testing whether the data sets $F(t)$ and $F(t-1)$ or any data set created from any time window including $F(t)$ are coming from different distributions or not, which is known as statistical hypothesis testing. This connection is widely applied in solving change detection problems, e.g. (14; 23). The obvious question here is which test can tell us whether $\mathcal{D}(t)$ is different from $\mathcal{D}(t-1)$ and if this difference necessarily and sufficiently implies that a change has occurred. In the language of statistical hypothesis testing, the test should ideally show only true changes, that is have no *false positives* and indicate all of them, that is have no *false negatives*. However, statistical hypothesis testing methods regularly require that the samples $F(t)$ are independent from $F(t-1)$. This most likely is not the case if the samples come form a moving population of an evolutionary algorithm. The data set $F(t)$ includes the fitness value of an evolving population and represents two types of interfering population dynamics. An evolving population moves (ideally and in the best case) monotonically towards the optima and in doing so changes its mean and standard deviation. Such a convergence behavior of the EA which is desired and the intended working mode is again a statistical phenomenon. Moreover, the fitness values of $F(t)$ are a direct result of the values of $F(t-1)$ and therefore can hardly be regarded as independent of each other. A second aspect is the reaction of a change in the fitness landscape, which more likely can be seen as independent if the dynamics is a stochastic process. For all these reasons we look for an alternative to statistical hypothesis testing. So, we intend to use ideas from artificial immunology for solving the change detection problem in dynamic fitness landscapes.

4. The immunological change detector

Artificial immune systems (AIS) are soft computing algorithms that take their inspiration from and mimicking working principles and functions of their biological counterparts (43; 44). AIS date back to the 80s (11) and were initiated by an increasing theoretical understanding of the natural immune system in connection with a strong interest in utilizing biological processes for computational proposes. These algorithms are capable of adaption, learning and memory and have been applied to problem solving in areas as different as classification, pattern recognition and data mining/analysis (6; 13; 18; 43). Among the different types of AIS, negative selection algorithms acclaimed a prominent role in solving so–called anomaly detection (7; 10; 13; 18; 42). Here, anomaly detection means to distinguish the normal behavior of a dynamic process, usually characterized by some (external) model, from anomalies defined by deviations from that model. In the following, we review negative selection and show how it can be used for detecting change in dynamic fitness landscapes.

Negative selection is anchored at the concept of a shape space that represents the observable features of the dynamic process for which a change in behavior needs to be detected. Within that shape space, we define a set of self elements that stem from the normal behavior. From these self elements, in turn, a set of detectors is derived that must not match any sample of the self set, usually by using some training data. Subsequently, the detectors are taken to decide if an incoming new feature data from the dynamic process is normal (self) or not (non–self). Thus, negative selection mimics the self/non–self discrimination of the natural immune system, see Fig. 1 which shows self and non–self elements in a two–dimensional shape space. We now describe the main components of the negative selection algorithm: shape space, affinity measure, detector generation and detection process.

i.) Shape space. The shape space of a negative selection algorithm is a representation of the data coming from the dynamic process under study and can be either a string over a finite alphabet (for instance a binary string, which has been used in a large number of previous works, see e.g. (18)) or real–valued (13). As the base for the change detection, the fitness distribution $F(t)$, is real–valued it seems straightforward to use a real–valued shape space $\mathcal{S} = [0,1]^m$ here, where m is its dimension. Dimensionality of the shape space is an important parameter influencing computational effort and performance of the detection scheme (42). The dimensionality of the fitness distribution $F(t)$ equals the number of individuals in the population μ. So, for the reason given above, it appears sensible to pre–process the data from the fitness distribution with the aims of both reducing dimensionality and extracting the most meaningful information about when the landscape has changed.

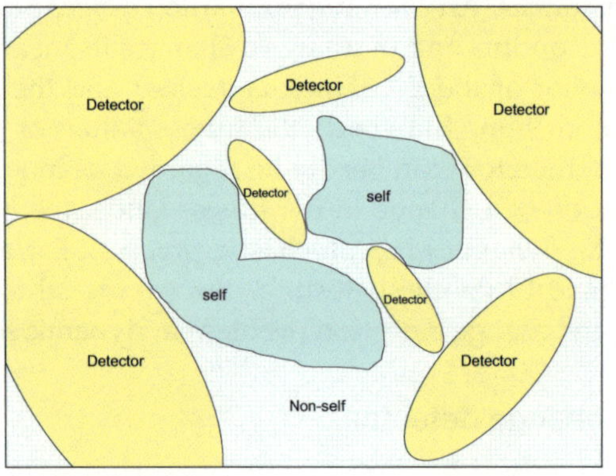

Fig. 1. Self and non–self elements and detectors for a two–dimensional shape space.

Among the several conceivable ways to do the pre–processing, we here consider the following scheme. The distributions $F(t)$ and $F(t-1)$ are independently sorted according to their fitness values. Then the $\frac{m}{2}$ highest and $\frac{m}{2}$ lowest ranked elements of both sorted distributions are taken, the elements coming from $F(t-1)$ are subtracted from the ones from $F(t)$ and finally these calculated quantities (which reflect the difference between two consecutive fitness distributions) are normalized to the interval $[0,1]$. Hence, the result is a point in the m–dimensional shape space. The given procedure of pre–processing the data is motivated by the common sense arguments that a change in the fitness landscape particularly affects the magnitude of the best and the worst fitness values and also that their relative difference from one generation to the subsequent one is telling if either a standard evolutionary search or a reaction to a landscape change has taken place. Note that by this pre–processing a metric on the fitness distributions is defined.

ii.) Affinity measure. The affinity measure states the degree of matching and recognition between elements (that are points) in the shape space. In other words, the affinity measure describes to what degree elements in the shape space differ. Every element in the shape space is defined by its center point $c \in [0,1]^m$ and a matching radius r. According to their function in the immunological detection and classification process, there are three types of elements in the shape space:

(a) self elements $se = (cs, rs)$ that are samples known to belong to the self space (usually from a training data set),

(b) detectors $dt = (cd, rd)$ that are derived from the self elements and must not match them, and

(c) incoming data samples $id = (ci, ri)$ that must be classified as belonging to either the self set or not.

Self elements, detectors and incoming data are also known by their immunological motivated terms self cells, antibodies and antigens, respectively. There is a large number of different affinity measures, see e.g. (18) for an overview. We here use Euclidean distance so that there is a match if $\|c_i - c_j\| < r_i + r_j$, with the indices i, j denoting different elements of the shape space.

iii.) Detector generation. In detector generation, self elements that come from training data with known self/non-self discrimination are used to calculate detector center points and radii. Similarly to the situation in computing the affinity measure, there is a multitude of different detector generation mechanisms, see e.g. (18). In some initial experiments (which are not reported here for sake of brevity), a scheme mainly using ideas from v–detectors (17) had shown best results and is considered here. This scheme has the advantage to address the problem of coverage of the non–self space in the generation process and to maximize the size of individual detectors to achieve a larger coverage. This comes at the cost of making the number of detectors actually created a (not predicable) result of the generation process and not a parameter to be set initially.

The scheme works like this. Input is a collection of self elements se_j, with $j = 1, 2, \dots \#_{se}$, and $\#_{se}$ the total number of self elements. Further, we set a target coverage α and calculate a quantity $h = \frac{1}{1-\alpha}$. Then, the following steps are repeated. A candidate detector point and its radius are generated as a realization of a uniformly distributed random variable. It is tested if the detector matches any of the self elements. If so, its radius is shrunk so that any match is abolished. If not so, the radius is enhanced to the limit of any match. After that it is tested if the candidate detector with its updated radius is entirely covered by a detector that already passed this test. If so, the candidate is discarded, otherwise it is saved to the set of detectors that passed the coverage test. These steps are repeated until candidate detectors cannot pass the coverage test h times in a row. The saved detector candidates are accepted for the change detection process.

iv.) Detection process. After the training time in which detectors are generated as described above, the immunological change detector can be used for deciding if a change point according to eq. (5) has been reached or not by monitoring a metric defined on the fitness distributions $F(t)$ and $F(t-1)$. The necessary pre–processing is the same as the one given for the training phase above in Sec. 4.i. So, an incoming data sample $id(t) = (ci(t), ri)$ is produced every generation t, where the center point comes from the pre–processing and the self–radius ri is a quantity that defines the sensitivity of the detector, is to be set in initializing the immunological change detector and will be examined in the numerical experiments reported below. The affinity function is calculated by using a Euclidean distance measure

$$w(t) = \sum_{j=1}^{\#_{det}} \text{aff}(id(t), dt_j), \tag{7}$$

where $\#_{det}$ is the total number of detectors dt_j, the individual affinities

$$\text{aff}(id(t), dt_j) = \begin{cases} \beta \| ci(t) - cd_j \| & \text{if} \quad \| ci(t) - cd_j \| < rd_j \\ | ri - rd_j | & \text{if} \quad \| ci(t) - cd_j \| < rd_j + ri \end{cases}$$

and β is a weighting factor. From the values $w(t)$, a change point can be concluded. Therefore, a threshold value $\bar{w}$ has to be set and a $w(t) > \bar{w}$ indicates a change.

v.) Performance evaluation. To evaluate the success and the quality of the change detection, the method of receiver–operating characteristics (ROC) curves can be used, e.g. (12). ROC curves are a tool for organizing and visualizing classifications together with their performances. So, they can be used to analyze and depict the relative trade–offs between benefits of the schemes (correctly identified instances according to the classification) and costs (incorrect identifications). That makes them particularly useful to assess change detection schemes. The classification here is between positive and negative change detections. Hence, we can define the following performance metrics. If there is a positive detection and a change in the fitness landscape has happened, it is counted as *true positive* (tp), if a change happened but is not detected, it is a *negative positive* (np). If, on the other hand, no change has happened and the detection is negative, it is a *true negative* (tn), a positive detection in this situation yields a *false negative* (fn). For this two–by–two change classification, we obtain as the elements of performance metrics: the tp rate

$$tp \approx \frac{\text{correctly identified changes}}{\text{total changes}} \tag{8}$$

and $fn = 1 - tp$ as well as the fp rate

$$fp \approx \frac{\text{incorrectly identified changes}}{\text{total non changes}} \tag{9}$$

and $tn = 1 - fp$. In the ROC plot, the tp rate is given (on the ordinate) versus the fp rate (on the abscissa). Hence, the tp and fp rates for the immunological change detector for a given threshold value $\bar{w}$ give a point in the ROC space; ROC curves are obtained by plotting the rates for varying the threshold value $\bar{w}$.

5. Experimental results

In the following we report numerical experiments with the change detection schemes described above. In the experiments, we use as dynamic fitness landscape a "field of cones on a zero plane", where N cones with coordinates $c_i(k)$, $i = 1, \cdots, N$, are moving with discrete time $k \in \mathbb{N}_0$. These cones are distributed across the landscape and have randomly chosen initial coordinates $c_i(0)$, heights h_i, and slopes s_i, see Fig. 2. So, we get

$$f(x,k) = \max\left\{0, \max_{1 \leq i \leq N} \left[h_i - s_i \|x - c_i(k)\|\right]\right\}, \tag{10}$$

where the number of cones is $N = 50$ and its dimension $n = 2$. The dynamics of the moving sequence for the cones' coordinates is mostly normally random, that is each $c_i(k)$ for each k is an independent realization of a normally distributed random variable. In the last set of experiments we also consider different kinds of dynamics, namely regular, circle–like (and hence completely predictable) dynamics where the cones' coordinates form a circle and so return to the same place in search space after a certain amount of time, and chaotic dynamics where the cones' coordinates follow the trajectory of a nonlinear dynamical system with chaotic behavior, see (30) for details of this kind of setting of landscape dynamics.

Further, we employ an EA with a fixed number of $\lambda = 48$ individuals that uses tournament selection of tournament size 2, a fitness–related intermediate sexual recombination (which is operated λ times and works by choosing two individuals randomly to produce offspring that is the fitness–weighted arithmetic mean of both parents) and a standard mutation with the mutation rate 0.1. Note that the choice of the EA is of secondary importance as long as it

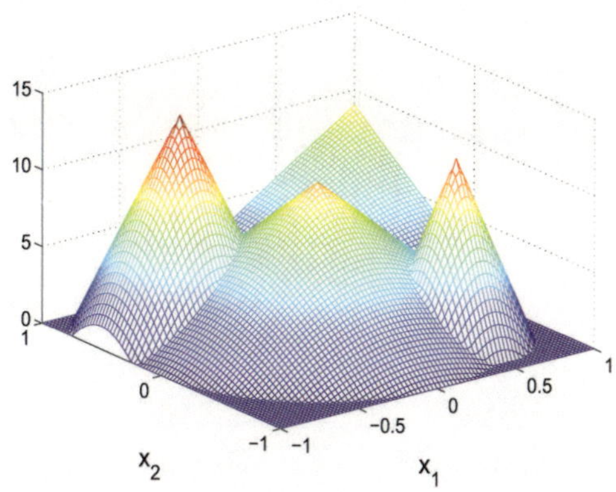

Fig. 2. Fitness landscape (10) for $n = 2$ and $N = 4$.

solves the DOP with some success. The immunological change detector was implemented as described in Sec. 4; we set $\beta = 5$.

Fig. 3 shows the detection process by monitoring the affinity function $w(t)$ calculated according to eq. (7), for shape space dimension $m = 8$, coverage $\alpha = 0.999$ and self radius $ri = 0.2$. We here use a training time of 20 generations. We see that even for this small training set, spikes in $w(t)$ can be used as indication for changes in the fitness landscape. As results of a second set of experiments, we give the ROC curves for varying dimension m and coverage α, see Fig. 4. Here, training time is 400 generations with total 1000 generations taken into account, self radius is $ri = 0.2$ and change frequency $\gamma = 20$. The tp and fp rates are calculated according to the eqs. (8) and (9) and are means over 100 repetitions. From the ROC curves we can deduce that the lower left point $(0,0)$ represents a change detection that never produces any positive decision. It makes neither a false positive error nor yields any true positives. Likewise but opposite, a detection represented by the upper right point $(1,1)$ only produces positive decisions with only true positives but also false positive errors in all cases. The line between these two points in the ROC space can be regarded as expressing a purely random guessing strategy to decide on whether or not a change has happened. Any classification that is represented by a point below that line is worse than random guessing, while classifications above are better, the more so if the point is more north–westwards of another, with the point $(0,1)$ expressing perfect classification.

With this in mind, we see from Fig. 4 that good detection results are achieved as we obtain curves that climb from the point $(0,0)$ vertically for a considerable amount of threshold values towards $(0,1)$ before bending off to $(1,1)$. Further, it can be seen in Fig. 4a that a higher coverage rate produces slightly better results, but the differences are not dramatic. Also, varying the shape space dimension leads to no substantial increasing in the detection success. The curve for $m = 8$ is even slightly lower than that for $m = 6$.

An important feature of the v–detector design used in this paper is that we get detectors with variable size but also that their exact number is not known beforehand. The number is a statistically varying result of the creating process and thus becomes a quantity that can be verified and studied experimentally. Fig. 5a shows the number of detectors $\#_{det}$ depending on the shape space dimension m, while Fig. 5b gives $\#_{det}$ over the average detector radii

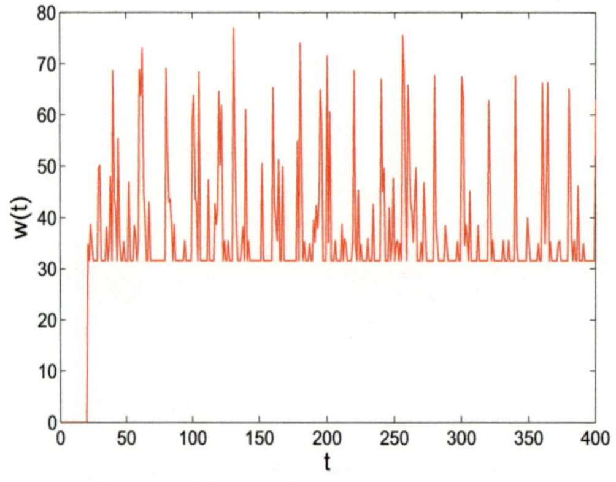

Fig. 3. Detection process for $\gamma = 20$, shape space dimension $m = 8$, coverage $\alpha = 0.999$ and self radius $ri = 0.2$.

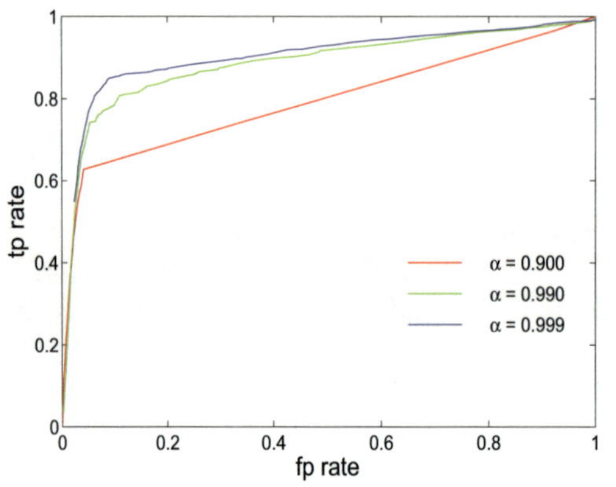

a

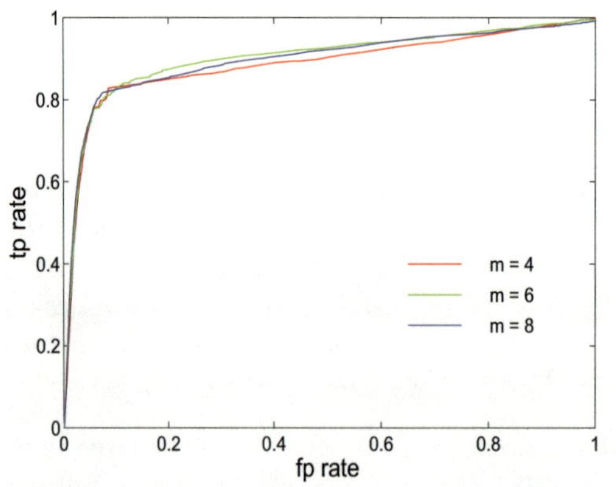

b

Fig. 4. ROC curves for: a) varying coverage α; b) varying shape space dimension m.

r_d. Both figures show a scatter plot for 20 subsequent detector generations each. It can be seen that generally the larger the coverage α and the dimension m the more detectors are produced. Both facts appear quite logical as higher coverage requires more detectors, and higher dimension means larger generalized volume to be filled by the detectors. For dimensions becoming larger also the actual numbers of detectors are more spread, that is they increase in their range of variation. For $m = 8$, for instance, and $\alpha = 0.900$ the difference between the lowest value ($\#_{det} = 15$) and the highest ($\#_{det} = 33$) is 18, while for $m = 4$ the maximal difference is 8. Results that allow a similar interpretation can also be found for the number of detectors over the average detector radii r_d, see Fig. 5b. Smaller coverage α produces not only a smaller number of detectors but also detectors with smaller average radii, albeit the range of radii overlap. A possible explanation is that for a higher coverage a larger number of detectors candidates are produced and tested, and hence it becomes more likely that such with larger radii are finally found and selected.

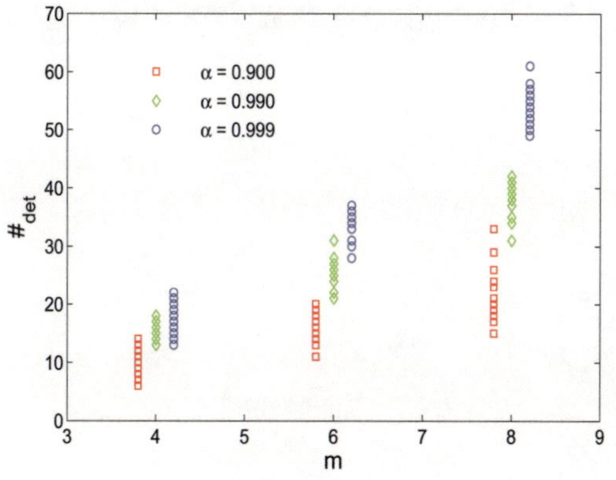

a

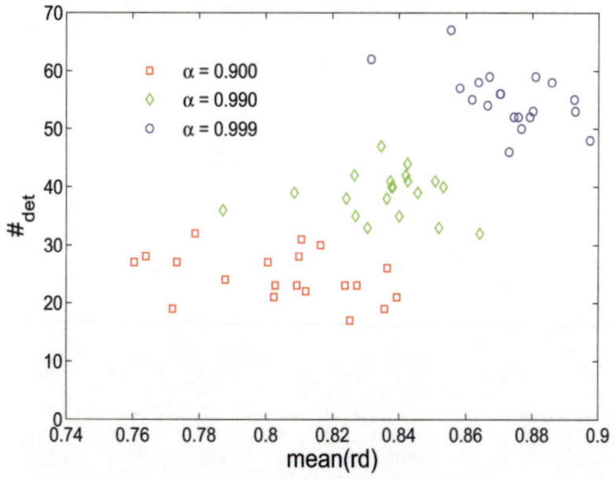

b

Fig. 5. Number of detectors $\#_{det}$ for different coverage α depending on: a) shape space dimension m; b) average detector radius mean(r_d) .

In a next experiment we study the effect of varying the self radius ri together with the influence of different kind of landscape dynamics. To get a numerical evaluation of the ROC curves, we calculate the area under the ROC curve (AUC), which is a measure for the detection success (12). Since the AUC is a fraction of the unit square, its values are $0 \leq \text{AUC} \leq 1$. Moreover, since random guessing gives the diagonal line in the unit square, a well–working change detection should have values $\text{AUC} > 0.5$. Fig. 6 shows the AUC over the self radius

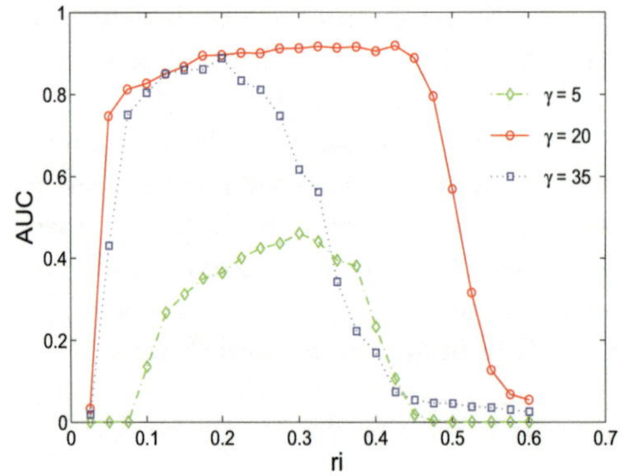

a

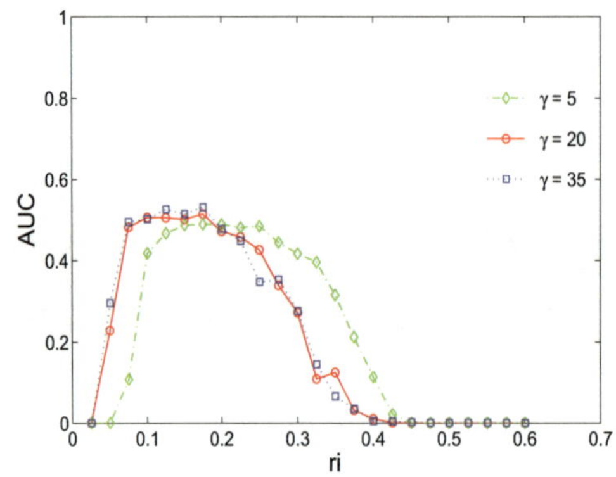

b

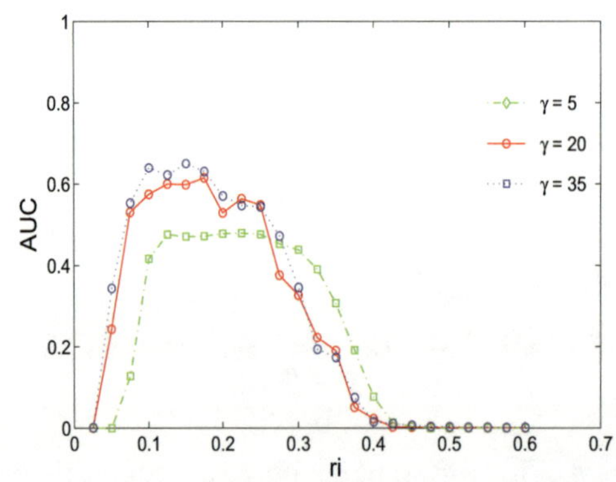

c

Fig. 6. AUC over self radius ri for different γ and different kinds of landscape dynamics, shape space dimension $m = 8$ and coverage $\alpha = 0.999$: a) random landscape dynamics; b) cyclic landscape dynamics; c) chaotic landscape dynamics.

ri for different change frequencies γ, shape space dimension $m = 8$ and coverage $\alpha = 0.999$, with Fig. 6a giving the results for random landscape dynamics, and Fig. 6b and Fig. 6c for regular dynamics (circle) and chaotic dynamics. The AUC is again the mean over 100 runs. We can generally see a reverse bath tube curve that indicates that a certain interval of ri is best. In some cases there is no significant differences in the performance within this interval, for instance for random dynamics and $\gamma = 20$, while for others, for instance random dynamics and $\gamma = 5$, a clear maximum can be observed. Further, the performance is generally better for random dynamics than for regular or chaotic, and a very fast landscape dynamics, $\gamma = 5$, may produce rather inferior detection results. These results appear to be a little bit surprising as it is know that for the optimization results for regular and chaotic dynamics we do not find such significant differences (33; 35). A possible explanation is that for random dynamics in the landscape the composition of the population is more homogeneous and the population dynamics more random–like. This in turn leads to better detector design and hence more effective change detection.

6. Conclusions

We have presented an immunological approach for solving the change detection problem in dynamic fitness landscape. A negative selection algorithm has been used to decide on whether or not the fitness landscape has changed. This is solely done with fitness information from the population on a sample base. Numerical experiments evaluated by receiver–operating characteristics (ROC) curves have shown the efficiency of the scheme. An important feature of the approach is that it does not directly uses any statistical test on which requirements could be imposed regarding the independence of the samples. In future work it would be interesting to compare and combine the immunological change detector with statistical tests. This could be connected with a study of dynamic fitness landscapes with higher dimension and complexity.

7. References

[1] T. Bäck. *Evolutionary Algorithms in Theory and Practice: Evolution Strategies, Evolutionary Programming, Genetic Algorithms.* Oxford University Press, New York Oxford, 1996.

[2] P. A. N. Bosman and H.Poutré. Computationally intelligent online dynamic vehicle routing by explicit load prediction in an evolutionary algorithm. In: T. P. Runarsson, H. G. Beyer, E. Burke, J. J. Merelo Guervós, L. D. Whitley, X. Yao (eds.), Parallel Problem Solving from Nature–PPSN IX, Springer–Verlag, Berlin Heidelberg New York, 312–321, 2006.

[3] J. Branke. *Evolutionary Optimization in Dynamic Environments*, Kluwer, Dordrecht, 2002.

[4] L. N. de Castro and J. Timmis. *Artificial Immune Systems: A New Computational Intelligence Approach*, Springer–Verlag, Berlin Heidelberg New York, 2002.

[5] J. E. Cohen. Mathematics is biology's next microscope, only better; Biology is mathematics' next physics, only better. PLoS Biol 2(12): e439. doi:10.1371/journal.pbio.0020439, 2004.

[6] D. Dasgupta. *Artificial Immune Systems and their Applications*, Springer–Verlag, Berlin Heidelberg New York, 1999.

[7] P. D'haeseleer, S. Forrest and P. Helman. An immunological approach to change detection: Algorithms, analysis and implications. In: *Proc. 1996 IEEE Symposium on Security and Privacy*, IEEE Computer Society, Los Alamitos, CA, 110–119, 1996.

[8] A. E. Eiben and J. E. Smith. *Introduction to Evolutionary Computing.* Springer–Verlag, Berlin Heidelberg New York, 2003.

[9] A. P. Engelbrecht. *Fundamentals of Computational Swarm Intelligence,* Wiley, Chichester, 2006.

[10] F. Esponda, S. Forrest and P. Helman. A formal framework for positive and negative detection schemes. *IEEE Trans. Syst. Man Cybern.,* B34: 357–373, 2004.

[11] J. D. Farmer, N. H. Packard and A. S. Perelson. The immune system, adaption, and machine learning. *Physica,* D22: 187–204, 1986.

[12] T. Fawcett. An introduction to ROC analysis. *Pattern Recognition Letters,* 27: 861–874, 2006.

[13] F. Gonzalez and D. Dasgupta. Anomaly detection using real–valued negative selection. *Genetic Programming and Evolvable Machines,* 4: 383–403, 2003.

[14] J. G. De Gooijer. Detecting change–points in multidimensional stochastic processes. *Computational Statistics & Data Analysis,* 51: 1892–1903, 2006.

[15] J. I. van Hemert and J. A. La Poutré. Dynamic routing problems with fruitful regions: Models and evolutionary computation. In: X. Yao, E. Burke, J. A. Lozano, J. Smith, J. J. Merelo Guervós, J. A. Bullinaria, J. Rowe, P. Tino, A. Kabán, H. P. Schwefel (eds.), *Parallel Problem Solving from Nature–PPSN VIII,* Springer–Verlag, Berlin Heidelberg New York, 692–701, 2004.

[16] J. Leo van Hemmen. Biology and mathematics: A fruitful merger of two cultures. *Biol. Cybern.,* 97: 1–3, 2007.

[17] Z. Ji and D. Dasgupta. Estimating the detector coverage in a negative selection algorithm. In: H. G. Beyer et al. (eds.), *Proc. Congress on Genetic and Evolutionary Computation, GECCO 2005,* ACM Press, New York, 281–288, 2005.

[18] Z. Ji and D. Dasgupta. Revisiting negative selection algorithms. *Evolutionary Computation,* 15: 223–251, 2007.

[19] Y. Jin and J. Branke. Evolutionary optimization in uncertain environments–A survey. *IEEE Trans. Evol. Comput.,* 9: 303–317, 2005.

[20] L. Kallel, B. Naudts and C. R. Reeves. Properties of fitness functions and search landscapes. In: L. Kallel, B. Naudts, A. Rogers (eds.), *Theoretical Aspects of Evolutionary Computing,* Springer–Verlag, Berlin Heidelberg New York, 177–208, 2001.

[21] E. F. Keller. A clash of two cultures. *Nature,* 445: 603, 2007.

[22] J. Kennedy, R. C. Eberhart and Y. Shi. *Swarm Intelligence,* Morgan Kaufmann, San Francisco, CA, 2001.

[23] D. Kifer, S. Ben-David and J. Gehrke. Detecting change in data streams. In: M. A. Nascimento et al. (eds.), *Proc. VLDB 2004,* Morgan Kaufmann, San Francisco, 180–191, 2004.

[24] R. Mendes and A. Mohais. DynDE: Differential Evolution for dynamic optimization problems. In D. Corne (ed.), *Proc. Congress on Evolutionary Computation, IEEE CEC 2005,* IEEE Press, Piscataway, NJ, 2808–2815, 2005.

[25] Z. Michalewicz. *Genetic Algorithms + Data Structures = Evolution Programs.* Springer–Verlag, Berlin Heidelberg New York, 1996.

[26] R. W. Morrison and K. A. De Jong. Triggered hypermutation revisited. In: A. Zalzala et al. (eds.), *Proc. Congress on Evolutionary Computation, IEEE CEC 2000,* IEEE Press, Piscataway, NJ, 1025–1032, 2000.

[27] R. W. Morrison. *Designing Evolutionary Algorithms for Dynamic Environments*, Springer–Verlag, Berlin Heidelberg New York, 2004.

[28] T. T. Nguyen and X. Yao. Benchmarking and solving dynamic constrained problems. In: A. Tyrrell (ed.), *Proc. Congress on Evolutionary Computation, IEEE CEC 2009*, IEEE Press, Piscataway, NJ, 690–697, 2009.

[29] G. Paun, G. Rozenberg and A. Salomaa. *The Oxford Handbook of Membrane Computing*, Oxford University Press, Oxford, 2010.

[30] H. Richter. A study of dynamic severity in chaotic fitness landscapes. In: D. Corne (ed.), *Proc. Congress on Evolutionary Computation, IEEE CEC 2005*, IEEE Press, Piscataway, NJ, 2824–2831, 2005.

[31] H. Richter. Evolutionary optimization in spatio–temporal fitness landscapes. In: T. P. Runarsson, H. G. Beyer, E. Burke, J. J. Merelo Guervós, L. D. Whitley, X. Yao (eds.), *Parallel Problem Solving from Nature–PPSN IX*, Springer–Verlag, Berlin Heidelberg New York, 1–10, 2006.

[32] H. Richter. Coupled map lattices as spatio–temporal fitness functions: Landscape measures and evolutionary optimization. *Physica*, D237: 167–186, 2008.

[33] H. Richter and S. Yang. Memory based on abstraction for dynamic fitness functions. In: M. Giacobini et al. (eds.), *EvoWorkshops 2008: Applications of Evolutionary Computing*, Springer–Verlag, Berlin Heidelberg New York, 597–606, 2008.

[34] H. Richter. Detecting change in dynamic fitness landscapes. In A. Tyrrell (ed.), *Proc. Congress on Evolutionary Computation, IEEE CEC 2009*, IEEE Press, Piscataway, NJ, 1613–1620, 2009.

[35] H. Richter and S. Yang. Learning behavior in abstract memory schemes for dynamic optimization problems. *Soft Computing*, 13: 1163–1173, 2009.

[36] H. Richter. Memory design for constrained dynamic optimization problems. In: C. Di Chio et al. (eds.), *Applications of Evolutionary Computation - EvoApplications 2010*, Springer–Verlag, Berlin Heidelberg New York, 552–561, 2010.

[37] H. Richter. Evolutionary optimization and dynamic fitness landscapes: From reaction–diffusion systems to chaotic CML. In: I. Zelinka, S. Celikovsky, H. Richter, G. Chen (eds.), *Evolutionary Algorithms and Chaotic Systems*, Springer–Verlag, Berlin Heidelberg New York, 409–446, 2010.

[38] D. P. Rowbottom. Models in biology and physics: What's the difference? *Found. Sci.*, 14: 281–294, 2009.

[39] A. Simões and E. Costa. Variable–size memory evolutionary algorithm to deal with dynamic environments. In: M. Giacobini et al. (eds.), *EvoWorkshops 2007: Applications of Evolutionary Computing*, Springer–Verlag, Berlin Heidelberg New York, 617–626, 2007.

[40] T. Smith, P. Husbands, P. Layzell and M. O'Shea. Fitness landscapes and evolvability. *Evolut. Comput.*, 10: 1–34, 2002.

[41] P. F. Stadler and C. R. Stephens. Landscapes and effective fitness. *Comm. Theor. Biol.* 8: 389–431, 2003.

[42] T. Stibor, J. Timmis and C. Eckert. A comparative study of real–valued negative selection to statistical anomaly detection techniques. In: C. Jacob et al. (eds.) *Artificial Immune Systems: Proc. ICARIS-2005*, Springer–Verlag, Berlin Heidelberg New York, 262–275, 2005.

[43] J. Timmis, M. Neal and J. Hunt. An artificial immune system for data analysis. *Biosystems*, 55: 143–150, 2000.

[44] J. Timmis, A. Hone, T. Stibor and E. Clark. Theoretical advances in artificial immune systems. *Theoretical Computer Science,* 403: 11–32, 2008.

[45] R. Tinós and S. Yang. A self–organizing random immigrants genetic algorithm for dynamic optimization problems. *Genetic Programming and Evolvable Machines,* 8: 255–286, 2007.

18

Modelling the Innate Immune System

Pedro Rocha, Alexandre Pigozzo, Bárbara Quintela,
Gilson Macedo, Rodrigo Santos and Marcelo Lobosco
Federal University of Juiz de Fora, UFJF
Brazil

1. Introduction

The Human Immune System (HIS) is a complex network composed of specialized cells, tissues, and organs that is responsible for protecting the organism against diseases caused by distinct pathogenic agents, such as viruses, bacteria and other parasites. The first line of defence against pathogenic agents consists of physical barriers of skin and the mucous membranes. If the pathogenic agents breach this first protection barrier, the innate immune system will be ready for recognize and combat them. The innate immune system is therefore responsible for powerful non-specific defences that prevent or limit infections by most pathogenic microorganisms.

The understanding of the innate system is therefore essential, not only because it is the first line of defence of the body, but also because of its quick response. However, its complexity and the intense interaction among several components, make this task extremely complex. Some of its aspects, however, may be better understood if a computational model is used. Modelling and simulation help to understand large complex processes, in particular processes with strongly coupled influences and time-dependent interactions as they occur in the HIS. Also, *in silico* simulations have the advantage that much less investment in technology, resources and time is needed compared to *in vivo* experiments, allowing researchers to test a large number of hypotheses in a short period of time.

A previous work (Pigozzo et al. (2011)) has developed a mathematical and computational model to simulate the immune response to Lipopolysaccharide (LPS) in a microscopic section of a tissue. The LPS endotoxin is a potent immunostimulant that can induce an acute inflammatory response comparable to that of a bacterial infection. A set of Partial Differential Equations (PDEs) were employed to reproduce the spatial and temporal behaviour of antigens (LPS), neutrophils and cytokines during the first phase of the innate response.

Good modelling practices require the evaluation of the confidence in the new proposed model. An important tool used for this purpose is the sensitivity analysis. The sensitivity analysis consists of the study of the impact caused by the variation of input values of a model on the output generated by it. However, this study can be a time consuming task due to the large number of scenarios that must be evaluated. This prohibitive computational cost leads us to develop a parallel version of the sensitivity analysis code using General-purpose Graphics Processing Units (GPGPUs). GPGPUs were chosen because of their ability to process many streams simultaneously. This chapter describes the GPU-based implementation of the sensitivity analysis and also presents some of the sensitivity analysis results. Our experimental results showed that the parallelization was very effective in improving the sensitivity analysis performance, yielding speedups up to 276.

The remainder of this chapter is organized as follows. Section 2 includes the background necessary for understanding this chapter. Section 3 describes the mathematical model implemented. Section 4 describes the implementation of the GPU version of the sensitivity analysis. Section 5 presents some of the results of the sensitivity analysis and the speedup obtained. Section 7 presents related works. Our conclusions and plans of future works are presented in Section 8.

2. Background

2.1 Biological background

The initial response of the body to an acute biological stress, such as a bacterial infection, is an acute inflammatory response (Janeway et al. (2001)). The strategy of the HIS is to keep some resident macrophages on guard in the tissues to look for any signal of infection. When they find such a signal, the macrophages alert the neutrophils that their help is necessary. The cooperation between macrophages and neutrophils is essential to mount an effective defence, because without the macrophages to recruit the neutrophils to the location of infection, the neutrophils would circulate indefinitely in the blood vessels, impairing the control of huge infections.

The LPS endotoxin is a potent immunostimulant that can induce an acute inflammatory response comparable to that of a bacterial infection. After the lyse of the bacteria by the action of cells of the HIS, the LPS can be released in the host, intensifying the inflammatory response and activating some cells of the innate system, such as neutrophils and macrophages.

The LPS can trigger an inflammatory response through the interaction with receptors on the surface of some cells. For example, the macrophages that reside in the tissue recognize a bacterium through the binding of a protein, TLR4, with LPS. The commitment of this receptor activates the macrophage to phagocyte the bacteria, degrading it internally and secreting proteins known as cytokines and chemokines, as well as other molecules.

The inflammation of an infectious tissue has many benefits in the control of the infection. Besides recruiting cells and molecules of innate immunity from blood vessels to the location of the infected tissue, it increases the lymph flux containing microorganisms and cells that carry antigens to the neighbours' lymphoid tissues, where these cells will present the antigens to the lymphocytes and will initiate the adaptive response. Once the adaptive response is activated, the inflammation also recruits the effectors cells of the adaptive HIS to the location of infection.

2.2 General-Purpose computation on Graphics Processing Units - GPGPUS

NVIDIA's Compute Unified Device Architecture (CUDA)(NVIDIA (2007)) is perhaps the most popular platform in use for General-Purpose computation on Graphics Processing Units

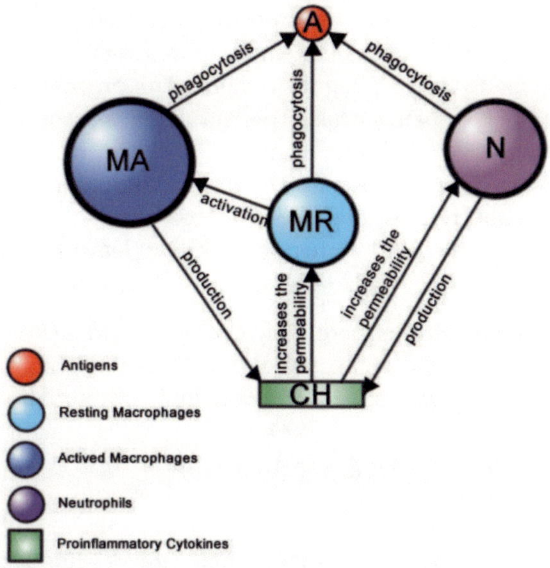

Fig. 1. Relationship between the components.

(GPGPUs). CUDA includes C software development tools and libraries to hide the GPGPU hardware from programmers.

In CUDA, a parallel function is called kernel. A kernel is a function callable from the CPU and executed on the GPU simultaneously by many threads. Each thread is run by a *stream processor*. They are grouped into blocks of threads or just blocks. A set of blocks of threads form a grid. When the CPU calls a kernel, it must specify how many threads will be created at runtime. The syntax that specifies the number of threads that will be created to execute a kernel is formally known as the execution configuration, and is flexible to support CUDA's hierarchy of threads, blocks of threads, and grids of blocks.

Some steps must be followed to use the GPU: first, the device must be initialized. Then, memory must be allocated in the GPU and data transferred to it. The kernel is then called. After the kernel has finished, results must be copied back to the CPU.

3. Mathematical model

The model proposed in this chapter is based on a set of Partial Differential Equations (PDEs) originally proposed by Pigozzo et al. (2011). In the original work, a set of PDEs describe the dynamics of the immune response to LPS in a microscopic section of tissue. In particular, the interactions among antigens (LPS molecules), neutrophils and cytokines were modelled. In this chapter, a simplified model of the innate immune system using ODEs is presented to simulate the temporal behaviour of LPS, neutrophils, macrophages and cytokines during the first phase of the immune response. The main differences between our model and the original one (Pigozzo et al. (2011)) are: a) the current model does not consider the spatial dynamics of the cells and molecules and b) the macrophages in two stages of readiness, resting and activated, are introduced in the current model.

Figure 1 presents schematically the relationship between macrophages, neutrophils, proinflammatory cytokines and LPS. LPS cause a response in both macrophages and neutrophils, that recognize LPS and phagocyte them. The process of phagocytosis induces, in a rapid way, the apoptosis of neutrophils. This induction is associated with the generation of reactive oxygen species (ROS) (Zhang et al. (2003)). The resting macrophages become activated when they find LPS in the tissue. The pro-inflammatory cytokine is produced by both active macrophages and neutrophils after they recognize LPS. It induces an increase in the endothelial permeability allowing more neutrophils to leave the blood vessels and enter the infected tissue.

Our set of equations is given below, where *RM*, *AM*, *A*, *N* and *CH* represent the population of resting macrophages, activated macrophages, LPS, neutrophils and pro-inflammatory cytokines, respectively. The dynamics of LPS is modelled with Equation 1.

$$\begin{cases} \frac{dA}{dt} = -\mu_A A - (\lambda_{N|A}.N + \lambda_{AM|A}.AM + \lambda_{RM|A}.RM).A \\ A(0) = 20 \end{cases} \tag{1}$$

The term $\mu_A A$ models the decay of LPS, where μ_A is its decay rate. The term $-(\lambda_{N|A}.N + \lambda_{AM|A}.AM + \lambda_{RM|A}.RM).A$ models the phagocytosis of LPS by macrophages and neutrophils, where $\lambda_{N|A}$ is the phagocytosis rate of neutrophils, $\lambda_{AM|A}$ is the phagocytosis rate of active macrophages, and $\lambda_{RM|A}$ is the phagocytosis rate of resting macrophages.

Neutrophils are modelled with Equation 2.

$$\begin{cases} permeability_N = (P_N^{max} - P_N^{min}).\frac{CH}{CH+keqch} + P_N^{min} \\ source_N = permeability_N.(N^{max} - N) \\ \frac{dN}{dt} = -\mu_N N - \lambda_{A|N} A.N + source_N \\ N(0) = 0 \end{cases} \tag{2}$$

The term $permeability_N$ uses a Hill equation (Goutelle et al. (2008)) to model how permeability of the endothelium of the blood vessels depends on the local concentration of cytokines. Hill equations are also used, for example, to model drug dose-response relationships (Wagner (1968)).

The idea is to model the increase in the permeability of the endothelium according to the concentration of the pro-inflammatory cytokines into the endothelium. In the Hill equation, P_N^{max} represents the maximum rate of increase of endothelium permeability to neutrophils induced by pro-inflammatory cytokines, P_N^{min} represents the minimum rate of increase of endothelium permeability induced by pro-inflammatory cytokines and *keqch* is the concentration of the pro-inflammatory cytokine that exerts 50% of the maximum effect in the increase of the permeability. The term $\mu_N N$ models the neutrophil apoptosis, where μ_N is the rate of apoptosis. The term $\lambda_{A|N} A.N$ models the neutrophil apoptosis induced by the phagocytosis, where $\lambda_{A|N}$ represent the rate of this induced apoptosis. The term $source_N$ represents the source term of neutrophil, that is, the number of neutrophils that is entering the tissue from the blood vessels. This number depends on the endothelium permeability

($permeability_N$) and the capacity of the tissue to support the entrance of neutrophils (N^{max}), that can also represent the blood concentration of Neutrophils.

The dynamics of cytokine is presented in Equation 3.

$$\begin{cases} \frac{dCH}{dt} = -\mu_{CH}CH + (\beta_{CH|N}N + \beta_{CH|AM}AM).A.(1 - \frac{CH}{chInf}) \\ CH(0) = 0 \end{cases} \tag{3}$$

The term $\mu_{CH}CH$ models the pro-inflammatory cytokine decay, where μ_{CH} is the decay rate. The term $(\beta_{CH|N}N + \beta_{CH|AM}AM).A$ models the production of the pro-inflammatory cytokine by the neutrophils and activated macrophages, where $\beta_{CH|N}$ and $\beta_{CH|AM}$ are the rate of this production by neutrophils and macrophages, respectively.

Equation 4 presents the dynamics of the resting macrophages.

$$\begin{cases} permeability_{RM} = (P^{max}_{RM} - P^{min}_{RM}).\frac{CH}{CH+keqch} + P^{min}_{RM} \\ source_{RM} = permeability_{RM}.(M^{max} - (RM + AM)) \\ \frac{dRM}{dt} = -\mu_{RM}RM - \lambda_{RM|A}.RM.A + source_{RM} \\ RM(0) = 1 \end{cases} \tag{4}$$

The term $permeability_{RM}$ models how permeability of the endothelium of the blood vessels to macrophages depends on the local concentration of cytokines. The term $\mu_{RM}RM$ models the resting macrophage apoptosis, where μ_{RM} is the rate of apoptosis.

Finally, the dynamics of activate macrophages is presented in Equation 5.

$$\begin{cases} \frac{dAM}{dt} = -\mu_{AM}AM + \lambda_{RM|A}.RM.A \\ AM(0) = 0 \end{cases} \tag{5}$$

The term $\mu_{AM}RM$ models the activated macrophage apoptosis, where μ_{RM} is the rate of apoptosis.

4. Implementation

The sensitivity analysis consists in the analysis of impacts caused by variations of parameters and initial conditions of the mathematical model against its dependent variables (Saltelli et al. (2008)). If a parameter causes a drastic change in the output of the problem, after suffering a minor change in its initial value, it is thought that this parameter is sensitive to the problem studied. Otherwise, this variable has little impact in the model. The sensitivity analysis is used to improve the understanding of the mathematical model as it allows us to identify input parameters that are more relevant for the model, i.e. the values of these parameters should be carefully estimated. In this chapter we use a brute force approach to exam the influence of the 19 parameters present in the equation and two of the initial conditions. A small change in the value of each parameter is done, and then the model is solved again for this new parameter set. This process is done many times, since all combinations of distinct values of parameters and initial conditions must be considered. We analyse the impact of changing one coefficient at a time. The parameters and initial conditions were adjusted from -100% to + 100% (in steps of 2%) of their initial values, except for some parameters, that were also adjusted from -100% to + 100%, but in steps of 20%. The combination of all different set of parameters and initial conditions give us a total of 450,000 system of ODEs that must be evaluated in this work.

The sequential code that implements the sensitivity analysis was first implemented in C. Then the code was parallelized using CUDA. The parallel code is based on the idea that each combination of distinct values of parameters and initial conditions can be computed independently by a distinct CUDA thread. The number of threads that will be used during computation depends on the GPU characteristics. In particular, the number of blocks and threads per block are chosen taking into account two distinct values defined by the hardware: a) the warp size and b) the maximum number of threads per block.

The forward Euler method was used for the numerical solution of the systems of ODEs with a time-step of 0.0001 days. The models were simulated to represent a total period equivalent to 5 days after the initial infection.

5. Experimental evaluation

In this section the experimental results obtained by the execution of both versions of our simulator of the innate system, sequential and parallel, are presented. The experiments were performed on a 2.8 GHz Intel Core i7-860 processor, with 8 GB RAM, 32 KB L1 data cache, 8 MB L2 cache with a NVIDIA GeForce 285 GTX. The system runs a 64-bits version of Linux kernel 2.6.31 and version 3.0 of CUDA toolkit. The *gcc* version 4.4.2 was used to compile all versions of our code. The NVIDIA GeForce 285 GTX has 240 stream processors, 30 multiprocessors, each one with 16KB of shared memory, and 1GB of global memory. The number of threads per block are equal to 879, and each block has 512 threads. The codes were executed 3 times to all versions of our simulator, and the average execution time for each version of the code is presented in Table 1. The standard deviation obtained was negligible. The execution times were used to calculate the speedup factor. The speedup were obtained by dividing the sequential execution time of the simulator by its parallel version.

Sequential	285 GTX	Speedup Factor
4,315.47s	15.63s	276.12

Table 1. Serial and parallel execution times. All times are in seconds.

The results reveal that our CUDA version was responsible for a significant improvement in performance: a speedup of 276 was obtained. This expressive gain was due to the embarrassingly parallel nature of computation that must be performed. In particular, the same computation must be performed for a huge amount of data, and there are no dependency and/or communication between parallel tasks.

6. Simulation

To study the importance of some cells, molecules and processes in the dynamics of the innate immune response, a set of simulations were performed for distinct values of parameters and initial conditions. Table 2 presents the initial conditions and the values of the parameters used in the simulations of all cases. Exceptions to the values presented in Table 2 are highlighted in the text.

The complete set of equations that has been simulated, including the initial values used, are presented by Equation 6:

$$\begin{cases} \frac{dA}{dt} = -\mu_A A - (\lambda_{N|A}.N + \lambda_{AM|A}.AM + \lambda_{RM|A}.RM).A \\ A(0) = 20|40 \\ \\ permeability_N = (P_N^{max} - P_N^{min}).\frac{CH}{CH+keqch} + P_N^{min} \\ source_N = permeability_N.(N^{max} - N) \\ \frac{dN}{dt} = -\mu_N N - \lambda_{A|N} A.N + source_N \\ N(0) = 0 \\ \\ permeability_{RM} = (P_{RM}^{max} - P_{RM}^{min}).\frac{CH}{CH+keqch} + P_{RM}^{min} \\ source_{RM} = permeability_{RM}.(M^{max} - (RM + AM)) \\ \frac{dRM}{dt} = -\mu_{RM} RM - \lambda_{RM|A}.RM.A + source_{RM} \\ RM(0) = 1 \\ \\ \frac{dAM}{dt} = -\mu_{AM} AM + \lambda_{RM|A}.RM.A \\ AM(0) = 0 \\ \\ \frac{dCH}{dt} = -\mu_{CH} CH + (\beta_{CH|N} N + \beta_{CH|AM} AM).A.(1 - \frac{CH}{chInf}) \\ CH(0) = 0 \end{cases} \tag{6}$$

It should be noticed that in this case two distinct initial values for $A(0)$ will be used: $A(0) = 20$ and $A(0) = 40$.

The sensitivity analysis has shown that two parameters are relevant to the model: the capacity of the tissue to support the entrance of new neutrophils (N^{max}) and the phagocytosis rate of LPS by neutrophils ($\lambda_{N|A}$).

N^{max} is the most sensitive parameter in the model. The capacity of the tissue to support the entrance of new neutrophils is directed related to the permeability of the endothelial cells, which form the linings of the blood vessels. If a positive adjustment is made in the parameter related to the permeability, then there are more neutrophils entering into the tissue. This larger amount of neutrophils into the tissue has many consequences: first, more cells are phagocyting, so the amount of LPS reduces faster. Second, a smaller amount of resting macrophages becomes active, because there is less LPS into the tissue. Third, a larger amount of cytokines are produced, since neutrophils are the main responsible for this production. If a negative adjustment is made, the inverse effect can be observed: with a smaller amount of neutrophils in the tissue, more resting macrophages become active. Also, a smaller amount of cytokines are produced.

Figures 2 to 6 illustrate this situation. It can be observed that the LPS decays faster when N^{max} achieves its maximum value.

Parameter	Value	Unit	Reference
N_0	0	cell	estimated
CH_0	0	cell	estimated
A_0	20	cell	estimated
RM_0	1	cell	estimated
AM_0	0	cell	estimated
μ_{CH}	7	$1/day$	estimated
μ_N	3.43	$1/day$	estimated
μ_A	0	$1/day$	Su et al. (2009)
μ_{RM}	0.033	$1/day$	Su et al. (2009)
μ_{AM}	0.07	$1/day$	Su et al. (2009)
$\lambda_{N\|A}$	0.55	$\frac{1}{cell.day}$	Su et al. (2009)
$\lambda_{A\|N}$	0.55	$\frac{1}{cell.day}$	Su et al. (2009)
$\lambda_{AM\|A}$	0.8	$\frac{1}{cell.day}$	Su et al. (2009)
$\beta_{CH\|N}$	1	$\frac{1}{cell.day}$	estimated
$\beta_{CH\|AM}$	0.8	$\frac{1}{cell.day}$	estimated
N^{max}	8	$cell$	estimated
MR^{max}	6	$cell$	estimated
P_N^{max}	11.4	$\frac{1}{day}$	based on Price et al. (1994)
P_N^{min}	0.0001	$\frac{1}{day}$	estimated
P_{RM}^{max}	0.1	$\frac{1}{day}$	estimated
P_{RM}^{min}	0.01	$\frac{1}{day}$	estimated
$chInf$	3.6	$cell$	based on de Waal Malefyt et al. (1991)
$keqch$	1	$cell$	estimated
$\lambda_{RM\|A}$	0.1	$\frac{1}{cell.day}$	estimated

Table 2. Initial conditions, parameters and units.

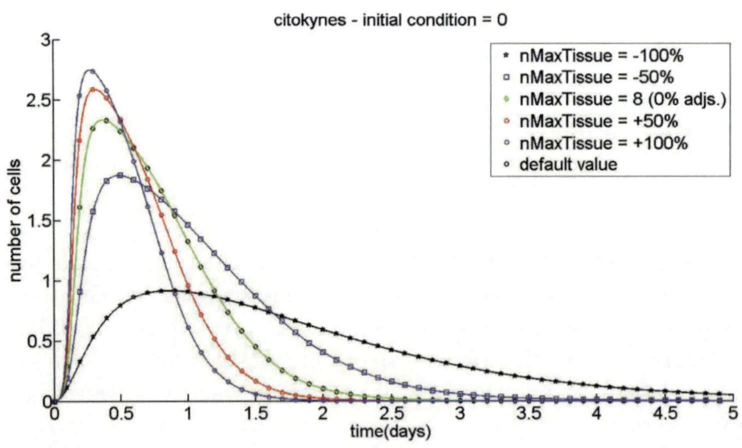

Fig. 2. Temporal evolution of cytokines with $A(0) = 20$ and for distinct values of N^{max}.

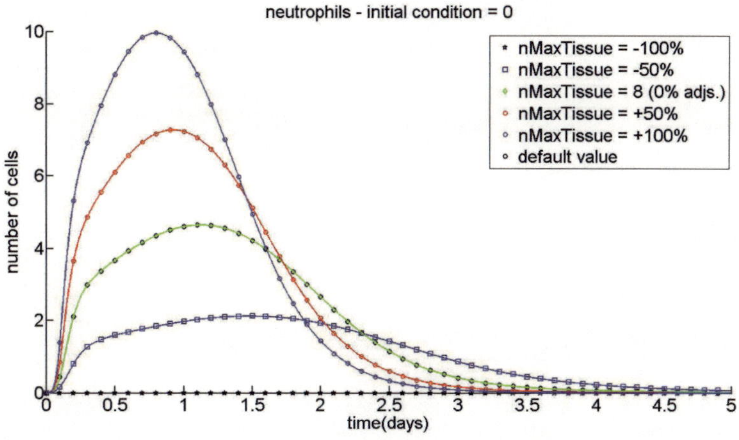

Fig. 3. Temporal evolution of neutrophils with $A(0) = 20$ and for distinct values of N^{max}.

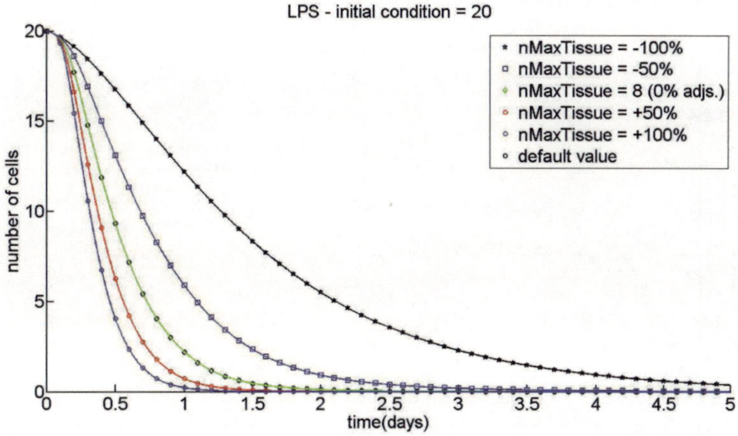

Fig. 4. Temporal evolution of LPS with $A(0) = 20$ and for distinct values of N^{max}.

In the second scenario, with the double of LPS and starting with just one resting macrophage, it can be observed that bringing more neutrophils into the tissue do not reduce the number of resting macrophages that become active. This happens due to the larger amount of LPS in this scenario when compared to the previous one. The larger amount of activated macrophages also explains why the amount of cytokines in this scenario is larger than in the previous one. Figures 7 to 11 present the complete scenario.

The third scenario presents the results obtained when the initial amount of LPS is again equal to 20. This scenario revels that the second most sensitive parameter is $\lambda_{N|A}$. $\lambda_{N|A}$ is responsible for determining how effective is the phagocitosis of the neutrophils in tissue. It can be observed in Figures 12 to 16 that a negative adjustment in this tax makes the neutrophil response to be less effective against LPS, while a positive adjustment in the tax makes the neutrophil response to be more effective. Resting macrophages and activated macrophages are also affected by distinct values of $\lambda_{N|A}$. Increasing the value of $\lambda_{N|A}$ causes the neutrophils

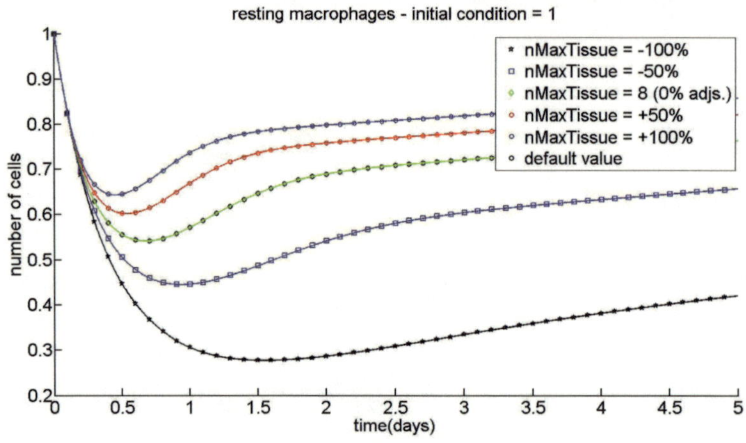

Fig. 5. Temporal evolution of resting macrophages with $A(0) = 20$ and for distinct values of N^{max}.

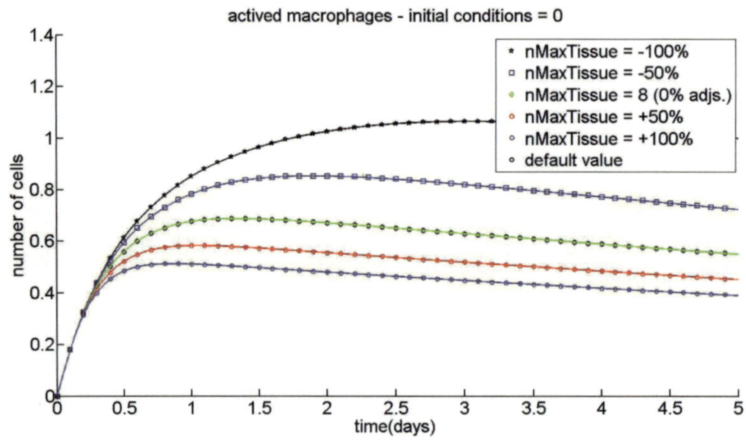

Fig. 6. Temporal evolution of activate macrophages with $A(0) = 20$ and for distinct values of N^{max}.

to produced more cytokines, so more macrophages can migrate into the tissue through blood vessel, and also there are more cells into the tissue that can phagocyte LPS.

The last scenario is presented by Figures 17 to 21. In this scenario, the amount of LPS is doubled when compared to the previous one. It can be observed that distinct values used as initial conditions for LPS only changes how long it takes to the complete elimination of LPS. It can also be observed that both macrophages populations are affected by the larger amount of LPS. In particular, the amount of macrophages is slightly higher in this scenario due to the larger amount of LPS.

7. Related works

This section presents some models and simulators of the HIS found in the literature. Basically two distinct approaches are used: ODEs and PDEs.

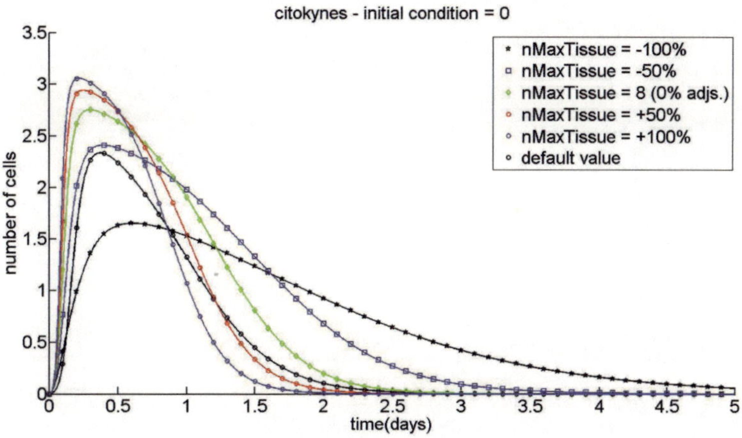

Fig. 7. Temporal evolution of cytokines with $A(0) = 40$ and for distinct values of N^{max}.

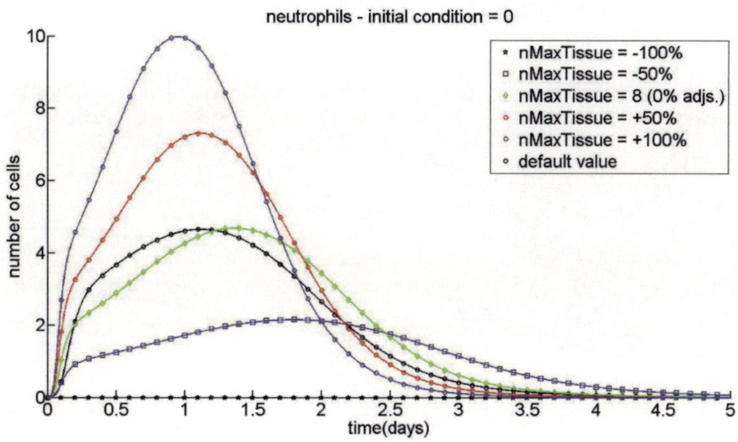

Fig. 8. Temporal evolution of neutrophils with $A(0) = 40$ and for distinct values of N^{max}.

7.1 ODEs models

A model of inflammation composed by ODEs in a three-dimensional domain considering three types of cells/molecules has been proposed by Kumar et al. (2004): the pathogen and two inflammatory mediators. The model was able to reproduce some experimental results depending on the values used for initial conditions and parameters. The authors described the results of the sensitivity analysis and some therapeutic strategies were suggested from this analysis. The work was then extended (Reynolds et al. (2006)) to investigate the advantages of an anti-inflammatory response dependent on time. In this extension, the mathematical model was built from simpler models, called reduced models. The mathematical model (Reynolds et al. (2006)) consists of a system of ODEs with four equations to model: a) the pathogen; b) the active phagocytes; c) tissue damage; and d) anti-inflammatory mediators.

A new adaptation of the first model (Kumar et al. (2004)) was proposed to simulate many scenarios involving repeated doses of endotoxin (Day et al. (2006)). In this work the results

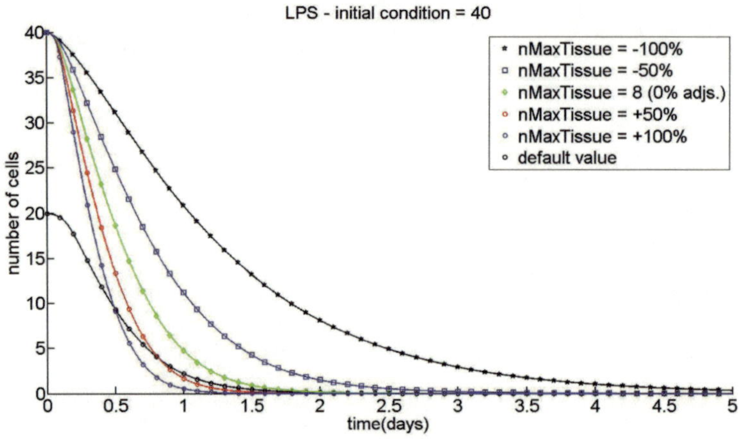

Fig. 9. Temporal evolution of LPS with $A(0) = 40$ and for distinct values of N^{max}.

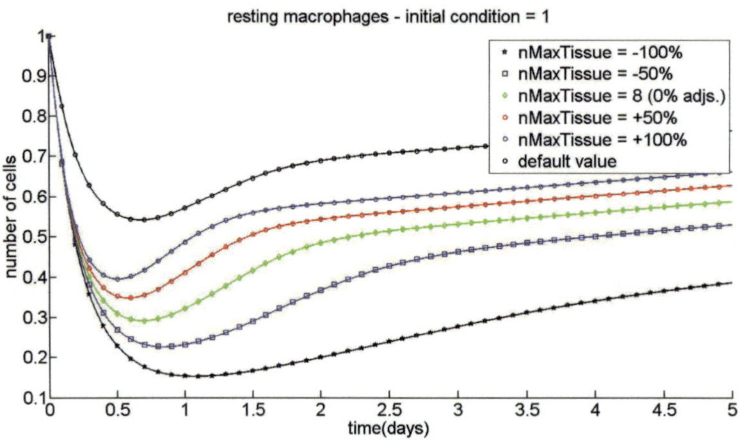

Fig. 10. Temporal evolution of resting macrophages with $A(0) = 40$ and for distinct values of N^{max}.

obtained through experiments with mouse are used to guide the *in silico* experiments seeking to recreate these results qualitatively.

A one-dimensional model to show if and when leukocytes successfully defend the body against a bacterial infection is presented in Keener & Sneyd (1998). A phase-plane method is then used to study the influence of two parameters, the enhanced leukocyte emigration from bloodstream and the chemotactic response of the leukocytes to the attractant.

Finally, one last work (Vodovotz et al. (2006)) developed a more complete system of ODEs of acute inflammation, including macrophages, neutrophils, dendritic cells, Th1 cells, the blood pressure, tissue trauma, effector elements such as iNOS, NO_2^- and NO_3^-, pro-inflammatory and anti-inflammatory cytokines, and coagulation factors. The model has proven to be useful in simulating the inflammatory response induced in mice by endotoxin, trauma and surgery or surgical bleeding, being able to predict to some extent the levels of TNF, IL-10, IL-6 and reactive products of NO (NO_2^- and NO_3^-).

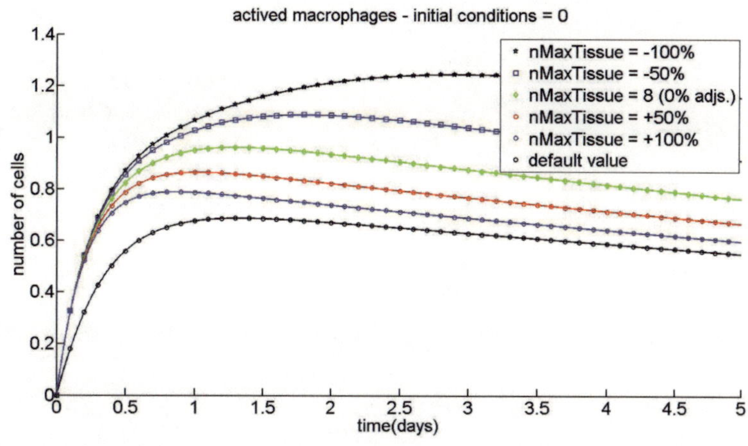

Fig. 11. Temporal evolution of activate macrophages with $A(0) = 40$ and for distinct values of N^{max}.

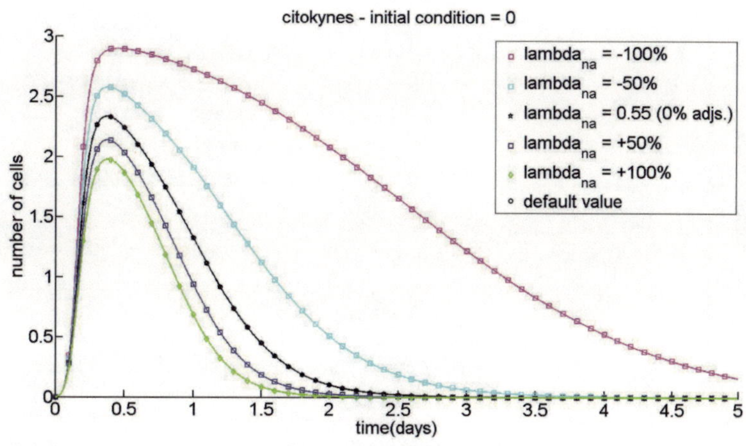

Fig. 12. Temporal evolution of cytokines with $A(0) = 20$ and for distinct values of $\lambda_{N|A}$.

7.2 PDEs models

The model proposed by Su et al. (2009) uses a system of partial differential equations (PDEs) to model not only the functioning of the innate immune system, as well as the adaptive immune system. The model considers the simplest form of antigen, the molecular constituents of pathogens patterns, taking into account all the basic factors of an immune response: antigen, cells of the immune system, cytokines and chemokines. This model captures the following stages of the immune response: recognition, initiation, effector response and resolution of infection or change to a new equilibrium state (*steady state*). The model can reproduce important phenomena of the HIS such as a) temporal order of arrival of cells at the site of infection, b) antigen presentation by dendritic cells, macrophages to regulatory T cells d) production of pro-inflammatory and anti-inflammatory cytokines and e) the phenomenon of chemotaxis.

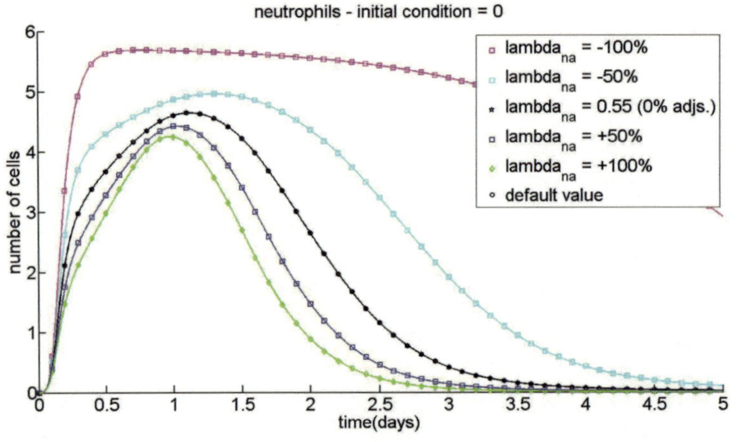

Fig. 13. Temporal evolution of neutrophils with $A(0) = 20$ and for distinct values of $\lambda_{N|A}$.

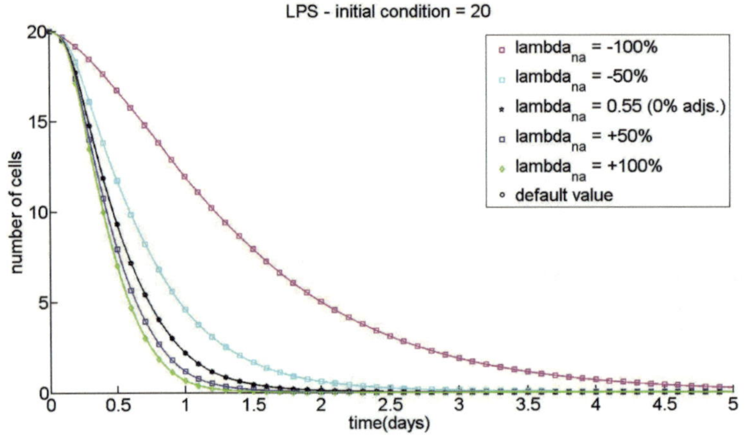

Fig. 14. Temporal evolution of LPS with $A(0) = 20$ and for distinct values of $\lambda_{N|A}$.

Pigozzo et al. (2011) present a PDE model to simulate the immune response to lipopolysaccharide (LPS) in a microscopic section of a tissue, reproducing, for this purpose, the initiation, maintenance and resolution of immune response.

7.3 Other works

Several proposals which attempt to model both the innate and the adaptive HIS can be found in the literature. An ODE model is used to describe the interaction of HIV and tuberculosis with the immune system (Denise & Kirschner (1999)). Other work focus on models of HIV and T-lymphocyte dynamics, and includes more limited discussions of hepatitis C virus (HCV), hepatitis B virus (HBV), cytomegalovirus (CMV) and lymphocytic choriomeningitis virus (LCMV) dynamics and interactions with the immune system (Perelson (2002)). An ODE model of cell-free viral spread of HIV in a compartment was proposed by Perelson et al. (1993). Another interesting work tries to integrate the immune system in the general physiology of the host and considers the interaction between the immune and neuroendocrine system

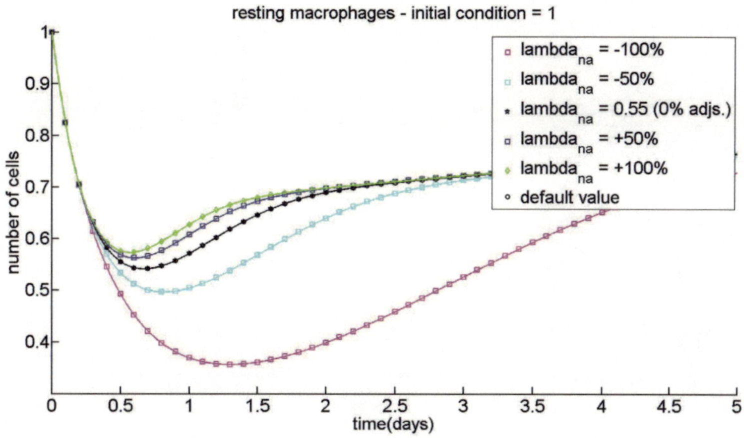

Fig. 15. Temporal evolution of resting macrophages with $A(0) = 20$ and for distinct values of $\lambda_{N|A}$.

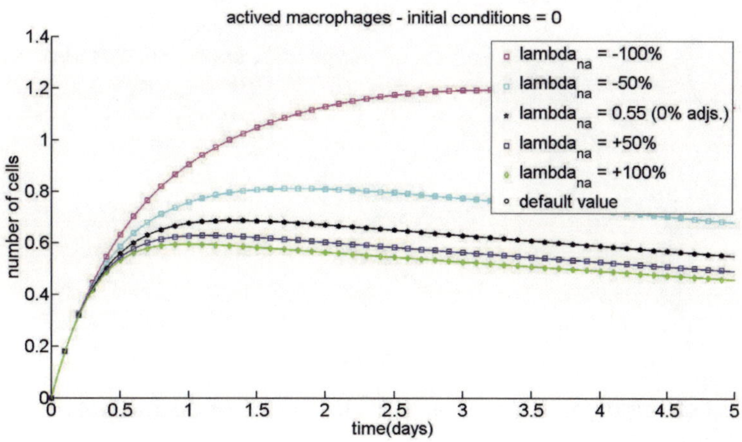

Fig. 16. Temporal evolution of activate macrophages with $A(0) = 20$ and for distinct values of $\lambda_{N|A}$.

(Muraille et al. (1996)). Klein (1980) presents and compares three mathematical models of B cell differentiation and proliferation.

ImmSim (Bezzi et al. (1997); Celada & Seiden (1992)) is a simulator of the HIS that implements the following mechanisms: immunological memory, affinity maturation, effects of hypermutation, autoimmune response, among others. CAFISS (a Complex Adaptive Framework for Immune System Simulation) (Tay & Jhavar (2005)) is a framework used for modelling the immune system, particularly HIV attack. SIMMUNE (Meier-Schellersheim & Mack (1999)) allows users to model cell biological systems based on data that describes cellular behaviour on distinct scales. Although it was developed to simulate immunological phenomena, it can be used in distinct domains. A similar tool is CyCells (Warrender (2004)), designed to study intercellular relationships.

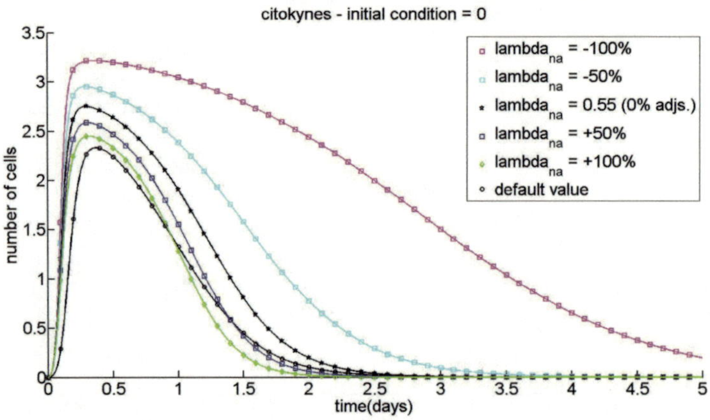

Fig. 17. Temporal evolution of cytokines with $A(0) = 40$ for distinct values of $\lambda_{N|A}$.

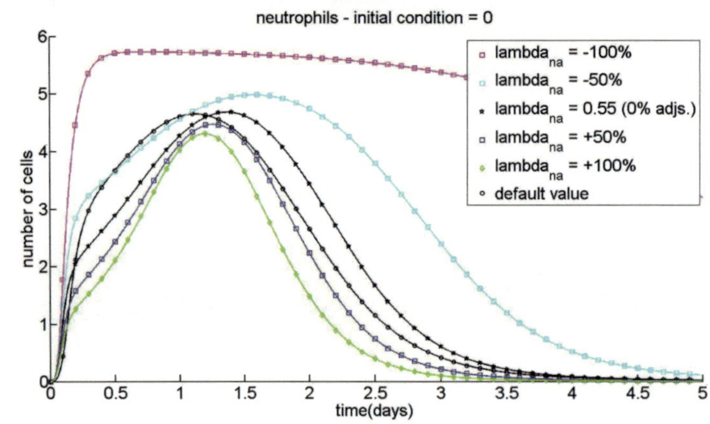

Fig. 18. Temporal evolution of neutrophils with $A(0) = 40$ for distinct values of $\lambda_{N|A}$.

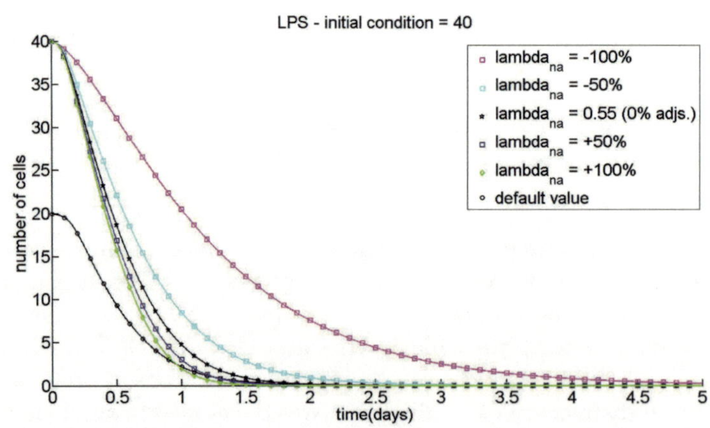

Fig. 19. Temporal evolution of LPS with $A(0) = 40$ for distinct values of $\lambda_{N|A}$.

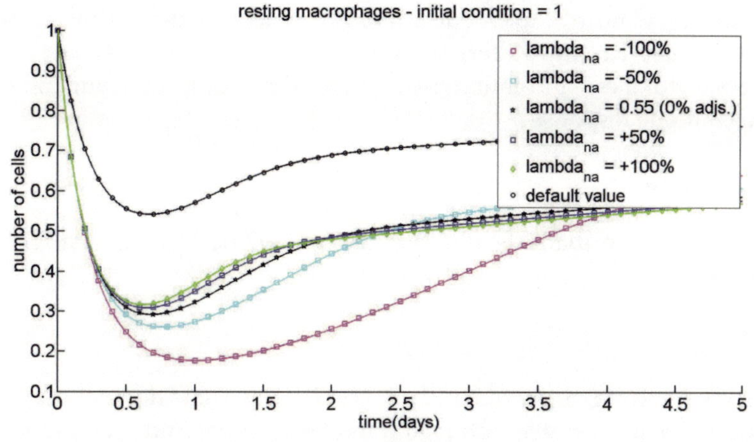

Fig. 20. Temporal evolution of resting macrophages with $A(0) = 40$ for distinct values of $\lambda_{N|A}$.

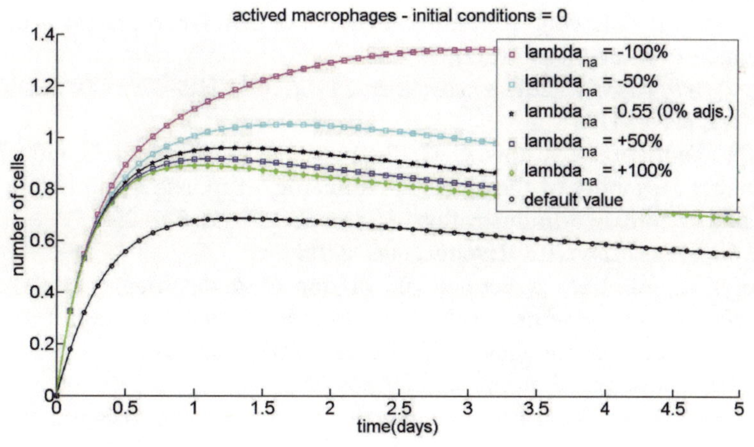

Fig. 21. Temporal evolution of activate macrophages with $A(0) = 40$ for distinct values of $\lambda_{N|A}$.

8. Conclusion and future works

In this chapter we presented the sensitivity analysis of a mathematical model that simulates the immune response to LPS in a microscopic section of a tissue. The results have shown that the two most relevant parameters of the model are: the capacity of the tissue to support the entrance of more neutrophils and the phagocytosis rate of LPS by neutrophils.

The sensitivity analysis can be a time consuming task due to the large number of scenarios that must be evaluated. This prohibitive computational cost leads us to develop a parallel version of the sensitivity analysis code using GPGPUs. Our experimental results showed that the parallelization was very effective in improving the sensitivity analysis performance, yielding speedups up to 276.

As future works, we plan to implement a more complete mathematical model including, for example, new cells (Natural Killer, dendritic cells and the complement system), others proinflammatory cytokines, anti-inflammatory cytokine, molecules and others processes involved in the immune responses.

9. Acknowledgement

The authors would like to thank FAPEMIG, CNPq (479201/2010-2), CAPES and UFJF for supporting this study.

10. References

Bezzi, M., Celada, F., Ruffo, S. & Seiden, P. E. (1997). The transition between immune and disease states in a cellular automaton model of clonal immune response, *Physica A: Statistical and Theoretical Physics* 245(1-2): 145 – 163.
URL: *http://www.sciencedirect.com/science/article/B6TVG-3W34FV4-8/2/992f79c98f0d0e31f1bb36b3f524426d*

Celada, F. & Seiden, P. E. (1992). A computer model of cellular interactions in the immune system, *Immunology Today* 13(2): 56 – 62.
URL: *http://www.sciencedirect.com/science/article/B6VHW-4805SYB-P/2/074bd180cec587021d6ed7b96be84125*

Day, J., Rubin, J., Vodovotz, Y., Chow, C. C., Reynolds, A. & Clermont, G. (2006). A reduced mathematical model of the acute inflammatory response ii. capturing scenarios of repeated endotoxin administration., *J Theor Biol* 242(1): 237–256.
URL: *http://dx.doi.org/10.1016/j.jtbi.2006.02.015*

de Waal Malefyt, R., Abrams, J., Bennett, B., Figdor, C. & de Vries, J. (1991). Interleukin 10(il-10) inhibits cytokine synthesis by human monocytes: an autoregulatory role of il-10 produced by monocytes., *J Exp Med* 174(5): 1209–20–.
URL: *http://ukpmc.ac.uk/abstract/MED/1940799*

Denise & Kirschner (1999). Dynamics of co-infection with m. tuberculosis and hiv-1, *Theoretical Population Biology* 55(1): 94 – 109.
URL: *http://www.sciencedirect.com/science/article/pii/S004058099891382X*

Goutelle, S., Maurin, M., Rougier, F., Barbaut, X., Bourguignon, L., Ducher, M. & Maire, P. (2008). The hill equation: a review of its capabilities in pharmacological modelling, *Fundamental & clinical pharmacology* 22(6): 633–648.
URL: *http://dx.doi.org/10.1111/j.1472-8206.2008.00633.x*

Janeway, C., Murphy, K. P., Travers, P., Walport, M. & Janeway, C. (2001). *Immunobiology*, 5th ed. edn, Garland Science, New York and London.

Keener, J. & Sneyd, J. (1998). *Mathematical physiology*, Springer-Verlag New York, Inc., New York, NY, USA.

Klein, P. (1980). Mathematical models of antibody response, *Folia Microbiologica* 25: 430–438. 10.1007/BF02876697.
URL: *http://dx.doi.org/10.1007/BF02876697*

Kumar, R., Clermont, G., Vodovotz, Y. & Chow, C. C. (2004). The dynamics of acute inflammation, *Journal of Theoretical Biology* 230(2): 145–155.

URL: *http://www.sciencedirect.com/science/article/B6WMD-4D1TSCK-2/2/44a01fc313cd567f0861e5b6c36fc80f*

Meier-Schellersheim, M. & Mack, G. (1999). Simmune, a tool for simulating and analyzing immune system behavior.
URL: *http://www.citebase.org/abstract?id=oai:arXiv.org:cs/9903017*

Muraille, E., Thieffry, D., Leo, O. & Kaufman, M. (1996). Toxicity and neuroendocrine regulation of the immune response: A model analysis, *Journal of Theoretical Biology* 183(3): 285 – 305.
URL: *http://www.sciencedirect.com/science/article/pii/S0022519396902210*

NVIDIA (2007). Nvidia cuda programming guide, *Technical report*, NVIDIA Corporation.

Perelson, A. S. (2002). Modelling viral and immune system dynamics., *Nat Rev Immunol* 2(1): 28–36.
URL: *http://dx.doi.org/10.1038/nri700*

Perelson, A. S., Kirschner, D. E. & de Boer, R. (1993). Dynamics of hiv infection of cd4+ t cells, *Mathematical Biosciences* 114(1): 81 – 125.

Pigozzo, A. B., Macedo, G. C., dos Santos, R. W. & Lobosco, M. (2011). Implementation of a computational model of the innate immune system, *ICARIS*, pp. 95–107.

Price, T., Ochs, H., Gershoni-Baruch, R., Harlan, J. & Etzioni, A. (1994). In vivo neutrophil and lymphocyte function studies in a patient with leukocyte adhesion deficiency type ii, *Blood* 84(5): 1635–1639.
URL: *http://bloodjournal.hematologylibrary.org/cgi/content/abstract/bloodjournal;84/5/1635*

Reynolds, A., Rubin, J., Clermont, G., Day, J., Vodovotz, Y. & Ermentrout, G. B. (2006). A reduced mathematical model of the acute inflammatory response: I. derivation of model and analysis of anti-inflammation, *Journal of Theoretical Biology* 242(1): 220–236.
URL: *http://www.sciencedirect.com/science/article/B6WMD-4JMKWTP-2/2/5ae6086e6a080ecb9bfa17c6f2a947c9*

Saltelli, A., Ratto, M., Andres, T., Campolongo, F., Cariboni, J., Gatelli, D., Saisana, M. & Tarantola, S. (2008). *Global Sensitivity Analysis: The Primer*, 1 edn, Wiley.

Su, B., Zhou, W., Dorman, K. S. & Jones, D. E. (2009). Mathematical modelling of immune response in tissues, *Computational and Mathematical Methods in Medicine: An Interdisciplinary Journal of Mathematical, Theoretical and Clinical Aspects of Medicine* 10: 1748–6718.

Tay, J. C. & Jhavar, A. (2005). Cafiss: a complex adaptive framework for immune system simulation, *Proceedings of the 2005 ACM symposium on Applied computing*, SAC '05, ACM, New York, NY, USA, pp. 158–164.
URL: *http://doi.acm.org/10.1145/1066677.1066716*

Vodovotz, Y., Chow, C. C., Bartels, J., Lagoa, C., Prince, J. M., Levy, R. M., Kumar, R., Day, J., Rubin, J., Constantine, G., Billiar, T. R., Fink, M. P. & Gilles Clermont, K. (2006). In silico models of acute inflammation in animals.

Wagner, J. G. (1968). Kinetics of pharmacologic response i. proposed relationships between response and drug concentration in the intact animal and man, *Journal of Theoretical Biology* 20(2): 173 – 201.
URL: *http://www.sciencedirect.com/science/article/B6WMD-4F1Y9M7-N2/2/9bf7ec729de0947563c9645c61399a34*

Warrender, C. E. (2004). *Modeling intercellular interactions in the peripheral immune system*, PhD thesis, Albuquerque, NM, USA. AAI3156711.

Zhang, B., Hirahashi, J., Cullere, X. & Mayadas, T. N. (2003). Elucidation of molecular events leading to neutrophil apoptosis following phagocytosis, *The Journal of biological chemistry* 278: 28443–28454.

19

A Stochastically Perturbed Particle Swarm Optimization for Identical Parallel Machine Scheduling Problems

Mehmet Sevkli[1] and Aise Zulal Sevkli[2]
[1]*King Saud University, Faculty of Engineering, Department of Industrial Engineering, Riyadh*
[2]*King Saud University, College of Computer and Information Sciences, Department of Information Technology, Riyadh*
Kingdom of Saudi Arabia

1. Introduction

Identical parallel machine scheduling (PMS) problems with the objective of minimizing makespan (C_{max}) is one of the well known NP-hard [1] combinatorial optimization problems. It is unlikely to obtain optimal schedule through polynomial time-bounded algorithms. Small size instances of PMS problem can be solved with reasonable computational time by exact algorithms such as branch-and-bound [2, 3], and the cutting plane algorithm [4]. However, as the problem size increases, the computation time of exact methods increases exponentially. On the other hand, heuristic algorithms generally have acceptable time and memory requirements, but do not guarantee optimal solution. That is, a feasible solution is obtained which is likely to be either optimal or near optimal. The well-known longest processing time (LPT) rule of Graham [5] is a sort of so called list scheduling algorithm. It is known that the rule works very well when makespan is taken as the single criterion [6]. Later, Coffman et al. [7] proposed MULTIFIT algorithm that considers the relation between bin-packing and maximum completion time problems. Yue [8] showed that the MULTIFIT heuristic is not guaranteed to perform better than LPT for every problem. Gupta and Ruiz-Torres [9] developed a LISTFIT algorithm that combines the bin packing method of the MULTIFIT heuristic with multiple lists of jobs. Min and Cheng [10] introduced a genetic algorithm (GA) that outperformed simulated annealing (SA) algorithm. Lee et al. [11] proposed a SA algorithm for the PMS problems and compared their results with the LISTFIT algorithm. Tang and Luo [12] developed a new iterated local search (ILS) algorithm that is based on varying number of cyclic exchanges.

Particle swarm optimization (PSO) is based on the metaphor of social interaction and communication among different spaces in nature, such as bird flocking and fish schooling. It is different from other evolutionary methods in a way that it does not use the genetic operators (such as crossover and mutation), and the members of the entire population are maintained through out the search procedure. Thus, information is socially shared among individuals to direct the search towards the best position in the search space. In a PSO algorithm, each member is called a particle, and each particle moves around in the multi-dimensional search space with a velocity constantly updated by the particle's experience, the experience of the particle's neighbours, and the experience of the whole swarm. PSO was first introduced to optimize various continuous nonlinear functions by Eberhart and Kennedy [13]. PSO has been successfully applied to a wide range of applications such as automated drilling [14], home care worker scheduling [15], neural network training [16], permutation flow shop sequencing problems [17], job shop scheduling problems [18], and task assignment [19]. More information about PSO can be found in Kennedy et al. [20].

The organization of this chapter is as follows: Section II introduces PMS problem, the way how to represent the problem, lower bound of the problem and overview of the classical PSO algorithm. The third section reveals the proposed heuristic algorithm. The computational results are reported and discussed in the fourth section, while the fifth section includes the concluding remarks.

2. Background

2.1 Problem description

The problem of identical parallel machine scheduling is about creating schedules for a set $J = \{J_1, J_2, J_3, \ldots, J_n\}$ of n independent jobs to be processed on a set $M=\{M_1, M_2, M_3, \ldots, M_m\}$ of m identical machines. Each job should be carried out on one of the machines, where the time required for processing job i on a machine is denoted by p_i. The subset of jobs assigned to machine M_i in a schedule is denoted by S_{M_i}. Once a job begins processing, it must be completed without interruption. Furthermore, each machine can process one job at a time, and there is no precedence relation between the jobs. The aim is to find a permutation for the n jobs to machines from set M so as to minimize the maximum completion time, in other words the makespan. The problem is denoted as $P||C_{max}$, where P represents identical parallel machines, the jobs are not constrained, and the objective is to obtain the minimum length schedule. An integer programming formulation of the problem that minimize the makespan is as follows: [5]

$$min\ y$$

subject to:

$$\sum_{j=1}^{m} x_{ij} = 1, \quad 1 \le i \le n, \tag{1}$$

$$y - \sum_{i=1}^{n} p_i x_{ij} \ge 0, \quad 1 \le j \le m \tag{2}$$

where the optimal value of y is C_{max} and x_{ij}=1 when job i is assigned to machine j, otherwise x_{ij}=0.

2.2 Solution representation and lower bound

The solution for the PMS problem is represented as a permutation of integers Π= *{1,..., n}* where Π defines the processing order of the jobs. As mentioned in the text above, three versions of the PSO algorithm are compared in terms of solution quality and CPU time.

In continuous based PSO by Tasgetiren et al. [17], PSO_{spv} , particles themselves do not present permutations. Instead, the SPV rule is used to derive a permutation from the position values of the particle. In discrete PSO by Pan et al.[21] and the proposed algorithm (SPPSO), on the other hand, the particles present permutations themselves.

Jobs	1	2	3	4	5	6	7	8	9
p_i	7	7	6	6	5	5	4	4	4

Table 1. An example of 9-job × 4-machine PMS problem

For all of the three algorithms, the process of finding makespan value for a particle can be illustrated by an example. Namely, let's assume a permutation vector of Π= *{1 8 3 4 5 6 7 2 9}*. By considering 4 parallel machines and 9 jobs, whose processing times are given in Table 1, the makespan value of the given vector is depicted in Figure 1.

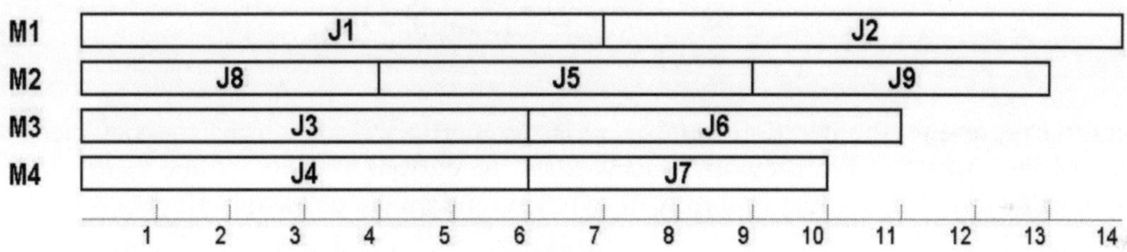

Fig. 1. Shedule generated from random sequence

According to the schedule, each value of the vector is iteratively assigned to the most available machine. First four elements of the permutation vector (1,8,3,4) are assigned to the four machines respectively. The remaining jobs are assigned one by one to the first machine available. For instance, 5 goes to second machine (M_2), since it is the first machine released. If there is more than one available machine at the time, the job will be assigned randomly (ties can be broken arbitrarily). The makespan value of the given sequence is $C_{max}(\Pi)=14$, as can easily be seen in figure 1.

The lower bound for $P||C_{max}$ is calculated as follows [22]:

$$LB(C_{\max}) = \max\left\{\left\lceil \frac{1}{m}\sum_{i=1}^{n} p_i \right\rceil \;\; ; \;\; \max_i\{p_i\}\right\} \tag{3}$$

It is obtained by assuming that preemption is not allowed. If $C_{max}(\Pi)=LB(C_{max})$, the current solution(Π) is optimum. So, lower bound will be used as one of the termination criteria throughout this chapter. The lower bound of the example presented in Table 1 can be calculated as:

$$LB(C_{\max}) = \max\left\{\left\lceil \frac{1}{4}\sum_{i=1}^{9} p_i \right\rceil \; ; \; \max_i\{p_i\}\right\} = \max(12;7) = 12$$

2.3 Classic Particle Swarm Optimization

In PSO, each single solution, called a particle, is considered as an individual, the group becomes a swarm (population) and the search space is the area to explore. Each particle has a fitness value calculated by a fitness function, and a velocity to fly towards the optimum. All particles fly across the problem space following the particle that is nearest to the optimum. PSO starts with an initial population of solutions, which is updated iteration-by-iteration. The principles that govern PSO algorithm can be stated as follows:

- n dimensional position ($X_i = (x_{i1}, x_{i2}, \ldots, x_{in})$) and velocity vector ($V_i = (v_{i1}, v_{i2}, \ldots, v_{in})$ for i^{th} particle starts with a random position and velocity.
- Each particle knows its position and value of the objective function for that position. The best position of ith particle is donated as $P_i = (p_{i1}, p_{i2}, \ldots, p_{in})$, and the best position of the whole swarm as, $G = (g_1, g_2, \ldots, g_n)$ respectively. The PSO algorithm is governed by the following main equations:

$$\begin{aligned} v_{in}^{t+1} &= wv_{in}^{t} + c_1 r_1 (p_{in}^{t} - x_{in}^{t}) + c_2 r_2 (g_i^{t} - x_{in}^{t}), \\ x_{in}^{t+1} &= v_{in}^{t+1} + x_{in}^{t} \end{aligned} \qquad (4)$$

where t represents the iteration number, w is the inertia weight which is a coefficient to control the impact of the previous velocities on the current velocity. c_1 and c_2 are called learning factors. r_1 and r_2 are uniformly distributed random variables in [0,1].

The original PSO algorithm can optimize problems in which the elements of the solution space are continuous real numbers. The major obstacle for successfully applying PSO to combinatorial problems in the literature is due to its continuous nature. To remedy this drawback, Tasgetiren et al. [17] presented the smallest position value (SPV) rule. Another approach to tackle combinatorial problems with PSO is done by Pan et al. [21]. They generate a similar PSO equation to update the particle's velocity and position vectors using one and two cut genetic crossover operators.

3. The proposed Stochastically Perturbed Particle Swarm Optimization algorithm

In this chapter, a stochastically perturbed particle swarm optimization algorithm (SPPSO) is proposed for the PMS problems. The initial population is generated randomly. Initially, each individual with its position, and fitness value is assigned to its personal best (i.e., the best value of each individual found so far). The best individual in the whole swarm with its position and fitness value, on the other hand, is assigned to the global best (i.e., the best particle in the whole swarm). Then, the position of each particle is updated based on the personal best and the global best. These operations in SPPSO are similar to classical PSO algorithm. However, the search strategy of SPPSO is different. That is, each particle in the swarm moves based on the following equations.

$$\begin{aligned} s_1 &= w^t \oplus \eta(X_i^t) \\ w^{t+1} &= w \cdot \beta \\ s_2 &= c_1 \oplus \eta(P_i^t) \\ s_3 &= c_2 \oplus \eta(G^t) \\ X_i^{t+1} &= best(s_1; s_2; s_3) \end{aligned} \tag{5}$$

At each iteration, the position vector of each particle, its personal best and the global best are considered. First of all, a random number of U(0,1) is generated to compare with the inertia weight to decide whether to apply *Insert* function(η) to the particle or not.

Insert function(η) implies the insertion of a randomly chosen job in front (or back sometimes) of another randomly chosen job. For instance, for the PMS problem, suppose a sequence of {3, 5, 6, 7, 8, 9, 1, 2, 4}. In order to apply *Insert* function, we also need to derive two random numbers; one is for determining the job to change place and the other is for the job in front of which the former job is to be inserted. Let's say those numbers are 3 and 5 (that is, the third job will move in front of the fifth. In other words, job no.6 will be inserted in front of job no.8 {3, 5, <u>6</u>, 7, <u>8</u>, 9, 1, 2, 4}). The new sequence will be {3, 5, 7, <u>8</u>, <u>6</u>, 9, 1, 2, 4}.

If the random number chosen is less than the inertia weight, the particle is manipulated with this *Insert* function, and the resulting solution, say s_1, is obtained. Meanwhile, the inertia weight is discounted by a constant factor at each iteration, in order to tighten the acceptability of the manipulated particle for the next generation, that is, to diminish the impact of the randomly operated solutions on the swarm evolution.

The next step is to generate another random number of U(0,1) to be compared with c_1, cognitive parameter, to make a decision whether to apply *Insert* function to personal best of the particle considered. If the random number is less than c_1, then the personal best of the particle undertaken is manipulated and the resulting solution is spared as s_2. Likewise, a third random number of U(0,1) is generated for making a decision whether to manipulate the global best with the *Insert* function. If the random number is less than c_2, social parameter, then *Insert* is applied to the global best to obtain a new solution of s_3. Unlike the case of inertia weight, the values of c_1 and c_2 factors are not increased or decreased iteratively, but are fixed at 0.5. That means the probability of applying *Insert* function to the personal and global bests remains the same. The new replacement solution is selected among s_1, s_2 and s_3, based on their fitness values. This solution may not always be better than the current solution. This is to keep the swarm diverse. The convergence is traced by checking the personal best of each new particle and the global best. As it is seen, proposed equations have all major characteristics of the classical PSO equations. The following pseudo-code describes in detail the steps of the SPPSO algorithm.

It can be seen from the pseudo-code of the algorithm that the algorithm has all major characteristics of the classical PSO, the search strategy of the algorithm is different in a way that the new solution is selected among s_1, s_2 and s_3, based on their fitness values. The selected particle may be worse than the current solution that keep the swarm diverse. The convergence is obtained by changing the personal best of each new particle and the global best.

```
Begin
   Initialize particles (population) randomly
   For each particle
      Calculate fitness value
      Set to position vector and fitness value as personal best (Pi^t)
      Select the best particle and its position vector as global best(Gt)
   End
   Do{
      Update inertia weight
      For each particle
       Apply insert with the probability of inertia weight (s1)
       Apply insert to (Pi^t) with the probability of c1 (s2)
       Apply insert to (Gt) with the probability of c2 (s3)
       Select the best one among the s1,s2 and s3
       Update personal best (Pi^t)
      End
      Update global best (Gt)
   }While (Maximum Iteration is not reached)
  End
```

Fig. 2. Pseudo code of the proposed SPPSO algorithm for PMS problem

4. Computational results

In this section, a comparison study is carried out on the effectiveness of the proposed SPPSO algorithm. SPPSO was exclusively tested in comparison with two other recently introduced PSO algorithms: PSO_{spv} algorithm of Tasgetiren et al. [17] and DPSO algorithm of Pan et al. [21]. Two experimental frameworks, namely E1 and E2, are considered implying the type of discrete uniform distribution used to generate job-processing times. That is, the processing time of each job is generated by using uniform distribution of U[1,100] and U[100,800] for experiments E1 and E2 respectively. All SPPSO, PSO_{spv} and DPSO algorithms are coded in C and run on a PC with the configuration of 2.6 GHz CPU and 512MB memory. The size of the population considered by all algorithms is the number of jobs (n).

For SPPSO and DPSO, the social and cognitive parameters were taken as $c_1 = c_2 = 0.5$, initial inertia weight is set to 0.9 and never decreased below 0.40, and the decrement factor β is fixed at 0.999. For the PSO_{spv} algorithm, the social and cognitive parameters were fixed at $c_1 = c_2 = 2$, initial inertia weight is set to 0.9 and never decreased below 0.40, and the decrement factor β is selected as 0.999. The algorithms were run for $20000/n$ iterations. All the there algorithms were applied without embedding any kind of local search.

The instances of problems were generated for 3, 4, 5, 10, 20, 30, 40, 50 machines and 20, 50, 100, 200, and 500 jobs. In order to allow for the variations, 10 instances are generated for each problem size. Hence, the overall number of instances added up to 350. The measures considered in this chapter are mainly about the solution quality. The performance measure is a relative quality measure, C/LB, where C is the result achieved (makespan) by the algorithm and LB is the lower bound of the instance which is calculated in Eq.(3). Once C catches LB, the index results 1.0, otherwise remains larger.

		PSO_{spv}			DPSO			SPPSO		
m	n	min	avg	max	min	avg	max	min	avg	max
3	20	1.000	1.000	1.000	1.000	1.000	1.000	1.000	1.000	1.000
	50	1.000	1.000	1.000	1.000	1.000	1.000	1.000	1.000	1.000
	100	1.000	1.000	1.000	1.000	1.000	1.000	1.000	1.000	1.000
	200	1.000	1.000	1.000	1.000	1.000	1.000	1.000	1.000	1.000
	500	1.000	1.000	1.000	1.000	1.000	1.000	1.000	1.000	1.000
4	20	1.000	1.000	1.000	1.000	1.000	1.000	1.000	1.000	1.000
	50	1.000	1.000	1.000	1.000	1.000	1.000	1.000	1.000	1.000
	100	1.000	1.000	1.000	1.000	1.000	1.000	1.000	1.000	1.000
	200	1.000	1.000	1.000	1.000	1.000	1.000	1.000	1.000	1.000
	500	1.000	1.000	1.000	1.000	1.000	1.000	1.000	1.000	1.000
5	20	1.000	1.001	1.005	1.000	1.001	1.005	1.000	1.001	1.005
	50	1.000	1.000	1.002	1.000	1.000	1.000	1.000	1.000	1.000
	100	1.000	1.000	1.001	1.000	1.000	1.000	1.000	1.000	1.000
	200	1.000	1.000	1.000	1.000	1.000	1.000	1.000	1.000	1.000
	500	1.000	1.000	1.000	1.000	1.000	1.000	1.000	1.000	1.000
10	20	1.050	1.091	1.168	1.050	1.091	1.168	1.050	1.091	1.168
	50	1.000	1.002	1.004	1.004	1.005	1.008	1.000	1.001	1.004
	100	1.000	1.001	1.002	1.002	1.003	1.005	1.000	1.000	1.002
	200	1.001	1.002	1.002	1.001	1.002	1.002	1.000	1.001	1.001
	500	1.001	1.001	1.002	1.001	1.001	1.001	1.000	1.000	1.001
20	50	1.015	1.026	1.050	1.033	1.043	1.053	1.009	1.024	1.050
	100	1.007	1.009	1.013	1.025	1.029	1.037	1.004	1.009	1.013
	200	1.006	1.007	1.010	1.013	1.015	1.018	1.004	1.006	1.008
	500	1.004	1.006	1.007	1.006	1.007	1.009	1.002	1.003	1.005
30	50	1.066	1.154	1.266	1.076	1.161	1.266	1.066	1.154	1.266
	100	1.013	1.022	1.028	1.043	1.061	1.072	1.019	1.029	1.039
	200	1.009	1.017	1.021	1.032	1.037	1.043	1.014	1.017	1.020
	500	1.009	1.011	1.015	1.011	1.016	1.021	1.008	1.009	1.011
40	50	1.282	1.538	1.707	1.282	1.538	1.707	1.282	1.538	1.707
	100	1.033	1.047	1.067	1.084	1.115	1.142	1.042	1.055	1.061
	200	1.021	1.028	1.034	1.054	1.067	1.075	1.028	1.035	1.042
	500	1.016	1.019	1.022	1.025	1.030	1.031	1.016	1.020	1.026
50	100	1.070	1.088	1.114	1.156	1.184	1.220	1.070	1.097	1.140
	200	1.036	1.044	1.053	1.081	1.096	1.106	1.049	1.057	1.065
	500	1.023	1.027	1.030	1.034	1.043	1.046	1.028	1.032	1.035
Average		**1.019**	**1.033**	**1.046**	**1.029**	**1.044**	**1.058**	**1.020**	**1.034**	**1.048**

Table 2. Results for experiment E1:p~U(1,100)

		PSO_{spv}			DPSO			SPPSO		
m	**n**	**min**	**avg**	**max**	**min**	**avg**	**max**	**min**	**avg**	**max**
3	20	1.000	1.000	1.000	1.000	1.000	1.000	1.000	1.000	1.000
	50	1.000	1.000	1.000	1.000	1.000	1.000	1.000	1.000	1.000
	100	1.000	1.000	1.000	1.000	1.000	1.000	1.000	1.000	1.000
	200	1.000	1.000	1.000	1.000	1.000	1.000	1.000	1.000	1.000
	500	1.000	1.000	1.000	1.000	1.000	1.000	1.000	1.000	1.000
4	20	1.000	1.001	1.001	1.000	1.000	1.001	1.000	1.000	1.001
	50	1.000	1.000	1.000	1.000	1.000	1.000	1.000	1.000	1.000
	100	1.000	1.000	1.000	1.000	1.000	1.000	1.000	1.000	1.000
	200	1.000	1.000	1.000	1.000	1.000	1.000	1.000	1.000	1.000
	500	1.000	1.000	1.000	1.000	1.000	1.000	1.000	1.000	1.000
5	20	1.001	1.002	1.003	1.001	1.002	1.003	1.001	1.001	1.002
	50	1.000	1.000	1.000	1.000	1.000	1.000	1.000	1.000	1.000
	100	1.000	1.000	1.000	1.000	1.000	1.000	1.000	1.000	1.000
	200	1.000	1.000	1.000	1.000	1.000	1.000	1.000	1.000	1.000
	500	1.000	1.000	1.000	1.000	1.000	1.000	1.000	1.000	1.000
10	20	1.046	1.071	1.128	1.040	1.068	1.128	1.040	1.068	1.128
	50	1.001	1.003	1.005	1.003	1.006	1.010	1.001	1.002	1.003
	100	1.000	1.001	1.001	1.003	1.004	1.004	1.001	1.001	1.001
	200	1.000	1.000	1.001	1.001	1.002	1.003	1.000	1.001	1.001
	500	1.000	1.000	1.000	1.000	1.001	1.002	1.000	1.000	1.001
20	50	1.022	1.067	1.113	1.026	1.037	1.054	1.011	1.019	1.025
	100	1.012	1.016	1.021	1.012	1.023	1.029	1.006	1.006	1.007
	200	1.002	1.005	1.010	1.011	1.014	1.017	1.003	1.003	1.004
	500	1.000	1.001	1.002	1.005	1.007	1.009	1.001	1.002	1.003
30	50	1.080	1.122	1.195	1.096	1.128	1.195	1.080	1.123	1.195
	100	1.016	1.029	1.043	1.038	1.055	1.065	1.012	1.015	1.016
	200	1.012	1.017	1.022	1.027	1.033	1.037	1.008	1.010	1.012
	500	1.005	1.006	1.007	1.012	1.015	1.017	1.005	1.007	1.008
40	50	1.268	1.378	1.534	1.268	1.378	1.534	1.268	1.378	1.534
	100	1.024	1.069	1.095	1.077	1.093	1.102	1.022	1.029	1.036
	200	1.016	1.022	1.028	1.046	1.057	1.066	1.015	1.019	1.021
	500	1.009	1.010	1.011	1.022	1.025	1.027	1.011	1.012	1.014
50	100	1.034	1.052	1.084	1.121	1.154	1.166	1.047	1.060	1.084
	200	1.007	1.011	1.022	1.076	1.086	1.099	1.026	1.032	1.035
	500	1.001	1.003	1.007	1.034	1.039	1.044	1.015	1.019	1.022
Average		**1.016**	**1.025**	**1.038**	**1.026**	**1.035**	**1.046**	**1.016**	**1.023**	**1.033**

Table 3. Results for experiment E2:p~U(100,800)

		PSO$_{spv}$				DPSO				SPPSO			
		p~U(1,100)		p~U(100,800)		p~U(1,100)		p~U(100,800)		p~U(1,100)		p~U(100,800)	
m	n	nopt	CPU	nopt	CPU	nopt	CPU	nopt	CPU	nopt	CPU	nopt	CPU
3	20	10	0.008	10	0.266	10	0.014	10	0.308	10	0.005	10	0.241
	50	10	0.015	10	0.571	10	0.008	10	0.077	10	0.003	10	0.029
	100	10	0.038	9	2.020	10	0.010	10	0.091	10	0.005	10	0.023
	200	10	0.310	9	8.054	10	0.044	10	0.239	10	0.019	10	0.062
	500	10	3.172	10	57.143	10	0.259	10	1.437	10	0.083	10	0.180
4	20	10	0.112	1	1.007	10	0.201	3	0.383	10	0.096	4	0.406
	50	10	0.013	2	0.836	10	0.055	7	0.294	10	0.024	10	0.202
	100	10	0.027	9	1.676	10	0.059	8	0.355	10	0.019	10	0.126
	200	10	0.202	9	4.391	10	0.115	7	0.865	10	0.053	10	0.239
	500	10	3.169	10	11.438	10	1.085	10	3.635	10	0.234	10	0.485
5	20	7	0.206	0	0.603	8	0.218	0	0.363	9	0.233	0	0.430
	50	9	0.084	8	0.678	10	0.134	1	0.274	10	0.052	5	0.286
	100	8	0.028	5	2.308	10	0.199	3	0.424	10	0.072	9	0.255
	200	9	0.408	9	4.877	10	0.397	2	1.023	10	0.127	9	0.357
	500	6	3.177	9	15.739	10	2.502	3	4.576	10	0.453	9	0.720
10	20	0	0.414	0	0.429	0	0.374	0	0.401	0	0.559	0	0.449
	50	5	0.799	0	0.922	0	0.322	0	0.329	8	0.344	0	0.399
	100	4	0.778	1	2.853	0	0.512	0	0.542	8	0.354	0	0.435
	200	0	0.208	1	10.314	0	1.189	0	1.259	5	0.630	0	0.673
	500	0	3.194	5	52.414	0	4.869	0	5.207	2	1.347	0	1.439
20	50	0	0.960	0	1.514	0	0.438	0	0.446	0	0.450	0	0.471
	100	0	2.840	0	2.883	0	0.627	0	0.650	0	0.510	0	0.551
	200	0	10.385	0	10.671	0	1.397	0	1.451	0	0.806	0	0.862
	500	0	52.525	0	67.284	0	5.334	0	5.643	0	1.750	0	1.853
30	50	0	1.636	0	1.631	0	0.459	0	0.469	0	0.485	0	0.504
	100	0	2.842	0	2.898	0	0.643	0	0.674	0	0.561	0	0.607
	200	0	10.495	0	11.330	0	1.455	0	1.532	0	0.906	0	0.972
	500	0	59.247	0	66.154	0	5.550	0	5.940	0	1.978	0	2.324
40	50	0	1.684	0	1.636	0	0.497	0	0.522	0	0.518	0	0.590
	100	0	2.984	0	2.873	0	0.699	0	0.742	0	0.620	0	0.726
	200	0	10.625	0	10.531	0	1.568	0	1.667	0	1.022	0	1.164
	500	0	59.573	0	65.551	0	5.829	0	6.292	0	2.244	0	2.548
50	100	0	3.658	0	3.626	0	0.813	0	0.861	0	0.697	0	0.745
	200	0	10.702	0	10.556	0	1.680	0	1.763	0	1.140	0	1.247
	500	0	65.759	0	65.793	0	6.117	0	6.465	0	2.521	0	2.844
Total		**148**		**117**		**148**		**94**		**172**		**126**	
Average			**8.922**		**14.385**		**1.305**		**1.634**		**0.598**		**0.727**

Table 4. Results for both experiments

The results for the instances with different sizes are shown in Table 3 and Table 4, where the minimum, average and maximum of the C/LB ratio are presented. Each line summarizes the values for the 10 instances of each problem size, where 10 replications are performed for each instance.

The result for the experiment E1, in which processing times are generated by using U(1,100) are summarized in Table 2. In this experiment, it is found that the minimum, average and maximum values of the ratios are quite similar for SPPSO and PSO_{spv}. On the other hand, SPPSO and PSO_{spv} performed better than DPSO.

The result for the experiment E2 in which processing times are generated by using U(100,800) are summarized in Table 3. In this experiment, there is also no significant difference between SPPSO and PSO_{spv}. However, in terms of max ratio performance SPPSO performed slightly better than PSO_{spv}. In addition, PSO_{spv} and SPPSO are also better than DPSO for all the three ratios in this experiment.

Table 4 shows the number of times the optimum is reached within the group (nopt) for each algorithm and their average CPU times in seconds for each experiment. Total number of optimum solutions obtained by PSO_{spv}, DPSO and SPPSO for the both experiment are summarized as (148,148,172) and (117, 94,126) respectively. Here, the superiority of SPPSO over PSO_{spv} and DPSO is more pronounced in terms of number of total optimum solutions obtained.

In terms of the average CPU, SPPSO shows better performance than PSO_{spv} and DSPO. SPPSO (0.598, 0.727) is about 15 times faster than PSO_{spv} (8.922, 14,395) and about 2 times faster than DPSO (1.305, 1.634) in both experiments.

5. Conclusion

In this chapter, a stochastically perturbed particle swarm optimization algorithm (SPPSO) is proposed for identical parallel machine scheduling (PMS) problems. The SPPSO has all major characteristics of the classical PSO. However, the search strategy of SPPSO is different. The algorithm is applied to (PMS) problem and compared with two recent PSO algorithms. The algorithms are kept standard and not extended by embedding any local search. It is concluded that SPPSO produced better results than DPSO and PSO_{spv} in terms of number of optimum solutions obtained. In terms of average relative percent deviation, there is no significant difference between SPPSO and PSO_{spv}. However, they are better than DPSO.

It also should be noted that, since PSO_{spv} considers each particle based on three key vectors; position (X_i), velocity (V_i), and permutation (Π_i), it consumes more memory than SPPSO. In addition, since DPSO uses one and two cut crossover operators in every iteration, implementation of DPSO to combinatorial optimization problems is rather cumbersome. The proposed algorithm can be applied to other combinatorial optimization problems such as flow shop scheduling, job shop scheduling etc. as future work.

6. References

[1] Garey MR, Johnson DS (1979) Computers and intractability: a guide to the theory of NP completeness. Freeman, San Francisco, California

[2] Van deVelde, S. L. (1993) "Duality-based algorithms for scheduling unrelated parallel machines". ORSA Journal on Computing, 5, 192–205.

[3] Dell Amico, M., Martello, S. (1995) "Optimal scheduling of tasks on identical parallel processors", ORSA Journal on Computing 7, 191-200.

[4] Mokotoff, E. (2004). "An exact algorithm for the identical parallel machine scheduling problem", European Journal of Operational Research, 152, 758–769.

[5] Graham, R. L., (1969). "Bounds on multiprocessor timing anomalies. SIAM", Journal of Applied Mathematics, 17, 416-429.

[6] Blazewicz, J ., Ecker, K., Pesch, E., Schmidt, G., and Weglarz, J., (1996), "Scheduling Computer and Manufacturing Systems". (Berlin: Springer).

[7] Coffman EG, Garey MR, Johnson DS, (1978). "An application of bin-packing to multi-processor scheduling". SIAM Journal of Computing 7, 1–17.

[8] Yue, M., (1990) "On the exact upper bound for the MULTIFIT processor algorithm", Annals of Operations Research, 24, 233-259

[9] Gupta JND, Ruiz-Torres AJ (2001) "A LISTFIT heuristic for minimizing makespan on identical parallel machines". Prod Plan Control 12:28–36

[10] Min, L.,Cheng, W.(1999) "A genetic algorithm for the minimizing the makespan in case of scheduling identical parallel machines", Artificial Intelligence in Engineering 13, 399-403

[11] Lee WC, Wu CC, Chen P (2006) "A simulated annealing approach to makespan minimization on identical parallel machines". Intelligent Journal of Advanced Manufacturing Technology 31, 328–334.

[12] Tang L,, Luo J. (2006) "A New ILS Algorithm for Parallel Machine Scheduling Problems", Journal of Intelligent Manufacturing 17 (5), 609-619

[13] Eberhart, R.C., and Kennedy, J., (1995) "A new optimizer using particle swarm theory, Proceedings of the Sixth International Symposium on Micro Machine and Human Science", Nagoya, Japan, 1995, 39-43.

[14] Onwubolu, G.C. and M. Clerc. (2004). "Optimal Operating Path for Automated Drilling Operations by a New Heuristic Approach Using Particle Swarm Optimisation." International Journal of Production Research 42(3), 473-491

[15] Akjiratikarl,C., Yenradee,P., Drake,P.R. (2007), "PSO-based algorithm for home care worker scheduling in the UK", Computers & Industrial Engineering 53(4), 559-583

[16] Van den Bergh, F. and A.P. Engelbecht. (2000). "Cooperative Learning in Neural Networks Using Particle Swarm Optimizers." South African Computer Journal 26, 84-90.

[17] Tasgetiren, M.F., Liang, Y.C., Sevkli, M. and Gencyilmaz, G, (2007) "Particle Swarm Optimization Algorithm for Makespan and Total Flowtime Minimization in Permutation Flowshop Sequencing Problem", European Journal of Operational Research 177 (3), 1930-1947

[18] Sha,D.Y., Hsu, C-Y, (2006) "A hybrid particle swarm optimization for job shop scheduling problem", Computers & Industrial Engineering, 51(4),791-808

[19] Salman, A., I. Ahmad, and S. Al-Madani. (2003). "Particle Swarm Optimization for Task Assignment Problem." Microprocessors and Microsystems 26, 363-371.

[20] Kennedy, J., R.C. Eberhart, and Y. Shi. (2001). Swarm Intelligence, San Mateo, Morgan Kaufmann, CA, USA.

[21] Pan, Q-K, Tasgetiren, M.F., and Liang,Y-C, (2008) A discrete particle swarm optimization algorithm for the no-wait flowshop scheduling problem, Computers & Operations Research, Vol.35(9), 2807-2839.
[22] Pinedo, M. (1995) Scheduling: theory, algorithm, and systems, Prentice hall, Englewood cliffs, New Jersey

Part 4

Hybrid Bio-Inspired Computational Algorithms

20

Performance Study of Cultural Algorithms Based on Genetic Algorithm with Single and Multi Population for the MKP

Deam James Azevedo da Silva[1], Otávio Noura Teixeira[2] and Roberto Célio Limão de Oliveira[1]
[1]*Universidade Federal do Pará (UFPA),*
[2]*Centro Universitário do Estado do Pará (CESUPA)*
Brazil

1. Introduction

Evolutionary Computation (EC) is inspired from by evolution that explores the solution space by gene inheritance, mutation, and selection of the fittest candidate solutions. Since their inception in the 1960s, Evolutionary Computation has been used in various hard and complex optimization problems in search and optimization such as: combinatorial optimization, functions optimization with and without constraints, engineering problems and others (Adeyemo, 2011). This success is in part due to the unbiased nature of their operations, which can still perform well in situations with little or no domain knowledge (Reynolds, 1999). The basic EC framework consists of fairly simple steps like definition of encoding scheme, population generation method, objective function, selection strategy, crossover and mutation (Ahmed & Younas, 2011). In addition, the same procedures utilized by EC can be applied to diverse problems with relatively little reprogramming.

Cultural Algorithms (CAs), as well as Genetic Algorithm (GA), are evolutionary models that are frequently employed in optimization problems. Cultural Algorithms (CAs) are based on knowledge of an evolutionary system and were introduced by Reynolds as a means of simulating cultural evolution (Reynolds, 1994). CAs algorithms implements a dual mechanism of inheritance where are inherited characteristics of both the level of the population as well as the level of the area of belief space (culture). Algorithms that use social learning are higher than those using individual learning, because they present a better and faster convergence in the search for solutions (Reynolds, 1994). In CAs the characteristics and behaviors of individuals are represented in the Population Space. This representation can support any population-based computational model such as Genetic Algorithms, Evolutionary Programming, Genetic Programming, Differential Evolution, Immune Systems, among others (Jin & Reynolds, 1999).

Multidimensional Knapsack Problem (MKP) is a well-known nondeterministic-polynomial time-hard combinatorial optimization problem, with a wide range of applications, such as cargo loading, cutting stock problems, resource allocation in computer systems, and economics (Tavares et al., 2008). MKP has received wide attention from the operations research community, because it embraces many practical problems. In addition, the MKP can be seen as a general model for any kind of binary problems with positive coefficients (Glover & Kochenberger, 1996).

Many researchers have proposed the high potential of the hybrid-model for the solution of problems (Gallardo et al., 2007). The algorithms presented in this work to solve MKP are a combination of CAs with a Multi Population model. The Multi Population model is the division of a population into several smaller ones, usually called the island model. Each sub-population runs a standard sequential evolution proceeds, as if it were isolated from the rest, with occasional migration of individuals between sub-populations (Tomassini, 2005).

In order to conduct an investigation to discover improvements for MKP, this work is centered in the knowledge produced from CAs through the evolutionary process that utilizes a population-based Genetic Algorithm model, using various MKP benchmarks found in the literature. In addition, there is an interest in investigating how to deal with the Cultural Algorithms considering a population-based in Genetic Algorithms.

So as to compare test results, we implemented the follows algorithms: the standard cultural algorithm with Single Population (also known as standard CA or CA-S) and Cultural Algorithm with Multi Population defined as CA-IM with two versions: CA-IM_1 which has fixed values for genetic operators (recombination and mutation) and CA-IM_2 which does not have fixed values for genetic operators because these values are generated randomly. In order to evaluate the performance of the CA-IM algorithms, some comparison testing will be conducted with other two algorithms based on Distributed GA, called DGA and DGA-SRM (Aguirre et al., 2000).

The outline of the paper is as follows: in Section 2, a description with formal definition of the MKP problem and an overview of Cultural Algorithms are presented. Section 3 shows an alternative approach that explores the multi population model with Cultural Algorithms and explores how the interaction process occurs among various sub-populations. Our experimental results are shown in Section 4 and finally we show some conclusions in Section 5.

2. Background

Since the introduction of the Knapsack problems some algorithm techniques such as brute force, conventional algorithms, dynamic programming, greedy approach and approximation algorithm have been proposed (Ahmed & Younas, 2011).

Evolutionary algorithms (EAs) have been widely applied to the MKP and have shown to be effective for searching and finding good quality solutions (Chu & Beasley, 1998). It is important to note that MKP is considered a NP hard problem; hence any dynamic programming solution will produce results in exponential time. In the last few years, Genetic Algorithms (GAs) have been used to solve the NP-complete problems and have shown to be very well suited for solving larger Knapsack Problems (Fukunaga & Tazoe, 2009; Gunther, 1998; Sivaraj & Ravichandran, 2011). For larger knapsack problems, the efficiency of approximation algorithms is limited in both solution quality and computational cost (Ahmed & Younas, 2011). Spillman's experiment, which applies the GA to the knapsack problem, shows that the GA does not have a good performance in relatively small size problem, but works quite well in problems that include a huge number of elements (Spillman, 1995). There are many packing problems where evolutionary methods have been applied. The simplest optimization problem and one of the most studied is the one-dimensional (zero–one or 0-1) knapsack problem (Ahmed & Younas, 2011), which given a knapsack of a certain capacity, and a set of items, each one having a particular size and value, finds the set of items with maximum value which can be accommodated in the knapsack. Various real-world problems are of this type: for example, the allocation of communication channels to customers who are charged at different rates (Back et al., 1997).

During a study of 0-1 knapsack, a number of extensions and variants have been developed such as (Ahmed & Younas, 2011): Multiple Knapsack Problems (MKP), Multidimensional Knapsack Problems (MDKP), Multi Choice Knapsack Problems (MCKP) and Multiple Choice Multidimensional Knapsack Problems (MMKP). It is also important to consider other extensions such as (Chu & Beasley, 1998): Multiconstraint Knapsack Problem, and also the term "Multidimensional Zero-one Knapsack Problem". Using alternative names for the same problem is potentially confusing, but since, historically, the designation **MKP** has been the most widely used (Chu & Beasley, 1998). Consequently, Multidimensional Knapsack Problem (MKP) is the designation selected for this work. In our previous research it was introduced a Multi Population Model on the cultural structure identified as "Multi Population Cultural Genetic Algorithm" (MCGA) (Silva & Oliveira, 2009). In MCGA model several sub-populations are connected with as ring structure, where the migration of individuals occurs after a generation interval (according to the migration based on parameter interval) with best-worst migration policy implementation. The results were satisfactory in relation to other algorithms in the literature. In another research two versions of Distributed GA (DGA) are presented as follows: standard Distributed GA (DGA) and an improved DGA (DGA-SRM), which two genetic operators are applied in parallel mode to create offspring. The term SRM represents "Self-Reproduction with Mutation", that is applied to various 0/1 multiple knapsack problems so as to improve the search performance (Aguire et al., 2000). Hybridization of memetic algorithms with Branch-and-Bound techniques (BnB) is also utilized for solving combinatorial optimization problems (Gallardo et al., 2007). BnB techniques use an implicit enumeration scheme for exploring the search space in an "intelligent" way. Yet another research utilizes adaptive GA for 0/1 Knapsack problems where special consideration is given to the penalty function where constant and self-adaptive penalty functions are adopted (Zoheir, 2002). Fitness landscape analysis techniques are used to better understand the properties of different representations that are commonly adopted when evolutionary algorithms are applied to MKP (Tavares et al., 2008). Other investigation utilizes multiple representations in a GA for the MKP (Representation-Switching GA) know as RSGA (Fukunaga, 2009). Other recent works consider two heuristics and utilize them for making comparisons to the well-known multiobjective evolutionary algorithms (MOEAs) (Kumar & Singh, 2010). While comparing MOEAs with the two heuristics, it was observed that the solutions obtained by the heuristics are far superior for larger problem instances than those obtained by MOEAs.

2.1 Multidimensional Knapsack Problem

As mentioned earlier, the MKP is a well-known nondeterministic-polynomial time-hard combinatorial optimization problem, with a wide range of applications (Tavares et al., 2008). The classical 0-1 knapsack problem is one of the most studied optimization and involves the selection of a subset of available items having maximum profit so that the total weight of the chosen subset does not exceed the knapsack capacity. The problem can be described as follows: given two sets of n items and m knapsacks constraints (or resources), for each item j, a profit p_j is assigned, and for each constraint i, a consumption value r_{ij} is designated. The goal is to determine a set of items that maximizes the total profit, not exceeding the given constraint capacities c_i. Formally, this is stated as follows (Tavares et al., 2008):

Maximize
$$\sum_{j=1}^{n} p_j x_j \,, \tag{1}$$

Subject to
$$\sum_{j=1}^{n} r_{i,j} x_j \le c_{i,} \quad \mathrm{i} = 1,\ldots,m \tag{2}$$

$$x_j \in \{0,1\}, \ \mathrm{j} = 1,\ldots.,n \tag{3}$$

With
$$p_j > 0 \,,\ r_{i,j} \ge 0 \ \text{and} \ c_i \ge 0 \tag{4}$$

The knapsack constraint is represented by each of the m constraints described in Eq. (2). The decision variable is the binary vector x $=(x_1,\ldots,x_n)$. Each item j is mapped to a bit and when $x_j = 1$, the corresponding item is considered to be part of the solution. The special case of $m = 1$ is generally known as the Knapsack Problem or the Unidimensional Knapsack Problem.

For single constraint the problem is not strongly NP-hard and effective approximation algorithms have been developed for obtaining near-optimal solutions. A review of the single knapsack problem and heuristic algorithms is given by Martello and Toth (Martello & Toth, 1990). Exact techniques and exhaustive search algorithms, such as branch-and-bound, are only of practical use in solving MKP instances of small size since they are, in general, too time-consuming (e.g., instances with 100 items or less, and depending on the constraints).

2.2 Evolutionary approach for the MKP

In a resolution of specific problems that implements an Evolutionary Algorithm, as for example, a simple Genetic Algorithm (GA), it is necessary the definition of five components (Agapie et al., 1997). The first component is the genotype or a genetic representation of the potential problem (individual representation scheme). The second is a method for creating an initial population of solutions. The third is a function verifying the fitness of the solution (*objective function* or *fitness function*). The fourth are genetic operators and the fifth are some constant values for parameters that are used by the algorithm (such as population size, probability of applying an operator, etc.).

2.2.1 Genotype

The natural representation of the MKP would be the binary representation, in which every bit represents the existence or not of a certain element in the Knapsack. A bit set to 1 indicates that the corresponding item is packed into the knapsack and a bit set to 0 indicates that it is not packed. Hence a typical population of two individuals for a six elements in Knapsack would be represented as showed in Figure 1. Thus, each element has an identification that is given by the bit index.

In Figure 1 (a) there are three elements in the knapsack, corresponding to the following positions: 1, 4 and 6. In Figure 1 (b) there are four elements in the knapsack, whose positions are: 2, 3, 5 and 6.

1	2	3	4	5	6
1	0	0	1	0	1

a)

1	2	3	4	5	6
0	1	1	0	1	1

b)

Fig. 1. Knapsack example for two chromosomes.

2.2.2 Initial population

The population is the solution representation that consists of a set of codified chromosomes. There are many ways to generate the initial population such as random chromosome or chromosome with the solution closer to the optimum. In most applications the initial population is generated at random.

2.2.3 Evaluation function

In GA each individual is evaluated by fitness function. Some individuals produce more children than others due to their fitness. By this mechanism, individuals that have chromosomes with better fitness have better chances of leaving their genes. This leads to better average performance of the whole population as generations proceed (Ku & Lee, 2001). A feasible vector solution x needs to satisfy constraint (2), otherwise it is infeasible. Hence, a penalty is applied to all infeasible solutions in order to decrease their corresponding "fitness". Therefore, the two types of evaluation functions used in this research are based on static (constant) and adaptive penalty functions. The standard evaluation function for each individual is given by the following expressions:

$$\text{Evaluation }(x) = \sum_{i=1}^{i=n} (x[i] \times p[i]) - Pen(x) \tag{5}$$

$$\text{Maximum Profit Possible (MaxP)} = \sum_{i=1}^{i=n} p[i] \tag{6}$$

A vector solution x is optimal when Evaluation (x) =MaxP.

2.2.4 Genetic operators

To implement the GA process, many factors should be considered such as the representation scheme of chromosomes, the mating strategy, the size of population, and the design of the genetic operators such as selection, mutation and recombination (Ku & Lee, 2001).

i. **Selection** - is an operator that prevents low fitness individuals from reproduction and permits high fitness individuals to offspring more children to improve average fitness of population over generations. There are various selections types, such as stochastic remainder, elitism, crowding factor model, tournament, and roulette wheel.
ii. **Recombination or Crossover** - is an operator that mixes the chromosomes of two individuals. Typically two children are generated by applying this operator, which are similar to the parents but not same. Crossover causes a structured, yet randomized exchange of genetic material between solutions, with the possibility that the "fittest" solutions generate "better" ones. A crossover operator should preserve as much as possible from the parents while creating an offspring.
iii. **Mutation** - introduces totally new individuals to population. It helps extend the domain of search and will restrain the diversity of the population. Mutation involves the modification of each bit of an individual with some probability Pm. Although the mutation operator has the effect of destroying the structure of a potential solution, chances are it will yield a better solution. Mutation in GAs restores lost or unexplored genetic material into the population to prevent the premature convergence of the GA.

The tournament is the selection type chosen for this work since it is more used and it presents good performance. For a binary representation, classical crossover and mutation operators can be used, such as n-point crossover or uniform crossover, and bit-flip mutation. In CAs the influence of information from Belief Space on recombination and mutation process such as: best chromosome or set of best chromosomes information is expected.

2.2.5 Constant values parameters

An Evolutionary Algorithm involves different strategy parameters, e.g.: mutation rate, crossover rate, selective pressure (e.g., tournament size) and population size. Good parameter values lead to good performance. There are three major types of parameter control (Eiben & Smith, 2008):

- **deterministic**: a rule modifies strategy parameter without feedback from the search (based on some type of a counter);
- **adaptive**: a feedback rule based on some measure monitoring search progress (quality);
- **self-adaptative**: parameter values evolve along with the solutions; encoded onto chromosomes they undergo variation and selection.

The implementation of a deterministic parameter control is easier, provided that the parameter values used are tested to verify the best performance.

2.3 Cultural algorithms

Cultural Algorithms (CAs) have been developed so as to model the evolution of the cultural component of an evolutionary computational system over time as it accumulates experience

(Reynolds & Chung, 1996). As a result, CAs can provide an explicit mechanism for global knowledge and a useful framework within which to model self-adaptation in an EC system. The CAs are based on knowledge of an evolutionary system that implements a dual mechanism of inheritance. This mechanism allows the CAs to explore as much microevolution as macroevolution. Microevolution is the evolution that happens in the population level. Macroevolution occurs on the culture itself, i.e. the belief space evolution. The belief space is the place where the information on the solution of the problem is refined and stored. It is acquired through the population space over the evolutionary process. The belief space has the goal to guide individuals in search of better regions. In the CAs evolution occurs more quickly than in population without the mechanism of macroevolution. The characteristics and behaviors of individuals are represented in the Population Space and as mentioned earlier the population space can support any population-based computational model such as Genetic Algorithms among others (Jin & Reynolds, 1999). The communications protocols dictate the rules about individuals that can contribute to knowledge in the Belief Space (function of acceptance) and how the Belief Space will influence new individuals (Function of Influence), as shown in Figure 2.

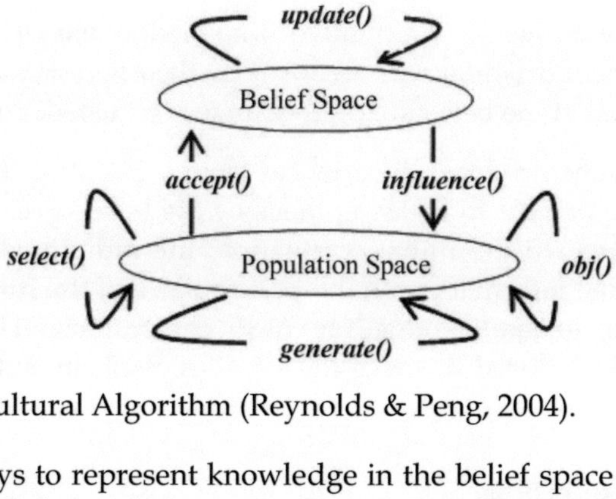

Fig. 2. Framework of Cultural Algorithm (Reynolds & Peng, 2004).

The two most used ways to represent knowledge in the belief space are (Reynolds & Peng, 2004): Situational Knowledge and Normative Knowledge. Situational Knowledge represents the best individuals found at a certain time of evolution and it contains a number of individuals considered as a set of exemplars to the rest of the population. The number of exemplars may vary according to the implementation, but it is usually small. For example, the structure used to represent this type of knowledge is shown in Figure 3. Each individual is stored within its parameters and fitness value (Iacoban et al. 2003).

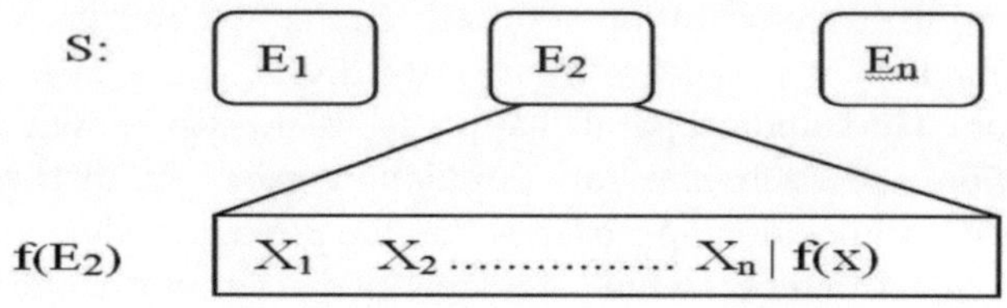

Fig. 3. Representation of Situational Knowledge.

The Situational Knowledge is updated when the best individual of the population is found. This occurs when its fitness value exceeds the fitness value of the worst individual stored.

Normative Knowledge represents a set of intervals that characterize the range of values given by the features that make the best solutions (Iacoban et al., 2003).

Figure 4 shows the structure used by Reynolds and his students, where are stored the minimum and maximum values on the individual's characteristics.

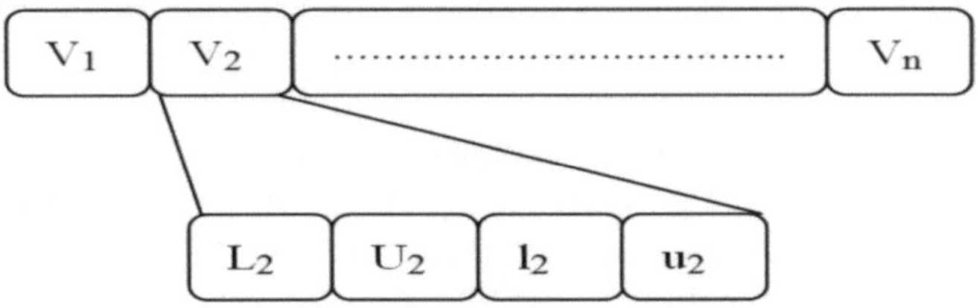

Fig. 4. Representation of Normative knowledge

These intervals are used to guide the adjustments (mutations) that occur in individuals. With these minimum values, (li) and maximum (ui), the fitness values are also stored. This value results from the individuals that produced each extreme Li and Ui respectively.

The adjustment of the range of Normative Knowledge varies according to the best individual. That is, if the individual was accepted by the *acceptance function* and its range is less than the range stored in the belief space, the range is adjusted, and vice versa.

The resolution of problems produces experiences from individuals in the population space, which are selected to contribute to the acceptance by the belief space, where the knowledge is generalized and stored. In the initial population, the individuals are evaluated by the fitness function. Then, the information on the performance of the function is used as a basis for the production of generalizations for next generations. The experiences of the individuals selected will be used to make the necessary adjustments on the knowledge of the current belief space.

2.4 Parallel Genetic Algorithms

The definition of Parallel Genetic Algorithms (PGAs) is related with execution of various GAs in parallel mode. The main goal of PGAs is to reduce the large execution times that are associated with simple genetic algorithms for finding near-optimal solutions in large search spaces and to find better solutions.

The PGAs can be implemented through two approaches (Sivanandam, 2007): standard parallel approach and the decomposition approach. In the first approach, the sequential GA model is implemented on a parallel computer by dividing the task of implementation among the processors. The standard parallel approaches are also known as *master-slave GAs.* In the decomposition approach, the full population exists in distributed form. Other characteristic in the decomposition approach is that the population is divided into a number of sub-populations called demes. Demes are separated from one another and individuals compete only within a deme. An additional operator called migration is used to move the individuals from one deme to another. If the individuals can migrate to any other deme, the model is called *island model* or *Multiple-population GAs* when implemented in parallel or distributed environments (Braun, 1991). Migration can be controlled by various parameters like migration rate, topology, migration scheme like best/worst/random individuals to migrate and the frequency of migrations (Sinvanadam, 2007).

Other authors classify Parallel Genetic Algorithm in four main categories (Aguirre & Tanaka, 2006): global master-slave, island, cellular, and hierarchical parallel GAs. In a global master-slave GA there is a single population and the evaluation of fitness is distributed among several processors. The important characteristic in a global master-slave GA is that the entire population is considered by genetic operators as selection, crossover and mutation. An island GA, also known as coarse-grained or distributed GA, consists of several sub-populations evolving separately with occasional migration of individuals between sub-populations. A cellular category also known as "fine-grained GA" consists of one spatially structured population, whose selection and mating are restricted to a small neighborhood. The neighborhoods are allowed to overlap permitting some interaction among individuals. Finally, a hierarchical parallel GA category, combines an island model with either a master-slave or cellular GA. The global master-slave GA does not affect the behavior of the algorithm and can be considered only as a hardware accelerator. However, the other parallel formulations of GAs are very different from canonical GAs, especially, with regard to population structure and selection mechanisms. These modifications change the way the GA works, affecting its dynamics and the trajectory of evolution. For example, the utilization of parameters as sub-population size, migration rate and migration frequency are crucial to the performance of island models. Cellular, island and hierarchical models perform as well as or better than canonical versions and have the potential of being more than just hardware accelerators (Aguirre & Tanaka, 2006). A new taxonomy about PGAs is also presented by Nowostawski and Poli (Nowostawski & Poli, 1999).

In recent studies about MKP Silva and Oliveira (Silva & Oliveira, 2009) have shown that good results are reached in the benchmark tests when taking into consideration the implementation of sub-populations and the migration process from the island model. The results presented were better than canonical version of Cultural Algorithm in most cases.

2.5 Island model (Multi Population Genetic Algorithms)

Multi population Genetic Algorithms (MGAs) or Island Model, is an extension of traditional single-population Genetic Algorithms (SGAs) by dividing a population into several sub-populations within which the evolution proceeds and individuals are allowed to migrate from one sub-population to another. Different values for parameters such as selection, recombination and mutation rate can be chosen for each sub-population. Normally, the basic island model uses the same values for these parameters in all sub-populations.

In order to control the migration of individuals, several parameters were defined such as: (i) the communication topology that defines the connections between sub-populations, (ii) a migration rate that controls how many individuals migrate, and (iii) a migration interval that affects the frequency of migration. In addition, migration must include strategies for migrant selection and for their inclusion in their new sub-populations (Aguire, 2000).

The sub-populations size, communication topology (its degree of connectivity), migration rate and migration frequency are important factors related to the performance of distributed GAS. In general, it has been shown that distributed GAs can produce solutions with similar or better quality than single population GAs, while reducing the overall time to completion in a factor that is almost in reciprocal proportion to the number of processors (Aguire, 2000).

In the island model GA, the sub-populations are isolated during selection, breeding and evaluation. Islands typically focus on the evolutionary process within sub-populations before migrating individuals to other islands, or conceptual processors, which also carry out an evolutionary process. At predetermined times, during the search process, islands send and receive migrants to other islands. There are many variations of distributed models, e.g. islands, demes, and niching methods, where each requires numerous parameters to be defined and tuned (Gustafson, 2006).

An example of the communication topology, can be defined as a graph in which the sub-populations *Pi* (i = 0, 1,..., K - 1) are the vertices and each defined edge Li,j specifies a communication link between the incident vertices Pi and Pj (neighbor sub-populations) (Aguire, 2000). In general, assuming a directed graph for each defined link Li,j we can indicate the number of individuals Ri,j that will migrate from P to Pj (migration rate) and the number of generations M between migration events (migration interval). The communication topology and migration rates could be static or dynamic and migration could be asynchronous or synchronous.

Various strategies for choosing migrants have been applied. Two strategies often used to select migrants are selection of the best and random selection. For example, the migration can implement a synchronous elitist broadcast strategy occurring every M generation. Each sub-population broadcasts a copy of its R best individuals to all its neighbor sub-populations.

Hence, every sub-population in every migration event receives migrants. Figure 5 illustrates a communication topology +l+2 island model in which each sub-population is linked to two neighbors (L = 2). In this example, the sub-population P0 can send individuals only to P1 and P2 and receive migrants only from P4 and P5.

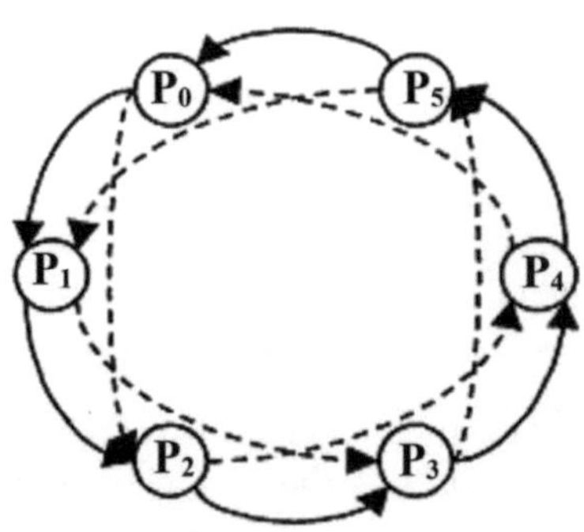

Fig. 5. +1+2 communication topology.

3. Cultural Island Model (CA-IM)

In this section is presented an approach about the communication topology for migration process implemented in a Cultural Algorithm based on the island model. As noted earlier in the classical island model implementation, there are sub-populations connected with as ring structure. Individuals in classical island model are migrated after every migration-interval (M) among generations and the best-worst migration policy is used.

The approach utilized in this work is an adaption and implementation of the island model on the cultural structure here identified as "Cultural Island Model" (CA-IM), briefly introduced in Silva & Oliveira (Silva & Oliveira, 2009). The implementations have become simple because the same CAs structures were used as much the evolutionary structure as the belief space that is the main characteristic present in CAs.

The main characteristic present in CA-IM is the link between main belief spaces (from main population) and secondary belief space (from multi population). They store information about independent evolution for main population and sub-populations respectively, i.e. the cultural evolutions occur in parallel among the main population and the sub-populations of the islands. The link of communication between two *Belief Spaces,* allows migration between the best individuals stored in the cultural knowledge structure implemented. Figure 6 shows the framework correspondent to the proposed structure.

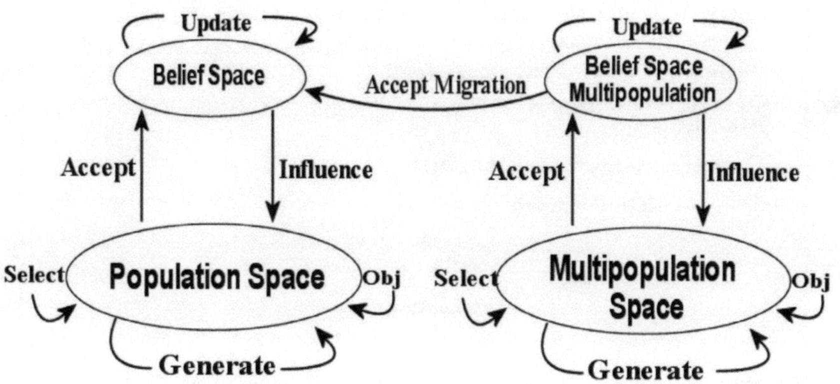

Fig. 6. Framework of model proposed

Migrations from islands occur through *Belief Space Multipopulation* structure that perform the communication process among sub-populations and send the best individuals through *Accept Migration*. It occurs in a predefined interval whose parameter is *M* (every *M* generation) where the best individuals are evaluated by acceptance function and updated in each belief space. The migration from *Belief Space Multipopulation* to *Main Belief Space* is implemented as a number of individuals which are considered as a set of exemplars to the rest of the population (Situational Knowledge).

It is important to note that CA-IM provides a continuous verification between the last solution (optimum value) found and the current solution. Then, it computes the number of generations where don't occur improvements. Thus, if the distance between the last generation, where the current solution was found, and the current generation is high then the sub-populations are eliminated and recreated randomly. As for CA-IM, there is a fixed difference for this occurrence in the range of 60 to 100 generations. If a new solution is not found in this range, then the sub-populations of the islands (Multipopulation Space) as well as the cultural information about all sub-populations (Belief Space Multipopulation) are recreated randomly by algorithm.

3.1 Mutation and recombination

In mutation operation the cultural knowledge (such as situational knowledge) as well as the standard binary mutation operation (known as "bit-flip mutation") is utilized. If the cultural knowledge is utilized during the mutation process, the mutated chromosome genes are replaced by the best genes from chromosome stored in situational knowledge with P_M probability, otherwise, the genes are inverted by bit-flip mutation. The chromosome chosen among a set of chromosomes from situational knowledge can be the best chromosome or a random chromosome.

The bit-flip mutation is a common operation applied in evolutionary algorithms to solve a problem with binary representation. Consequently, each bit from current mutated chromosome is flipped, i.e. the value of the chosen gene is inverted also with probability of mutation P_M. Figure 7 shows the pseudo-code of mutation utilized by CA-IM.

```
CA-IM_Mutation
1- Get initial Parameters:
  • PM (Probability of Mutation);          • C (Current Chromossome);
  • S[] (Situational Knowledge);           • Sbest (best chromosome of S[]);
  • Srandom= random chromosome of S[];
2- Create C '(Chromossome Mutation)
  If (random<=0.5)
  {
     for (int i=0; i<genotypeLength; i++)
     {
          if (random <=PM)
          {
               if (random <=0.5)
                    C'[i]=Sbest[i];
               else
                    C'[i]=Srandom[i];
          }
     }
  }
  else
  {
     for (int i=0; i<genotypeLength; i++)
     {
        If (random <=PM)
           C'= flip(C, i);
     }
  }
3- Return C';
```

Fig. 7. Mutation pseudo-code.

In recombination operation the cultural knowledge as well as the standard binary recombination operation (known as "uniform recombination") is also utilized. In the uniform recombination the bits are randomly copied from the first or from the second parent to genes in the offspring chromosomes, in any sequence of ones and zeros. Figure 8 shows the pseudo-code of CA-IM recombination.

If the cultural knowledge is utilized during the recombination process, the chromosome genes are replaced by the best genes from chromosome stored in situational knowledge with P_R probability. Otherwise, the genes are replaced with genes from their parents. Here only the best chromosome is chosen from situational knowledge during the recombination process.

```
CA-IM_Recombination
1- Get initial Parameters:
  • PR (Probability of Recombination);
  • C1 (Current Chromosome -1);        // Parents Chromosomes
  • C2 (Current Chromosome -2);        // Parents Chromosomes
  • S [ ] (Situational Knowledge);
  • Sbest=best chromosome of S [ ];

2- Create C1' and C2' // Offsprings Chromosome Recombination )
   for (int i=0; i<genotypeLength; i++)
   {
      If (random<= PR)
      {
         If (random <=0.5)
         {
            if (random<= 0.5)
            {
               C1'[i] = Sbest[i];
               C2'[i] = Sbest[i];
            }
            else
            {
               C1'[i] = C2[i];
               C2'[i] = Sbest[i];
            }
         }
         else
         {
            C1'[i] = C2[i];
            C2'[i] = C1[i];
         }
      }
      else
      {
         C1'[i] = C1[i];
         C2'[i] = C2[i];
      }
   }
3- Return Sons (C1' and C2');
```

Fig. 8. Recombination pseudo-code.

4. Experimental results and discussion

To evaluate the performance of the proposed algorithm CA-IM, a comparison of various tests with Distributed Genetic Algorithms utilizing the same knapsack problems was carried out. To make a comparison two kinds of algorithms based in Distributed GAs (Aguirre et al., 2000): (i) A Distributed canonical GA (denoted as DGA), and (ii) a Distributed GA-SRM (denoted as DGA-SRM) were utilized. The SRM term means "Self-Reproduction with Mutation", and introduces diversity by means of mutation inducing the appearance of beneficial mutations.

For the CA-IM algorithm there are two versions: CA-IM_1 and CA-IM_2. The only difference is that CA-IM_1 has a fixed rate for mutation and recombination, while CA-IM_2 has a random rate for mutation and recombination. The standard CA (CAs) is the Cultural Algorithm with single population.

4.1 DGA and DGA-SRM

The DGA works with various 0/1 multiple knapsack problems (NP hard combinatorial) which from previous efforts seem to be fairly difficult for GAs (Aguirre et al., 2000). Those algorithms were evaluated on test problems which are taken from the literature. The problem sizes range from 15 objects to 105 and from 2 to 30 knapsacks and can be found in OR-Library (Beasley, 1990). The knapsack problems are defined by: problem *(n, m)* where *n* represents the number of objects and *m* represents the number of knapsacks. Each knapsack has a specific capacity as well each object has a specific weight. For example, Weing7 (105, 2) represents a MKP with 105 objects and 2 knapsacks.

Every experiment presented here has a similar capacity to the work described in DGA and DGA-SRM (Aguire et al., 2000) such as: population size, number of function evaluations in each run and a total of 100 independent runs. Each run uses a different seed for the random initial population. To improve understanding of DGA and DGA-SRM algorithms, some parameters and symbols are presented:

- The maximum size of the population is represented by λ_{total} (fixed in 800);
- The parent and offspring population sizes are represented by μ and λ respectively;
- The parameter K represents the number of sub-populations (partitions). Hence, λ ***K**=* λ_{total} (maximum=800);
- The parameter ***M*** is the number of generations between migration events (migration interval) ;
- The symbol **N** represents the number of times the global optimum was found in the 100 runs;
- The symbol τ represents a threshold (utilized for control of a normalized mutant's survival ratio).
- The symbol ***T*** represents the number of function evaluations in each run;
- *Average* is the average of the best solutions and *Stdev* is the standard deviation around *Average*, respectively;

In DGA and DGA-SRM, each sub-population broadcasts a copy of its ***R*** best individuals to all of its neighbor sub-populations. Hence, every sub-population in every migration event receives λ_m = L x R migrants, where L is the number of links. When there is no migration and the sub-populations evolve in total isolation, the values corresponding to such a characteristic are denoted by X in the table. The results for knapsack problem Weing7 for DGA and DGA-SRM is shown in the Table 1 (Aguirre et al., 2000).

K	λ_m / λ	DGA						DGA-SRM					
		L R	λ	**M**	**N**	**Average**	**Stdev**	μ	λ	**M**	**N**	**Average**	**Stdev**
8	0.10	5 2	100	5	0	**1094423.4**	433.38	50	100	80	63	1095421.44	30.84
8	0.05	5 1	100	5	0	1093284.95	733.24	50	100	100	66	1095423.58	29.84
8	0.01	1 1	100	5	0	1089452.96	1082.41	50	100	80	77	**1095430.51**	26.51
8	X	X	100	X	0	1087385.56	1729.4	50	100	X	60	1095419.80	30.86

Table 1.The best results for Weing7 (105, 2) by DGA and DGA-SRM (λ_{total} =800; T=8x10^5).

According to Table 1 the best value found in *Average* is equal to 1094423.4, for DGA and 1095430.51 for DGA-SRM. Table 1 also indicates that the DGA-SRM improves the results in relation to DGA. Table 2 shows the results found for others knapsack problems by DGA and DGA-SRM. In order to simplify the results shown in Table 2, the following configuration parameters should be considered: K = 16 sub-populations and $\mu = 25$ (Aguirre et al., 2000).

Problem (n, m)	λ_m / λ	DGA						DGA-SRM (τ =0.35)				
		LR	λ	M	N	Average	Stdev	λ	M	N	Average	Stdev
Petersen6 (39,5)	0.01	1 1	50	5	0	**10506.90**	26.11	50	140	77	10614.82	5.82
Petersen7 (50,5)	0.10	5 1	100	5	0	1093284.95	733.24	50	40	89	16535	5.94
Sento1 (60, 30)	0.10	5 1	100	5	0	1089452.96	1082.41	50	40	98	7771.78	1.54
Sento2 (60, 30)	0.10	5 1	100	5	0	1087385.56	1729.4	50	40	84	8721.32	2.11

Table 2. The best results for other problems by DGA and DGA-SRM (λ_{total} = 800; T=4x10^5).

4.2 CA-IM_1

For the algorithm proposed (CA-IM) various parameters and symbols are also considered such as:

- The parameter ***P*** is the size of main population;
- The parameter P_M is the probability of mutation and P_R probability of recombination.
- The number of islands is ***K*** (number of sub-populations);
- The parameter α is the percentage which defines the size of the population of each island at function of ***P***.
- The sub-population size in each island is ***SI***, since ***SI*** = α ****P***.
- The percentage of best individuals in Situational Knowledge on population space is represented by SK_P and the percentage of best individuals in Situational Knowledge on multi population space is represented by SK_M.
- The parameter ***M*** is the number of generations between migration events (migration interval). Here ***M*** determines the interval of influence from the islands population through the Situational Knowledge.
- The symbol ***T*** represents the number of function evaluations in each run;
- The symbol ***N*** represents the number of times the global optimum was found in the 100 runs.
- *Average* is the average of the best solutions and *Stdev* is the standard deviation around *Average;*
- *Average of generations* is the average of the generations whose best solution was found in each run.

For the tests carried out for CA-IM_1, the selection chosen was tournament, whose value is 3, the mutation rate (P_M) is 0.025 and recombination rate (P_R) is 0.6. The situational knowledge configurations are: SK_P=*0.2* and SK_M=0.5. Table 3 shows the results found by CA-IM_1, whose best value found in *Average* is 1095445 (the optimal value) and in the *Average of Generations* is 44.49. All values reached have optimum value. However, if *Average of Generations* is low in relation to total of generations, then this means that the optimum is found in few generations.

As it is shown in Table 3, it is possible to observe that CA-IM outperforms DGA-SRM for any configuration such as the number of sub-populations (islands) and size of sub-population. Similarly, CA-IM also exhibits higher convergence reliability than DGA-SRM with higher values for *N* and *Average* with smaller *Stdev*. These results show that the CA-IM produces higher performance for all utilized parameters.

P	K	α	SI	M	N	Average of Generations	Average	Stdev
400	8	0.125	50	20	100	52.9	1095445	0.0
400	8	0,125	50	05	100	**44.49**	**1095445**	0.0
100	7	1.0	100	05	100	68.87	1095445	0.0

Table 3. The best results for **Weing7** (105, 2) by CA-IM_1 (λ_{total} =800 and T=8x10^5).

A new result "Average of Generations" was introduced so as to evaluate other type other type of performance whose value represents the average of generations that the optimum value was found for 100 independent runs for each problem presented. Particularly, it occurs when *M* is low and *K* is high (see result for Average of Generations). This means that a larger number of islands with small populations produce better convergence.

According to Table 3 the best value found in *Average* is 1095445 (the optimal value) while the *Average of generations* is 44.49 that means a low value, considering that 500 generations was utilized in each run which T=4x10^5. This represents 500 generations with a population size equal to 800 (including all subpopulations). Table 4 shows the results for others MKPs found by algorithm CA-IM_1.

Problem (n, m)	P	K	α	SI	M	N	Average of Generations	Average	Stdev.
Petersen6 (39,5)	400	8	0.125	50	20	100	30.22	10618.0	0.0
Petersen6 (39,5)	400	4	0,25	100	05	100	**26.29**	10618.0	0.0
Petersen7 (50,5)	400	8	0.125	50	20	100	78.49	16537.0	0.0
Petersen7 (50,5)	400	4	0,25	100	05	100	**71.51**	16537.0	0.0
Sento1 (60,30)	400	8	0.125	50	20	100	100.21	7772.0	0.0
Sento1 (60,30)	400	4	0,25	100	05	100	**87.44**	7772.0	0.0
Sento2 (60,30)	400	8	0.125	50	20	99	185.19	8721.81	0.099
Sento2 (60,30)	400	4	0,25	100	05	100	**166.12**	87722.0	0.0

Table 4. The best results for other problems by CA-IM_1 (λ_{total} = 800, T=4x10^5).

Thereby, it is possible to observe that CA-IM_1 outperforms DGA-SRM. Similarly, CA-IM_1 also exhibits higher convergence reliability (higher values of *N* and *Average* with smaller *Stdev*) than DGA-SRM. These results show that the CA-IM_1 is able to find global optimal for MKP, taking into consideration the tests results with 100% success.

The problem that presented greater difficulty was Sento2, that presented in some cases optimal values near to 100% such as N=98 and N=99. Even with results of *N* < 100 they are still better than the results obtained in the chosen benchmarks. In the meantime, the implementation of some adjustments allows CA-IM_1 to reach N=100 for Sento2.

4.3 CA-IM_2

For the tests carried out for CA-IM_2 the selection chosen was tournament whose value is 3. The mutation rate (P_M) is a random value in a specific interval: P_M= [0.01, 0.5]. The Recombination rate (P_R) is also a random value in an interval: P_R= *[0.1,* 0.99]. The situational knowledge configurations are: SK_P*=0.2* and SK_M=0.5. The CA-IM_2 results are presented in

Table 5 that shows the results for Weing7 and in Table 6 that shows the results for others knapsack problems.

P	K	α	SI	M	N	Average of Generations	Average	Stdev
400	8	0.125	50	20	100	**70.48**	1095445	0.0
400	8	0,125	50	05	100	72.72	1095445	0.0
100	7	1.0	100	05	100	107.11	1095445	0.0

Table 5. The best results for Weing7 (105,2) by CA-IM_2 (λ_{total} =800, T=8x10^5).

Problem (n, m)	P	K	α	SI	M	N	Average of Generations	Average	Stdev.
Petersen6 (39,5)	400	8	0.125	50	20	100	37.89	10618.0	0.0
Petersen6 (39,5)	400	4	0,25	100	05	100	**33.39**	10618.0	0.0
Petersen7(50,5)	400	8	0.125	50	20	100	81.46	16537.0	0.0
Petersen7(50,5)	400	4	0,25	100	05	100	**74.38**	16537.0	0.0
Sento1(60,30)	400	8	0,25	50	20	98	**112.55**	7771.75	1.7717
Sento1(60,30)	400	4	0,25	100	05	100	126.46	7772.0	0.0
Sento2(60,30)	400	8	0.125	50	20	71	183.35	8720.0	3.7199
Sento2(60,30)	400	4	0,25	100	05	88	**173.53**	8721.38	2.1732

Table 6. The best results for other problems by CA-IM_2 (λ_{total} = 800, T=4x10^5).

The implementation of random rate for mutation and recombination in CA-IM_2 doesn't produce satisfactory results in comparison to CA-IM_1, as it is shown in Table 6. In addition, the *Average of Generations* from algorithm CA-IM_2 is greater than CA-IM_1 for all knapsack problems. However, in comparison to CA-IM_1, there are few differences in results for Weing7 as is shown in Table 3 and Table 5.

4.4 CA-S (Standard CA)

For CA-S we also utilized the same configuration such as: tournament value=3, P_M= 0.025 and P_R = 0.6. The situational knowledge configuration is equal to 0.2 (SK_P=0.2). Every experiment presented here also consists of 100 independent runs and each run uses a different seed for the random initial population.

Problem (, m)	P	N	Average	Stdev.
Petersen6 (39,5)	800	97	10617.58	2.4002
Petersen7 (50,5)	800	81	16533.7	6.8703
Sento1 (60,30)	800	100	7772.0	0.0
Sento2 (60,30)	800	82	8721.14	2.4495
Weing7 (105,2)	800	100	1095445.0	0.0

Table 7. The best results for all knapsack problems by CA-S (T=4x10^5).

Table 7 shows the results from standard Cultural Algorithm (CA-S) that utilizes single population. According to results, the CA-S reaches optimum average for 100 runs only for Sento1 and Weing7. However, the results from CA-S for Petersen6, Pertersen7 and Sento2 outperform the results presented by DGA-SRM.

5. Conclusion

This work presented a Cultural Algorithm (CA) with single population (CA-S) and multi population (CA-IM) in order to improve the search performance on MKP. It was observed that CA-S improves the convergence reliability and search speed. However, CA-S is not enough to reach global optimum for most problems presented. Our cultural algorithm implementation with island model (CA-IM_1 and CA-IM_2) allows the migration among islands sub-populations and main population through belief space structures that represent the cultural knowledge available in Cultural Algorithms.

The results have shown that the CA-IM_1 is better than CA-IM_2 for the benchmarks selected. The results have also shown that the CA-IM_1 and CA-IM_2 perform the optimum search and reach optimum values equally or above the ones reached by algorithms DGA and DGA-SRM that were chosen for comparison. The positive results obtained, give support the idea that this is a desirable approach for tackling highly constrained NP-complete problems such as the MKP. In addition, it is possible that the hybridization of cultural algorithms based on population of GA with local search techniques improves the results obtained by standard CAs. In a future work, a study will be done about the behavior of the sub-populations that are eliminated and recreated randomly. In addition a local search will be implemented to CAs as much for standard CA (single population) as for CA-IM (multi population) so as to verify improvements on these algorithms.

6. Acknowledgments

This research was supported by the CAPES (Coordenação de Aperfeiçoamento do Pessoal de Ensino Superior, Brazil) and by FAPESPA (Fundação de Amparo à Pesquisa do Estado do Pará, Brazil).

7. References

Adeyemo, J.A. (2011). Reservoir Operation using Multi-objective Evolutionary Algorithms-A Review, In: *Asian Journal of Scientific Research*, Vol.4, No. 1, pp.16-27, February 2011, ISSN 19921454.

Agapie, A., Fagarasan, F. & Stanciulescu, B. (1997). A Genetic Algorithm for a Fitting Problem, In: *Nuclear Instruments & Methods in Physics Research Section A*, Vol. 389, No. 1-2, April 1997, pp. 288-292, ISSN 0168-9002.

Aguirre, H. E. & Tanaka, K. (2006). A Model for Parallel Operators in Genetic Algorithms, In: *Springer Book Series Studies in Computational Intelligence, Parallel Evolutionary Computations* , Nedjah, N., Alba, E. & Macedo M., L., pp.3-31, Springer, ISBN 9783540328391, Berlin Heidelberg.

Aguirre, H. E., Tanaka, K., Sugimara, T. & Oshita, S. (2000). Improved Distributed Genetic Algorithm with Cooperative-Competitive Genetic Operators, In: *Proc. IEEE Int.*

Conf. on Systems, Man, and Cybernetics, Vol.5, ISBN 0-7803-6583-6, pp. 3816-3822, Nashville, TN, USA, October 8-11 2000.

Aguirre, H. E., Tanaka, K. & Sugimura, T. (1999). Cooperative Model for Genetic Operators to Improve GAs In: *International Conference on Information Intelligence and Systems*, ISBN 0-7695-0446-9, pp. 98–106, Bethesda, MD, USA, 31 Oct. - 03 Nov., 1999.

Ahmed, Z. & Younas I. (2011). A Dynamic Programming based GA for 0-1 Modified Knapsack Problem, In: *International Journal of Computer Applications*, Vol. 16, No.7, February, 2011, pp. 1–6, ISSN 09758887.

Back, T., Fogel D. B. & Michalewicz Z., (Ed(s).). (1997). *Handbook of Evolutionary Computation*, Oxford University Press, ISBN 0-7503-0392-1, UK.

Beasley, J. E. (1990). Multi- Dimensional Knapsack Problems, In: *OR-library*, Date of Access: September 2011, Available from: http://people.brunel.ac.uk/~mastjjb/jeb/orlib/mknapinfo.html.

Braun, H. (1991). On Solving Traveling Salesman Problems by Genetic Algorithms, In: *Parallel Problem Solving from Nature – Proceedings of 1st Workshop*, Vol. 496 of Lecture Notes in Computer Science, H.P. Schwefel and R. Manner, Vol. 496, pp. 129-133, Springer, ISBN 3-540-54148-9, Dortmund, FRG, October 1-3 1990.

Chu, P. C. & Beasley J. E. (1998). A Genetic Algorithm for the Multidimensional Knapsack Problem, In: *Journal of Heuristics*, vol. 4, no. 1, June 1998, pp. 63–86, ISSN:1381-1231.

Eiben, A. E. & Smith, J.E. (2008). *Introduction to Evolutionary Computing*, Springer, Second edition, ISBN 978-3-540-40184-1, Amsterdam, NL.

Fukunaga, A. S. & Tazoe, S. (2009). Combining Multiple Representations in a Genetic Algorithm for the Multiple Knapsack Problem, In: *IEEE Congress on Evolutionary Computation*, ISBN 978-1-4244-2958-5, pp. 2423 - 2430, Trondheim, 18-21 May, 2009.

Gallardo, J. E., Cotta C. & Fernández A. J. (2007). On the Hybridization of Memetic Algorithms With Branch-and-Bound Techniques, In: *IEEE Transactions on Systems, Man, and Cybernetics, Part B*, Vol. 37, No. 1, February 2007, pp. 77-83, ISSN 1083-4419.

Glover, F. & Kochenberger, G. A. (1996). Critical Event Tabu Search for Multidimensional Knapsack Problems, In: *Meta-Heuristics: Theory and Applications*, Osman, I.H. & Kelly, J.P., pp. 407-427, Springer, ISBN 978-0-7923-9700-7, Boston, USA.

Gunther, R. R. (1998). An Improved Genetic Algorithm for the Multiconstrained 0–1 Knapsack Problem, In: *Evolutionary Computation Proceedings. IEEE World Congress on Computational Intelligence*, ISBN 0-7803-4869-9, pp.207-211, Anchorage, AK, May 4-9 1998.

Gustafson, S. & Burke, E.K. (2006). The Speciating Island Model: An Alternative Parallel Evolutionary Algorithm, In: *Journal of Parallel and Distributed Computing*, Vol. 66, No. 8, August 2006, pp. 1025-1036, ISSN 07437315.

Iacoban, R., Reynolds, R. & Brewster, J. (2003). Cultural Swarms: Modeling the Impact of Culture on Social Interaction and Problem Solving, In: *IEEE Swarm Intelligence Symposium*. ISBN 0-7803-7914-4, pp. 205–211, University Place Hotel, Indianapolis, Indiana, USA, April 24-26 2003.

Jin, X., & Reynold, R. G. (1999). Using Knowledge-Based System with Hierarchical Architecture to Guide the Search of Evolutionary Computation, In: *Proceedings of the 11th IEEE International Conference on Tools with Artificial Intelligence*, ISBN 0-7695-0456-6, pp. 29–36, Chicago, Illinois, November 08-10 1999.

Ku, S. & Lee, B. (2001). A Set-Oriented Genetic Algorithm and the Knapsack Problem, In: *Proceedings of the Congress on Evolutionary Computation*, ISBN 0-7803-6657-3, pp. 650–654, Seoul, South Korea, May 27-30 2001.

Kumar, R. & Singh, P. K. (2010). Assessing Solution Quality of Biobjective 0-1 Knapsack Problem using Evolutionary and Heuristic Algorithms, In: *Applied Soft Computing*, Vol. 10, No 3, June 2010, pp. 711 - 718, ISSN 1568-4946.

Martello, S. & Toth, P. (1990). *Algorithms and Computer Implementations*, John Wiley & Sons, ISBN 0471924202, New York.

Nowostawski , M. & Poli , R. (1999). Parallel Genetic Algorithm Taxonomy, In: *Proceedings of the Third International conference on knowledge-based intelligent information engineering systems*, ISBN 0780355784, pp. 88-92, Adelaide, August 1999.

Reynolds, R. G., & Peng, B. (2004). Cultural Algorithms: Computational Modeling of How Cultures Learn to Solve Problems, In: *Seventeenth European Meeting on Cybernetics and Systems Research*, ISBN 3-85206-169-5, Vienna, Austria, April 13-16 2004.

Reynolds, R. G. & Chung C. (1996). The Use of Cultural Algorithms to Evolve Multiagent Cooperation, In: *Proc. Micro-Robot World Cup Soccer Tournament*, pp. 53–56. Taejon, Korea, 1996.

Reynolds, R. G. (1994), An Introduction to Cultural Algorithms, In: *Proceedings of the Third Annual Conference on Evolutionary Programming,* ISBN 9810218109, pp. 131-139, San Diego, California, February 24-26 1994.

Reynolds, R. G. (1999). Chapter Twenty-Four; Cultural Algorithms: Theory and Applications, In: *New Ideas in Optimization*, Corne, D., Dorigo, M. & Glover F., pp. 367-377, McGraw-Hill Ltd., ISBN 0-07-709506-5, UK, England.

Silva, D. J. A. & Oliveira R. C. L. (2009). A Multipopulation Cultural Algorithm Based on Genetic Algorithm for the MKP, In: *Proc. of the 11th Annual conference on Genetic and evolutionary computation,* ISBN 978-1-60558-325-9, pp. 1815-1816, Montreal, Québec, Canada, July 8-12 2009.

Sivanandam, S.N. & Deepa, S. N. (2007). *Introduction to Genetic Algorithms,* (1st), Springer, ISBN 978-3-540-73189-4, New York.

Sivaraj, R. & Ravichandran,T. (2011). An Improved Clustering Based Genetic Algorithm for Solving Complex NP Problems, In: *Journal of Computer Science,* Vol. 7, No. 7, May 2011, pp. 1033-1037, ISSN 15493636.

Spillman, R. (1995). Solving Large Knapsack Problems with a Genetic Algorithm, In: *IEEE International Conference on Systems, Man and Cybernetics*, Vol. 1, ISBN 0-7803-2559-1, pp 632 -637, Vancouver, BC, Canada, October 22-25 1995.

Tavares, J., Pereira, F. B. & Costa, E. (2008). Multidimensional Knapsack Problem: A Fitness Landscape Analysis, In: *IEEE Transactions on Systems, Man and Cybernetics, Part B: Cybernetics*, Vol. 38, No. 3, June 2008, pp.604-616, ISSN 1083-4419.

Tomassini, Marco (2005). *Spatially Structured Evolutionary Algorithms: Artificial Evolution, Space and Tim - Natural Computing Series* (1st), Springer, New York, Inc., ISBN 3540241930, Secaucus, NJ, USA.

Zoheir, E. (2002). Solving the 0/1 knapsack Problem Using an Adaptive Genetic Algorithm, In: *Artificial Intelligence for Engineering Design, Analysis and Manufacturing*, Vol.16, No. 1, January 2002, pp.23-30, ISSN 08900604.

21

Using a Genetic Algorithm to Solve the Benders' Master Problem for Capacitated Plant Location

Ming-Che Lai[1] and Han-suk Sohn[2,*]
[1]*Yu Da University,*
[2]*New Mexico State University*
[1]*Taiwan*
[2]*USA*

1. Introduction

The capacitated plant location problem (CPL) consists of locating a set of potential plants with capacities, and assigning a set of customers to these plants. The objective is to minimize the total fixed and shipping costs while at the same time demand of all the customers can be satisfied without violating the capacity restrictions of the plants. The CPL is a well-known combinatorial optimization problem and a number of decision problems can be obtained as special cases of CPL. There are substantial numbers of heuristic solution algorithms proposed in the literature (See Rolland et al., 1996; Holmberg & Ling, 1997; Delmaire et al., 1999; Kratica et al., 2001; He et al., 2003; Uno et al., 2005). As well, exact solution methods have been studied by many authors. These include branch-and-bound procedures, typically with linear programming relaxation (Van Roy & Erlenkotter, 1982; Geoffrion & Graves, 1974) or Lagrangiran relaxation (Cortinhal & Captivo, 2003). Van Roy (1986) used the Cross decomposition which is a hybrid of primal and dual decomposition algorithm, and Geoffrion & Graves (1974) considered Benders' decomposition to solve CPL problem. Unlike many other mixed-integer linear programming applications, however, Benders decomposition algorithm was not successful in this problem domain because of the difficulty of solving the master system. In mixed-integer linear programming problems, where Benders' algorithm is most often applied, the master problem selects values for the integer variables (the more difficult decisions) and the subproblem is a linear programming problem which selects values for the continuous variables (the easier decisions). If the constraints are explicit only in the subproblem, then the master problem is free of explicit constraints, making it more amenable to solution by genetic algorithm (GA). The fitness function of the GA is, in this case, evaluated quickly and simply by evaluating a set of linear functions. In this chapter, therefore, we discuss about a hybrid algorithm (Lai et al., 2010) and its implementation to overcome the difficulty of Benders' decomposition. The hybrid algorithm is based on the solution framework of Benders' decomposition algorithm, together with the use of GA to effectively reduce the computational difficulty. The rest of

* Corresponding Author

this chapter is organized as follows. In section 2 the classical capacitated plant location problem is presented. The applications of Benders' decomposition and genetic algorithm are described in sections 3 and 4, respectively. In Section 5 the hybrid Benders/genetic algorithm to solve the addressed problem is illustrated. A numerical example is described in Section 6. Finally, some concluding remarks are presented in Section 7 followed by an acknowledgment and a list of references in Sections 8 and 9, respectively.

2. Problem formulation

The classical capacitated plant location problem with n potential plants and m customers can be formulated as a mixed integer program:

$$\text{CPL: Min} \sum_{i=1}^{m} F_i Y_i + \sum_{i=1}^{m}\sum_{j=1}^{n} C_{ij} X_{ij} \tag{1}$$

$$\text{Subject to } \sum_{i=1}^{m} X_{ij} \geq D_j, \quad j = 1,\ldots n \tag{2}$$

$$\sum_{j=1}^{n} X_{ij} \leq S_i Y_i, \quad i = 1,\ldots m \tag{3}$$

$$X_{ij} \geq 0\ , i = 1,\ldots m;\ j = 1,\ldots n \tag{4}$$

$$Y_i \in \{0,1\}, \quad i = 1,\ldots m \tag{5}$$

Here, Y is a vector of binary variables which selects the plants to be opened, while X is an array of continuous variables which indicate the shipments from the plants to the customers. Fi is the fixed cost of operating plant i and Si its capacity if it is opened. Cij is the shipping cost of all of customer j's demand Dj from plant i. The first constraint ensures that all the demand of each customer must be satisfied. The second constraint ensures that the total demand supplied from each plant does not exceed its capacity. As well, it ensures that no customer can be supplied from a closed plant.

3. Benders' decomposition algorithm

Benders' decomposition algorithm was initially developed to solve mixed-integer linear programming problems (Benders, 1962), i.e., linear optimization problems which involve a mixture of either different types of variables or different types of functions. A successful implementation of the method to design a large-scale multi-commodity distribution system has been described in the paper of Geoffrion & Graves (1974). Since then, Benders' decomposition algorithm has been successfully applied in many other areas, for example, in vehicle assignment (Cordeau et al., 2000, 2001), cellular manufacturing system (Heragu, 1998), local access network design (Randazzo et al., 2001), spare capacity allocation (Kennington, 1999), multi-commodity multi-mode distribution planning, (Cakir, 2009), and generation expansion planning (Kim et al., 2011). Benders' algorithm projects the problem onto the Y-space by defining the function

$$v(Y) = \sum_{i=1}^{m} F_i Y_i + \text{Min} \sum_{i=1}^{m} \sum_{j=1}^{n} C_{ij} X_{ij} \tag{6}$$

$$\text{Subject to} \sum_{i=1}^{m} X_{ij} \geq D_j, \quad j = 1, \ldots n \tag{7}$$

$$\sum_{j=1}^{n} X_{ij} \leq S_i Y_i, \quad i = 1, \ldots m \tag{8}$$

$$X_{ij} \geq 0, i = 1, \ldots m; j = 1, \ldots n \tag{9}$$

and restating the problem (CPL) as

$$\underset{Y \in \{0,1\}^m}{\text{Min}} \; v(Y) \tag{10}$$

We will refer to the evaluation of $v(Y)$ as the (primal) subproblem, a transportation LP whose dual LP problem is

$$v(Y) = \sum_{i=1}^{m} F_i Y_i + \text{Max} \sum_{i=1}^{m} S_i Y_i U_i + \sum_{j=1}^{n} D_j V_j \tag{11}$$

$$\text{Subject to } -U_i + V_j \leq C_{ij} \quad \text{for } i = 1, \ldots m; j = 1, \ldots n \tag{12}$$

$$U_i \geq 0, \quad i = 1, \ldots m; \quad V_j \geq 0, \quad j = 1, \ldots n \tag{13}$$

If $\psi = \{(\hat{U}^k, \hat{V}^k), k=1,\ldots,K\}$ is the set of basic feasible solutions to the dual subproblem, then in principle $v(Y)$ could be evaluated by a complete enumeration of the K basic feasible solutions. (The motivation for using the dual problem is, of course, that ψ is independent of Y.) That is,

$$v(Y) = \sum_{i=1}^{m} F_i Y_i + \underset{k=1,2,\ldots K}{\text{Max}} \left\{ \sum_{i=1}^{m} S_i \hat{U}_i^k Y_i + \sum_{j=1}^{n} D_j \hat{V}_j^k \right\} = \underset{k=1,2,\ldots K}{\text{Max}} \left\{ \alpha^k Y + \beta^k \right\} \tag{14}$$

where $\alpha_i^k \equiv F_i + S_i \hat{U}_i^k, \beta^k \equiv \sum_{j=1}^{n} D_j \hat{V}_j^k$.

The function $v(Y)$ may be approximated by the underestimate

$$\underline{v}_T(Y) \equiv \underset{k=1,2,\ldots T}{\text{Max}} \left\{ \alpha^k Y + \beta^k \right\} \tag{15}$$

where $T \leq K$. Benders' decomposition alternates between a master problem

$$\underset{Y \in \{0,1\}}{\text{Min}} \; \underline{v}^T(Y) \tag{16}$$

which selects a trial Y^k, and the subproblem, which evaluates $v(Y^k)$ and computes a new linear support $\alpha^k Y+\beta^k$ using the dual solution of the transportation subproblem. The major effort required by Benders' algorithm is the repeated solution of the master problem, or its mixed-integer LP equivalent,

$$\text{Min } Z \tag{17}$$

$$\text{Subject to } Z \geq \alpha^k Y + \beta^k, \quad k = 1,\ldots T \tag{18}$$

$$Y_i \in \{0,1\} \tag{19}$$

One approach to avoiding some of this effort is by suboptimizing the master problem, i.e., finding a feasible solution of the linear system

$$\hat{Z} > \alpha^k Y + \beta^k, \quad k = 1,\ldots T \tag{18}$$

$$Y_i \in \{0,1\}, \quad i = 1,\ldots m \tag{19}$$

i.e., Y such that $\underline{v}^T(Y) < \hat{Z}$, where $\hat{Z}$ is the value of the incumbent at the current iteration, i.e., the least upper bound provided by the subproblems. (By using implicit enumeration to suboptimize the master problem, and restarting the enumeration when solving the following master problem, this modification of Benders' algorithm allows a single search of the enumeration tree, interrupted repeatedly to solve subproblems.) For more information on the problem and the application of Benders' algorithm for its solution, refer to Salkin et al. (1989).

4. Genetic algorithm

Genetic algorithm (GA) has been effective and has been employed for solving a variety of difficult optimization problems. Much of the basic ground work in implementing and adapting GAs has been developed by Holland (1992). Since then, a large number of papers have appeared in the literature, proposing variations to the basic algorithm or describing different applications. In many cases, the GA can produce excellent solutions in a reasonable amount of time. For certain cases, however, the GA can fail to perform for a variety of reasons. Liepins & Hilliard (1989) have pointed out three of these reasons: (1) choice of a representation that is not consistent with the crossover operator; (2) failure to represent problem-specific information such as constraints; and (3) convergence to local optima (premature convergence). The first reason for failure, a representation inconsistent with the crossover operator, is most easily illustrated by an example of the traveling salesman problem, in which the crossover operator simply fails to preserve the feasible permutation in most cases. The second reason for failure is the inability to represent problem specific information such as constraints in an optimization problem. In general, for constrained problems, there is no guarantee that feasibility will be preserved by crossover or mutation, or even that a randomly-generated initial population is feasible. A broad range of approaches have been used in the literature to remedy this situation. However, there is no single mechanism that has performed consistently well in handling constrained problems with genetic algorithms (Reeves, 1997). The most direct solution is simply to ignore this problem. If an infeasible solution is encountered, it may be assigned a very low fitness value to increase the chance that it will "die off" soon. But sometimes, infeasible solutions are close to the optimum by any reasonable distance measure. Another direct solution is to modify the objective function by incorporating a penalty function which reduces the fitness by an amount which varies as the degree of infeasibility. Unfortunately, not all penalty functions work equally well, and care must be exercised in their choice (Liepins & Hillard, 1989). If the penalty is too small, many infeasible solutions are allowed to enter the population pool; if it is too large, the search is confined to a very small portion of the search space. Another increasingly popular technique for coping with infeasibility is the use of repair algorithms. These heuristic algorithms accept infeasible solutions but repair them in order to make them feasible before inserting them into the population. We can find various repair algorithms in the context of the traveling salesman problem in the literature (Goldberg & Lingle, 1985; Oliver et al., 1987; Chatterjee et al., 1996). Several practical questions arise, such as whether it should be the original offspring or the repaired version that should be used in the next generaion, and whether the entire randomness should be sacrificed because of the adoption of the repair methods. The third reason for failure is convergence to local optima (premature convergence). This condition occurs when most strings in the population have similar allele values. In this case, applying crossover to similar strings results in another similar string, and no new areas of the search space are explored (Levine, 1997). Many improvements to the genetic algorithms help to avoid premature convergence, such as thorough randomization of initial populations, multiple restart of problems, and appropriate parameter settings, i.e., carefully adjustment of the mutation rate and a suitable population size.

Most researchers agree that, to guarantee success of an application of genetic algorithms, the representation system is of crucial importance. The difference between a successful application and an unsuccessful one often lies in the encoding. Kershenbaum (1997) pointed out that an ideal encoding would have the following properties: (a) It should be able to represent all feasible solutions; (b) It should be able to represent only feasible solutions. (An encoding that represents fewer infeasible solutions is generally better than one that represents a large number of infeasible solutions. The larger the number of representable infeasible solutions, the more likely it is that crossover and mutation will produce infeasible offspring, and the less effective the GA will become.); (c) All (feasible) solutions should have an equal probability of being represented; (d) It should represent useful schemata using a small number of genes that are close to one other in the chromosome. (It is generally very difficult to create an encoding with this property a priori, since we do not know in advance what the useful schemata are. It is, however, possible to recognize the presence of short, compact schemata in solutions with high fitness and thus to validate the encoding after the fact. This is important for recognizing successful GA applications.); and (e) The encoding itself should possess locality, in the sense that small changes to the chromosome make small changes in the solution. Kershenbaum also pointed out taht although some of these properties conflict (often making tradeoffs), to the extent taht those properties can be achieved, the genetic algorithms are likely to work well. In this section, we focus on the design of the GA approach for the master problem of CPL problem. More discussion of some of these as well as definitions and some of the basic GA terminology that is used in this section can be found in Goldberg (1989) and Davis (1991). The implementation of GA is a step-by-step procedure:

4.1 Initialization

Initialization is to generate an initial population. The population size and length of "chromosome" depends on the users' choice and other requirements of the specific problem. To start, we usually have a totally random population. Each random string (or "chromosome") of the population, representing a possible solution for the problem, is then evaluated using an objective function. The selection of this objective function is important because it practically encompasses all the knowledge of the problem to be solved. The user is supposed to choose the proper combination of desirable attributes that could be best fit to his purposes. In CPL problem, the variable Y is a vector of binary integers. It is easily to be coded as a string of binary bit with the position #*i* corresponding to the plant #*i*. For example, Y = (0 1 1 0 1 0 0) means that plants #1, 4, 6 and 7 are not open and plants 2, 3 and 5 are open. In our GA, a population size of 50 was used and the fitness function is evaluated quickly and simply by evaluating a set of linear functions, i.e., $\underline{v}_T(Y) \equiv \max_{k=1,2,\ldots T} \{\alpha^k Y + \beta^k\}$.

4.2 Selection

Selection (called "reproduction" by Goldberg) starts with the current population. Selection is applied to create an intermediate population or mating pool. All the chromosomes in the mating pool are waiting for other operations such as crossover and/or mutation to create the next population. In the canonical genetic algorithm, selection is made according to the fitness. The fitness could be determined by many ways. For example, the fitness could be assigned according to probability of a string in the current population (Goldberg, 1989), a string's rank in the population (Baker, 1985; Whitley, 1989), or simply by its performance of scores. In our GA, the latter case is used, i.e., a string with an average score is given one mating; a string scoring one standard deviation above the average is given two matings; and a string scoring one standard deviation below the average is given no mating (Michalewicz, 1998).

4.3 Crossover and mutation

We use a standard single-point crossover method. The duplicated strings in the mating pool are randomly paired off to produce two offspring per mating. The crossover location of the strings is generally chosen at random but not necessary always the case. For example, the distribution for selection the crossover point of the GenJam system, an interactive genetic algorithm jazz improviser, which was developed by Dannenberg for the Carnegie Mellon MIDI Toolkit, is biased toward the center of the chromosome to promote diversity in the population. If a crossover point is too near one end of the chromosome or the other, the resulting children are more likely to resemble their parents. This will lead the GenJam system to repeat itself when two nearly identical phrases happen to be played close to one another in the same solo and it does not seem desirable for GenJam to perform in that way. The role of mutation is to guarantee the diversity of the population. In most case, mutation alters one or more genes (positions in a chromosome) with a probability equal to the mutation rate. Typically, but not always, mutation will flip a single bit. In fact, GenJam's mutation operators, on the other hand, are more complex than flipping a bit. They adopt several standard melodic development techniques, such as transposition, retrograde, rotation, inversion, sorting, and retrograde-inversion. Because these operators are all musically meaningful, they operate at the event level rather than on individual bits (Biles, 2001).

4.4 Replacement

After the process of selection, crossover, and mutation, the current population is replaced by the new population. Those successful individuals of the each generation are more likely to survive in the next generation and those unsuccessful individuals are less likely to survive. In our GA, we use the incremental replacement method (See Beasley et al., 1993), i.e., only the new individuals whose fitness values are better than those of the current will be replaced. Thus, the individuals with the best fitness are always in the population.

4.5 Termination

In general, a genetic algorithm is terminated after a specified number of generations or when fitness values have converged. Our GA terminates when there has been no improvement in the best solution found for 100 iterations.

5. Hybrid Benders/Genetic algorithm

The basic idea of Benders' partitioning algorithm for mixed-integer linear problems is to decompose the original problem into a pure integer master problem and one or more subproblems in the continuous variables, and then to iterate between these two problems. If the objective function value of the optimal solution to the master problem is equal to that of the subproblem, then the algorithm terminates with the optimal solution of the original mixed-integer problem. Otherwise, we add constraints, termed Benders' cuts, one at a time to the master problem, and solve it repeatedly until the termination criteria are met. A major difficulty with this decomposition lies in the solution of the master problem, which is a "hard" problem, costly to compute.

For the addressed CPL problem, however, the constraints are explicit only in the subproblem and the master problem is free of explicit constraints. Thus, the master problem is more amenable to solution by GA.

Lai et al. (2010) introduced a hybrid Benders/Genetic algorithm which is a variation of Benders' algorithm that uses a genetic algorithm to obtain "good" subproblem solutions to the master problem. Lai and Sohn (2011) conducted a study applying the hybrid Benders/Genetic algorithm to the vehicle routing problem. Below is a detailed description of the hybrid algorithm and it is illlustrated in Fig. 1 as well.

Step 1. Initialization. We initialize the iteration counter k to zero, select initial trial values for the vector of binary variables Y which selects the plants to be opened.

Step 2. Primal Subsystem. We evaluate the value of $v(Y)$ by solving a tranportation linear programming problem whose fesible region is independent of Y.

Step 3. Generation of Benders' Cut. We compute a new linear support using the dual solution of the transportation subproblem and increment k by 1.

Step 4. Primal Master system by GA. A trial location paln Y is to be computed by implementing a GA whose solution delivers both a feasible investment plan and a lower bound to the minimal cost for the equivalent program.

4a. Initialization. We initialize the variable Y as a string of binary bit with the position $\#i$ corresponding to the plant $\#i$. We generate initial population and their fitness function are evluated as well.

4b. Genetic Operations. We perform a standard single-point crossover approach. The mutation operation to guarantee the diversity of the population is performed as well. The current population is replaced by the new population through the incremental replacement method.

4c. Termination. We terminate the GA if no improvement within 100 iterations.

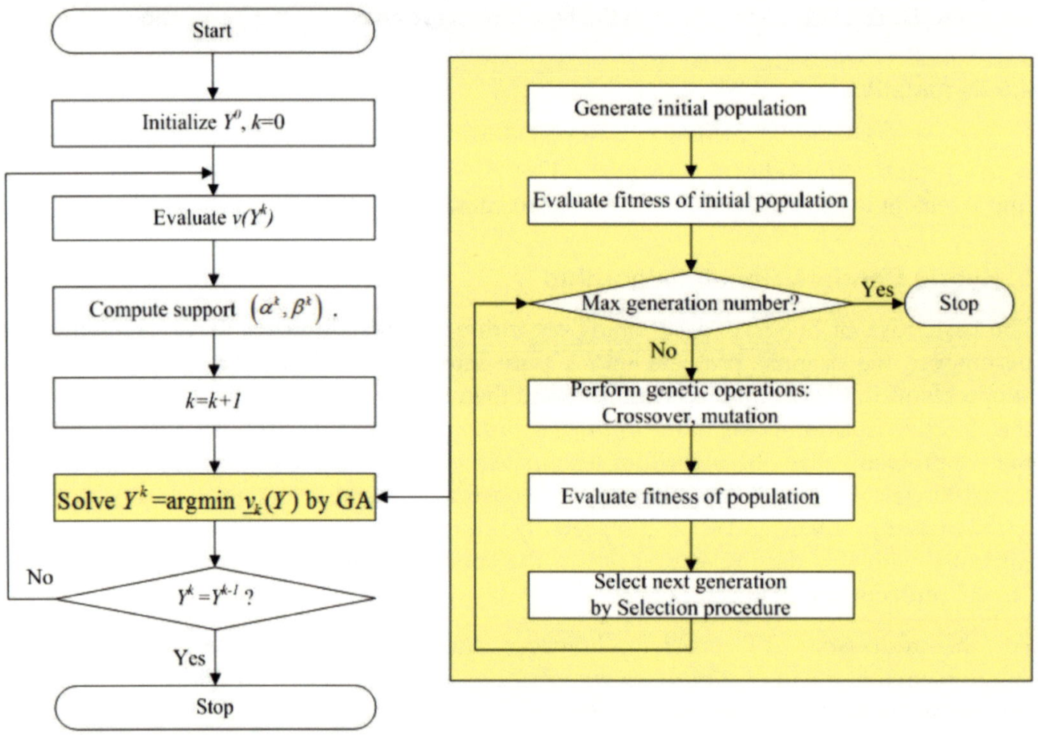

Fig. 1. Flowchart of the Hybrid Benders/Genetic Algorithm

This hybrid algorithm would avoid other traditional search methods, i.e., branch-and-bound, which were used in the master problem. It will search the solution space in parallel fashion and take advantage of the "easy" evaluation of the fitness function.

6. Example

To illustrate the hybrid algorithm discussed in the earlier section, we use a randomly-generated problem with 20 plant sites and 50 customers. Fifty points in a square area were randomly generated, and the first 20 of these points were designated as both demand points and potential plant sites (see Fig. 2).

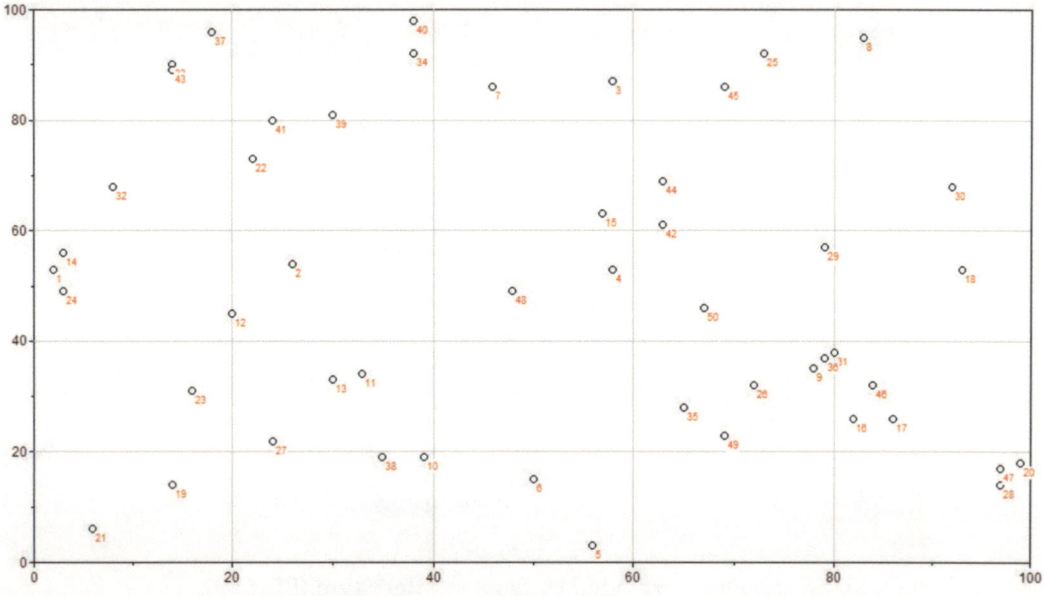

Fig. 2. Fifty Randomly Generated Points

The transportation cost between two points is proportional to the Euclidean distance between them. Three variations of Benders' algorithm were applied to this plant location problem: (1) Optimization of master problem using implicit enumeration (BD-Opt); (2) Suboptimization of master problem using implicit enumeration (BD-Subopt); and (3) Suboptimization of master problem using a genetic algorithm (Hybrid BD/GA). In each case, the problem was not solved to completion, but was terminated after solving 50 subproblems.

First, an implicit enumeration algorithm was used to optimize Benders' master problem. Fig. 3 shows the values of the upper and lower bounds, i.e., the solutions of the subproblems and master problems, respectively. The incumbent solution, which was found at iteration #10, is shown in Fig. 4 and requires opening 11 plants with a total cost of 5398, of which 2619, or 48.5%, are fixed costs of the plants and the remaining costs are transportation costs. The greatest lower bound at this stage is 4325, so that the gap is approximately 19.9% when the algorithm was terminated.

Secondly, the algorithm was restarted and again 50 iterations were performed, but suboptimizing the master problem using implicit enumeration. Fig. 5 shows the progress of this case. Because the master problem was suboptimized, no lower bound is available. After 50 iterations, the incumbent solution shown in Fig 6, which requires opening seven plants, has a total cost of 5983, of which 1710, or approximately 28.6%, are fixed costs of the plants. It is important to note, of course, that although the quality of the incumbent solution is somewhat inferior to that found by optimizing the master problem, the computational effort is miniscule compared to that required when the master problem is optimized.

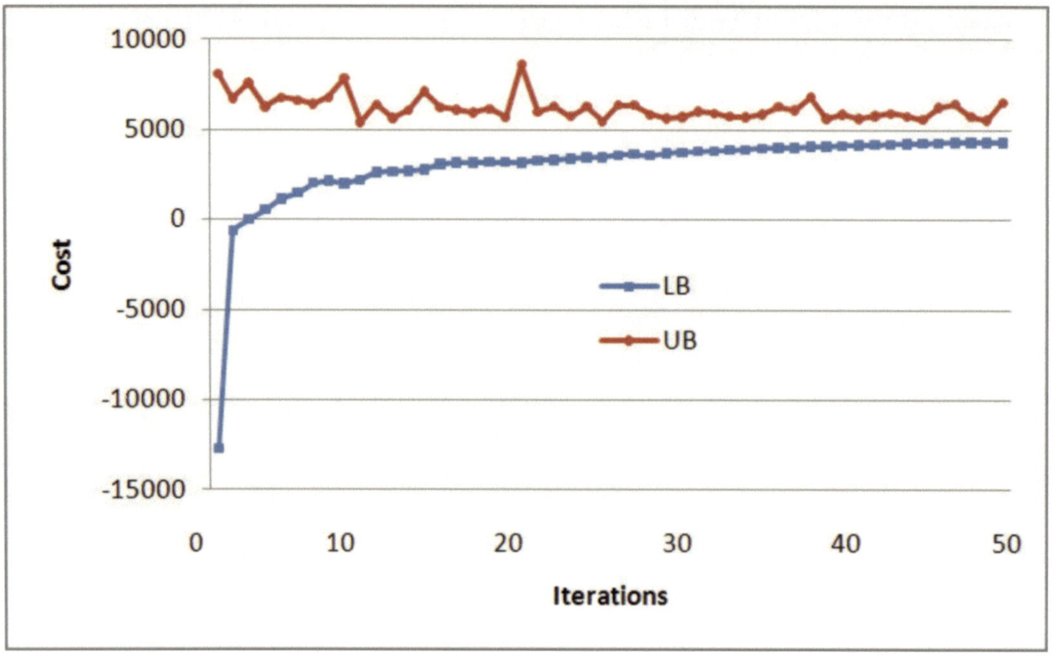

Fig. 3. Upper and lower bounds provided by Benders' algorithm (BD-Opt).

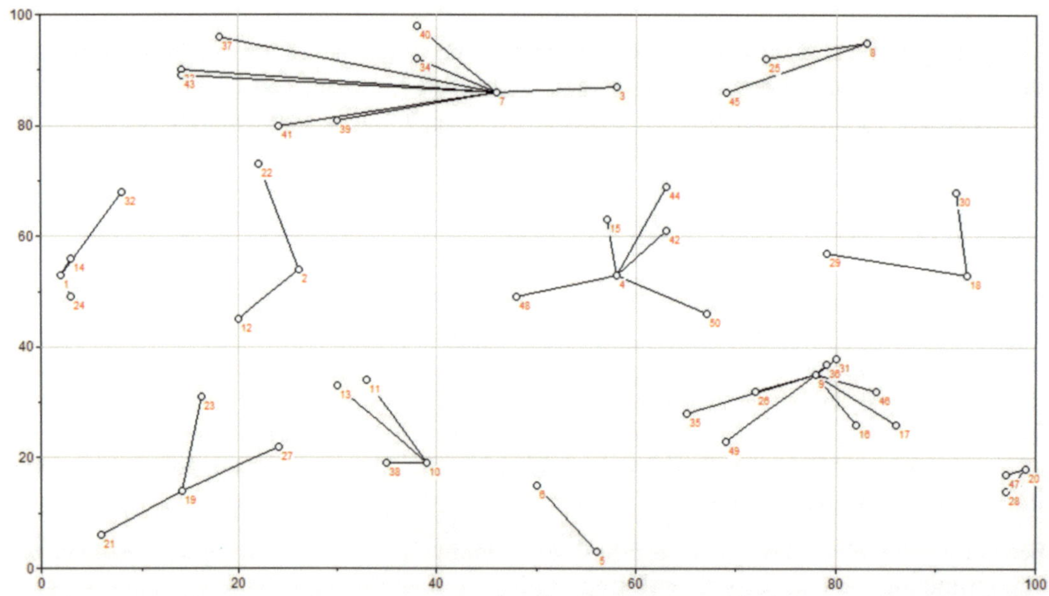

Fig. 4. Incumbent Solution Found by Benders' algorithm (BD-Opt).

Finally, the algorithm was again restarted, and 50 trial solutions were evaluated by the subproblems, this time using a genetic algorithm, so that the master problem is again suboptimized to generate the trial solutions. Each master problem was terminated after 40 trial solutions better than the incumbent have been found (or after a maximum of 100 generations) at which time all those solutions better than the incumbent were evaluated. (After each subproblem, the trial solutions are re-evaluated, using the updated master problem cost function, $\underline{v}^T(Y)$, and only those with cost less than the incumbent are evaluated by the subproblem.)

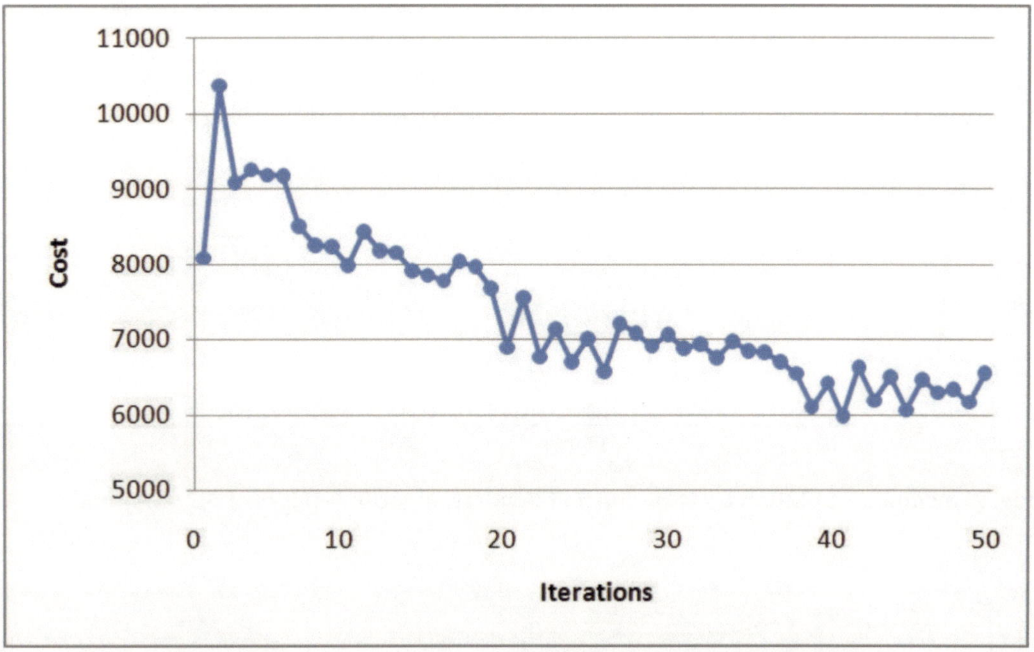

Fig. 5. Subproblem solutions of variation 2 of Benders' algorithm (BD-Subopt).

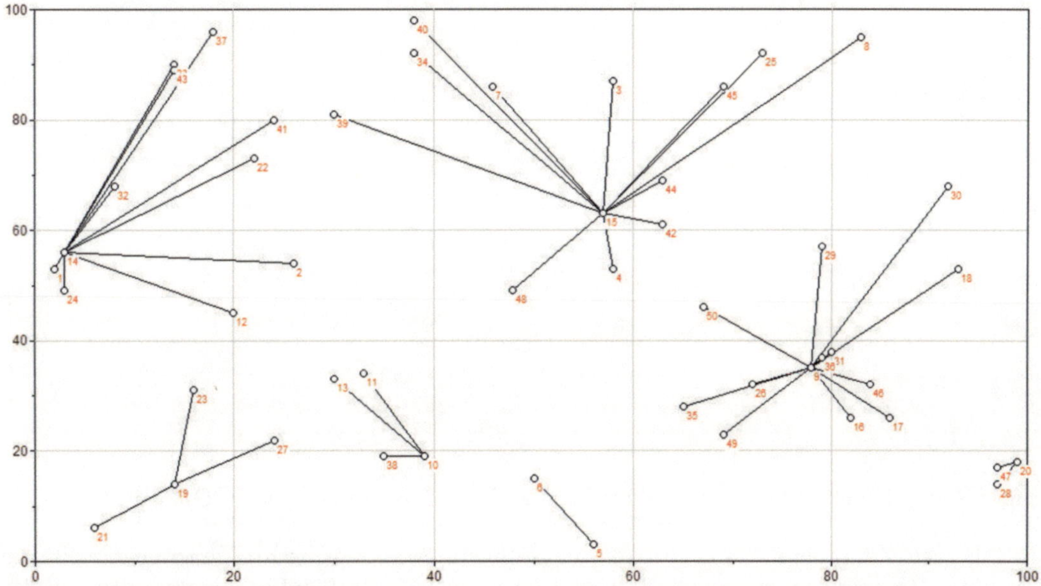

Fig. 6. Incumbent Solution Found by variation 2 of Benders' algorithm (BD-Subopt).

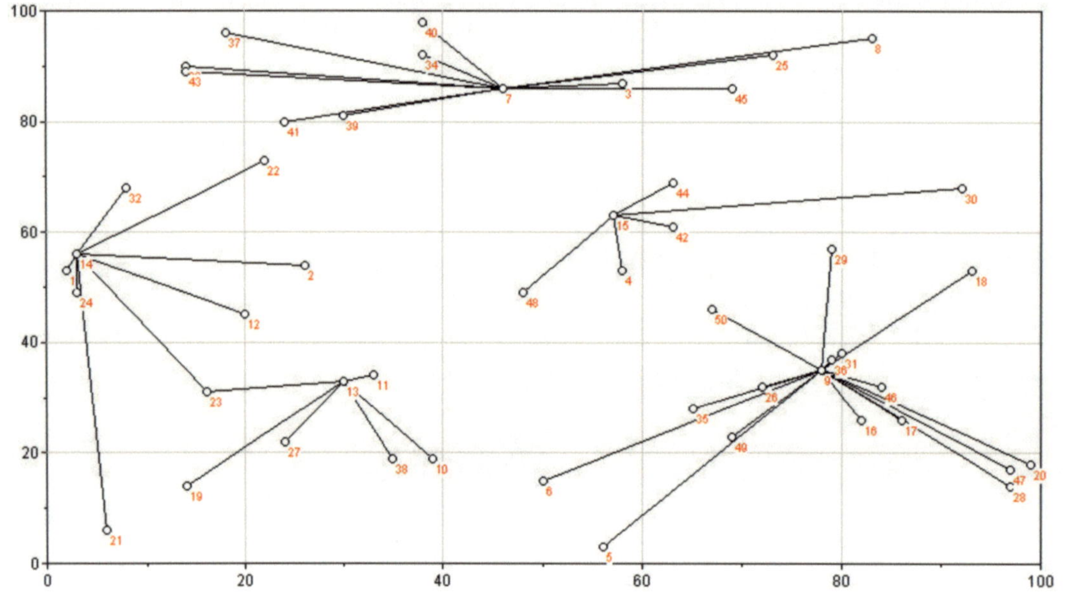

Fig. 7. Incumbent Solution by variation 3 of Benders' algorithm (Hybrid BD/GA) *trial 1*.

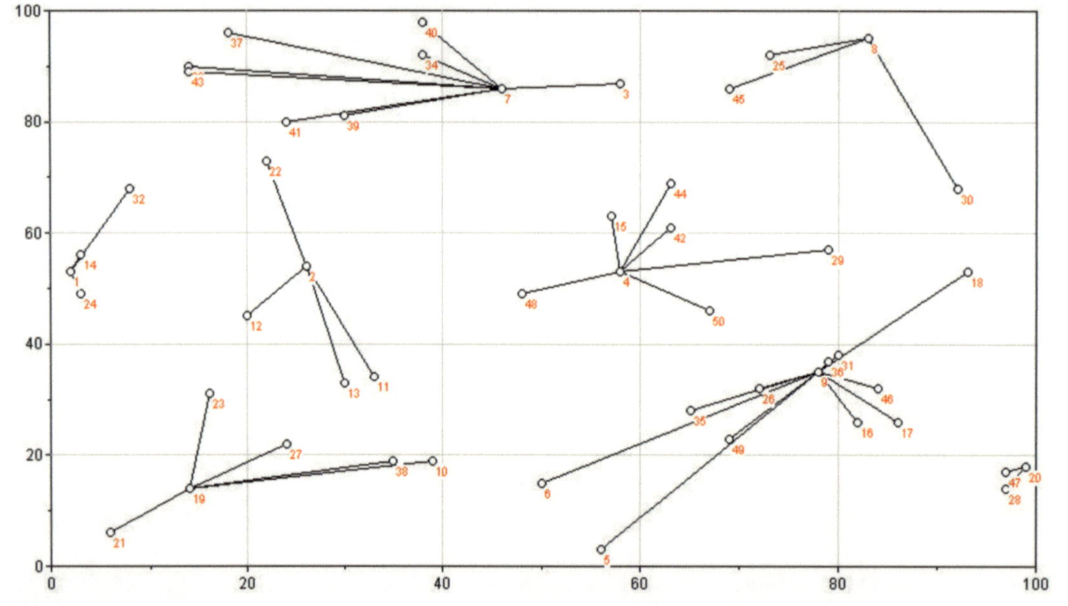

Fig. 8. Incumbent Solution by variation 3 of Benders' algorithm (Hybrid BD/GA) *trial 2*.

In this case, it happens that only 7 master problems were required to generate the 50 trial solutions. (A population size of 50 was used, with 75% probability of crossover and 1% probability of mutation.)

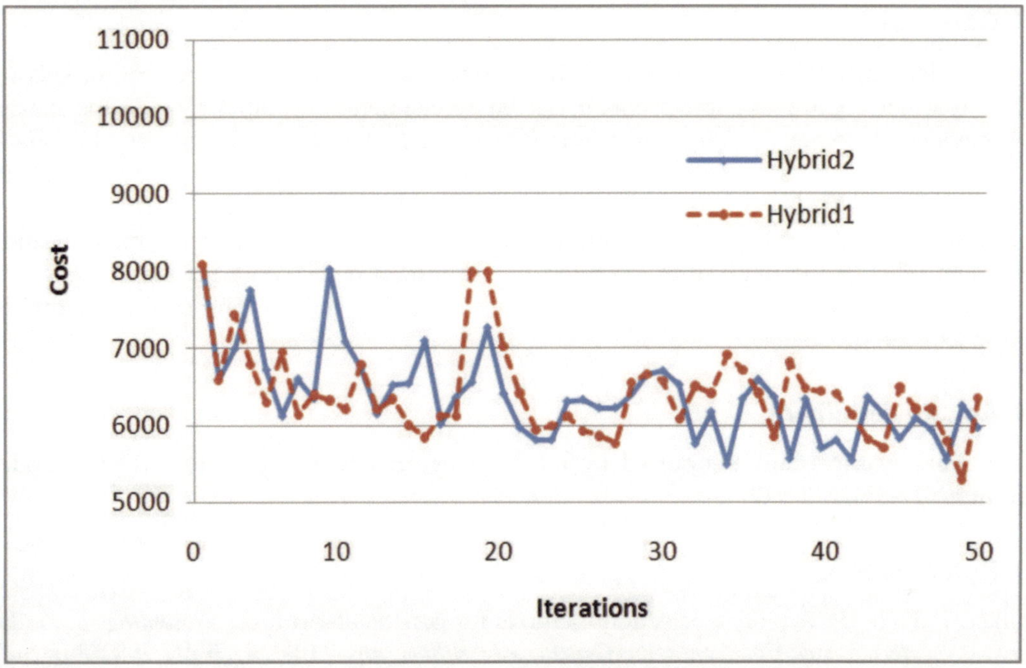

Fig. 9. Upper bounds provided by Benders' subproblems in variation 3 (Hybrid BD/GA).

The best of the 50 trial solutions was found at iteration 49, with a total cost of 5303, of which 988 (or approximately 18.6%) were fixed costs. Five plants were opened in this solution (see Fig. 7). Again, because the master problem is being suboptimized, no lower bound is available from the algorithm. Due to the random nature of the genetic algorithm, a second run of this variation was performed and found another incumbent solution (see Fig. 8). Fig. 9 shows the progress of two trials of the hybrid algorithm, i.e., the upper bounds provided by the subproblems.

Variation of Benders' algorithm	Incumbent total cost	Fixed costs	% fixed costs	# plants open
BD-Opt	5398	2619	48.5%	11
BD-Subopt	5983	1710	28.6%	7
Hybrid BD/GA, *trial 1*	5303	988	18.6%	5
Hybrid BD/GA, *trial 2*	5491	1856	33.8%	8

Table 1. Summary of results of variations of Benders' algorithm

As well, Table 1 summarizes the results obtained by these three variations of Benders' algorithm (terminated after 50 subproblems have been solved). Remarkably, in these results we observe no significant degradation of the quality of the solution when the master problem is suboptimized using a genetic algorithm, compared to optimizing the master problem and suboptimizing it by implicit enumeration.

7. Conclusion

In this chapter, we have demonstrated that Benders' decomposition algorithm for solving the capacitated plant location problem can be accelerated substantially when the master problem is solved heuristically. The hybrid Benders/GA algorithm is a variation of Benders' algorithm in which, instead of using a costly branch-and-bound method, a genetic algorithm is used to obtain "good" subproblem solutions to the master problem. The numerical example shows that the hybrid algorithm is effective to solve the capacitated plant location problem. The results imply that the hybrid algorithm is much more practical when only near-optimal solutions are required. Future work could extend the proposed algorithm to other location problems.

8. Acknowledgment

This work was partially supported by the US Department of Agriculture (USDA under grant #2011-38422-30803).

9. References

Baker, J. E. (1985). Adaptive selection methods for genetic algorithms. *Proceedings of the 1st International Conference on Genetic Algorithms*, pp. 101-111, ISBN 0-8058-0426-9, Pittsburgh, PA, USA, July, 1985.

Beasley, D.; Bull, D. R. & Martin, R. R. (1993). An Overview of Genetic Algorithms: Part 1, Fundamentals. *University Computing*, Vol. 15, No. 4, pp. 170-181.

Benders, J. F. (1962). Partitioning Procedures for Solving Mixed-Variables Programming Problems. *Numerische Mathematik*, Vol. 4, pp. 238-252.

Biles, J. A. (2001). GenJam: evolution of a jazz improviser. In: *Creative Evolutionary Systems (The Morgan Kaufmann Series in Artificial Intelligence)*, P. J. Bentley & D. W. Corne (Ed.), pp. 165-188, Morgan Kaufmann, ISBN 978-1558606739, SanFrancisco, CA, USA.

Cakir, O. (2009). Benders decomposition applied to multi-commodity, multi-mode distribution planning. *Expert Systems with Applications*, Vol. 36, pp. 8212-8217.

Chatterjee, S.; Carrera, C. and Lynch, L. (1996). Genetic algorithms and traveling salesman problems. *European journal of operational research*, Vol. 93, No. 3, pp. 490-510.

Cordeau, J.-F.; Soumis, F. & Desrosiers, J. (2000). A Benders decomposition approach for the locomotive and car assignment problem. *Transportation science*, Vol. 34, No. 2, pp. 133-149.

Cordeau, J.-F.; Soumis, F. & Desrosiers, J. (2001). Simultaneous assignment of locomotives and cars to passenger trains. *Operations research*, Vol. 49, No. 4, pp. 531-548.

Cortinhal, M. J. & Captivo, M. E. (2003). Upper and lower bounds for the single source capacitated location problem. *European journal of operational research*, Vol. 151, No. 2, pp. 333-351.

Davis, L. (1991). *Handbook of Genetic Algorithms*, Van Nostrand Reinhold Company, ISBN 978-0442001735, New York, USA.

Delmaire, H.; Di´az, J. A. & Ferna´ndez, E. (1999). Reactive GRASP and tabu search based heuristics for the single source capacitated plant location problem. *INFOR*,

Canadian Journal of Operational Research and Information Processing, Vol. 37, pp. 194-225.

Geoffrion, A. M. & Graves, G.W. (1974). Multicommodity distribution system design by Benders decomposition. *Management science*, Vol. 20, No. 5, pp. 822-844.

Goldberg, D. E. (1989). *Genetic Algorithms in Search, Optimization, and Machine Learning*, Addison-Wesley Professional, ISBN 978-0201157673, Boston, MA, USA.

Goldberg, D. E. & Lingle, R. J. (1985). Alleles, loci and the traveling salesman problem, *Proceedings of the 1st International Conference on Genetic Algorithms*, pp. 154-159, ISBN 0-8058-0426-9, Pittsburgh, PA, USA, July, 1985.

He, S.; Chaudhry, S. & Chaudhry, P. (2003). Solving a class of facility location problems using genetic algorithms. *Expert Systems*, Vol. 20, No. 2, pp. 86-91.

Heragu, S. S. & Chen, J. (1998). Optimal solution of cellular manufacturing system design: Benders' decomposition approach. *European journal of operational research*, Vol. 107, pp. 175-192.

Holland, J. H. (1992). *Adaptation in Natural and Artificial Systems: An Introductory Analysis with Applications to Biology, Control, and Artificial Intelligence*, A Bradford Book, ISBN 978-0262581110, Cambridge, MA, USA

Holmberg, K.. & Ling, J. (1997). A Lagrangean heuristic for the facility location problem with staircase costs. *European journal of operational research*, Vol. 97, No. 1, pp. 63-74.

Kennington, J. L. & Whitler J. E. (1999). An efficient decomposition algorithm to optimize spare capacity in a telecommunications network. *INFORMS Journal on computing*, Vol. 11, No. 2, pp. 149-160.

Kershenbaum, A. (1997). When genetic algorithms work best. *INFORMS Journal on computing*, Vol. 9, No. 3, pp. 254-255.

Kim, H.; Sohn, H. & Bricker, D.L. (2011). Generation expansion planning using Benders' decomposition and generalized networks. *International Journal of Industrial Engineering*, Vol. 18, No. 1, pp. 25-39.

Kratica, J.; Tosic, D.; Filipovic, V. & Ljubic, I. (2001). Solving the simple plant location problem by genetic algorithm. *RAIRO Operations Research*, Vol. 35, pp. 127-142.

Levine, D. (1997). Genetic algorithms: a practitioner's view. *INFORMS Journal on computing*, Vol. 9, No. 3, pp. 256-259.

Lai, M.; Sohn, H.; Tseng, T. & Chiang, C. (2010). A Hybrid Algorithm for Capacitated Plant Location Problems. *Expert Systems with Applications*, Vol. 37, pp. 8599-8605.

Lai, M. & Sohn, H. A Hybrid Algorithm for Vehicle Routing Problems. (2011) working paper.

Liepins, G. E. & Hilliard, M. R. (1989). Genetic algorithms: foundations and applications. *Annals of operations research*, Vol. 21, pp. 31-58.

Michalewicz, Z. (1998). *Genetic Algorithms + Data Structures = Evolution Programs*, Springer, ISBN 978-3540606765, New York, USA

Oliver, I. M.; Smith, D. J. & Holland, J. R. (1987). A study of permutation crossover operators on the traveling salesman problem. *Proceedings of the 2nd International Conference on Genetic Algorithms*, pp. 224-230, ISBN 0-8058-0158-8, Hillsdale, NJ, USA, July, 1985.

Randazzo, C.; Luna, H. & Mahey, P. (2001). Benders decomposition for local access network design with two technologies. *Discrete mathematics and theoretical computer science*, Vol. 4, pp. 235-246.

Reeves, R. C. (1997). Genetic algorithms for the operations researcher. *INFORMS Journal on computing*, Vol. 9, No. 3, pp. 231-250.

Rolland, E.; Schilling, D. A. & Current, J. R. (1996). An efficient tabu search procedure for the p-median problem. *European Journal of Operational Research*, Vol. 96, pp. 329-342.

Salkin, H. M.; Mathur, K. & Haas, R. (1989). *Foundations of Integer Programming*, Appleton & Lange, ISBN 978-0130550392, New York, USA

Uno, T.; Hanaoka, S. & Sakawa, M. (2005). An application of genetic algorithm for multi-dimensional competitive facility location problem. *Proceedings of IEEE International Conference on Systems, Man and Cybernetics*, pp. 3276-3280, ISBN 0-7803-9298-1, Big Island, Hawaii, USA, October 12, 2005

Van Roy, T. J. (1986). A cross decomposition algorithm for capacitated facility location. *Operations Research*, Vol. 34, pp. 145-163.

Van Roy, T. J. & Erlenkotter, D. (1982). Dual-based procedure for dynamic facility location. *Management Science*, Vol. 28, pp. 1091-1105.

Whitley, D. (1989). The GENITOR algorithm and selective pressure: Why rank-based allocation of reproductive trials is best. Proceedings of the 3rd International Conference on Genetic Algorithms, pp. 116-121, ISBN 1-55860-066-3, Fairfax, Virginia, USA, June 1989.